The Historical Archaeology Laboratory Handbook
Volume 3: Nineteenth and Twentieth Century Materials

Edited by John M. Chenoweth

SOCIETY *for* HISTORICAL ARCHAEOLOGY

A Society for Historical Archaeology Publication

The Historical Archaeology Laboratory Handbook Volume 3: Nineteenth and Twentieth Century Materials

© 2016 Society for Historical Archaeology
13017 Wisteria Drive #395
Germantown, MD 20874, U.S.A.

Edited by John M. Chenoweth

Library of Congress Control Number: 2016944270

Cover Design by Dylan Telerski and Knic Pfost.

www.sha.org

Contents

Part II: Metal and Small Finds

Preface: Citations to the Original Publications

The editor and the SHA would like to extend their deepest gratitude to the authors whose work has been collected here and to the original publishers who have given permission for the works to be reprinted. Full original citations to the reprinted chapters are included below.

ADAMS, WILLIAM HAMPTON, AND SARAH JANE BOLING
1989   Status and Ceramics for Planters and Slaves on Three Georgia Coastal Plantations. Historical Archaeology 23(1):69-96.

ANDERSON, ADRIENNE
1968   The Archaeology of Mass-Produced Footwear. Historical Archaeology 2:56-65.

BALLIN, TORBEN BJARKE
2012   'State of the Art' of British Gunflint Research, with Special Focus on the Early Gunflint Workshop at Dun Eistean, Lewis. Post-Medieval Archaeology 46(1):116-142.

BEAUDRY, MARY C., JANET LONG, HENRY M. MILLER, FRASER D. NEIMAN, AND GARRY WHEELER STONE
1983   A Vessel Typology for Early Chesapeake Ceramics: the Potomac Typological System. Historical Archaeology 17(1):18-43.

BELL, EDWARD L.
1990   The Historical Archaeology of Mortuary Behavior: Coffin Hardware from Uxbridge, Massachusetts. Historical Archaeology 24:54-78.

BINFORD, LEWIS R.
1962   A New Method of Calculating Dates from Kaolin Pipe Stem Samples. Southeastern Archaeological Conference Newsletter 9(1):19-21.

BRADLEY, CHARLES S.
2000   Smoking Pipes for the Archaeologist. In Studies in Material Culture Research. K. Karklins, ed. Pp. 104-133. Rockville, MD: Society for Historical Archaeology.

BUSCH, JANE
1981   An Introduction to the Tin Can. Historical Archaeology 15(1):95-104.

—

1987   The Second Time Around: A Look at Bottle Reuse. Historical Archaeology 21(1):67-80.

CHENOWETH, JOHN M.
2006   "What'll Thou Have": Quakers and the Characterization of Tavern Sites in Colonial Philadelphia. Northeast Historical Archaeology 35:77-92.

COHEN-WILLIAMS, ANITA G.
1992   Common Majolica Types of Northern New Spain. Historical Archaeology 26(1):119-130.

DETHLEFSEN, EDWIN, AND JAMES DEETZ
1966   Death's Heads, Cherubs, and Willow Trees: Experimental Archaeology in Colonial Cemeteries. American Antiquity 31(4):502-510.

DUNNING, PHIL
2000   Composite Table Cutlery from 1700 to 1930. In Studies in Material Culture Research. K. Karklins, ed. Pp. 32-45. Rockville, MD: Society for Historical Archaeology.

GLEICHMAN, PETER J., AND DOCK M. TEEGARDEN
2005   Cartridges, Caps, and Flints: A Primer for Archaeologists. Southwestern Lore 71(3):3-27.

GRIFFITHS, DOROTHY M.
1978   Use-Marks on Historic Ceramics. Historical Archaeology 12:68-81.

GUSSET, GÉRARD
2000   A Preliminary Annotated Bibliography on Electrical Artifacts In Studies in Material Culture Research. K. Karklins, ed. Pp. 134-140. Rockville, MD: Society for Historical Archaeology.

HARRIS, JANE E.
2000   Eighteenth-Century French Blue-Green Bottles from the Fortress of Louisbourg, Nova Scotia. In Studies in Material Culture Research. K. Karklins, ed. Pp. 233-258. Rockville, MD: Society for Historical Archaeology.

HILL, ERICA
1995   Thimbles and Thimble-Rings from the Circum-Caribbean Region, 1500-1800: Chronology and Identification. Historical Archaeology 29(1):84-92.

JONES, OLIVE R.
1971   Glass Bottle Push-Ups and Pontil Marks. Historical Archaeology 5(1):62-73.

—

1993   Commercial Foods, 1740-1820. Historical Archaeology 27(2):25-41.

—

2000   A Guide to Dating Glass Tableware: 1800 to 1940. In Studies in Material Culture Research. K. Karklins, ed. Pp. 141-232. Rockville, MD: Society for Historical Archaeology.

KARKLINS, KARLIS
1982   Guide to the Description and Classification of Glass Beads History and Archaeology. Histoire et Archéologie. [Parks Canada] 59:83-117.

KELLY, ROGER E., AND MARSHA C. S. KELLY
    1977   Brick Bats for Archaeologists: Values of Pressed Brick Brands. Historical Archaeology 11:84-89.

KENMOTSU, NANCY
    1990   Gunflints: A Study. Historical Archaeology 24(2):92-124.

KIDD, K. E., AND M. A. KIDD
    1970   A Classification System for Glass Beads for the Use of Field Archaeologists. Canadian Historic Sites, Occasional Papers in Archaeology and History 1:45-89.

LIGHT, JOHN D.
    2000   A Field Guide to the Identification of Metal. In Studies in Material Culture Research. K. Karklins, ed. Pp. 3-19. Rockville, MD: Society for Historical Archaeology.

LINDSEY, BILL
    2006   Overview of BLM's Historic Glass Bottle Identification and Information Website. Technical Briefs in Historical Archaeology 1:16-20.

LOCKHART, BILL
    2004   An Annotated Bibliography of Bottle Manufacturer's Marks. SHA Newsletter 37(4):10-13.

    —
    2006   The Color Purple: Dating Solarized Amethyst Container Glass. Historical Archaeology 40(2):45-56.

LORRAIN, DESSAMAE
    1968   An Archaeologist's Guide to Nineteenth Century American Glass. Historical Archaeology 2:35-44.

MARTIN, ANN SMART
    1989   The Role of Pewter as Missing Artifact: Consumer Attitudes Towards Tablewares in Late 18th Century Virginia. Historical Archaeology 23(2):1-27.

MAXWELL, D. B. S.
    1993   Beer Cans: A Guide for the Archaeologist. Historical Archaeology 27(1):95-113.

MILLER, GEORGE L.
    1991   A Revised Set of CC Index Values for Classification and Economic Scaling of English Ceramics from 1787 to 1880. Historical Archaeology 25(1):1-25.

    —
    2000   Telling Time for Archaeologists. Northeast Historical Archaeology 29:1-22.

MILLER, GEORGE L., AND CATHERINE SULLIVAN
    1984   Machine-Made Glass Containers and the End of Production for Mouth-Blown Bottles. Historical Archaeology 18(2):83-96.

MYERS, ADRIAN T.
    2010   Telling Time for the Electrified: An Introduction to Porcelain Insulators and the Electrification of the American Home Technical Briefs in Historical Archaeology 5:31-42.

NEWMAN, T. STELL
    1970   A Dating Key for Post-Eighteenth Century Bottles. Historical Archaeology 4:70-75.

OLSEN, STANLEY J.
    1963   Dating Early Plain Buttons by their Form. American Antiquity 28(4):551-554.

PRIESS, PETER J.
    2000   Historic Door Hardware. In Studies in Material Culture Research. K. Karklins, ed. Pp. 46-95. Rockville, MD: Society for Historical Archaeology.

ROCK, JAMES
    1984   Cans in the Countryside. Historical Archaeology 18:97-111.

ROSS, DOUGLAS E.
    2009   Identification and Dating of Japanese Glass Beverage Bottles. Technical Briefs in Historical Archaeology 4:7-17.

ROSS, LESTER A., AND JOHN D. LIGHT
    2000   A Guide to the Description and Interpretation of Metal Files. In Studies in Material Culture Research. K. Karklins, ed. Pp. 20-31. Rockville, MD: Society for Historical Archaeology.

SAMFORD, PATRICIA M.
    1997   Response to a Market: Dating English Underglaze Transfer-Printed Wares. Historical Archaeology 31(2):1-30.

SCHARFENBERGER, GERARD P.
    2004   Recent Evidence for Broad Window Glass in Seventeenth-and Eighteenth-Century America. Historical Archaeology 38(4):59-72.

SINGLEY, KATHERINE R.
    1981   Caring for Artifacts After Excavation: Some Advice for Archaeologists. Historical Archaeology 15(1):36-48.

SOUTH, STANLEY
    1964   Analysis of the Buttons from Brunswick Town and Fort Fisher. Florida Anthropologist 17(2):113-133.

    —
    1971   Evolution and Horizon as Revealed in Ceramic Analysis in Historical Archaeology. Conference on Historic Site Archaeology Papers 6(2):71-106.

    —
    1978   Pattern Recognition in Historical Archaeology. American Antiquity 43(2):223-230.

SPRAGUE, RICK
2003   China or Prosser Button Identification and Dating. Historical Archaeology 36(2):111-127.

SPUDE, CATHY
n.d.   Common 20th Century Artifacts - A Guide to Dating, Society for Historical Archaeology Research Resources Website, http://www.sha.org/index.php/view/page/20thCent_artifacts, accessed August 12, 2014.

STUART, IAIN
2005   The Analysis of Bricks from Archaeological Sites in Australia. Australasian Historical Archaeology 23:79-88.

SUSSMAN, LYNNE
1977   Changes in Pearlware Dinnerware, 1780-1830. Historical Archaeology 11:105-111.

—
2000   Objects vs. Sherds: A Statistical Evaluation. In Studies in Material Culture Research. K. Karklins, ed. Pp. 96-103: Society for Historical Archaeology.

TURNBAUGH, WILLIAM, AND SARAH PEABODY TURNBAUGH
1977   Alternative Applications of the Mean Ceramic Date Concept for Interpreting Human Behavior. Historical Archaeology 11(1):90-104.

VOSS, BARBARA L., AND REBECCA ALLEN
2000   Guide to Ceramic MNV Calculation Qualitative and Quantitative Analysis. Technical Briefs in Historical Archaeology 5:1-9.

WALL, DIANA DIZEREGA
1991   Sacred Dinners and Secular Teas: Constructing Domesticity in Mid-19th-Century New York. Historical Archaeology 25(4):69-81.

WEILAND, JONATHAN
2009   A Comparison and Review of Window Glass Analysis Approaches in Historical Archaeology. Technical Briefs in Historical Archaeology 4:29-40.

WELLS, TOM
1998   Nail Chronology: The Use of Technologically Derived Features. Historical Archaeology 32(2):78-99.

WHITE, CAROLYN L.
2009   Knee, Garter, Girdle, Hat, Stock, and Spur Buckles from Seven Sites in Portsmouth, New Hampshire. International Journal of Historical Archaeology 13(2):239-253.

WHITE, JOHN R.
1978   Bottle Nomenclature: A Glossary of Landmark Terminology for the Archaeologist. Historical Archaeology 12:58-67.

WILKIE, LAURIE
1996   Glass-Knapping at a Louisiana Plantation: African-American Tools? Historical Archaeology 30(4):37-49.

—
2000   Culture Bought: Evidence of Creolization in the Consumer Goods of an Enslaved Bahamian Family. Historical Archaeology 34(3):10-26.

Introduction to Volume Three: 19th and 20th Century Materials

John M. Chenoweth

As noted at the beginning of Volume Two, the last two volumes of this collection focus on the identification of different kinds of archaeologically-recovered materials. Again, the volumes are divided chronologically (because many historic sites contain objects only from certain time periods) and into rough groupings by material (since this is where most artifact analysis begins).

Volume III focuses on chronologically later materials: those produced and used mainly during the 19th and 20th centuries. At this time, ceramics become much more diverse and complex, and gaining a mastery of 19th-century ceramic types is the work of a lifetime. Decoration becomes particularly important at this time, and for some purposes decoration eclipses the question of "ware" (Majewski and O'Brien 1987; Miller 1980). Decoration is one focus for Samford (1997, III:2)[1]. Refer to the primer on historic ceramics in Volume I of this collection for more on ceramic types and decorations and consult Majewski and O'Brien (1987) as a starting place for a deeper understanding of 19th and 20th century ceramics. Another kind of ceramic, the brick, has been important for centuries, but new manufacturing techniques are introduced during this time, and bricks begin to be regularly marked with stamped identifications that can provide a wealth of information. Although these marks are often quite local, examples of interpretation and identification included here (Kelly and Kelly 1977, III:3; Stuart 2005, III:4) should help researchers explore the brickmaking industries of their own areas.

Before the 19th century, most glass was free blow or blown into a simple mold, and bottles were comparatively difficult to acquire and so were reused many times. In the 19th century, bottles begin to be made by a variety of semi-mechanized and mechanized techniques that left different marks on the finished products; these changes increased bottle availability and thus their frequency within archaeological sites. When coupled with new variations in form, glass vessels provide a great deal of dating and use information (Jones 2000, III:7; Lockhart 2006, III:12; Lorrain 1968, II:10; Newman 1970, III:8; Ross 2009, III:9). With these new techniques, bottles could be made with embossed designs and words more easily as well. This produced a huge variety of marks which are indexed on several websites. The first of Lockhart's two chapters (Lockhart 2004, III:11) provides an overview of one of these websites, which is an excellent place to begin efforts to identify a particular mark.

As in Volume II, the second half of this volume contains information on a wide variety of "small finds." Some of these, such as metal files (Ross and Light 2000, III:14) and coffin hardware (Bell 1990, III:13) existed long before the 19th century. However, these two chapters—some of the best discussions of these artifacts available—focus on materials and types primarily from the 19th century onwards, which is why they are included in this volume. Other materials considered in this section, such as "tin" cans (Busch 1981, III:15; Maxwell 1993, III:17; Rock 1984, III:16), are innovations of the 19th century, at least as mass-produced objects frequently found archaeologically. Also included here are pieces considering footwear (Anderson 1968, III:18), the dizzying variety of objects associated with guns (Gleichman and Teegarden 2005, III:19), and "prosser" buttons, a kind of ceramic button popular during this time (Sprague 2003, III:20). The earliest common electrical objects are introduced in the end of the 19th century and so two pieces (Gusset 2000, III:21; Myers 2010, III:22) are included to help analyze fragments of these systems. A final piece (Spude n.d., III:23), appropriately reprinted from the SHA website, considers even more recent artifacts, such as foils and plastics.

[1] References to works included in The Historical Archaeology Laboratory Handbook will be given to their original publication followed by a Roman numeral indicating the volume within the handbook and then an Arabic numeral giving the chapter within that volume.

References

ANDERSON, ADRIENNE
1968   The Archaeology of Mass-Produced Footwear. Historical Archaeology 2:56-65.

BELL, EDWARD L.
1990   The Historical Archaeology of Mortuary Behavior: Coffin Hardware from Uxbridge, Massachusetts. Historical Archaeology 24:54-78.

BUSCH, JANE
1981   An Introduction to the Tin Can. Historical Archaeology 15(1):95-104.

John M. Chenoweth

GLEICHMAN, PETER J., AND DOCK M. TEEGARDEN
    2005   Cartridges, Caps, and Flints: A Primer for
            Archaeologists. Southwestern Lore 71(3):3-27.

GUSSET, GÉRARD
    2000   A Preliminary Annotated Bibliography on Electrical
            Artifacts. In Studies in Material Culture Research.
            K. Karklins, ed. Pp. 134-140. Rockville, MD:
            Society for Historical Archaeology.

JONES, OLIVE R.
    2000   A Guide to Dating Glass Tableware: 1800 to
            1940. In Studies in Material Culture Research. K.
            Karklins, ed. Pp. 141-232. Rockville, MD: Society
            for Historical Archaeology.

KELLY, ROGER E., AND MARSHA C. S. KELLY
    1977   Brick Bats for Archaeologists: Values of Pressed
            Brick Brands. Historical Archaeology 11:84-89.

LOCKHART, BILL
    2004   An Annotated Bibliography of Bottle Manufacturer's
            Marks. SHA Newsletter 37(4):10-13.

    2006   The Color Purple: Dating Solarized Amethyst
            Container Glass. Historical Archaeology 40(2):45-
            56.

LORRAIN, DESSAMAE
    1968   An Archaeologist's Guide to Nineteenth Century
            American Glass. Historical Archaeology 2:35-44.

MAJEWSKI, TERESITA, AND MICHAEL J. O'BRIEN
    1987   The Use and Misuse of Nineteenth-Century English
            and American Ceramics in Archaeological Analysis.
            Advances in Archaeological Method and Theory
            11:97-209.

MAXWELL, D. B. S.
    1993   Beer Cans: A Guide for the Archaeologist. Historical
            Archaeology 27(1):95-113.

MILLER, GEORGE L.
    1980   Classification and Economic Scaling of 19th-
            Century Ceramics. Historical Archaeology 14:1-40.

MYERS, ADRIAN T.
    2010   Telling Time for the Electrified: An Introduction
            to Porcelain Insulators and the Electrification of
            the American Home. Technical Briefs in Historical
            Archaeology 5:31-42.

NEWMAN, T. STELL
    1970   A Dating Key for Post-Eighteenth Century Bottles.
            Historical Archaeology 4:70-75.

ROCK, JAMES
    1984   Cans in the Countryside. Historical Archaeology
            18:97-111.

ROSS, DOUGLAS E.
    2009   Identification and Dating of Japanese Glass Beverage
            Bottles. Technical Briefs in Historical Archaeology
            4:7-17.

ROSS, LESTER A., AND JOHN D. LIGHT
    2000   A Guide to the Description and Interpretation of
            Metal Files. In Studies in Material Culture Research.
            K. Karklins, ed. Pp. 20-31. Rockville, MD: Society
            for Historical Archaeology.

SAMFORD, PATRICIA M.
    1997   Response to a Market: Dating English Underglaze
            Transfer-Printed Wares. Historical Archaeology
            31(2):1-30.

SPRAGUE, RICK
    2003   China or Prosser Button Identification and Dating
            Historical Archaeology 36(2):111-127.

SPUDE, CATHY
    n.d.   Common 20th Century Artifacts – A Guide to
            Dating, Society for Historical Archaeology Research
            Resources Website, http://www.sha.org/index.php/
            view/page/20thCent_artifacts, accessed August 12,
            2014.

STUART, IAIN
    2005   The Analysis of Bricks from Archaeological Sites
            in Australia. Australasian Historical Archaeology
            23:79-88.

Part I:

Ceramics and Glass

PATRICIA M. SAMFORD

Response to a Market: Dating English Underglaze Transfer-Printed Wares

ABSTRACT

At the end of the 18th century, the Staffordshire pottery industry began transfer printing designs on refined earthenwares. Gaining immediate acceptance from both the British and American markets, printed earthenwares remained immensely popular until the mid-19th century. Hundreds of printed patterns were produced, and these patterns formed distinctive decorative styles based on central motifs and borders. Using characteristics of datable, marked vessels as a database, this study establishes a chronology for dating printed earthenwares based on decorative styles and color.

Introduction

Ceramics are one of the primary dating tools used by archaeologists working on 18th- and 19th-century North American sites. Over the last several decades, research combining primary documents, such as potters' invoices, trade catalogs, and store accounts, with archaeological data has created a greater understanding of the variety of ceramics available to American consumers during these periods. Information on characteristics such as body composition, glaze type, and decorative attributes is often available in potters' records, allowing accurate date ranges to be assigned. Often, identifying and dating ceramics using evidence from documents is critical, since the majority of individual ceramic vessels were not marked by their manufacturers. While greater effort has gone into developing dating schemes and discovering the social functions of colonial-period ceramics, a growing body of research on 19th-century wares has also developed. In addition to creating classification and dating tools for post-colonial ceramics (Price 1979; Majewski and O'Brien 1987), work has focused on the availability and marketing of ceramics in North America (Miller and Hurry 1983; Miller 1984), household expenditure patterns (Miller 1980), and the effects of ethnicity, gender, and economic class on ceramic purchasing patterns (Baker 1978; Felton and Schulz 1983; Wall 1994).

This paper develops a dating scheme for one particular type of English pottery produced primarily from the late 18th to the mid-19th centuries. The technique of transfer printing designs under the glaze on ceramics, which revolutionized the Staffordshire ceramic industry, enabled complex decoration to be applied quickly and relatively inexpensively. It also allowed uniformity of design between vessels, something not possible with painted decorations. Thousands of designs were manufactured in a variety of colors and styles, with the Staffordshire potters producing patterns they hoped would be in demand by consumers both in England and abroad. While some patterns, such as Blue Willow, Asiatic Pheasants, and Canova, were extremely popular and manufactured by a number of potteries, the production span of most patterns was short-lived and limited to one potter. These designs reflected the larger social and decorative trends taking place within England and North America.

This study uses marked vessels to establish the chronological ranges for the major decorative styles on printed wares. Information from these dated vessels documents a series of styles that began at a point in time, rose to a level of popularity, and declined in frequency as other styles became more popular. Chronological information on motifs, used in conjunction with data on print color, vessel form, and manufacturing innovations, can assist archaeologists in refining date ranges for archaeological assemblages that contain printed wares. Such a dating tool is valuable because of the problems encountered in dating many 19th-century assemblages, where the majority of the ceramic assemblage is generally undecorated or minimally decorated white earthenware and white granite. Since printed wares were popular for almost a hundred years, they are common on late 18th- and 19th-century archaeological sites. Because the intent is to create a dating tool for archaeologists, the focus of this study is underglaze printed patterns on commonly available vessels forms. Data were not gathered on vessels decorated with overglaze printing, which are rarely found in 19th-century archaeological contexts and are less common overall.

This paper begins with a discussion of the various printing processes which have been used on pottery and a brief historical overview of printing on English ceramics. This section is followed by an explanation of the study methods and the composition of the database. Results of the study follow and are divided into sections on identifying and dating central motifs, border patterns, ink colors, and printing techniques. Discussed separately are ceramics decorated using flown colors.

Before discussing dating, it is important for the reader to understand the technical processes involved in printing on ceramics. Some technological advances in the printing process and materials used resulted in discernible evidence which can be used to help date printed wares. These advances and how to recognize their use on printed wares are discussed.

The Transfer Printing Process

Transfer printing, which involved the transferring of a design engraved into a copper plate via tissue paper or a glue bat to a ceramic vessel, was first used beginning in the 1750s (Coysh and Henrywood 1982:8). There were two primary types of printing on ceramics: prints applied over the final glaze and prints applied onto bisque-fired earthenware prior to glazing. Early efforts in printing were on vessels which had already received a final glazing. Printing over the glaze was known by three names: bat printing, cold printing, and overglaze printing (Copeland 1980:26–27; Majewski and O'Brien 1987:141).

Overglaze printing was used as a decorative technique on tin-glazed earthenware tiles in the 1750s, as well as on porcelain and, slightly later, on creamware (Holdway 1986:24–25). It soon thereafter began to be used as a means of decorating earthenware vessels and was generally restricted to high-status items such as tea wares or large jugs printed to order in Liverpool. Most of these earlier earthenwares were printed over the glaze in black on creamware bodies and were probably done using a technique known as bat printing. Developed in the third quarter of the 18th century, this technique used the transfer, in oil, of the engraved design to a thin sheet, or bat, of glue (des Fontaines 1966:102; Drakard and Holdway 1983:11). This glue bat was placed, oiled side down, on the glazed pottery surface, leaving the design in oil (Halfpenny 1994a:46). Powdered enamels were then dusted onto the oil. The design was fixed into place by firing the pottery in a low-temperature kiln. The powdered enamel colors most suitable for bat printing were black, red, chocolate-brown, and purple (Holdway 1986:22). Because the design was placed over the lead glaze, which slightly blurred the ink in underglaze printing, bat printing allowed a great level of detail.

As a technique for decorating ceramics, bat printing was firmly established by 1805 and stayed popular for several decades (Halfpenny 1994a:57). Bat printing was suitable for irregularly shaped vessels, because the flexible glue bat could be easily fitted along convex surfaces where tissue paper designs would have to be folded. This technique was most effective with small vessels like mugs or teapots, since it was difficult to work with large glue bats (Halfpenny 1994a:46). The process was also unsuitable for transferring continuous border patterns (Drakard and Holdway 1983:11). Bat printing was also known as cold printing, since the engraved copper plates used in this technique were not heated before being charged with oil (Majewski and O'Brien 1987:141).

The development of a printing process for ceramics using the transfer of an inked design by paper allowed a wider range of vessel forms to be decorated. Underglaze, or hot process, printing on earthenwares did not begin in England until Thomas Turner's first attempts around 1780 (Coysh 1970), but was quickly adopted by other Staffordshire potters. Spode was printing under the glaze on earthenwares by 1784 (Drakard and Holdway 1983). The process of printing on ceramics allowed standardization of decoration, permitting complex designs to be created quickly and in larger quantities. Using this technique, a design was first engraved onto a copper plate (Coysh and Henrywood 1982:8). After the plate was heated to help thin and spread the ink, it was then inked with a thick mixture of boiled linseed oil, powdered flint, and metallic oxide or some other coloring agent. Ink color was determined by the metallic oxide: cobalt produced a blue color; manganese and cobalt, shades of purple, brown, and red; and chromium oxide, maroon (Williams 1975:131–132). Black was produced by adding manganese and cobalt to brown tints made with iron, chromium, and zinc, and greens were made using chromium oxide (Majewski and O'Brien 1987:139–140). Excess ink was removed from the copper plate, leaving the color only in the engraved areas of the design. A dampened tissue paper, which was placed over the copper plate and the inked design, was then transferred by passing the plate and paper through the rollers of a press (Coysh and Stefano 1981:12). After being lifted from the copper plate, this tissue paper was cut apart if necessary, and pressed, inked side down, onto the porous ware (biscuit fired, but still unglazed), which absorbed the ink (des Fontaines 1966:102). The ceramic item was then fired at a low temperature to burn off the linseed oil and set the coloring agent. Next the vessel was dipped in liquid glaze and refired in a glost oven (des Fontaines 1966:102).

Although the process of transfer printing involved a series of steps, all but the initial carving of the design on a copper plate could be accomplished by minimally skilled labor. These plates, done by expert engravers, would have to be made to fit each vessel form and size desired in the pattern, but, as the engraved plates could be used repeatedly, the most substantial cost in this form of decoration was up front. While some manufacturers retained full-time engravers on staff, many of the smaller potteries purchased their engraved plates from independent workshops (Coysh and Stefano 1981:15; Halfpenny 1994b:61). Popular designs were frequently sold to more than one manufacturer, with small changes often made (Gurujal 1988:16). Additionally, some potters sold or traded their used

copper plates to other potteries (Halfpenny 1994b:65). Copper plates engraved for transfer onto ceramics had to be engraved more deeply than those used for book illustrations, since the heat of the glost oven lightened the colors of the ink and the biscuit ware absorbed more ink than paper (des Fontaines 1966:101; Coysh 1970:7). The more deeply the plate was engraved, the darker the color of the resulting print.

In the late 18th century and the early years of the following century, a limited number of factories were producing printed wares; consequently, printed wares were expensive relative to other decorated and undecorated English ceramics. George Miller's (1980) research on the economic scaling of 19th-century ceramics has shown that printed wares were three to five times the cost of undecorated cream-colored earthenwares (CC) in the 1790s. By the mid-19th century, however, the relative price of printed wares had dropped to within one to two times the cost of undecorated wares. While at first only the members of the upper economic classes could afford to purchase printed wares, by 1842, a group of New York pottery dealers considered that Staffordshire wares were now so inexpensive that they were within reach of the poorest (Ewins 1990:8).

Despite the fact that the technique of transfer printing under the glaze had been possible for over two decades, it was not until after the War of 1812 that printed wares began to appear in great numbers in America, as indicated by New York invoices for pottery (Miller 1994:38). This increase in consumption of printed wares following the War of 1812 was probably the result of a major fall in ceramic prices (Miller et al. 1994:234–238). Large fortunes were being amassed in the growing cities of the northern Atlantic coast, and the westward expansion also created new markets for the products of Staffordshire (Tracy 1963:19, 23). After the opening of the American market in the years following the war, Staffordshire potters found a willing market in the American consumer, and pottery in hundreds of patterns made the journey across the Atlantic Ocean to grace the tables of the New Republic. Almost 43% of the plates and soup plates ordered by New York merchants between 1838 and 1840 were printed (Miller 1994:34). Printed wares remained popular until around the mid-19th century, when they gave way to undecorated or minimally decorated white earthenwares and ironstones for a time. Printed wares in certain colors, such as flow mulberry, continued to remain popular into the 1860s, and, beginning around 1870, printed wares enjoyed a revival which lasted until the use of decals became popular in the early 1900s (Majweski and O'Brien 1986:145, 147).

Methods

The date ranges for printed earthenwares given in this study were derived using a process related to seriation, a technique particularly valuable on sites where pottery and other sensitive cultural traits are common. Using changes in stylistic attributes of pottery and other material culture has figured prominently in archaeological literature (Petrie 1972[1904]; Spier 1917; Kroeber and Strong 1924; Dethlefsen and Deetz 1966; Marquardt 1978). Seriation involves ordering units based on similarity. Basic to its theoretical focus is the assumption that a given attribute originates at a specific time, becomes gradually and increasingly common, and is slowly replaced by a different attribute (Clarke 1968:205). Seriation assumes that the popularity of an attribute or trait is transient in nature; experiencing one peak in frequency of occurrence. Arrangement of these attributes over time produces an overlapping effect. For example, as one attribute wanes in frequency, the frequency of another may be increasing. By using this technique to analyze decorative attributes on marked and datable examples of ceramics, it is possible to see changes in stylistic motifs over time. Once these different motifs can be assigned a date range of production, it is then possible to date unmarked fragments from archaeological contexts.

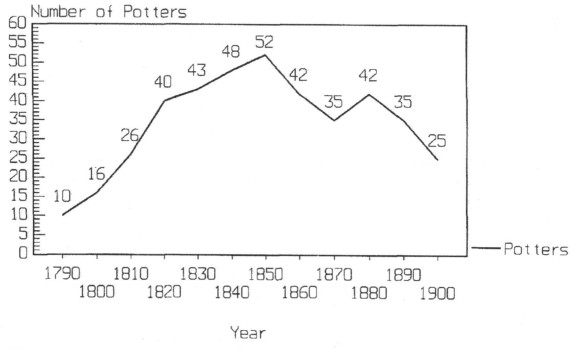

FIGURE 1. The number of potters producing printed wares increased dramatically in the first decades of the 19th century, peaked at mid-century, and enjoyed a brief resurgence in the 1880s.

The study sample included 3,250 pottery vessels made by 176 different British pottery firms. The majority of these potteries were located in Staffordshire, the leading world supplier of decorative and utilitarian ceramics at that time (Tracy 1963:108). Several Scottish firms were also included in the sample. The greatest number of firms producing printed wares as at least one of their products occurred between 1835 and 1855, with a high of 52 of the sampled potteries in business in 1845 (Figure 1).

Information on decorative motifs and other attributes was cataloged into a Paradox database that allowed sorting by various categories. In order to qualify for inclusion in the database, each vessel had to meet several prerequisites. Each had to be marked in a way that would allow it to be positively attributed to a specific maker. Most contained printed or impressed manufacturers' marks, as shown in Geoffrey Godden's (1964) *Encyclopaedia of British Pottery and Porcelain Marks*. Some vessels contained no maker's mark, but did have printed or impressed registry marks, which allowed the manufacturer to be identified by using registry records. To be included in the database, the use-span of the mark, as defined in Godden (1964), or the total operation span of the potter's firm had to date to less than 40 years, in order to maintain greater temporal control. This meant that several important firms, including William Adams and Sons, Ltd. (1769–present) and Josiah Wedgwood (1759–present) could not be included in the sample.

Data for this study were gleaned from a number of primary and secondary sources. These sources are listed below, and the manner in which the data were gathered for each is given.

Primary documents consisted of potters' invoices for wares that were shipped to the United States in the first half of the 19th century. These documents usually contained information about vessel form, size, decoration, color, and pattern name. Published photographs or actual vessels in these patterns by the same manufacturers were located in order to gather the information on decorative attributes, such as central

and border motifs, as well as vessel shape, molded motifs, and the like. Primary documents used in this study were contained within the Joseph Downs Collection of Manuscripts and Ephemera at the Henry Francis DuPont Winterthur Museum, and in the U.S. Customs House Papers (1790–1869) for the Port of Philadelphia, held at the University of Delaware and available on microfilm at Winterthur. The sources used at Winterthur included the Printed Bills Collection (Box 3, Pottery and Glassware Folder) and the Gallimore Collection in the Joseph Downs Collection (71x166.1–.68). Additionally, information on printed pottery as discussed by Ann Eatwell and Alex Werner (1991) was used.

Collections of marked, printed ceramics were examined at the Colonial Williamsburg Foundation Department of Collections and Department of Archaeological Research, at the Smithsonian Museum of American History, and at the Henry Francis DuPont Winterthur Museum. Several sizeable private collections of printed earthenwares were also cataloged, including those of George L. Miller, Ann Smart Martin, and Robert Hunter.

The following secondary sources were used for data gathering. These sources contained photographs of the patterns cataloged, as well as information on makers and marks. In some instances, color and size information was also available. These sources included Robert Copeland (1980), A. W. Coysh (1970, 1972), A. W. Coysh and R. K. Henrywood (1982, 1989), David Drakard and Paul Holdway (1983), Ellouise Baker Larsen (1975[1950]), Sam Laidacker (1938, 1951), Veneita Mason (1982), Silber and Fleming's 1882 trade catalogue (in Bosomworth 1991), and Petra Williams (1971, 1973, 1978). Several archaeological publications and reports were also used where there was a body of information about marked printed earthenwares. These works were David L. Felton and Peter D. Schulz (1983) and Lynne Sussman (1979).

Several minor problems were encountered in using the secondary sources. In the printed sources, every pictured pattern with a known manufacturing range of less than 40 years was recorded. In instances where photographs were not clear enough to adequately identify the pattern type, no information was recorded. Additionally, the research interests of the scholars who have published on printed wares have introduced some potential biases. There has been great interest in blue printed wares and patterns depicting American buildings, landscapes, and historical events. Consequently, many of the published sources concentrate on these limited categories (Camehl 1948[1916]; Larsen 1975[1950]; Fennelly 1967; Copeland 1982; Coysh and Henrywood 1982, 1989). Other sources are more comprehensive in terms of a representative sample (Laidacker 1938, 1951; Williams 1971, 1973, 1978).

In addition to makers' mark data, information was collected on central design motifs, border (or marley) decorations, ink color, vessel shape, measurements, and additional decorative attributes. Many of these decorative attributes,

such as engraving techniques, were in fact closely linked to technological innovations in the ceramic industry. For those vessels recovered from archaeological excavations, data were also collected on the context from which each was recovered.

To arrive at the date ranges presented in the results section of this report, the beginning and end production dates for each vessel within a category were listed. The sum of all beginning production dates in each category was totaled and divided by the number of examples to arrive at a mean beginning date. The same was done with the end production dates, thus providing a date span for a period of peak production. In general, the results revealed a peak production range of between 15 and 20 years for each design or decorative category. Also shown in each table are the inclusive ranges of production for each type or category, based on the earliest beginning and latest ending dates for marks. In cases where a specific pattern was listed in more than one vessel form by the same potter, the

TABLE 1
DATE RANGES FOR CENTRAL DESIGNS ON PRINTED WARES

Design	N	Mean Beginning and End Production Dates		Range of Production
Chinese	22	1797	1814	1783–1834
British Views	401	1813	1839	1793–1868
Chinoiserie	33	1816	1836	1783–1873
Pastoral	88	1819	1836	1781–1859
Exotic Views	214	1820	1842	1793–1868
American Historical	49	1826	1842	1785–1880
American Views	192	1826	1838	1793–1862
Floral				
Sheet Patterns	7	1826	1842	1795–1867
Central Floral	56	1833	1849	1784–1869
Classical	104	1827	1847	1793–1868
Romantic	376	1831	1851	1793–1870
Gothic	20	1841	1852	1818–1890
Japanese	44	1882	1888	1864–1907
No Central	11	1868	1878	1845–1920

Note. Mean beginning and end dates for all the tables in this paper reflect the period of highest production for these wares, while range of production is based on the earliest beginning date and latest end date of the manufacturers making them.

pattern was only counted once in order to avoid weighting the data. For example, the pattern Marble by John Ridgway (ca. 1830–1855) was listed 30 times in the database, once for each vessel form in which it was available. In calculating dates for central or border motifs, however, this pattern was only listed once.

Results

Analysis did show that significant dating differences occurred in many of the decorative attributes on printed earthenwares. The results discussed below are divided into central motifs, border designs, print color, and other decorative techniques.

Central Motifs on Printed Earthenwares

Staffordshire printed wares can be seen as commercial and industrial art that reflected social and decorative trends of the time (Krannert Art Museum 1988:4). A series of revivals influenced design and the decorative arts in England and Europe in the 18th and 19th centuries. These revivals of classical, romantic, and gothic tastes were just as important in American design as they were in England. Even after the two wars that pitted the United States against England, Americans continued to look to England, as well as France, for guidance in fashion and refined taste (Cooper 1993:11). In general, upper-class Americans, who traveled and read more extensively than did their middle-class counterparts, were the first purveyors of fashionable decorative arts and home furnishings in America. The presence of fashionable items in the home, particularly those displaying exotic scenes of faraway lands, conveyed messages about one's place in the world and one's knowledge of culture, history, and travel. Interestingly, many of the design motifs and stylistic trends of the 19th century were influenced by the findings of archaeological excavations of English medieval churches and monuments and on classical-period sites. In many ways, the industrial environment and development of technologies that allowed transfer printing as a means of decorating ceram-

ics were the phenomena being reacted against in many of the design motifs seen on these printed wares; this is especially true of the romantic patterns.

Central design motifs have been divided into 13 different categories, corresponding to decorative trends evident in the 19th century and based on examining printed vessels. Analysis showed distinct temporal differences in the periods of peak production for most of these stylistic motifs. Table 1 lists the categories used and the period of peak production for each of these central motifs. A discussion of each type follows.

Chinese and Chinoiserie

The western fascination with things Chinese had long preceded the advent of underglaze printing on earthenwares. Trade with the East had introduced the West to tea, spices, fine silks, embroidery, lacquered items, and porcelain (Jarry 1981). For decades, consumers desirous of owning expensive Chinese porcelains, but unable to afford them, contented themselves with painted renditions of Chinese-style designs on less costly ceramics, in particular tin-glazed earthenwares. Later in the 18th century, English import duties on porcelain went through a series of increases,

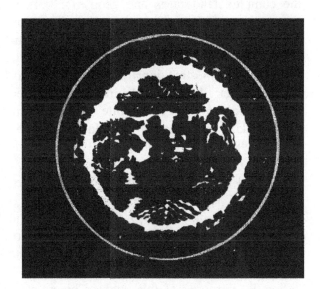

FIGURE 2. Early printed patterns were primarily based directly on Chinese porcelains, like the Broseley pattern shown here on bone china, maker unknown. (Photo by P. Samford; courtesy of George L. Miller.)

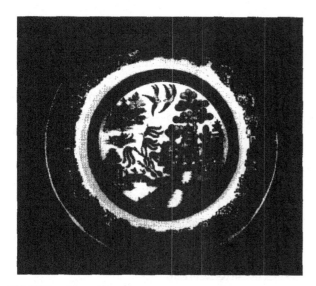

FIGURE 3. Blue Willow was the most commonly produced pattern, popular with both English and North American potters. This example was manufactured by the Buffalo Pottery Company (1916–present) of New York. (Photo by P. Samford; courtesy of George L. Miller.)

reaching 109 percent by 1799 (Copeland 1982:7), and even those who had been able to drink their tea or serve dinner guests from porcelain found it increasingly difficult to obtain replacements and additions to their services. With the advent of printed underglaze designs in blue on white-bodied earthenwares, production of the complex landscapes and geometric borders common on Chinese porcelains became more cost efficient. Additionally, the whiteness of the newly developed pearlware body and glaze were well-suited to the traditionally blue Chinese motifs. In fact, the Staffordshire potters called Wedgwood's new "Pearl white" bodied ware "China glaze" in imitation of Chinese porcelain (Miller 1987). The combination of Chinese style designs and vessel forms with the China glaze was aimed at filling a niche previously occupied by Chinese porcelain. Copies of original Chinese designs, such as Broseley, Buffalo, and Mandarin, printed on English earthenware provided a sufficient, albeit poorer quality, substitute for Chinese porcelain.

For the purposes of this study, Chinese-style printed wares have been divided into two categories—those based directly on Chinese designs and those based on interpretations of Chinese patterns. The earliest printed earthenware designs were copied directly from Chinese porcelain motifs, such as the Buffalo and Broseley patterns (Figure 2). Perhaps the most enduring of the Chinese-style patterns was Blue Willow (Figure 3). Based on the Mandarin pattern, it was first introduced around 1790 by Josiah Spode (Copeland 1980:33). The Blue Willow pattern has been made by numerous potters since its introduction, and at times its name was synonymous with that of printed wares. The peak ranges of production of marked Chinese designs fall between 1797 and 1814, but these wares were the dominant types from the introduction of underglaze printing in Staffordshire in 1784 until 1814. As time passed, elements such as figures in western dress and western architectural features began to appear (Impey 1977:11; Coysh and Henrywood 1982:9). The term "chinoiserie" is used here to designate all styles based on European interpretations of oriental designs (Impey 1977:10). Chinoiserie designs were most commonly produced between 1816 and 1836.

Because this was a period of experimentation with the new method of underglaze printing on earthenwares, late 18th- and early 19th-century Chinese-style and chinoiserie printed earthenwares designs generally appear two dimensional and in one shade of blue (Coysh and Henrywood 1982:9). Common decorative motifs found on printed Chinese-style and chinoiserie earthenwares include pagodas, temples, weeping willow trees, cherry blossoms, orange trees, figures in eastern dress, junks and sampans, and

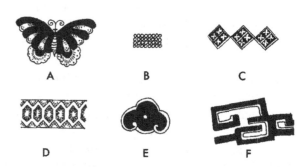

FIGURE 4. These motifs are among those commonly found on Chinese and chinoiserie-style printed wares: a, butterfly; b, fish roe; c, lozenges; d, honeycomb; e, Joo-I; and f, key motif (after Copeland 1980).

FIGURE 5. New York from Heights Near Brooklyn (James and Ralph Clews, 1818–1834) is a typical American view. The combined use of line and stipple engraving give it a soft, watercolor-like appearance (Larsen Collection, Smithsonian Institution).

Chippendale-style fencework. The marleys or rim designs on chinoiserie-style earthenwares are often densely printed geometric designs with butterflies, key motifs, honeycombing, and latticing (Figure 4). Although the penchant for chinoiserie persisted throughout the 19th century, disenchantment with the exoticism of this style occurred in mid-century (Jacobson 1993:178). The opening of Japan to the west in the latter part of the 19th century and the subsequent interest in Japanese design sparked a revival of interest in chinoiserie (Jacobson 1993:202).

British Views

Between ca. 1815 and 1840, potters produced a number of designs depicting English cities, colleges, estates, and country homes. In the early 19th century, as the British empire expanded, patriotism increased, and the Napoleonic Wars made travel in Europe and other parts of the world more dangerous, numerous books were published portraying the beauty of Great Britain and its buildings. These prints were the primary sources for British views produced on pottery (Coysh and Stefano 1981:7). Enoch Wood and Sons (1818–1846) produced a series of over 50 known views based on the prints of John

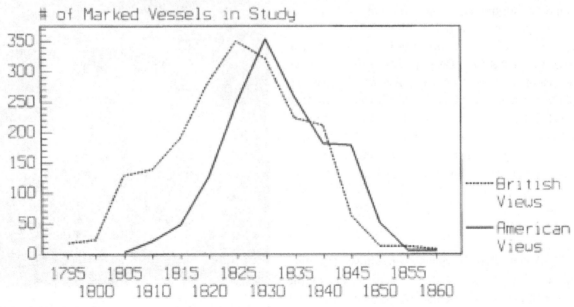

FIGURE 6. Graph illustrating how the production of American views skyrocketed after the end of the War of 1812 and the Embargo of 1807.

TABLE 2
DATE RANGES FOR AMERICAN VIEWS

Color	N	Mean Beginning and End Production Dates		Range of Production
Dark Blue	65	1822	1836	1810–1850
Black	31	1826	1839	1810–1854
Brown	21	1830	1840	1818–1854
Light Blue	23	1830	1843	1818–1854
Reds/Purples	52	1828	1838	1818–1854

Preston Neale, published in a book entitled *Views of the Seats of Noblemen and Gentlemen in England, Wales, Scotland, and Ireland* (1818–1829). Other series of British views on earthenwares include "Metropolitan Scenery" by Goodwins and Harris (1831–1838), and "Picturesque Scenery" and the "Select Views" series by Ralph Hall (1822–1849).

Often a different design was engraved for each vessel form in a set; in the Grapevine Border series, over 50 different designs were used by Enoch Wood and Sons on one of their dinner services (Laidacker 1951:93). In many instances, the engravings or aquatints were not copied exactly; studies have shown that elements were added or subtracted from the published sources in order to create a better fit with the shape of the ceramic vessel intended for decoration (Maguire 1988:4). Despite this artistic license, the passage of the Copyright Act of 1842, which made it illegal to copy book illustrations, dealt a fatal blow to the British views category (Coysh and Henrywood 1982:11). This category peaks in production popularity around 1823, with mean beginning and end dates of 1813 and 1839.

American Views

Similar to British views were those depicting American scenes. By the second decade of the 19th century, many of the Staffordshire potteries were encountering financial difficulties brought about in large part by the effects of the Napoleonic Wars, the Embargo of 1807, and the War of 1812. As a result of these events, there had been little direct trade between Britain and the United States between 1808 and 1815, and ceramic manufacturers were understandably anxious to reestablish North American trade ties after the close of the War of 1812. Staffordshire potters found a willing and ready market for their products with the flourishing population and rising middle class of the early 19th-century United States.

Many Staffordshire potters appealed specifically to the American market by creating series of views depicting American landmarks, such as churches, hotels and resorts, government build-

FIGURE 7. The Monopteros pattern (John Rogers and Son, ca. 1814–1836) is an example of an exotic view with a border that is a continuation of the main scene. (Photo by P. Samford; courtesy of George L. Miller.)

FIGURE 8. The Monopteros pattern in Figure 7 was based on this print taken from Thomas Daniell's *Oriental Scenery*.

ings and homes, city vistas, and natural wonders (Figure 5). The production of these wares began in 1815, almost immediately after the reestablishment of trade with the United States, and showed a rapid increase in production, peaking in 1831 (Figure 6). As with British views on ceramics, published prints were used as the primary source materials. In some cases, the potters sent engravers or artists to America to document the latest architecture and monuments. In 1818, for example, William Wall sent English potter Andrew Stevenson sketches of some of America's most important buildings (Gurujal 1988:16). Engraver William Birch moved from England to Philadelphia in 1794, where he published *Views of Philadelphia and Country Seats*

in the United States (Bloom 1988:36). Ellouise Larsen's research has turned up almost 800 American scenic and historical views (Larsen 1975[1950]). The sheer quantity of American views recorded to date suggests that they were popular, but, like the British views category, their production was essentially brought to an end by the 1842 Copyright Act. Analysis shows that the production of British and American views, although already on the decline, does taper off considerably after 1842 and ceases completely by the mid-1850s.

Distinguishing between British and American views, particularly at the sherd level, may be difficult. In general, both British and American views show a high degree of skill and detail in engraving, with the finished vessels displaying an almost watercolor-like appearance. While it does appear that many of the American views produced and exported to the United States—and disproportionately recorded in this survey due to the attention they have been given by scholars and collectors—were printed in dark blue, they were also available in other colors, such as light blue, brown, black, purple, and pink. In general, the copper plates produced for these other colors do not appear to have been engraved with the

FIGURE 9. The Palestine pattern (William Adams, 1769–present) is an example of a composite exotic view. (Photo by P. Samford; courtesy of George L. Miller.)

FIGURE 10. Patterns with classical motifs, such as Canova (Thomas Mayer, ca. 1826–1838), contain columned temples, urns, and draped figures. (Photo by P. Samford; courtesy of George L. Miller.)

attention to detail and tonal gradations evident in the slightly earlier dark blue American views. Table 2 illustrates date ranges for various print colors on American views.

A smaller, but nonetheless important, category of American ceramics created by the Staffordshire potteries specifically for the American market included designs featuring military battles, heroes, and special events. One of the more popular subjects of these historical views was General Lafayette's triumphant return visit to the United States in 1824 (Larsen 1975[1950]:57). These patterns are generally well documented in secondary literature and can be dated fairly easily, but data suggest that the majority of American historical views were produced between 1826 and 1838.

Exotic Views

In the early 19th century, the expanding British colonization of India and other foreign countries sparked a great deal of interest in places outside Great Britain (Bloom 1988:33). For the wealthy, travel to exotic places was not difficult, and "The Grand Tour" of Europe was standard for young men (Coysh and Henrywood 1989:8). But for most Victorians, the cost of travel was prohibitive and the desire to learn about and experience foreign lands had to be satisfied through published travel diaries and books of engravings. As with American and British views, the Staffordshire potters took advantage of published illustrations of cities, monuments, and landscapes in places like India, the Middle East, and even the Arctic to provide them with subjects for their wares. For example, the Monopteros pattern (Figure 7) by John Rogers and Son (1815–1842) was based on a print entitled "Remains of an Ancient Building near Firoz Shah's Cotilla, Delhi" (Figure 8) taken from Thomas Daniell's *Oriental Scenery* (Coysh and Henrywood 1982:157). Additionally, some Staffordshire potters sent engravers to Italy, Greece, and India to produce drawings for pottery design (Bloom 1988:32).

The exotic views category encompasses all designs that contain motifs of foreign architec-

ture, ruins, and nonnative animals such as elephants or tigers. These scenes could either be based on published engravings of actual places, as was common before 1842, or could be more fanciful, romantic interpretations of exotic places. An example of a composite interpretation of an exotic view is the pattern entitled Palestine (Figure 9) by William Adams and Sons Ltd. (1769–present). The exotic buildings shown are well in the background, and the focus of the view is on the tent and eastern-garbed figures in the foreground. The scene portrayed is romanticized and lacks the distinct architectural detail present on views of actual foreign locales. The mean beginning and end dates for the production of exotic views were 1820 and 1842.

Classical

Archaeological excavations at the ancient cities of Herculaneum, Pompeii, and similar sites were one of the driving factors behind the Greek Revival style of the late 18th and early 19th centuries (Cooper 1993:10). Archaeological reports were used as source material by architects

FIGURE 11. The Messina pattern, by Edward Challinor (1853–1862), shows figures and water in the foreground and buildings typical of Romantic patterns in the background. (Photo by P. Samford; courtesy of George L. Miller.)

and designers, and the purity of line and form of ancient Greece and Rome began to replace the excesses of the baroque and rococo styles (Tracy 1963:12). Classical motifs were particularly embraced by Americans, with the use of these motifs in architecture and art perceived as a way for the new nation to join the ranks of great past civilizations (Bushman 1993:16). Appearing in America by the first decade of the 19th century, the classical style was dominant during the emergence of the new middle class, whose desire for fashionable objects helped spread the influence of classical motifs in the decorative arts (Cooper 1993:11; Bushman 1993:14). The taste for classical furnishings had begun to wane by the 1840s, and was replaced in popularity by Gothic Revival themes (Cooper 1993:12).

Since classical motifs permeated every aspect of the decorative arts, Staffordshire potters were not immune to the economic opportunities afforded by using these motifs. Many of their designs from this time period feature classical elements such as columned temples, urns, draped figures, and acanthus leaves. Prints of Greek and Roman ruins were often the inspiration for these designs (Bloom 1988:33). A well-known example of a classical motif is the Canova pattern (Figure 10). Antonio Canova (1757–1822), an Italian neoclassical sculptor, was popular in England. Legend has it that his heart was placed in a neoclassical urn after his death, and the Canova pattern prominently features just such an urn (Williams and Weber 1986:59; Coysh and Henrywood 1989:46). Classically-inspired motifs on English earthenwares enjoyed a brief period of popularity between 1827 and 1847.

Romantic

The 19th-century Romantic movement in England and Europe influenced music, art, literature, and even social and political thought (Meijer 1959:38). Stressing emotion and intuition over tradition and reason, the Romantic movement arose in opposition to the classical revival and in response to the increasing industrialization sweeping through England. Humans were seen as subordinate to the all-powerful but

FIGURE 12. The Girl at the Well (John Heath, 1809–1823) is representative of pastoral patterns. (Photo by P. Samford.)

benign forces of nature. One of the manifestations of this movement was evident in garden design. The formal, geometric gardens of the 17th and early 18th centuries began to be replaced by expansive parklands whose relaxed style evoked wilderness.

Given the interest in nature, it is perhaps not surprising that much of the decorative art associated with the Romantic movement contains depictions of the landscape. Landscape painting continued as a means of expression, and nature was a favorite subject for the newly developing field of photography (Millard 1977; Vaughan 1978). Certain picturesque elements were predominant in romantic imagery; mountains, waterfalls, trees, cottages, and castles evoked images that excited the Victorian imagination. Philosopher Friedrick von Schelling wrote in 1796 on viewing Heidelburg Castle, "The castle hovers above the town and dominates it completely, increasing the romanticism of this moment" (quoted in Sandkuhle 1970:66).

Ceramics printed with Romantic-style motifs typically follow a formula: they were generally bucolic scenes containing several elements (Coysh and Henrywood 1982:11). In the background were generally one or more stylized buildings, whose fanciful nature or lack of distinguishing architectural detail indicated that they were not depictions of actual buildings. In the mid-ground was usually a water source such as a river or lake, and the foreground contained small human figures or animals, generally placed there to provide a sense of scale. Nature in the form of trees, mountains, or wooded valleys completed the Romantic formula (Figure 11). Research has suggested that elements from different sources were combined in some Romantic views (Bloom 1988:34). Many of the names given to Romantic patterns bear little or no resemblance to the subject portrayed on the vessel, but were chosen instead to help boost sales (Coysh and Henrywood 1989:8). For example, the pattern Scinde began production after this part of India was annexed in 1845 (Coysh and Henrywood 1982:11). Camden, a geometric pattern produced by Ridgway, was inspired by Sir Charles Pratt, the first Earl of Camden. With a number of towns in the United States and several in Australia named Camden, Ridgway may have been banking on export sales for this pattern (Coysh and Henrywood 1989:46). Many patterns were named after European cities and

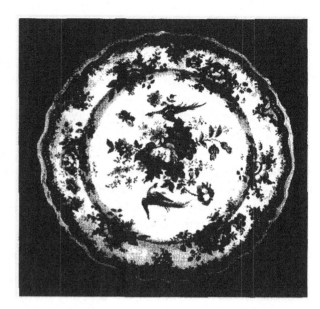

FIGURE 14. Asiatic Pheasants (Ralph Hall and Company 1822–1849) was one of the most commonly █████████████ patterns. Its border consists of a discontinuous repeating floral motif. (Photo by P. Samford; courtesy of George L. Miller.)

towns, like the Roselle—registered in 1848 by John Meir and Son—and the Geneva—Joseph Heath, 1845–1853—patterns (Coysh and Henrywood 1989:8). Romantic views, although remaining popular throughout the 19th century, were at their peak of highest production ca. 1831 to 1851.

Pastoral

Closely related to Romantic views were those which have been given the designation of pastoral. These views depicted generally rural-based scenes containing detailed views of farm animals, such as cows or horses, or persons engaged in working pursuits, such as milking cows, chopping wood, or drawing water from a well (Figure 12). In the pastoral category, the focus of the view was on the activities of the figures portrayed prominently and in detail in the foreground. Pastoral views were at their peak of production between 1819 and 1836.

Gothic Revival

FIGURE 13. The pattern Gothic Ruins by Davenport (ca. 1793–1887) is typical of Gothic motifs. (Photo by P. Samford.)

The Gothic Revival style, an offshoot of the Romantic period, began as a literary movement and gained popularity through the works of authors like Sir Walter Scott. Using the Middle Ages as inspiration, the Gothic Revival drew upon the design motifs depicted in medieval illuminated manuscripts and in archaeological publications that described Gothic medieval monuments (Vaughan 1978:127). In many ways a reaction against the severity and formality of classicism, the Gothic style reinterpreted many of the themes and motifs that had been predominant in the Middle Ages and stressed irregularity, drama, melancholy, and unity with nature. The year 1820 is given as the beginning of the Gothic Revival in England, and it flourished throughout the middle of the 19th century in England and America (Addison 1938:60; Howe and Warren 1976:5). The Gothic style influenced home and garden design—country homes with turrets, towers, and crenelated walls began to spring up in Britain and the United States, naturalistic garden landscaping became common, and gardens and estates were embellished with picturesque ruins. For example, Prospect Hill, an estate in Norwalk, Connecticut, was converted from a Greek Revival style to a Gothic style during the late 1840s (Howe and Warren 1977:91).

The Gothic Revival style enjoyed its greatest popularity in Britain, where it influenced design

FIGURE 16. The asymmetry of the Melbourne pattern by Gildea and Walker (1881–1885) is typical of Japanese-influenced motifs of the late 19th century. (Photo by P. Samford; courtesy of George L. Miller.)

between around 1820 and 1870 (Addison 1938:60, 94). It particularly appealed to the British, since they felt that this style, with its overtones of castles and medieval churches, was more in keeping with British national character than that of the classical style (Germann 1972:182). In mid-19th century Britain, many public and private buildings, especially churches, were constructed in the Gothic style. The publication of numerous design books, such as Pugin and Willson (1895[1821]) and Alexander Jackson Davis (1980[1838]), helped familiarize people with the Gothic style. Although the Gothic Revival began as a primarily literary movement, it permeated every aspect of the decorative arts, with Gothic motifs finding their way onto pottery, bottles, wallpaper, bird houses, and the like (Howe and Warren 1976:9). In the United States, the Gothic Revival style was at its most popular in the mid-19th century, from about 1840 to the outbreak of the Civil War (Davies 1976:5). Additionally, the Great Exposition of 1851 brought added exposure of the Gothic Revival style with the medieval exhibit held in the Crystal Palace (Addison 1938:85).

Given its popularity, it was inevitable that Gothic designs would find their way into the

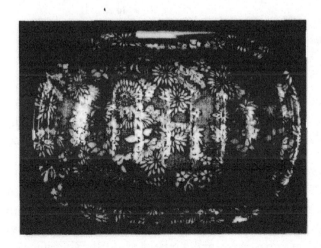

FIGURE 15. This 20th-century soapdish by an unknown maker displays a floral sheet pattern. On this example, the tissue paper used to transfer the inked design is still in place and is peeling away along the upper edge of the vessel. (Photo by George L. Miller.)

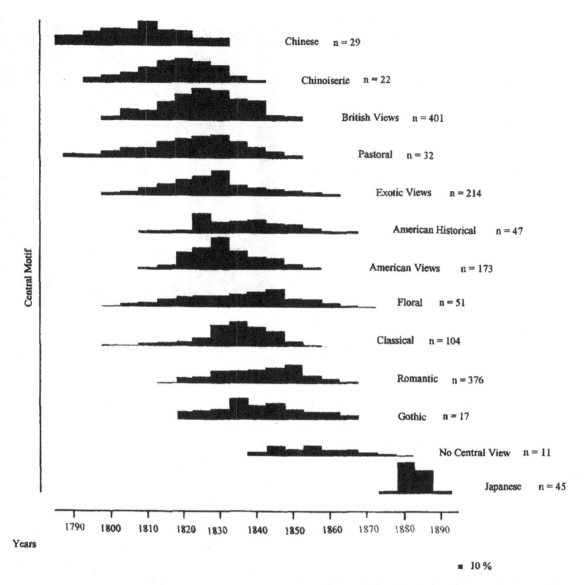

FIGURE 17. This graph illustrates the overlapping periods of production for central designs on printed wares. Bars represent percentage of total patterns produced during five-year intervals. (Illustration by Jane Eastman.)

engravings of the Staffordshire potters. From the mid-1830s through ca. 1860, Davenport of Longport (ca. 1793–1887) printed a series entitled "Scott's Illustrations," based on the novels of Sir Walter Scott. Another Gothic pattern, Fonthill Abbey, was inspired by the country estate of the same name, built between 1796 and 1799 for author William Beckford (Addison 1938:50). Structural flaws caused the house to collapse in 1825, and it subsequently and rather appropriately became the subject for a Gothic-style dinner service produced by James and Ralph Clews between 1818 and 1834 (Coysh and Henrywood 1982:144). This pattern was also produced by Enoch Wood (1818–1846) and Ralph Stevenson (ca. 1810–1832).

Gothic Revival patterns on Staffordshire earthenwares are characterized by depictions of church and other building ruins, structures with architectural details such as arches, turrets, towers, bastions, and crenelated walls (Figure 13). Gothic designs were most commonly produced on pottery after the more composite Romantic views began to decline in production, with peak

TABLE 3
CHARACTERISTIC MOTIFS ON CENTRAL DESIGNS

Central Designs	Motifs
Chinese/Chinoiserie	1. Pagodas/temples 2. Willow trees 3. Junks/sampans 4. Orange trees 5. Figures in eastern garb 6. Chippendale fencing
American and British Views	1. Building or landscape feature displayed prominently with attention to specific detail.
American Historical	1. Detailed scenes of military battles, or special events, such as treaty signings, and war ships. 2. State seals or coats of arms bearing U.S. state names.
Exotic Views	1. Animals not indigenous to America or the British Isles, such as camels, tigers, and elephants. 2. Exotic architecture, such as mosques, minarets, etc. 3. Figures in foreign garb.
Romantic	1. Small figures in foreground, strolling, fishing, etc. 2. Water source such as river or pond in mid-ground. 3. Fanciful building in background. 4. Gazebos or pavilions in foreground.
Classical	1. Urns 2. Acanthus leaves 3. Columned temples 4. Figures in classical garb 5. Greek key elements
Floral	1. Central Floral—group of flowers located in center of plate or vessel, usually surrounded by unengraved (white) area. 2. Sheet Floral—a small repeating pattern, usually of flowers, across the entire surface of the vessel.
Pastoral	1. Rural-based scenes with focus on animals or people working.
Gothic	1. Architectural ruins. 2. Buildings with turrets, arches, towers, or battlements.
Japanese	1. Prunus branches 2. Fans 3. Asymmetrical designs, often on ivory-dyed ceramic body 4. Birds/plants 5. In-filled half circles

TABLE 4
DATE RANGES FOR
MARLEY DESIGNS ON PRINTED WARES

Marley Type	N	Mean Beginning and End Production Dates		Range of Production
Continuation				
Main Scene	38	1815	1837	1784–1903
Continuous Repeating:				
Floral	858	1820	1836	1784–1856
Geometric	105	1818	1829	1784–1864
Other	164	1825	1848	1784–1910
Linear	44	1842	1858	1820–1891
Noncontinuous Repeating:				
Floral	121	1829	1843	1799–1894
Vignettes:				
Floral	49	1832	1848	1802–1889
Scene	132	1832	1847	1790–1889
Object	27	1838	1849	1809–1889

years of manufacture between 1841 and 1852. Central Gothic designs are often accompanied by border motifs that contain scrolled or arched designs against a background of concentric circles or lines, as shown in Figure 19.

Floral

Floral motifs were popular transfer-print subjects for potters throughout the course of the 19th century. Temporal differences were apparent, however. The most prevalent floral designs had a central floral motif, generally accented with a floral printed marley or border (Figure 14). The peak years of production for central floral patterns were 1833–1849. Another type of floral pattern is that with an overall repeating design, known as a sheet pattern (Figure 15). These were most commonly produced between 1826 and 1842.

FIGURE 18. This unmarked classical pattern with a vignette border, was imported to the United States by the Davenport Brothers of New York. (Photo by P. Samford; courtesy of George L. Miller.)

Japanese Aesthetic

The opening of trade with Japan to the west in the mid-19th century sparked the popularity of Japanese-style designs in British decorative arts that occurred in the 1870s and 1880s (Pickford 1983:153). Intrigued by the perceived romanticism and exoticism of Japan, westerners began purchasing Japanese prints, fabrics, and lacquer (Meech 1989:19). British manufacturers, inspired by the exhibits displayed at the 1862 International Exhibition, saw the monetary potential of "Japonisme" or the "taste for things Japanese" and began to produce a number of household and decorative items in this style (Sato and Watanabe 1991:14, 127). Japanese-inspired designs formed one component of the aesthetic movement, where decorative emphasis was on asymmetry and imagery that combined birds and butterflies with exotic flowering plants (Bosomworth 1991:8). Many of the Japanese-inspired earthenwares are printed in brown, black, red, or green on ivory-dyed ceramic bodies. Common design motifs on Japanese aesthetic vessels are fans, half circles filled with decorative patterns, prunus blossoms, bamboo, birds, and butterflies in asymmetrical collage-like effects (Figure 16).

Summary

In summary, the data from marked vessels support temporal patterning of central designs on printed wares. Each of the central motifs exhibited a peak range of production that generally spanned about 20 years. Designs based on Chinese porcelains were the earliest motifs to appear on Staffordshire earthenwares, followed by anglicized variations of these designs. Blue printing on a white background, in imitation of Chinese porcelain, was standard for these early Chinese-influenced patterns. As technological advances occurred that allowed greater detail in engraving and a wider range of colors to be produced, potters began to broaden the range of designs. These motifs can be readily related to major decorative trends occurring in England and the United States during the 19th century (Table 3). Scenes depicting places in North America and

FIGURE 19. The Venus pattern, by Podmore, Walker, and Company (1834–1859), has a border with a continuous repeating linear pattern. (Photograph by P. Samford; collection of the author.)

Britain were also among the earliest designs used by the potteries; these gave way to fanciful Romantic, Pastoral, and Gothic scenes after the Copyright Act of 1842 made it illegal to use published prints as sources for the engravers. Classical designs enjoyed a brief span of popularity coinciding with the Greek Revival in the United States. Japanese-inspired designs were popular after Japan was opened to the West toward the end of the 19th century. Figure 17 illustrates the overlapping periods of production for each of the different central motifs. The graph for each motif type shows what percentage of the total number of patterns, in the study sample, were in production at different times. For example, of the 214 different exotic views patterns in production between 1793 and 1868, a total of 133, or 67 percent, of the patterns were being produced in 1830. Some of the graphs show short, sharp peaks of production for motifs, such as Japanese-inspired designs, while others show slower, longer periods of production.

Borders on Printed Wares

Another key to dating printed wares lies within the border, or marley, designs that served as a frame around the central decorative element on many vessel forms. Inspiration for border design appears to have been drawn from many sources, including lace and wallpaper (Coysh 1970:7; Postlewait 1988:21). While some borders were distinctive to one particular manufacturer, popular patterns were often imitated, and potter attribution based on border style can be dangerous (Postlewait 1988:20). Marley designs, however, do fall into several easily characterizable categories with distinct production periods (Table 4).

Continuation of Main Scene

These rather uncommon transfer-print treatments are found on plates, dishes, and other flat vessel forms and are distinct in that there is no separate border motif (Figure 7). The central design continues to the rim of the flatware vessel, although the border area is often "framed" with a tree or other vegetation which is part of the main design. This treatment appears to have been restricted to British, American, and exotic views. Enoch Wood and Sons used this treatment in their Italian Scenery series, as did James

and Ralph Clews in their Foliage and Scroll Border series. This border treatment is most common on vessels produced between 1815 and 1837, corresponding well with the dates for these American, British, and exotic views.

Geometric

Geometric borders are those whose primary elements consist of unbroken, repeating patterns of lozenges, honeycombs, butterflies, Joo-I, and key motifs (Figures 3, 4). These designs are found most typically in conjunction with Chinese and chinoiserie central motifs and have a peak range of production between 1818 and 1829.

Floral

Floral borders fall most readily into two types: those with continuous repeating motifs whose patterns run unbroken around the marley (Figure 5), and those whose floral motifs are broken by unprinted white areas or areas with a light or airy background pattern (Figure 14). The marleys with noncontinuous floral motifs were most commonly produced between 1829 and

TABLE 5
DATE RANGES FOR COLOR ON PRINTED WARES

Color	N	Mean Beginning and End Production Dates		Range of Production
Dark blue	122	1819	1835	1802–1846
Medium blue	120	1817	1834	1784–1859
Black	49	1825	1838	1785–1864
Brown	69	1829	1843	1818–1869
Light blue	89	1833	1848	1818–1867
Green	21	1830	1846	1818–1859
Red	20	1829	1842	1818–1880
Purple	56	1827	1838	1814–1867
Lavender	13	1830	1846	1818–1871
Mulberry	29	1837	1852	1818–1870
Pink	52	1827	1842	1784–1864
Two color printing	18	1831	1846	1818–1866
Brown on ivory body	24	1881	1888	1873–1895
Black on ivory body	26	1883	1889	1879–1890

1843. Those with boldly printed, unbroken floral borders date somewhat earlier, with peak production occurring between 1820 and 1836.

Vignettes or Reserves

In the 1830s and 1840s, marley designs incorporating small oval or oblong cartouches enclosing a variety of designs became popular (Figure 18). These vignettes, usually found in conjunction with floral elements, were often printed on white granite bodies (Teresita Majewski 1996, pers. comm.). Floral vignettes were most often produced between 1832 and 1848. Vignettes containing objects such as musical instruments or statuary were common between 1838 and 1849, and those with scenes or landscapes had a peak production range of 1832 to 1847.

Linear

During the later decades of printed ware popularity, a border treatment that has been designated as a continuous repeating linear element was common. With a period of peak production ranging from 1842 to 1858, this border treatment consisted of closely spaced concentric lines running around the rim of the marley. These concentric lines served as a background for discontinuous floral or scroll marley motifs (Figure 19).

Summary

In summary, while there are not as many distinct marley motifs as there are central design motifs, several recognizable themes occur which show temporal patterning. Specific types of marley decoration appear to be related to central motif: Chinese and chinoiserie central motifs usually have geometric repeating borders; continuous floral motifs are typical of American, British, and exotic views, as is the less common treatment where there is no distinct border. Later central motifs, such as Romantic, pastoral, Gothic, and floral, are usually characterized by

FIGURE 20. This plate, depicting the pattern Ulysses Weeps at the Song of Demodocus, by Joseph Clementson (1839–1864) is an example of a negative pattern. It is part of the Classical Antiquities Series, and was registered on 13 March 1849. (Photo by P. Samford; courtesy of George L. Miller.)

noncontinuous floral marleys, or those with floral and vignette elements.

Colors on Printed Wares

Underglaze printed vessels produced at the end of the 18th century and into the first several decades of the following century were primarily blue in color. At that time, cobalt was the only coloring agent that could withstand the high heat of the glost oven without excessive blurring (Coysh 1970:7). Blue was undoubtedly the most popular color for printed decoration on English earthenwares; in addition to the dark blue typical of the early period of transfer wares, a variety of lighter shades was also common.

As technology improved and glazes became clearer, other colors began to be developed successfully for underglaze printing. Various combinations of metallic oxides produced different colors; for example, a mixture of manganese, copper, and cobalt produced a black printed transfer (Williams 1975:131). Simeon Shaw wrote:

Very recently several of the most eminent Manufacturers have introduced a method of ornamenting Table and Dessert Services, similarly to Tea Services, by the Black Printers using red, brown and green colours, for beautiful designs of flowers and landscapes; on Pottery greatly improved in quality, and shapes formed with additional taste and elegance. This pottery has a rich and delicate appearance, and owing to the Blue Printed having become so common, the other is now obtaining a decided preference in most genteel circles (Shaw 1900[1829]:234–235).

Consumers could purchase matching dinner, tea, or toilet sets in an assortment of colors. In August of 1833, Philadelphia merchants S. & T. Tams purchased from potters Job and John Jackson table, tea, and toiletwares of the pattern "Clyde Scenery" in purple, pink, brown, and blue (U.S. Customs House Papers 1790–1869). The following year, the same pottery firm shipped "Clyde Scenery" printed in green to the United States (Downs Collection Bill of Lading).

Black appears to have been among the first successful colors other than blue, but was followed by various shades of brown, purple, green, red, and lavender. The color brown was used in printing prior to 1829, but it became more common in the 1830s (Miller 1984:44). The peak periods of production for green, red, and brown wares confirmed the mean beginning date of

1829 (Table 5). Red was one of the more difficult colors to produce successfully (Williams 1975:133). For the purposes of this analysis, dark red or maroon printed vessels have been included with the "red" category, while a distinction was made between purple wares and those more of a mulberry, or brownish purple, color. Appendix A lists the Munsell color values used for each color designation in this study (Munsell 1929).

Printing in two or more colors was introduced around 1840 (Honey 1952:622–623). Generally, the central design of a vessel would be depicted in one color, and the border in a contrasting color. The production of these vessels could involve two different copper plates, one for each ink color, or a single copper plate where different colored oils were applied to different parts of the engraved design (Halfpenny 1994c:69–70). When multicolored prints were first produced, multiple firings, one for each color, were required (Majewski and O'Brien 1987:143). By 1848, however, blue, red, and yellow could be fixed in a single firing. Four years later potters could also fix brown and green colors at the same time (Hughes and Hughes 1968:54). The most commonly appearing color combination in the study's database was red and green.

Some printed wares display a type of polychrome decoration known as clobbering, consisting of colored enamels—pinks, greens, yellows, reds—hand-applied as highlights over the final lead glazing (Coysh and Henrywood 1982:87). Clobbering is generally restricted to small areas along the rim or marley of the vessel and is a technique quite distinct from one practiced somewhat later in the century of printing a design with larger areas intended to be filled with enamels. Clobbering used as a decorative technique most commonly appears on vessels manufactured after 1840.

Other Printing Techniques

Engraving technology, field dots, negative printing, and flown colors are other technologies, addressed briefly below.

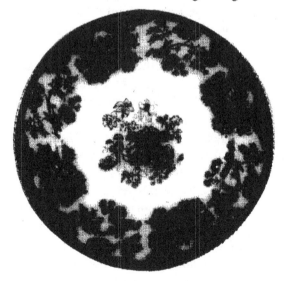

FIGURE 21. Persian Rose, a flow pattern by W. Baker and Company (1839–1932), shows the soft blurring typical of the flow process. (Photo by George L. Miller.)

TABLE 6
DATE RANGES FOR ENGRAVING ELEMENTS ON PRINTED WARES

Technique	N	Mean Beginning and End Production Dates		Range of Production
Line Engraving	13	1797	1812	1785–1833
Field Dots	34	1816	1841	1790–1853
Negative Print	13	1821	1840	1802–1864

Engraving Technology

Improvements in the materials used in the engraving process changed the look of printed wares in the first decade of the 19th century. During the first several decades of printing as a decorative technique, the tissue paper used for transferring the inked design to the bisque-fired vessel was coarse and thick. Due to poor paper quality, engraving of the copper plates had to be rendered in thick lines to enable the paper to absorb the ink and resulted in finished wares (Figure 3) with little or no tonal value (Whiter 1970:142). After the 1803 invention of the Fourdrinier paper machine, capable of producing finer quality tissue, artists employed by the potteries enjoyed more freedom in engraving techniques. Line engraving could be combined with stippling to allow fine tone gradations in color and three-dimensional shading of the entire surface (Figure 5). The use of combined line and stipple engraving began around 1807, with ceramic vessels showing a mastery of the technique by the end of the first decade of the century (Coysh and Henrywood 1982:9). Vessels in the study sample with simple line engraving showed a peak production range between 1797 and 1812 (Table 6). The use of line and stipple

TABLE 7
DATE RANGES FOR FLOWN COLORS ON PRINTED WARES

Type	N	Mean Beginning and End Production Dates		Range of Production
Flow Blue				
Chinoiserie landscape	38	1841	1854	1828–1867
Romantic	15	1849	1863	1830–1920
Chinoiserie floral	10	1839	1856	1834–1887
Central floral	17	1890	1904	1862–1929
No central design	18	1891	1908	1878–1920
Flow Mulberry	25	1840	1858	1828–1867

combination engraving continued throughout the remainder of the period of printed ware popularity.

Field Dots

With this decorative element, the marley design is printed on a background, or field, of small white dots against the colored ground. Of the examples used in this study, 88 percent (30 out of 34) were on vessels with British or American views as their central motif. The use of field dots was typical of the firms of Enoch Wood and Sons (1818–1846), Ralph Stevenson (1810–1832), and Andrew Stevenson (1816–1830).

Negative Print

This category includes vessels which have been printed "in reverse" to typical vessels. For example, the background of the vessel will be blue and the design elements will appear in white (Figure 20). This treatment appears to have been uncommon, and the sample size from this study was quite small (N = 13). The period of peak production for these vessels was 1821 to 1840.

Flow Blue and Other Flown Wares

In the early 1830s, a new process for decorating ceramics was introduced by the Staffordshire potters (Williams 1984). It was not until the 1840s, however, that flown decorated wares were available in any quantity in the U.S. market (Collard 1967:118; Miller 1991:9) Believed to produce a softer visual effect than the mechanical look of the standard underglaze printing technique, flown colors on earthenwares were achieved by placing a cup with a volatizing solution, such as lime or chloride of ammonia, in the saggars during the glaze firing of traditionally printed wares. These chemicals caused the printed color to flow outside the original pattern lines and produce a soft, halo-like effect (Williams 1984). While a misty or cloudy effect was produced in lighter colored pieces, designs in some of the more heavily printed or darker flown pieces were almost completely obscured from view.

The popularity of flown wares was enormous and long-lived, with production continuing from the early 19th century well into the 20th century. There seem to have been two periods of popularity for flow blue ceramics, one period falling in the mid-19th century (1840s and 1850s) and the other at the end of the same century (ca. 1890–1904). Several distinctive stylistic motifs occur within each of these periods (Table 7). Earlier patterns tended to have chinoiserie themes, with landscapes most common between 1841 and 1854. Chinoiserie florals—peonies, chrysanthemums, lotus blossoms, and butterflies were typical elements—were at their peak range of production between 1839 and 1856. Designs with a romantic theme were popular slightly later, and were more typically produced between 1849 and 1863. At the end of the 19th century, floral designs predominated (Figure 21). They consisted of either small central non-chinoiserie flowers with a corresponding floral marley, or vessels decorated only with a border and no central motif. The period of highest popularity for these later central floral patterns fell between 1875 and 1886. Vessels with no central motif, but with a marley design in flown colors, were most popular between 1891 and 1908. The marley designs on flow decorated vessels of all types were generally discontinuous repeating floral patterns.

Although blue was by far the most popular color for flown decorated wares, vessels were printed in mulberry (also called puce), brown, black, and green (Collard 1967:118). Blue remained a popular color throughout the period of flow production, while the manufacture of mulberry-colored vessels was much more temporally restricted. The period of heaviest production of mulberry-printed flow vessels fell between 1841 and 1858. Not enough data were collected on other flow colors to establish date ranges. The use of gold gilt as a decorative element on flown wares began in the 1860s (Mason 1982:9).

Conclusions

In a segment of *Eliza Cook's Journal*, entitled "The New Crockery Shop," Cook addressed the role of printed ceramics in the middle-class household:

> Poussins may arise; Claudes may paint their glorious landscapes; Raphaels their divine countenances; but pictures such as these are not always accessible; and even when accessible, not always intelligible to mental faculties, wholly or partially uneducated. But a well-shaped jug, or cup with a hanging bunch of flowers, or pastoral landscapes on them, in these our days of cheap and cheapening art, in relation to domestic life, can go every where; and the germ of many a great intelligence will be fostered, by thus placing the true foundation of progressive art in ALL the forms which minister to the conveniences of every-day life. The vital impulse necessary to artistic love and artistic excellence may be given to the child by the figure on his dinner-plate. . . .Neat tea services have likewise led to many a well scrubbed table, a cleaner hearth, a cheerfuller fireside. . . .and such sound comforts as lead men and women from the gin shops (Cook 1849:37–38).

While certainly not all purchasers of printed wares would have endowed their crockery with the significance that Eliza Cook did, the proliferation of motifs and individual patterns on printed earthenwares attests to their popularity. Not immune to the desires of consumers, Staffordshire potters tried a variety of decorative techniques to attract new markets and stimulate purchases of their wares. The design motifs that they chose to use reflected the larger decorative trends of the day, and, as this study illustrates, their manufacture dates closely paralleled them. As seen earlier in Simeon Shaw's 1829 quotation, new colors were developed because blue printed wares had become so commonplace they no longer attracted a genteel clientele. As the market among the wealthy for printed wares became saturated toward the end of the first quarter of the 19th century, the potters, desirous of appealing to the middle classes, cut the cost of printed wares by decreasing the size and amount of detail in the engravings. The soft, watercolor-like effect typical of American, British, and early exotic views gave way to smaller and more two-dimensional prints. By the end of

the 1850s, production of printed wares was tapering off as molded white granite and other minimally decorated wares were becoming more popular. The introduction of decals as a means of decorating ceramics beginning in the late 19th century may have also played a role in the decline of printed decoration (Majewski and O'Brien 1987:147; Majewski 1996, pers. comm.). Underglaze printing did continue, but by the end of the 19th century, the most common printed designs in the study sample were floral or geometric border designs surrounding an undecorated central area.

Researchers using this dating tool should keep in mind that the dates provided in this paper are dates of peak production for specific motifs, colors, or engraving techniques. Ceramics found in archaeological contexts will have a use-span which will need to be considered during analysis. Future research could address the question of how production date ranges correlate with date ranges for use of ceramic items.

Additional studies on printed wares could include linking vessel form with design motifs and other decorative attributes to see if a time lag exists between the appearance of motif types on teawares, and other costly, high-status vessel forms, and those of humbler ceramics, such as chamberpots, basins, and ewers. Additionally, larger sample sizes for some categories used in this study, particularly print colors, could help confirm or refine the date ranges shown here. In addition, dates from this study, used in conjunction with archaeological data on well-documented sites could help determine whether motif and color preferences exist regionally or socioeconomically. Work in Texas (Pollan et. al. 1996), Alaska (Jackson 1991), California (Felton and Schulz 1983), and the Pacific Northwest (Chapman 1993) would be good comparisons for sites excavated east of the Mississippi.

Using the results of this study, it is possible to look at central design motifs and other decorative and technological details on printed wares and date them with greater accuracy than previously possible. Although archaeologists may not find a large enough portion of a vessel to determine the central motif, the elements listed in

Table 4 are useful for picking out likely elements in these motifs. Fortunately, marley designs and vessel color are much easier to assign based on small sherds. Using the dating tools given here, either singly or in combination, should provide another means by which late 18th- and 19th-century sites can be dated.

ACKNOWLEDGMENTS

I would like to thank the reviewers, who, to my great delight, decided to waive their anonymity when sending their comments. They were Meta Janowitz, Teresita Majewski, and George L. Miller. Their careful editing and greater knowledge of English ceramics caught my mistakes and helped me flesh out the paper in more than one area. Any errors, however, are entirely my responsibility. I also would like to acknowledge the generous support of the Henry Francis DuPont Winterthur Museum, for providing me with a research fellowship that allowed me time to gather additional data and write up the results of this research. The staff of the museum was supportive in every way. I would like in particular to thank Ann Smart Martin, Patricia Elliott, Amanda Lange, Eleanor Thompson, Mary Elise Haug, Iris Snyder, Gail Stanislaw, Mary Alice Cicerale, Bert and Ellen Denker, and Kate Hutchins. I would also like to thank the staff of the Smithsonian Museum of American History, who allowed me the opportunity to use the catalog files of the Larsen collection; and the departments of Collections and Archaeological Research at the Colonial Williamsburg Foundation for access to their collections of printed earthenwares. George L. Miller, Ann Smart Martin, and Robert Hunter shared their private collections for cataloging; I am also in their debt. Thanks go as well to Jane Eastman, Vincas P. Steponaitis, and Amy Earls. R. P. Stephen Davis, Patrick Livingood, and Tom Maher, all of the Research Laboratories of Anthropology at the University of North Carolina, and David Muraca at the Colonial Williamsburg Foundation, fielded computer questions for me. Last, but far from least, I am grateful to George L. Miller, who was the driving force behind this project in all of its phases. His inspiration, support, and, at times, less than gentle pushing have ensured that the results of this research are available.

REFERENCES

ADDISON, AGNES
1938 *Romanticism and the Gothic Revival.* Richard R. Smith, NY.

BAKER, VERNON G.
1978 Historical Archaeology at Black Lucy's Garden, Andover, Massachussetts: Ceramics from the Site of a Nineteenth-Century Afro-American. *Papers of the Robert S. Peabody Foundation for Archaeology*, Vol. 8. Phillips Academy, Andover, MA.

BLOOM, LINDA S.
1988 Exotic Scenes. In *At Home and Abroad in Staffordshire*, pp. 32–34. University of Illinois, Champaign.

BOSOMWORTH, DOROTHY
1991 *The Victorian Catalogue of Household Goods.* Portland House, NY.

BUSHMAN, RICHARD
1993 Popular Culture and Popular Taste in Classical America. Introduction. *Classical Taste in America 1800–1840*, by Wendy A. Cooper, pp. 14–23. Abbeville Press, NY.

CAMEHL, ADA WALKER
1948 *The Blue-China Book: Early American Scenes and History Pictured in the Pottery of the Time.* Reprint of 1916 edition. Tudor, NY.

CHAPMAN, JUDITH SAUNDERS
1993 French Prairie Ceramics: The Harriet D. Munnick Archaeological Collection, ca. 1820–1860: A Catalog and Northwest Comparative Guide. *Anthropology Northwest* 8. Department of Anthropology, Oregon State University, Corvallis.

CLARKE, DAVID
1968 *Analytical Archaeology.* Methuen, London.

COLLARD, ELIZABETH
1967 *Nineteenth-Century Pottery and Porcelain in Canada.* McGill University Press, Montreal, PQ.

COOK, ELIZA
1849 The New Crockery Shop. *Eliza Cook's Journal*, pp. 20–25, 36–38. John Owen Clarke, London.

COOPER, WENDY A.
1993 *Classical Taste in America, 1800–1840.* Abbeville Press, NY.

COPELAND, ROBERT
1980 *Spode's Willow Pattern and Other Designs After the Chinese.* Rizzoli, NY.
1982 *Blue and White Transfer Printed Pottery.* C. I. Thomas and Sons, Haverfordwest.

COYSH, A. WILLIAM
1970 *Blue and White Transfer Ware, 1780–1840.* Charles

E. Tuttle, Rutland, VT.

1972   *Blue-Printed Earthenware, 1800–1850*. Charles E. Tuttle, Rutland, VT.

COYSH, A. WILLIAM, AND RICHARD K. HENRYWOOD
1982   *A Dictionary of Blue and White Printed Pottery, 1780–1880*, Vol. 1. Baron, Suffolk.
1989   *The Dictionary of Blue and White Printed Pottery, 1780–1880*, Vol. 2. Antique Collectors Club, Woodbridge, Suffolk.

COYSH, A. WILLIAM, AND FRANK STEFANO, JR.
1981   *Collecting Ceramic Landscapes; British and American Landscapes on Printed Pottery*. Lund Humphries, London.

DANIELL, THOMAS
1816   *Oriental Scenery: 150 Years of the Architecture, Antiques, and Landscape Scenery of Hindoostan*. Published by the author, London.

DAVIES, JANE B.
1976   Introduction. *The Gothic Revival Style in America, 1830–1870*, by Katherine S. Howe and David Warren, pp. 1–9. Museum of Fine Arts, Houston, TX.

DAVIS, ALEXANDER JACKSON
1980   *Rural Residence*. Reprint of 1838 edition. Da Capo Press, NY.

DES FONTAINES, UNA
1966   Ceramic Transfer-Printing Techniques, 1750–1850. *The Eleventh Wedgwood International Seminar*, pp. 100–103. Henry Ford Museum, Dearborn, MI.

DETHLEFSEN, EDWIN, AND JAMES DEETZ
1966   Death's Heads, Cherubs, and Willow Trees: Experimental Archaeology in Colonial Cemeteries. *American Antiquity* 31(4):502–510.

DRAKARD, DAVID, AND PAUL HOLDWAY
1983   *Spode Printed Ware*. Longman, NY.

EATWELL, ANN, AND ALEX WERNER
1991   A London Staffordshire Warehouse—1794–1825. *Journal of the Northern Ceramic Society* 8:91–124.

EWINS, NEIL M. D.
1990   *Staffordshire Ceramic Trade with North America, ca. 1780–1880*. Unpublished B.A. thesis, Staffordshire Polytechnic, Stoke.

FELTON, DAVID L., AND PETER D. SCHULZ
1983   The Diaz Collection: Material Culture and Social Change in Mid-Nineteenth-Century Monterey.

California Archaeological Reports 23. California Department of Parks and Recreation, Sacramento.

FENNELLY, CATHERINE
1967   *Something Blue: Some American Views on Staffordshire*. The Meriden Gravure, Meriden, CT.

GERMANN, GEORG
1972   *Gothic Revival in Europe and Britain: Sources, Influences, and Ideas*, translated by Gerald Onn. Lund Humphries, London.

GODDEN, GEOFFREY
1963   *British Pottery and Porcelain, 1780–1850*. Baker, London.
1964   *Encyclopaedia of British Pottery and Porcelain Marks*. Crown, NY.

GURUJAL, L. CHAVONNE HOYLE
1988   The Historical Development of the Staffordshire Transfer Ware Process. In *At Home and Abroad in Staffordshire*, pp. 12–17.   University of Illinois, Champaign.

HALFPENNY, PAT A.
1994a Bat Printing on 19th-Century Porcelain. In *Penny Plain, Twopence Coloured; Transfer Printing on English Ceramics, 1750–1850*, edited by Pat A. Halfpenny, pp. 45–58. Stoke-on-Trent City Museum and Art Gallery, Stoke.
1994b Underglaze Blue Printed Ware. In *Penny Plain, Twopence Coloured; Transfer Printing on English Ceramics, 1750–1850*, edited by Pat A. Halfpenny, pp. 61–68. Stoke-on-Trent City Museum and Art Gallery, Stoke.
1994c Colour and Multi-Colour Transfer-printed Pottery. In *Penny Plain, Twopence Coloured; Transfer Printing on English Ceramics, 1750–1850*, edited by Pat A. Halfpenny, pp. 69–74. Stoke-on-Trent City Museum and Art Gallery, Stoke.

HOLDWAY, PAUL
1986   Techniques of Transfer Printing on Cream Coloured Earthenware. In *Creamware and Pearlware*, edited by Terence A. Lockett and Pat A. Halfpenny, pp. 20–23. Print George Street Press, Stoke-on-Trent.

HONEY, W. B.
1952   *European Ceramic Art from the End of the Middle Ages to about 1815*. Faber and Faber, London.

HOWE, KATHERINE, AND DAVID B. WARREN
1976   *The Gothic Revival Style in America, 1830–1870*. Museum of Fine Arts, Houston, TX.

HUGHES, BERNARD, AND THERLE HUGHES
1968 *English Porcelain and Bone China, 1743–1850.* Frederick A. Praeger, NY.

IMPEY, OLIVER
1977 *Chinoiserie; The Impact of Oriental Styles on Western Art and Decoration.* Charles Scribner's Sons, NY.

JACKSON, LOUISE M.
1991 *Nineteenth-Century British Ceramics: A Key to Cultural Dynamics in Southwestern Alaska (Russian America).* Ph.D. dissertation, Department of Anthropology, University of California, Los Angeles. University Microfilms International, Ann Arbor, MI.

JACOBSON, DAWN
1993 *Chinoiserie.* Phaidon Press, London.

JARRY, MADELEINE
1981 *Chinoiserie; Chinese Influence on European Decorative Arts, 17th and 18th Centuries.* Vendome Press, NY.

KRANNERT ART MUSEUM
1988 *At Home and Abroad in Staffordshire.* Exhibit catalog. Krannert Art Museum, University of Illinois, Champaign.

KROEBER, ALFRED L., AND WILLIAM STRONG
1924 The Uhle Pottery Collections from Ica. *University of California Publications in American Archaeology and Ethnology* 21(3):95–133.

LAIDACKER, SAM
1938 *The Standard Catalogue of Anglo-American China from 1810 to 1850.* Sam Laidacker, Scranton, PA.
1951 *Anglo-American China, Part 2.* Sam Laidacker, Bristol, PA.

LARSEN, ELLOUISE BAKER
1975 *American Historical Views on Staffordshire China.* Reprint of 1950 edition. Doubleday, NY.

MAGUIRE, EUNICE D.
1988 What's in a Name? In *At Home and Abroad in Staffordshire*, pp. 2–10. Krannert Art Museum, University of Illinois, Champaign.

MAJEWSKI, TERESITA, AND MICHAEL J. O'BRIEN
1987 The Use and Misuse of Nineteenth-Century English and American Ceramics in Archaeological Analysis. *Advances in Archaeological Method and Theory* 11:97–207. Michael B. Schiffer, editor. Serial Publication Series. Academic Press, NY.

MARQUARDT, WILLIAM H.
1978 Advances in Archaeological Seriation. *Advances in Archaeological Method and Theory* 1:257–314.

Michael B. Schiffer, editor. Serial Publication Series. Academic Press, NY.

MASON, VENEITA
1982 *Popular Patterns of Flow Blue China with Prices.* Wallace-Homestead, Des Moines, IA.

MEECH, JULIA
1989 Japonisme at the Turn of the Century. In *Perspectives on Japonisme; The Japanese Influence on America*, edited by Phillip D. Cate, pp. 18–28. Rutgers University Press, New Brunswick, NJ.

MEIJER, E. R.
1959 On the Romantics and Their Times. In *The Romantic Movement; Fifth Exhibition to Celebrate the Tenth Anniversary of the Council of Europe*, pp. 38–43. Arts Council of Great Britain. Shenval Press, London.

MILLARD, CHARLES
1977 Images of Nature: A Photo-Essay. In *Nature and the Victorian Imagination*, edited by U. C. Knoepflmacher and G. B. Tennyson, pp. 3–26. University of California Press, Berkeley.

MILLER, GEORGE L.
1980 Classification and Economic Scaling of 19th-Century Ceramics. *Historical Archaeology* 14:1–40.
1984 George M. Coates, Pottery Merchant of Philadelphia, 1817–1831. *Winterthur Portfolio* 19(1):37–92.
1987 Origins of Josiah Wedgwood's "Pearlware." *Northeast Historical Archaeology* 16:83–95.
1991 A Revised Set of CC Index Values for Classification and Economic Scaling of English Ceramics from 1787 to 1880. *Historical Archaeology* 25(1):1–25.
1994 New York Earthenware Dealers and the Country Trade in the Nineteenth Century. Manuscript on file, University of Delaware Center for Archaeological Research, Newark.

MILLER, GEORGE L., AND SILAS D. HURRY
1983 Ceramic Supply in an Economically Isolated Frontier Community: Portage County of the Ohio Western Reserve, 1800–1825. *Historical Archaeology* 17(2):80–92.

MILLER, GEORGE L., ANN SMART MARTIN, AND NANCY S. DICKINSON
1994 Changing Consumption Patterns: English Ceramics and the American Market from 1770 to 1840. In *Everyday Life in the Early Republic*, edited by Catherine E. Hutchins, pp. 219–248. Winterthur Museum, Winterthur, DE.

MUNSELL COLOR COMPANY
1929 *Munsell Book of Color.* Baltimore, MD.

PETRIE, WILLIAM M. F.
1972 *Methods and Aims in Archaeology.* Reprint of 1904 edition. Benjamin Blom, NY.

PICKFORD, IAN
1983 *Silver Flatware: English, Irish, and Scottish, 1660–1980.* Baron, Woodbridge, Suffolk.

POLLAN, SANDRA D., W. SUE GROSS, AMY C. EARLS, JOHNNEY T. POLLAN, JR., AND JAMES L. SMITH
1996 *Nineteenth-Century Transfer-Printed Ceramics from the Townsite of Old Velasco (41BO125), Brazoria County, Texas: An Illustrated Catalogue.* Prewitt and Associates, Austin, TX.

POSTLEWAIT, DEBORAH S.
1988 Borders on Transfer Ware. In *At Home and Abroad in Staffordshire*, pp. 20–22. Krannert Art Museum, University of Illinois, Champaign.

PRICE, CYNTHIA
1979 Nineteenth-Century Ceramics in the Eastern Ozark Border Region. *Southwest Missouri State University Center for Archaeological Research Monograph Series* 1. Center for Archaeological Research. Springfield, MO.

PUGIN, A. W., AND E. J. WILLSON
1895 *Specimens of Gothic Architecture.* Reprint of 1821 edition. John Grant, Edinburgh.

SANDKUHLE, H. J.
1970 *F. W. J. Schelling.* Stuttgart.

SATA, TOMOKO, AND TOSHIO WATANABE
1991 The Aesthetic Dialogue Examined. In *Japan and Britain; An Aesthetic Dialogue, 1850–1930*, edited by Tomoko Sato and Toshio Watanabe, pp. 14–17. Lund Humphries, London.

SHAW, SIMEON
1900 *History of the Staffordshire Potteries.* Hanley. Reprint of 1829 edition. Scott and Greenwood, London.

SPIER, LESLIE
1917 An Outline for a Chronology of Zuni Ruins. *Anthropological Papers of the American Museum of Natural History* 18 (part 3). American Museum of Natural History, NY.

SUSSMAN, LYNNE
1979 Spode/Copeland Transfer-Printed Patterns Found at 20 Hudson's Bay Company Sites: Canadian Historic Sites. *Occasional Papers in Archaeology and History* 22. Parks, Canada, Ottawa, ON.

TRACY, BERRY
1963 *Classical America, 1815–1845.* Baker, Newark, NJ.

U.S. CUSTOMS HOUSE PAPERS
1790–1869 *United States Customs House Papers, Philadelphia, Pennsylvania.* University of Delaware, Newark. Microfilm.

VAUGHAN, WILLIAM
1978 *Romantic Art.* Oxford University Press, NY.

WALL, DIANA DIZEREGA
1994 *The Archaeology of Gender: Separating the Spheres in Urban America.* Plenum Press, NY.

WHITER, LEONARD
1970 *Spode: A History of the Family, Factory and Wares from 1733 to 1833.* Barrie and Jenkins, London.

WILLIAMS, PETRA
1971 *Flow Blue China: An Aid to Identification.* Fountain House East, Jeffersontown, KY.
1973 *Flow Blue China II.* Fountain House East, Jeffersontown, KY.
1975 *Flow Blue China and Mulberry Ware.* Fountain House East, Jeffersontown, KY.
1978 *Staffordshire Romantic Transfer Patterns: Cup Plates and Early Victorian China.* Fountain House East, Jeffersontown, KY.

WILLIAMS, PETRA, AND MARGUERITE R. WEBER
1986 *Staffordshire II; Romantic Transfer Patterns: Cup Plates and Early Victorian China.* Fountain House East, Jeffersontown, KY.

WILLIAMS, SUSAN R.
1984 Flow-Blue. *Antiques* 126(4):923–931.

PATRICIA M. SAMFORD
RESEARCH LABORATORIES OF ANTHROPOLOGY
UNIVERSITY OF NORTH CAROLINA
CHAPEL HILL, NC 27599-3120

Patricia Samford

APPENDIX A
MUNSELL COLOR DESIGNATIONS

Dark Blue			Red		
7.5 PB 2.5/10	7.5 PB 2.5/8	5 PB 3/8	10RP 3/10	10RP 4/12	
2.5 PB 3/7	7.5 PB 2/6				
			Maroon		
Medium Blue			7.5RP 3/6	7.5RP 3/8	2.5R 3/10
7.5 PB 3.5/12	2.5 PB 4/10		5R 2/8		
Light Blue			Mulberry		
7.5B 7/6	7.5B 9/4	2.5PB 8/6	5RP 3/4	5RP 2/4	5RP 2/6
2.5PB 7/8			5RP 2/8	2.5R 2/6	2.5R 2/4
Purple			Brown		
7.5P 5/8	7.5P 5/10	7.5P 4/6	2.5Y 4/4	2.5Y 3/4	2.5Y 3/2
5RP 3/6	7.5RP 2/2	10R 3/4	7.5YR 3/6	7.5YR 3/4	7.5YR 3/2
			7.5YR 2/4		
Lavender					
7.5P 7/8	7.5P 7/6	7.5P 6/8	Green		
7.5P 6/10			2.5BG 3/6	2.5BG 3/8	2.5BG 4/8
			2.5BG 4/6	2.5BG 3/4	5BG 4/8
Pink			10GY 3/6	10GY 4/8	7.5GY 3/6
5RP 6/8	5RP 7/8	5RP 6/10			
10RP 6/6					

The Historical Archaeology Laboratory Handbook

ROGER E. KELLY
MARSHA C. S. KELLY

Brick Bats for Archaeologists: Values of Pressed Brick Brands

ABSTRACT

Impressed names, letters, or symbols on construction bricks produced from the 1880s to the 1940s may be useful data for analytical or interpretive aspects of historical archaeology and sister disciplines. As an artifact having wide range of type, impressed "brands," geographical distribution, and cultural use, such bricks were manufactured by now-obsolete methods. Primary documentary sources for the identification of manufacturing companies, duration of specific "brands," and past distribution systems are industry publications, government documents, and business directories.

Introduction

Although based in antiquity, the high-volume production of cheap, industrially-made burned building bricks is only a little over a century old in North America. To be sure, hand manufacture of bricks was common during the 17th and 18th centuries in European colonies north of Mexico. Early patents for brick-making devices were issued during the late 18th Century, and by the 1860s numerous, high-volume, and reliable brick-making machines had been developed in the United States as well as in Western European counties (McKee 1973, Gurcke 1976). Many American, English, and French machines were illustrated and described in the pages of *Scientific American* during the 1860s and 1870s. In 1976, the Centennial Exposition at Philadelphia featured a wide variety of machines from Canada, England, and the United States. Each model illustrated a somewhat different process of changing prepared clay blends to solid, modular building units. At this time and later, two basic automated procedures were used (see Dezettel 1972: 11; Baker 1909: 34):

A. Clay, tempering materials, and water were mixed in a pug-mill, then extruded into a thick ribbon of "stiff mud" which was then cut into modular units, dried, and burned;

B. Clay blends were mixed with less water, then pressed into molds with sufficient force to form modular units which then could be burned or fired without long drying periods.

From the 1870s to post World War II years, brick manufacturing technology expanded as demands grew, clay deposits were located and exploited, and distribution systems were developed. As noted by McKee, "when brick-making became an industry, most cities had at least one brick plant (1973: 41)," indicating a great variety within the industry and particularly the need for identifying marks or "brands." By the early 20th century, the Hudson River Valley lead in production within the United States, furnishing up to 20% of that nation's brick from over 200 plants and yards (State of New York 1951, De Noyelles 1974. By World War I, midwestern states of Illinois, Indiana, and Ohio were equalling New York production rates, and California manufacturers were supplying Western states' markets (Richardson 1917: 257–59). Development of oil and gas recovery methods from Kansas City to Coffeyville, Kansas, highly influenced the establishment of a mid-continent brick industry from the 1890s to 1920 (Pfalser 1974:7). Brick production reached 12.8 billion units in 1925, but the depression and other factors had reduced production to less than 3 billion units in 1945 (Gunsallus and others 1946). After World War II changes in economics and technology, new building media and tastes, and higher transportation costs changed the brick industry in the United States from its pre-1940 directions.

To the archaeologist working in an historic site yielding bricks of pre-World War II periods, the products of the industry offer very considerable potential for anthropological archaeology and other interdisciplinary endeavors, especially in architectural history and industrial archaeology. At least four aspects need discussion:

Roger E. Kelly and Marsha C. S. Kelly

1. The types and sizes of bricks as manufactured;
2. The "brands" or identifying marks on bricks;
3. Historic and other sources useful in research; and
4. Potential analytical and interpretive uses of such data.

Brick Typology

Although a recent elaborate typology for English brick has been developed by L. S. Harley (1974), the writers do not propose a typological scheme for American bricks at this time; use of the terminology of the industry is accepted rather than attempting to impose an archaeological classification. Industrial typology classed bricks according to three characteristics—methods of molding or pressing, position in the kiln, and intended use (see Baker 1909: 35–37, Richardson 1917: 351–54). Here the interest is in machine-made "stiff mud" pressed brick and their "brands" although it is recognized that makers' marks are found on earlier "soft mud" bricks, both machine and hand-molded (Lazarus 1965). It has been noted by McKee recently that the term "pressed brick" is erroneously applied to bricks of uniform appearance, but in reality "some machines, even at an early date, moulded the clay at one stage of the operation and compressed it further at another stage (1976: 88)." The burning or firing process yields "body" or "hard" bricks which are well-fired and "soft" or "salmon" bricks which are underfired and are usually lighter in color. In construction use terminology, archaeologists are interested in "common brick" which are usually "body" or "salmon" bricks, "face brick" which are harder, colored in shades of red-brown, and hard "fire" or "refractory" bricks which are light yellow, cream, or tan. Archaeologists may find "pavers" or paving bricks in either thin square or blocky rectangular forms, the former were called "Roman" or "Norman" paving bricks, depending on the square dimensions.

The visable color differences of bricks results from the inclusion of iron oxides, silicates of lime, carbonates of lime, magnesia, alumina oxides, or alkalies in the clay blends (Turner 1950: 144). "Common" or "face" bricks are reddish-brown from the "common" clays used in manufacturing process. Paving bricks are also usually of this type. "Fire" bricks are lighter in shades of yellow or cream because of the higher alumina oxide or silica inclusions in the "fire," "china," or "ball" clays used (Turner 1950: 143).

The use of bricks in different construction features has provided a terminology of function. Face brick are those to be used in exterior surfaces while fire brick are employed in the construction of fireplces, incinerators, and other locations of high temperature. "Compass brick" were those having one long edge or side shorter than the opposite edge or side and were employed in shaft linings (Baker 1909: 37). "Feather-edge brick" were those having one short edge or end thinner than the opposite edge or end and were used in building arches (Baker 1909: 37). A half-standard brick made as a unit was called a "soap brick" by at least one major West Coast brick maker while a longitudinal portion of a standard brick was called a "split" by the same company (Gladding, McBean, and Company 1923).

Lastly, collectors use the "brand" as a name and refer to examples as "Alamo bricks" or use a symbol from the "brand" as in "sunflower bricks" (see Pfalser 1974: 8 and Figure 1). This taxonomy is sometimes merged with industry form names but often does not distinguish between color, function, kiln location or size.

Except for speciality forms, the modular brick size of 2 × 4 × 8 inches for a standard brick has been used since the 1880s when the National Brick-makers' Association (1887) and the National Traders and Builders' Association (1889) adopted 8¼ × 4 × 2¼ inches for common brick and 8⅜ × 4⅛ × 2¼ inches for face brick (Baker 1909: 46–47). But such standards were not legal during the turn-of-the-century and dimensions actually varied with the individual manufacturer or producer (Baker 1909: 46). Professional standards on international levels and local building codes now regulate size, strength, and grade of bricks manufactured. Foreign brick makers during the early 20th century also varied widely in basic size, often as much as three inches from American sizes (Baker 1909: 46). As William Lazarus (1965) and Stanley South (1964) have shown, size is an important attribute for observation, but size alone cannot be used for dating purposes even though some accuracy of ethnic identification is possible in some time periods. The typology of Harley includes categories based on attributes of method of manufacture, size, weight, color, and other characteristics to which numerical code values are assigned (1974). As with other fragmentary artifacts, it is possible to determine at least functional characteristics from brick bats, if not actual manufacturer and date, by observing color, size, and method of molding as well as a complete or partial "brand."

Brick "Brands"

During the decades from about 1870 to about 1950, many manufacturers stamped one or more of the surfaces of common, face, fire, and paving brick with a "brand" or empressed identification. The development of high production brick machines coincided with the use of "brands" since the name or logo of the company or its location could be pressed into the brick surface as part of the manufacturing process. But not every finished brick bore an impressed mark; in fact in some geographical regions, common or fire brick were usually impressed but paving brick were not, yet in the Kansas area, street and sidewalk paving brick were impressed but construction brick were not (see DeNoyelles 1972, 1974; Pfalser 1974). The marks, or "brands" as the industry termed the labels, were impressions made in the unburned brick by a metal imprint die attached to the rear or backing panel of brick molds. Such dies could be changed readily,

and many brick yards apparently used a variety of dies, depending on the type of bricks under production at a given time. Die makers usually cast simple dies, lettered or using a logo, but sometimes reverses in letters such as N or S gave the brick face an unusual appearance (Pfalser 1974: 30). Often the screws holding the die to the backing panel or the mold may be seen as faint marks (see LAPBCo brick in Figure 1).

The use of "brands" is said to have served three purposes: to save a small amount of raw material, to provide a better bond with mortar layers, and to advertize the maker's product by identifying it by distinctive names or initials (DeNoyelles 1974, Pfalser 1974). Sometimes the "brand" was enclosed within an indented rectangle ¼ to ½ inch deep (see PBY and LAPBCo bricks in Figure 1); such deep

FIGURE 1. Varieties of pressed brick "Brands." Length of "Zenith" brick in 8 inches.

indentations were thought to save additional raw materials (DeNoyelles 1978, pers. comm.). Usually, the "brand" was impressed into one of the two larger surfaces or "faces" of the bricks, but some Kansas manufacturers used end impressed "brands" for paving bricks (Pfalser 1974: 8)..

As may be seen in Figure 1, the actual placement and type of "brand" varys widely. Five types of impressions seem to occur frequently; these are:

1. Family names of plant owners such as BENNETT, ROSE, BROPHY or CARY (see DeNoyelles 1974);
2. Initials of Company names, including multiple family names as owners such as DFjr&Co for Denton Fowler, Jr. & Co. (De Noyelles 1972) or PBY for Phoenix Brick Yard (Figure 1);
3. Place names which identify location of the plant or yard such as GALLUP or ALAMO (see Figure 1). Sometimes both the town and the company name will be included as in CANEY BRICK CO. VITRIFIED CANEY KAS (Pfalser 1978: 8);
4. "Nicknames" or trade names such as ZENITH, TROJAN, KEYSTONE, or PREMIER (Figure 1);
5. Combinations of symbols or logo designs with letters as in the ABCO with cresent or the oval enclosure with GMB (Figure 1).

Lettering styles used were usually simple, block forms with or without serifs, arranged in straight or curving lines although words or letters may be enclosed by diamond or curvilinear scroll (Figure 1). Letters or symbols vary from 1 inch to 1½ inch high and were usually impressed only ¼ to ½ inch deep. At least once brick "brands" were used for nonindustry identification. In 1908, Dr. Samuel Crumbine, Kansas State Health Officer from 1902 to 1923, arranged for Kansas brick makers to imprint "DON'T SPIT ON THE SIDEWALK" on sidewalk paver bricks as an effort to reduce the spread of tuberculosis.

These bricks were made by several manufacturers in Kansas and now are prized collectors' items (Pfalser 1974: 31).

Research Sources

To an historical archaeologist working in either marine or terrestrial sites yielded branded bricks, the identification of a company of origin, city of manufacture, and duration of a specific mark or "brand" is of course valuable data, but determination of such facts may be laborious. To assemble a definitive list of "brands" and their meanings in time and space is a Herculean task since the stylistic practice was widespread in many regions. Fortunately, Daniel DeNoyelles has compiled such an inventory list for the Hudson River Valley from the 1830s to 1950 which should be very useful for bricks found in sites of Eastern States.

To compile such inventories for other regions, use of the following types of documentary sources would be helpful.

A. Local or state governmental documents from the bureaus of mines or official state mineralogists' office reports since clay mining and manufacturing or structural clay products are discussed in terms of company name, location, production rate, processes used, and dates of operation. Dietrich (1928), State of New York (1951).
B. Local commercial directories, telephone books, regional histories, and company catalogs held in historical libraries. Membership lists of chambers of commerce are useful also. Such familiar sources to historical archaeologists are usually accessible.
C. Industry publications which are periodicals (*Brickbuilder, American Architect, Brick and Clay Record,* or *Brick and Tile* are examples), textbooks and manuals (Baker 1909, Richardson 1917, Phillips and Byrne 1908, Dezettel 1972) or technical report (Gunsallus and others 1946). Karl Gurcke (1976) has compiled an excellent bibliography of such literature.

Although some historical archaeologists have described bricks and kilns or "clamps," particularly in sites within Eastern and Southeastern states, it is difficult to find an archaeological report containing identifications of branded bricks. A short report by Gillio and Scott (1971) describing a Denver area site is an exception. Architectural history and historic architecture literature such as Harley J. McKee's publications (1973, 1976) and articles by Carroll (1976) and Loth (1974) are useful to an understanding of historic periods of brick use. At least one useful article has appeared in a hobby or collectors' magazine (see Pfalser 1974).

Since regional and local variation of bricks and their "brands" is complex, individual collectors may be identified for consultation. The authors are cognizant that a network of collectors specialize in branded bricks as a hobby activity, and in 1975, advertizements in *Antiques* offered a Coffeyville, Kansas, brick for $4.95 postpaid. Daniel DeNoyelles maintains a large and extensive identified collection for New York areas while I. L. Pfalser and others possess collections from the Kansas-Oklahoma area. At least one organized collection exists in New Mexico.

Analytical Uses of Brick Data

As with other classes of common historic artifacts from excavations or other projects such as nails, bottles, ceramics, or metal objects, bricks, and their "brands" can be adapted for many research designs. Identifiable in fragmentary form and long-lasting, brick brands may illustrate economic networks between urban and rural areas of the region. As late as the mid-1940s, locally produced bricks were usually for a market area from 100 to 300 miles from a plant location, hence useful in a regional or areal research design (Gunsallus and others 1946: 8). Brick shipments and sales were usually in crates of 1000 by rail or truck and may be traced in company records (Gladding, McBean, and Company 1923). It may be possible to utilize

distribution histories in illustrating changes in networks and loci as well as chronological stability. Foreign trade may be indicated by the Canadian brick in Figure 1.

Since brick structures are both material and labor expensive, the social status of occupants or builders may be documented by testable hypotheses involving other artifact classes. Although re-use of bricks is an important capability which may lead to ambiguous interpretations of chronology, principles of field and dating observations as in dendrochronology or other artifact studies should be used to avoid errors due to recycling of bricks. Remodelling of structures by later inhabitants may be reflected in branded bricks and may reveal different cultural patterns for the use of space. Of course, brick "brands" may help date structural fabric or a deposit and building dates will help date the branded bricks in the absence of documentary records.

The manipulation of bricks into bonding systems which changes through time may also be important to both the historical archaeologist and the historic architect (McKee 1973: 48; Ferro 1976). Preservation methods and technology for in-place brick fabric may also be used for archaeological specimens which are sometimes friable or soft due to weathering. As horizon markers representing a period of industrial practice now obsolete, branded bricks will likely be encountered and utilized by historical archaeologists increasingly in the future. It is recommended that bricks and their "brands" be recorded and that compilation of manufacturers with years of production be accomplished on a local basis so that the full analytical potential of these artifacts be realized.

ACKNOWLEDGEMENTS

We appreciate the information gained from Daniel DeNoyelles (Thiells, New York), John P. Wilson (Las Cruces, New Mexico), Karl Gurcke (Moscow, Idaho), and Ann Howard (San Francisco, California). We are responsible for factual and interpretive statements. A preliminary version of this paper was read at the 1977 Society for Historic Archaeology meetings, Ottawa.

Roger E. Kelly and Marsha C. S. Kelly

REFERENCES

BAKER, IRA O.
1909 *A Treatise on Masonry Construction.* Wiley and Sons, New York.

CARROLL, ORVILLE W.
1976 Early Brick Laws in Massachusetts. *Association for Preservation Technology, Bulletin* 8: 20–23. Ottawa.

DeNOYELLES, DANIEL
1972 Charles Ellery Hall's *Story of Brick* (originally published in 1905 by the Building Trades Employees Association. New York). Privately reprinted. Thiells, New York.
1974 *Brick Brands and Manufacturers of the Hudson River and the Metropolitan New York City Market.* Privately printed. Thiells, New York.

DIETRICH, W. F.
1928 The Clay Resources and the Ceramic Industry of California. *Division of Mines, State of California.* Bulletin 99. Sacramento.

DEZETTEL, LOUIS M.
1972 *Masons and Builders Library* 2. Indianapolis.

FERRO, MAXIMILIAN L.
1976 *Evolution of Masonry Construction in American Architectural Styles.* ServiceMaster Industries, Inc. Downers Grove, Illinois.

GILLIO, DAVID AND DOUGLAS SCOTT
1971 Archeological Tests of the Forney Site, Denver, Colorado. *Colorado Anthropologist* 3(2): 24–34. Boulder.

GLADDING, McBEAN, AND COMPANY
1923 *Price List No. 50.* Los Angeles, San Francisco, and Oakland.

GUNSALLUS, BROOKE L. AND OTHERS
1946 Manufacturing Brick and Tile to Serve Your Community. *Industrial (Small Business) Series* 49. United States Department of Commerce. Washington.

GURCKE, KARL
1976 Notes Toward A Bibliography of Bricks. Department of Sociology/Anthropology. University of Idaho, Moscow.

HARLEY, L. S.
1974 A Typology of Brick with Numerical Coding of Brick Characteristics. *Journal of the British Archaeological Association,* 3d Series; 38: 63–87. London.

LAZARUS, WILLIAM C.
1965 A Study of Dated Bricks in the Vicinity of Pensacola, Fla. *Florida Anthropologist,* 18: 2, Part 2, pp. 69–84. Gainsville.

LOTH, CALDER
1974 Notes on the Evolution of Virginia Brickwork from the Seventeenth Century to the Late Nineteenth Century. *Association for Preservation Technology, Bulletin* 6: 82–119. Ottawa.

McKEE, HARLEY J.
1973 *Introduction to Early American Masonry, Stone, Brick, Mortar, and Plaster.* National Trust for Historic Preservation. Washington.
1976 Brick and Stone; Handicraft to Machine. In *Building Early America.* Edited by Charles E. Peterson, pp. 74–95. Chilton Book Company, Radnor, Pennsylvania.

PFALSER, I. L.
1974 Bricks of the Mid-Continent Room. *Relics* 7(5): 4–8, 30–31. Austin.

PHILLIPS, ALFRED E. AND AUSTIN T. BYRNE
1908 *Masonry Construction.* Chicago.

RICHARDSON, CHARLES H.
1917 *Building Stones and Clays: A Handbook for Architects and Engineers.* University of Syracuse, New York.

SOUTH, STANLEY
1964 Some Notes on Bricks. *Florida Anthropologist,* 17(2): 67–74. Gainsville.

STATE OF NEW YORK
1951 *The Clays and Shales of New York State.* Department of Commerce, State of New York, Albany.

TURNER, MORT D.
1950 Clays. In *Mineral Commodities of California,* edited by Lauren A. Wright, pp. 142–150. Bulletin 156, Division of Mines, State of California,
1951 Clay and the Ceramic Industry of the San Francisco Bay Counties. In *Geologic Guidebook of the San Francisco Bay Counties,* edited by Elisabeth L. Egenhoff and Oliver E. Bowen Jr., pp. 247–252. Bulletin 154, Division of Mines, State of California. San Francisco.

ROGER E. KELLY
NATIONAL PARK SERVICE
450 GOLDEN GATE AVENUE
SAN FRANCISCO, CALIFORNIA 94102

The Historical Archaeology Laboratory Handbook

The Analysis of Bricks from Archaeological Sites in Australia

IAIN STUART

In the context of renewed interest in artefact analysis in Australian historical archaeology, this paper discusses the methods and attributes that have been used to analyse bricks in the past, and concludes by suggesting a standard set of attributes for future analysis.

INTRODUCTION

The practice of historical archaeology in Australia in recent years has refocused on the analysis of material evidence, in particular on artefact analysis from large urban excavations. While precise reasons for this change are unclear, what has been evident is that the change has resulted in the examination of the results of large salvage excavations and a fundamental critique and review of archaeological practice in the area of artefact cataloguing and analysis (e.g. Crook et al. 2000). Two outcomes of this process of reflection have been the identification of the need for better methods of identifying and cataloguing material evidence and the need to develop the analytical potential of material evidence through 'mid-range' theory, which would enable questions posed in research designs to be evaluated (Murray and Mayne 2002, Murray 2002).

This paper presents a review of the practice of analysing clay building bricks from Australian archaeological sites. Its aim is to look at current archaeological practice and make suggestions about ways of improving the methods used with the intention of producing results that contribute to the understanding of the past. In doing this, it is the intent of this paper to contribute to the analysis of a class of artefacts commonly found on most post-contact archaeological sites and to the overall improvement in historical archaeological practice.

REVIEW OF CURRENT PRACTICE IN THE ANALYSIS OF BRICKS

In order to understand how bricks have been analysed, a brief review of archaeological reports was undertaken. The report review was not intended to cover every project in which a brick was found, as not all projects were thought likely to have the resources or the need to intensively analyse bricks. Rather, an attempt was made to examine final reports of major projects where the analysis of bricks was undertaken, drawing upon examples either in: the author's personal library, the Godden Mackay Logan report library or in the library of the NSW Heritage Office. The review was based on a highly selective sample from a limited geographical area, and no doubt could be criticised on that basis. However, the purpose of the review was to identify whether there was an 'archaeological practice' for brick analysis. The reports examined are listed in Appendix One.

The review looked at each report in order to answer the following questions:

- What was the aim of the analysis and how did it fit into the overall research aims of the project?
- How was the collection made?
- What attributes were recorded and how were these decided?

- What reference was made to supporting material such as related studies, historical research, etc?

The answers varied considerably, although the variance was not necessarily over time but between the consulting groups working on each project, suggesting that there is a certain approach to research design and analysis that could be called analytical practice, adopted by each of the major consulting groups as a de facto house style. In some cases, the analytical practice seems not to have varied over the last ten years despite all the discussion in the discipline over that time.

Aims of the analysis and fit with the research aims of the project

The analysis of bricks was mostly considered as part of a broader analysis of building materials in general. Notably, specific research questions relating to building materials were rarely posed in most reports. Two examples of reports where such questions were asked are the work at Corinella (Victoria) and the Queen's Arms Inn (Western Sydney). The work at Corinella, which was aimed at locating evidence of the 1826–1828 settlement site, is an example of directly tying brick analysis into research aims. A team of specialists was used to attempt to identify some of the 10 000 bricks brought to the settlement from Sydney as a way of locating the settlement site (Coutts 1985; McConnell and Edwards 1983). Casey & Lowe's excavation of the site of RH/46, the Queen's Arms Inn, identified four specific questions about the nature of the building, which the building material analysis addressed (Casey & Lowe 1995). In contrast to these examples, detailed analysis of building materials and the typology of bricks developed during the archaeological excavations at the Cumberland/Gloucester Street site was only loosely tied into the overall research aims for the project (Barnes 1999). Some archaeological projects, however, never really progressed beyond the cataloguing of bricks, although in the analysis of archaeological contexts, bricks were used for dating strata (e.g. Higginbotham 1992).

How was the collection made?

On most excavations, there was a large degree of formal and informal discarding of bricks owing to the sheer numbers and weight of bricks. There was little quantification of the sampling process involved in creating the sample of bricks used for analysis (Casey & Lowe 1995 is a rare example where this was done), although the fact that the artefacts analysed represent a sample was regularly acknowledged in most reports. Noting that artefacts are a sample is of little utility unless some description of the universe from which they were sampled from is made. This raises a further point, in that no attempts seem to have been made to record bricks from 'demolition layers' or from 'in situ' structural features, such as walls, and to integrate that data into the overall analysis of building material.

What attributes were recorded and how were these decided?

The published brick analysis from First Government House (Sydney) by the late Sue Pearson is one of the earliest available brick analyses, being undertaken in 1987 or 1988. Pearson developed her analysis based on earlier building materials research by George Gibbons (1980a, 1980b), described further below (Pearson 1988:1). Pearson's report includes a copy of the data sheet for recording building materials (Pearson 1988:9) and, from the sheet, it can be seen that length, width and thickness were recorded along with colour, using the Munsell Soil colour chart as a standard. Three attributes derived from Gibbons' research were recorded: body texture, constituents, and surface features. The type of brick was identified as being sandstock, fire brick, or CB (whatever that was). Frogs and other markings were also recorded. Use of these attributes seem to have been adopted as common practice in Sydney. A further procedure is the development of 'type series' in which the cataloguing of identical numbers of the same bricks are referred back to an 'ideal type', which is a distinct type of artefact within a broader class of artefacts. While this is an understandable approach in the context of an item that was mass produced (a brick machine would produce 1800 to 2500 identical bricks per hour), it is often difficult to ascertain the key attributes of the type in question, from the published reports.

The bricks from the 1983 and 1984 excavations at Corinella were measured in three dimensions: length, width and thickness, and weighed. Frogs and manufacturers' marks were also recorded. The project director, Dr Peter Coutts, determined what attributes were to be recorded and the level of precision required. Coutts referred to Gibbons' work and to research by a post-graduate student at the University of Sydney, Robert Varman. The attributes used seemed self-evident to the author, who undertook the initial cataloguing. Coutts then involved McConnell (a geo-archaeologist) and Edwards (a ceramicist) for a more specialist analysis of the bricks. McConnell and Edwards recorded the same basic set of attributes from the collection but also used a wider range of other attributes in their attempt to separate out any bricks made in Sydney. These attributes were mostly related to the composition of the bricks and were standard analytical techniques for the analysis of inorganic material (McConnell and Edwards 1983:3). The reason for choosing these techniques was simple: the authors searched for similar projects, found none, and then sought advice from experts who admitted that they had no experience with the question of sourcing bricks. Hence, they adopted a default position in order to undertake the analysis (McConnell and Edwards 1983:3).

What is notable from all the reports is that the basic attributes were taken as given, passed down from prior reports such as Pearson's. No attempt has been made to review critically the basic attributes of length, width, thickness, colour, brick type, and weight. These seem to be 'self evident' attributes (except for weight) that are passed down from one set of artefact cataloguers to another.

References to supporting material

Most of the reports on brick analysis in the 1980s refer to the work of George Gibbons, from the Department of Applied Geology, NSW Institute of Technology. In 1980 Gibbons undertook an important early study into the nature of bricks as a building material. Two reports on bricks are available (Gibbons 1980a, 1980b) although locating copies is difficult. It should be noted that Gibbons' work was part of a broader study on the conservation of building materials funded by the NSW Heritage Office, rather than specific research into bricks. Gibbons also lectured to historical archaeology students on building materials. Judging by citations and acknowledgements, Gibbons' reports were widely read and utilised by other archaeologists working in Sydney (e.g. Dillane 1992) and Gibbons was consulted as a technical expert in matters relating to bricks by many of those working on brick analysis (e.g. McConnell and Edwards 1983).

The only other consistent reference to supporting historical material was to Warwick Gemmell's *And So We Graft from Six to Six* (Gemmell 1986). This was an excellent summary history of brick making in NSW but was not intended as a technical study or an exhaustive study of the topic. Other relevant sources seem have been overlooked or ignored in brick analysis. For example, Patterson's recent report on Building Materials from the Casselden Place (Melbourne) excavations (Patterson 2004) does not refer to Miles Lewis' on-line work *Australian Building: a Cultural Investigation* that has a whole chapter on bricks and is a standard reference on building material in Australia (Lewis 2000).

There are no references in any of the archaeological studies reviewed to Australian Standards, which define technical specifications of bricks, nor their immediate British predecessors. Neither has there been any reference to technical material on the manufacture and use of bricks such as could have been obtained, from either the then Brick Research and Development Institute in Melbourne or the later Clay Brick and Pavers Institute. Certain technical illustrations ultimately sourced to Dobson's (1895) *Rudimentary Treatise on Bricks and Tiles* have been widely used to illustrate brick-making technology.

Surprisingly, there is no reference in the reviewed reports to two relevant archaeological studies on bricks: Harley's (1974) article *A Typology of Brick …* and Gurcke's (1987) *Bricks and Brickmaking: A Handbook for Historical Archaeology*. Gurcke's work in particular was aimed at historical archaeology, although in the American context, and is particularly strong in explaining the brick production process and in demonstrating non-metrical attributes of bricks related to their production. Harley's work is of less relevance for Australia but at the time analysis of bricks was beginning in Australia it was one of the few typological studies available.

During the 1980s and early 1990s Robert Varman was undertaking a doctorate at the University of Sydney on building material as means of dating archaeological sites, focusing on bricks and nails (Varman 1993). However, it is unclear from his thesis how his work engages with similar work undertaken by Gibbons, or with archaeological investigations in Sydney. On the evidence of citations in the reports reviewed, there seems to be little interest in the results of his research in studies undertaken since it became available.

In summary, the analysis of bricks has rarely been highlighted in research designs for archaeological excavations. There is little evidence of a systematic strategy to collect information on bricks from archaeological sites, while generally only a sample of the bricks on a site has been analysed. The methods of analysis have been largely a matter of repeating practices established in the early 1980s and do not seem to have been reviewed in the light of technical information about the manufacture of bricks or other information relating to the history of the brick industry. There is evidence of a standard practice of analysing or cataloguing bricks in Australian archaeology. This can be characterised as using a standard set of metrical attributes, (length, width, thickness and colour) as well as separating bricks based on manufacturing techniques and manufacturers' markings, although the attributes relating to these categories of evidence are poorly researched.

RESEARCH DIRECTIONS

Lest anyone think that the first brick has been cast unduly or rashly, the author freely confesses to undertaking such analysis of bricks in the manner characterised above. The issue is not one of assigning blame, but how to move on to improved methods. As a way of developing the potential of brick analysis, research directions to which they might contribute and the possibilities for contributing to a broader series of archaeological and historical research questions are discussed below.

Identification and dating of bricks

Firstly, the most obvious research direction lies in the identification and dating of bricks. Being able to assign a date to a brick type helps in the identification, assessment and interpretation of historical archaeological sites. In the context of survey, knowing the date of a brick can help in dating a particular site or site feature in the field. In archaeological excavations they may be used to date stratigraphic features, as well as to date structural elements in archaeological approaches to standing structures. If the bricks are of a special shape or type such as firebricks, they can also help in identifying the function of specific sites or site features.

Research into the broad chronologies of brick manufacturing (both manufacturers and the technology used) and brick markings is necessary if bricks are to be used as a tool for dating. Manufacturers frequently marked their bricks with their names or brand names and these can be dated by reference to historical documents. Gemmell gives a very general but useful list of brick makers in Sydney and surrounding areas (1986:62–84), while Gibbons provides a list of brick manufacturers and their marks in NSW dating from 1855 (1980a:65–70). Varman has also produced a detailed list of mainly Sydney brick manufacturers (1993:82–138). It would be interesting to collate all this information and put it in a more accessible forum.

For Victoria, there are several papers on the brick and tile industries which provide a useful source of information on brick manufacturers (Bain and Spencer-Jones 1952a, 1952b, 1953). These could be supplemented by research into trade directories and other sources to produce a list of Victorian brick makers. No doubt similar basic lists could be established for other states and regions.

From manufacturers' catalogues and other trade documents it is evident that in addition to the standard rectangular brick most manufacturers produced 'specials': bricks of non-standard shapes for which they could charge a premium. These shapes were a mixture of decorative items such as 'bullnose' (used for capping wall tops) and functional items such as crown bricks used for keystones in arches. Information about how a special brick would be used in a structure or in an industrial process can be obtained from trade literature.

Attributes that have been used to determine the date of manufacture of bricks are: the nature of the frog, manufacturers' marks (typically located in the frog), and brick size (a more detailed discussion is provided in a following section). The manufacturing process used to make the brick has also been suggested as a means of dating, and this is expressed in the term 'brick type' (i.e. sandstock, machine

made … etc). Shape has been the primary attribute used to identify special bricks types, although some types of firebricks also have a number impressed in them indicating the standard shape type.

Building quality

Another research direction is the issue of building quality, a point previously raised by Barnes (1999). In his research discussion on the bricks from the Cumberland/Gloucester Street excavations in the Rocks, Barnes drew attention to the building regulations in Sydney at the time and the extent to which buildings on the site complied (1999:173–174). However, concerned as it was with bricks and building material in isolation from their role as part of the site's architecture, his analysis failed to address the issue raised. The question of building quality is one that remains to be addressed, especially for urban areas where at least the perception of poor building quality by slum landlords is rife. Barnes saw quality as being linked to compliance with the regulations for brick construction in Sydney, but this approach may be limited due to the general lack of regulations across Australia until comparatively recently. Assessment of quality might involve notions of regular size, colour and conformity with known standards for brick manufacture (see below).

Buildings archaeology

Buildings archaeology is the analysis of buildings and other built structures through archaeological means including: analysis of building materials, construction techniques, building style and building stratigraphic sequences. It aims to treat the whole building as an item of material culture, just as their contents and underfloor deposits would be. Despite having a well-developed methodology for integrating architectural and archaeological evidence (e.g. Davies and Buckley 1987, Davies and Egloff 1984), the development of buildings archaeology as a separate area of archaeological research in Australia is embryonic. Architecture is not simply the backdrop onto which artefacts are deposited; architecture shapes the space in which humans interact and, just as much as any transfer-printed ceramic bowl, architecture expresses through its design and decoration notions of social status, order, taste, class and so on. In American historical archaeology, there is a tradition of integrating material evidence and architecture (both built and landscape) as shown for example in the works of Leone (1988) and Deetz (1977) and in the general appropriation of Henry Glassie's *Folk Housing in Middle Virginia* (1979) as an almost archaeological study.

Bricks were often an important part of architectural design and formed key elements of some architectural styles, particularly as polychrome brickwork and in the dominance of red brick and terracotta tiles and finials for the various Federation styles (Apperly et al. 1989). Part of the design effect was the colour of the brick and its quality. It is known that architects had special requirements for quality bricks for use in building facades. These were: colour, even texture on the face and straight arrises. Bricks with these qualities were sold as facing bricks. Evidence from bricks, in the form of colour and quality, points to the nature of the architecture on a particular site.

An important consideration is the location of bricks of particular types in relation to the structural elements on a particular site. Facing bricks typically were used on a building's façade and common bricks were used for interior, side and rear external walls. Context is therefore important in arguing that particular bricks form part of the architectural style of a particular building or not. It may be critical to understand from where on an archaeological site the bricks being analysed come from.

There is also the related question of the recycling of bricks. In the context of research at Corinella, where the bricks from the 1828 settlement were removed by subsequent settlers, much time was spent examining nearby early homestead sites and structures looking for recycled bricks. Shortages of material are presumed to be the prime reason for recycling bricks in Australia, however this may be a simplistic assumption. The issue of identifying recycling of building material in general has been discussed by Windsor (2004). Windsor (2004:4) notes that the key for identifying recycling is the context of the material suspected of being recycled. Removal of mortar with a high cement content is very difficult from bricks and so recycled bricks may have bits of old mortar adhering to them. There is, however, no recognised method for identifying recycled bricks.

Bricks in industrial archaeological research

Bricks in themselves are material evidence of the techno-logical nature of the brick industry in a particular area and at a particular time. From the examination of a brick, evidence of manufacturing techniques and production quality in the brick industry can be ascertained. This often forms a useful counterpoint to documentary evidence, which is often in the form of a manufacturer's own assessment of their product. The location of bricks from a particular manufacturer on archaeological sites can point to trade networks. Bricks provide evidence of the nature of the brick industry that complement or even challenge the documentary evidence.

ATTRIBUTES FOR BRICK ANALYSIS

The broad attributes used in brick analysis are now discussed in detail in order to identify key metrical and non-metrical data that can be used in the analysis of bricks (see also Appendix 2). This discussion is based upon historical information relating to the production of bricks and technical information on current brick making practice.

Bricks and their parts

A brick is defined as a solid or perforated block of material moulded from clay or cement used for building (typically bonded masonry), industrial or paving purposes (after McLaglan 1978; Milton 1994).

The longest axis of a brick is the length, the second longest axis is the width, and the narrowest axis is called the height. Bricks frequently have an indentation on the top surface, called a 'frog' (Fig. 1). Occasionally there were frogs on the top and bottom of bricks – referred to as double frogged. Frogs in machine-made bricks may have a raised section across their middle – this is called the bridge. Often frogs contain raised, conical lumps, originally used to identify the machine making the brick for quality control purposes, although for the archaeologist deciphering these markings may be a challenge. Bricks can also be perforated with holes running from top to bottom. Bricks with holes running through from head to head are hollow bricks. Wire cut bricks have no frogs but have perforations. Further definitions are provided in Appendix 2.

Bricks are laid with the longest axis facing outwards to form a stretcher or the width axis facing outwards to form a 'header'. Two headers plus mortar equals a 'stretcher'. This ratio is critical in the construction of masonry structures using bricks, as the mortar joints in the bond cannot overlap without significantly weakening the structure. However, buildings are

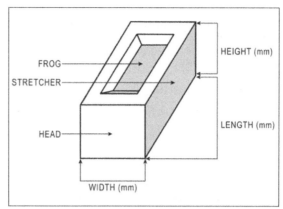

Fig. 1: The parts of a brick.

not often designed with walls that are the correct size for bricks to fit in. Typically, a brick wall requires parts of a brick, called 'closers', to be used to make up the length. Closers are defined as 'a brick less than full size used to bring the end of a wall to a vertical face' (Scully 2001:7). Half bricks and quarter bricks are used in this way. Scully (2001:7) also identified 'bevelled closers', 'king closers' and 'queen closers'. Nangle et al. (1951:93) identify a queen closure as being a brick halved along its longest axis, while a king closure is 'a brick with its head cut off so as to reduce its head to show as a quarter brick on the surface of a wall'.

A bricklayer simply made closures with a sharp blow from the trowel on a normal sized brick or used a mechanised brick cutter. This created a near-vertical straight edge that would assist in identifying closures from simply broken bricks.

Counting bricks

It is important to quantify how many bricks one has in a collection or sample to allow comparison to other collections or samples. However, relying on simple counts produces meaningless data; to say a collection has 15 bricks and 10 green bottles is nice but of little relevance. The idea of weighing artefacts is sometimes put forward as a way of making meaningful comparisons (e.g. in the City Link report by Wilson 1990), but this too is meaningless unless the specific gravity of all artefacts is the same. Nevertheless, the problem of how to get an overview of the brick collection remains.

The basic analytical unit is a whole brick, although as discussed above, half bricks, closures and special shapes (relatively easy to identify based on manufacturers' cata-logues) can form part of the collection. A simple counting of bricks, half bricks, closures and specials could be easily made.

Bricks are also amenable to being analysed using the 'type series' approach especially as they were manufactured and sold as quantities of the same type. The type series approach identifies each different brick as a type and describes the brick based on certain attributes, typically size, method of manu-facture, frog shape, manufacturer, etc). Identical items of the same type are simply counted and can be discarded. Two bricks of each type should be kept to allow one for accession as part of a permanent collection and the other to be sampled should analysis of the fabric be undertaken.

A simple approach to quantifying bricks would seem to be identifying numbers of brick types and the numbers of bricks, half bricks, and closures in each type. This would be relatively easy to do with a high level of precision. A further level of meaning would be added if brick types were identified during excavation and related to features on the site, so that the end result could be say 35 bricks of type A that are known to have come from a wall foundation and 67 bricks of type C that have come from a well. Such an approach could be easily applied across a site and include bricks not typically collected, such as bricks in fill deposits and in architectural features.

Size – does it matter?

The question of the relationship between brick size and date of production has been of interest to Australian archaeologists as it is believed that bricks became larger over time (Jeans 1983: 103). It would appear that Gibbons was pursuing this question but, from his interim report, no strong pattern over time was demonstrated (1980a:29). According to Searle, in Great Britain (or England, it is not clear which) brick sizes were regulated from 1625 until the repeal of the tax on bricks after which 'manufacturers made bricks of any size they pleased' (Searle 1956:12). Lewis discussed brick size, arguing that 'brickmakers brought moulds with them' when coming to Australia which established an Australian size, although he noted that 'variation is considerable' (Lewis 2000:6.01.10). Lewis also suggested an approximate date of 1860 when brick sizes became more standardised, although if Searle's view is correct, English sizes varied after 1850, which presumably would have been reflected in Australian sizes. It has also been suggested that when the Hoffman Brick Company in Victoria commenced manufacturing, in 1870, it introduced a 9 in x 4.5 in x 3in sized brick which was larger than the size in general use in Victoria at that time (Parsons 1970:419). This was referred to as the 'German' size, although the brick machines were in fact British. Certainly, with the introduction of mechanisation through brick presses and better quality kilns it became possible to produce bricks of a consistent size and to develop an industry-wide standard.

In 1904, The Royal Institute of British Architects and the Institute of Clayworkers agreed to a standard set of brick sizes giving minimum and maximum dimensions (Searle 1920: 20–21). In 1941, the first British Standard for clay building bricks was produced (Searle 1956:32–33), but by then the first Australian Standard for Building Bricks had been issued as AS A21 in 1934. The 1941 British brick sizes were slightly different from the Australian Standard, being 2mm shorter and 4mm wider and a length/width ratio of 0.5 rather than 0.48. A standard 'traditional' brick is defined in the 1984 Australian Standard as being 230 mm x 110 mm x 76 mm (AS 1225–1984). The Australian Standard allows for a variation of +/- 90mm in the length of 20 bricks; for a variation of +/- 50mm in the width of 20 bricks and a variation of +/- 50 mm in a height of 20 bricks. A modular brick standard has also been introduced with metric dimensions being 290 mm x 90mm x 90mm changing the length width ratio to from 2:1 to 3:1. However, these modular bricks are usually cement bricks rather than clay bricks (Scully 2001:6; Ward-Harvey 1984:34).

It is not necessarily the size of a brick that is critical – it is the relationship between the length (the stretcher) and the width (the header) that is important in brickwork. Two headers plus mortar should fit on a stretcher so the length width ratio should be just under 0.5. Australian Standard AS 1225 notes that 'length shall not be less than 1.5 times width'. As previously discussed, length is the longest axis on a complete brick. In archaeological analysis, the dimensions of a brick should be measured as if the brick was complete, which in most cases should be easily determined from an examination of surfaces. The rationale behind this is to help distinguish closures from broken bricks.

Given the variation allowed in modern brick production, precision in the measurement of bricks is not particularly important. Measuring to the nearest 2mm seems a useful archaeological standard which should detect significant variation. Clearly, an analysis that placed great emphasis on variations of less than the current manufacturing tolerances would be spurious. Major variations in brick size are unlikely as this would throw out the whole system of building structures and tie the builder into a single source for the bricks.

Another attribute occasionally measured in bricks is weight, but it is not clear if weighing bricks achieves any analytical purpose. As brick production was mechanised, greater density of clay material could be achieved, thus weight could distinguish between hand made and machine-made bricks. However, other morphological features of bricks could do this just as well. At the moment there seems to be no compelling reason to weigh bricks.

Colour

Bricks were deliberately coloured for decoration. In many cases the desired colour was achieved by selecting the appropriate clay body such as kaolin, or by adding material such as manganese or iron when the clay was being pugged (Searle 1921: 7–10). Generally this occurred in the mechanised era where greater control on colour could be obtained by adding material to the clay and by controlled burning in the kiln (Rowden 1964: 30). Before mechanisation and in particular with Scotch or Colonial kilns or clamps, the process of burning was not uniform and bricks were discoloured in the kilns. This colouring was a guide to potential strength and durability, with bricks being roughly graded according to colour. It can be seen therefore that brick colour is a mixture of deliberate preparation of clay bodies and burning in the kiln.

Munsell Soil Colour charts have been used for recording colours on bricks (e.g. Gibbons 1980) and some standard colour charts for recording earthenware pottery are also useful. The disadvantage of all these charts is that the full range of potential colours is unlikely to be contained within the one chart. This is particularly the case with the Munsell Soil Colour Charts, which are an extract from the Munsell Book of Colour specifically designed for recording soils. The important point to stress is that some sort of reference standard, be it the Munsell standard or the Australian or British Colour Standards, should be used to record brick colour. Whatever standard is used should be noted in any catalogues or reports so there is no doubt which standard was used.

Bricks are rarely uniform in colour: even monochrome bricks show minor variations in hue. Generally, these can be discounted and the dominant colour recorded but deliberate mottling effects were produced which should be recorded. The standards for recording mottles and other colour patterns in soils in The Australian Soil and Land Survey Field Handbook (McDonald et al. 1990:114–115) are a useful way of recording mottling in bricks.

Evidence of manufacture

There are four types of manufacturing process used to make bricks: Hand Manufacture, Mechanical extrusion (also called Stiff-mud in American literature), Semi Dry Press and Stiff Plastic. Detailed descriptions of manufacturing processes can be found in the literature (Brick Industry Association 1989, Dobson 1895, Goodson 1962, Gurcke 1987, Searle 1920, 1921, 1956) and it is not proposed to discuss these in detail.

In the context of identifying evidence of manufacture, it is of relevance to note that there is little obvious difference in the bricks made by Semi Dry Press and the Stiff Plastic method and the author has not been able to find clearly definable attributes to separate bricks made by these processes. Because the processes are similar, the bricks have similar moisture contents when green and typically have the same type of repress. The raw material types are usually different but this is not reflected in the surface morphology of the brick.[1] It is possible that further discussion may assist in developing attributes to distinguish bricks made by these two processes.

A summary of the manufacturing processes and related attributes found on bricks is presented in Table 1. Most of these attributes can be simply recorded as being present or absent. The shape and number of perforations in an extruded brick should also be recorded as these vary widely. From the 1880s onwards bricks became more decorative. Extruded bricks in particular have decorative textures and patterns on their sides which were important in establishing different product lines. Some attempt should be made to record these patterns, as well as frogs and manufacturers' marks. Frog shapes should be recorded with reference to standard geometric shapes or dictionaries of ornament. The lettering in manufacturers' marks should be recorded along with font size and type, if this can be established.

Quality of bricks

Quality is a difficult concept to apply in any analysis as it is such a subjective term (see Pirsig 1974 for elaboration). Yet quality is identified as being a critical concept in the research directions discussed above. It is not the production of bricks, so much as their nature and quality, that allows many potential research questions to be addressed. Therefore, some approach to the issue must be made. In contemporary society, quality is seen in relation to some form of standard or benchmark. In relation to manufactured goods, this is usually some form of

Australian Standard or Industry Code of Practice providing parameters that the item has to meet for it to be considered to be of good quality. If an item exceeds these parameters to a great extent, it might be considered to be of 'excellent' quality. This assumes that the standards being used actually represent 'quality'.

If the aim of the analysis is to understand the past, the quality of an item must be assessed in the context of our understanding of what that quality may have meant in the past. For clay bricks, this can be partially be established based on historical documents such as standards, legislation, technical manuals, professional journals and information on building practice from sources such as newspapers or diaries. Much of this information for bricks generally dates from the twentieth century. The question of quality in nineteenth-century bricks has not been researched to any great extent. It is also important to think of attributes that will not be altered by the brick entering the archaeological record and its subsequent recovery. Despite these difficulties some attributes are put forward as indicating the quality of an individual brick.

Four main attributes indicative of quality are presented: consistent shape, straight lines, consistent colour and good even firing. These are discussed below; however other attributes may emerge following further research.

A consistently rectangular shape is desirable as the brick should be a rectangle with parallel straight edges. If a brick does not have parallel edges, it is not much use as a brick, although a small amount of distortion in a brick could be covered up by mortar during the construction of a wall. Note that some special bricks are deliberately curved or wedged and these should not be confused with poor quality bricks.

Table 1: Summary of processes and attributes.

Manufacturing Process	Attribute	Comments
Hand Made Pugged clay, termed the clot, is thrown into a mould on a table, pressed in and excess clay cut off from the top of the mould. The formed brick is then knocked out of the mould and stacked for drying prior to firing in the kiln.	Thumbprint	There are at least seven explanations for thumbprints: irrespective of which if any is correct, thumbprints are exclusively found on hand made bricks.
	Hack Mark	A thin raised line along the stretcher side of the brick formed by stacking green bricks for drying.
	Sand struck	To release the clot from the mould it was sometimes dusted with fine sand which adhered to the clot and is burnt with it.
	Wet Struck	To release the clot from the mould, it was sometimes wet producing a series of distinct but ill-defined vertical lines along the stretcher edge.
	Strike	To scrape off excess clay from the mould a board was used leading a series of parallel lines running along the top of longest axis of the brick known as a strike.
Mechanical Extrusion The clay is mixed inside the brick press through a series of pug mills and augers and extruded through a rectangular nozzle out onto a table where the billet of clay is cut into brick. This is usually done by wire, hence the name "wire cut".	Perforation	All bricks with perforations through the body of the brick have been extruded.
	Wire Cut mark	Semi-circular lines along the top and bottom of the brick.
	Texture	The stretcher and header sides are frequently decorated.
Semi-Dry Press Clay (or shale) was ground to powder, then a measured amount of powder mixed with water is pushed into a mould which is then compressed at least twice to form a brick. The material was consolidated into a brick by the pressure.	Circular mark	Circular marks on the top and bottom surface of the brick.
	General appearance	Denser brick with sharper edges and smoother faces.
Stiff Plastic Clay was ground to powder and mixed with some water. It fed intoa mould in which the clot is compressed to form a brick.	Circular mark	Circular marks on the top and bottom surface of the brick.
	General appearance	Denser brick with sharper edges and smoother faces.

Architects picked facing bricks for their straight edges (arrises) and smooth faces (see evidence by George Pender to the Industrial Court's Enquiry into the price of bricks, Court Reporting Office 1939:52). Faces should be smooth and free of even hairline cracks for a facing brick (Searle 1920:13–14).

Consistent colour is important as a quality in the decorative use of bricks, as well as being an indicator of the quality of burning. A blue brick for example results from poor firing and possibly indicates that the brick is unsound. The colour should be even across the brick unless some particular type of colour effect is being attempted.

Good consistent firing is indicated by colour, lack of distortion, lack of evidence of over-firing (e.g. the brick turning to glass) and by a clear ringing sound when two bricks are hit together (Nagel 1955:87). Under-fired bricks called 'callows' have a tendency to crumble and hold water (i.e. increased porosity due to lack of vitrification) (Nagel 1955:86–87, Searle 1920:14). Over-fired bricks tend to be more likely to fracture.

Unfortunately, quality assessment is not this simple. Anecdotal evidence suggests for example that the Glen Innes brickworks were deliberately making over-burnt clinkers or blue bricks to sell to Sydneysiders for feature walls in renovated houses (apparently in Balmain). Clifton-Nubrick's 'tumbled range' of Semi-Dry pressed bricks was produced by tumbling perfectly good green bricks to remove their sharp edges, so in this case a presumed measure of quality was not a straight edge. They also produced an 'old world classic' clinker brick 'inspired from our glorious past' (Nubrick 1988). This is a salutary warning that one manufacturer's poor quality brick can be another's key selling point and that such analysis needs to proceed with care.

When constructed into masonry, bricks can exhibit efflorescence or surface fretting of the brick itself. Efflorescence is usually caused by ground water, wet mortar, or even salt laden air depositing salts which are absorbed into the brick pores in solution. As the brick dries the salt crystalizes, and where this occurs near the surface of the brick, the structure of the brick may fail, causing fretting. Salts can also cause staining of the brick masonry (see Zsembery 2001). While the bricks themselves are generally considered not to be a source of salt attack (due to the nature of clays in Australia) the porosity of the brick is a contributing factor, allowing the salt to penetrate in solution. Generally, efflorescence is not a sign of poor quality bricks.[2]

CONCLUSIONS

Ultimately, the brick attributes used will depend on the underlying research design and the nature of the brick collection. However some basic approaches to brick analysis are proposed below.

The recording and analysis of bricks should, *inter alia*, be considered during the research design development and planning phase of an archaeological program so that appropriate data collection is planned and can be accommodated in field and laboratory work. The recording of bricks from both standing structures on a site as well as archaeological deposits should be undertaken as a way of systematically obtaining information on bricks from a particular site. It seems inadequate to consider only bricks collected during excavation and ignore bricks in structures.

Ultimately, it is recognised that the nature and level of collecting and recording of bricks will vary between each project. Accompanying a basic recording of bricks should be a discussion of the recording strategy so that it is clear which part of the overall deposit of bricks on a site was sampled or was not sampled. It is important that a record be kept of decisions regarding the collection of brick samples and any attributes analysed so that future researchers can gain insight into the processes that led to the archaeological collection.

At a minimum, the basic recording of bricks should aim to identify the numbers of bricks, half bricks and closures, the variety of bricks types (including fire bricks and special bricks) on a site and their archaeological or structural context. It is recommended that a sample of each brick type be kept. Typically, two bricks should be a minimum for each type as this allows one brick to be sampled if required.

A suggested set of attributes for describing brick types is presented in Table 2. These can be utilised in a simple database. In addition, photographs of each brick type can be taken and added to the database. In the author's experience,

Table 2: Suggested attributes for describing brick types.

Attribute		Comments
Manufacture of brick	Use attributes in Table 1 to determine the method of manufacture.	
Part of brick	Identify whether it is a whole brick, half brick, closer or special.	There are standard shapes and sizes in manufacturers' catalogues, which will help identify some brick shapes.
Dimensions	Measure the three axis to nearest mm.	It is very easy to measure a brick if you set up a simple measuring board using graph paper and a straight edge.
Length width ratio	Ratio of length over width can easily be calculated on a spreadsheet.	Useful for detecting odd-shaped bricks.
Is a frog present?	Yes/No	If yes, describe with reference to a standard shape note whether it is bridged or otherwise marked. Measurement of frog dimensions is often useful where it is likely there are different types of brick with the same frog shape.
Are two frogs present?	Yes/No	As above.
Record manufacturers marks	Simply record all characters recording spaces and unreadable characters.	
Colour	Identify the main colour of the brick and the colour of any other features such as mottling.	Use an appropriate colour standard. Mottling can be described using the method in MacDonald et al. (1990:114-115). Note consistency of colour.
Quality attributes	Straight edges.	Place along straight edge.
Quality attributes	Rectangular shape.	Use a builders square.
Quality attributes	Clear ringing sound when two are banged together.	Watch fingers!
Quality attributes	Colour and "glassy patches".	Evidence of poor firing
Manufacturing attributes	Record attributes in Table 1.	Record as presence/absence and detail as necessary.

once all the forms and measuring guides are established, the description of a brick is relatively quick and uncomplicated. The longest part in the process is the cleaning of the brick, which is recommended to make the colours and attributes more visible. Water is the best cleaning agent with a light scrub (be careful as some bricks can be quite soft).

The potential for using the recording of bricks as a means of answering detailed questions about a site has been identified, although how this potential is utilised has to be left to the individual researcher or research team and depends on the specifics and context of the site and the broader research program involved.

ACKNOWLEDGEMENTS

This paper's origins lie in a failed venture, the 'Historic Brick Collection', established at the late Victoria Archaeological Survey. The topic of brick analysis was taken up in meetings on standards in historical archaeology organised by the NSW Heritage Office and at a round table meeting on brick at the 2000 Society for Historical Archaeology conference organised by Larry Burr. I would like to acknowledge the assistance of Martin Gibbs, Jane Cummins-Stuart, Richard Mackay and an anonymous referee in improving the quality of this paper.

ENDNOTES

1. The Stiff Plastic process was typically used in Melbourne while the Semi Dry pressed process was typically used in Sydney.

2. An interesting exception to this rule is the bricks from Port Arthur. Hutton, in discussing the problem of salt attack and deterioration of brickwork at Port Arthur, identified salt in the fabric of the brick itself that and suggested this was due to clay pugging in salt water (1981:158). Poor firing (it was estimated the bricks were fired to c400°C) contributed to the deterioration, as the temperature reached did not melt the sea salts, which remained in the body of the brick after firing.

BIBLIOGRAPHY

APPERLY, R., IRVING, R. and P. REYNOLDS 1989. *A Pictorial guide to identifying Australian Architecture*, Angus and Robertson Publishers, North Ryde.

BAIN, A.D.N. and D. SPENCER-JONES 1952a. 'Melbourne Brick and Tile Industry, Part 1'. *The Mining and Geological Journal*, 4:20–28.

BAIN, A.D.N. and D. SPENCER-JONES 1952b. 'The Melbourne Brick and Tile Industry, Part 2'. *The Mining and Geological Journal*, 4:13–20.

BAIN, A.D.N. and D. SPENCER-JONES 1953. 'Melbourne Brick and Tile Industry, Part 3 – Tiles'. *The Mining and Geological Journal*, 5:24–29.

BARNES, K. 1999. *Building Materials Artefact Report*, vol. 4 Specialist Artefact Reports The Cumberland/Gloucester Streets Site, The Rocks: Archaeological Investigation Report, Report prepared for the Sydney Cove Authority by Godden Mackay Logan Pty Ltd, Sydney.

BRICK INDUSTRY ASSOCIATION 1989. *Technical Notes on Brick Construction 9A – Manufacturing, Classification, and Selection of Brick, Classification, Part 2*. vol. 2005: Brick Industry Association, Renton, Virginia, USA.

CASEY & LOWE. 1995. *Archaeological Excavation RH/46: Queens Arms Inn & Rouse Hill Post Office*: Report for the Rouse Hill Infastructure Project, by Casey & Lowe for Brayshaw MacDonald Pty. Ltd.

COMMITTEE BD/26, BURNT CLAY AND SHALE BUILDING BRICKS 1984. *Australian Standard: Clay Building Bricks AS 1225–1984*.The Standards Association of Australia, Sydney.

COURT REPORTING OFFICE 1939. *Transcripts of Evidence 1900–1960, Brick Inquiry, Newcastle and Wollongong*. SR 6/2071, State Records of NSW. Sydney

COUTTS, P.J.F. 1985. *Report on Archaeological Investigations at the 1826 Settlement Site – Corinella*, Victoria Archaeological Survey, Melbourne.

CROOK, P., LAWRENCE, S. and M. GIBBS 2002. The role of artefact catalouges in Australian historical archaeology: a framework for discussion, *Australasian Historical Archaeology*, 20:26–38.

DAVIES, M. and K. BUCKLEY 1987. *Archaeological Procedures Manual*, Department of Lands Parks and Wildlife, Hobart.

DAVIES, M. and B. EGLOFF 1984. The Commandants' Residence at Port Arthur: An Archaeological Perspective. *Archaeology at ANZAAS. Canberra: Canberra Archaeological Society*, ed. by Graham Ward: 46–55. Canberra: Canberra Archaeological Society.

DEETZ, J. 1977. *In Small Things Forgotten: the Archaeology of Early American Life*, Anchor Books Doubleday, New York.

DILLANE, S. 1992. Report on the Building Material Artefacts. *Little Pier Street Precinct Archaeological Excavations, Volume 4 Specialist Report*, ed. by Ltd Godden Mackay Pty. Sydney: Godden Mackay.

DOBSON, E. 1895. *A Rudimentary Treatise on the Manufacture of Bricks and Tiles containing an outline of the principles of brickmaking*. Crosby Lockwood and Son, London (revised edition).

GEMMELL, W. 1986. *'And so we graft from six to six'*. Angus and Robertson Publishers, Sydney.

GIBBONS, G.S. 1980a. *Research Grant: Materials Studies for Building Restoration: Second Quarterly Report*. Sydney: Report to the NSW Heritage Council by G.S. Gibbons, Department of Applied Geology, The NSW Institute of Technology.

GIBBONS, G.S. 1980b. *Research Grant: Materials Studies for Building Restoration: Third Quarterly Report*. Sydney: Report to the NSW Heritage Council by G.S. Gibbons, Department of Applied Geology, The NSW Institute of Technology.

GLASSIE, H. 1979. *Folk housing in Middle Virginia: A structural analysis of historic Artefacts*, University of Tennessee Press, Knoxville.

GOODSON, F.J. 1962. *Clay Preparation and Shaping*, Brick Development Association Limited, United Kingdom.

GURCKE, K. 1987. *Bricks and Brickmaking: A Handbook for Historical Archaeology*, University of Idaho Press, Moscow, Idaho.

HARLEY, L.S. 1974. 'A Typology of Brick: with numerical coding of Brick characteristics'. *Journal of the British Archaeological Association, 3rd Series*, 38:63–87.

HIGGINBOTHAM, E. 1992. *Report on the Archaeological Excavation of the site of Westfield Shoppingtown, Aird Street, Parramatta, NSW*: Report for Westfield.

HUTTON, J.T. 1981. Clays and Bricks of the Penal Settlements at Port Arthur and Maria island, Tasmania, *Papers and Proceedings of the Royal Society of Tasmania*, 115:153–161.

JEANS, D. 1983. 'The building Industry: Materials and Styles' in *Industrial Archaeology in Australia: Rural Industry*, ed. by Judy. M. Birmingham, R. Ian Jack and Dennis Jeans. Richmond: Heinemann Publishers Australia Pty. Ltd.

LEONE, M.P. 1988. The Georgian order as the Order of Mercantile Capitalism in Annapolis, Maryland. *The Recovery of Meaning: Historical Archaeology in the Eastern United States*, ed. by M. P. Leone and P. B. Potter: 235-261. Washington, D.C.: Smithsonian Institution Press.

LEWIS, M.B. 2000. *Australian Building a Cultural Investigation*, http://www.abp.unimelb.edu.au/staff/milesbl/dbmenu.html, Accessed July 2005.

McCONNELL, A. and I. EDWARDS 1983. *Interim Report, Corinella Historical Brick Analysis*. Report 1983/7 Unpublished Report Series, Victorian Archaeological Survey.

McDONALD, R.C., ISBELL, R.F., SPEIGHT, J.G., WALKER, J. and HOPKINS, M.S. 1990. *Australian Soil and Land Survey: Field Handbook*, C.S.I.R.O., Canberra.

McLAGAN, D.S. (ed.) 1978. *A Glossary of Building and Planning Terms in Australia* National Committee on Rationalised Building, National Capital Development Commission, Canberra.

MILTON, H. J. (ed.) 1994. *A Glossary of Building Terms*, National Committee on Rationalised Building, Standards Australia and Suppliers Index Pty. Ltd., Sydney.

MURRAY, T. 2002. But that was long ago: theory in Australian historical archaeology, *Australasian Historical Archaeology* 20:8–14.

MURRAY, T. and A. MAYNE 2002. *Cassleden Place Development Archaeological Investigation works Phases 1 and 2: Full Research Design*. Melbourne: Prepared for Godden Mackay Logan in association with the Archaeological Program La Trobe University and Austral Archaeology.

NANGLE, J, NANGLE, J.E.T. and A. NANGLE. 1951. *Australian Building Practice: A Treatise for Australian Students of Building Construction, Builders. Architects ... etc.*, Fifth Revised and Enlarged Edition, William Brooks and Co Limited, Sydney.

NUBRICK 1988. Advertising pamphlets for 'The Classic Range', 'Nubrick Brick Range' and 'A Taste of Nubrick Pavers', collected by the author.

PARSONS, T.G. 1982. The Brick Manufacturing Industry 1870 to 1890: The Hoffman Patent Steam Brick Company Limited and the Northcote Brick Company Limited, Unpublished PhD Thesis, Monash University.

PATTERSON, L. 2004. Building Materials. *Casselden Place, 50 Lonsdale Street, Melbourne, Archaeological Excavations, Research Archive Report*: 681–717: Report to ISPT and Heritage Victoria by Godden Mackay Logan, La Trobe University and Austral Archaeology.

PEARSON S. 1988. Building Materials Analysis, First Government House Site, Sydney. Canberra: Anutech Pty. Ltd.

PIRSIG, R.M. 1974. *Zen and the Art of Motorcycle Maintenance: an Inquiry into Values*, Bodley Head, London.

ROWDEN, E. 1964. *The Firing of Bricks*, Brick Development Association Limited, United Kingdom.

SCULLY, M. 2001. *CBPI Brick and Paver Dictionary*. vol. 2005: Clay Brick and Paver Institute, Baulkham Hills NSW.

SEARLE, A.B. 1920. *Modern Brickmaking*. 2nd Edition, Scott Greenwood & Son, London.

SEARLE, A.B. 1921. *The Clay Workers Handbook*. 3rd Edition, Charles Griffin and Company Ltd., London.

SEARLE, A.B. 1956. *Modern Brickmaking*. 4th Edition, Ernest Benn Limited, London.

VARMAN, R. 1993. Bricks and Nails: Building Materials as Criteria for Dating in Sydney and Environs from 1788, A Documentary Survey and Assessment of Dating Potential, Department of Prehistoric and Historical Archaeology, University of Sydney: Doctor of Philosophy.

WARD-HARVEY, K. 1984. *Fundamental Building Materials*, Sakoga Pty Ltd & the RAIA, Sydney.

WINDSOR, I.J. 2004. *The Use and Reuse of Building Material in the Archaeological Record*, on-line paper, accessed 13th June 2006.

ZSEMBERY, S. 2001. *Manual 2: The Properties of Clay Masonry Units* 2005: Clay Brick and Paver Institute, Baulkham Hills NSW.

APPENDIX ONE: ARCHAEOLOGICAL REPORTS REVIEWED

BAIRSTOW, D. 1997. *Grace Brothers, Broadway, Historical Archaeology Report*: Report for Walker Civil Engineering.

BARNES, K. 1999. *Building Materials Artefact Report*, vol. 4 Specialist Artefact Reports The Cumberland/Gloucester Streets Site, The Rocks: Archaeological Investigation Report, Report prepared for the Sydney Cove Authority by Godden Mackay Logan Pty Ltd, Sydney.

CASEY & LOWE 1995. *Archaeological Excavation RH/46: Queens Arms Inn & Rouse Hill Post Office*: Report for the Rouse Hill Infrastructure Project, by Casey & Lowe for Brayshaw MacDonald Pty.Ltd.

CASEY & LOWE 1995. *Archaeological Excavation Paragon Iron Foundry, Bulwara Road Pyrmont*, report for Meriton Apartments.

CASEY & LOWE 2004. *Archaeological Testing and Monitoring cnr George and Harris Streets Parramatta*: Report for Champion Legal on behalf of Vipena.

CONNAH, G. 1997. *The Archaeology of Lake Innes House: Investigating the visible evidence 1993–1995*, Connah Canberra, Canberra.

CONNAH, G. 2002. *The 2001 Excavations at Lake Innis estate, Port Macquarie, NSW*: Report to the Heritage Council of NSW.

COUTTS, P.J.F. 1985. *Report on Archaeological Investigations at the 1826 Settlement Site – Corinella*, Victoria Archaeological Survey.

CULTURAL RESOURCE MANAGEMENT n.d. *Archaeological Investigations, Lucan Park Homestead Site, M7 Motorway, Eastern Creek*, Report by CRM to Abi Leighton Joint Venture.

CULTURAL RESOURCE MANAGEMENT 2002. *Archaeological Investigations, Transgrid site Haymarket*, Report by CRM to Transgrid.

DILLANE, S. 1992. Report on the Building Material Artefacts. *Little Pier Street Precinct Archaeological Excavations, Volume 4 Specialist Report*, ed. by Godden Mackay Pty. Ltd. Sydney: Godden Mackay.

HIGGINBOTHAM, E. 1987. *79 George Street, Parramatta, N.S.W.*, Consultant Archaeological Services.

HIGGINBOTHAM, E. 1990. *Historical and Archaeological analysis of the former 'Red Cow' Inn. Proposed Site of Multi-storey Car Park, Erby Place, Parramatta, N.S.W.*, Consultant Archaeological Services.

HIGGINBOTHAM, E. 1992. *Report on the Archaeological Excavation of the site of Westfield Shoppingtown, Aird*

Street, Parramatta, NSW: Report for Westfield.

HIGGINBOTHAM, E. 1997. *Report on the Archaeological excavation of Richmond Marketplace bounded by March, Paget, Lennox and east Market Streets, Richmond*: Report for Restika & Partners Pty. Ltd.

HIGGINBOTHAM, E. 2003. *Report on the Archaeological excavation of Waringo Hut near Cadia*: Report to Cadia Holdings by Edward Higginbotham & Associates Pty. Ltd.

HIGGINBOTHAM, E. 2005. *Report on the Archaeological excavation of part of Cadia Mining Village near Orange, NSW*: Report to Cadia Holdings by Edward Higginbotham & Associates Pty. Ltd.

McCONNELL, A. and I. EDWARDS. 1983. *Interim Report, Corinella Historical Brick Analysis*. Report 1983/7 Unpublished Report Series, Victorian Archaeological Survey.

PATTERSON, L. 2004. Building Materials. *Casselden Place, 50 Lonsdale Street, Melbourne, Archaeological Excavations, Research Archive Report*: 681–717: Report to ISPT and Heritage Victoria by Godden Mackay Logan, La Trobe University and Austral Archaeology.

PEARSON, S. 1988. Building Materials Analysis, First Government House Site, Sydney. Canberra: Anutech Pty. Ltd.

TUCK, D. 1998. Building Material and Metal Artefacts Report. *Angel Place Project 1997 Archaeological Excavation Vol 2 Specialist Reports*, ed. by Godden Mackay Pty. Ltd. Sydney.

WILSON, A. 1990. *Archaeological Investigations of the City Link Development Site, Footscray 1989*, City of Footscray.

APPENDIX TWO:
GLOSSARY OF BRICK TERMS

Term	Description	Source
	Brick Manufacturing	
Dry pressed	Machine made (generic term)	Nangle 1951:86
Extruded	Bricks made by extruding from a brick press and being cut by wire (wire cut).	Scully 2001:6
Plastics	Machine made or wire cut	Nangle 1951:86
Re-pressed	Brick made by extruding clay with a 14% to 17% moisture content into a mould to give a clot that is compacted and repressed (Stiff Plastic brick)	Scully 2001:6
Sandstock	Hand made (generic term)	Nangle 1951:86
Semi-dry pressed	Clay ground to powder compressed to brick, 10%-19% water.	Goodson, 1962, Searle 1956
Stiff- plastic	Powdered clay mixed with water and compressed into a stiff paste, 10-14% water.	Goodson, 1962; Searle 1956
	Types of Brick	
Air	Perforated bricks used for ventilation.	Maclagan 1978:10
Callows	Underburnt bricks, underfired brick.	Maclagan 1978:11, Nangle 1951:86, Scully 2001:6
Clinkers	Misshapen and over burnt bricks, produced by firing to the point of complete vitrification.	Maclagan 1978:11, Nangle 1951:86-87, Scully 2001:6
Common	Any brick made primarily for building purposes and not especially treated for texture or colour; reject facing bricks of a quality suitable for use where they will not be visible in the finished wall.	Maclagan 1978:11, Scully 2001:6
Commons, Picked, Selected	The best of ordinary of common bricks. Maclagan 1978:11, Scully	Maclagan 1978:11
Dough-boy	Callow brick	2001:6
Faced	Best quality bricks used for face or external work or for other special work.	Maclagan 1978:11
Fire brick	Brick made from refractory clay that will withstand high temperatures.	
Hard-fired/ burned	Brick fired at high temperatures to near vitrification.	Scully 2001:6
Heeler	Face bricks of normal length and width with a height of approximately half that of an ordinary brick.	Maclagan 1978:11
Ordinary	Good common bricks.	Nangle 1951:86-87
Picked	The best quality bricks among the common bricks – typically specially picked out.	Nangle 1951:86-87
O.K.	Open kiln bricks, made by dry-pressed process and burned in the 'old type of kiln' (not sure what this means – possibly Scotch kilns or down draft kilns).	Nangle 1951:86-87
Double-pressed	Typically wire cuts that have been repressed, often used for facing	Nangle 1951:86-87
Double frogged	Bricks with frogs on both sides, typically made during the late 19th c.	Stuart
Enamelled bricks	Bricks that are glazed.	Nangle 1951:86-87
Texture Bricks	Special brick – marketed under different trade names; bricks with patterned sides usually wire cut.	Maclagan 1978:11, Nangle 1951:86, 88
Modular brick	Brick with dimensions that are a multiple of a 100mm module.	Scully 2001:6
Modulated brick	Brick with dimensions in length and width that are a multiple of a 100mm module but whose height is less than a module; several are required to achieve a multi-module.	Scully 2001:6
Run of kiln brick	Ungraded and unsorted bricks from a single kiln.	Scully 2001:16

Overview of BLM's Historic Glass Bottle Identification and Information Website

Bill Lindsey

ABSTRACT

The United States Bureau of Land Management (BLM) is creating a comprehensive internet website devoted to the dating and typing of glass bottles produced in the United States and to some degree Canada between 1800 and the 1950s. The BLM website provides information allowing users to determine a likely manufacturing date range and use for most U.S.-made bottles or substantial fragments. The website also provides in-depth information on an array of subjects related to the manufacturing of bottles. Currently, the BLM website is almost complete, with full completion expected in 2007, although most sections are fully useable now.

Introduction

The Unites States Bureau of Land Management (BLM) administers and manages the largest land base of any entity in the United States—261 million acres of public lands located almost exclusively in the American West and Alaska. Part of the mission of the BLM is the management and preservation of cultural and heritage resources found on public lands, both prehistoric and historic.

Discovering, studying, and understanding the evidence of past human influences on the land provides the BLM background information that is critically important in the process of determining appropriate land uses today and in the future. Many historic sites located on public lands contain information important to the understanding of a particularly vibrant era in American history—the trans-Mississippi migration and settlement of the American West. The recording, interpretation, and protection of historic sites are critical and mandated missions of the agency. The proper study and understanding of historic sites on public lands entails the use of analytical tools that assist in dating and interpreting occupation details and time period of a given site or landscape. Among the most common artifacts found on historic sites are discarded bottles and bottle fragments.

Currently, the information needed to have a reasonable chance at dating, typing or determining the likely use of historic bottles is scattered in hundreds of different, usually narrowly focused, professional and avocational publications, many of which are difficult to nearly impossible to obtain. A good example of a high quality but narrowly defined work is the classic *Bottle Makers and Their Marks* by the late Julian Toulouse (1971).

Few attempts have been made at consolidating these diverse works into a single user-friendly guide. Probably the most notable attempt was *The Parks Canada Glass Glossary* (Jones and Sullivan 1989). The *Intermountain Antiquities Computer System (IMACS) Guide*, to which BLM was a contributor, was another effort to create an interpretive aid for historic artifact identification through a section on bottles (University of Utah 1992). Both of these guides were attempts "… to provide archaeologists with a manual for a standard approach to arriving at historical artifact function and chronology" (University of Utah 2001). They are useful works but dated and constrained in scope. In addition, neither has been updated in recent years; Jones and Sullivan is out of print and largely unavailable.

BLM's Historic Glass Bottle Identification and Information Website

Simply stated, the BLM's Historic Bottle Website is an attempt to combine, consolidate, and interpret all pertinent and available historic bottle-related information into one source using the most modern and flexible of publishing forums, the internet <*http://www.blm.gov/historic_bottles/index.htm*>. This website is intended to provide a user-friendly information source that will allow both the cultural professional and general public a chance at greater understanding of the history and evolution of historic bottles in the United States and, to a lesser degree, Canada.

This history of American glass bottles touches on and connects with the transition from a craft-based to industrial based economy, 18th and 19th century technological change, the settlement of the United States, cultural patterns and changes, and more.

Nominally, the BLM has justified and facilitated the preparation of the Historic Bottle Website as an extension of agency responsibilities intended to assist internal and external cultural professionals, other employees, contractors, and volunteers in the pursuit of agency goals in the BLM's cultural resources management programs. The website does, however, have much broader external appeal and is already being accessed extensively by archaeologists, government and private institutions, and individuals throughout the world.

The information found on the BLM's Historic Bottle Website is presented via the Internet for several reasons. First, to answer or address questions related to the dating and typing of a bottle, an extensive amount of information must be presented in a way that is easily accessible to the user. A major benefit of using the Internet to accomplish this task is the ability to use hundreds or thousands of illustrative pictures—an attribute that would not be possible or affordable if in book form. The Internet also allows for ease of revising or adding new information as it becomes available. As soon as the information is incorporated into the webpage and reloaded on the BLM server, it is available to everyone immediately, another attribute not possible with a printed publication. Finally, the ability of the Internet to reach more potential users than any other communication medium makes it a most powerful tool for education and enlightenment today.

Goals of the Historic Bottle Website

The Historic Bottle Website is primarily designed for field archaeologists trying to identify and date bottles or bottle fragments that are found during cultural surveys and excavations in the United States and more generally for anyone trying to date a bottle, determine what it was used for, or begin a search for information on historic bottle types and technologies. Second, it is intended to provide a teaching resource for educators dealing with the subject of bottles in historic archaeology and material culture studies.

The overriding goal of the Historic Bottle Website is to enable a user to answer two primary questions about most utilitarian bottles and jars produced in the United States and Canada between the early 1800s and 1950s (see Figure 1 for a range of these types). These include:

1. What is the age of the bottle? (bottle dating)
2. What type of bottle is it? (bottle identification or typology)

The site also assists the user with three additional and related bottle questions:

3. What technology, techniques, or processes were used to manufacture the bottle?
4. Where did the bottle come from, where was it made and what is its distribution in the United States?
5. Where can more information on historic bottles and bottle manufacturing technologies be found?

How to Use the Historic Bottle Website

If a user is attempting to determine the approximate manufacturing date or age of a bottle or fragment with diagnostic features, the first page to visit is the Bottle Dating page and related subpages <*www.blm.gov/historic_bottles/dating. htm*>. This group of pages leads a user through a series of questions about the physical or morphological characteristics of historic bottles that helps to narrow down the age of an item. These pages are the major hub of the website and the best place to start a search. Also linked to the Bottle Dating page is a subpage called Examples of Dating Historic Bottles that tracks different bottles through a dating and general information quest to illustrate how the website works.

If a user is interested in identifying what a bottle was likely used for or what type of bottle it is, the Bottle Typing/Diagnostic Shapes page and related subpages should be visited < *www.blm.gov/historic_bottles/typing. htm*>. These include bottle type-specific subpages with extensive style and dating information. Beyond Bottle Dating and Bottle Typing, numerous other specialty pages cover various aspects of historic bottles in greater depth including Bottle Finishes and Closures, Bottle

Figure 1. Grouping of historic American-made bottles dating from the 1830s to 1930s. (Photo by author, 2003.)

Bases, Bottle Body Characteristics and Mold Seams, Bottle Glass Color and Glassmaking and Glassmakers. The site also provides an extensive Bottle Glossary and a comprehensive Reference Sources/Bibliography.

None of the Historic Bottle Website pages are fully inclusive since related information is typically spread over many pages. For example, there is information pertinent to dating bottles on virtually every page within the website, not just the Bottle Dating complex of pages. The title of any given page gives the predominant theme of that page and would be the first place to start when pursuing information on that particular subject. Because the processes of bottle dating and identification can be complex, there is a need for many web pages incorporating an abundance of descriptive information. Users need to spend some time viewing different pages.

Attributes and Limitations of the Historic Bottle Website

Since there were several hundred thousand different bottles produced in the United States between 1800 and the 1950s, it is beyond the capability of this or any website or book to provide more than a fraction of data and information related to historic bottles (Fike 1987). The BLM website primarily helps a user determine some key facts about a bottle—approximate age and function—based on observable physical characteristics.

Historic Bottle Website users will note that bottles produced in the United States are strongly emphasized. This geographical limitation is followed for the following reasons.

1. The art and science of bottle dating and typing is a very complex subject when focus is upon the history

of glassmaking for one specific country, in this case the United States. To cover all or most of the world would entail research that is well beyond the funding available for this project and knowledge base of the website's author. A broader geographical scope would entail the creation of a massive website with so many exceptions and regional variations as to significantly reduce the utility found in just focusing on American made bottles.

2. During the late-19th and early-20th centuries (1890 to 1920), American bottle manufacturing technology generally progressed faster than European and Asian glassmaking. This resulted in European and Asian bottles from the early-20th century showing some manufacturing-based traits that would date them as 20 or 30 years older if they had been produced in the US.

3. The Bureau of Land Management is an agency of government that manages lands exclusively in the United States - lands that are virtually all in the American West and Alaska. The bottles most likely to be found during cultural surveys on these lands are those produced in the United States. Although foreign produced bottles are found with regularity during surveys, they are typically a minority.

4. The United States government funds The Historic Bottle Website and it is appropriate that BLM place its emphasis on bottles with most interest to American citizens.

That said, the information on this website is generally applicable to many bottles produced in Canada since its glassmaking history closely parallels that of the United States. In fact, a significant amount of information used in the creation of this website was produced by Canadian historic archaeologists and collectors. It should be noted, however, that there are manufacturing and stylistic trends for Canadian bottles that parallel English bottle making and styles, particularly with many liquor, soda, and beer bottles (Watson and Skrill 1971; Watson et al. 1972; Urquhart 1976; Unitt 1980a, 1980b). What is generally true for Canada to the north is not necessarily true for Mexico to the south. Mexico was slower to implement new techniques and processes and in fact, continued to use mouth-blown processes

for many utilitarian bottles well into the mid-20th century.

Future of the Historic Bottle Website

Currently, the basic structure and content of the *Historic Bottle Website* is almost complete, with most portions fully functional to users pursuing historic bottle information relative to the noted goals. This website will also be, in a sense, always a work in progress as it is the intention of the website author to continually update, refine, and broaden the website's information base in the future with the ultimate goal of allowing all users an ever increasing opportunity to gain substantive information on the majority of bottles produced in the United States between 1800 and the 1950s. New or newly found information will always become available and will be incorporated into the site periodically and indefinitely. It is expected that the BLM will facilitate and sponsor this website on the internet indefinitely.

REFERENCES

Fike, Richard E.
1987   *The Bottle Book: A Comprehensive Guide to Historic Embossed Medicine Bottles.* Gibbs M. Smith, Inc., Peregrine Smith Press, Salt Lake City, UT.

Jones, Olive, and Catherine Sullivan
1989   *The Parks Canada Glass Glossary for the Description of Containers, Tableware, Flat Glass, and Closures.* National Historic Parks and Sites Branch, Parks Canada, Ottawa, Ontario, Canada.

Toulouse, Julian H.
1971   *Bottle Makers and Their Marks.* Thomas Nelson, Inc., New York, NY.

Unitt, Doris, and Peter Unitt
1980a   *Across Canada Bottle Price Guide*, revised edition. Clock House Publications, Peterborough, Ontario, Canada.

1980b   *Bottles in Canada.* Clock House Publications, Peterborough, Ontario, Canada.

University of Utah
1992   *Intermountain Antiquities Computer System User's Guide*, Bottle section, Part
472. University of Utah, Salt Lake City
<http://www.anthro.utah.edu/imacs.html>.

2001   Introduction. In *Intermountain Antiquities Computer System User's Guide*. University of Utah,
Bureau of Land Management, U.S. Forest Service
<http://www.anthro.utah.edu/imacs.html>.

Urquhart, Olive
1976   *Bottlers and Bottles, Canadian*. S. & O. Urquhart,
Toronto, Ontario, Canada.

Watson, George, and Robert Skrill
1971   *Western Canadian Bottle Collecting*. Hume Comp-
ton, Nanaimo, British Columbia, Canada.

Watson, George, Robert Skrill, and Jim Heidt
[1972–1973]   *Western Canadian Bottle Collecting, Book 2.*
Evergreen Press, British Columbia, Canada.

Bill Lindsey
Bureau of Land Management
Klamath Falls Resource Area
2795 Anderson Ave., Building 25
Klamath Falls, OR 97603
<William_Lindsey@or.blm.gov>

GEORGE L. MILLER
CATHERINE SULLIVAN

Machine-Made Glass Containers and the End of Production for Mouth-Blown Bottles.[1]

ABSTRACT

Between 1880 and 1920 a major revolution in the production of glass containers transformed the glass industry and launched an ancient craft into a modern "mechanized engineering activity" (Meigh 1960:25). The number of patents for and improvements of semi-automatic and automatic bottle blowing machines in this period is very confusing. This discussion is an attempt to outline these developments with an emphasis on their chronology and impact on bottle and jar production. Although this discussion is limited to containers, it should be borne in mind that similar mechanization was occurring in other branches of the glass industry.

Introduction

During the late 19th century, improvements in the finish portion of glass containers in combination with the development of convenient, reliable closures, helped increase the demand for glass commercial containers. Two very important closures were the crown top for bottles and the Phoenix cap for jars, both patented in 1892 (Lief 1965:17–20). During this same period, automatic canning and bottling machinery was being developed, along with better knowledge of sterilization and a wider availability of refrigeration (Hampe & Wittenberg 1964:115–21). All of these developments were part of a broad change in food consumption patterns and emerging brand-name products.

Statistics illustrating the impact of these developments on glass container demand and production for Canada and England are very limited; however, in the United States, container produc-

tion increased 50 per cent between 1899 and 1904, that is, before the development of the fully automatic machine (Barnett 1926:70). From 1897 to 1905 the number of hand bottle-blowers in the United States increased from 6000 to 9000, which matches the 50 per cent increase in glass container production (Barnett 1926:71). By 1919 the amount of glass containers produced was 180 per cent higher than the number produced in 1904 (Barnett 1926:70, 89). The increasing market for glass containers helped provide the capital necessary for mechanization and the drive for its success.

All glass-blowing machines (semi-automatic and automatic) that have been successfully taken into production, have involved three separate molding steps. These involve a ring mold which shapes the finish, a parison or part-size mold to give initial shape to the hot glass, and a blow or full-size mold to form the container's final shape, size and any embossed letters or designs it might have. Machine production follows these steps:

1. A gob of molten glass enters the ring and parison mold and is forced by air pressure, suction, or a plunger to take the shape of the full-sized finish mold and that of the part-sized parison mold. The role of the parison mold is to distribute the glass into the shape needed for blowing the full-sized container.
2. With the finish ring mold still attached, the parison mold is removed. In some cases, the body of the parison is allowed to elongate.
3. The full-sized or blow mold is joined to the ring mold around the parison and the bottle is blown to full size by air pressure.

While both semi-automatic and automatic machines went through the above steps, there was a fundamental difference recognized by the glass industry. Semi-automatic machines were supplied with gobs of molten glass and operated by semi-skilled laborers. Fully automatic machines, on the other hand, gathered glass directly from the furnace and all processes in molding and blowing were independent of human labor. Semi-automatics were limited in their production capacity by the speed with which the worker could feed glass to the machine and run the machine through the molding sequence. Limited production capacity and the cost of labor led to the elimination of

[1]This article is reprinted by permission of Park Canada, Ottawa, Ontario k1A1G2, from *Research Bulletin* Number 171.

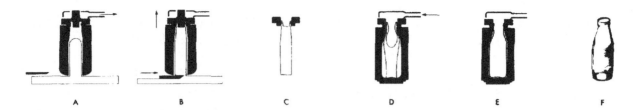

FIGURE 1. The Owens suction-and-blow process (*Drawing by S. Epps*). A. Gob sucked up into blank mold; B. Neck formed and gob sheared off at base; C. Blank (parison) shape with ring mold still attached; D. Blank shape transferred to full size mold; E. Final shape blown; F. Finished bottle

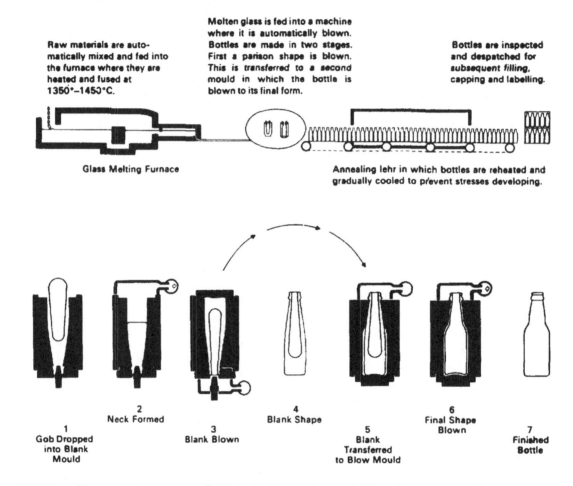

FIGURE 2. Blow-and-blow process (Published with permission of *Glass Manufacturers Federation 1973:25*).

semi-automatic machines in favor of the more productive automatic bottle-blowing machines.

In the hand-blowing process, the glass blower gathered a gob of molten glass on the blow pipe, shaped it and then blew it into shape with or without molds. After the vessel was fully blown, the bottle was disconnected from the blowpipe and then the neck was shaped. Because the mouth of the container was the last part completed, it became known as the finish. A major development

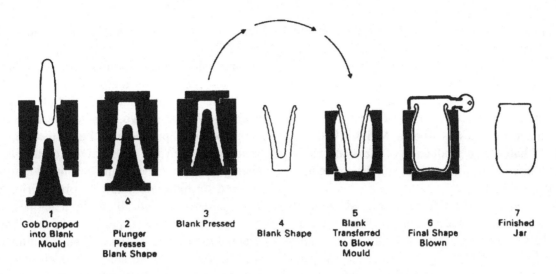

FIGURE 3. Press-and-blow process (*Glass Manufacturers Federation* 1973:25).

towards machine-made glass bottles was the recognition that the finish had to be the first part formed rather than the last. It is the finish that provides the momentary connection of the glass to the machine for blowing of the container. Two American patents, Gillender's in 1865 and Atterbury's in 1873, both described molding processes where the finish was formed as the first part of machine blowing; however, neither of these patents seems to have come into production (Barnett 1926:67).

Two semi-automatic blowing machines were developed in the 1880s—one, by Philip Arbogast, patented in 1881 in the United States, and the other, by Howard Ashley, patented in 1886 in England (Meigh 1960:26–27). Use of machines was limited by strong glass blowers' unions in their respective countries. Arbogast's machine established the principle of using a parison and a blow mold in a press-and-blow method which formed wide-mouthed containers. Use of his machine did not enter large scale production until 1893 when it was used in a non-union shop to make vaseline jars, and, later, fruit and other jars as well (Meigh 1960:27). The Ashley machine used a blow-and-blow process with a parison and full-sized mold to produce small-mouthed containers (Meigh 1960:28). Its successful application to mass production of containers did not take place until 1899 (Meigh 1960:27).

After the development of these prototypes, several other machines were developed in quick succession. These have been well described by Edward Meigh (1960) in "The development of the automatic glass bottle machine: a story of some pioneers." The 1890s was a period of revolution in glass technology; however, the new technology did not begin to cut down on the number of hand glass blowers until after 1905, because expanding demands for glass containers accommodated both the new technology and the old (Barnett 1926:71). This situation could not last forever.

In 1903 Michael Owens of the Libbey Glass Works in Toledo, Ohio, patented his fully automatic glass-blowing machine. He had been making a series of improvements towards machine-blown bottles since 1898 (Meigh 1960:29–31). The machine Owens developed was a major advance over the semi-automatic machines, and in 1903 The Owens Bottle Machine Company was organized with a capital of $3,000,000 to license rights to the machine to various glass companies for production of specific types of bottles (Walbridge 1920:67–68). By 1909 three other companies had taken up licences to use the machine and had put 46 machines into production (Scoville 1948:105, 115). Their success with the machine and further improvements by Owens increased the number of glass companies taking out licences. In the two years from September 1909 to September 1911, the number of Owens machines in production doubled from 51 to 103.

Between 1903 and 1923, Owens designed a series of 12 automatic bottle-blowing machines which increased productivity and expanded the types of containers that could be produced from three-ounce bottles to carboys (Meigh 1960:33). By 1917 half of the production of glass containers in the United States was done on Owens machines (Barnett 1926:88).

The spread of the Owens Bottle Machine to other countries was fairly rapid. In 1906 a licence from the Owens Company was issued to the Canadian Glass Manufacturing Company for a glass works in Hamilton, Ontario (King 1965:90). By 1914 there were 60 Owens machines in Europe (Barker 1968:317).

During the period when the Owens machine was being developed, semi-automatic machines were being improved and automatic feeding devices were being invented. These devices, such as the Brooke's continuous stream-feeding device and the Peiler Paddle Gob Feeder, transformed semi-automatics into automatic glass bottle-blowing machines (Meigh 1960:35–40). They were much simpler than Owens machines and much less costly to build and operate. The feeding devices took a small amount of glass to the machines, whereas the Owens device took the whole machine to the glass. Owens machines could weigh up to 120 tons and were raised and lowered by counterweights to suck up the molten glass (Walbridge 1920:93). Each arm of the Owens machine was dipped into a revolving circular tank furnace to suck glass up into the mold. Each mold-filling required the whole machine to move up and down (Figure 1). Some Owens machines had up to 15 arms and could produce 350 gross pint bottles in 24 hours, production equal to the output of 50 glass workers (Meigh 1960:33).

While the Owens machine was highly successful in large production runs, it was of limited use for short runs due to the necessity of shutting down the whole machine to change a mold on any one arm. As well, the larger the Owens machine, that is the greater the number of arms, the larger the revolving tank needed, which meant that fuel costs were higher for the more complex machines (Meigh 1960:34).

Rapid adoption of machines for manufacturing glass containers was a matter of economics. Semi-automatic and automatic glass bottle-blowing machines worked in two ways to lower the cost of glass container production. First, mechanization greatly increased the productivity of the workers making glass containers, and second, it eliminated the need for highly-skilled craftsmen. Prior to the development of bottle-blowing machines, glass blowers were very well paid, for their skills were essential to produce bottles and jars. Minimal skill was needed to operate semi-automatic machines, and the fully automatic machines almost completely replaced laborers.

In terms of productivity, the machines greatly increased output of containers per man-hour. Boris Stern's 1927 study of *Productivity of Labor in the Glass Industry* established that semi-automatic machines were between 42 and 171 per cent more productive per man-hour than hand production methods and that fully automatic machines were between 642 and 3806 per cent more productive than hand manufacture (1927:8). These ranges relate to the size of containers being produced and differences in the capacity of the various types of bottle-blowing machines.

The same study indicates that the labor cost per gross of bottles produced on the semi-automatics were from 23 to 52 per cent cheaper than hand-blown bottles. Labor costs per gross of bottles produced on fully automatic machines were between 90 and 97 per cent lower than hand-blown bottles (Stern 1927:8). Lower labor costs were of course offset by the capitalization necessary to acquire the machines.

Development of the Semi-Automatics into Automatic Bottle-Blowing Machines

Semi-automatic bottle-blowing machines which began development before the Owens machine had their significance eclipsed by the speed and efficiency of the Owens machine. The step needed to make the semi-automatic fully automatic was the development of automatic feeding devices. One of the earliest such devices to be successfully developed was the Brooke's stream feeder, patented in 1903 (Scoville 1948:182–83). Between 1911 and 1915 the Graham Glass Company adapted the stream feeder to their semi-automatic machine. When it became apparent that the Graham Glass Company had developed a workable automatic glass-blowing machine, the Owens company bought them out. However, attempts to further the production of this machine met with limited success (Scoville 1948:182–83). Brooke's feeder used a gravity flow of glass in a stream from the glass furnace. The flow was husbanded in a cup until the desired quantity was collected and it was then dumped into the mold. Cooling of the glass in the cup caused it to be stringy and often entrapped air blisters. These defects did not stop Hazel-Atlas from using a stream feeder to produce pressed jar lids (Meigh 1960:36).

The Hartford-Fairmont Feeding Devices

An engineering firm in Hartford, Connecticut, and a glass company in Fairmont, West Virginia, were incorporated in 1914 to develop an automatic feeding device to be used with semi-automatic bottle-blowing machines (Meigh 1960:36–37). The engineer who developed the feeding device was Karl E. Peiler, with an engineering background from the Massachusetts Institute of Technology rather than from the glass industry. The first successful feeder he developed used a fire clay paddle to push a gob of molten glass from the furnace onto a metal chute kept moist to create a cushion of stream for the gob to ride on into the mold (Meigh 1960:37–38). In 1915 this device was put into use for the production of milk bottles and Hartford-Fairmont began marketing it to other glass manufacturers.

The gob feeder was limited to the production of wide-mouth glass containers. To overcome this limitation, Peiler created an improved gob feeder, a Paddle-needle Feeder that came into production in 1918 (Meigh 1960:38). It had a lip on the tank furnace with a hole at its base, through which a plunger needle fed the glass. Success of Peiler's feeding devices led to their wide usage. In fact, the Owens Company entered into an agreement with Hartford-Fairmont and became a major lessee of gob feeders in 1924 (Meigh 1960:39). By 1925, in the United States, the gob feeders working with various glass bottle- and jar-blowing machines were producing approximately 8,500,000 gross of glass containers as compared to roughly 12,500,000 gross by the Owens machine (Scoville 1948:185).

Use of the gob feeders with bottle-blowing machines involved mechanical alignment of parison and blow molds, usually by means of one or two rotating tables. This complexity was simplified by the I.S. or Individual Section Machine developed by Henry Ingle of the Hartford Empire Company in 1925 (Meigh 1972:62). Instead of moving molds to the feeding device, the I.S. feeder had a bank of parison and blow molds in a straight line on a fixed-bed plate. Gobs of hot glass were delivered to each mold in sequence and any one section of the machine could be shut down to change the molds without stopping production in the other sections (Meigh 1972:62–64). This was a great advantage over other automatic machines and by 1960 there were 1250 I.S. machines in production (Meigh 1960:47).

Because the various machines with gob feeders were less expensive than the Owens machine and more versatile for small orders, they began to supersede the Owens machine during the 1920s. Sometime between 1927 and 1930, the number of glass containers produced on gob feeder machines surpassed the amount produced on the Owens machines (Meigh 1972:57). By 1947, in the United States, it is estimated that only 30 per cent of production was on the Owens machine while the gob feeders produced 67 per cent of the glass containers (Phillips 1947:188–89). Meigh estimates that over 90 per cent of world production of glass containers by the early 1970s was produced on gob feeder machinery (Meigh 1972:58). Whether any Owens machines are still in production today is not clear from the literature. In Canada the Owens machine stopped being used at Dominion Glass Company in about 1945.

Impact of the Machine-made Glass Container

The impact of automatic machine production of glass containers was extensive and rapid. Hand production of bottles and jars declined rapidly from the second decade of the 20th century. For archaeologists, two immediate questions come to mind: when did hand production stop, and what characteristics might be used to identify bottles from the various machines that came into production? Much broader than these questions is the impact of cheap glass containers on society.

The period of overlap for hand and machine production is fairly long. Types of bottles being blown by hand were continually being reduced as semi-automatic, automatic, and feeding device machines were developed. Barnett's *Chapters on Machinery and Labor* (1926) estimates the number of hand glass bottle-blowers working in the United States during the period when bottle-blowing machinery was being developed:

Year	No. of Blowers	Page Ref.
1896	6229	83
1897	6000	70
1905	9000	71
1917	2000	90
1924	1000	86

Declines in the number of bottle blowers were occurring at a time when glass container production was rapidly increasing. Once again, Barnett provides the statistics on container production used below:

Year	No. of Gross Produced	Page Ref.
1899	7,777,000	70
1904	11,942,000	89
1909	12,313,000	89
1914	19,288,000	89
1917	24,000,000 est.	89
1919	22,289,000	89
1924	18,000,000 est.	85

The drop in production reflected in the figures for 1919 and 1924 was caused by prohibition which began in 1919 in the United States. Rising glass container production from the beginning of the 20th century was of course related to increased use of semi-automatic and later fully automatic bottle-blowing machines: in 1900 there were 80 semi-automatic machines producing wide-mouthed glass containers; by 1904 when Owens machines came into production there were 200 semi-automatics in production and the number increased to a high of 459 in 1916 (Barnett 1926:69, 92). After that, the Owens machine and gob feeding devices adapted to existing machines cut into bottle production by semi-automatics. By 1924 there were only 72 semi-automatics in production (Barnett 1926:111). Impact of the automatics is reflected in a 1927 government study by Boris Stern, *Productivity of Labor in the Glass Industry*, which states that:

> In 1926, out of 25 bottle plants inspected only one plant was found using the semi-automatic to a large extent. In another plant the semi-automatic was found standing by the furnace but dismantled and ready to be displaced by an automatic. In still another plant a semi-automatic machine had recently been consigned to the scrap heap (Stern 1927:35).

Adoption of Owens machines was retarded by the leasing system used by the Owens Company. In the 1905–06 period there were only eight Owens machines in production. By 1916–17 there were 200 in production (Barnett 1926:88). It was shortly after this period that the gob-feeding devices and the Individual Section Machine began making inroads on the market serviced by Owens machines. As mentioned earlier, by 1917 the Owens machine was producing half of the glass containers made in the United States. The other half was produced by 2000 hand blowers and 2000 operators of semi-automatic machines. According to Barnett, the 12,000,000 bottles produced by glass blowers and semi-automatic machine operators in 1917 was equal to the 12,000,000 bottles produced by 9000 glass blowers and 1000 semi-automatic machine operators in 1905 (Barnett 1926:88–89). Stated as mathematical equations, these figures come out as follows:

1905

9000 blowers' production + 1000 machine workers' production = 12,000,000 gross

1917
2000 blowers' production + 2000 machine workers' production = 12,000,000 gross

Assuming that productivity for blowers remained the same and solving the above equations gives the following results:

Hand-blown   Semi-automatic
1905 7,714,000 gross + 3,286,000 gross = 12,000,000 gross
1917 1,500,000 gross + 10,500,000 gross = 12,000,000 gross

Total 1917 production
1,500,000 gross by hand blown methods
10,500,000 gross by semi-automatics
12,000,000 gross by Owens machines

These figures are rather rough, but they suggest that hand-blown containers made up between 5 and 10 per cent of all the bottles and jars produced in the United States in 1917.

One of the myths about the Owens bottle-blowing machine is that it greatly lowered the cost of glass containers and thus expanded the demand for them. In reality, the price of bottles made on Owens machines fell only about 15 per cent from 1905 to 1914 (Barnett 1926:130). Thus, the cost of production was a marginal consideration in expanding the use of glass containers. More important was that machines could produce highly standardized, reliable finishes and sizes that could be used on the automatic machines that filled the containers. These developments combined to meet and change consumer demands for products put up in glass containers.

The types of bottles produced on the Owens machine were limited to those for which there was a fairly large demand. Stern's 1927 report sums up the machine-made bottle market as follows:

The principle advantage of the machine lies in mass production. The high cost of making the necessary number of molds and the time required in adjusting the machine and changing molds make it uneconomical for large machines to work on orders less than 1,000 gross of bottles. Even for the smaller six-arm machines the order has to be at least 250 gross to make production economical. Hence the smaller orders, especially those below 100 gross, necessarily go to the hand plants. Among bottles of this kind the principle place is occupied by perfumery and toilet ware, individually shaped bottles being used as a means of identifying and advertising their contents.

As a competitive factor in the bottle branch of the glass industry hand production is absolutely non existent. At best it fills the gaps left by the machine and must therefore be considered as supplementary to the machine rather than competitive (1927:55).

Some idea of just how costly the molds for the Owens machine were is given in B. E. Moody's *Packaging in Glass:*

A 'single' mould, i.e., the equipment required for one head on a machine, consists of at least nine separate parts, . . . and a complete set for a six-head machine could cost well over £1000. It is clearly vital that the bottle maker should be able to obtain a long working life from the moulds; a single mould may be capable of producing something like a million bottles before it has to be scrapped (1963:21).

The minimum number for an economical run of glass containers appears to have increased between 1927 and 1963 when Moody wrote his book. He states that:

We have seen above that it is not an economic proposition to run a bottle machine for short periods, and generally a run of about three days would be regarded as an absolute minimum. The output from a modern bottle machine might be in the region of 100 to 1200 gross per day, depending on the size of the bottle and size of machine, so the minimum number of bottles which can be made economically in a run is of the order of 1,000 gross (1963:20).

The economics of machine production changed the characteristics of bottles. Prior to machine domination of glass container production, the industry produced a wide variety of bottles and jars for small companies such as local breweries and soft drink bottlers. Through the use of plate molds, glass manufacturers made distinctive bottles for small pharmacies and medicine companies. These small-run orders were not compatible with machine production. Barnett summarizes the situation in 1926.

Many articles put up in glass containers have a small market and the orders of the makers of these articles are for only a small number of bottles. The Owens machine is an instrument of large scale production, and the manufacturers who were using the older methods of manufacture—hand and semi-automatic—were able, therefore, to hold the orders for small lots of special bottles. This advantage has been less

important in recent years, as the small user of glass containers, in order to secure cheaper bottles, has become willing to
use standard sizes and to rely on the label for his distinctive
mark (1926:91).

Hand-blown tradition for commercial containers
was still going on in 1934 for "small orders and
oddly-shaped bottles" (Jerome 1934:106).

World War II further consolidated the standardization of glass containers when the American
federal government, with the glass manufacturers,
reduced the number of types and varieties of bottles to maximize production.

Prior to the war, there were many odd shapes and sizes of
bottles. War standardization, and elimination of small sizes,
provided an increased output with the same production
machinery. Janssen stated in 1946 that a return to the prewar
pattern would cut output by 20% in grossage, or 40% in
gallonage (Holscher 1953:375).

Hand-blowing of commercial containers in the
United States probably was close to non-existent
by World War II, and in the period between the
World Wars it was limited to odd shaped containers, perfumery, toiletware and carboys.

Machine-made Glass Containers in England

Information for countries other than the United
States is not as easy to locate. In England, according to Angus-Butterworth, mechanization of the
glass industry was fairly complete by 1924
(Angus-Butterworth 1948:177–78). Mechanical
production of glass containers in England began
with the use of the Ashley semi-automatic machine
in Castleford in 1887. Further modifications produced several models, one of which, the Plank
machine, had 20 units in commercial operation by
1889. A semi-automatic jar machine was in production in the early 1890s, and before the end of
the 19th century, three factories had put bottle
machines into operation and a further three or four
had used jar machines (Turner 1938:251–52).

Shortly after the Owens automatic bottle-
blowing machine was developed in the United
States, the Owens Company attempted to lease
rights to it in Europe. Not finding a buyer, they

formed the Owens European Bottle Machine Company and built a factory at Manchester, England,
which was in production by 1907 (Meigh
1960:34). Successful demonstration of the
machine's capabilities in the mass production of
cheap glass containers convinced the European
manufacturers to speedily form a cartel, the Eu-
ropaischer Verband der Flaschen-fabriken Gesell-
schaft (E.V.), to purchase the European rights to
the Owens machine for 12 million gold marks
(Meigh 1960:34). The English part of the cartel
was the British Association of Glass Bottle Manufacturers Ltd.

The E.V. cartel was interested in minimizing the
impact of the Owens machine on glass production
and union resistance to it. Therefore, they set goals
of 10 per cent of glass container production for the
first year with an increase of 5 per cent for the
following two years of each country's production
(Barker 1968:317). If they had continued to increase at the rate of 5 per cent a year, then 100 per
cent automation would have occurred around
1925. Angus-Butterworth suggests that by 1924
the English glass container industry was under
"fairly complete mechanization" (1948:177–78).
Supporting this is Meigh's statement that the English glass container industry was fully automated
by the early 1920s (1960:34). However, Meigh,
writing in 1934, indicates that a small number of
hand-blown bottles was being produced in England
for "special bottles and those used in small
quantities" (1934:123–24).

One of the English companies that continued
hand production on a large scale was Beatson,
Clark & Company Ltd., a large manufacturer of
druggists' ware. Their production in 1929 was 98
per cent mouth-blown and 2 per cent semi-
automatic, with an output of 1100 gross per week
(Beatson, Clark & Co. Ltd. 1952:40). While this
seems like a large production, it would be less than
one per cent of the British glass container production which was over eight million gross in 1928
(Meigh 1960:43). In 1929 Beatson, Clark and Co.
began building a glass works capable of fully automatic production and by 1949, 80 per cent of their
production was fully automatic, 19 per cent semi-
automatic and less than 1 per cent mouth-blown

(Beatson, Clark & Co. Ltd. 1952:30–40). As in the United States, it was the pharmaceutical and cosmetic bottles that were the last types to be mouth-blown.

Machine-made Glass Containers in Germany

For the rest of Europe, the history of the transition to machine-made glass is much more sketchy. Germany had the largest glass container production in Europe prior to the introduction of the Owens machine and was the major shareholder in the E.V. cartel formed in 1907 to purchase European rights to the Owens machine (Barker 1968:317). Before the Owens machine came on the scene, a very successful device known as the Schiller Semi-Automatic, a press-and-blow machine, was in 1906 put into commercial use in Germany. Between 1906 and 1932, it is claimed, 1150 Schiller Semi-Automatic bottle-making machines were installed throughout Europe, 223 of them in Germany itself (Turner 1938:257).

The first Owens fully-automatic bottle-blowing machine was installed in Germany in 1907, the year the E.V. cartel was formed (Turner 1938:58). As mentioned earlier, the E.V. cartel attempted to minimize the impact of the Owens machine by limiting its production to 10 per cent of the glass containers for the year of introduction with 5 per cent increases for the following two years. If this schedule were followed by Germany, then roughly 40 per cent of German bottle production by 1914 would have been made on fully-automatic machines. In 1914, half of the 60 Owens machines authorized by the E.V. cartel were in Germany (Barker 1968:317), a higher proportion than the original agreed-upon distribution of machines based on pre-machine production for each country in the cartel. This suggests that Germany may have been ahead of England in the proportion of Owens machine-made bottles being produced. What happened to the German glass industry during World War I is not clear, and it is difficult to say when mouth-blown bottle production ended in Germany.

Machine-made Glass Containers in France

Prior to the introduction of Owens machines into Europe, the French production of glass containers almost equalled English production, making France the third largest European producer of such wares (Barker 1968:317). Like manufacturers in the United States, England, and Germany, the French had developed a successful semi-automatic bottle machine. Claude Boucher began developing his machine in 1894 and was successful by 1897 (Turner 1938:253). According to Henrivaux, the Boucher bottle machine was used in countries other than France, and he estimates world-wide production by this machine to have been in excess of 200,000 bottles in 1909 (Henrivaux 1909:395). Unfortunately, figures are not given for French production of machine-made vs. hand-made glass containers.

French glass manufacturers joined the E.V. cartel in 1907 and then withdrew from the agreement (Barker 1968:317). How long they remained outside the cartel is not clear; however, the first Owens machine was installed in France in 1910, following installations in England, Germany, Holland, Austria, and Sweden (Turner 1938:258). How fast the French industry converted to mechanized bottle production is not clear from the literature consulted.

Machine-made Glass Containers in Canada

Information on the transition of the Canadian glass industry from a craft to an automated industrial activity is very limited. For example, the available literature provides little information on the introduction of semi-automatic bottle machines into the Canadian market and no quantitative information on their output. The dramatic technological developments in the United States probably entered Canada much faster than England, due to physical proximity, the constant flow of information carried by glass workers moving between Canada and the U.S., and contact between the unions involved in setting wages in both countries.

For example, one of the early manufacturers of semi-automatic machines was Frank O'Neill (of Toledo, Ohio) who had one of his jar-lid power presses operating in Ontario by around 1901 (Scoville 1948:333 n42). Newspapers from Wallaceburg, Ontario, for 24 September, 1903, report fruit jar-making machines at the Sydenham Glass Works but unfortunately do not mention the type of machine being used (Stevens 1967:29). Among the types of semi-automatic machines documented in use in Canada are the O'Neill, Teeple-Johnson, Olean, and Lynch machines (Stevens 1967:20, 21, 54, 55, 88, 90, 91; King 1965:89; Meigh 1960:40). The relationship of Frank O'Neill with the Canadian glass manufacturers appears to have been fairly significant. After selling his United States interests in the O'Neill Machine Company in Toledo in 1912, he set up the O'Neill European Machine Company factory in Montreal (Meigh 1960:40). How much impact the semi-automatic machines had on hand-blown production of glass containers and how rapidly they spread in Canada is not documented in the literature.

Information on the introduction of the Owens machine to Canada is better documented, due to the leasing structure set up by the Owens Company, and, no doubt, also because of the great costs involved. Rights to the Owens automatic machine for Canada were secured before the European rights were leased. In 1906, for $104,900, the Canadian Glass Manufacturing Company purchased exclusive Canadian container rights on the Owens bottle machine (Scoville 1948:141, Table 14). This company was established specifically to lease Owens machines to operating glass plants in Canada. One of the prime movers in the company was George A. Grier who had acquired control of the Diamond Glass Company and changed its name to Diamond Flint Glass Company (King 1965:90). The first Owens machines in Canada were set up in the Hamilton Glass Works in 1906 (Stevens 1967:9–10).

Control of container rights for the Owens machines was instrumental in the amalgamation of Diamond Flint Glass, Sydenham Glass Company, and the Canadian Glass Company into the Domin-

ion Glass Company in 1913 (King 1965:90). This was the dominant Canadian glass company until the founding of Consumers Glass Company in 1917 (Stevens 1967:54–55). By that time the feed-and-flow devices discussed earlier were being adapted to semi-automatics, such as the O'Neill, Hartford, and Lynch machines, which made them competitive with the Owens machine, and they were a great deal cheaper (Meigh 1960:39).

How long it took bottle-blowing machines to replace bottle blowers in Canada is not well documented. Because the Dominion Glass Company had a practical monopoly on glass production in Canada, it was not a case of hand factories competing against mechanized factories. When Dominion Glass built its new glassworks in Redcliff, Alberta, in 1913, the company combined production on the Owens machine with hand-blown shops. In 1915 the Redcliff operation had an Owens ten-arm machine, a lamp chimney machine, and three bottle shops in operation (Stevens 1967:69). The bottle shops would have produced orders that were too small for production on the Owens machine. Most likely these included such types as pharmaceutical bottles, cosmetic wares and probably demijohns. By the mid-1920s the amount of glassware being hand-blown in Canada was very small, as was the case in the United States and England. Gerald Stevens describes the declining role of glass blowers at the Redcliff plant in the 1930s:

> Mechanization was to take its toll. A jurisdictional issue arose in 1937 and the last of the glass blowers declared a lengthy strike. Eventually, they returned to work, "but things were never the same. Their time had run out and they and their skills and songs are gone." (Stevens 1967:69–70).

According to E. G. Davis, manager of the Dominion Glass Works plant at Wallaceburg, Ontario, there were no glass blowers employed in Canadian glass factories in 1959 and the last hand-blowing operation at the Wallaceburg works was in about 1942 (Stevens 1967:91).

The Owens machine in Canada began being replaced by the Individual Section Machine in the 1940s (King 1965:91).

Discussion and Chronological Summary

For the purposes of archaeology, the machine-made bottle provides an excellent, readily-identifiable time marker. Because all semi-automatic and automatic bottle-blowing machines work on the principle of forming the finish first as an attachment to the blowing machine, and the use of a parison mold followed by a full-size mold, identification of the differences between bottles made on the various machines is limited. The major exception to this is the Owens scar.

Characteristics of Machine-made Bottle Manufacture

1. A large number of mold seams, particularly related to the finish.
2. Finish seams:—horizontal mold seam encircling the neck-finish junction. This seam must appear with other machine-made characteristics; an 1860 patent for hand-blown bottles features this seam (Toulouse 1969:584).—1 or 2 horizontal mold seams around the top of the finish or lip caused by a neck-shaping plug and a collar to guide it. On beer and beverage bottles these seams have sometimes been fire-polished off, so other evidence must be sought.—continuous vertical mold seams up the side of the body and over the finish (Figures 4 and 6).
3. Body seams:—wandering vertical "ghost" mold seams on the body of the container, left by the parison mold halves, which join the full-sized mold seams at the finish. A "ghost" seam is certain proof of machine manufacture (Toulouse 1969:585) (Figure 5).
4. Base:—either cup or post bottom mold seams can appear on machine-made bottles and should not be confused with the mouth-blown versions.
   —Owens scar, a distinctive, circular mark with "feathery" edges, caused by the shears that cut off the gob of glass in the suction

FIGURE 4. *a & b.* Two bottles showing typical machine-produced mold seams, including on *b* a "ghost" seam from the parison mold on the body (*Photo by R. Chan; Drawing by D. Kappler*).

machines. An Owens scar is usually off-center and may sometimes even extend onto the heel. It dates from 1904 until at least 1969 (Toulouse 1969:582) (Figure 8).
—valve mark. A non-symmetrical indented groove on the base, found on wide-mouthed containers and milk bottles. 1930s into 1950s (Toulouse 1969:583) (Figure 7).
—"ghost" seam from the base part of the parison mold.

The main difference between semi-automatic and automatic machines was the degree of mechanization and thus the rate of production, not the appearance of the container. Bottles produced by either method should look the same and have similar "typical" seams and evidence of manufacture.

Roughly speaking, the chronology of mechanization for production of glass containers is as follows:

FIGURE 5. Close-up view of a wandering 'ghost' mold seam on the body of a container (*Photo by R. Chan*).

FIGURE 6. Close-up view of a container finish, showing the large number of seams left by the mold parts (*Photo by R. Chan*).

A. Semi-automatic machines for wide-mouthed containers: commercial production begins 1893, peak ca. 1917, end ca. 1926.

B. Semi-automatic machines for production of narrow-mouthed containers: commercial production begins 1889, peak ca. 1917, end ca. 1926.

C. Fully-automatic production on the Owens machine for narrow- and wide-mouth containers: commercial production begins 1904; by 1917 they were producing half of the bottles in the United States; began being replaced by feeders in the 1920s; end of production around the late 1940s or early 1950s.

D. Semi-automatic made automatic by flow-and-feed devices: introduced in 1917, continued to grow in importance and offered an inexpensive alternative to the Owens machine.

E. The Individual Section Machine: developed in 1925; by the 1940s this had become the machine most commonly used in producing bottles.

Hand-blown bottles, as discussed earlier, lasted into the 1930s but only for small run types such as pharmaceutical bottles, cosmetic wares and demi-

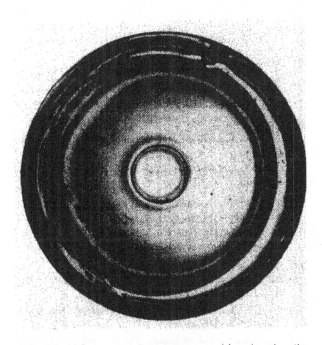

FIGURE 7. Owens suction scar caused by shearing the glass when the mold is full. The shears leave a cooled glass surface, creating a scar from the cutting action; a also shows the base and heel mold seams from the parison mold (*Drawing by D. Kappler; Photo by R. Chan*).

johns. Their quantities would be very small in any post-1920 archaeological assemblage.

REFERENCES

ARGUS-BUTTERWORTH, L. M.
  1948 *The Manufacture of Glass.* Pitman Publishing Corporation, New York.

BARKER, T. C.
  1968 The Glass Industry. In *The Development of British Industry and Foreign Competition: 1874–1914, Studies in Industrial Enterprise,* edited by Derek H. Aldocroft, pp. 307–25. University of Toronto Press, Toronto.

BARNETT, GEORGE E.
  1926 *Chapters on Machinery and Labor.* Harvard University Press, Cambridge.

BEATSON, CLARK & CO. LTD.
  1952 *The Glass Works Rotherham: 1751–1951.* Beatson, Clark & Co. Ltd., Rotherham, England.

THE GLASS MANUFACTURERS FEDERATION
  1973 *Making Glass.* Glass Manufacturers Federation, London.

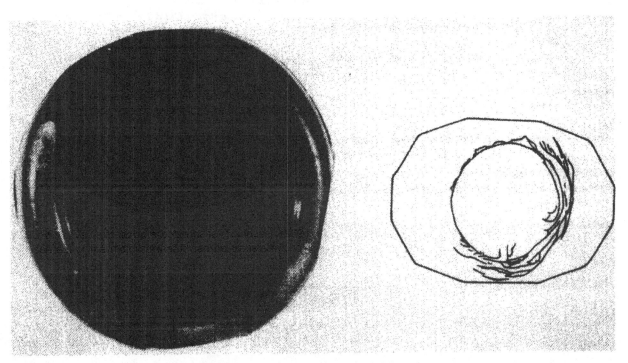

FIGURE 8. Valve mark on a bottle base. Toulouse (1969:583) says that this mark is caused by a valve that ejects the parison out of the mold so that it can be transferred to the blow mold for completion (*Photo by R. Chan*).

HAMPE, EDWARD C., JR., AND MERLE WITTENBERG
1964   *The Lifeline of America: Development of the Food Industry.* McGraw-Hill Book Company, New York.

HENRIVAUX, JULES
1909   Fabrication mecanique des bouteilles. *La Nature* 37:392–95.

HOLSCHER, H. H.
1953   Feeding and Forming. In *Handbook of Glass Manufacture: A Book of Reference for the Plant Executive, Technologist and Engineer*, compiled and edited by Fay V. Tooley, pp. 299–388. Ogden Publishing Co., New York.

JEROME, HARRY
1934   *Mechanization in Industry.* National Bureau of Economic Research, New York.

KING, THOMAS B.
1965   History of the Canadian Glass Industry. *Journal of the Canadian Ceramic Society* 34:86–91.
1977   19th century Bottle Moulds. *Glasfax 10th Anniversary Seminar, June 11, 1977*, pp. 53–59. Montreal.

LIEF, ALFRED
1965   *A Close-up of Closures: History and Progress.* Glass Containers Manufacturers Institute, New York.

MEIGH, EDWARD
1934   Notes on the Design of Glass Bottles. *Journal of the Society of Glass Technology* 18:122–127.
1960   The Development of the Automatic Glass Bottle Machine: A Story of Some Pioneers. *Glass Technology* 1:25–50.
1972   *The Story of the Glass Bottle.* C. E. Ramsden & Co. Ltd., Stoke-on-Trent, England.

MOODY, E. B.
1963   *Packaging in Glass.* Hutchinson, London.

PHILLIPS, C. J.
1947   *Glass the Miracle Maker: Its History, Technology and Applications.* Pitman Publishing, New York.

SCOVILLE, WARREN C.
1948   *Revolution in Glassmaking: Enterpreneurship and Technological Change in the American Industry 1880–1920.* Harvard University Press, Cambridge.

STERN, BORIS
1927   *Productivity of Labor in the Glass Industry.* Bulletin of the United States Bureau of Labor Statistics No. 441. Government Printing Office, Washington, D.C.

STEVENS, GERALD
1961   *Early Canadian Glass.* McGraw-Hill, Ryerson, Toronto.
1967   *Canadian Glass: c. 1825–1925.* Ryerson Press, Toronto.

TOOLEY, FAY V. (COMPILER AND EDITOR)
1953   *Handbook of Glass Manufacture: A Book of References for the Plant Executive, Technologist and Engineer.* Ogden Publishing Co., New York.

TOULOUSE, JULIAN HARRISON
1967   When did hand bottle blowing stop? *The Western Collector* 5 (8):41–45.
1969   A Primer on Mold Seams. *The Western Collector* 7 (12):578–587.

TURNER, W. E. S.
1938   The early Development of Bottle Making Machines in Europe. *Journal of the Society of Glass Technology.* 22:250–58.

WALBRIDGE, WILLIAM S.
1920   *American Bottles Old & New: A Story of the Industry in the United States.* The Owens Bottle Company, Toledo.

GEORGE L. MILLER
SENIOR LABORATORY ANALYST
OFFICE OF EXCAVATION AND CONSERVATION
COLONIAL WILLIAMSBURG FOUNDATION
WILLIAMSBURG, VIRGINIA 23185

CATHERINE SULLIVAN
1600 LIVERPOOL COURT
PARKS CANADA
OTTAWA, ONTARIO K1A 1G2

OLIVE R. JONES

A Guide to Dating Glass Tableware: 1800 to 1940

Introduction

Between 1800 and 1940, the glass industry production method in North America and Europe changed from predominantly mouth-blown to predominantly machine-made. At the beginning of this period, successful glass production was based on practical observation and experience but, step by step, the knowledge base changed to mechanical and scientific expertise. Hand-in-hand with changing production methods came changes in tableglass decorating technologies and new glass formulas. Increased mechanization and innovations provided lower-priced tableglass which significantly increased the number of consumers who could afford glass and, at the same time, increased the choices available to consumers.

Tableglass was made and purchased not only to be used but to be seen, motivations similar to those for choosing ceramic tablewares, furniture, and other domestic furnishings. Motifs and tableglass shapes often reflected the decorative arts movements of the 19th and early 20th centuries. At the same time, some motifs and shapes remained in production regardless of fashion. For example, tumblers decorated with vertical panels were made throughout the entire 1800-1940 period. Some tableglass was made with no surface decoration; some was completely covered with decoration; some motifs were pictorial, others were geometric or abstract. Increasingly, between 1825 and 1940, consumers could choose from a number of different styles and a variety of price ranges. Prestigious and expensive hand-cut or hand-engraved motifs were imitated in inexpensive mold-blown, pressed, or acid-etched glasses while inexpensively cut and engraved tableglass competed with pressed and acid-etched glasses. Consumers chose tableglass that reflected their purchasing power, aesthetic preferences, and social position. However, in any one household, the tableglass probably represented a range of prices, a variety of styles, and different levels of service. In the same household, as with ceramic tablewares, one might also expect to find a mix of older and newer glassware.

During the 140 years covered by this guide, the goods produced by glass manufacturers reflected changes in drinking patterns and in food service. For example, tumbler usage increased as non-alcoholic drinks–such as soda water, water, lemonade, and fruit juices–became the drinks of choice for many consumers. The American habit of drinking tea from the saucer led to the production and use of glass cup plates between the late 1820s and about 1860. Celery glasses reflected the practice of serving celery stalks at the table. Salt shakers were introduced in the 1860s, and gradually became the dominant form for serving salt, although small individual open salts continued to be sold. Inns and taverns had always served food and drink but it was not until the 1840s that glass manufacturers started offering "bar tumblers" and decanters with "bar lips" for commercial use. By the early 20th century, suppliers offered a wide range of wares specifically for commercial use by restaurants, hotels, clubs, ocean liners, and railroads (Budde & Westermann 1913).

At the beginning of the 19th century, American markets were supplied with some domestically made glass and with glass imported from continental Europe and Britain (Lanman 1969:15-48; Wilson 1994[2]:769-772). Although glass manufacturers in the United States faced fierce competition from Europe and a shortage of experienced workmen, they were able to establish the basis for a successful American glass industry during the first 25 years of the 19th century. During the second quarter of the century, American glass factories began to compete seriously with foreign producers (Davis 1949:35-41, 50-64, 65-71) and by mid-century, the industry was firmly established. However, imported glasswares continued to be an important part of the American marketplace, particularly in mouth-blown and hand-decorated wares.

From the 1760s until the 1840s, the Canadian market was served almost entirely by British-made products, but after Great Britain adopted free trade in 1845, the Canadian market was opened to American and European products (Jones 1986a, 1986b, 1986c, 1986d, 1992). Attempts to manufacture glass in Canada began in the 1840s, but the companies survived only briefly. In the 1870s, a glass factory in Hamilton, Ontario, was able to operate successfully for a number of years, but it was not until the 1890s that the Canadian glass industry truly became established (King 1987:front and back flyleaves). The primary tableglass products were pressed and machine-blown tablewares. Canadian cut glass firms operating in the early 20th century used imported blanks; Henry Birks & Sons, for example, used French and American blanks (Henry Birks & Sons 1903:8).

While the country of origin was sometimes used as a selling point, it is important to understand that the glass industry of the 19th and early 20th centuries was an international one (Great Britain 1907). Successful technological advances, decorative innovations, and decorative motifs were immediately copied by manufacturers and decorators in other countries, not just by rival firms. After the success of the 1851 London Great Exhibition, subsequent international exhibitions encouraged the diffusion of technology and styles throughout the western world.

From 1800 to 1940, the tableglass industry was one of innovation, invention, eclecticism, revivals, and imitation, particularly after about 1850, when interest in industrial design led to the establishment of design schools and of museums such as the Victoria and Albert Museum in London and the Musée des arts décoratifs in Paris. This interest led glassware designers to pillage the past for inspiration. For example, engraved glassware shown at the Paris Exhibition in 1878 highlighted classical motifs, but also included Arabian, Assyrian, Byzantine, Egyptian, Persian, Indian, Chinese, Japanese, Celtic, Medieval (Gothic Revival revisited), Renaissance, and 18th-century styles (Morris 1978:95-96). Colonial, Adam, or Georgian revival styles, which imitated patterns of the first 30 years of the 19th century, began to appear in the early 20th century and continued well into the 1930s. At the same time, the glass industry was a conservative one, with many shapes and motifs staying in production for decades. While it is possible to give introductory dates for many changes, it is more difficult to establish end

dates. Certain types of decorative motifs faded but never entirely disappeared, or they survived in a simplified form, or reappeared in a modified version or as a conscious revival which never quite matched the original. It is safest to assume that no motif or style disappeared for good. Nevertheless, it is possible to identify trends and to place individual pieces of tableglass within a context.

Technological innovations were also an integral part of the manufacturing and decorating techniques introduced between 1800 and 1940. However, while one part of the industry adopted new technology other parts did not, depending on the markets served by the manufacturer. Hand-blown and hand-decorated glassware existed alongside pressed glassware and, finally, machine-blown tablewares. For example, from about 1820 to 1860, trailed glass threads as decoration were applied to wares made in window and bottle glass factories in the United States. The process was mechanized in the 1860s, but hand-trailing continued to be used on glassware at the high end of the market (see Glass on Glass).

Morris (1978:14) summarizes the table glass industry at the end of the 19th century as follows:

Towards the end of the Victorian period production had crystallized into three main streams catering for different social strata with widely differing tastes. At the top end of the scale were richly cut and engraved table glass and expensive novelties such as "cameo" glass, for the high class trade and for export. Plainer, simpler glass, often historically based on earlier styles catered for those of aesthetic taste and for devotees of the Arts and Crafts movement. The third stream, the cheapest end of production, included pressed glass (sometimes in imitation of the current styles of cut glass, but often in entirely independent styles) and innumerable styles of fancy glass and novelties catering for the vast mass of the public.

With the large volume of detailed information available on tableglass manufactured between 1800 and 1940, no attempt has been made to duplicate these details. Instead, this guide will summarize datable attributes, introduce the primary and secondary sources, and provide guidance as to which sources have additional information on a specific decorative or manufacturing process. Discussion centers on American, British, and Canadian glass, with some information given on Bohemian and other continental

European glass. Emphasis is placed on less expensive tablewares as these are found most frequently in archaeological contexts.

The guide is organized in three sections. The first introduces the secondary and primary literature available for research. The second concentrates on method of decoration, providing introductory dates for technological innovations, and, where appropriate, discusses the motifs popular in different time periods. The third section discusses tableware forms, illustrates examples of these forms, and, for stemware and decanters, provides additional dating information.

Researching Glass Tablewares

Secondary Sources

Numerous books and articles have been written on the tableglass produced during the 1800-1940 period. However, coverage is uneven and reflects the interests and needs of 20th-century collectors. It is often difficult to follow the history of a specific type of tableware if it is not considered collectible. For example, a great deal of research has been done on American mold-blown tableglass of the first half of the 19th century, but very little on glassware decorated this way in Britain at the same time or in either country during the second half of the century. Most books concentrate on glassware made in a specific country, such as the United States, Canada, or Ireland, and frequently on production at a specific factory or in a specific region. However, most pay little attention to the types of glassware used in a region or country, regardless of manufacturing origins. While it is difficult to get a complete picture of glassware used in a particular country or region from these sources, they nevertheless offer useful dating information for archaeologists.

Fueled by interest in Colonial and Federal America, collectors and dealers in the early 20th century began researching the history of "early American glass." Many researchers, like Knittle (1927), Lee (1944, 1958), and McKearin and McKearin (1948), sought to identify the products of known American factories of the 19th century. Both Palmer (1993a:13-39) and Wilson (1994[1]:17-20) provide useful discussions of the early history of glass collecting in the United States, and the often symbiotic relationships between dealers and collectors. Researchers such as Revi (1959, 1964), Wilson (1972, 1994), Innes (1976), Heacock and Bickenheuser (1978), Spillman (1981, 1982), Welker and Welker (1985), and Palmer (1993a) have expanded on the earlier work by refining and redefining the conclusions reached by earlier researchers and by studying other parts of the industry. In the 1970s, collecting interests expanded to include common tableglass of the 1920s and 1930s, and books began to appear on this glass (Weatherman 1974; Florence 1995a, 1995b, 1996). Within the last twenty years researchers have begun publishing on tableglass produced in the United States after 1940 (Weatherman 1978; Florence 1992; Rogove and Steinhauer 1993; Measell 1994b). The high end of the glass market, such as brilliant cut glass and art glass, has also been the subject of much study in the last 30 years (Revi 1965; Farrar and Spillman 1979; Spillman 1989, 1996). Dozens of publications exist on individual American companies that made glassware in the late 19th and 20th centuries and whose products are of interest to collectors (Stout 1972; Fauster 1979; Husfloen 1992:130-148, 186-190). Organizations, such as the Early American Glass Club and the Sandwich Historical Society have active publishing programs which encourage new scholarship; these two produce *The Glass Club Bulletin* (Spillman et al. 1993) and *The Acorn*, respectively.

Academic studies of American glass production have primarily been in the economic and labor history tradition and generally lack details concerning products made by the industry (Scoville 1948; Davis 1949; Zembala 1984). These are important resources for understanding the context in which the American glass industry operated, although they are less useful for identifying and dating individual objects. Theses by American curators trained in decorative arts offer a great deal more information on objects produced in American factories (Lanman 1968; Baker 1986; Leinicke 1986; Nelson 1988; Blaszczyk 1995).

Organized or systematic research into Canadian glass production began under the impetus of Stevens (1967) and MacLaren (1968) and continued with work by Unitt and Unitt (1969), Holmes (1974, 1987), King (1987), and others (Holmes and Jones 1978). Although Stevens and MacLaren had begun researching the history of Canada's glass industry in the early 1960s, it was the Canadian centennial (1967) which spurred wider interest in Canadian-made glass. As the Canadian industry did not even begin until the 1840s, and was not on a firm footing until the 1870s, the bulk of the glassware discussed dates from the 1870s to 1920. Since the demise of the *Glasfax Newsletter* in the late 1970s and the *Canadian Antiques Collector* in the late 1980s, there is no obvious publishing venue for new research on Canadian tableglass.

For most of the 20th century, researchers studying glassware manufactured in Britain and Ireland had little interest in tableglass made after 1830. The first book on British Victorian glass appeared in 1961 (Wakefield 1961), but it was virtually the only one until the late 1970s, when several important studies began to appear (Morris 1978; Lattimore 1979; Wakefield 1982; Slack 1987; Thompson 1989; Hajdamach 1991). In the late 1980s British researchers began to publish work on 20th-century British glass (Tyne and Wear County Council Museums 1983; Dodsworth 1987; Crowe 1989; Jackson 1997; Launert 1997). Both British glass collectors' organizations, the Glass Circle and the Glass Association, publish newsletters and periodic journals (*The Glass Circle* and *Glass Cone*, respectively) which are encouraging new research.

Continental European studies on the glass of the 19th and early 20th centuries have tended to concentrate on the high end of the market or on specific factories, such as Baccarat and Lalique in France or Val St. Lambert in Belgium (Philippe 1975). The cheaper wares, which were certainly sold in North America (Lanman 1969), have received less attention and very little has been published in English. However, some publications are available (Charleston 1965; Lanman 1969; Buchwald and Schlüter 1975; Mucha 1979; Drahotova 1983), and comparative discussions in both Hajdamach (1991:81-94) and Wilson (1994[2]:523-526) highlight the key role Bohemian glass styles played in British and American glass production and decoration in the 19th century.

Documentary Sources

TECHNICAL BOOKS

Books written by practicing glassmakers such as Pellatt (1849), Jarves (1865), and Bontemps (1868) provide much useful and accurate information on glassmaking practices of their own time. They are less trustworthy when discussing manufacturing techniques and products from earlier eras, such as Roman or Venetian glass.

NEWSPAPER ADVERTISEMENTS

Advertisements published in newspapers have been heavily used by such researchers as Wilson (1972, 1994), Jones and Smith (1985), and Palmer (1993a) for understanding products either made or used in North America during the 18th and early 19th centuries.

PATTERN BOOKS, PRICE LISTS, AND GLASSWARE CATALOGUES

Some illustrated pattern books exist from the early 19th century, although most of them are undated (Charleston 1965; Lanmon 1969:29-47; Westropp 1978:232-233, Plates x-xiv; Wolfenden 1987, 1992; Hajdamach 1991:45-56; McFarlan 1992; Pattern Book n.d.). Unillustrated price lists dating to the first half of the 19th century give an idea of the range of products that were made by different branches of the glass industry, although it is difficult to be certain what the glasses looked like from the descriptions (e.g., the 1829 list in Hughes [1958:24-25] and Sullivan [1985]). It was only in the 1840s that published, illustrated glassware catalogues began to appear (Wakefield 1968; Spillman 1983). In the 1860s, several American companies making pressed glass published illustrated catalogues (Watkins 1970 [or Spillman 1997]; Innes 1976:298-311; M'Kee and Brothers 1981). From the 1870s onward, more catalogues were published and/or have survived. Several glass catalogues were reprinted in the 1970s, and parts of others are available in various publications. Microfiche or microfilm copies of catalogues are available from The Juliet K. and Leonard S. Rakow Research Library of The Corning Museum of Glass (Corning 1987), the Winterthur Library (McKinstry 1984), and the Peabody Essex Museum (1794-1819) in Salem, Massachusetts.

RETAIL CATALOGUES

These generally date from the 1890s onward. Wholesale distributors, such as Butler Brothers, assembled glassware assortments for retail stores and their catalogues generally show a wider range of glassware than the large North American catalogue shopping stores such as Sears Roebuck, Montgomery Ward, or T. Eaton Co. (Toronto). For example, glassware offered in Eaton's catalogues between 1889 and 1940 tended to be conservative, generally offering only one or two choices in either object or style, with essentially two price ranges; one for the low end and one for a moderately high end market. English catalogues include Silber and Fleming (1990), *The Victorian Catalogue of Household Goods* (1991), and *Yesterday's Shopping* (Army and Navy Stores 1969). Price lists and retail catalogues provide useful comparative data concerning price variations between differently manufactured and/or decorated glasswares.

DESIGN REGISTERS

In 1839, the British Patent system began to include designs and, in 1842, the British Design Register system was set up (Morris 1978:190; Slack 1987:21-22). In subsequent years many glass designs were registered. Thompson (1989) extracted the glass designs registered between 1842 and 1908, and has itemized, and often illustrated, patterns registered by the principal manufacturers of pressed glass. Slack (1987:135-198), whose typewritten list for the years 1842 to 1883 is easier to read than the photocopied originals shown in Thompson, has also listed the design registers until 1900. Edgley (1996) compiled a list of glass registration numbers for the years 1908 to 1945. From 1842 to 1883, the design mark embossed in the glass is diamond-shaped like those on ceramics and metalwares. After 1883, the mark is simply "Rd" followed by a number.

PATENTED DESIGNS AND PROCESSES

From the late 1820s, submissions to the American patent office have contained information about the pressing process (Zembala 1984; Wilson 1994[1]:265-285) and, from the late 1860s (Innes 1976:299), pressed glassware designs. Among the authors who have published design patent illustrations are Revi (1964), Innes (1976), and Welker and Welker (1985). Along with catalogues, these records form the basis for dating American pressed patterns of the late 1860s to 1890s. Descriptions and illustrations of several different decorative processes developed in England can be found in Hajdamach (1991).

GOVERNMENT DOCUMENTS

Other government documents providing information on the glass industry include reports on industries, and investigations into tariff regulations, child labor, and excise administration (Britain between 1745 and 1845). Examples include Great Britain (1835, 1865, 1907), Weeks (1886), and United States Senate (1911). These reports are useful for understanding how the glass industry operated and occasionally offer details useful for dating.

ARCHIVAL MATERIAL

Archival materials from glass factories, including design books and business correspondence, are available and much new work is continuing to be done using these sources. Three examples of new work are Spillman (1996) on recently available material from the T. G. Hawkes firm in Corning, New York; Evans et al. (1995) on the Whitefriars factory in London, England; and Blaszczyk's (1995) work in the Corning Glass Company archives, Corning, New York, on the development of Pyrex.

EXHIBITION CATALOGUES

Beginning with the 1851 exhibition in London, exhibition catalogues illustrated and commented on the glass entries from many different countries. While these entries usually featured the finer, more elaborate end of the market, less expensive ordinary glassware echoed the themes shown at the world's fairs. As one commentator noted, concerning the Pellatt and Company products shown at the 1862 exhibition:

> Their costlier works are of rare excellence: these are to be regarded, however, rather as examples of what they can do than what they continually produce, for Messrs. Pellatt are extensive manufacturers of every class and order of "table glass;" and the same good taste and sound judgement that have produced more expensive objects, have been exercised to form and decorate such as are within the reach of persons of ordinary means (*The Art-Journal* 1862:128).

TRADE JOURNALS

Beginning in the mid 1870s, trade journals such as the English *Pottery Gazette and China and Glass Trades Review*, subsequently referred to as the *Pottery Gazette*, and the *American Crockery and Glass Journal* began to appear. Welker and Welker (1985:490-491) summarize the publishing histories of American glass trade journals. *The Canadian Pottery and Glass Gazette* was published briefly in the first decade of the 20th century.

Glassware

COMPANY NAMES AND TRADEMARKS

Embossed company names in blown-molded glassware appeared in wares manufactured by Irish glass factories, dating from ca. 1790 to 1820 (Figure 64*a*) (Warren 1981:71-98, 199-200). Several pressed salts made in the late 1820s had company names embossed on them (McKearin and McKearin 1948:Plate 165, Nos. 1-3, Plate 142, No. 4; Wilson 1994[1]:295-297). English trademark legislation came into effect January 1876, and shortly afterwards several English pressed-glass firms used trademarks embossed in the glass to identify their wares (Slack 1987:133-134). Peterson (1968) illustrates American glass marks, who registered them, and how they were applied: embossed, etched, stamped, or labeled. Acid-etched marks were used primarily by cut-glass firms around 1900. Pullin (1986) includes European and North American marks, and King (1987:247-250) shows Canadian marks, primarily for containers. Dodsworth (1987:109-110) illustrates early-20th-century English marks.

ARCHAEOLOGICAL EXCAVATIONS

Dated archaeological contexts provide information on glassware used at the same time and place and may contribute to refinements in dating. However, the chief contribution archaeological material makes is for understanding social contexts in which glassware was used, such as work groups (Jones and Smith 1985) or ethnic affiliation. Studied in combination with ceramic and metal tablewares, food and beverage storage containers, and food preparation items, glassware helps in understanding food and beverage choices and different levels of service at the table of consumers.

Excavations on glass factory sites have also been a technique used in the United States and Canada to identify products from specific factories (Stevens 1967; MacLaren 1968; White 1974; Starbuck 1986). With the exception of Starbuck's work at the New England Glassworks in Temple, New Hampshire, a great deal of this work has, unfortunately, consisted of digging holes on the sites, finding glass fragments, and concluding that whatever was found was made at the factory. Glass batches require the use of cullet, which can come from anywhere, thus this may or may not be a valid conclusion. Sheeler (1978) discusses the thorny issue of cullet and how many sherds of a specific pattern or bottle style are needed to state that it was made at the factory. Certainly glass scrap from manufacturing processes is more likely to reflect wares made at the factory, rather like wasters found during excavations at ceramic factories.

GLASSWARE

Handling and closely examining glassware is one of the best ways to develop expertise concerning manufacturing and decorating techniques, and how glass from different periods looks and feels. Archaeological collections provide the best context but often are too fragmentary to provide information concerning the appearance of complete pieces. Museum collections (Spillman 1981; Palmer 1993a; Wilson 1994), private collections, and antique shops and shows all provide opportunities to refine our knowledge of how to date glass and are particularly useful for hands-on knowledge of glassware illustrated in secondary sources.

Decorative Techniques

Colored Glass

Although many different glass colors were known and used by glassmakers, colorless glass has been the primary choice for tableware for 500 years. Nonetheless, colored tableglass has been fashionable at different periods.

Coming into the 19th century, colors in production were cobalt blue, amethyst, emerald green, and opaque white. Early-19th-century tablewares made in bottle and window glass factories in the United States also came in aqua, dark green, and amber shades (Figure 8) (Wilson 1994[1]:73-88, 153-160. These colors were caused by iron and other impurities in the sand, not by deliberate attempts to create them. On the other hand, colorless glass *is* a deliberate choice achieved partly by adding certain metallic oxides to the glass batch which change or mask the colorizing effects of any impurities (Jones and Sullivan 1989:12-13).

In the late 1820s, Bohemian glassmakers began to experiment with color and developed a gold ruby glass (an intense transparent red), as well as black, opaque sealing-wax red, cornflower blue, opaque white, apple green, and turquoise. By the early 1830s, glassmakers had learned how to use uranium which gives glass a distinctive lime-yellow or lime-green color. In the 1840s, translucent colors, sometimes called alabaster or clam broth, in white, pink, aqua, and green were introduced. Although these colored glasses were introduced at the high end of the market, some were also made in pressed glass. Most distinctive of all were the cased glasses composed of two or three layers of differently colored glass which were cut or engraved to expose the colors under the surface layer. In archaeological contexts, these layered glasses are usually window glass or lighting devices, particularly lampshades, although vase and tableware fragments are occasionally encountered, and usually date closer to 1900. Yellow and red stains introduced in the 1830s were used as cheaper versions of cased glass. For colored illustrations, see Spillman (1981:Plates 1-16), Drahotova (1983:166-167, Plates 122-128), Hajdamach (1991:81-94, 104), and Wilson (1994[1]:249-263).

In the 1880s, colored glass once again became fashionable, from the cheapest to the most expensive wares, with an astonishing array of colors made possible by the introduction of new glass formulas and new decorative techniques, including many which are outside the scope of this guide (Revi 1959; Hajdamach 1991:249-329). The prevailing theme from the 1880s onward seems to have been "more is better." Exuberantly decorated glass stayed popular into the 20th century, as can be seen by the water and lemonade sets offered by Butler Brothers in 1910 (Figure 1). Colored glasses made in this period include the following:

1. Transparent colors. In the 1880s, red became a very popular color but uranium yellow/green, amber, aqua, pale blue, and grass green (ca. 1900) were also produced.

2. Opaque colors (Figure 2). Opaque white pressed glass was relatively common before the 1870s, but in the later 1870s, British and American manufacturers expanded the opaque glass repertoire to include yellow, ivory, greens, blue, turquoise, and black (Spillman 1982:185, 190; Slack 1987).

3. Heat-sensitive glasses (Figure 3). For batches containing arsenic, uranium, or gold, the glass was cooled slightly and then reheated to change its color wherever the heat was applied and the glass was thickest. This meant that shaded colors could be made in transparent or opaque glass, shading from ruby to amber, pink to yellow, transparent blue to opalescent blue, or vice-versa. Pressed glass patterns sometimes had protuberances, such as hobnails, so that the tips would be a different color than the base. Developed in the United States in 1883, the formulas spread like wildfire, with many different color combinations tried out, including cased glasses in which the outer layer changed color but the inner did not. Even in fragments, the graduated colors of heat-sensitive glass make it easy to identify.

4. Cased or flashed glasses. New in this period was the treatment of layered glasses using hot glass techniques, which took advantage of the transparent and translucent properties of glass and of the new heat-sensitive glasses. Cutting, engraving, and acid-etching continued to be used on layered glasses. Extremely complex technical processes were used. For example,

FIGURE 1. Selection of jugs from the 1910 Butler Brothers catalogue which illustrates the variety of decoration offered from the 1880s until World War I, including colorless, green, blue, and ruby glass; opalescent and iridescent glass; enameling; and gilding as well as pressed, engraved, and etched patterns in geometric, naturalistic, and abstract motifs. With almost no exceptions, the glass is covered in decoration. One of the characteristic jug shapes in the early 20th century was a small handle placed in the center of the tall body which was often waisted (wider at the top and base and narrow through the middle) (Butler Brothers 1910:401). (Courtesy of Collins Kirby Art & Antiques, Fort Payne, Alabama.)

FIGURE 2. Opaque glassware: *left*, creamer in opaque turquoise blue, called Vitro-Porcelain glass, introduced ca. 1885, made by Tyne Flint Glass Works, South Shields, England (Slack 1987:107); *right*, creamer in opaque white glass, probably English. (Photo by Peter Lockett, private collection; digital image by Rock Chan.)

shaded opalescent glassware (Figure 1, center, bottom two rows), which featured opalescent white patterns such as coin dots, swirls, and hobnails against a colored ground, was accomplished by layering a heat-sensitive colorless glass over a colored ball of non-heat-sensitive glass. The vessel was blown in a pattern mold, the glass cooled slightly and then reheated to "strike" the opalescent white (Revi 1959:32-34; Spillman et al. 1994:70,74-75). Cased glass

refers to two or more layers of glass of equal thickness; flashed glass refers to a thin layer of colored glass over a thicker layer, usually colorless (Jones and Sullivan 1989:52-53).

5. Marbled glasses (Figure 4). In the late 1870s, English pressed-glass manufacturers reintroduced marbled glasses–generally opaque white mixed with transparent purple, blue, green, pink, and brown–which are characterized by swirled color variations (Slack 1987:34, 51, 93, 94). These types of glasses were also made in the United States.

6. Solarized glasses. Colorless pressed glass tableware made after 1864 in the new soda-lime glass (see Glass Composition) can be found with a purplish tint. Manganese, used to decolorize the glass, produces a photo-sensitive glass which begins to turn purple after prolonged exposure to ultraviolet rays. Solarized glass is most common from the 1870s to World War I, but some 18th-century French table glass is also affected. Although also decolorized with manganese, colorless potash-lead glasses are not affected by sunlight.

In the late 1920s, a new color palette was developed for the U.S. and Canadian market: transparent pastel colors in pink, green, yellow, and blue; transparent dark blue and deep red;

FIGURE 3. Pressed creamers made in heat-sensitive glass patented in 1889, by George Davidson & Co., Gateshead-on-Tyne, England (Slack 1987:74, 76-80): *left*, Primrose Perline, a yellow transparent glass shading into translucent/opaque yellow; *right*, Blue Perline, an "electric" transparent blue glass shading into translucent/opaque blue. (Photo by Peter Lockett, private collection; digital image by Rock Chan.)

Olive R. Jones

FIGURE 4. Pressed salt in marbled glass, called Blue Malachite, introduced in the late 1870s by Sowerby's Ellison Glass Works, Gateshead-on-Tyne, England. (Photo by Peter Lockett, private collection; digital image by Rock Chan.)

and black. These colors are distinctive and, combined with motifs from the period, can easily be distinguished from earlier colors after some experience with real examples (Weatherman 1974; Spillman 1982:15, 90; Florence 1995a, 1996).

Applied Colors

Glass could also be colored by enameling, gilding, or staining, which are cold techniques that do not need to be done in a glasshouse, and by exposing hot glass to metallic chlorides which is done at the time of manufacture.

ENAMELING

In this process, vitreous colors combined with an adhesive are applied to a glass surface and then reheated between 700° and 900° F (370° and 480° C), fusing them to the surface and burning off the adhesive. The technique is an old one which was particularly favored by decorators in the German/Bohemian regions of Europe. Enameling was one of the popular decorative techniques used from the 1880s into the early 20th century (Figure 5).

Beginning in the late 1920s, enameling once again became popular for beverage wares in North America (Figures 14, 69) and was done partly by hand and, after the mid 1930s, also

by machine. Several techniques were used, including turning glass against a wheel filled with paint, using a rubber stamp, rolling glass in paint or enamel dust, by silk screen technique (Weatherman 1978:5-6), or by using a transfer to outline the pattern which was filled in by hand (Golledge 1987:29-30, 56-59). Motifs used in the 1930s, and often later, included colored horizontal or swirled bands in red, yellow, black, white, jade green, or navy blue; playing card motifs (hearts, clubs, diamonds, and spades); sailboats, checkerboards, tulips, polka dots, Spanish dancers, "Mexican theme," polar bears, fighting cocks (cocktails), and Scotty dogs. Generally at least two colors were used. One pattern, which had raised frosting on the lower half of the pitcher and tumblers with a narrow red band above it, was described in this way: "The frosting gives this Beverage Set a very cold appearance and the red bands give a colorful cheerful effect . . ." (Weatherman 1978:91). "Colorful cheerful effect" sums up this whole range of wares.

GILDING

Gilding is done by applying a layer of gold leaf, paint, or dust to the glass surface, which may then be fired or unfired (Newman 1977:131-132). Unfired gilding can be easily rubbed off and appears to be the type used in the 1890s and later for cheaply decorated wares (Figures 5, 89) where it was applied around the rim, in bands, or to highlight parts of pressed patterns (Measell 1994a:127-130, 165). As an alternative to gilding, some used iridescent gold (Figure 93).

STAINING

Using silver chloride to produce a yellow stain was developed in 1820 and a red stain in 1840 (Newman 1977:293). The technique was a cheap imitation of cased or flashed glasses. From the late 1880s and into the 20th century, red and yellow stains became popular ways to color cheap pressed wares (Figure 6). The stains do not adhere well to the glass surface and are usually worn or scraped off. Ruby staining was often used for cheap souvenir wares which exhibit crudely engraved designs and wording that celebrate famous attractions, special occasions, and sentiments.

IRIDESCENT GLASS

In the 1870s, another distinctive color development was iridescent glass which was produced by exposing hot glass to metallic chlorides. Depending on the color of the base glass and the composition of the fumes, the surface of the glass became iridescent in colors such as ambers, blues, or greens. As pressed-glass manufacturers were usually prompt to imitate more expensive techniques, it is puzzling that pressed iridescent glass, called "carnival" by collectors, was not made until 1905 (Figure 1) (Spillman 1982:51, 65, 286-289; Measell 1994a:132-136, 153-155, 163-168). After that date American, European, and even Australian glass companies made carnival glass and it continued to be a well-known product past the 1930s.

DEPOSIT-WARE

Bonding silver onto glassware was being done by 1880 (Revi 1959:198-201; Hajdamach 1991:287-289), and continued into the 1930s. Patterns offered in the T. Eaton Co. catalogues around 1914 were in sinuous art-nouveau styles, while those in the 1930s resembled acid-etched patterns of the period.

Glass Composition

The basic glass compositions of potash-lime, potash-lead, and soda-lime continued during the 1800-1940 period. Potash and soda are fluxes added to the glass batch to lower the melting point of sand. Lime and lead are also fluxes but their primary purpose is to make glass stable after it is cool (Jones and Sullivan 1989:10-12). However, determining glass composition is difficult without expensive time-consuming tests. Although shortwave and longwave ultraviolet lights are useful tools for archaeologists to sort glass fragments of different composition (Jones and Sullivan 1989:12), determining what the fluorescences actually mean is impossible without further tests. For example, in contexts dating to the second half of the 19th century, a purple fluorescence in colorless glass fragments probably indicates the presence of lead in the composition. However, no chemical analyses have been done to confirm this. Purple fluorescence has been found on both tablewares and lamp chimneys. Be cautious when reading documentary material as words such as "flint" and "crystal" are sometimes used to suggest higher quality glass than is

justified, such as the "pure crystal glass" offered by Montgomery Ward & Co. (1901:45). These terms describe colorless glass of good quality but not necessarily with any lead content. Only if the source states that the glass contains lead can one assume that it does; e.g., "Pure thin lead blown glass" (Butler Brothers 1905:147). Another term found in early-20th-century literature is "pot metal" which refers to glass melted in a pot furnace rather than a tank furnace. Pot metal was of better quality (Rosenhain 1908:109-110).

It is impossible to use glass composition to determine date and country of origin because of the international nature of the glass trade in the 19th and 20th centuries and the lack of hard base-line data. Some datable composition changes are known, most of which are related to color, such as the introduction of heat-sensitive glasses and uranium for yellow/green glass (see Colored Glass).

One important composition change is related to American pressed glass. From the introduction of mechanically pressed glass in the late 1820s, American manufacturers used potash-lead glass. Lead glass has a high refractive index which was considered desirable in pressed glassware. Its luster compensated for deficiencies in pressing technology, particularly in the early years, and it echoed the luster and weight of cut glass. Lead glass, however, sets up slowly; that is, it remains fluid longer than soda-lime glass which meant that in the pressing process, glass had to remain in the mold longer for the glass to "set." The ingredients for lead glass were also comparatively expensive. In 1864, William Leighton in West Virginia developed a formula for soda-lime glass. The formula substituted bicarbonate of soda for the type previously used. It produced glass which resembled lead glass, but was lighter in weight, and could be made for one-third the cost of lead glass (Wilson 1994[2]:522). Within a few years, most American pressed-glass factories had switched to the new formula. Patterns made from the 1840s into the late 1860s and early 1870s can be found in both lead and soda-lime glasses, depending on the date of manufacture. Patterns introduced after the late 1860s, however, were only made in soda-lime glasses.

English manufacturers also altered their pressed-glass formulas, as an 1888 article in the *Pottery Gazette* indicates, by retaining a small

FIGURE 5. Jug decorated with pink, white, blue, and brick red enameling; gilding; optic molding; and a crimped rim. Crimping tools were introduced about 1874, but came into widespread use in the 1880s (Hajdamach 1991:297-300). The handle was first applied at the base and pulled up to the rim. The jug has optic-molded panels on its interior (see Optic-Molded Glass). The absence of mold lines indicates that the second, full-size, mold was a turn mold. There is a rough pontil mark on the base, demonstrating that the pontil continued in use in the tableglass industry long after the mid 19th century, when alternative tools had come into use (Hajdamach 1991:34-36). Based on the combination of decorative techniques and overall style, the jug dates from the 1880s to early 20th century, and was probably made in Bohemia, although American firms also made similar wares (Measell 1994a:127). (Photo by Rock Chan, Parks Canada collection.)

amount of lead in the formula (Slack 1987:47, 50).

HEAT-RESISTANT GLASSES

Borosilicate glasses have a low coefficient of expansion which makes them suitable for coping with extreme temperature changes. Formulas for this type of glass were developed in the early 20th century to make specialty products such as railway lanterns and battery jars.

PYREX

By 1910, Corning Glass Works had developed several different borosilicate glass formulas for railway signal lenses, lantern globes, and battery jars. The new formulas were so effective that the rate of breakage dropped dramatically and sales of replacement lenses and globes plummeted. The company began searching for alternative uses for its borosilicate glasses. Between 1911 and 1915, Corning Glass Works concentrated on developing a chemically stable, safe, chip-proof glass suitable for baking, on determining the right product mix, and on developing a product with consumer appeal (Blaszczyk 1995:489-521). In 1915, after four years of research, the company had perfected its formula and began to sell casseroles and baking dishes, custard cups, loaf pans, cake dishes, and pie plates (Rogove and Steinhauer 1993:70-83). Other items followed, such as teapots in 1922, measuring cups in 1925, and refrigerator dishes in 1929. Sales were brisk from the beginning. In its 1917 fall catalogue, the T. Eaton Co. showed the new baking dishes, placed in a silver-plated holder: "Silver plated casserole, lined with transparent oven glass, cut glass cover. Glass will stand heat of the oven, fitted in silver-plated pierced design bright burnished seven-inch frame" (T. Eaton Co. 1917-18:289).

FIGURE 6. The Red Block pattern, introduced in the mid 1880s, was made by several American firms and reissued several times during the 1890s by the United States Glass Company (Jenks and Luna 1990:432-433). This is a sugar bowl in colorless glass with a scratched and worn red stain around the rim and on the top of the blocks; the handles were pressed at same time as the body. (Photo by Rock Chan, Parks Canada collection.)

Pyrex Casserole, Cut-glass Cover
30-1601. Handsome Casserole with a real Pyrex glass lining, cut glass cover, pierced design frame with conventional ornamentation, wood handle diameter about 8 ins. Pyrex glass is transparent and will stand the heat of the oven. Would be appreciated as a gift; most moderately priced. Price, delivered **7.25**

FIGURE 7. An early offering of Pyrex by T. Eaton Co., with cut decoration on the cover, and placed in a silver-plated holder for service at the table. (T. Eaton Co. 1918-19:359; reproduced with the kind permission of The T. Eaton Company Limited, Toronto; digital image by George van der Vlugt.)

The 1918 Spring/Summer catalogue noted that the glass casserole would not chip or break from the heat, that it did not absorb odors, was easy to keep clean, and "with proper care will last indefinitely" (Figure 7) (T. Eaton Co. 1918:225). The casserole and its electro-plated frame cost $6.00. Eaton's catalogues continued to offer both pie plates and casseroles until 1940, with frequent design changes. In the Eaton's catalogues, Pyrex competed with, and soon replaced, white-lined brown earthenware baking dishes called Guernseyware.

In 1922, Corning had plants in Europe and Britain manufacturing Pyrex (Tyne and Wear County Council Museums 1983:8), but Canadian production did not begin until 1946 (King 1987:192).

Pyrex sales slowed down in the 1920s for a number of reasons: high prices, stagnant designs, and breakage which resulted when Pyrex was not treated properly. It was considered expensive and had not reached lower income consumers except as wedding presents. Company research showed that the middle-class market was saturated (Blaszczyk 1995:649-651; 660-662). Through the 1930s, the company worked at lowering its prices, at redesigning products, and at developing a glass that could be placed directly on the burner.

PYREX FLAMEWARE

Alterations in glass formulas produced an aluminosilicate glass which could be used on top of the stove. It was made from 1936 to 1979. Between 1936 and 1946, the glass had a bluish tone to it to distinguish it from Pyrex (Rogove and Steinhauer 1993:100).

Molded trademarks and green stamped marks for Pyrex and Flameware can be found in Rogove and Steinhauer (1993:67-69), although they do not date most of them.

FIRE-KING GLASSWARE

Borosilicate glasses were also developed by other firms. "FIRE-KING" is the trademark used by the Anchor Hocking Glass Corporation between 1942 and 1976. Kilgo et al. (1991) illustrate and date the different forms and decorations produced under this trademark, but the most familiar product is the translucent white or green coffee mug.

Glass on Glass

Placing glass onto glass can be part of the process of making an object, such as attaching a stem, foot, or handle, or it can be a decorative technique. It was a common decorative technique during two periods: initially during the first half of the 19th century and again, at the higher end of glass production, during and beyond the 1880s.

DOUBLE GATHERS

With the exception of cased or flashed glass, double gathers were usually done on the lower part of the body and could be plain or decorated by ribbing or tooling (Figures 8, 42 [nos. 16 and 21], 48, 74*f*). Often combined with a flaring rim, objects decorated by this technique echo classical Greek-urn shapes. Pillar molding, which has bold protuberant ribs, does not have an obvious second layer, and dates from the 1830s to ca. 1870 (Wilson 1994[1]:195-196).

LOOP OR FESTOON GLASS

"A thread—generally opaque white but sometimes blue or red, was trailed horizontally around

FIGURE 8. Glass threading and "lily pad" decoration applied to the lower body of hollowares, such as bowls, pitchers, and vases, was done in bottle- and window-glass houses in New England, New York state, and possibly, in 1840, in a short-lived factory at Mallorytown, Ontario. As a group, the tablewares manufactured in these factories were made in shades of aqua, green, and amber, and date from ca. 1820 to 1860 (Spillman 1982:Nos. 122-123; Palmer 1993a:174-179; Wilson 1994[1]:46, 142-144). (Courtesy of The Corning Museum of Glass, Corning, New York.)

the body of a piece and then, after reheating, pulled up and then down" (Wilson 1994[1]:94, 147-150). The technique was used in the 18th century and again in the United States around 1840.

THREADED GLASS

This is another old technique which continued in use in the early 19th century in North America, primarily for tablewares made in bottle and window glass factories. The threads used were the same color as the body of the glass and were applied by trailing a thin stream of glass onto the object as it was rotated by the glassmaker (Figure 8, far right). In 1876, a machine for threading was patented in England and subsequently several other machines were developed. Usually in a different color from the base glass, these threads are distinguished by their consistent size, the mechanical regularity of application, and were used to cover all or parts of an object (Figure 9). Combining threading with other decorative techniques, glassmakers produced amazing variations on the theme over the next few decades (Hajdamach 1991:273-283).

TRAILED GLASS

In the 1880s, under the influence of Rustic styles and Japonism, and at the higher end of the glass market, glassmakers applied asymmetrically crude (often decorated by ribbing) trails or irregularly shaped buttons of differently colored glass over a glass piece already decorated in other ways. Sometimes they added pointy feet or handles (Hajdamach 1991:Color Plate 30).

Blown Glass

Mouth-blown glassware is shaped by blowing air through a blowpipe into hot glass and manipulating it with various types of tools into whatever style is desired. *Free-blown* glassware is made without using molds but may still be decorated in some way by tooling or adding glass (Figures 8, 39 [tumblers]), or by cold techniques like cutting, engraving, acid-etching, enameling, or gilding. *Mold-blown* glass is shaped and decorated by the use of some type of mold (Jones and Sullivan 1989:50-54, 23-33). *Semi-automatic machine-blown* tableware production began in 1897 for tumblers, finger bowls, lemonade glasses, and stemware using a machine developed originally for blowing light bulbs and lamp chimneys (Scoville 1948:97-98, 133-135, 152-154, 195-196). These were turn- or paste-mold machines so they left a highly polished surface with no visible mold lines. The role of *automatic machines* in blown tableware production in the 1920s and 1930s has not been discussed in detail in the sources used (Scoville 1948; Weatherman 1974; Dodsworth 1987), but it is doubtful if details of manufacturing technology will provide much refinement in dating objects whose patterns can be dated and assigned to specific factories.

Even after the introduction of machines, mouth-blown glassware continued to be made because, as Davis (1949:227) points out in connection with the pressed-glass trade, hand production is profitable for items not made in large enough quantities to justify mechanized production and also to supply a market which values "hand-made" glassware. For example, from the late 1930s and into the 1950s, American industrial designer Russel Wright used American hand factories to manufacture his designs for department stores catering to middle-class shoppers (Blaszczyk 1993:2-22). Unfortunately most of these American hand factories faced financial difficulties in the 1940s and 1950s, and many had closed by the early 1970s. Not without difficulties, hand production continues in Britain, Ireland, and parts of continental Europe.

It is frequently difficult to determine how individual pieces of tableglass were made if there are no obvious signs of mold use. Glassmakers made free-blown wares, and used fire-polishing or turn molds to eliminate mold lines and dulled surfaces, resulting in glasses with the same look. It is likely that products blown in semi-automatic or automatic machines can be identified with more research.

PATTERN-MOLDED GLASS

Pattern molding, in which the glass parison is blown into a patterned mold and then removed and blown to full-size, is not a technique which translates to machine production. It is a very old technique and was still in use in the first

FIGURE 9. Footed goblet with an engraved bowl, a colorless applied frill at the stem and bowl junction, and a foot decorated with cranberry threads applied by machine. Based on these decorative methods, the goblet dates no earlier than the 1880s. (Photo by Peter Lockett, private collection; digital image by Rock Chan.)

half of the 19th century for tablewares, particularly tumblers, and jelly and wine glasses (Figures 10, 85). Although various types of diamond patterns were used in the 18th century, the 19th-century motifs are primarily ribs, rib/flutes, and rib/panels. The technique, which gives a diffuse look to motifs, was still a useful decorative technique for art glass in the last quarter of the 19th century. Pattern molding can be identified by the corresponding profiles on the interior and exterior surface: a rib on the outside can be felt as a rib on the inside.

CONTACT-MOLDED GLASS

In this process, glass is blown into a full-size open-and-shut mold which can shape and

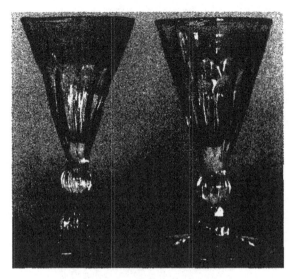

FIGURE 10. Wine glasses with drawn stems with bowl, knop, and step decorated by pattern molding. This style of drawn stem–with a knop and a step–is shown in the 1840 Apsley Pellatt catalogue as a "six-fluted ball stem" (Wakefield 1968:52). (Photo by Olive Jones, private collection.)

decorate it at the same time. In comparison to labor-intensive techniques such as cutting and engraving, it produces a decorated item with minimum effort and can imitate cut and engraved motifs successfully, although the resulting pattern is more diffuse. Contact molding can be identified by comparing the profiles of the interior and exterior surface: a rib on the outside corresponds to a depression on the inside. With some exceptions, the role of contact molding in forming and decorating tableglass was not discussed in the sources used.

From ca. 1790 to ca. 1820, several Irish glasshouses used a full-size partial mold for decorating the base and lower body of decanters, finger bowls, and other vessels. Generally, the lower body is decorated with ribs/flutes which, on the base, become rays encircling an undecorated center which may or may not have a molded company name on it (Figure 64a) (Warren 1981:71-98, 199-200). Warren is unclear as to whether a dip mold or a hinged mold was used for these objects, although both are feasible.

"Blown three mold" is an American collectors' term for a wide range of decorated tablewares blown in full-size open-and-shut molds from about 1810 to 1840s (Figures 11, 48). The molds usually consisted of three vertical parts

and a base part (Wilson 1994[1]:168-171, 205, 214-247). The earlier patterns imitated cut-glass styles, primarily vertical rib/diamond combinations. In 1814, Rundell stated in her book on domestic cookery: "Those who wish for trifle dishes, butter stands, &c. at a lower charge than cut glass, may buy them in molds, of which there is a great variety that looks extremely well if not placed near the more beautiful article" (Wilson 1994[1]:170).

From the 1820s to 1840s, there appeared densely packed vertical ribs and patterns with more flowing lines consisting of scrolls, fans, arches, guilloches, peacock eyes (or comets), and rosettes. Characteristic of all these patterns is overall coverage in the molded parts. McKearin and McKearin (1948:240-331) provide comprehensive analysis of the blown three-mold patterns and have assigned numbers to each pattern which subsequent authors continue to use. Colors produced were colorless, aqua, amber, cobalt blue, purple, and olive green.

Fully mold-blown Anglo-Irish tablewares made during the first half of the 19th century have not been studied as thoroughly as American ones. Anglo-Irish factories made tablewares with vertical rib/diamond patterns, possibly earlier than the American examples (Warren 1981:200-212; McNally 1982:112-113; Jones and Smith 1985:32, 73). The factories, however, also seem to have produced other types of patterns, particularly for tumblers. Included in an 1829 list of prices for the English flint-glass trade are a number of molded items: cruets and castors, decanters, blow-over and blow-back dishes and salts (see Blow-over Molds), liquor bottles, and tumblers with "molded, star or ornamental bottom" (Hughes 1958:24-25). Tumblers with molded ribs, with star bursts on the base, are examples of this type of decoration (Figure 12) (Brooks 1987:11, 15, 18) and were probably blown in a partial full-size mold similar to the marked Irish pieces. The discrepancy between American and British coverage of the "blown three-mold" group makes it difficult to compare products. Was this a decorative technique little used in the English glass industry or, as seems more likely, is its absence in the secondary literature based on a lack of interest by English researchers and collectors? Did much of this type of glassware find its way across the Atlantic from the 1920s to the 1950s,

FIGURE 11. Examples of blown-three-mold glass attributed to New England and Midwestern factories. The creamer and decanter on the left are in the "baroque" style while the other decanter and sugar bowls are in the "geometric" style which imitates cut glass motifs of the early 19th century (Figure 40). The colorless decanter is of lead glass. Both covers on the sugar bowls have pontil marks on top of the finial. (Courtesy of The Corning Museum of Glass, Corning, New York.)

and become transformed into "early American glass?"

After the mid-19th century, the use of contact molding for decorating tableware becomes less clear. Some American products can be identified, such as molasses cans, bar bottles, or colognes made in bold patterns similar to pressed patterns of the 1850s and 1860s (Wilson 1994[2]:523, 540-545). From the 1870s onward, the principal type of contact molding used seems to have been optic molding (below) although some contact molding continued (Figure 13). It is likely that pressing (see Pressed Glass) had become the dominant technique for making and decorating cheaper tablewares, a position pressed wares held until the development in the late 1890s of semi-automatic machines to make blown-molded, but undecorated, tumblers and stemware. A commentator in the *National Glass Budget* made the following observations on the new machine, which Michael J. Owens had developed and the Rochester Tumbler Company had bought the rights to use:

When the Owens machine was introduced and it was proven that the output of punch tumblers could be greatly increased and the cost of production radically reduced, there was no alternative left the Rochester Company between acquiring the right to use the machine, or practically abandon, not only the hand manufacture of punch tumblers, but, since the machine blown punch tumbler contains less metal, is of lighter weight, (freight advantage), and can therefore be made and sold much cheaper than a pressed tumbler, also abandon the manufacture of pressed tumblers, their specialty, or sink all their investment and possessions in vainly competing for a few brief years with a more formidably equipped, and unconquerable antagonist, or turn their entire plant over, for the manufacture of such specialty as did not exist (*National Glass Budget* 1897:1).

The commentator went on to compare the output of each system: a hand blower could make about 700 punch tumblers in the same period as the machine made between 1800 and 2000 tumblers. Comparative costs were 50¢ per hundred compared to less than 6¢ per hundred. As this was a semi-automatic machine there was still considerable human involvement but it was

Olive R. Jones

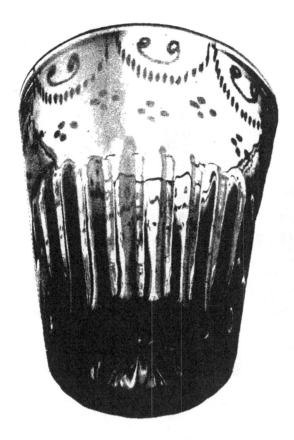

FIGURE 12. Colorless lead glass tumbler decorated by contact molding on the base and body and by sketchily-done engraving on the upper body, similar in execution to Bohemian-style engraving often found on tumblers. As this is of lead glass and the ribs and flutes were executed by contact molding, the tumbler was likely made in England sometime during the first half of the 19th century. Similar Bohemian-style tumblers would have been made in potash-lime glass and decorated by pattern-molding (Figure 85). The pontil mark consists of rough bits of glass around the resting point. (Photo by Rock Chan, private collection.)

less skilled and lower-paid work. It is likely that the tumblers shown in the Butler Brothers (1914:324A) catalogue were made in a semi-automatic machine: "9 ½ oz. LEAD BLOWN TABLE TUMBLERS. Just think of it! We have a half million of these tumblers in stock and we'll sell them all before the month is out. Are you one of the lucky buyers?" The tumblers were tapered, completely plain, thinly blown, and cost 23 ½ ¢ cents per dozen.

The next obvious group of tableware decorated by contact molding is found in the late 1920s and 1930s. In the Butler Brothers (1929, 1930) catalogues, thin blown tumblers, stemware, and water sets are offered in greater variety than in

previous catalogues and the term "thin blown" is highlighted (Figure 14). Designers of the period used the flexibility offered by contact molding to produce patterns with distinctive modern looks (Weatherman 1974:48; Florence 1995a:182).

BLOW-OVER MOLDS

In this technique, glass is blown into the mold and then burst off, which leaves a thinner edge, or blown over, which leaves a thicker edge (Figure 15) (Pellatt 1849:96). The technique was used to make objects in which the rim could be cut and polished, such as salts or open dishes, or ground for a fitment, such as castor and cruet bottles. The finish or rim was ground or polished when the glass was cold, thus it was not necessary to use a pontil to hold the object while it was being made. On small dishes the glass can be so thick that the inner surface is smooth, without the concave/convex relationship between the interior and exterior surface so characteristic of contact molding (Wilson 1994[1]:205). Using descriptions in American period documents, Wilson (1994[1]:171-173, 205-213) dates the technique ca. 1810 to ca.

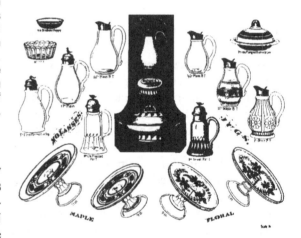

FIGURE 13. The pint Rose pattern jug (center right) was blown in a mold while the jugs adjacent to it in Maple and Jewel patterns were pressed (Pennsylvania Glassware 1972:30). Molasses or syrup jugs are characterized by metal covers, often of Britannia metal and often patented, which regulated the flow of viscous liquid (Spillman 1982:192-194). They were introduced at least as early as the 1850s (Figure 22), and continued to be offered into the 1930s (Butler Brothers 1930:n.p.). Salvers in Maple and Floral patterns are also shown on this page. (Courtesy of the Juliet K. and Leonard S. Rakow Research Library of The Corning Museum of Glass, Corning, New York.)

1830. Its inclusion in Pellatt's book suggests, however, that it was still in use, at least in British glasshouses, into the 1840s. For vessels with glued-on fitments or screw tops, such as molasses jugs, or salt and pepper shakers, the burst-off technique continued to be used into the 20th century. For this use it was not always necessary to grind the finish and without the metal covers, one can sometimes note the horizontal mold line at the top and the thin burst

off remnants (Spillman 1982:No. 185; Jones and Sullivan 1989:91; Lyon 1994:71-74).

TURN-MOLDED GLASS

It is likely that some tablewares from the 1870s onward were blown in turn molds. The turn mold is a full-size multi-part mold that is coated with a paste which is moistened before blowing the object. During the blowing process,

FIGURE 14. The majority of the jugs and tumblers in these water and beverage sets are described as "blown" and clearly the horizontal-rib patterns, such as IC-1851 and IC-1047, are best made by blowing into a full-size mold. Technically, the horizontal nature of these patterns would make it feasible to blow the jugs and tumblers in turn or paste molds, to eliminate mold lines. In the same catalogue, berry bowls and nappies, and cream and sugar sets are all pressed, mostly in older, less-adventurous patterns than these (Figure 61) (Butler Brothers 1930:n.p.). (Courtesy of Collins Kirby Art & Antiques, Fort Payne, Alabama.)

FIGURE 15. Glass dish made in the blow-over method. Its roughly ground rim and undecorated surface indicate that it was to be used as a liner, probably for a silver or silver-plated dish. Generally open vessels made in this technique have a flat or decorated and polished rim. (Photo by Rock Chan, Parks Canada collection.)

the object is rotated, riding on a thin cushion of steam which imparts a shiny surface and eliminates mold marks (Figure 5) (Jones and Sullivan 1989:30-31). The technique is suitable for mouth-blowing or machine production, and was used for making bottles, lamp chimneys, and light bulbs as well as tablewares.

OPTIC-MOLDED GLASS

Optic molding is a technique in which the glass is blown into a small patterned mold and then transferred to a full-size undecorated mold and blown. The pattern, usually consisting of panels, ribs, or circular protrusions, is transferred to the inside of the object (Jones and Sullivan 1989:32-33). When the full-size mold is a turn mold or dip mold, no mold lines appear on the piece. Tumblers blown in this way have been found on 18th-century French colonial sites in North America, but the major use of the technique in tableware dates from the 1880s into the 20th century where it was used principally for drinking glasses and jugs (Figures 5, 14) (Diamond Flint Glass Company 1904:25; Butler Brothers 1910:408; Wilson 1994[2]:605-974). It is one which translates into machine production as it involves the use of two molds, a process familiar to 20th-century glass manufacturers. In addition to optic molding, glasses are often decorated with enameling, gilding, needle etching, and light cutting. In the 1905, 1910, and 1914 Butler Brothers catalogues, optic molding was not common; however, in the 1925, 1929, and 1930 catalogues, for both tumblers and stemware, it is the dominant decorative

technique. Continental European glassmakers are still making optic-molded tableware.

COMPRESSED AIR

In the early 1830s, Robinet—a glassblower at Baccarat in France—invented a mechanical pump which supplied sufficient air pressure to enable French manufacturers to produce complex patterns with crisp definition. This technique was largely used in European glass houses, particularly in France. Air was used rather than a plunger, thus it may be possible to feel the characteristic surface on blown contact molding (Spillman 1982:164). The French patterns are generally very detailed and often resemble American pressed lacy patterns. Examples of this type of glass from Launay Hautin & Cie ca. 1840 catalogues are published in Innes (1976:299-300) and copies of complete catalogues are available on fiche from The Juliet K. and Leonard S. Rakow Research Library of The Corning Museum of Glass. English manufacturers also used this technique (Figure 16) (Hajdamach 1991:96-97).

Pressed Glass

PINCHING

During the 18th century, specialized branches of the British glass industry used hand-held pinchers to form small objects such as chandelier drops and fob seals. By the end of the century, vessel manufacturers used the technique to form decanter stoppers and feet for salts and bowls (Figure 17) (Jones and Sullivan 1989:33-35). These techniques continued to be used at least into the late 1820s. In 1828, Thomas Leighton, of the Boston & Sandwich Glass Company, sent examples of articles to his colleague in Scotland: "We make them the Same as you Make the Square feet. the Mould Lifts with 2 ha[n]dles and opens at the Corners" (Spillman 1992:6). The surface was ruffled, hence the pinched elements were decorated, usually with ribbing, and flat parts, such as edges and resting surfaces or feet, were cut and polished.

MECHANICAL PRESSING

Pressed glass is formed in a multi-part mold in which glass is pushed into the mold by a plunger powered by a screw or lever mechanism. At its simplest, the whole object can be shaped and decorated quickly and cheaply with very little skill as only the correct amount of glass needs to be dropped into the mold. Initially mechanical pressing was developed in the United States in the mid-1820s to manufacture glass furniture knobs. By 1828, however, the technique was being used to make a variety of tableware forms, and firms making the new wares were already having to protect their designs from competitors (Nelson 1988:48-62, 98). Both the technique and the products spread quickly. By 1831, Apsley Pellatt in London was taking out a patent for pressed glass and in 7 June 1832, the *Brockville Gazette* (Ontario), advertised "75 Casks American pressed Glass Ware, consisting of Sugar bowls, Creams, Salts, Preserve Dishes, Fruit, and Stand dishes, 3, 4, 5, 6, 7, 8, and 9 Inch Plates, 110 Dozen Glass Knobs" (Jones 1992:11). Plates and open bowls or dishes

FIGURE 16. Cream or milk jug in thick, heavy lead glass may have been formed by compressed air as the inner surface follows the contour of the outer surface. The top has been fire-polished, however, to form the pouring lip which may have altered the relationship between the inner and outer surfaces. As well, the glass is close to 1 cm (0.4 in.) thick which may also affect the profile of the inner surface as thick glass retains heat longer than thin glass. Handle was applied first at the rim and then looped down to the lower body; it has a cut and polished base with impressed starburst and scalloped rim. Probably English, mid-19th century. (Photo by Rock Chan, Parks Canada collection.)

had not been a strong product line in the glass industry prior to mechanical pressing but open forms, including salts, were particularly suited to the pressing technique. Rectangular and square objects require effort to make freeblown, however, along with blown contact molding (Figure 64*d*), pressing expanded the range of angular forms which could be made quickly and cheaply. Until the late 1830s, the traditional backbone products of the glass industry–stemware, tumblers, and decanters–were not made by pressing because of difficulties in making a vessel with a thin upper part (see Tumblers) as well as narrow-mouthed vessels.

Manufacturers very quickly figured out how to make multi-part objects, such as lamps and even decanters, by attaching different parts to each other with thin wafers of hot glass, sometimes by pressing one part and blowing another, or by using multi-part open-topped molds with subsequent retooling to form the object (Figures 18, 19) (Wilson 1994[1]:278-280). Throughout the 19th century glass manufacturers, machinists, and engineers continued to invent time-saving and cost-cutting improvements in the process of pressing (Scoville 1948; Davis 1949:226-229; Zembala 1984; Slack 1987:14-20; Wilson 1994[1]:265-285). Wilson (1994[1]:289-517) documents manufacturing processes in his descriptions of pressed pieces in the Toledo Museum, one of the few authors to do so. In 1917, automatic feeders were introduced to the pressed-glass trade and bit by bit, other parts of the process were mechanized. However, hand plants continued to make pressed specialized products whose production runs were too small for machines (Davis 1949:226-229).

Pressed glass is usually described by its decorative motifs because pressing not only shaped the object but also decorated it. The motifs possible in this technique ranged anywhere from plain to highly decorated; they could mimic simple or complex geometric cut-glass patterns or the realism of engraved patterns. Complex cut and engraved patterns took hours to make; pressed imitations took seconds.

PRESSED GLASS, 1827-CA. 1850

Pressed glass of this period is generally covered in decoration; the decoration is bold,

Olive R. Jones

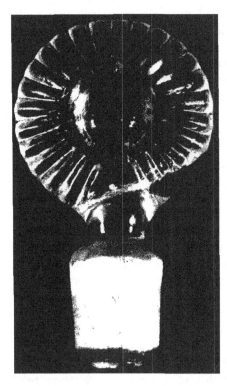

FIGURE 17. Decanter stopper made by pinching. (Photo by George Lupien, Parks Canada collection.)

detailed, and well-defined, with crisp edges. The glass sparkles because it is made of lead glass, which has high refractive qualities, and because it is covered by over-all patterns which provide many surfaces for light to catch. The dense patterns also serve to hide imperfections left by the pressing technique such as shear marks, which appear as cracks in the glass, and dulled surfaces caused by under-heated molds.

The earliest pressed glass, dating 1827 to ca. 1830 or 1835 (Spillman 1981:37-44; Wilson 1994[1]:276, 292-312), was decorated with imitation Anglo-Irish cut motifs: strawberry diamonds, crosscut waffle squares, and fans. Dating for these patterns is based on the absence of mold lines associated with the use of a cap ring, introduced about 1830, which was a mold part that formed and controlled the thickness of an object's rim (McKearin and McKearin 1948:345; Nelson 1990:44-48).

From about 1830 until ca. 1850 (Figure 20) (Wilson 1994[1]:278), the patterns are known as "lacy" because of the presence of dots, diamonds, or lines on the background. Thousands of pattern variations exist which imitate cut and

FIGURE 18. Pressed glass made in multi-part open-topped molds (from left to right): *Celery* in the Diamond Point or Sharp Diamond pattern which was made from the late 1840s to ca. 1870. Three mold lines, hidden in the pattern, extend from foot to rim although they were eliminated at the rim when it was fire-polished. Made in colorless lead glass, the piece is very heavy. As no pontil mark appears on the piece, a snap case or other holder was used to hold it while the rim was fire-polished. *Decanter* in the Ashburton pattern which was introduced at least as early as 1848, and continued to be made into the 1880s (Watkins 1970:151-152, 157-159; Husfloen 1992:32; Wilson 1994[1]:280, 285, n. 69). Narrow-mouthed vessels like this were pressed in a mold with a plain, flat base part, three or four body parts bearing the decoration, and above them an undecorated one-piece cylindrical mold part (Wilson 1994[1]:478). Held by a pontil, the cylindrical part was reheated and tooled to form the shoulder, neck, and lip. Mold lines encircle the heel and follow the edges of the body pattern and across the top of the design. As this piece was empontiled, the pontil mark has been ground away and then polished, resulting in a smooth, circular depression. The one-piece cylindrical upper part in the mold made it possible to make complex objects without mold lines showing on the undecorated part and was adaptable to different forms, including stemware bowls and feet. An American patent illustrating this concept was taken out in 1847 (Wilson 1994[1]:271), and pressed items, such as goblets, shown in this guide with no mold marks on the upper undecorated surface were made in this type of mold and subsequently fire-polished. *Creamer* in Ribbed Leaf pattern (Figure 24) in which the upper part was initially formed in the same way as the Ashburton decanter, reheated, and tooled to form the pouring lip. Three vertical mold lines are hidden on the vertical ribs and extend down over the foot where a fourth mold part was used to shape the bottom of the foot. A horizontal mold line encircles the top of the pattern. The handle was initially applied at the top and looped down to be attached on the lower body. No pontil was used. Made of lead glass, the piece dates 1864 to ca. 1875. (Photo by Rock Chan, Parks Canada collection.)

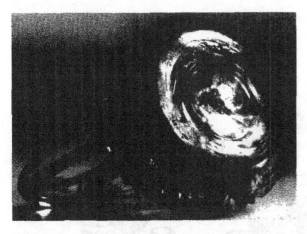

FIGURE 19. Narrow-mouthed vessels made in cut-and-shut molds were pressed upside down with a large band of undecorated glass at the base of the object. After withdrawing the object from the mold, the glass at the base was tooled inward and cut off which left a swirled crease on the base. The technique was developed in the 1870s (Innes 1976:66-67) and is most commonly found on cruets and molasses jugs. (Photo by Rock Chan, Parks Canada collection.)

engraved patterns and/or reflect decorative arts movements of the period. Motifs include classical (acanthus leaves, palmettes, cornucopia, oak leaves, shells and scrolls, feathered leaf shapes), gothic revival (arches, rosettes, quatrefoils, lancets, hairpins), folk art (hearts, tulips), historical/realistic (ships, eagles, buildings), peacock eye (later called comet), guilloches, thistles, and pineapples (McKearin and McKearin 1948:Plates 144-175).

Lacy-type patterns were also made in Europe, either by pressing or compressed air, and their production continued past mid-century (Spillman 1981:358-359).

PRESSED GLASS, CA. 1840-1870S

Pressed panel tumblers, introduced in the late 1830s (see Tumblers), seem to have been the first products made in a new style, now called geometric. During the 1840s, many new patterns were introduced in both the United States

FIGURE 20. Covered sugar bowl, open dish, cup plate, salt, and plate decorated by "lacy"-type pressed patterns produced in American factories between 1830 and ca. 1850. They are characterized by crisp, well-defined patterns against a textured ground and are of lead glass. The cup plate, center front, shows the *Chancellor Livingston* which operated between New York City and Providence, Rhode Island, until 1834, when it was decommissioned (Spillman 1981:137) (Courtesy of The Corning Museum of Glass, Corning, New York.)

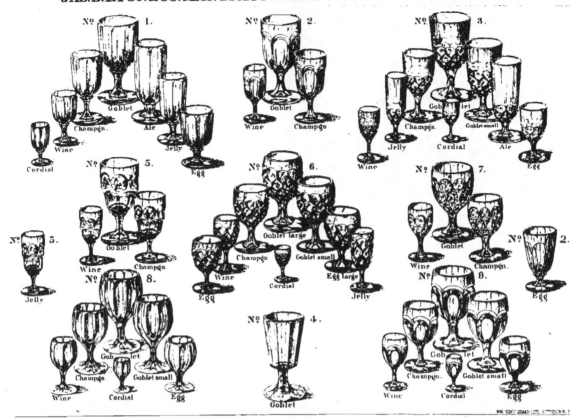

Nº 116 Water Street (five Doors below Monongahela House) Pittsburgh, Pa.

FIGURE 21. Page from the O'Hara Flint Glass Works catalogue which illustrates examples of geometric styles, sizes, and different functions of the stemware made by this firm (O'Hara Flint Glass Works 1861:3). Patterns are: No. 1 - Huber; No. 2 - Hotel; No. 3 - New York; No. 4 - Bohemian; No. 5 - Ashburton; No. 6 - Cincinnati; No. 7 - St. George; No. 8 - Huber; and No. 9 - O'Hara. Several patterns of this type continued to be made past the 1870s. Patterns resembling New York, for example, were still being made into the 1920s. (Courtesy of the Juliet K. and Leonard S. Rakow Research Library of The Corning Museum of Glass, Corning, New York.)

and Britain which imitated cut-glass motifs, particularly panels, flutes, round or oval facets, hexagons, diamonds, cross-hatching, and miters (Figures 21-23). During the 1850s, advertisements in Montreal newspapers by the Boston & Sandwich Glass Company and other American glass manufacturers showed both the range of objects and the range of patterns in the new style (Figure 22) (Jones 1992:10, 13-15). One piece of evidence suggests that the new styles in pressed glass competed head to head with cut glass and may even have forced the lowering of some cut-glass prices. An advertisement in the *Montreal Transcript* (1842) stated that it had "English Cut Dishes, as cheap as American pressed." The geometric style was produced in both Britain and the United States (Morris 1978:190-197; Spillman 1982:416-417; Slack 1987). Although its patterns were less detailed than the lacy ones, they nevertheless tended to cover all or most of the vessel surface up to the rim. The glass is thick, heavy, and of potash-lead composition. It is not clear if lacy patterns continued to be made during the 1850s and 1860s in the United States.

PRESSED GLASS, CA. 1865-1880S

In 1864, William Leighton developed a new soda-lime formula (see Glass Composition) which was considered a satisfactory visual substitute for potash-lead glasses. Most American pressed glass manufacturers had switched to the new formula within a few years because it was so

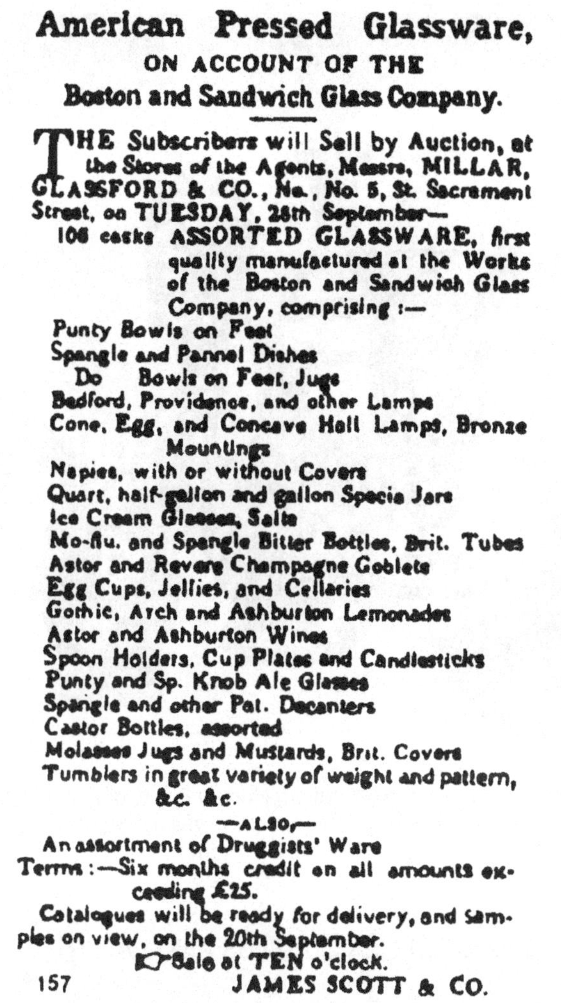

American Pressed Glassware,
ON ACCOUNT OF THE
Boston and Sandwich Glass Company.

THE Subscribers will Sell by Auction, at the Stores of the Agents, Messrs. MILLAR, GLASSFORD & CO., No., No. 5, St. Sacrament Street, on TUESDAY, 28th September— 106 casks ASSORTED GLASSWARE, first quality manufactured at the Works of the Boston and Sandwich Glass Company, comprising :—
Punty Bowls on Feet
Spangle and Pannel Dishes
  Do   Bowls on Feet, Jugs
Bedford, Providence, and other Lamps
Cone, Egg, and Concave Hall Lamps, Bronze Mountings
Napies, with or without Covers
Quart, half-gallon and gallon Specia Jars
Ice Cream Glasses, Salts
Mo-flu. and Spangle Bitter Bottles, Brit. Tubes
Astor and Revere Champagne Goblets
Egg Cups, Jellies, and Cellaries
Gothic, Arch and Ashburton Lemonades
Astor and Ashburton Wines
Spoon Holders, Cup Plates and Candlesticks
Punty and Sp. Knob Ale Glasses
Spangle and other Pat. Decanters
Castor Bottles, assorted
Molasses Jugs and Mustards, Brit. Covers
Tumblers in great variety of weight and pattern, &c. &c.
—ALSO,—
An assortment of Druggists' Ware
Terms :—Six months credit on all amounts exceeding £25.
Catalogues will be ready for delivery, and samples on view, on the 20th September.
☞Sale at TEN o'clock.
157   JAMES SCOTT & CO.

FIGURE 22. Named patterns from the Boston & Sandwich Glass Company include Punty, Spangle, Panel, Astor, Revere, Gothic, Arch, and Ashburton. The list includes a wide range of tablewares, including specialized forms with Britannia-metal tubes or covers (Montreal Gazette 1852:3).

much cheaper to produce. A comment in the *Crockery and Glass Journal* in 1879 about a newly introduced pattern extolled the visual appeal of pressed glass: "Every line in the design is a component part of an exquisite group and when this entire set of twenty-four pieces is placed on a well-spread table, the crystalline effect is beautiful" (Wilson 1994[1]:281).

Several different types of motifs were introduced during the ca. 1865-1880s period (Figures 24-25). Generally, the orientation of the patterns was horizontal; they circled the object rather than going from rim to base. *Geometric patterns* from the 1850s and 1860s continue, particularly honeycomb, facets, panels, and

V-shaped ribs. *Plain patterns* left most of the object undecorated except for decorative elements on the rim, finial, stem, or foot. Blank areas could be decorated with engraving (Figure 49) or, from the 1880s onwards, by staining. *Naturalistic patterns*, such as fruit, flowers, leaves, animals, hands, shells, baskets, and people, were used on finials, stems, and on the main body of the piece. The motifs stood out from the background and most typically went around the object. *Textured patterns* had stippled grounds with raised dots or frosted areas in contrast with smooth shiny areas. This type of design began in the mid 1860s (Morris 1978:194-196), and the effect was achieved by molding, acid-etching, engraving, or sandblasting. Many of these types of patterns continued to be made into the 1890s and later. Beginning in the 1870s, handles began to be pressed in the mold, rather than being applied by the glassmaker in a separate operation.

PRESSED GLASS, 1880S AND LATER

During the 1880s, color innovations became an important feature of pressed glass, including not just the glass (see Color), but also ruby and yellow stains, enamels, and gilding. Motifs introduced in the 1870s continued to be made, but several design changes were introduced in the late 1870s and early 1880s (Figures 26-29). The most prominent change concerned the orientation of patterns which switched from a horizontal to a vertical orientation. *Naturalistic patterns* featuring fruit and flowers, birds, animals, people, and scenes had a vertical orientation and were often confined in panels. Many new floral and leaf designs were shallower and less sculptured than the 1870s ones. Patterns in *contrasting textures* continued to be popular. *Rustic* designs were characterized by handles, feet, and finials disguised as twigs or branches. *Hobnails*, featuring protuberant rounded or pointed circles on the body of vessels, were often made in heat-sensitive glass. *Japonism* motifs were asymmetrical, with designs enclosed in parallelograms rather than squares or rectangles, and included such things as fans, butterflies, and swallows. Square bowls and plates were made under the same influence. *Plain* patterns often had a heavy band of decoration at the base in sharp contrast to an undecorated

FIGURE 23. Called Comet in period catalogues, collectors also call this type of pattern Horn of Plenty or Peacock Eye (Wilson 1994[1]:483). It dates mid-to-late 1850s into the 1870s. This group illustrates the range of shapes produced in a single pattern, including lamps. (Courtesy of The Corning Museum of Glass, Corning, New York.)

body. Some earlier *Geometric* patterns continued to be made. *Brilliant patterns* imitated brilliant cut patterns (Figure 26) (see Cut Glass). They were in production almost immediately after 1882, and continued to be a dominant style in pressed glass for much of the 20th century.

Patterns produced in English factories followed themes similar to those produced in American and Canadian factories, such as imitation cut patterns (Figure 52), rustic and Japonic patterns, contrasting textures, and naturalistic patterns. The naturalistic patterns tend to have a crisper, more sculptured look to them than North American examples, and often include realistically shaped vessels (Figures 2-4) (Slack 1987). Evidence for English production in the late 1870s and 1880s comes from the design registers, trademarked pieces, catalogues, and *The Pottery Gazette*. Partly because so much of the production is easily identified, and partly because of its attractiveness, glass from this period has been popular for both collectors and researchers.

PRESSED GLASS, 1890S AND LATER

In 1891, 18 companies in the American Midwest amalgamated to become the United States Glass Company although, after a devastating strike between 1893 and 1896, several of the original factories closed. By 1904, only six remained, plus three additional specialized plants (Revi 1964:306, 308). Production from this new company included new designs and reissues of many older patterns from its member factories (Figures 27-29). Catalogue pages from the U.S. Glass Company are illustrated throughout Revi (1964), in *Pennsylvania Glassware* (1972:133-156), and Heacock and Bickenheuser (1978). These catalogues serve as a snapshot of American pressed glass production in the 1890s, for both patterns and vessel shapes. A number of independent glass firms, however, continued to make pressed tablewares during the 1890s and first decade of the 20th century (Husfloen 1992:130-146).

During the 1890s and the first decade of the 20th century, consolidation also took place in the Canadian industry with several smaller factories being taken over by Diamond Glass which became the Dominion Glass Company in 1913 (Figure 30) (King 1987:84, 107-126).

Although a good variety of new patterns was issued, dozens of best-sellers from previous decades continued in wide production. Sometimes they were given a face lift by the addition of color, such as ruby and amber staining, and the application of flashy gold or colored enamel trim to highlight the design" (Husfloen 1992:102-103).

Colored glassware, including transparent and opaque colors and "marbled" colors, continued to be popular. Introduced into pressed-glass production in the early years of the 20th century was "Carnival glass" which featured iridescent golds, blues, and greens (Figure 1), and was often decorated with fruit or flower motifs.

From the patterns shown in the catalogues of the U.S. Glass Company, of Butler Brothers (Figures 1, 79), and of retail firms such as Montgomery Ward & Co. and T. Eaton Co., it is clear that imitation cut patterns and geometric patterns dominated the pressed-glass market

FIGURE 24. Although the Ribbed Bell-Flower or Ribbed-Leaf pattern has been attributed to several manufacturers and even to a ca. 1850 date, the 1864 M'Kee catalogue is the first dated documentary evidence for its production (M'Kee and Brothers 1981:29-31). The pattern does not appear in M'Kee's 1859-1860 illustrated catalogue, while the 1864 catalogue illustrates 42 pieces, strongly suggesting a new pattern. The style of decoration, with naturalistic motifs going around the object, as well as the contrast between a smooth pattern against a heavily patterned background, supports the view that this is a pattern introduced in the mid 1860s. Objects shown here include the "set" consisting of creamer, covered sugar, spooner, and covered butter, as well as a tumbler, different stemware, a plate, and pitcher. (Courtesy of The Corning Museum of Glass, Corning, New York.)

FIGURE 25. Examples of pressed-glass patterns of the 1870s (from left to right): *Footed sugar* in the Princess Feather or Rochelle pattern which appears in the ca. 1875 catalogue of Bakewell Pears & Co. It has three feathered medallions with a crosshatched center and a stippled ground. Patterns of this type bear some resemblance to lacy pressed patterns of the second quarter of the 19th century. *Goblet* with patterns similar to Nova Scotia Grape and Vine or Grape Band were introduced about 1870 and exhibit typical 1870s realistic decoration going around the vessel (Maple and Floral salvers in Figure 13). *Goblet* in a plain panel pattern of a type in production for decades. *Goblet* in Lion Head pattern, introduced ca. 1877, which consists of a plain undecorated bowl with panels supporting the bottom of the bowl, three lions' heads on the stem, and a cabled foot rim. The stem and foot are frosted by acid etching. *Creamer* in the Jacob's Ladder pattern which was patented in 1876, and was in production as late as 1907, in both Canada and the United States (Jenks and Luna 1990:297). This pattern has a vertical orientation which presages the patterns introduced in the 1880s. *Jug* in Victor or Shell and Jewel pattern was introduced in the 1870s but continued in production into the 20th century, and in Canada into the 1920s although the later Canadian versions have a flat rim (Figure 30). It is characterized by bold, high-relief glossy motifs against a stippled ground. (Photo by Rock Chan, Parks Canada collection.)

FIGURE 26. The Daisy and Button pattern, in imitation of the brilliant-cut Russian pattern, was a perennial favorite produced by many companies. Note the square celery and bowl in the lower left corner, an 1880s design change which reflected the angular forms of Japanism (Hobbs Glass Company n.d.). (Courtesy of The Winterthur Library, Printed Book and Periodical Collection.)

FIGURE 27. Examples of tumbler patterns offered by the United States Glass Company (1894) in an undated catalogue of the 1890s as reissues of patterns originally produced by member companies in the 1880s (Revi 1964:18-22, 54-61, 67-68, 86-90, 125-127, 148-151, 163-171, 216-223, 270-276). In this group, the patterns cover most of the body. Some have stiff, formal repeats (**top far right, bottom center**). Other motifs include imitation cut diamonds, swirled ribs, swirled rosettes, a meander (in the **far right of the last row** called Ribbon Candy), and one naturalistic vertical pattern enclosed in a frame which is called Fan and Butterfly. (Courtesy of the Juliet K. and Leonard S. Rakow Research Library of The Corning Museum of Glass, Corning, New York.)

from the 1890s to the 1920s. In the early 20th century, several American firms marketed these patterns under trade names such as Prescut (M'Kee; patented 1904), Plunger-cut (Heisey; patented 1906), and Nu-cut (Imperial; patented 1914) (Wilson 1994[2]:642). Although some new patterns featuring plants and flowers were introduced during these 30 years, usually for iridescent-glass patterns, they were far fewer in number, and "realistic" patterns, featuring such things as coins, were even fewer (Husfloen 1992:104). As a rule, patterns were oriented vertically on the piece, and as they tend to be narrower than patterns from earlier periods, the necessary repeats around the object often give a stiff, formal look to the patterns (Figures 27, 31).

Brilliant cut patterns included stars, pinwheels, Xs, strawberry diamonds, buzz-saws, fans, curved miter cuts, and crosshatching (Figure 32). In 1905, Butler Brothers offered a new pressed pattern: "Heavy pure crystal glass in beautiful new deep cut pattern copied from the latest genuine cut glass design, brilliantly fire polished" (Butler Brothers 1905:141). *Vertical ribs and panels* (Figure 29) were a common motif, sometimes plain, sometimes decorated, sometimes alternating plain and decorated, and were often outlined in

FIGURE 28. More from the 1890s U.S. Glass Company catalogue. The top row features (left to right): Magic, a rosette-type pattern, Fish-scale or Coral with alternating matte and shiny surfaces, and Brazil or Paneled Daisy which is a naturalistic pattern with vertical orientation and enclosed in a panel. The other patterns are largely imitation cut motifs including, in the middle row, diamond or square patterns composed of deep V-shaped grooves. (Courtesy of the Juliet K. and Leonard S. Rakow Research Library of The Corning Museum of Glass, Corning, New York.)

notches, beading, or cross-hatching. *Swirled ribs and panels* (Figure 29) helped give movement to an otherwise repetitive and stiff pattern. *Squares and diamonds* (Figure 28) created by V-shaped grooves formed a comparatively plain group of patterns. *Rosettes* (Figure 27), a round "floral" pattern consisting of a center and "petals," were also made during this period. *Meander, serpentine, and guilloche* (Figure 31) formed sinuous patterns, often combining both vertical and horizontal movement. *Naturalistic* patterns (Figure 27), featuring flowers, vines, leaves, or fruit, were oriented vertically and usually confined within panels although some patterns were placed over the panel edges. *Rococo revival* styles (Figure 33) appeared in both

pressed and acid-etched glassware in the early 1890s, with designs characterized by curving asymmetrical figures, scrolls, shells, and patterns with names such as "Louis XV" (Revi 1964:269). Beginning in the early 1900s, relatively plain paneled patterns, called "colonial" (Figures 34, 93), represented a growing interest in plainer patterns associated with Colonial revival aesthetics.

PRESSED GLASS, CA. 1920-1940

From the early years of the 20th century, in response to Colonial revival tastes, some pressed glass had been offered in comparatively plain patterns. The bulk of pressed glass, however, carried the heavily patterned look of the late

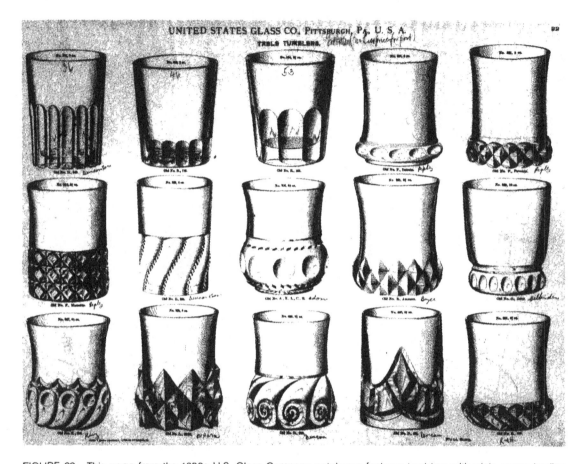

FIGURE 29. This page from the 1890s U.S. Glass Company catalogue features tumblers with plain upper bodies and imitation cut patterns on the lower body which often swells out at the base, a characteristic feature of this time period. (Courtesy of the Juliet K. and Leonard S. Rakow Research Library of The Corning Museum of Glass, Corning, New York.)

FIGURE 30. A group of Canadian patterns produced ca. 1900 to 1920s (Rottenberg and Tomlin 1982). From left to right: *Covered butter* in Stippled Swirl and Star is an example of the swirled-rib type of pattern; *Jug* in Maple Leaf pattern is a naturalistic-type pattern with a large well-defined motif, reminiscent of patterns from the 1880s; *Sugar bowl* in Nugget pattern, a Canadian version of Victor first produced in the 1870s, and reissued by the U.S. Glass Company in the 1890s, and still in production in the United States in the early 20th century and in Canada until the 1920s (Figure 25); *Covered sugar* which illustrates the vertical-type patterns (Beaded Oval and Fan No. 1) with an undecorated oval outlined by beading, another characteristic feature of the ca. 1900-1920 period; *Footed nappy* in Beaded Oval and Fan No. 2 pattern which is a brilliant-cut imitation; *Jug* in Athenian pattern which has a large bold motif placed on a textured ground and, like Maple Leaf, harks back to patterns of the 1880s; *Covered butter* in Bow Tie pattern, consisting of overlapping vertical ovals and small horizontal ovals decorated with crosshatching which form a horizontal row through the center of the vertical ovals. (Photo by Rock Chan, Parks Canada collection.)

Victorian period. By the late 1920s and into the 1930s, however, it was largely replaced by a lighter look which, although often profusely decorated, was achieved through the use of light colors, thinner transparent glass, shallow decoration, and clean lines (Figures 35-37). Pressed patterns tended to echo acid-etched or engraved designs, the lighter cut patterns introduced around 1910, and even blown glassware. Interest in the Colonial or Georgian period brought revivals of cut and pressed patterns of the 1820-1840 period and reinterpretations of neo-classical motifs. New vessel forms introduced during this period were serving plates with handles in the center, grill plates with three dividers molded in the glass, cups and saucers, soup bowls, and dinner and salad plates (Figure 59). Although introduced before the turn of the century, specialized plates or trays for such things as cheese and crackers, spoons, bonbons, olives, and mayonnaise were common. The impression from the Butler Brothers catalogues is that by 1929-1930, machine-blowing had become more prominent than pressing for making jugs, tumblers, and stemware.

Beginning in the mid to late 1920s, pressed glass (and blown glass) is most easily recognized by its color palette: pastel pinks, ambers, lime and emerald greens, blues, deep intense blue and red, amethyst, and opaque colors including white, custard, and black (Florence 1995a, 1996). "Carnival" glass also continued to be made. *Brilliant cut patterns* (Figures 38, 61) continued to be offered although in much smaller variety and were commoner in "company" pieces, such as berry bowls, vases, and sugar and cream sets. Often referred to as "colonial," *vertical panels* were staple patterns, in varying heights, widths, with rounded or square tops, or going from top to bottom of the object (Figure 34). *Horizontal panels/ribs*, sometimes combined with vertical ribs, were completely new to pressed tableware and reflected art deco aesthetics. This type of combination was also found in blown glassware (Figure 14). *Squares* or *hexagons* assumed more of an art deco look although they had been introduced earlier (Figures 28, 36). Overall patterns, such as *bull's-eyes, hobnails, and crackle*, continued to be produced (Figure 55). *Acid-etched* designs featuring florals, borders, festoons,

OUR "BIG BRILLIANT"
TABLE SET ASSORTMENT.
Large full size sets at a price usually charged for small ones.

C1030—Asst. comprises: 6 sets each of 3 patterns, all footed, one with large double handles. Each set consists of covered butter dish, sugar bowl, spoon holder and cream pitcher, all in rich new crystal patterns. Total 18 sets in bbl. (Bbl. 35c.)
Per set. 16½c

NEW "MAGNIFICENT" TABLE SET ASST.
Positively the most beautiful set ever offered at a 50c price

C1034—Three elaborate and brilliant genuine cut glass patterns, all extra large, heavy and massive, richly finished and polished. 4 sets of 3 patterns. Total 12 sets in bbl. (Bbl. c)
Per set. 32c

FIGURE 31. Selections from the 1905 Butler Brothers catalogue: *upper*, intertwined-type pattern contrasted with one of the stiff vertical patterns; *lower*, pattern featuring guilloche with central rosette, a meander-type pattern and a brilliant-cut-type pattern (Butler Brothers 1905:142). (Courtesy of Collins Kirby Art & Antiques, Fort Payne, Alabama.)

hanging pendants, medallions, and other vaguely neoclassical-inspired designs were shallowly pressed and imitated popular acid-etched motifs (Figures 35, 37, 82). *Lacy* patterns imitating pressed lacy glass of the 1830-1850 period were part of Colonial revival esthetics.

Cut Glass

Cut glass is a cold decorating technique and as such can be done in a glass factory, in a cutting shop, or by individuals (Kaellgren 1993; Palmer 1993b, 1993c; Spillman 1996). It was a decorating technique favored by, but not exclusive to, the English, and enhanced the lustrous light-transmitting properties of potash-lead glass.

The surface of the glass is cut away by grinding with wheels and grit. Polishing is accomplished by using increasingly finer abrasives and polishing wheels. In the 19th century, the edges of the cut motif are generally crisp, the cut surface is shiny, and the wheel marks can be seen on some pieces. For most cut glass, there is a difference in surface texture between the cut and uncut areas. In the early 20th century, however, acid baths began to be used for polishing, replacing the laborious and time-consuming wheel work (Hajdamach 1991:178; Wilson 1994[2]:640). As acid removes the surface, it also removes the marks of the wheel and softens the sharp edges so characteristic of earlier cutting. Motifs in cut glass tend to be geometric, based on straight line cuts, although curved lines and ribs are possible.

"Rich cut glassware" or "elegant cut glassware" were phrases used over and over in 19th-century Canadian newspaper advertisements because cut glassware, whether consisting of elaborate designs or simple panels, had an immediately recognized prestige which it still retains. From the 1790s onward, the constant imitation of cut-glass-inspired motifs in both contact-molded patterns and in the pressed glass industry attest to the popularity of the cut-glass look. Cut glass imported from Great Britain and Bohemia or made in the United States served the American market while Canadians used British cut glass almost exclusively. By the early 20th century, several Canadian firms were using imported blanks from Europe and the United States to make cut glass. Blanks are pieces of glass produced to be decorated by cutting or engraving.

For much of the 19th century, glassware cut in simple motifs, such as panels, flutes, miters, and facets, was the standard offering in the market. More elaborate cut patterns, however, were fashionable in different periods.

Variously called Georgian, Regency, or Anglo-Irish, patterns featuring V-shaped miter cuts were characteristic of British and American cut glass from ca. 1800 to the 1840s (Figures 39-42). In addition to flat cuts forming panels, cutters used

FIGURE 32. Jug in imitation brilliant-cut design which exhibits its characteristic complex motifs and the overall exuberance of decoration. (Photo by Rock Chan, Parks Canada collection.)

a V-shaped wheel to produce a repertoire of motifs consisting of V-shaped grooves, fields of plain diamonds or strawberry diamonds, blazes (straight or diagonal), fans, splits, and swirls (McFarlan 1992:1-12).

Beginning in the late 1820s and 1830s, a new vertical look was introduced into cut glass. This style had broad flute cuts which tended to go all the way up the body of the vessel to meet similar cuts coming down the neck and shoulder (Figure 42).

By mid-19th century, cut glass was characterized by simple bold motifs such as broad panels, large facets, and deep miter cuts (Wilson 1994[2]:523), similar to those seen in pressed glass (Figures 21, 23), generally on thickly blown glass (Figure 43). "Between 1851 and 1860 Stevens and Williams, for example, recorded over 1,000 cut glass designs in their pattern books. The majority of these patterns consisted of flutes, hollows, miters, prisms and fan scallops . . ." (Figure 87) (Hajdamach 1991:359). Vessels covered with elaborate cut

designs were shown at the 1851 exhibition, but these were certainly not bread-and-butter wares (*The Art-Journal* 1851:32, 70, 138-139, 174-175). As glassware became lighter in the late 1860s and 1870s, cut motifs tended to be shallow and simple (Figure 44) (Boston & Sandwich Glass Co. 1992).

From 1882 until 1915 and later, elaborately cut glass, known as brilliant cut glass, was fashionable. The first of it, in the Russian pattern, was patented in 1882, by a cutter working for T. G. Hawkes & Co. of Corning, New York, although many other glass companies also made it (Figure 26) (Spillman 1982:29; 1996:239-241). Brilliant cut glass featured stars, hobstars, strawberry-diamonds, fans, sunbursts, pinwheels, Xs, and curved V-shaped miters deeply cut into thick, heavy blanks and, in the earlier years, covering the entire object. "The characteristic feature of the work itself was the exact mathematical precision to which the cutters aspired. Usually composed of bold groupings of relatively small elements, the decoration gave an effect of great richness" (Wakefield 1982:45). Cut in the United States, Canada, Britain, and Bohemia, brilliant cut glass became a standard of social and material success

FIGURE 33. Covered sugar in opaque white glass in a rococo-revival-type pattern, although it is a subdued and rather stiff rendition in contrast to some of the acid-etched versions (Figure 56). (Photo by Rock Chan, Parks Canada collection.)

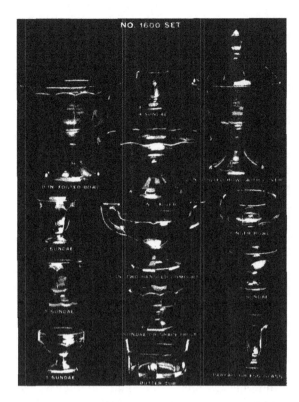

FIGURE 34. Innumerable patterns with vertical panels, called Colonial, were made by many companies from ca. 1900 onward, and they are one of the long-lived "looks" of the 20th century. These patterns were part of the Colonial revival movement and both the names used and the shapes made echoed early 19th-century styles. For example, the high squared handles on the compote imitate early-19th-century Georgian silver forms. Two forms offered as a parfait or egg glass and as a sundae or grapefruit glass suggest that the same shape could be used for different purposes. Dessert glasses, particularly individual serving bowls, become far more obvious in early-20th-century catalogues. For example, in addition to the six sundae variants on this page, the company also offered three other styles in different sizes (Stevens 1967:164-167). Figure 34 is taken from an undated catalogue of the Jefferson Glass Company, a Canadian company which operated from ca. 1912 to 1925 (Rottenberg and Tomlin 1982:10). (Photo by Rock Chan; original in Dominion Glass Company Limited papers in the National Archives of Canada, Ottawa.)

and was popular as giftware, particularly for weddings. For example, in the early years of the 20th century, Henry Birks & Sons of Montreal offered "ATTRACTIVE WEDDING GIFTS IN CUT GLASS" which featured boxed versions of water sets comprising a carafe and six tumblers, cream and sugar sets sometimes in combination with a berry bowl, or a berry bowl with six small bowls (Henry Birks & Sons 1906:94-95). Over the next 20 years,

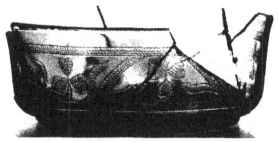

FIGURE 35. Bowl, 4 in. (10 cm), in lime green glass in Cloverleaf pattern which was made between 1930 and 1936 by the Hazel Atlas Glass Company (Florence 1996:38-41). (Photo by Rock Chan, Parks Canada collection.)

both technological innovations and changes in the patterns lowered the price of brilliant cut glassware (Farrar and Spillman 1979:13-15; Wilson 1994[2]:635-643). In the 1880s, the patterns on individual pieces tended to consist of a single motif, but later ones generally had a mixture of motifs. "On glass with a repeat design, . . . it is especially important that the cutting be perfectly even, the lines parallel, and that all points of the design meet properly. With mixed motifs, you may overlook poor cutting . . ." (Spillman 1982:262). Blown or

FIGURE 36. Footed sherbet in pink glass showing an imitation cut pattern in which V-shaped grooves intersect to form diamonds. This is the Waterford pattern made by Anchor Hocking between 1938 and 1944 (Florence 1996:225-226), although it resembles patterns from the 1890s shown in Figure 28. (Photo by Rock Chan, Parks Canada collection.)

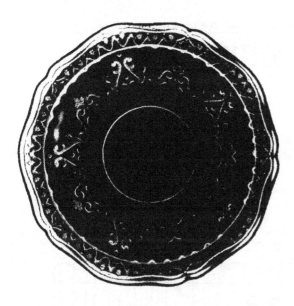

FIGURE 37. Saucer in pale amber glass with a pattern imitating acid-etched designs, including the frosted surface. This is the Patrician pattern made by Federal Glass Company, 1933 to 1937 (Florence 1996:168-169). (Photo by Rock Chan, Parks Canada collection.)

molded blanks with patterns already roughed out virtually eliminated the preliminary roughing process. Pressed glass imitations of brilliant cutting were a successful part of the marketplace from the 1880s into the 1920s (Figure 32), and, in the opinion of some, were partly responsible for the demise of brilliant cut glass (Wilson 1994[2]:643).

About 1900, brilliant cut styles were joined by a light, shallow cut style with simple floral/ fruit/leaf and stem designs which left most of the surface uncut (Figure 45). Flowers were stylized, facing outward with a round center and petals coming out from it. Sometimes this type of cutting was offered in a "gray" finish; it was left unpolished, like copper wheel engraving or acid-etched designs. Shallowly cut glass could be done on the thin light glass so widely used up to and during the 1930s, and on Pyrex (Figures 7, 82, 94). This type of cutting significantly lowered the price of cut glass, offering its prestige to a lower economic range, but it also appealed to consumers who wanted a lighter look. Conscious imitations of early 19th-century glasswares also affected cut glass (Figure 46).

Engraved Glass

As with other cold-decorating techniques, engraving can be done independently from the glass factory. It was a technique favored by, but not exclusive to, German/Bohemian decorators.

Like cutting, engraving involves the cutting away of glass by using abrasives and wheels, but the wheels are smaller and capable of producing a much greater variety of motifs than the cutting process. Generally, the surface is left unpolished, providing a matte surface in contrast to the original glossy surface. As engraving is flexible, it can be shallow to accommodate very thin glass or deeply incised for a rich carved look. Many different levels of engraving were done, from simple motifs (Figures 44, 46-51, 88) to complex scenes covering the whole vessel; from sketchy quickly-done motifs (Figures 12, 85) to superbly executed imitations of period prints requiring hundreds of hours of work. Engraving was so adaptable, it could be used to produce personal mementoes as well as large-scale commercial works.

In the early 19th century, Bohemian engravers favored motifs in the Federal or neoclassical style, such as swags, festoons, knots, hanging tassels, stars, bouquets, closely packed rows of tiny vertical flowering plants, narrow bands with small oval or round cut and polished facets, and floral sprays (Lanman 1969:29-47; Spillman 1982:No. 101; Pattern Book n.d.). Similar motifs were adapted by engravers working in the United States and were produced up to ca. 1840 (Figure 47) (Innes 1976:166-171). Also in the first 40 years of the 19th century, engravers working in Britain and the United States made commemorative glasses for places, events, ships, buildings, and clubs, as well as for individuals, engraving people's names or initials, and dates. They also engraved words such as "wine" or "spirits," and idyllic scenes (Wakefield 1982:80-86; Hajdamach 1991:149-156).

Most authors discuss high-end engraved glassware of the mid to late 19th century, which featured complex, finely executed patterns done by famous engravers, often for international exhibitions (Morris 1978:76-100; Hajdamach 1991:156-173). Rock crystal engraving, which has polished surfaces, was introduced in the 1880s, and "intaglio" engraving, which is deep engraving done by stone wheels and produces larger bolder patterns, came in about 1900 (Wakefield 1982:94, 98, 102). Elaborately engraved glassware was still being made in the 1920s and 1930s (Farrar and Spillman

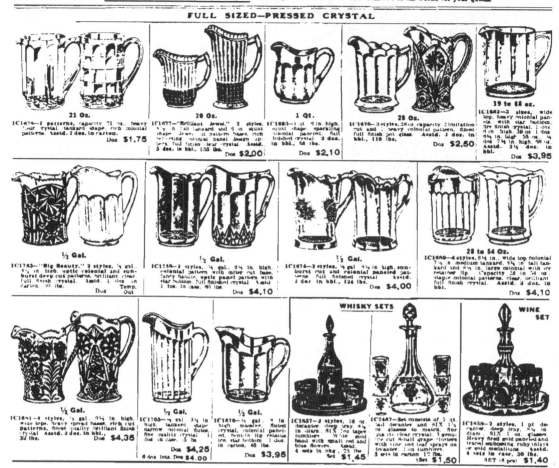

FIGURE 38.   Selection of jugs from the Butler Brothers (1925) catalogue showing pressed designs.   Note the variety of vertical panels offered, all called Colonial.   The distinctive short, squat jug in the center of the top row was shown in their 1914 catalogue as was an ice water pitcher featuring a bent-in lip designed to hold back ice, which became generally available as refrigerators became more common.   (Courtesy of Collins Kirby Art & Antiques, Fort Payne, Alabama.)

1979; Spillman 1982:No. 33, No. 275, No. 307; 1996).

In the 1870s, it is possible to pick up the threads of less expensive engraved glasses through catalogue illustrations and glassware (Figures 49-51) (Bakewell, Pears & Co. 1875:43, 44; Boston & Sandwich Glass Co. 1992). Borders, horizontal bands of floral/leaf/fruit motifs, sprays of flowers, and monograms enclosed in wreaths seem to have been standard ware. The role of simpler engraved patterns past 1900 is not clear as simple cut, acid-etched, and enameled patterns seem to have fulfilled the role

they had played in the past. Although Butler Brothers included some engraved tumblers in their 1905, 1910, and 1914 catalogues, there seems to be no engraving in the 1925, 1929, and 1930 catalogues (Butler Brothers 1905:147, 150, 1910:403-404, 1914:318-319).

Frosted Glass (Textured Glass)

Terminology for these techniques is difficult to sort out as both period documents and 20th-century authors have used the same terms inconsistently.

FIGURE 39. Lynn-molded and cut glassware (from left to right): Both *tumblers* are decorated by a hot-glass technique known as Lynn molding which leaves irregularly spaced, shallow, horizontal grooves around an object. Examples have been found in archaeological contexts in Canada dating from the late 18th to early 19th century. *Decanter* decorated with cut panels on the shoulder and lower body, as well as tiny vertical V-shaped grooves. Although the cutting elements are vertical, they are placed in bands around the object, which, when combined with the applied neck rings, give the decanter a squat horizontal look. Ringed decanters with this tapered-body shape date from the late 18th century into the 1840s (Figure 64 *left*); *Stemware* with a centrally knopped stem and a bucket bowl was the dominant style during the first half of the 19th century and continued to be made during the second half of the 19th century, although in far fewer numbers (Figure 74). Two glasses are decorated with cut panels, and the large goblet on the right has angled blazes as well. All cut glassware from archaeological sites of this period tends to be comparatively plain. (Photo by Rock Chan, Parks Canada collection.)

ROUGHED GLASS

A fashion for contrasting textures began in the 1840s and 1850s (Morris 1978:25-26). It consisted of a gray granular ground with shiny pattern superimposed on it or of a textured pattern against a shiny ground (Figure 51). Several different techniques were used to achieve these results:

1. Grinding the glass surface with a wheel and leaving it unpolished, like engraving, or by using stone wheels normally used for cut glass but eliminating the polishing steps (Figure 52). In some examples, the horizontal lines left by the wheel can be seen. This technique was superseded by pressing and acid etching beginning in the late 1860s and 1870s.

2. Acid etching, in which the surface etched by the acid was left matte, leaves "a very fine, uniform, flat texture" (Hajdamach 1991:184). A "white" acid finish, which results in a frosted silky surface, is achieved by neutralizing hydrofluoric acid with an alkali salt (Figure 53). As acid cuts into the glass evenly, if the pattern has sufficient depth, one can observe an almost right-angled edge to the roughed surface leading up to the smooth surface.

3. Sand blasting, in which sand is directed against glass by air pressure, was developed in the late 1860s and early 1870s. The areas to be left undecorated were protected by an overlay resist and a stencil or cut-out design was used to make the pattern. The technique was used to decorate or label windows, lampshades, and

FIGURE 40. Jug, attributed to a New York glasshouse, decorated in the Anglo-Irish style of cutting which features horizontal and vertical miter cuts, diamonds with crosshatching, and flat panels. Inexpensive imitations of these motifs were done by contact molding. (Courtesy of The Corning Museum of Glass, Corning, New York.)

drinking glasses and generally left a coarser surface with less detailed design than other methods (Figure 54) (Hajdamach 1991:374-378).

4. Pressing, in which the texture was molded into the glass (Figures 25, 30).

CRACKLED GLASS

Fissures or cracks in the glass were made by several techniques:

1. During the manufacturing process, the hot glass is plunged into cold water, reheated, and expanded. The process produces glass "irregularly veined, [having] marble-like projecting dislocations, with intervening fissures" (Pellatt 1849:116-117). Although the resulting glass is full of cracks it is, as Pellatt states, "perfectly sonorous." Called crackled glass, or sometimes ice-glass, Pellatt introduced it to the English market in the mid-19th century as an imitation of an earlier Venetian technique.

2. During manufacture, the object is rolled in crushed glass which adheres to the exterior surface and, when expanded by blowing, forms a rough surface with smooth veins (Revi 1959:61-64; Spillman 1982:95). Collectors have

FIGURE 41. Cut glass attributed to the Pittsburgh area, ca. 1820 to 1850, which shows different combinations of motifs associated with the Anglo-Irish repertoire. The cut motif on the celery vase, second from the left, was imitated by an English firm in the 1930s (Figure 69). (Courtesy of The Corning Museum of Glass, Corning, New York.)

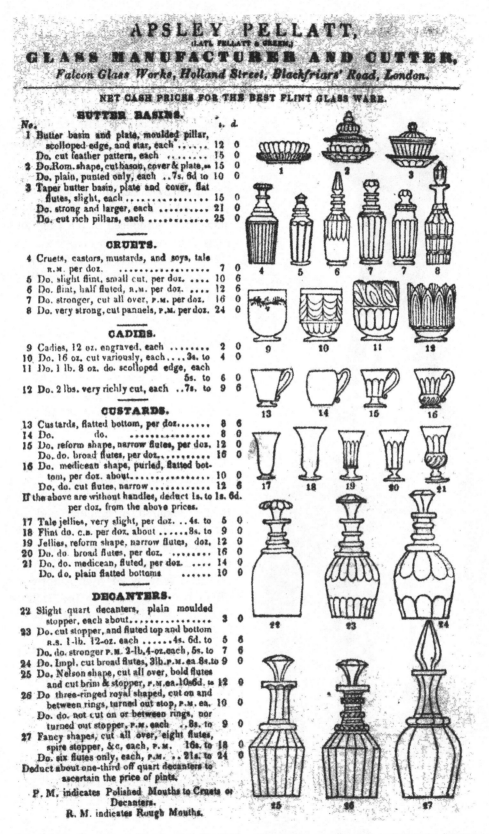

APSLEY PELLATT,
(LATE PELLATT & GREEN,)
GLASS MANUFACTURER AND CUTTER,
Falcon Glass Works, Holland Street, Blackfriars' Road, London.

NET CASH PRICES FOR THE BEST FLINT GLASS WARE.

BUTTER BASINS.

No.		s.	d.
1	Butter basin and plate, moulded pillar, scolloped edge, and star, each	12	0
	Do. cut feather pattern, each	15	0
2	Do. Rom. shape, cut bason, cover & plate,	15	0
	Do. plain, punted only, each .. 7s. 6d to	10	0
3	Taper butter basin, plate and cover, flat flutes, slight, each	15	0
	Do. strong and larger, each	21	0
	Do. cut rich pillars, each	25	0

CRUETS.

No.		s.	d.
4	Cruets, castors, mustards, and soys, tale R.M. per doz.	7	0
5	Do. slight flint, small cut, per doz.	10	6
6	Do. flint, half fluted, R.M. per doz.	12	6
7	Do. stronger, cut all over, P.M. per doz.	16	0
8	Do. very strong, cut pannels, P.M. per doz.	24	0

CADIES.

No.		s.	d.
9	Cadies, 12 oz. engraved, each	2	0
10	Do. 16 oz. cut variously, each.... 3s. to	4	0
11	Do. 1 lb. 8 oz. do. scolloped edge, each 5s. to	6	0
12	Do. 2 lbs. very richly cut, each ..7s. to	9	6

CUSTARDS.

No.		s.	d.
13	Custards, flatted bottom, per doz.	8	6
14	Do. do.	8	0
15	Do. reform shape, narrow flutes, per doz.	12	0
	Do. do. broad flutes, per doz.	16	0
16	Do. medicean shape, purled, flatted bottom, per doz. about	10	0
	Do. do. cut flutes, narrow	12	6

If the above are without handles, deduct 1s. to 1s. 6d. per doz. from the above prices.

No.		s.	d.
17	Tale jellies, very slight, per doz. ..4s. to	5	0
18	Flint do. C.B. per doz. about ......8s. to	9	0
19	Jellies, reform shape, narrow flutes, doz.	12	0
20	Do. do. broad flutes, per doz.	16	0
21	Do. do. medicean, fluted, per doz.	14	0
	Do. do. plain flatted bottoms	10	0

DECANTERS.

No.		s.	d.
22	Slight quart decanters, plain moulded stopper, each about	3	0
23	Do. cut stopper, and fluted top and bottom R.S. 1-lb. 12-oz. each ......4s. 6d. to	5	6
	Do. do. stronger P.M. 2-lb. 4-oz. each, 5s. to	7	6
24	Do. Impl. cut broad flutes, 3lb. P.M. ea. 8s. to	9	0
25	Do. Nelson shape, cut all over, bold flutes and cut brim & stopper, P.M. ea. 10s6d. to	12	0
26	Do. three-ringed royal shaped, cut on and between rings, turned out stop, P.M. ea.	10	0
	Do. do. not cut on or between rings, nor turned out stopper, P.M. each ..8s. to	9	0
27	Fancy shapes, cut all over, eight flutes, spire stopper, &c. each, P.M. 16s. to	18	0
	Do. six flutes only, each, P.M. .. 21s. to	24	0

Deduct about one-third off quart decanters to ascertain the price of pints.

P. M. indicates Polished Mouths to Cruets or Decanters.
R. M. indicates Rough Mouths.

FIGURE 42. First page of Apsley Pellatt's 1840 catalogue showing three decanters in the bottom row which are decorated with a broad flute-style of cutting. (Courtesy of the Juliet K. and Leonard S. Rakow Research Library of The Corning Museum of Glass, Corning, New York.)

Olive R. Jones

FIGURE 43. Decanter and stopper in heavy lead glass with deep-cut finger flutes on the body alternating with a curved uncut surface, cut vertical panels on the neck, and a deeply cut star on the base. This decanter resembles some produced in Britain in the late 1830s and 1840s (Hajdamach 1991:52; Morris 1978:19, 28). (Photo by Rock Chan, Parks Canada collection.)

called this technique "overshot," but Nelson (1992:13, 15, 17-18) notes that the Boston & Sandwich Glass Company called glassware decorated by this technique "frosted;" ground surfaces were called "roughed;" vessels with ground surfaces decorated by wheel-polished designs were called "Frosted and Bright;" and the term "etched" was used for acid-etched designs.

3. Using pressed patterns to imitate glassware decorated by either of the above methods. The Tree of Life pattern, resembling overshot technique, was introduced in the late 1860s, and versions of it continued in production into the 1890s (Jenks and Luna 1990:524-525). Twentieth-century versions included Spider Web in carnival glass (Spillman 1982:197) and crackle glass (Figure 55).

Acid-etched Glass

A glass object is coated with a compound which resists the action of hydrofluoric acid; a design is incised through the resist; and the glass is placed in an acid bath or in fumes where the acid attacks the exposed glass surface. Afterwards, the resist is removed from the glass. Depending on the mixture in the acid bath, the surface can be made silky smooth, shiny, frosted, textured, or granular, and, depending on the time in the acid, the glass can be etched shallowly or deeply. More complex designs can be done by etching sequentially.

The discovery of hydrofluoric acid and its effect on glass dates to the 18th century, but until the middle of the 19th century, it was regarded more as a curiosity than a viable commercial proposition. In the 1850s, both Benjamin Richardson and John Northwood began experimenting with different parts of the process, including the resist material, ways of transferring the pattern through the resist, and the acid mixture itself. In those early years, and later, acid-etching could involve a great deal of handwork, sometimes making it as expensive as engraving (Morris 1978:113-126; Hajdamach 1991:175-201).

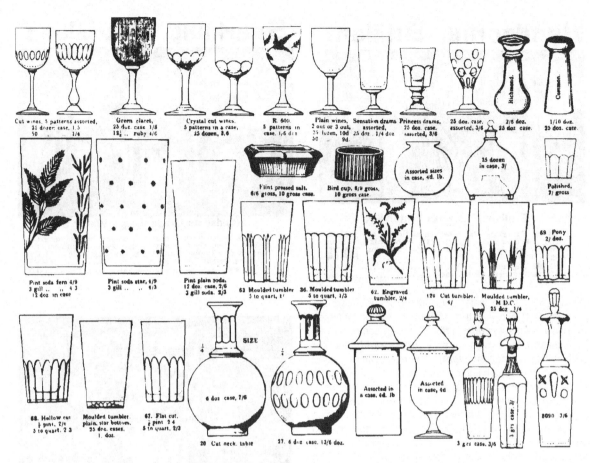

FIGURE 44. Selection of plain, cut, and engraved stemware and tumblers offered by M. Davis & Co. in the *Pottery Gazette* (1881:near 817). Bicolored glasses, like the claret glass in the top row, third from the left, with green or red bowls and colorless stems and feet, date from ca. 1850 to World War I. In marked contrast to brilliant-cut glass, these designs are plain, traditional, and vary little from earlier periods. It is not clear if the molded tumblers are pressed or blown-molded. Also shown in the lower right corner are three castor and cruet bottles decorated by cutting (Courtesy of The British Library, London; digital image by George van der Vlugt.)

NEEDLE ETCHING BY TEMPLATE

In 1861, Northwood developed a template machine for tracing patterns through the resist, which made it possible to produce complex patterns of great delicacy, comparable to engraving (Figure 56) (Morris 1978:116, 118; Hajdamach 1991:179-182).

NEEDLE ETCHING BY LATHE

In the mid 1860s, Northwood developed a geometric etching machine for incising a design through the resist (Hajdamach 1991:182-184). The apparatus resembled a lathe and was capable of producing repeating patterns, such as a Greek key design or a continuous band of overlapping circles (Figure 57) (Boston & Sandwich Glass Co. 1992:Plate 27). A host of repeating patterns

followed and were still in production in the 1930s. This type of decoration was particularly suited for thinly blown glassware popular from the 1870s into the 1930s, and is often found in conjunction with optic molding (Figure 94, *bottom left*).

PLATE ETCHING

Through a complicated process similar to transfer printing on ceramics, the resist was put on paper and transferred to the glass, leaving the pattern open. The rest of the glass was then covered in the resist as well so that the vessel could be dipped in acid. This process was developed in the 1850s (Hajdamach 1991:196-197). A simpler process, in which the acid pattern was put on paper and then applied to the glass, was developed in the 1870s

Olive R. Jones

Handsome, Brilliant

Brilliant Cut-glass Water Set

11-321. Cut-glass Water Set, consisting of one jug, capacity one quart, and standing 8½ inches high, and six tumblers. Has beautifully cut design. Shipping weight 15 lbs. Price **10.75**
11-322. Jug only. Price **5.65**
11-323. Tumblers. Price, each **85c**

FIGURE 45. Three water sets offered by T. Eaton Co. (1918/19:514) showing the difference in price between the brilliant-cut set (**upper left**), which is a comparatively plain pattern, the simple-cut style (**upper right**), and the brilliant-pressed pattern (**right**). The new style of cutting tended to be done on lighter glass, not only cutting costs at the factory and cutting shop, but also shipping costs. The cut grape water set continued for a long time in Eaton's catalogues, being offered intermittently until 1930-31 when the price had fallen to $1.25 per set. The pattern also appeared on individual tumblers, fruit bowl and nappy sets, and decanter or cordial sets. (Reproduced with the kind permission of The T. Eaton Company Limited; digital image by George van der Vlugt.)

Sparkling Cut-Glass

Handsome Grape-design Water Set

11-324. Seven-piece Water Set, with a handsome grape design cut on clear blanks. Light-weight tumblers. Set consists of 6 tumblers and 1 jug, capacity 3 pints. Shipping weight 7 lbs. Price **2.50**
11-400. Extra Tumblers, per half-dozen. Price.... **1.00**

7-piece Water Set

11-336. Seven-piece Crystal Glass Water or Lemonade Set: made of extra heavy, clear crystal glass with an attractive and handsome "Prescut" design. Set consists of 1-qt. jug and 6 tumblers. Shipping weight 12 lbs. Price, per set **1.75**

(Hajdamach 1991:197-198). Patterns done by this type of process tended to be pictorial (Figure 58).

Tableware Forms

Glass tableware is part of a whole group of objects of different materials that are used to serve and consume food and beverages. Identifying their function from fragments, therefore is important for archaeologists interested in studying foodways. This section of the guide briefly discusses tableware forms made between 1800 and 1940, and, when appropriate, provides guidance for dating attributes.

Glass tableware was used in a variety of settings. Different meals and occasions, such as breakfast or dinner, afternoon tea or evening tea, formal or informal, required different assemblages (Williams 1985). If the meal were eaten at

home, it may have had a different composition than meals eaten at the workplace, taverns, restaurants, or hotels. As well, social class influenced both the selection of objects and the cost level of the choice:

"Fortunately," replied Monsieur, to whom this aside had been addressed, "the persons who consider Champagne, japonicas, and attar of roses necessaries of life are very well able to provide cut-glass receptacles for them. But isn't it worth one's while to be proud of a country where every artisan's wife has her tumblers, her goblets, her vases, of pressed glass, certainly, but 'as good, to her mind, as cut,' to quote our friend? And don't you think it better that twenty-two thousand dozen pressed tumblers should be sold at ten cents apiece than one-third that number of cut ones at thirty cents, leaving all those who cannot pay the higher

122   *The Historical Archaeology Laboratory Handbook*

E 9686
GOBLET
Height 5½"
12 - each

E 9686
CHAMPAGNE
Height 4¾"
10 - each

E 9686
CLARET
Height 4½"
9 - each

E 9686
COCKTAIL
Height 4½"
7 6 each

E 9686
PORT
Height 4"
7 - each

E 9686
SHERRY
Height 4"
7 - each

E 9686
LIQUEUR
Height 3½"
6 - each

E 9686
FINGER BOWL
Dia 5"
11 6 each

E 9686
½-PINT TUMBLER
Height 3½"
7 6 each

E 9686
GRAPE FRUIT GLASS
Dia 4"
9 - each

E 9686
CELERY OR FLOWER VASE
Height 8"
21 - each

E 9686
QUART DECANTER
Height 11½"
90 - pair

E 9686
QUART JUG
Height 6½"
30 - each

FIGURE 46. This type of design, with the bowl bulging out over a constricted base, is reminiscent of Anglo-Irish styles of the 1820s (Figure 74*e*) and is a good example of the top-heavy look in glass which came in with Colonial revival and art deco styles, and which, to a certain extent, still persists. Hillston Crystal produced a variety of 18th- and 19th-century styles as revivals or as reproductions (Hill-Ouston Co. 1936:81). Virtually the same pattern, without the engraving, was produced in pressed glass by Hocking about 1930, and called "Georgian" (Figure 95) (Weatherman 1974:140). (Author's collection; digital image by George van der Vlugt.)

price to drink out of . . ." (Austin 1991:84).

The structure of a meal, such as one with a soup course, followed by one or two meat and vegetable courses and finally a dessert, necessitated the use of different vessels. Until about the middle of the 19th century, it had been customary to place the serving dishes on the table in a balanced and aesthetic manner so that guests served themselves and each other. Beginning about mid-century, however, a new style was introduced into North America, called *service à la russe*, which had the serving dishes placed on a side table and the food carved and brought to the table by servants (Williams 1985:149-155). Flowers, ornaments, vases, or ornamental scenes were placed in the center of the table. Although the method of service changed the location of the serving pieces, it did not necessarily affect their number or variety. At the other end of the scale, individuals or households living a marginal existence may have had little or no glass.

Beverage service also varied from situation to situation, depending on place, the consumers, and the occasion. It was not necessarily associated with the consumption of food or even with a table.

Sets or services of glassware decorated in the same way and with the same motifs were available in the early 19th century (Warren 1981:224-239; Gray and Gray 1987:11-18). Until the middle of the 19th century, sets tended to be confined to things that were used together, such as paired decanters, drinking glasses, cruet sets, dessert glasses, glassware for traveling

FIGURE 47. The engraved motifs of swags, bows, stars, and hanging pendants were typical neoclassical motifs favored by Bohemian engravers of the first half of the 19th century, as was the contrast in texture between the polished leafy branches and flower against the matte surface of the unpolished swag. The three-ring decanter shape, pressed mushroom stopper, lead-glass composition, and ground and polished pontil mark point either to an English origin for the decanter or to an American imitation of an English style. As with all cold-decorating techniques, like cutting and engraving, the decoration could be done anywhere and was not necessarily part of a glass factory operation. Independent cutters and engravers operated in cities such as New York, Philadelphia, and Baltimore, decorating domestic and/or imported glass, or whatever glass their customers wanted (Palmer 1993b, 1993c). Although this decanter is attributed to the American Midwest, as Wilson (1994[1]:197) points out in connection to a similarly engraved celery in lead glass, attributions to specific areas have been based on the presence of glass houses capable of producing this type of ware and on the fact that in the early days of collecting, from the 1920s to the 1950s, objects of this type were being found in certain locations. (Courtesy of The Corning Museum of Glass, Corning, New York.)

FIGURE 48. A group of engraved glasses, attributed to the Pittsburgh area, dating ca. 1815-1840s (Innes 1976:154-164; Spillman 1982:71, 130), from left to right: *Covered sugar bowl* with galleried rim. The bowl is decorated with an engraved berry-and-leaf design; the cover with a leaf-wreath design. *Celery* decorated with a blown-three-mold baroque-style design on the lower body and engraved with daisies and leaves. *Celery* with a ribbed double gather of glass at the base of the bowl, and above it, an engraved scene with house, pots of flowers, and birds. Below the scene is a rough band decorated with shallow cut and polished round facets, and beneath that a swag with pendants and stars. *Jug* decorated by 12 contact-molded ribs and an engraved floral/leaf/berry design. The handle is hollow and the pontil mark unground. (Courtesy of The Corning Museum of Glass, Corning, New York.)

chests, and matching bottom plates for butter tubs or finger bowls. When one considers the similarity of cut, engraved, or blown-glassware patterns available in the first half of the 19th century, however, consumers certainly had the choice to purchase different forms in the same or similar patterns if they wished to do so. As the century progressed, larger groups of matching glassware became more common, particularly in pressed glass where as many as 42 different pieces were offered in a single pattern (Figures 23-24) (Jenks and Luna 1990). Although the compositions of the groups sometimes changed over time, forms used together continued to be sold together, including pressed glass "sets" consisting of butter, sugar, creamer and spooner, cruet and castor sets, salt and pepper shakers, beverage sets consisting of a jug and six glasses, decanter sets of a decanter and six glasses, or a large berry bowl with six nappies.

It was not until the late 1920s and 1930s, that the equivalent range of tableware forms found in ceramics was made in glass (Florence 1995a, 1996). During this period, glass manufacturers introduced cups and saucers for hot beverages as well as dinner and salad plates in the same patterns as other glass tableware. Nevertheless, it is clear from catalogues of the period, such as those of T. Eaton Co., that serving pieces did not have to match each other or the drinking glasses or plates. Hostesses could use their prized glassware pieces, perhaps received as wedding gifts, as special embellishment for the table. Another group introduced in the early 20th century (Butler Brothers 1910:407), although not included in this guide, were matched kitchenwares used in the storage and preparation of food, such as pantry jars, measuring cups, and, later, refrigerator dishes and mixing bowls (Florence 1995b), some of which may have ended up on informal dining tables.

Specific dating factors for glass tableware forms are more difficult to develop than for the manufacturing and decorative techniques for a number of reasons. Most glass publications, with the exception of Spillman (1981; 1982), Warren (1981:105-198), Jones and Smith (1985), and Palmer (1993a), are not organized by functional form. Establishing date ranges for specific forms requires one to piece together information from a number of sources–dated examples in the secondary literature, and primary sources in both published literature and in documentary collections. Information found in documents is not straightforward, however. It is frequently impossible to match glassware shapes with those mentioned in unillustrated documents. Nouns and their modifiers vary from one document to another both in the same period and over time. American and British usage varies. It is not clear how closely the names used in documents reflected how consum-

ers used that form. Manufacturers even offered different uses for the same form (Figure 34).

With some exceptions, most tableglass forms made in 1800 were still in production in 1940. Starting in the 1880s, however, a number of specialized shapes were introduced which were seldom entirely new but were rather an adaptation of forms already in production. While some shapes underwent stylistic changes, became static, and then changed again, others remained relatively static for long periods of time. Some shapes, such as plates, were in production throughout the whole period under discussion, but their roles on the dinner table changed. Other forms became more specialized over time. As with the decorative motifs, once a form was introduced, it tended to remain in production although sometimes its use became far more

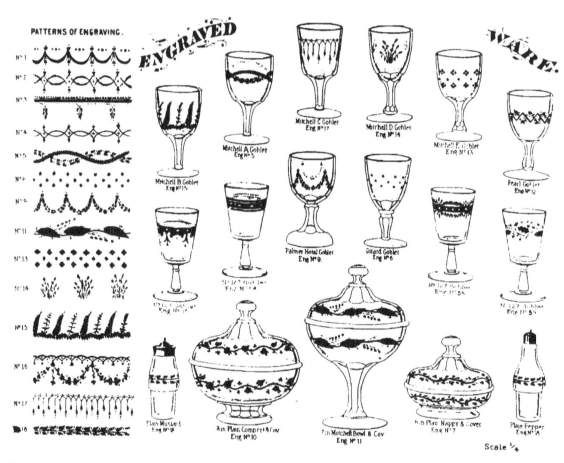

FIGURE 49. Page from the King, Son & Company catalogue, early 1870s, which shows simple engraving on glassware made in plain pressed patterns such as Mitchell. The motifs are horizontal and some echo the swags, floral sprays, hanging pendants, and bands seen on Bohemian-style engravings of the early 19th century (*Pennsylvania Glassware* 1972:38). (Courtesy of the Juliet K. and Leonard S. Rakow Research Library of The Corning Museum of Glass, Corning, New York.)

FIGURE 50. Blown cruet decorated with cut vertical panels on neck, a small cut facet on top of the handle, a cut starburst on base, and engraved fern pattern on the body. Ferns were a long-lived and popular engraved motif from the 1860s onward, after publication in the late 1850s of John Moore's book on ferns (Morris 1978:82). Sketchy fern motifs like this one show up in catalogues of the 1870s and 1880s (Figure 88). As indicated by the swelling at the base of the handle, it was attached first at its base and then brought up and attached at the neck. This method was introduced in the late 1860s and became the dominant technique by the 1880s (Spillman 1982:79; Hajdamach 1991:274). The earlier method was to attach the upper part of the handle first (Figure 16) and pull it down towards the base. The squat jug style of cruet with handle and globular body was in production by the 1880s (Spillman 1982:190-191) and became the common cruet style in the 20th century. (Photo by Rock Chan, Parks Canada collection.)

restricted, such as with open salts, or its production faded away, such as with the celery vase. In the following discussions, more-detailed dating guides have been offered for stemmed drinking glasses and decanters as these are forms likely to be found in archaeological contexts. Other forms are discussed generally as they are found less frequently.

Bowls, Dishes, and Trays

As a general guide, *bowls* have curved sides, *dishes* have straight sides and are usually shal-

lower than bowls, and *trays* are flat or almost flat (footed examples are called salvers); all three styles were made without a foot, with a foot, with a foot and stem, and with or without a cover. Bowls were made throughout the period but in increasing variety and quantity after the mid-19th century, particularly in pressed glass (Figures 13, 20, 23, 26).

This group of glassware was used primarily for food service, but it also included pieces for individual use. Common throughout the 1800-1940 period was the use of bowls for serving cold food such as salads, vegetables, or different types of desserts. Bread trays, often with wheat themes, were made in the 1870s and 1880s. Celery trays were introduced in the 1890s, and spoon trays, oval pickle dishes, small olive or bonbon dishes (often with a single small round handle), and mayonnaise bowls appeared at about the same time (Figure 59) (Spillman 1982:248-289). A standard offering in 20th-century catalogues was the berry set consisting of a bowl with six matching nappies but the same bowl, without the nappies, was also sold as a salad bowl (Figures 60-61).

Castors, Cruets, and Covered Pots

Serving vessels for condiments included a range of vessels (see Salts). *Cruets* were for

FIGURE 51. Page from early 1870s King, Son & Company Catalogue showing engraved patterns (Figure 49), including sprays and an initial enclosed in a wreath, and "frosted and cut" patterns (bottom half) (*Pennsylvania Glassware* 1972:39). (Courtesy of the Juliet K. and Leonard S. Rakow Research Library of The Corning Museum of Glass, Corning, New York.)

FIGURE 52. Sugar bowl made by Percival Vickers & Co. of Manchester in design registered 7 May 1873 and marketed as St. Petersburg into the 1880s (Slack 1987:161; Yates 1987:35). The bowl was completely pressed and the exterior surface roughed by wheel grinding, as evidenced by horizontal striations left by the wheel visible in the close-up. (Photo by Rock Chan, private collection.)

sugar, cayenne, and were fitted with a perforated top (Figure 49). The exterior upper neck surface was usually ground so that the top could be glued on; later versions had screw threads to accommodate a threaded cover. *Covered pots* were for wet condiments such as mustard, horseradish, and pickles. Specific forms were made for mustards and pickles during the 19th century (Wakefield 1968:50-51; Jones and Smith 1985:69-70, 74-77). In the late 19th and early 20th century, other *specialized forms* were

FIGURE 53. Pressed goblet in Lion Head pattern in which the stem and foot have been acid etched, leaving a frosted surface that is satiny to the touch. Pattern dates to the late 1870s. (Photo by Rock Chan, Parks Canada collection.)

liquids such as oil and vinegar, and prepared sauces, and had a pouring spout, a stopper and ground (or ground and polished) bore, and sometimes a handle (Figures 44, 50). *Castors* were for powdered substances such as pepper,

FIGURE 54. Sand-blasted designs from a ca. 1900 United States Glass Company catalogue. (Courtesy of the Juliet K. and Leonard S. Rakow Research Library of The Corning Museum of Glass, Corning, New York.)

offered, including a bowl for mayonnaise (Spillman 1981:Bowls), elaborate stands for highly decorated pickle jars, and a small single-handled dish for olives or bonbons. Commercially prepared foods could be placed on the table in their original *bottles or jars*, and by 1900, some silverware firms even offered special holders for things such as Maclaren's Imperial Cheese jars, and Lea and Perrins, Tabasco, or Harvey's Sauce bottles (Rainwater 1973; Langbridge 1975). It was, of course, practical to leave food in its original container, but the commercial package with its label and distinctive look also attested to the quality of the condiments being served.

Although condiment containers were used by themselves, the popular and acceptable way for most of the 19th century was to put them together in a stand made of wood, silver, silver plate, or Britannia metal. After electroplating was introduced in the 1840s, the market for silver-plated cruet stands expanded, and they became standard on middle-class tables. The condiments offered varied, depending on the meal and household, so that stands held different assemblages of containers. Newspaper advertisements, production and sales documents, and numerous patterns in catalogues attest to the popularity of cruet stands and specialized glasses for condiments (M'Kee and Brothers 1981; Wilson 1994[1]:228). In Canadian newspaper advertisements in the mid-19th century, they are

mentioned frequently; e.g., "Cruet stands with 3,4,5,6,7 bottles of surpassing elegance, being quite new designs" (*Montreal Gazette* 1867).

Two types of stands were available. The first had a flat base and cage-type holders for straight-sided castors, cruets, and pots (Figures 42, 44). These types were made throughout the 19th century. About 1880, a squat bottle with a globular body and handle was introduced and also put in this type of holder (Figure 50) (Spillman 1982:190-191). This shape became the standard one for oil and vinegar. The second type of stand had the castors, cruets, and pots suspended in a holder, either a flat circular piece with holes for the bottles or an open frame. Containers for this type have a narrow cylindrical lower body and an upper body that swells out over the holder (Figure 49). This type was probably introduced during the mid-19th century as examples are shown in the 1858 catalogue of the Rogers Brothers Mfg. Co. (*Victorian Silverplated Holloware* 1972:34-36). Although early 20th-century catalogues, such as the 1901 Montgomery Ward & Co. catalogue, show elaborate cruet stands, they were on their way out for middle-class households.

During the early 20th century, cruet stands were replaced by smaller sets or by individual dishes, such as salt and pepper shakers, mayonnaise bowls, pickle dishes, pickle jars in elaborate stands, small handled oil and vinegar cruets sometimes in a stand, or salt and pepper shakers with one vinegar or oil cruet in a small handled stand, often made of glass (Butler Brothers 1910:406). For example, T. Eaton Co. (1914-1915:219) advertised a simple stand holding both a vinegar and an oil bottle, and salt and pepper shakers. On the same page were illustrated a stand holding two jam dishes, and an elaborate stand holding a covered pickle jar. Individual pieces or small sets were ideal candidates for presents or wedding gifts so that a relatively modest table might sport one or two more elaborate and expensive condiment dishes.

Celeries

Celeries–substantial footed vases with a tall bowl–were used to serve celery on the table (Figures 18, 23, 48). The first dated evidence for their production appears in 1820, in an

Olive R. Jones

FIGURE 55. Examples of crackled glass offered by Butler Brothers (1929:255) although the method used to achieve the effect is ambiguous as they describe it as "embossed cracked effect" or as "all-over genuine crackled design." (Courtesy of The Fenton Art Glass Company, Williamstown, West Virginia.)

The Historical Archaeology Laboratory Handbook

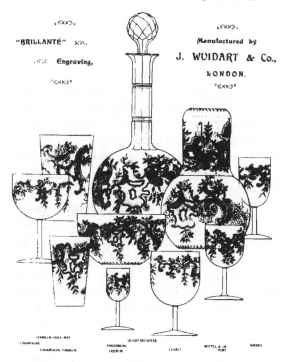

The "New LOUIS XV." Suite of Crystal Glass

"BRILLANTÉ" Engraving,

Manufactured by
J. WUIDART & Co.,
LONDON.

FIGURE 56. Drinking glass set with a needle-etched design, probably using a template, in a rococo revival design called "New Louis XV" (*Pottery Gazette* 1894:before 49). (Courtesy of The British Library, London; digital image by George van der Vlugt.)

advertisement from Virginia which offered celery stands along with a variety of other products (Wilson 1994[1]:173). From that period on, they became standard offerings in advertisements, glassware price lists, and catalogues. For much of the 19th century, growing celery was a labor-intensive task, making it expensive, and its presence on a table was a sign of prestige. Commercially grown, self-blanching celery was available by the 1880s, however, so that its status diminished thereafter (Williams 1985:109-111). Although the tall, footed celery glass was still offered around 1900 and later, it had become old fashioned:

> Why does not some inventive woman give us a pretty celery glass? asks a society writer. The old tall vase is, I am told, 'out of fashion,' and it is now supposed to be more correct to hand it round upon a flat dish, which, from every point of view, is a mistake (*Pottery Gazette* 1893:4).
> Who . . . has not mentally anathematized the old fashioned tall celery glass, from which it is almost impossible to remove one stalk without dragging two

or three more out upon the spotless damask? (Palmer 1993a:270).

Flat dishes for celery were shallow, rectangular or oval (Figure 59) (Higgins & Seiter 1899:27). Vertical celery glasses were still offered, however, without stem and often unfooted, and sometimes with a shorter body, more closely resembling spoon holders (Figure 62). As late as 1936, this later style of "flower or celery vase" was still available (Hill-Ouston Co. 1936:39).

Cups

Small handled cups usually with hemispherical bowls, sometimes footed, were in production throughout the 140-year period discussed in this guide and were used in a variety of ways. The

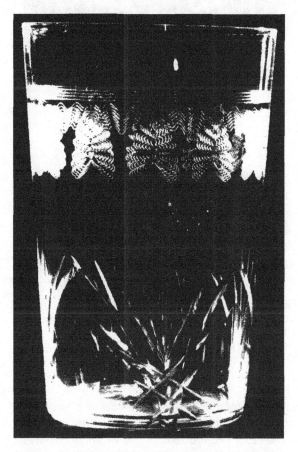

FIGURE 57. Blown tumbler decorated around the rim with needle-etched pattern typical of the relentless repeats of the lathe-type process and on the lower body by cutting. This glass is thin and light, of a type introduced in the 1870s, but far more pervasive in North American markets between 1900 and into the 1930s, after the introduction of semi-automatic machines. (Photo by Rock Chan, private collection.)

FIGURE 58. Pressed goblet decorated by plate etching. Detailed patterns were possible using this technique. Although the etching has no depth there is a discernible difference in surface texture. (Photo by Rock Chan, Parks Canada collection.)

most common seems to have been for desserts, primarily custard or, by the late 19th century, for sherbet (Figure 63). Cups or small handled mugs were also used for drinking lemonade, and, starting around 1900, were part of punch sets with a large matching bowl. There do not seem to be any obvious differences in the illustrated documents between dessert cups or cups for drinking. In the late 1920s, cups and saucers for hot beverages were introduced

(Figure 59). Mugs in opaque white or green heat-resistant glass for drinking coffee appeared in the 1930s (Spillman 1982:69).

Decanters

Decanters were produced throughout the 1800-1940 period (Figures 64-69). As temperance became more and more acceptable, however, many households made the choice not to drink liquor, replacing alcohol with tea or cold beverages, such as water or lemonade, for social and family occasions (Williams 1985:134-140). The T. Eaton Co., whose founder Timothy Eaton was a staunch opponent of both alcohol and tobacco, generally did not include decanters in its catalogues although they did sell wine glasses as late as 1908. In the catalogues of the late 1920s and early 1930s, after the repeal of prohibition in Canada, the company sold a set labeled "cordial set" or "decanter set" which consisted of a "Seven-Piece Decanter Set of generous size in the popular cut grape design. Bottle and six glasses for . . . $1.00" (T. Eaton Co. 1930:286). The accompanying tumblers, also sold separately, were "Bell-shaped Optic Tumblers. Strong, fine glass in graceful optic cut grape design. Have smoothly rounded edges. Popular tall, slender shape. Price dozen . . . 84¢" (T. Eaton Co. 1930:286). In comparison, one or more lemonade or water sets, consisting of a jug and a half dozen tumblers, were always included in the catalogue and the design changed regularly. Eaton's customers, from personal experience, included a large clientele which chose to serve their guests tea or cold non-alcoholic drinks. In comparison, the Army and Navy Store catalogue for 1907 offered over two dozen different "table glass services" consisting of decanters, stemware, and finger bowls as well as one and one-half dozen spirits bottle styles, and another two dozen jug styles for drinks such as claret cup, champagne, etc. (Army and Navy Stores 1969:923-924, 936-938). These offerings ranged from plain thicker wares for regimental and naval messes to elaborately cut and engraved wares. It is clear from the glassware offered in this catalogue that their clientele included those who expected formal and elaborate table settings and who served alcohol as a matter of course, a well-established British military tradition (Jones and Smith 1985). Drinking sets,

FIGURE 59. Selection of serving pieces from the 1930 Butler Brothers catalogue as well as cups, saucers, and plates for individual service (Butler Brothers 1930:n.p.). (Courtesy of Collins Kirby Art & Antiques, Fort Payne, Alabama.)

with decanter and matching glasses or decanter and matching tumblers, were also offered in American catalogues in the 20th century but in fewer numbers (Figure 38). Only a handful of the late higher-end 1920s and 1930s drinking sets shown in Florence (1995a) had decanters, although a few had cocktail shakers and some had ice buckets. This glassware catered to a middle-class clientele which shopped in department and gift stores and might be expected to use decanters. On the other hand, all the traditional drinking sets (Figure 46) in the English 1936 Hill-Ouston Co. catalogue had decanters, although cocktail sets in trendier designs (Figure 69) were also featured in the catalogue. Cocktail shakers, with a wide mouth, cover, and pouring lip, were introduced in the 1930s.

From the late 1840s onward, *pressed decanters* were made for both domestic and commercial use including those made with bar lips and a specialized stopper suitable for pouring (Figure 18, caption for decanter). Most bar-lipped decanters are associated with the geometric-style patterns which came in during the late 1840s and early 1850s. Without a pouring stopper of some type, it is very difficult to pour liquid successfully from these vessels. From the 1870s onward, decanters appear in far fewer numbers in the catalogues, if at all, and seem to have been made primarily for use in bars and restaurants. For example, in 1868, M'Kee and Brothers (1981:123-154) offered decanters in ten patterns but only one was shown with a glass stopper, and five had patent cork stoppers with bar lips. In the 1880 catalogue, only one decanter was shown (in the Huber pattern, introduced around 1850) and it is on the same page as bitters and bar bottles, suggesting it was used in the same setting (Stout 1972:85). The Bakewell Pears & Co. Glass Catalogue (1875:10-11) offered four decanters but, again,

Olive R. Jones

Berry Set
11-335. Seven-piece
Berry Set—one 8-in.
bowl and six 4½-in.
nappies, cut with an
attractive flower and
leaf design. Shipping
weight 6 lbs.
Price **5.00**
11-402. Bowl only.
Price 2.60
11-403. Extra Nap-
pies. Each..... 40c

FIGURE 60. Berry set offered by T. Eaton Co. (1918-19:514) in the lighter style cutting. The pressed set offered on the same page cost only $1.40. (Reproduced with the kind permission of The T. Eaton Company Limited; digital image by George van der Vlugt.)

these were placed with bitters and bar bottles. In the lists of vessels made in each pressed pattern in Jenks and Luna (1990), decanters are seldom mentioned but when they are, the patterns were introduced prior to 1870. Virtually none of the pressed-pattern sets made in the late 1920s and 1930s included decanters (Florence 1996).

Bar bottles appear to have been intended for use in commercial settings like bars and restaurants. They had tall bodies, with short necks, sometimes with bar lips and patented cork stoppers or sometimes with flanged lips and glass stoppers. Later examples were shaped more like bottles (Figure 68). Some catalogues show them with names such as Brandy or Whiskey cut or engraved on them, but most appear to have been plain. *Bitters bottles* were in production at least as early as the 1850s (Figure 22) and continued into the 20th century. They tend to be smaller than bar bottles because they contained strong flavorings such as peppermint, ginger, or bitters.

Comprehensive glassware drinking sets included different stemware shapes and sizes

FIGURE 61. Selection of berry bowls from the 1930 Butler Brothers catalogue in which older, heavily patterned pressed styles predominate, in contrast to the more modern designs offered in water and beverage sets (Figure 14) (Butler Brothers 1930:n.p.). Two new colors (pink and emerald green) join colorless and iridescent glass which were the only choices offered by the company in their 1925 catalogue. (Courtesy of Collins Kirby Art & Antiques, Fort Payne, Alabama.)

Spoon Holders and Celery Glasses

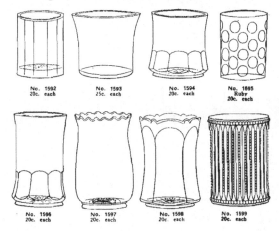

FIGURE 62. Shorter spoon holders and taller celery glasses from the Budde & Westerman (1913:45) hotel wares catalogue. In the 20th century celery glasses tended to be made without the stem and foot found on 19th-century examples. (Courtesy of George Miller.)

for different beverages, tumblers, finger bowls, water bottles or carafes, and sometimes matching tumblers set upside down over the top of the bottle (Figure 56), and sometimes narrow-mouthed "claret" jugs or wide-mouthed jugs for hard liquor.

The implications of finding decanters on sites need to be considered in both temporal and cultural contexts. Decanters are storage and serving containers, not commercial packages, thus they represent a level of service above the minimum, particularly during the 1800-1940 period when bottled wines, beers, and distilled liquors were commonplace. As the 19th century progressed, decanters represented an increasing level of formal service in either domestic or public settings, or, at least, a continuing level of service at certain strata of society. Depending on the time period and context, decanters may represent a masculine setting, such as a club, or army or navy mess, or may reflect different ethnic or socio-economic groups. Judging by the early-20th-century documentary evidence, Britons may have been more inclined to use decanters than either Americans or native-born Canadians. The decreasing presence of decanters in pressed glass, in comparison with the host of examples offered in cut, engraved, or acid-etched styles, suggests that, by the end of the 19th century, they were not used by lower-income groups. Finally, families and groups who did not drink

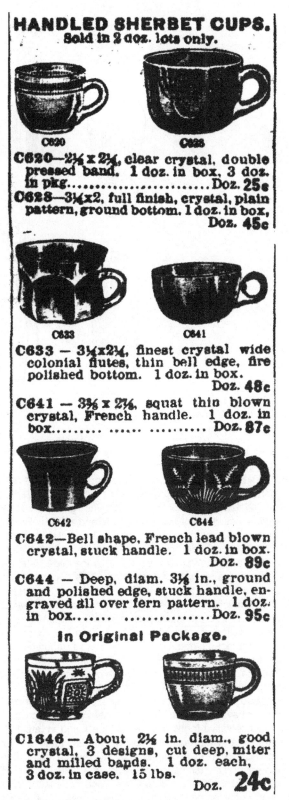

FIGURE 63. Handled sherbet cups from Butler Brothers (1914:319); footed sherbets without handles were also offered. (Courtesy of the Juliet K. and Leonard S. Rakow Research Library of The Corning Museum of Glass, Corning, New York.)

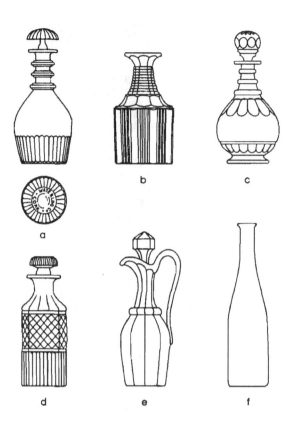

FIGURE 64. Examples of decanter styles, 1800 to ca. 1850: **a,** classic Anglo-Irish decanter shape between 1800 to 1840s. It is characterized by a pronounced flanged lip, tapered body, three applied and tooled neck rings, and came with a mushroom, lozenge, or target stopper. It may be undecorated or decorated by cutting, engraving, and contact molding. This example is decorated by contact-molded ribs on the lower body and base, on which is molded the words "Waterloo Co. Cork," one of many Irish glasshouse products marked in this way (Warren 1981:54-55, 71-98). This company was in business between 1815 and 1835. In British and American factories the shape continued in production after the mid century but the rings had basically disappeared by the 1850s (Figure 65**f**). The form with neck rings continued to be made, however, in Swedish and Danish glass factories after 1850 (Buchwald and Schlüter 1975:37-116 [16-18]; based on Warren 1981:91); **b,** by the mid to late 1820s, decanters with more cylindrical bodies were available as were examples without neck rings. This decanter illustrates the shape suited to the vertical broad-flute cutting style introduced in the late 1820s. The body is decorated with cut ribs alternating with ribs decorated with flutes. The decoration, however, still retains the elements of earlier horizontal bands on the shoulder and neck. Illustration based on WHR drawings discussed in Wolfenden (1987:22). Real example shown in Wakefield (1982:30); **c,** American style consisting of globe-shaped body on a foot, with or without the three applied neck rings, made undecorated, or with contact molded, cut and/or engraved decorations. This style was illustrated in several American newspaper advertisements between 1823 and 1831 (Innes 1976:139; Palmer 1993a:138; Wilson 1994[1]:176) and is considered to date ca. 1815 to 1840s. Without the neck rings, slenderized versions of the footed spherical body were made in the mid-19th century (Wakefield 1982:40; Hajdamach 1991:134). Based on Wilson (1994[1]:199); **d,** squared decanters decorated by engraving or cutting, or blown in plain or patterned contact molds were made for liquor stands and for cases or traveling trunks. Those for cases and trunks were usually decorated on the shoulder. Square decanters are very conservative forms and can still be found in late-19th-century catalogues. Based on mold-blown decanter in McKearin and McKearin (1948:252, GII-28, Plate 10, 264-265); **e,** claret decanter decorated with cut panels from base to lip in the broad flute style which dates from the late 1820s onwards. Claret decanters with taller, narrower bodies, tall narrow necks, pouring lips, and handles became a fixture in glass production from the 1840s onwards. This example is based on one in Pellatt's 1840 catalogue (Wakefield 1968:51; Warren 1984:122); **f,** tall narrow decanter dating from the 1840s onward. Dated examples in the literature are colorful and decorated in many different ways. Based on yellow opaline example decorated with transfer print in Hajdamach (1991:104). (Drawings by Dorothea Larsen.)

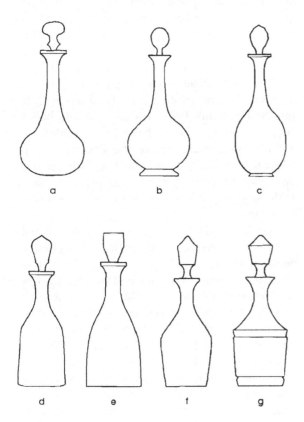

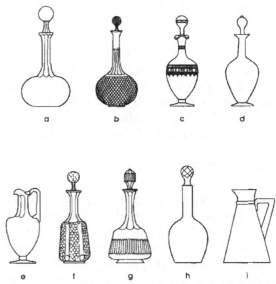

FIGURE 65. Examples of decanter styles ca. 1850-1870: **a,** decanters with long necks and spherical bodies continued in production from ca. 1850 into the 20th century (Figure 67). They often had vertical cut panels on the neck which emphasized the squatness of the body. Based on a decanter exhibited at the 1851 exhibition (*The Art-Journal* 1851:175); **b,** similar in style to a but with an applied foot. Based on a decanter made in London for the Viceroy of Egypt, 1854-1863 (Warren 1984:131); **c,** long-necked decanter with an ovoid body and applied foot (The Art-Journal 1851:175); **d,** decanter with body sloping outward towards the base, based on a decanter made in England about 1850 (Morris 1978:28); **e,** a pressed version of d with a less-defined neck as it curves into the long sloping shoulder; based on an illustration in the 1861 James B. Lyon & Company catalogue (Innes 1976:345); **f,** pressed decanter with body widening towards the shoulder. This form was in style from the early 19th century and continued in production at least as late as 1869 (based on Watkins 1970:158; Spillman 1997:95); **g,** pressed decanter with body widening towards the shoulder and an abrupt body and shoulder junction. This variant of **f** was introduced in the late 1840s (based on Watkins 1970:153; Spillman 1997:79). (Drawings by Dorothea Larsen.)

FIGURE 66. Examples of decanter styles 1870-1890: **a,** the long-necked decanter with globular body continued to be produced during this period and appears to have been the commonest shape. Decorated with cut panels, a subdued and slightly everted lip, and a globe-shaped stopper. This shape was also made as a claret jug, with a high handle and pouring spout. Based on Smart Brothers (1885:3); **b,** similar to a but with a foot. Based on M. Davis and Co. advertisement in Pottery Gazette (1881); **c,** shapes derivative of Greek pottery shapes, such as this one, were first introduced in the late 1840s and many examples were shown at the 1851 exhibition (Wakefield 1982:68). The decanter has an egg-shaped body, the characteristic trifoil lip, a cushion knop separating the body and foot, and a globe stopper. Based on Smart Brothers (1885:3); **d,** similar to c but without the cushion knop and with a plain everted lip. Based on Smart Brothers (1885:3); **e,** claret jug with handle and pouring lip imitating another Greek pottery shape. This style can be found with or without the cushion knop separating the body and foot. Based on Smart Brothers (1885:3); **f,** body widens from shoulder to base, the lower body curves in towards the foot, although on other examples in the catalogue the angle is much more abrupt. Based on Smart Brothers (1885:3); **g,** A squatter version of **f** and a style which appears to start in the 1880s. This example has a different stopper style, one which reflects the body shape. Based on Smart Brothers (1885:4); **h,** Not all decanters had an everted lip. In this example the lip is simply left flat on top. Based on example in the ca. 1874 Boston & Sandwich Glass Co. catalogue (1992:Plate 37); **i,** decanters with this straight tapered body were often decorated with vertical trails of glass. The shape was apparently introduced in the Stourbridge area in the early 1870s and continued in production until the end of the century (Wakefield 1982:117-118). Based on Smart Brothers (1885:5). (Drawings by Dorothea Larsen.)

Olive R. Jones

alcohol had little need of decanters. It appears that North American glass manufacturers and retailers had already responded to changing drinking patterns before the advent of prohibition in 1919.

Figures 64-69 are guides only to changing decanter styles, particularly after the middle of the 19th century when innovations in decoration became commonplace. It is clear that a strong conservative element resulted in the production of some decanter styles for over 60 years.

Dessert Glasses

Dessert glasses encompass a number of forms for individual service: small handled custard or sherbet cups (Figure 63), jelly glasses (Figure 42), small bowls or nappies, plates, and footed sherbets or sundaes (Figure 70). Serving pieces include large bowls and salvers (see Bowls), and plates (Figure 59).

Finger Bowls and Wine Glass Rinsers

There is some confusion as to how finger bowls and wine glass rinsers were used at the table. It is clear from English glass manufacturers' documents of the first half of the 19th century that they thought of finger bowls and wine glass rinsers as different. In his 1840 catalogue, Pellatt, for example, illustrated three styles of "finger-cups" but noted that the price for monteiths or wine coolers was an additional 10% (Wakefield 1968:51). In period illustrations and commentaries, however, the finger bowl style was also being used as a wine glass rinser.

These bowls held water which was used in three ways (Warren 1981:244-245; Lole 1993:2-4). According to some observers, it was a custom in England, dating from the mid to late 18th century, to rinse out one's mouth at the table using the water in the bowl and then spitting it back into the bowl. A second use was to rinse one's fingers before dessert was served. The third use was to rinse or cool a wine glass in the water. The latter use is one often seen in period illustrations where wine glasses are upended in bowls of water (Jones and Smith 1985:55-57). This practice continued at least into the early 1860s, as a photograph in the National Archives in Ottawa shows a table set at the governor's house in Halifax with each

place setting provided with a water bottle and tumbler turned upside down over it, two wine glasses (one colored), and a third resting in a bowl. During the second half of the 19th century, however, the only usage which remained was to rinse fingers, although even as late as 1865, an American etiquette guide still felt it necessary to caution diners not to rinse out their mouths (Williams 1985:41-42). Etiquette books suggest that the finger bowl be presented on a doily on a plate before the dessert course (Fenwick 1948:279). By the late 19th century and into the 20th century, their presence on a table suggests the presence of either servants or waiters.

The first style of bowl, generally considered wine-glass rinsers, is essentially a cylinder about 4 in. (10 cm) high and 4 in. (10 cm) in diameter. Some have one or two pouring lips or notches (Spillman 1982:272) which were used to support the stem of one or two wine glasses. Examples of this style in both glass and faience have been found on mid-18th-century French colonial sites in Canada. Both historic illustrations and documents make it clear they were intended to be used as wine glass rinsers or coolers. It is possible that the practice of rinsing or cooling wine glasses originated in France and was adopted in England during the 18th century. This style disappeared sometime during the first half of the 19th century.

The second bowl style, generally considered finger bowls, was a hemispherical bowl about 3 to 3 ½ in. (7.5 to 9 cm) high with a rim diameter of about 5 in. (13 cm). Period price lists often offer finger bowls in colored glass, and several examples found in early-19th-century contexts in Canada are in colorless, blue, or green glass. Finger bowls matched other tableware pieces (Figures 34, 56) (Weatherman 1974:278-279). By the early 20th century, finger bowls were about ½ in. (1.3 cm) shallower.

Pitchers, Jugs, and Beverage Sets

Pitchers and jugs were used to serve milk (see Sets), water, cider, beer, wines, and other alcoholic beverages. The two terms seem to have been used interchangeably. Their use increased dramatically in the 19th century and by the early 20th century, pitchers and jugs appear to have become the dominant form

CUT GLASS DECANTERS   CUT GLASS DECANTERS

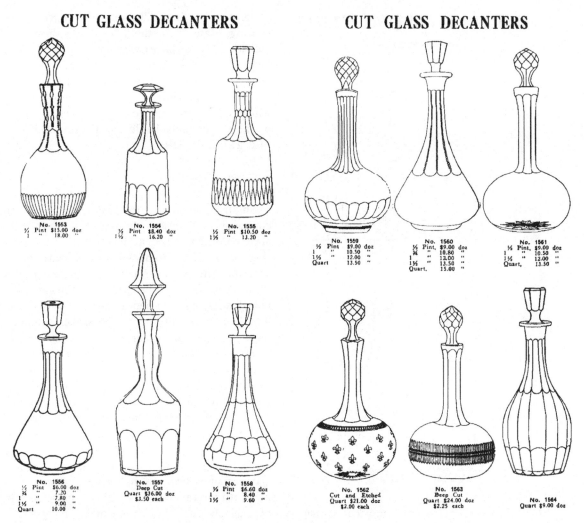

FIGURE 67. Decanters illustrated in Budde & Westerman (1913:39-40) showing the long-lived nature of some decanter shapes and decoration. (Courtesy of George Miller.)

for serving beverages. Water, lemonade, and other non-alcoholic beverages had replaced alcoholic beverages in many homes and public settings, and manufacturers and retailers responded by offering the water, lemonade, or beverage set, consisting of a half-gallon pitcher and six glasses, and sometimes a tray. These sets were decorated in an astonishing array of patterns and decorative techniques (Figures 1, 14, 38, 45) and were obviously comparable in both status and use to ceramic teawares. Guests who might not expect a meal would certainly expect to be offered a drink and perhaps a little snack.

Plates

Although glass plates were made from the 18th century onward, they were not common and, at least in the first half of the century, tended to be used as under-plates for butter tubs (Figure 42) or covered pickles, or as "ice plates" for serving ices, a popular dessert. In the 1830-1860 period, pressed-glass plates, called toddy plates by collectors, were made in 5 and 6 in. (13 and 15 cm) sizes, but their precise use is not clear. A common pressed or blown plate that was made between the late 1820s and

FLINT GLASS WORKING BOTTLES

(Capacity 26-28 oz.)

No. 1575
$1.50 doz

No. 1576
$3.00 doz

No. 1577
$3.00 doz

No. 1578
$5.00 doz

No. 1579
$5.00 doz

No. 1580
Cut Neck
$6.00 doz

No. 1581
Cut Olive & Flute
$7.00 doz

No. 1582
Cut Neck & Flute
$8.00 doz

FIGURE 68. Examples of bar bottles in Budde & Westerman (1913:42). (Courtesy of George Miller.)

about 1860, was the *cup plate* for which more than 800 pressed patterns have been identified (Figure 20) (Wilson 1994[1]:274-275). Between 3 and 4 in. (7.5 and 10 cm) in diameter, cup plates held the cup while a person sipped tea from the saucer (Spillman 1971:128-133). Visitors to the United States often commented on this habit. In comparison to the large number of shallow bowls or dishes, the ca. 1874 catalogue of the Boston & Sandwich Glass Company (1992:Plates 5, 19, 21, 24,31, 37, 39) offered very few plates. These included plates for serving ice cream, those with a domed cover for serving cheese or butter, and under-plates for cracker jars and butter tubs. Plates in pressed

patterns from the 1870s onward tended to be serving plates. In the late 1920s, however, individual eating plates were introduced in a full range of sizes, including ones divided into three sections (Figure 59). Also introduced during this period were serving plates with central handles which were either molded in the glass or made of metal and detachable (Spillman 1982:Nos. 212, 217, 218, 219).

Salts and Salt Shakers

Small open dishes for salt are one of the commoner tableware forms recovered from archaeological sites, at least until the 1870s (Figures 71-72). Some salts were made in the same patterns as other tableware pieces; others were made in distinctive patterns. Smaller individual salts began to appear in the catalogues in the 1860s. As salt and pepper shaker combinations became more common in the 1880s, larger open salts disappeared but individual salts, or "salt dips," continued to be offered, primarily in catalogues selling cut glass. They became the sign of formal service instead of everyday service. Salts were not traditionally part of the cruet or castor set, although pepper castors (or dusters) were. Salt shakers began to be made in the late 1850s, and by the 1880s, salt and pepper shaker sets had become common in both utilitarian pressed or blown glass and in expensively decorated pairs suitable for gifts.

Peterson (1970:50) outlined the steps which led to successful salt shakers and their common use: (1) molded screw threads for the finish, beginning in the late 1850s and early 1860s, which made it easier to keep salt away from the metal top; (2) mechanical devices to keep salt from caking and to facilitate the flow of salt, beginning in the late 1850s; (3) altering the nature of salt to keep salt from caking, beginning in the 1880s; and (4) changing the metals used in tops to ones less subject to corrosion.

Sets (Creamer, Sugar Bowl, Butter Dish, Spoon Holder)

Pressed "sets" are illustrated in many catalogues and consist of a *cream jug, sugar bowl, butter dish,* and *spoon holder* (Figure 71). The butter dish was often referred to as a covered

(text continues on p. 224)

FIGURE 69. Examples of cocktail and wine sets from Hill-Ouston (1936:105). Three of the sets are decorated with enameling and the cut set is an imitation of cut patterns of the second quarter of the 19th century (Figure 41). (Author's collection; digital image by George van der Vlugt.)

Olive R. Jones

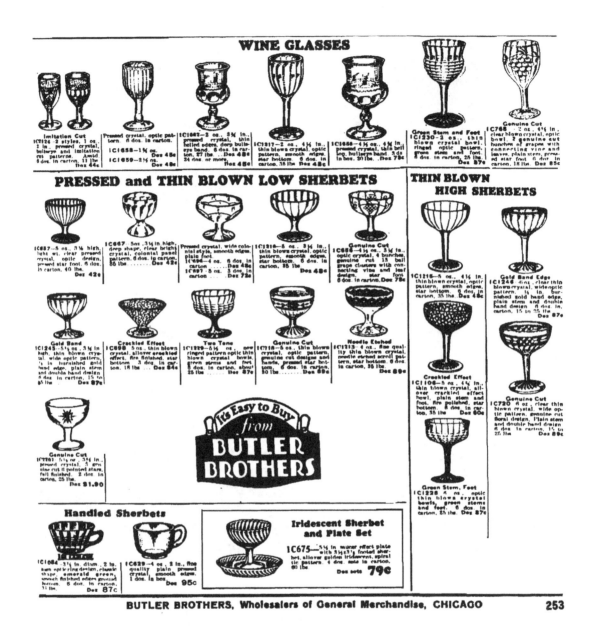

FIGURE 70. Examples of footed sherbets from Butler Brothers (1929:253). In this catalogue the sherbets are closer in style and decoration to the beverage glasses and sets than they are to berry bowls. In the 1930 catalogue (Figure 82) they are placed with other stemware. One possible explanation is that food was brought to the table already in sherbet dishes, whereas with berry bowl sets, food was presented first in the large bowl and served into individual bowls at the table. Although individual footed nappies or footed jellies were available as early as the 1870s (*Pennsylvania Glassware* 1972:35) it was not until the 20th century that the form became dominant and offered in such wide variety. (Courtesy of The Fenton Art Glass Company, Williamstown, West Virginia.)

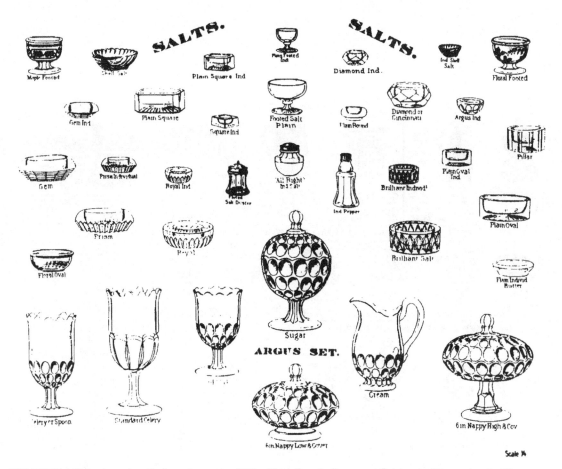

FIGURE 71. Selection of salts from the early 1870s King, Son & Company Catalogue (*Pennsylvania Glassware* 1972:29). Note the presence of "master salts" which were shared between diners, individual salts, salt dusters, and an individual pepper which matches neither of the salt dusters. Maple and Floral patterns were part of large tableware sets. (Courtesy of the Juliet K. and Leonard S. Rakow Research Library of The Corning

FIGURE 72. Salt and pepper shakers offered in the 1930 Butler Brothers catalogue showing both utilitarian sets in Colonial pattern and more decorative ones. Toothpick holders were introduced in the 1880s. (Courtesy of Collins Kirby Art & Antiques, Fort Payne, Alabama.)

FIGURE 73. Cream and sugar sets from Butler Brothers 1930 catalogue offered a mix of modern and older styles. By this time the paired cream and sugar were commoner than the four-piece sets including the butter and spooner, although one is still offered here in the center of the bottom row. Top right shows "new modernistic colonial design" with strong art deco elements including the inverse-shaped conical body with largest diameter at the rim, squared handles, and the squared motif. Although the look is more strongly associated with art deco, inverse cone-shaped bowls placed directly on the foot appear as early as 1916 in the Bryce Brothers' (1916:246) catalogue. (Courtesy of Collins Kirby Art & Antiques, Fort Payne, Alabama.)

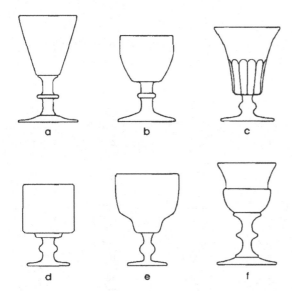

FIGURE 75. Drawn stemware styles, late 1770s to 1840s. The stem was generally drawn out from the bowl and attached to the foot. In contrast to earlier 18th-century drawn stems, this group is short, ranging from 9.5-12.0 cm (3¾- 4¾) in height: *a*, plain drawn stem with conical bowl, decorated by vertical cut panels, a type of decoration done from the 1780s onward (Jones and Smith 1985:39, 46). Based on Apsley Pellatt's 1840 catalogue (Wakefield 1968:52); *b*, plain stem, cup-shaped bowl, unfinished pontil mark, folded foot. Folded feet, with the edge of the foot folded under, were called "welted" in price lists, and were still being offered as late as 1832 (Sullivan 1985). Based on example in Wilson (1994[1]:187, No. 162) dated ca. 1815-1830; *c*, drawn stem with knop, conical bowl, decorated by pattern-molded panels (Figure 10). This is one of the newer stemware styles included in the 1840 Pellatt catalogue. Based on glasses in private collections and archaeological examples. (Drawing by D. Larsen.)

FIGURE 74. Centrally knopped stemware styles, ca. 1780-1840s. Called "button" stem in the documents, the style occurs with V-shaped, bladed or rounded knops, with or without a step at the foot, with or without a collar (or merese) under the bowl, and with different bowl shapes: *a-b*, bucket; *c,* bell; *d,* cylindrical; *e,* ogee; *f,* thistle. The bowls were decorated by cutting, usually panels, pattern-molding, contact-molding, engraving, and enameling. Although the basic style is simple, the different combinations of shape and decoration make it a complex group. It is not clear how datable the different combinations are. The picture is complicated by the fact that European glassmakers continued to make this type of stemmed drinking glass into the second half of the 19th century, generally in non-lead glass, and that it may never have entirely died out in English production (Figure 44) before revivals of the style were introduced in the 20th century (Spillman 1982:Nos. 8-9). Detailed descriptions: *a,* bucket-shaped bowl with engraved crest for the 13th Regiment of Foot who were stationed in Canada during the War of 1812-1814 (Jones and Smith 1985:114). Collar under the bowl, step at the stem, and ground and polished pontil mark. Height 11.0 cm (4 ½ in.) (Parks Canada collection); *b,* incurved bucket with no collar or step, unfinished pontil mark. Height 8.5 cm (3 ½ in.) (Parks Canada collection); *c-e,* based on Samuel Miller Waterford Glass House Patterns, dated ca. 1820-1830 (Warren 1970:41-42, 48). Several of the designs offered by this factory included star cuts on the base; *f,* the thistle shape is achieved by a double gather of glass on the lower part of the bowl and a strong outward curve on the upper part. The bowl resembles classical urns and is found on other glassware items such as jellies (Figure 42, nos. 16, 21) and celery vases (Figure 48) which date ca. 1830 to 1840s. Step and collar are present, pontil mark is unfinished. Height 10.0 cm (4 in.) (Parks Canada collection; drawing by D. Larsen.)

FIGURE 76. Stemware styles introduced in the mid to late 1830s. The point of interest on these stems has shifted from the center to below the bowl and at the foot. Although Hajdamach (1991:47-48) and Spillman (1989:39) suggest these styles were in production in the late 1820s, other evidence supports a late 1830s introductory date. For example, dated English price lists for 1829 and 1832 offer only button stems and plain stems and Irish factory drawings thought to date to the 1820s (Warren 1981:43-51) do not show this style. However, *b* resembles one style in the 1840 Pellatt catalogue and *a* reflects the long flute cuts going from foot to bowl also included there. Both *a* and *b* resemble stems styles from a Manchester factory catalogue hand dated to 1846 (Yates 1987:32, 39). All three drawings are based on examples in a Webb Richardson pattern book thought by Hajdamach (1991:47) to date between 1829 and mid 1830s, but which probably dates no earlier than the mid to late 1830s: *a,* curved stem which swells out under bowl and above foot. Vertical cut panels on the stem, going up onto the lower part of the bowl in the broad flute style of cutting; *b,* straight stem with knops at bowl and stem junction. Cut panels on bowl; *c,* straight stem with collar and knop under bowl and slight step at foot. Cut oval-shaped panels on bowl. (Drawing by D. Larsen.)

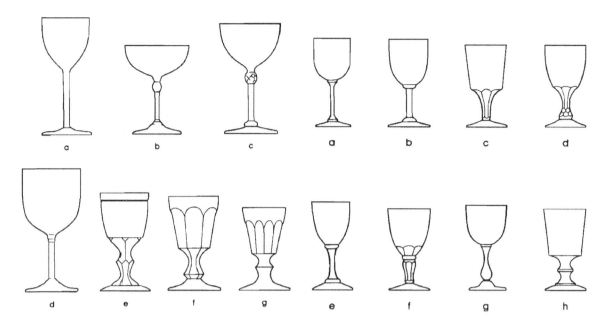

FIGURE 77. Examples of stemware styles 1850-1870: **a,** thin straight stem with rather flat foot and oval bowl. Profile of a wine glass accessioned at the Conservatoire National des Arts et Metiers in Paris in 1851, made by Apsley Pellatt's firm in London (based on Warren 1984:128, Figure 15); **b,** champagne glass characterized by an open shallow bowl, a style introduced about the middle of the 19th century and still associated with champagne. Profile of a glass given by Pellatt and Company to the Royal Scottish Museum in Edinburgh in 1864 (based on Warren 1984:128-129, Figure 17**d**); **c,** oval bowl on a thin straight stem with a knop near the bowl (and decorated by cut facets) and pronounced step at the base of the stem. The foot is relatively flat. Part of the same group as **b** (based on Warren 1984:129, Figure 17e); **d,** cylindrical bowl with curved bottom and a thin straight stem with a step at the foot. Part of the same group as b (based on Warren 1984:130, Figure 18**c**); **e,** stem is decorated by pressed vertical flutes which break at the central knop to form a serrated pattern. American pressed stemware of all types often has the knopped stem decorated in this way or with hexagonal facets. Based on Sharp Diamond pattern champagne glass made by the Boston & Sandwich Glass Company and shown in their 1868-1869 catalogue (Watkins 1970:153; Spillman 1997:79); **f,** bucket-shaped bowls continued in production in this period but definitely had lost their dominant position. Even in pressed glass, stems in this period had knops or swellings lower on the stem or near the bowl. Shown in the same catalogue as **e** (Watkins 1970:160, Figure 12; Spillman 1997:94); **g,** pressed New-Orleans-pattern cordial glass, one of the last remnants of the centrally knopped stems with bucket bowls so common during the first half of the 19th century. Shown in the same catalogue as e (Watkins 1970:160, Figure 12; Spillman 1997:94). (Drawings by Dorothea Larsen).

FIGURE 78. Examples of stemware styles 1870-1890. Not shown in this group is the hollow-stemmed champagne glass with saucer bowl which was introduced in the mid 1870s (Innes 1976:352; Boston & Sandwich Glass Company 1992:Plates 27, 37): **a,** stem is straight and thin with a collar under the bowl that in many illustrated examples is quite thin and sharp and with a step at the base of the stem (Figure 44) (based on *Pottery Gazette* 1881:817); **b,** stem is slightly thicker than the previous example, the collar and step correspondingly larger and rounded (Figure 44) *(Pottery Gazette* 1881:817); **c,** relatively straight stem that widens considerably under the bowl. Whether cut or pressed, the panels on the stem go just onto the base of the bowl, making a kind of base for the bowl to rise from. This is in contrast to the earlier styles where the panels extended onto the bowl, sometimes as much as three quarters of the way up (based on King, Son & Company catalogue dated early 1870s [Pennsylvania Glassware 1972:38]); **d,** similar to **c** this glass has a swelling, a pronounced step at the base of the stem, which could be decorated. The stem profile is curved rather than straight (based on King, Son & Company catalogue dated early 1870s [Pennsylvania Glassware 1972:38]); **e,** a common style for this period was the curved stem sometimes ending with a collar and/or step (Figure 44) *(Pottery Gazette* 1881:817); **f,** the inverted baluster stem was also made during this period, sometimes in a vestigial form (based on King, Son and Company catalogue, dated early 1870s [*Pennsylvania Glassware* 1972:38]); **g,** true baluster stem, with the swelling at the base of the stem, not just a step before the foot, is common in this period. The stem can be plain or decorated with panels or facets. The domed foot is unusual (Figure 44) *(Pottery Gazette* 1881:817); **h,** although examples of the centrally knopped stem with bucket bowl were rare, they were still in production; based on Greek Champagne glass in Bakewell Pears & Co. (1875:8).

Wine Glasses, Etc. *255

C75, 28c Doz. C86, 28c Doz. C79, 29c Doz. C83, 29c Doz. C76, 30c Doz. C73, 31c Doz.

	Doz.
C75, "Diamond" Wine—Imitation cut pattern..........	$0 28
C86, "Beaded Wine"—Beaded pattern with plain edge, cut stem.....................................	28
C79, "Bright" Wine—For wine and mantel............	29
C83, "Popular" Wine—You can double your money......	29
C76, "Mirror" Wine—Dot mirror pattern..............	30
C73, "Plain" Wine—Cut stem.........................	31

C82, 33c Doz. C80, 33c Doz. C87, 35c Doz. C88, 38c Doz. C78, 40c Doz.

C82, "Beaded Panel" Wine—Brilliant flared top.......	33
C80, "Pressed Band" Wine—Three mold bands....	33
C87, "Satin Cut" Wine—Cut glass pattern, fancy stem, star base...................................	35
C88, "Shapely" Wine — Panel pattern, flaring shape, fancy stem......	38
C78, "Sherry" Wine—For wine or toothpick glass	40

C95, 41c Doz. C81, 41c Doz. C84, 42c Doz. C89, 42c Doz. C366, 80c Doz.

C95, "Figured Panel" Wine—Figured and plain panels, fancy stem.........................	41
C81, "Cut Pattern" Wine—Cut stem.....	41
C84, "Floral Engraved" Wine—Regular size	42
C89, "Elite" Wine — Cut panel, fancy stem...	42
C366, "Reflector Wine Glass"—Burnished gold band............	80
C85, "Gold Prism" Wine — Gold lines and panels.	80
C367, "Gold Band" Cut Pattern Wine—Imitation cut stem and ¼-in. band of 18 karat gold top	80

C85, 80c Doz. C367, 80c Doz.

Cup Foot Wine Glasses. *254

C90, 39c Doz. C91, 39c Doz. C92, 41c Doz. C94, 42c Doz. C77, 43c Doz. C93, 43c D oz.

C90, "Engraved Band"—One wide and two narrow engraved bands.................	39
C91, Cut Stem Cordial Glass—Plain, imitation cut stem, cup foot	39
C92, Cut Stem Wine Glass—Medium size, plain, fancy stem......	41
C94, Plain Wine Glass—Unique stem.............	42
C77, "Banded Wine":—Cup foot. seamless banded wine.	43
C93, "Hoffman House" Wine Glass—Low shape. plain, slender stem, cup foot....................	43

Assortment of Wine Glasses. *243

C641, 29c Doz. C640, 30c Doz.

C641, "Staple" Wine Glass—1 doz. each of four patterns: colonial flute, bead panel, plain and flute and pressed band. Total 4 doz. in box, no charge for box .	29
C640, "Fancy" Wine Glass— Rich cut patterns. finished and fire polished. 1 doz. each of 4 patterns. 4 doz. in wood case. no charge for case.........................	30

FIGURE 79. Pressed wine glasses offered by Butler Brothers (1902:124). (Courtesy of the Juliet K. and Leonard S. Rakow Research Library of The Corning Museum of Glass, Corning, New York.)

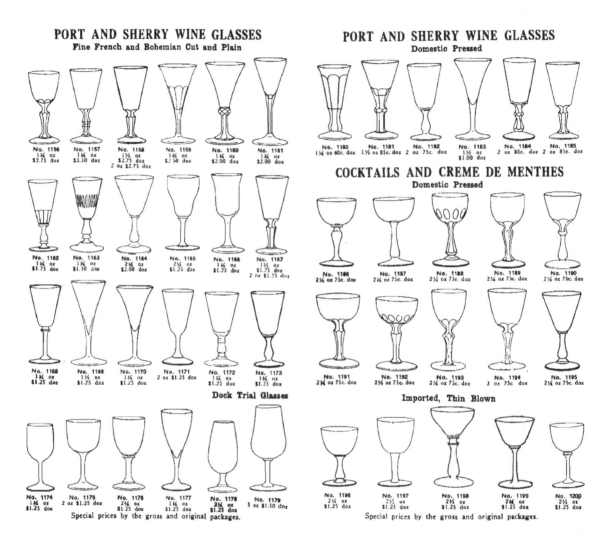

FIGURE 80. Selection of stemware from 1913 Budde & Westerman catalogue for hotelware. The catalogue illustrates the difference in price between blown, cut, and pressed wares. For example, No. 1159 plain blown cut stem cost $2.50 dozen, No. 1170 plain blown stem cost $1.25 dozen, No. 1183 plain pressed stem cost $1.00 dozen. Many of the stemware styles shown here and in other catalogues of the same period, such as Bryce Brothers (1916), continue to show styles first introduced between ca. 1850 and 1880 (Budde & Westermann 1913:11-12). A shift in styles is beginning to appear, however, in the number of conical, ogee, or trumpet-shaped bowls being offered. The look is more open and echoes 18th- and early-19th-century bowl shapes. (Courtesy of George Miller.)

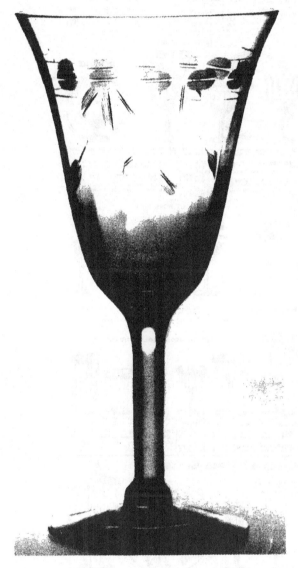

FIGURE 81. Blown stemware in pink glass, decorated by optic molded panels and lightly cut motif which has been left unpolished. This glass has a large bowl, with the bowl rim diameter of 3½ in. (9 cm) considerably larger than the foot rim diameter of 2¾ in. (7mm), and a comparatively long stem. Total height is almost 7 in. (17.2 cm). These proportions are characteristic of stemmed drinking glasses from the 1920s onward. The cut pattern was done by a gang wheel, introduced about 1913, which had a serrated surface so that a single cut could make a petal or leaf. The resulting pattern–which consists of a group of narrow parallel grooves or, when cut again at right angles, creates crosshatching–is distinctive (Farrar and Spillman 1979:14, 21). (Photo by Rock Chan; Parks Canada collection.)

FIGURE 82. Selection of stemware offered by Butler Brothers (1929:254). Notable features for the late 1920s and 1930s were the preference for thin glass, large open bowls decorated by different optic molded patterns and then by cutting, acid etching, or gilding. Different dark-colored feet or stems and feet (such as "Tiffin" stemware) were introduced in this period. The stemware offered includes goblets, wines, and sherbets, plus tumblers for iced tea. Stems are thin, plain, and comparatively tall. Several patterns have decorated feet. (Courtesy of Fenton Art Glass Company, Williamstown, West Virginia.)

FIGURE 83. Heavy goblet with molded stem applied to bowl and foot, neither of which have mold lines. No pontil mark, lead glass. Total height is 5 in. (12.5 cm). Probably English, mid-19th century (Morris 1978:108, 111). (Photo by Rock Chan, Parks Canada collection.)

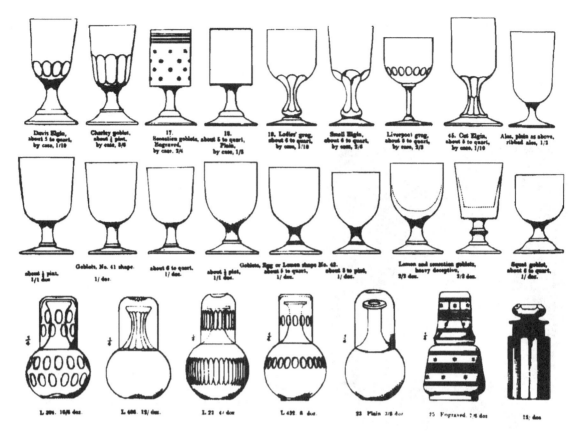

FIGURE 84. A selection of goblets and water bottles with their tumblers, called tumble-ups, inverted over the neck. The sizes of the bowls are indicated by how many would be needed to hold a quart of liquid–"about 5 to quart" (*Pottery Gazette* 1881:before 817). (Courtesy of The British Library, London; digital image by George van der Vlugt.)

FIGURE 85. Example of a Bohemian-style tumbler with pattern-molded panels and ribs, and sketchy engraving at the rim. Made of non-lead glass which, when compared with the heaviness of the tumbler in Figure 12, makes this tumbler extremely light. One feature which has been found on mid-18th-century examples excavated from French colonial sites in Canada is the rough grinding around the pontil mark. Tumblers such as this date from the mid 18th century into the early years of the 19th century. (Photo by Rock Chan, private collection.)

FIGURE 86. Text and accompanying illustrations from the 1861 catalogue of the O'Hara Flint Glass Works in Pittsburgh. The text lists capacity, pattern name, and other distinguishing features such as handled, heavy, table, or bar. Although 63 tumblers are illustrated in the catalogue, most are paneled patterns, along with two hexagonal patterns. Lists such as this one frequently mention bar tumblers, generally heavy and with a thicker base. Handled tumblers or mugs were offered throughout the 140 years covered by this guide. (Courtesy of the Juliet K. and Leonard S. Rakow Research Library of The Corning Museum of Glass, Corning, New York.)

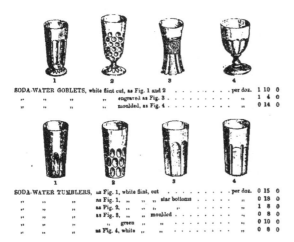

SODA-WATER GOBLETS, white flint cut, as Fig. 1 and 2 . . . . per doz. 1 10 0
" " " " engraved as Fig. 3 . . . . " 1 4 0
" " " " moulded, as Fig. 4 . . . . " 0 14 0

SODA-WATER TUMBLERS, as Fig. 1, white flint, cut . . . . per doz. 0 15 0
" " " as Fig. 1, " " " star bottoms . . . . . . " 0 18 0
" " " as Fig. 2, " " " " . . . . " 1 8 0
" " " as Fig. 3, " " moulded . . . . " 0 8 0
" " " " green " . . . . " 0 10 0
" " " as Fig. 4, white " . . . . " 0 8 0

FIGURE 87. Soda water glasses are taller and slimmer than other tumblers. The 1840 Apsley Pellatt price list illustrates an example (Wakefield 1968:52) so they were in production at least that early. Specialized glasses for soda water reflect the growing popularity of this type of beverage. In American sources, however, they were often referred to as lemonades and in the 20th century as iced tea glasses. This group, decorated by cutting, engraving, or molding, appears in S. Maw & Son (1866:260). (Private collection.)

FIGURE 88. A group of engraved tumblers offered by M. Davis, many of which exhibit the rather stiff vertical orientation of patterns introduced in the 1880s. The pattern in the bottom row with the swallows was inspired by Japanese motifs (*Pottery Gazette* 1884:before 817). (Courtesy of the British Library, London; digital image by George van der Vlugt.)

FIGURE 89. Tumbler in aqua glass decorated by optic molding, enameled floral/leaf sprays around a decal of Niagara Falls put on a white enamel ground, and gilding on the rim. The body surface has been lightly acid-etched to provide a matte surface for the enameling and to hide its less attractive back view. This tumbler represents Bohemian-style taste both in decorative techniques and motifs around the turn of the 20th century. It also represents a whole group of inexpensive souvenir ware produced at the same period. Although decals were introduced in North America during the 1890s, they were in use in continental Europe in the 1870s. The flat ground rim, disguised with gilding, is also a Bohemian feature found on drinking glasses. English glassblowers preferred to cut excess glass off from wide-mouthed wares, such as wine glasses or tumblers, with a pair of shears in a single operation. "In Bohemia and Germany, generally, the workmen are said not to be sufficiently skilful to use the shears; but the edges of bowls are blown in the rough, and cut smooth by the glass-cutter when cold, which leaves a flat and unsightly finish, far inferior to the round, smoothed edge of fire-polish after shearing" (Pellatt 1849:82). (Photo by Rock Chan, private collection.)

FIGURE 90. Jelly glasses for storing preserved jellies were in production at least by the early 19th century. Early examples were tumbler-shaped with a folded-in, slightly everted lip which held the oiled-paper or cloth covering in place (Wilson 1994[1]:186-187). These early 1870s examples from the King Company had glass or tin covers, and were intended for domestic use (*Pennsylvania Glassware* 1972:22). (Courtesy of the Juliet K. and Leonard S. Rakow Research Library of The Corning Museum of Glass, Corning, New York.)

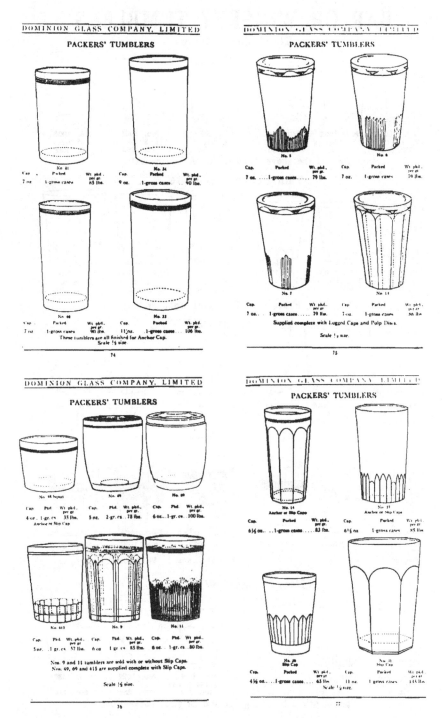

FIGURE 91. Packer's tumblers made by Dominion Glass Company were sold filled with mustard, jelly, and other foods, and then the consumer could use them as tumblers afterwards. These were suitable for Anchor Caps (with fine vertical ribs), lugged closure, or slip top (Dominion Glass Company 1915:74-77). The Anchor Cap was introduced in 1908 under the Sure Seal trade name and with some variations continued to be made into the 1960s (Bender 1986:77-79). Even fragments of these lips are easily identified. (Papers of Dominion Glass Company Limited, National Archives of Canada, Ottawa.)

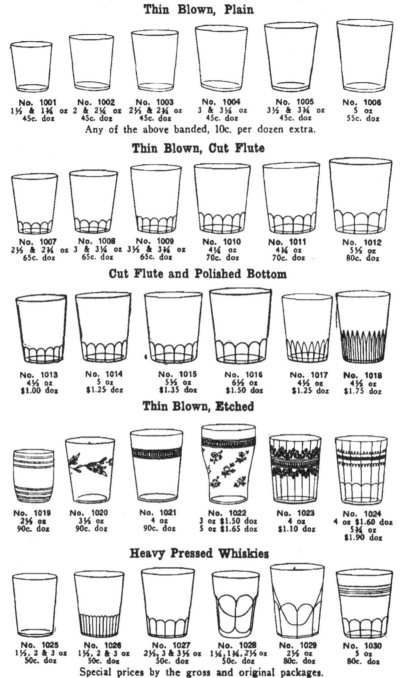

BAR OR WHISKEY TUMBLERS

Thin Blown, Plain

No. 1001	No. 1002	No. 1003	No. 1004	No. 1005	No. 1006
1½ & 1¾ oz	2 & 2¼ oz	2½ & 2¾ oz	3 & 3¼ oz	3½ & 3¾ oz	5 oz
45c. doz	45c. doz	45c. doz	45c. doz	45c. doz	55c. doz

Any of the above banded, 10c. per dozen extra.

Thin Blown, Cut Flute

No. 1007	No. 1008	No. 1009	No. 1010	No. 1011	No. 1012
2½ & 2¾ oz	3 & 3¼ oz	3½ & 3¾ oz	4¼ oz	4¾ oz	5½ oz
65c. doz	65c. doz	65c. doz	70c. doz	70c. doz	80c. doz

Cut Flute and Polished Bottom

No. 1013	No. 1014	No. 1015	No. 1016	No. 1017	No. 1018
4½ oz	5 oz	5½ oz	6½ oz	4½ oz	4½ oz
$1.00 doz	$1.25 doz	$1.35 doz	$1.50 doz	$1.25 doz	$1.75 doz

Thin Blown, Etched

No. 1019	No. 1020	No. 1021	No. 1022	No. 1023	No. 1024
2½ oz	3¼ oz	4 oz	3 oz $1.50 doz	4 oz	4 oz $1.60 doz
90c. doz	90c. doz	90c. doz	5 oz $1.65 doz	$1.10 doz	5¾ oz
					$1.90 doz

Heavy Pressed Whiskies

No. 1025	No. 1026	No. 1027	No. 1028	No. 1029	No. 1030
1½, 2 & 3 oz	1½, 2 & 3 oz	2½, 3 & 3½ oz	1¼, 1¾, 2½ oz	2½ oz	5 oz
50c. doz	50c. doz	50c. doz	50c. doz	80c. doz	80c. doz

Special prices by the gross and original packages.

FIGURE 92. Selection of tumblers offered to the restaurant and hotel trade which includes thinly-blown wares, heavy pressed wares, and cut or acid-etched decorations. The extra-thick glass in the two tumblers on the lower right in the last row is often found on pressed tumblers and probably dates as early as the mid-19th century (Budde & Westermann 1913:1). (Courtesy of George Miller.)

FIGURE 93. Tumbler in Athenia or Paneled 44 pattern, introduced by the United States Glass Company in 1912 (Peterson 1973:127-129). The T. Eaton Co. included a 4-piece table set in their 1914 catalogue (1914:110) which describes the pattern as "a combination of Colonial and Grecian border pattern with small floral design." Except for the flowers, the back to back 4s resemble Arts and Crafts motifs. The plain panels are decorated by gold iridescence. (Photo by Rock Chan, private collection.)

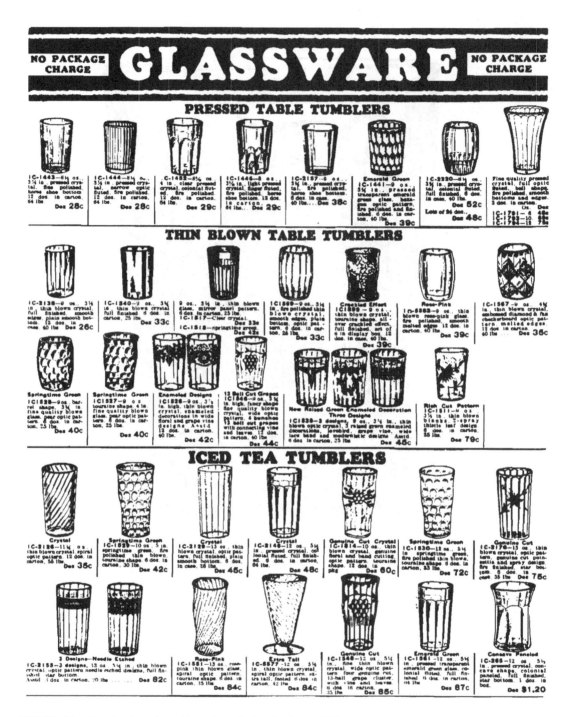

FIGURE 94. A selection of tumblers from Butler Brothers 1930 catalogue showing range of pressed and blown tumblers decorated by enameling, cutting, and acid-etching. (Courtesy of Collins Kirby Art & Antiques, Fort Payne, Alabama.)

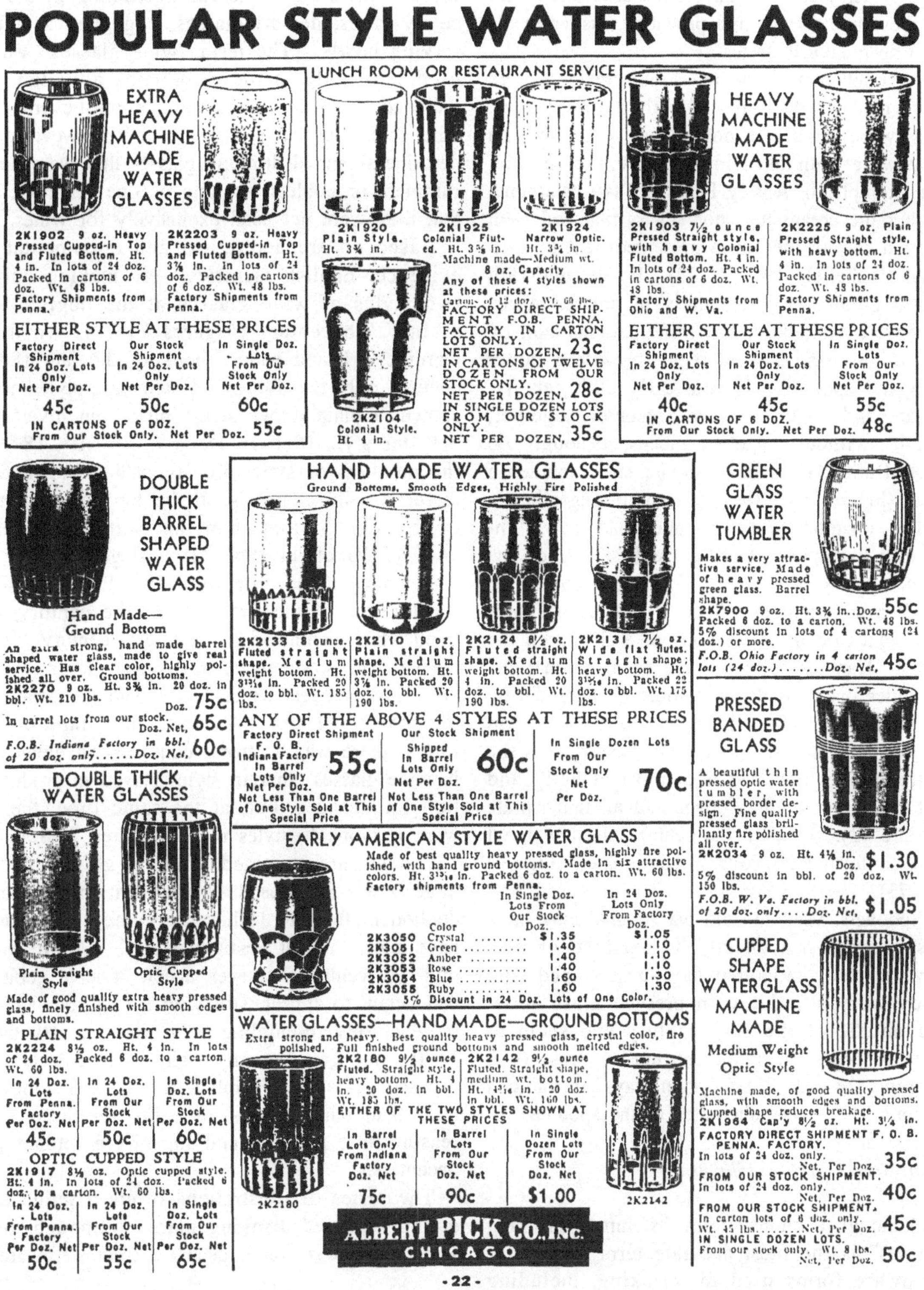

POPULAR STYLE WATER GLASSES

EXTRA HEAVY MACHINE MADE WATER GLASSES

2K1902 9 oz. Heavy Pressed Cupped-in Top and Fluted Bottom. Ht. 4 in. In lots of 24 doz. Packed in cartons of 6 doz. Wt. 48 lbs. Factory Shipments from Penna.

2K2203 9 oz. Heavy Pressed Cupped-in Top and Fluted Bottom. Ht. 3⅞ in. In lots of 24 doz. Packed in cartons of 6 doz. Wt. 48 lbs. Factory Shipments from Penna.

EITHER STYLE AT THESE PRICES

Factory Direct Shipment In 24 Doz. Lots Only Net Per Doz.	Our Stock Shipment In 24 Doz. Lots Only Net Per Doz.	In Single Doz. Lots From Our Stock Only Net Per Doz.
45c	50c	60c

IN CARTONS OF 6 DOZ. From Our Stock Only. Net Per Doz. 55c

LUNCH ROOM OR RESTAURANT SERVICE

2K1920 Plain Style. Ht. 3¾ in.

2K1925 Colonial Fluted. Ht. 3⅝ in.

2K1924 Narrow Optic. Ht. 3¾ in.

2K2104 Colonial Style. Ht. 4 in.

Machine made—Medium wt. 8 oz. Capacity

Any of these 4 styles shown at these prices:

Cartons of 12 doz. Wt. 60 lbs.

FACTORY DIRECT SHIPMENT F.O.B. PENNA. FACTORY IN CARTON LOTS ONLY. NET PER DOZEN, 23c

IN CARTONS OF TWELVE DOZEN FROM OUR STOCK ONLY. NET PER DOZEN, 28c

IN SINGLE DOZEN LOTS FROM OUR STOCK ONLY. NET PER DOZEN, 35c

HEAVY MACHINE MADE WATER GLASSES

2K1903 7½ ounce Pressed Straight style, with heavy Colonial Fluted Bottom. Ht. 4 in. In lots of 24 doz. Packed in cartons of 6 doz. Wt. 48 lbs. Factory Shipments from Ohio and W. Va.

2K2225 9 oz. Plain Pressed Straight style, with heavy bottom. Ht. 4 in. In lots of 24 doz. Packed in cartons of 6 doz. Wt. 48 lbs. Factory Shipments from Penna.

EITHER STYLE AT THESE PRICES

Factory Direct Shipment In 24 Doz. Lots Only Net Per Doz.	Our Stock Shipment In 24 Doz. Lots Only Net Per Doz.	In Single Doz. Lots From Our Stock Only Net Per Doz.
40c	45c	55c

IN CARTONS OF 6 DOZ. From Our Stock Only. Net Per Doz. 48c

DOUBLE THICK BARREL SHAPED WATER GLASS

Hand Made— Ground Bottom

An extra strong, hand made barrel shaped water glass, made to give real service. Has clear color, highly polished all over. Ground bottoms.

2K2270 9 oz. Ht. 3¾ in. 20 doz. in bbl. Wt. 210 lbs. Doz. 75c

In barrel lots from our stock. Doz. Net, 65c

F.O.B. Indiana Factory in bbl. of 20 doz. only......Doz. Net, 60c

HAND MADE WATER GLASSES

Ground Bottoms, Smooth Edges, Highly Fire Polished

2K2133 8 ounce. Fluted straight shape. Medium weight bottom. Ht. 3 13/16 in. Packed 20 doz. to bbl. Wt. 185 lbs.

2K2110 9 oz. Plain straight shape. Medium weight bottom. Ht. 3⅞ in. Packed 20 doz. to bbl. Wt. 190 lbs.

2K2124 8½ oz. Fluted straight shape. Medium weight bottom. Ht. 4 in. Packed 20 doz. to bbl. Wt. 190 lbs.

2K2131 7½ oz. Wide flat flutes. Straight shape; heavy bottom. Ht. 3 13/16 in. Packed 22 doz. to bbl. Wt. 175 lbs.

ANY OF THE ABOVE 4 STYLES AT THESE PRICES

Factory Direct Shipment F. O. B. Indiana Factory In Barrel Lots Only Net Per Doz. Not Less Than One Barrel of One Style Sold at This Special Price	Our Stock Shipment Shipped In Barrel Lots Only Net Per Doz. Not Less Than One Barrel of One Style Sold at This Special Price	In Single Dozen Lots From Our Stock Only Net Per Doz.
55c	60c	70c

GREEN GLASS WATER TUMBLER

Makes a very attractive service. Made of heavy pressed green glass. Barrel shape.

2K7900 9 oz. Ht. 3⅜ in..Doz. 55c

Packed 6 doz. to a carton. Wt. 48 lbs. 5% discount in lots of 4 cartons (24 doz.) or more.

F.O.B. Ohio Factory in 4 carton lots (24 doz.).......Doz. Net, 45c

PRESSED BANDED GLASS

A beautiful thin pressed optic water tumbler, with pressed border design. Fine quality pressed glass brilliantly fire polished all over.

2K2034 9 oz. Ht. 4⅛ in. Doz. $1.30

5% discount in bbl. of 20 doz. Wt. 150 lbs.

F.O.B. W. Va. Factory in bbl. of 20 doz. only....Doz. Net, $1.05

DOUBLE THICK WATER GLASSES

Plain Straight Style

Optic Cupped Style

Made of good quality extra heavy pressed glass, finely finished with smooth edges and bottoms.

PLAIN STRAIGHT STYLE

2K2224 8½ oz. Ht. 4 in. In lots of 24 doz. Packed 6 doz. to a carton. Wt. 60 lbs.

In 24 Doz. Lots From Penna. Factory Per Doz. Net	In 24 Doz. Lots From Our Stock Per Doz. Net	In Single Doz. Lots From Our Stock Per Doz. Net
45c	50c	60c

OPTIC CUPPED STYLE

2K1917 8½ oz. Optic cupped style. Ht. 4 in. In lots of 24 doz. Packed 6 doz. to a carton. Wt. 60 lbs.

In 24 Doz. Lots From Penna. Factory Per Doz. Net	In 24 Doz. Lots From Our Stock Per Doz. Net	In Single Doz. Lots From Our Stock Per Doz. Net
50c	55c	65c

EARLY AMERICAN STYLE WATER GLASS

Made of best quality heavy pressed glass, highly fire polished, with hand ground bottoms. Made in six attractive colors. Ht. 3 13/16 in. Packed 6 doz. to a carton. Wt. 60 lbs. Factory shipments from Penna.

	Color	In Single Doz. Lots From Our Stock Doz.	In 24 Doz. Lots Only From Factory Doz.
2K3050	Crystal	$1.35	$1.05
2K3051	Green	1.40	1.10
2K3052	Amber	1.40	1.10
2K3053	Rose	1.40	1.10
2K3054	Blue	1.60	1.30
2K3055	Ruby	1.60	1.30

5% Discount in 24 Doz. Lots of One Color.

WATER GLASSES—HAND MADE—GROUND BOTTOMS

Extra strong and heavy. Best quality heavy pressed glass, crystal color, fire polished. Full finished ground bottoms and smooth melted edges.

2K2180 9½ ounce Fluted. Straight style, heavy bottom. Ht. 4 in. 20 doz. in bbl. Wt. 185 lbs.

2K2142 9½ ounce Fluted. Straight shape, medium wt. bottom. Ht. 4 3/16 in. 20 doz. in bbl. Wt. 160 lbs.

EITHER OF THE TWO STYLES SHOWN AT THESE PRICES

In Barrel Lots Only From Indiana Factory Doz. Net	In Barrel Lots From Our Stock Doz. Net	In Single Dozen Lots From Our Stock Doz. Net
75c	90c	$1.00

2K2180

2K2142

CUPPED SHAPE WATERGLASS MACHINE MADE

Medium Weight Optic Style

Machine made, of good quality pressed glass, with smooth edges and bottoms. Cupped shape reduces breakage.

2K1964 Cap'y 8½ oz. Ht. 3¼ in.

FACTORY DIRECT SHIPMENT F. O. B. PENNA. FACTORY. In lots of 24 doz. only. Net. Per Doz. 35c

FROM OUR STOCK SHIPMENT. In lots of 24 doz. only. Net. Per Doz. 40c

FROM OUR STOCK SHIPMENT. In carton lots of 6 doz. only. Wt. 45 lbs........Net, Per Doz. 45c

IN SINGLE DOZEN LOTS. From our stock only. Wt. 8 lbs. Net, Per Doz. 50c

ALBERT PICK CO., INC. CHICAGO

- 22 -

FIGURE 95. Tumblers for restaurant and hotel use, most of rather thick glass. Note that the "Early American Style Water Glass" has a hand ground bottom. This pattern is a pressed example of a conscious revival of early-19th-century styles (Figures 46, 74***e***) (Albert Pick Company 1932:22). (Courtesy of George Miller.)

nappy. They seem to have been associated with hot beverage service and probably smaller meals such as breakfast or tea.

Although both sugar bowls and creamers were being made in the 18th and early 19th centuries, they were generally not paired, even though they were both used in hot beverage service. For example, in Apsley Pellatt's 1840 catalogue, neither the cream jugs nor sugars matched each other nor were they even presented next to each other (Wakefield 1968:50, 52). By the mid-19th century, however, particularly in pressed glass, they were available in the same patterns and, by the 1870s, were offered regularly with a butter dish and spooner. By the early 20th century, sugars and creamers were presented together, usually without the other pieces, although the 1930 Butler Brothers catalogue still includes a "set" (Figure 73). The 20th-century sugar bowls and cream pitchers were smaller than early-19th-century examples. During the first half of the 19th century, the covers for sugar bowls sat inside a galleried rim (Figure 11); later examples had ledges on the main body or a flange on the cover. Handles seem to have been optional.

Butter dishes underwent some changes during the 1800 to 1940 period. The dominant form during the first half of the 19th century was the butter tub, which had a cylindrical body and flat base, and often a cover and an under-plate (Figure 42). Later in the century, the low bowl or dish form with cover predominated (Figures 30, 73).

Spooners, used to hold tea spoons, may have a stem, may rest directly on the foot, or may have no foot and often have a scalloped rim. They were introduced in pressed glass about the middle of the 19th century and seem to have continued in production until at least 1930 (Figures 24, 62, 73). Spoon trays, introduced around 1900, were alternates to the spooner.

Stemmed Drinking Glasses

Although a clumsy term, "stemmed drinking glasses" is the most accurate term to use for stemware forms used for drinking, including wine glasses of different shapes and sizes (cordial, claret, hock, and champagne), ales, and larger drinking glasses called rummers or goblets. "Stemware" technically describes any glass vessel with a stem, including drinking glasses, celery vases, dessert glasses, egg glasses, and serving bowls. The term "wine glasses" was used frequently in the documents although it included stemware styles suitable for beverages other than wine. It is a useful term, however, to describe stemmed drinking glasses that were not rummers or goblets, as long as one remembers that they were not used exclusively for wines.

Based on archaeological and documentary evidence, English factories were making only two styles of wine glasses at the beginning of the 19th century (Figures 74-75). In the Gardiner's Island pattern book of the late 18th century, only two Bohemian stemware styles are shown, a plain drawn stem and a thin inverted baluster style (Pattern Book n.d.). By 1840, the numbers of stemware styles had begun to increase, with emphasis on the top and bottom of the stem, rather than the center (Figures 76-77) (Wakefield 1968:52). In general, they also tended to be proportionally taller than the short forms of the first half of the century, a trend which continued into the 20th century. By the late 1920s, stemware bowls were large, with tall stems and feet which had a diameter smaller than the bowl rim. As with other tableware forms, there was a strong conservative element in wine glasses wherein styles stayed in production for decades, but, at the same time, there were fashionable styles made (Figures 77-82).

Goblets are stemmed drinking glasses with large bowls (Figures 83-84). From their introduction in the late 18th century, they tended to have short, almost vestigial stems. Before the mid-19th century, however, a new style of goblet had begun to appear, still with a large bowl but more closely resembling wine glasses. By the 1870s, one gets the impression, particularly in pressed glass, that goblets were more widely used than wine glasses, probably for the same reasons that pitchers and jugs were replacing decanters.

The series of illustrations offers a guide to dating stemmed drinking glasses although the same styles were often used on other stemware.

Tumblers

Tumblers (Figures 85-95) are the commonest tableglass form found on archaeological sites and are the most difficult to date. The dominant decorative motif was the panel which seems to have been made in an astonishing array of variations in both cut and pressed glass and was offered throughout the 140 years covered by this guide. Other styles were offered, however, following the dominant decorative motifs of different periods as illustrations scattered throughout this guide demonstrate. A hint of the quantities and variety available is provided by an 1875 advertisement of the Rochester Tumbler Company which boasted that they produced more that 175 different patterns and 200,000 tumblers every 6 days (Innes 1976:59). This company specialized in tumblers and even sold its products to other glass companies (Innes 1976:58). Tumbler shapes were generally conical although cylindrical, waisted, and barrel-shaped ones were also made. Descriptions of tumblers in the catalogues included details such as capacity, weight (particularly in England), thickness, what was to be put in them (ale, whiskey, soda water, iced tea, lemonade), the appropriate setting (bar or table), the method of manufacture, and decoration. Blown tumblers were among the first tablewares to be manufactured by machine (see Blown Glass).

For the first half of the 19th century, lead, glass tumblers, whether made in England or the United States, dominated the North American market. They were plain or decorated by contact molding (Figure 12), cutting, and, after the late 1830s, by pressing. After the American Revolution, importation of Bohemian glassware into the United States increased and certain tumbler styles began appearing in quantity in the American marketplace (Lanman 1968, 1969; Bonasera 1998). Made of potash-lime glass, these tumblers have plain bodies or pattern-molded ribs partway up the body, sketchily engraved motifs either around the rim or in the center of the body, and often a roughly ground pontil mark (Figure 85). Rim motifs include crude squiggles, swags, small horizontal ovals filled with crosshatching, and larger motifs on the body including tulips or roses, birds and heart, or a two-handled basket with floral bouquet. These styles are much rarer in Canada around 1800, although similar examples dating to the middle of the 18th century have been found on French colonial sites in North America.

Pressed paneled tumblers (Figure 86) were introduced in the mid to late 1830s. In 1837, two glass companies exhibited fluted tumblers in Boston at the first exhibition held by the Massachusetts Charitable Mechanic Association (Watkins 1970:61). In England, the first production of a paneled tumbler is attributed to a talented machinist in 1836, who had figured out how to press a thin-topped vessel like a tumbler (*Pottery Gazette* 1885:903). Two pressed designs registered in England in 1840 showed different types of panels and mitered grooves suitable for goblets, tumblers, and other forms (Morris 1978:190-193). The immediate success of pressed tumblers is reflected in a comment about the New England Glass Company in 1838: "the only thing we press now is Tumblers . . . our men make 400 in six hours" (Spillman 1992:4). Pressed tumblers may have mold lines hidden in the pattern, but most do not have obvious lines on the body or base. Smooth surfaces on the undecorated rim portion of the tumbler were achieved by using an undecorated part in the mold and by fire-polishing. Pressed paneled tumblers often have a ground and polished resting surface, a feature which lasted well into the 1930s (Figure 95). The popularity of the pressed-panel tumbler is attested to by the host of variations shown in catalogues and by the frequency of their occurrence on archaeological sites.

Thin, light tumblers were being made as early as the 1870s. The Boston & Sandwich Glass Company (1992:Plate 4) illustrates examples decorated with acid-etched designs executed by the recently introduced needle-etching machine (see Acid-etched Glass). In 1877, a rival firm described wares from the Rochester Tumbler Company: "They were as thin as a sheet of paper and as clear as crystal, also destitute of any mold mark" (Innes 1976:60). Although Innes assumes these were pressed tumblers, the absence of mold lines suggests that they were blown in turn-paste molds. Thinly blown tumblers with acid-etched designs continued to be manufactured into the 1930s (Figure 94).

Conclusions

During the 140 years covered in this guide, a strong core of conservatism ran through the glass industry and its customer base while at the same time unprecedented technological developments in both manufacturing and decorative techniques increased the range of glass available at all levels of society in Canada, the United States, and elsewhere. Technical accomplishments went hand in hand with a willingness on the part of everyone to loot the past for design ideas and to capitalize on someone else's ideas and products. By the last quarter of the 19th century, consumers were faced with an astonishing array of choices, from traditional styles to the latest trends, from cheap to expensive, from colorless to extraordinary colors, from plain to highly decorated. Dating glassware from this mix ranges from precise beginning dates to decades-long time spans. End dates for technical processes, such as the use of the pontil, are impossible to determine because the tableware industry continued to use hand production methods even after the introduction of mechanized production. Decorative themes are possible to identify in certain time periods but many themes never went out of style and others were repeated several times during the 140-year period. Tableware forms, through changing shapes and through the introduction of specialized shapes, sometimes provide additional dating information.

Dating artifacts is a tool to help us understand the contexts in which objects were originally used. Certainly glass tableware can only be understood in comparison with other tableware forms in ceramic and metal. Archaeological collections should offer us something that the innumerable books on glass and ceramic antiques do not offer–an opportunity to understand how objects were used during their active life. By using tableware of all types from archaeological collections, it may be possible to identify assemblages associated with different groups of people; their domestic, work, and commercial lives; whether they lived in a rural or urban context, whether they favored traditional, up-to-date, or practical tableware; and how choices changed or remained the same through time.

REFERENCES

ALBERT PICK COMPANY
[1932] Untitled catalogue. Albert Pick Co., Chicago, IL.

ARMY AND NAVY STORES
1969 Yesterday's Shopping: The Army and Navy Stores Catalogue 1907, introduction by Alison Adburgham. David and Charles, Newton Abbot, Devon, England.

THE ART-JOURNAL
1851 The Crystal Palace Exhibition, Illustrated Catalogue, London 1851. Reprinted 1970, Dover Publications, New York, NY.
1862 The Art-Journal Illustrated Catalogue of the International Exhibition 1862. Reprinted 1973, EP Publishing, Wakefield, Yorkshire, England.

AUSTIN, JANE G.
1991 "Cullet": An Article reprinted from The Atlantic Monthly, September 1864. The Acorn, Journal of The Sandwich Glass Museum 2:75-91.

BAKER, GARY EVERETT
1986 The Flint Glass Industry in Wheeling, West Virginia: 1829-1865. Master's thesis, University of Delaware, Newark.

BAKEWELL, PEARS & CO.
[1875] Glass Catalogue, introduction by Lowell Innes. Reprinted 1977, Thomas C. Pears III, Pittsburgh, PA. [Dated ca. 1875 by Lowell Innes.]

BENDER, NATHAN E.
1986 Early 20th Century Commercial Closures. Paper presented at the Annual Conference on Historical and Underwater Archaeology, Sacramento, CA.

BLASZCZYK, REGINA LEE
1993 The Wright Way for Glass: Russel Wright and the Business of Industrial Design. The Acorn, Journal of The Sandwich Glass Museum 4:2-22.
1995 Imagining Consumers: Manufacturers and Markets in Ceramics and Glass, 1865-1965. Ph.D. dissertation, University of Delaware, Newark. University Microfilms International, Ann Arbor, MI.

BONASERA, MICHAEL C.
1998 The Bohemian Tradition in New York City: Glassware from Two Turn of the Nineteenth Century Deposits. Paper presented at the Annual Meeting of the Council for Northeast Historical Archaeology, Montreal, Quebec.

BONTEMPS, GEORGES
1868 Guide du Verrier, Traité historique et pratique de la fabrication des verres, cristaux, vitraux. Librairie du Dictionnaire des arts et manufactures, Paris, France.

BOSTON & SANDWICH GLASS CO.
1992 Reprint of the "c. 1874" Boston & Sandwich Glass Company Trade Catalog and Price List. The Acorn, Journal of The Sandwich Glass Museum 3:21-end.

BROOKS, JOHN A.
1987 *Glass Tumblers 1700-1900.* John A. Brooks, Rothley, Leicester, England.

BRYCE BROTHERS COMPANY
1916 *Catalogue of Lead Blown Glassware.* Bryce Brothers Company, Mount Pleasant, PA.

BUCHWALD, GUNNAR, AND MOGENS SCHLÜTER (EDITORS)
1975 *Kastrup and Holmegaard's Glassworks Denmark 1825-1975.* Kastrup and Holmegaard's Glassworks, Copenhagen, Denmark.

BUDDE & WESTERMANN
1913 *Budde & Westermann Catalogue No. 101: Department of Glassware and Supplies in General for Cafes, Clubs, Hotels, Restaurants, etc.* Budde & Westermann, New York, NY.

BUTLER BROTHERS
1902 *Spring 1902 "MISSIONARY" Edition of "Our Drummer."* Butler Brothers, New York, NY.
1905 *Glassware 1905,* Catalog No. 536, Glassware Department. Reprint, Antiques Research Publications, Mentone, AL.
1910 *Glassware 1910,* Fall 1910 catalog, Glass section. Reprint, Antiques Research Publications, Mentone, AL.
1914 "Our Drummer." Spring. Butler Brothers, New York, NY.
1925 *China & Glassware 1925,* Midwinter catalog, No. 2233. Reprinted 1968, Antiques Research Publications, Mentone, AL.
1929 "Our Drummer" is Our Salesman, August. Butler Brothers, Chicago, IL.
1930 *China & Glassware 1930,* Catalog No. 2749, October. Reprinted 1968, Antiques Research Publications, Mentone, AL.

CHARLESTON, ROBERT J.
1965 A Glass Pattern-Book of the Biedermeier Period. *VIIe Congrès International du Verre,* Paper 261. Brussels, Belgium.

THE CORNING MUSEUM OF GLASS
1987 *Guide To Trade Catalogs From The Corning Museum Of Glass.* Clearwater Publishing Company, New York, NY.

CROWE, KATE
1989 The French Connection: The Decorative Glass of James A. Jobling and Co. of Sunderland during the 1930s. *The Glass Circle* 6:32-45.

DAVIS, PEARCE
1949 *The Development of the American Glass Industry.* Harvard University Press, Cambridge, MA.

DIAMOND FLINT GLASS COMPANY LIMITED
1904 *Catalogue of Blown Tumblers, Plain and Decorated.* Diamond Flint Glass Company Limited, Montreal, Quebec.

DODSWORTH, ROGER (EDITOR)
1987 *British Glass Between the Wars,* exhibition catalogue. Dudley Leisure Services, Dudley, England.

DOMINION GLASS COMPANY
[1915] *Packers' Glassware Catalogue No. 11.* Dominion Glass Company Limited, Montreal, Quebec.

DRAHOTOVA, OLGA
1983 *European Glass.* Excalibur Books, New York, NY.

EDGLEY, JIM D. (COMPILER)
1996 *Registration Numbers 1908-1945.* The Glass Association, Kingswinford, West Midlands, England.

EVANS, WENDY, CATHERINE ROSS, AND ALEX WERNER
1995 *Whitefriars Glass: James Powell and Sons of London.* Museum of London, London, England.

FARRAR, ESTELLE SINCLAIRE, AND JANE SHADEL SPILLMAN
1979 *The Complete Cut & Engraved Glass of Corning.* Crown Publishers, New York, NY.

FAUSTER, CARL U.
1979 *Libbey Glass Since 1818: Pictorial History & Collector's Guide.* Len Beach Press, Toledo, OH.

FENWICK, MILLICENT
1948 *Vogue's Book of Etiquette: A Complete Guide to Traditional Forms and Modern Usage.* Simon and Schuster, New York, NY.

FLORENCE, GENE
1992 *Collectible Glassware from the 40's, 50's, 60's: An Illustrated Value Guide.* Collector Books, Paducah, KY.
1995a *Elegant Glassware of the Depression Era,* 6th edition. Collector Books, Paducah, KY.
1995b *Kitchen Glassware of the Depression Years,* 5th edition. Collector Books, Paducah, KY.
1996 *The Collector's Encyclopedia of Depression Glass,* 12th edition. Collector Books, Paducah, KY.

GOLLEDGE, CHRISTINE
1987 Stuart and Sons Limited (1918-1939). In *British Glass Between the Wars,* Roger Dodsworth, editor, pp. 28-31. Dudley Leisure Services, Dudley, England.

GRAY, CHERRY, AND RICHARD GRAY
1987 The Prince's Glasses, Some Warrington Cut Glass 1806-1811. *The Journal of the Glass Association* 2:11-18.

GREAT BRITAIN
1835 Commission of Inquiry into the Excise Establishment and into the Management and Collection of the Excise Revenue. Report No. 13: Glass. H.M.S.O., London, England.
1865 Parliament. Sessional Papers. Children's Employment Commission. Vol. 20. H.M.S.O., London, England.
1907 *Report of the Tariff Commission. Volume 6, The Glass Industry.* Reprinted 1972, Johnson Reprint Corporation, New York, NY.

Olive R. Jones

HAJDAMACH, CHARLES R.
1991   *British Glass 1800-1914.* Antique Collectors' Club, Woodbridge, England.

HEACOCK, WILLIAM, AND FRED BICKENHEUSER
1978   *Encyclopedia of Victorian Colored Pattern Glass: Book 5 U.S. Glass From A to Z.* Antique Publications, Marietta, OH.

HENRY BIRKS & SONS
1903   *Catalogue No. 12.* Henry Birks & Sons, Montreal, Quebec.
1906   *Catalogue No. 17.* Henry Birks & Sons, Montreal, Quebec.

HIGGINS & SEITER
1899   *China and Cut Glass, Higgins & Seiter 1899.* Reprinted 1971, The Pyne Press, Princeton, NJ.

HILL-OUSTON CO. LTD.
[1936] *Hillston Crystal Gifts, Catalogue No. 10.* Hill-Ouston Co. Ltd., Birmingham, England. [3 April 1936 stamped on catalog.]

HOBBS GLASS COMPANY
n.d.   Catalogue. The Winterthur Library, Printed Book and Periodical Collection, Winterthur, DE.

HOLMES, JANET
1974   Glass and the Glass Industry. In *The Book of Canadian Antiques,* Donald Blake Webster, editor, pp. 268-281. McGraw-Hill, Ryerson, Toronto, Ontario.
1987   *Patterns in Light. The John and Mary Yaremko Glass Collection.* Royal Ontario Museum, Toronto, Ontario.

HOLMES, JANET, AND OLIVE JONES
1978   Glass in Canada: An Annotated Bibliography. *Material History Bulletin* 6:115-148.

HUGHES, G. BERNARD
1958   *English Glass for the Collector 1660-1860.* Lutterworth Press, London, England.

HUSFLOEN, KYLE
1992   *Collector's Guide to American Pressed Glass, 1825-1915.* Wallace-Homestead Book Company, Radnor, PA.

INNES, LOWELL
1976   *Pittsburgh Glass 1797-1891: A History and Guide for Collectors.* Houghton Mifflin, Boston, MA.

JACKSON, LESLEY
1997   Automated Table Glass Production in Britain Since World War II. *The Journal of The Glass Association* 5:68-80.

JARVES, DEMING
1865   *Reminiscences of Glass-Making.* Reprinted 1968, Beatrice C. Weinstock, Great Neck, NY.

JENKS, BILL, AND JERRY LUNA
1990   *Early American Pattern Glass, 1850-1910.* Wallace-Homestead Book Company, Radnor, PA.

JONES, OLIVE
1986a   Glass Tablewares 1850-1870. Source Book. Manuscript, Parks Canada, Ottawa, Ontario.
1986b   Glass Tablewares 1870-1890. Source Book. Manuscript, Parks Canada, Ottawa, Ontario.
1986c   Glass Tablewares 1890-1914. Source Book. Manuscript, Parks Canada, Ottawa, Ontario.
1986d   Glass Tablewares 1890-1914. Source Book. Manuscript, Parks Canada, Ottawa, Ontario.
1992   Early American Glass in Canada, ca. 1820-1860. *The Glass Club Bulletin of The National Early American Glass Club* 168(Fall):3-16.

JONES, OLIVE R., AND E. ANN SMITH
1985   Glass of the British Military, 1755-1820. Parks Canada, *Studies in Archaeology, Architecture and History.* Ottawa, Ontario.

JONES, OLIVE R., AND CATHERINE SULLIVAN, WITH CONTRIBUTIONS BY GEORGE L. MILLER, E. ANN SMITH, JANE E. HARRIS, AND KEVIN LUNN
1989   The Parks Canada Glass Glossary for the Description of Containers, Tableware, Flat Glass, and Closures, revised edition. Parks Canada, *Studies in Archaeology, Architecture and History.* Ottawa, Ontario.

KAELLGREN, PETER
1993   Birmingham Cut Glass and the American Market; Examining an 1811 Account and its Context. In *Reflections on Glass: Articles from the Glass Club Bulletin,* Jane Shadel Spillman, Olive R. Jones, and Kirk J. Nelson, compilers, pp. 45-52. National Early American Glass Club, Silver Spring, MD.

KILGO, GARRY, DALE KILGO, JERRY WILKINS, AND GAIL WILKINS
1991   *A Collector's Guide to Anchor Hocking's "Fire-King" Glassware.* K&W Collectibles, Addison, AL.

KING, THOMAS B.
1987   *Glass in Canada.* Boston Mills Press, Erin, Ontario.

KNITTLE, RHEA MANSFIELD
1927   *Early American Glass.* The Century Company, New York, NY.

LANGBRIDGE, R. H. (COMPILER)
1975   *Edwardian Shopping: A Selection from the Army & Navy Stores Catalogues 1898-1913,* introduction by R. H. Langbridge. David & Charles, London, England.

LANMAN, DWIGHT P.
1968   Glass in Baltimore: The Trade in Hollow and Tablewares, 1780-1820. Master's thesis, University of Delaware, Newark.
1969   The Baltimore Glass Trade, 1780 to 1820. *Winterthur Portfolio* 5:15-48. Winterthur, DE.

LATTIMORE, COLIN R.
1979   *English 19th-Century Press-Moulded Glass.* Barrie & Jenkins, London, England.

LAUNERT, FREDERIKA
1997   The Survival of Traditional Design in Post-War Stourbridge Glass. *The Journal of The Glass Association* 5:61-67.

LEE, RUTH WEBB
1944   *Victorian Glass: Specialties of the Nineteenth Century,* 12th edition. Lee Publications, Wellesley Hills, MA.
1958   *Early American Pressed Glass: A Classification of Patterns Collectible in Sets Together with Individual Pieces for Table Decorations,* 34th edition. Lee Publications, Wellesley, MA.

LEINICKE, KRIS GAYMAN
1986   Production of the Boston and Sandwich Glass Company in the Year 1827. Master's thesis, State University of New York College at Oneonta.

LOLE, F. PETER
1993   The Royal Finger Bowls and Coolers Mystery. *Glass Circle News* 56(June):2-4.

LYON, KENNETH W.
1994   Re-Thinking Blown Three Mold (A Sub-category of Mold Blown Glass). *The Acorn, Journal of The Sandwich Glass Museum* 5:70-80.

MACLAREN, GEORGE
1968   Nova Scotia Glass, revised edition. *Nova Scotia Museum, Occasional Paper* 4, *Historical Series* 1. Halifax

McFARLAN, GORDON
1992   Early Nineteenth Century Patterns from the Ford Ranken Archive. *The Journal of the Glass Association* 4:1-12.

McKEARIN, GEORGE S., AND HELEN McKEARIN
1948   *American Glass.* Crown Publishers, New York, NY.

McKINSTRY, E. RICHARD
1984   *Trade Catalogues at Winterthur: A Guide to the Literature of Merchandising 1750 to 1980.* Garland Publishing, New York, NY.

M'KEE AND BROTHERS
1981   *Victorian Glass: Five Complete Glass Catalogs from 1859/60 to 1871,* introduction and text by Lowell Innes and Jane Shadel Spillman. Dover Publications, New York, NY.

McNALLY, PAUL
1982   Table Glass in Canada, 1700-1850. Parks Canada, *History and Archaeology* 60. Ottawa, Ontario.

MEASELL, JAMES S.
1994a   H. Northwood & Company 1902-1925. In *Wheeling Glass 1829-1939: Collection of the Oglebay Institute*

Glass Museum, Gerald I. Reilly, editor, pp. 23-168. Oglebay Institute, Wheeling, WV.
1994b   *New Martinsville Glass 1900-1944.* Antique Publications, Marietta, OH.

MONTGOMERY WARD & CO.
1901   *Catalogue and Buyers' Guide, No. 69,* undated reprint. Antiques Research Publications, Mentone, AL.

MONTREAL GAZETTE
1852   American Pressed Glass. *Montreal Gazette,* 1 September:3. Montreal, Quebec.
1867   *Montreal Gazette,* 7 November:3. Montreal, Quebec.

MONTREAL TRANSCRIPT
1842   China, Glass, and Earthenware. *Montreal Transcript,* 22 September:3. Montreal, Quebec.

MORRIS, BARBARA
1978   *Victorian Tableglass & Ornaments.* Barrie & Jenkins, London, England.

MUCHA, MIRIAM E.
1979   Mechanization, French Style Cristaux, Moule en Plein. *The Glass Club Bulletin* 126(September):3-8.

NATIONAL GLASS BUDGET
1897   Owens' Blowing Machine, Punch Tumbler Manufacture Revolutionized. *National Glass Budget,* 13 (23):1; 23 October.

NELSON, KIRK J.
1988   Progress Under Pressure: The Mechanization of the American Flint Glass Industry, 1820-1840. Master's thesis, University of Delaware, Newark.
1990   Early Glass Pressing Technology in Sandwich. *The Acorn, Journal of the Sandwich Glass Museum* 1:38-50.
1992   Introductory Note to the "c.1874" Catalog and Price List. *The Acorn, Journal of The Sandwich Glass Museum* 3:11-20.

NEWMAN, HAROLD
1977   *An Illustrated Dictionary of Glass.* Thames and Hudson, London, England.

O'HARA FLINT GLASS WORKS
1861   *Illustrated Catalogue and Prices of Flint Glassware, Manufactured by James B. Lyon & Co.* James B. Lyon & Co., Pittsburgh, PA.

PALMER, ARLENE
1993a   *Glass in Early America, Selections from the Henry Francis du Pont Winterthur Museum.* Henry Francis du Pont Winterthur Museum, Winterthur, DE.
1993b   Joseph Baggott, New York Glasscutter. In *Reflections on Glass: Articles from the Glass Club Bulletin,* Jane Shadel Spillman, Olive R. Jones, and Kirk J. Nelson, compilers, pp. 57-62. National Early American Glass Club, Silver Spring, MD.
1993c   Some Notes on Cutters and Engravers of Glass in Early America. In *Reflections on Glass: Articles from the Glass Club Bulletin,* Jane Shadel Spillman,

Olive R. Jones, and Kirk J. Nelson, compilers, 35-40. National Early American Glass Club, Silver Spring, MD.

PATTERN BOOK

n.d. Pattern Book for Glass Decanters, Tumblers, etc., late 18th century, which belonged to the Gardiner Family of Gardiner's Island. Property of Henry Francis du Pont Winterthur Museum Libraries, Winterthur, DE.

PEABODY ESSEX MUSEUM

1794-1819 Sample Books (candlesticks, tea-pots and other tableware of Sheffield plate and Britannia ware, Sheffield, England, 1794-1819?), 8 volumes. Peabody Essex Museum, Philips Library, Salem, MA.

PELLATT, APSLEY

1849 *Curiosities of Glass Making: With Details of the Processes and Productions of Ancient and Modern Ornamental Glass Manufacture.* Reprinted 1968, Ceramic Book Company, Newport, England.

PENNSYLVANIA GLASSWARE, 1870-1904

1972 *Pennsylvania Glassware, 1870-1904.* The Pyne Press, Princeton, NJ.

PETERSON, ARTHUR G.

1968 *400 Trademarks on Glass.* Washington College Press, Takoma Park, MD.

1970 *Glass Salt Shakers.* Wallace-Homestead Book Company, Des Moines, IA.

1973 *Glass Patents and Patterns.* Arthur G. Peterson, DeBary, FL.

PHILIPPE, JOSEPH

[1975] *Le Val-Saint-Lambert, ses cristalleries et l'art du verre en Belgique.* Librairie Halbart, Liège, Belgium.

POTTERY GAZETTE AND CHINA AND GLASS TRADES REVIEW

1881 M. Davis & Co. Supplement to *Pottery Gazette and China and Glass Trades Review,* 5(51):between 816 and 817, 1 October.

1884 M. Davis & Co. Supplement to *Pottery Gazette and China and Glass Trades Review,* 8(89):after 1292, 1 November.

1885 Trade Reminiscences. The First Pressed Tumbler. *Pottery Gazette and China and Glass Trades Review,* 1 August:903.

1893 Notes on Fancy Goods. *Pottery Gazette and China and Glass Trades Review,* 2 January:4.

1894 The "New Louis XV" Suite of Crystal Glass. Fancy Trades Supplement to *Pottery Gazette and China and Glass Trades Review,* 19(199):before 49, 1 January.

PULLIN, ANNE GEFFKEN

1986 *Glass Signatures, Trademarks and Trade Names from the Seventeenth to the Twentieth Century.* Wallace-Homestead Book Company, Radnor, PA.

RAINWATER, DOROTHY T. (EDITOR)

1973 *Sterling Silver Holloware.* The Pyne Press, Princeton, NJ.

REVI, ALBERT CHRISTIAN

1959 *Nineteenth Century Glass: Its Genesis and Development.* Thomas Nelson & Sons, New York, NY.

1964 *American Pressed Glass and Figure Bottles.* Thomas Nelson & Sons, New York, NY.

1965 *American Cut and Engraved Glass.* Thomas Nelson & Sons, New York, NY.

ROGOVE, SUSAN TOBIER, AND MARCIA BUAN STEINHAUER

1993 *Pyrex by Corning: A Collector's Guide.* Antique Publications, Marietta, OH.

ROSENHAIN, WALTER

1908 *Glass Manufacture.* Archibald Constable, London, England.

ROTTENBERG, BARBARA LANG, AND JUDITH TOMLIN

1982 Glass Manufacturing in Canada: a Survey of Pressed Glass Patterns. *National Museum of Man, Mercury Series, History Division, Paper* 33. Ottawa, Ontario.

S. MAW & SON

1866 *A Catalogue of Surgeons' Instruments & Appliances.* S. Maw & Son, London, England.

SCOVILLE, WARREN C.

1948 *Revolution in Glassmaking: Entrepreneurship and Technological Change in the American Industry.* Harvard University Press, Cambridge, MA.

SHEELER, JOHN

1978 Factors Affecting Attribution: The Burlington Glass Works. *Material History Bulletin* 6:31-51.

SILBER AND FLEMING

1990 *The Silber and Fleming Glass & China Book.* Wordsworth Editions, Ware, Hertfordshire, England.

SLACK, RAYMOND

1987 *English Pressed Glass 1830-1900.* Barrie & Jenkins, London, England.

SMART BROTHERS

[1885] Smart Brothers, in presenting to the Trade an entirely new edition of their Price List. Round Oak Glassworks, near Brierly Hill, Staffordshire, England. D. F. Taylor & Co., Birmingham, England. Fiche 93, Corning Museum of Glass, Corning, NY.

SPILLMAN, JANE SHADEL

1971 Documented Use of Cup Plates in the Nineteenth Century. *Journal of Glass Studies* 13:128-133.

1981 *American and European Pressed Glass in The Corning Museum of Glass.* The Corning Museum of Glass, Corning, NY.

1982 *Glass Tableware, Bowls & Vases.* Knopf, New York, NY.

1983 Pressed-glass Designs in the United States and Europe. *The Magazine Antiques* 124(1 July):130-139

1989 *White House Glassware: Two Centuries of Presidential Entertaining.* White House Historical Association, Washington, DC.

1992   The Leighton-Ford Correspondence. *The Acorn, Journal of The Sandwich Glass Museum* 3:3-10.

1996   *The American Cut Glass Industry: T. G. Hawkes and His Competitors.* Antique Collector's Club, Woodbridge, Suffolk, England.

1997   The New England Glass Company Catalog of Pressed Glass. *The Acorn, Journal of The Sandwich Glass Museum* 7:71-98.

SPILLMAN, JANE SHADEL, OLIVE JONES, AND KIRK NELSON
1993   *Reflections on Glass: Articles from the Glass Club Bulletin.* National Early American Glass Club, Silver Spring, MD.

SPILLMAN, JANE SHADEL, JAMES S. MEASELL, AND HOLLY H. MCCLUSKEY
1994   Glassmaking in South Wheeling 1845-1893 (Hobbs, Brockunier and Related Firms). In *Wheeling Glass 1829-1939: Collection of the Oglebay Institute Glass Museum,* Gerald I. Reilly, editor, pp. 39-91. Oglebay Institute, Wheeling, WV.

STARBUCK, DAVID S.
1986   The New England Glassworks: New Hampshire's Boldest Experiment in Early Glassmaking. *The New Hampshire Archeologist* 27(1).

STEVENS, GERALD
1967   *Canadian Glass c. 1825-1925.* Ryerson Press, Toronto, Ontario.

STOUT, SANDRA MCPHEE
1972   *The Complete Book of McKee Glass.* Trojan Press, North Kansas City, MO.

SULLIVAN, CATHERINE
[1985] Glass Tablewares 1800-1850, Source Book. Manuscript, Parks Canada, Ottawa, Ontario.

T. EATON CO.
1884- T. Eaton Catalogs, 1884-1952. Canadian Library
1952   Association Newspaper Microfilm Project, Ottawa, Ontario.

THOMPSON, JENNY
1989   *The Identification of English Pressed Glass.* Jenny Thompson, Kendal, Cumbria, England.

TYNE AND WEAR COUNTY COUNCIL MUSEUMS
1983   *Pyrex: 60 Years of Design.* Tyne and Wear County Council Museums, Sunderland, England.

UNITED STATES GLASS COMPANY
[1894] *United States Glass Co.'s Catalogue of Pressed Tumblers & Beer Mugs.* Pittsburgh, PA.

UNITED STATES SENATE
1911   Report on Condition of Woman and Child Wage-Earners in the United States in 19 Volumes, Vol. 3: Glass Industry. 61st Congress, 2nd Session, *Senate Executive Document* No. 645. Washington, DC.

UNITT, DORIS, AND PETER UNITT
1969   *Treasury of Canadian Glass.* Clock House Publications, Peterborough, Ontario.

THE VICTORIAN CATALOGUE OF HOUSEHOLD GOODS
1991   *The Victorian Catalogue of Household Goods.* Studio Editions, London, England.

VICTORIAN SILVERPLATED HOLLOWARE
1972   *Victorian Silverplated Holloware.* Wallace-Homestead Book Company, Des Moines, IA.

WAKEFIELD, HUGH
1961   *Nineteenth Century British Glass.* Faber and Faber, London, England.

1968   Early Victorian Styles in Glassware. In *Studies in Glass History and Design. Papers read to Committee B Session of the VIIIth International Congress on Glass, held in London 1st-6th July 1968,* R. J. Charleston, W. Evans, and A. E. Werner, editors, pp. 50-54. Gresham Press, Old Woking, Surrey, England.

1982   *Nineteenth Century British Glass,* revised edition. Faber and Faber, London, England.

WARREN, PHELPS
1981   *Irish Glass: Waterford-Cork-Belfast in the Age of Exuberance,* revised edition. Faber and Faber, London, England.

1984   Apsley Pellatt's Table Glass, 1840-1864. *Journal of Glass Studies* 26:120-135.

WATKINS, LURA WOODSIDE
1970   Pressed Glass of the New England Glass Company: An Early Catalogue at the Corning Museum. *Journal of Glass Studies* 12:149-164.

WEATHERMAN, HAZEL MARIE
1974   *Colored Glassware of the Depression Era,* volume 2. Weatherman Glassbooks, Springfield, MO.

1978   *The Decorated Tumbler.* Glassbooks, Springfield, MO.

WEEKS, JOSEPH D.
1886   *Report on the Manufacture of Glass.* United States, Department of the Interior, Census Office, Washington, DC.

WELKER, JOHN, AND ELIZABETH WELKER
1985   *Pressed Glass in America: Encyclopedia of the First Hundred Years, 1825-1925.* Antique Acres Press, Ivyland, PA.

WESTROPP, MICHAEL S. D.
1978   *Irish Glass: A History of Glass-making in Ireland from the Sixteenth Century,* revised edition, Mary Boydell, editor. Allen Figgis, Dublin, Ireland.

WHITE, HARRY HALL
1974   The Story of the Mantua Glass Works, parts 1-4. In *American Glass From the Pages of Antiques: 1. Blown and Molded,* Marvin D. Schwartz, editor, pp. 195-213. The Pyne Press, Princeton, NJ.

Olive R. Jones

WILLIAMS, SUSAN
    1985   *Savory Suppers & Fashionable Feasts: Dining in Victorian America.* Pantheon Books, New York, NY.

WILSON, KENNETH M.
    1972   *New England Glass and Glassmaking.* Thomas Y. Crowell Company, New York, NY.
    1994   *The Toledo Museum of Art: American Glass 1760-1930*, 2 volumes. Hudson Hills Press, New York, NY.

WOLFENDEN, IAN
    1987   The 'WHR' Drawings for Cut Glass and the Origins of the Broad Flute Style of Cutting. *The Journal of the Glass Association* 2:19-28.
    1992   Cut Glass in the Pattern Books of Matthew Boulton's Soho Manufactory. *The Journal of the Glass Association* 4:47-50.

YATES, BARBARA
    1987   The Glasswares of Percival Vickers & Co. Ltd., Jersey Street, Manchester, 1844-1914. *The Journal of the Glass Association* 2:29-40.

ZEMBALA, DENNIS MICHAEL
    1984   *Machines in the Glasshouse: The Transformation of Work in the Glass Industry, 1820-1915.* Ph.D. dissertation, George Washington University, Washington, DC. University Microfilms International, Ann Arbor, MI.

OLIVE R. JONES
MATERIAL CULTURE RESEARCH
ONTARIO SERVICE CENTRE
PARKS CANADA
1600 LIVERPOOL COURT
OTTAWA, ONTARIO K1A 0M5
CANADA

A Dating Key For
Post-Eighteenth Century Bottles

T. STELL NEWMAN

The Theory

Bottles produced in the United States after the eighteenth century may be rather precisely dated on the basis of recorded changes in bottle manufacture techniques. The bottle manufacture process was constantly improved throughout this period and the dates at which many of the new techniques appeared seem well established. Obviously, by knowing the invention dates of the various techniques used to produce any one bottle, it is possible to know that the bottle could not have been made prior to the latest dated technique used in its manufacture. This provides a "no earlier than" type of absolute date for the bottle, and for any coterminous archaeological level in which it is found.

The rapid improvement of bottle manufacture techniques resulted in the replacement of earlier, less efficient techniques, especially during the last half of the nineteenth century. Replacement techniques often came in at known dates and these also provide "no earlier than" dates for bottles manufactured by the new process. The date the improved technique was developed does not, unfortunately, provide a terminal "no later than" date for the earlier technique. One cannot simply use the date a replacement technique was developed as a terminal date for an archaeological level containing a bottle made with the replaced technique because of:

1. delays in particular bottle manufacturers changing over to the new technique;

2. the use of existing stocks of bottles made by an earlier technique after a new technique was developed;

3. storage time at the manufacturer's factory prior to shipment to the bottler;

4. delays in filling the bottles with the contents to be retailed;

5. transportation time to the site; and

6. the possibility of re-use of the bottle prior to final discard.

It is unlikely that the terminal date for the production of an older technique was substantially later than the date when the new manufacturing process was developed to replace it. The bottle manufacturing industry during the nineteenth century was highly competitive and new improvements were speedily adopted. The increasing demand for bottled products would quite likely have meant a fast turnover of bottle stocks, while the transportation system in the United States was able to distribute the bottles to the users without undue delay.

If the date of a replacement technique were increased by about ten years, a terminal date would be generated for archaeological levels containing bottles made with the replaced technique. Ten years seems adequate to allow for the time delays in American bottles reaching most archaeological sites in the United States.

Thus, two bracket dates are generated each time a manufacturing process is changed:

1. the introduction date of the first technique, and

2. its termination date based on adding ten years to the date of a replacement technique.

Volume 3   171

T. Stell Newman

The first date acts as the lower date before which the bottle is unlikely to have been made, while the second date is the general termination date for bottles having been made by the technique. For example, a bottle blown in a two-piece mold would not be expected to date before 1845. Since the two-piece mold was replaced by the automatic bottle making machine beginning in 1903, the bottle would have been unlikely to have been deposited in a site later than about 1913 (1903 + 10 years). Thus, the bottle was most likely deposited in a site between 1845 and 1913.

By using multiple manufacture traits it is possible to considerably refine this time span. For example, if the bottle described above were made with a snap case holding device, the dates would be 1855 to 1913, a ten year decrease in time span. If the bottle also had a crown cap, the dates would be from 1895 to the present. By using these dates in combination one can be reasonably sure that the bottle was deposited in a site between 1895 and 1913; hence, the level coterminous with the bottle most likely also dates from this time.

Use of the Bottle Dating Key

The bottle dating key presented here is based on a synthesis of data on bottle manufacture techniques given in the bibliography entries; however, sources are not shown on the key to preserve clarity. Some familarity with bottles and the manufacture techniques is necessary and this background may be obtained from sources in the bibliography.

The key poses questions about each bottle part that are to be answered by "yes" or "no". If an answer is "maybe" or "uncertain", then the "no" answer is to be used. "Yes" answers will route the reader to a date and then on to the next appropriate question. A "no" answer merely routes the reader to the next question. Directional arrows are provided to indicate the route where there might be confusion. Each major bottle part is dated separately; therefore fragments can be dated if they exhibit any of the traits covered by the key. By keeping track of the various dates produced, it is often possible to considerably refine the date for the whole bottle. Where two dates are given on the key, the first date is of the "no earlier than" type while the second is the date of a replacement technique increased by a factor of ten years to give a general termination date for the older technique.

The user is cautioned that this key is based upon generalizations and exceptions do exist. There are many variables affecting the termination date and this date must not be thought of as being infallable. An old saying may be appropriately revised as follows:

This bottle dating key is for the guidance of the wise and the obedience of fools.

References

FERRARO, PAT AND BOB
1966 *A Bottle Collector's Book.* Western Printing and Publishing Co., Sparks, Nevada.

KENDRICK, GRACE
1966 *The Antique Bottle Collector.* Edwards Brothers, Inc., Ann Arbor.

KENDRICK GRACE
1966 *Price Supplement to the Antique Bottle Collector.* Edwards Brothers, Inc., Ann Arbor.

LIEF, ALFRED
1965 *A Close-up of Closures: History and Progress.* Glass Container Manufacturers Institute, New York.

LORRAIN, DESSAMAE
1968 "An Archaeologist's Guide to Nineteenth Century American Glass." *Historical Archaeology 1968.* The Society for Historical Archaeology.

LUBRICATION
1962 "Blown Glass." *Lubrication,* Vol. 48, No. 8, pp. 109-128.

McKEARIN, GEORGE SKINNER AND HELEN
1959 *American Glass.* Crown Publishers, New York.

PUTNAM, H. E.
1965 *Bottle Identification.* H. E. Putnam, Fontana, California.

TIBBITTS, JOHN C.
1963 *Chips From the Pontil.* John C. Tibbitts, Sacramento.

TIBBITS, JOHN C.
1967 *John Doe, Bottle Collector.* The Little Glass Shack, Sacramento.

VAN RENSSELAER, STEPHEN
1969 *Early American Bottles and Flasks.* Revised Edition edited by J. Edmund Edwards. J. Edmund Edwards, Stratford.

YOUNT, JOHN T.
1967 *Bottle Collector's Handbook and Pricing Guide.* Action Printery, San Angelo, Texas.

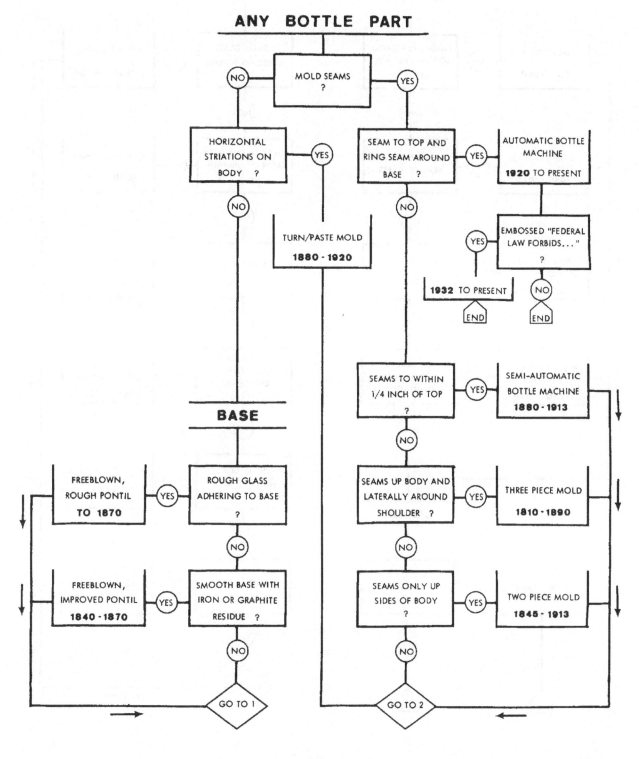

FIGURE 1.

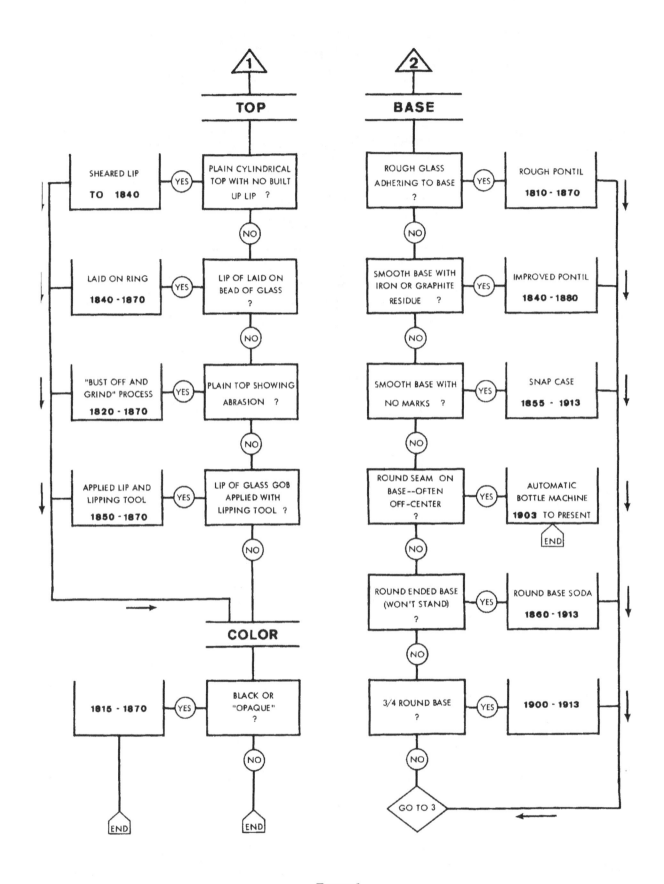

FIGURE 2

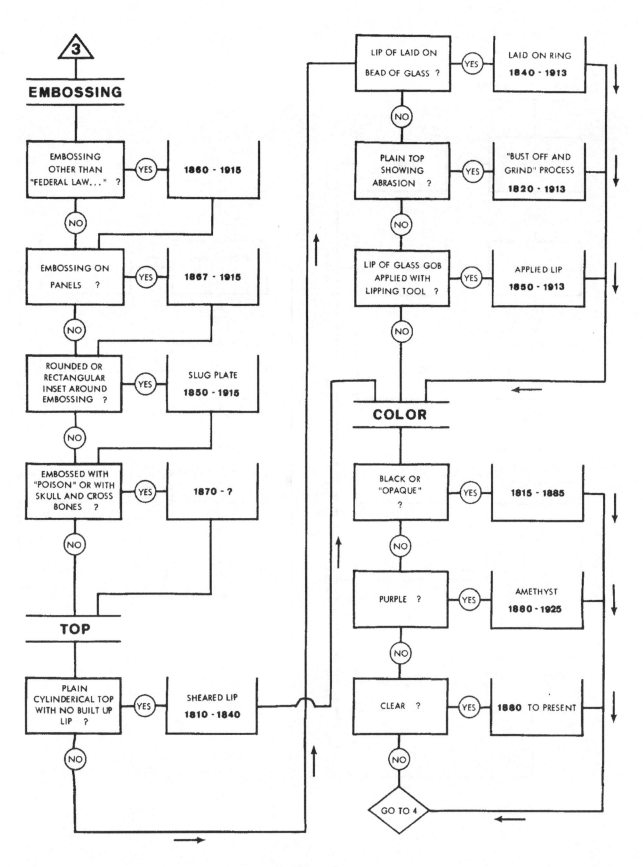

FIGURE 3

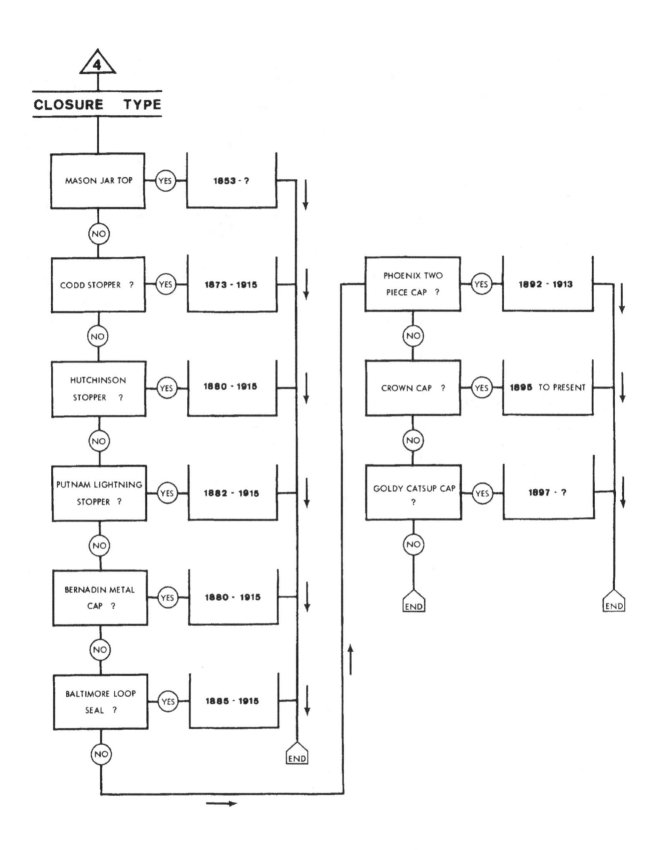

FIGURE 4

Identification and Dating of Japanese Glass Beverage Bottles

Douglas E. Ross

ABSTRACT

Japanese overseas migrants imported a variety of consumer goods from home, goods which have been recovered from Japanese, Chinese, and other archaeological sites. One class of imports granted only limited attention in the archaeological literature is glass beverage bottles, which are easily confused with their North American counterparts. Historical and archaeological data on identification and chronology of Japanese beer, soda, and sake bottles enhance their usefulness in dating sites and interpreting migrant lifeways.

Introduction

Accompanying the arrival of Chinese and Japanese migrants to North America and elsewhere, beginning in the late 19th century, was a diverse range of imported consumer goods that appears in abundance on archaeological sites. Ceramic table- and storage wares typically dominate the Asian components of these assemblages, but they also include beverage containers, smoking paraphernalia, pharmaceutical bottles, gaming pieces, coins, and articles associated with grooming and personal hygiene, among others. Existing archaeological literature addresses many of these artifact classes in depth, but one class receiving only limited attention is Japanese glass beverage bottles. In part, this may be a product of difficulties in distinguishing these vessels from bottles produced in Europe and North America, with which they share common morphology and manufacturing technology. In fact, in mixed assemblages or on sites without obvious Asian components, bottles of Asian origin may easily be confounded with their non-Asian counterparts. Nevertheless, in many cases it is possible to identify and date Asian specimens based on morphology and makers' marks, and to determine the bottles' probable contents. The following discussion outlines the manufacturing history and distinguishing characteristics of these vessels in an effort to enhance identification and interpre-

tive potential for archaeologists working on overseas Asian and non-Asian sites.

Although the archaeological literature on Japanese migrants and their descendants is still very modest, archaeologists have reported Japanese beer, soda, and sake bottles from sites in British Columbia, the western United States, and the Pacific Islands (Armstrong 1979; King and Parker 1984; Copp 1987; Costello and Maniery 1988; Tamir et al. 1993; Burton 1996; Greenwood 1996; Schaefer and McCawley 1999; Muckle 2001; Dixon 2004; Slaughter 2006; Ross 2009). This diverse range of sites is associated with Chinese and Japanese domestic and commercial deposits in urban and rural contexts, an urban neighborhood landfill, and World War II military fortifications and internment camps. In fact, most Asian-made beverage bottles found on Chinese sites are Japanese in origin. China did not industrialize as early as Japan and continued to ship most indigenous beverages in ceramic containers, manufacturing few Western-style beverage bottles until well into the 20th century (Godley 1986; Yang 2007).

Research for this report was conducted in conjunction with a study of Chinese and Japanese labor camps associated with an industrial salmon cannery (1885–1930) on Don and Lion islands along the Fraser River in British Columbia (Ross 2009). Before describing these bottles in detail, however, it is important to understand the history of alcohol and soft-drink production and consumption in Japan.

Alcoholic and Carbonated Beverages in Japan

Prior to the Meiji period (1868–1912), the dominant alcoholic beverage in Japan was sake, fermented from rice (14–16% alcohol). A stronger alcoholic beverage (25% or greater), known as *shochu*, distilled from a variety of materials including rice, barley, and sweet potatoes, was also common (Laker 1975:48; Perez 2002:195). Despite

Douglass E. Ross

the rise of large urban sake-brewing firms in the Tokugawa and Meiji periods, small-scale rural production for local consumption, including home brewing, remained widespread (Tanimoto 2006). Both before and during the Meiji period, brewers shipped sake in large wooden casks to urban shops, and customers purchased it in ceramic bottles, often bearing the name and address of the merchant (Kanzaki 1989:68–69; Kondo 1996:50; Gauntner 2002, 2004). The first glass sake bottles did not appear on the market until 1879, but the common 1 *sho* (1.8 L) bottles, usually sealed with lightning-type ceramic closures, began replacing wooden casks by the turn of the 20th century. By the end of the Taisho period (1912–1926) however, only a small proportion of sake was sold in glass bottles, and as late as 1940 only about 40% was bottled (Laker 1975:v; Gauntner 2004; Izumi 2005:27).

Production and consumption of beer and soda in Japan are a product of Meiji industrialization and Westernization. They are closely related to the broader processes through which Western foods were introduced and accepted into the Japanese diet in the late 19th and early 20th centuries. Laker's (1975, 1980) study of the role of entrepreneurs in the development of individual brewing companies between the 1870s and 1930s offers an abundance of valuable data. Unless otherwise noted, the following discussion relies exclusively on Laker's work, including Table 1, which provides a chronology of the major companies and brands of Japanese beer.

The first commercial brewers in Japan were an American and a German operating out of the Yokohama foreign settlement at the beginning of the 1870s. These and other foreigners were responsible for teaching local merchants how to brew beer and helped them open their own breweries. Brewers imported virtually all machinery, barley malt, yeast, and hops from Germany and the United States in these early years and for a long time afterwards; they even used empty beer bottles and wine barrels from imported beverages, along with cork stoppers strapped to the bottle with wire. Beer companies also purchased locally produced porcelain and glass bottles from a range of factories. In fact, development of glass manufacturing in Japan is closely tied to the rise of the beer industry. In the early years, the market for Japanese beer increased slowly and the product was largely a luxury item enjoyed by the rich (Laker 1975:30–40, 50–92, 246–247).

By 1906, the market for beer had increased significantly in Japan, due to a higher quality, standardized product sold at a lower cost and backed by extensive marketing. The earliest beers in Japan were English-style ales which were easier to brew, but joint stock companies increasingly turned to German-style lagers, which had a longer shelf life. Longevity was an asset for a developing industry that produced more than it could immediately sell. An attempt to monopolize the industry led to a merger of the three largest companies in 1906, which became the Dai Nippon Beer Company, later expanded by further mergers. By 1913, there were only four major firms left: Dai Nippon, the Kirin Beer Company, Kabuto Beer, and the Teikoku Beer Company. Dai Nippon dominated the Japanese beer industry until 1949, when American occupation authorities forced it to split into two companies, Asahi and Nippon. It was after 1906 that beer gained widespread popularity in Japan and companies approached self-sufficiency. They achieved this by sending technicians abroad and gaining increased control over the production of machines, bottles, and raw materials (Laker 1975:42–45, 156–177).

Two key problems associated with bottle manufacture were finding a low-cost means of mass production and a more efficient closure to replace the labor-intensive cork-and-wire method. Over the years breweries relied on a combination of imports and a series of local glass companies to supply their needs. Dai Nippon was a leader in expanding and reorganizing the bottle industry through purchase and consolidation. Starting in 1911, the company also introduced semi-automatic and automatic bottle-making machines from Europe and America. In that same year, it became the first Japanese company to introduce crown closures on its bottles, and others soon followed. In 1920, Dai Nippon purchased Nippon Glass Kogyo Company, founded in 1916, whose owner was the first to acquire machines and patent rights from the Owens Bottle Machine Company of Toledo, Ohio. By the 1920s, Dai Nippon was using either Graham or Owens machines in all its plants. Bottle sizes were not standardized until 1944, but beer was typically marketed in two sizes, with the larger size modeled after the London Bass Beer Company's 630.8 ml bottle, and the smaller size of half that volume. Laker notes that Dai Nippon often used different sizes of bottle at different breweries. By the 1930s, companies were even

9. Identification and Dating of Japanese Glass Beverage Bottles

Table 1. Major Japanese Beer Companies and Brands.

Company	Years Active	Brands (First Year)	Trademarks	Previous/Later Incarnations
Mitsuuroko Beer	1874–1901	Mitsuuroko (1874)		
Hakkosha Fermentation Company	1875–1893	Sakurada (1879)		Renamed Sakurada in 1890; became Tokyo Beer Company in 1893
Kaitakushi	1876–1886	Kaitakushi (1876) Sapporo (1886)		Sold to Okura in 1886, then to Sapporo in 1887
F. M. Beer Company	1881–1888	Tegata (1881)		
Asada Beer	1885–1910	Asada (1885)		
Japan Brewing Company	1885–1907	Kirin (ca. 1885)	Kirin	Sold to Kirin in 1907
Marusan Beer	1887–1906	Marusan (ca. 1887) Kabuto (ca. 1900)	Helmet	Renamed Nihon Daiichi, then Kabuto
Sapporo Beer Company	1887–1906	Sapporo (1886)		Merged into Dai Nippon in 1906
Hinode Beer	1890–1913	Hinode (1893)		Sold to Dai Nippon in 1913
Osaka Beer Company	1887–1906	Asahi (1892)	Sun rising from sea	Asahi name purchased from another brewer who had used it from ca. 1884; merged into Dai Nippon in 1906
Nippon Brewing Company	1887–1906	Yebisu (1889)		Merged into Dai Nippon in 1906
Tokyo Beer Company	1893–1907	Tokyo (ca. 1893)	Cockscomb	Sold to Dai Nippon in 1907
Tsingtao (China)	1903–1916	Tsingtao (ca. 1903)		Anglo-German brewery, sold to Dai Nippon in 1916
Dai Nippon Beer Company	1906–1949	Sapporo (1886) Asahi (1892) Yebisu (1889) Kabuto (ca. 1900) Tsingtao (ca. 1903) Union Season Vitamin Munchen	Sun (circle and dot)	Merger of Sapporo, Osaka, and Nippon in 1906; divided into Asahi and Nippon in 1949
Kirin Beer Company	1907–	Kirin (ca. 1885)	Kirin; KB monogram	Formerly Japan Brewery Company
Kabuto Beer	1907–1921	Kabuto (ca. 1900)	Helmet	Formerly Marusan, then Nihon Daiichi; merged into Nihon Beer Kosen in 1921
Teikoku Beer Company	1912–1929	Sakura (1913)		Company renamed Sakura in 1929
Takasago Beer Company (Taiwan)	1919–1939	Takasago (1920)		Sold to Dai Nippon, Kirin, and Sakura in 1939
Nichi-Ei	1920–1923, 1929–1934	Cascade (1920) Chiyoda Oraga (1930)		Sold to Dai Nippon in 1934
Nihon (Nippon) Beer Kosen Company	1921–1933	Kabuto (ca. 1900)		Merger of Nihon Seibin, Kabuto, and Teikoku Kosen in 1921; merged with Dai Nippon in 1933
Sakura Beer Company	1929–1943	Sakura (1913)		Merged with Dai Nippon in 1943

Source: Laker 1975.

grinding competitors' names off empty bottles and reusing them (Laker 1975:88, 247–262).

In addition to dominating the Japanese market, Dai Nippon created subsidiary companies in Korea and parts of China, occupied as a result of Japanese military expansion. As a result, export booms occurred during World War I and through the 1930s in Southeast Asia and the Pacific Islands. In 1916, following Japanese occupation of the German enclave in China, the company purchased the Tsingtao (Qingdao) brewery. This Anglo-German brewery had been operating since 1903 in the city of the same name. Dai Nippon and other beer companies also expanded into production of soft drinks and other non-alcoholic Western beverages, which began appearing in Japan in the 1870s. In 1907, the Teikoku Kosen Company established itself in Osaka with equipment purchased from the Apollinaris Soft Drink Company in England. It produced two soft drinks in dark green bottles with crown closures, Mitsuya (Three Arrows) and Kujaku (Peacock). Mitsuya cider became Japan's most popular soft drink. In 1921, the company merged with Kabuto Beer and the Nihon Bottle Manufacturing Company to become the Nihon Beer Kosen Company. It later merged with Dai Nippon in 1933 and became the largest soft-drink producer in the country. Dai Nippon had already introduced its own soft drinks: Ribbon Citron (1909), Ribbon Tansan (soda water) and Ribbon Raspberry (1914), and the orange-nectarine flavored Napolin (1923). In 1928 to 1929, Kirin brought out Kirin Lemon, Kirin Citron, Kirin Cider, and Kirin Tansan, although only the lemon sold well. The Teikoku Beer Company (later Sakura) produced Miyoshino Lemon and Miyoshino Cider from 1920 (Laker 1975:179–204).

Japanese Bottle Morphology

By combining archaeological and historical evidence, it is possible to provide a basic description of some of the most common Japanese beverage bottles. Morphological terms used here generally conform to those used on the Historic Glass Bottle Identification & Information Website (Society for Historical Archaeology 2009). In terms of size, the large and small Japanese beer bottles correspond to the range for quart-sized (22–30 oz., 650–887 ml) and pint-sized (11–16 oz., 325–473 ml) beer bottles in North America. For sake it is the smaller size (4 *go*, 720 ml) that corresponds to the North American quart bottle, and which is common on archaeological sites.

Sake Bottles

Many glass sake bottles found on North American sites are deep aqua blue in color, and have a champagne body style, with a ring finish and dimple holes for a porcelain lightning-type stopper, or a club sauce-like finish (Figures 1, 2). Some sake bottles also contain vertical embossed lines and makers' marks on the body and shoulder. A bottle recovered from a Japanese logging camp in the Seymour Valley in British Columbia displays the name of the Hakutsuru (White Crane) sake brewery founded in Osaka in 1743 (Muckle 2001; Hakutsuru Sake Brewing Co., Ltd. 2008). A lightning-type stopper from the Japanese fishing camp on Don Island, British Columbia is marked *Otsuka Seijou* (Otsuka Vintage) in blue transfer-printed characters, a sake brewery about which further details are needed (Ross 2009) (Figure 3). Slaughter (2006) identified remains of at least 20 glass sake jugs from Hawaiian breweries during a surface survey of Camp Amache, a Japanese internment camp in Colorado. They were typically clear, aqua, or green gallon jugs with small round handles on the shoulder and makers' marks embossed on the bases.

Merchants also shipped sake in cylindrical stoneware bottles, known as *saka-bin*, similar in shape to non-Asian champagne-style glass bottles with a bluish white or bluish grey exterior glaze (Stoltie 1995; Schaefer and McCawley 1999) (Figure 4). Such vessels are commonly associated with commercial establishments, and often have calligraphic, printed, or stamped marks of the sake brewer or retailer (Cort 1979:212; Jahn 2004:302). Some examples recovered from Mugu Fish Camp in California had remains of lead seals similar to those found on wine bottles (Schaefer and McCawley 1999). Remains of at least 152 *saka-bin*, in both large and small sizes, were recovered during salvage excavations in Walnut Grove, California (Costello and Maniery 1988:25). Japanese-style vessels known as *tokkuri* were also used, and consist of cylindrical or bulbous bottles of stoneware or porcelain with slender necks and a flaring rim, some with faceted or fluted sides (Stoltie 1995; Schaefer and McCawley 1999). Porcelain specimens generally function as domestic serving vessels.

Figure 1. Japanese beverage bottles from North American sites (*left* to *right*): Mitsuya Cider (turn mold, height 23.8 cm); Teikoku Beer (three-piece mold, height 29.9 cm); Dai Nippon Beer (Owens machine, height 28.7 cm); Hakutsuru Sake (three-piece mold, height 30.6 cm). (Photo by author, 2008.)

Figure 2. Machine-made Japanese *sake* bottle from Don Island with club sauce-like finish. (Photo by author, 2008.)

Figure 3. Porcelain lightning-type stopper from Don Island, marked "Otsuka Vintage." (Photo by author, 2008.)

Douglass E. Ross

Beer Bottles

Many Japanese beer bottles were mold blown in champagne or export body styles with mineral finishes, but after 1911 were also machine-made with crown finishes. Data from archaeological specimens suggest other manufacturing trends. Walnut Grove, California (Costello and Maniery 1988), Lovelock, Nevada (Armstrong 1979), and Don Island, British Columbia (Ross 2009) are pre-World War II Chinese and/or Japanese sites, and in all cases most beer bottles appear to be of the large size and amber in color. A Sakura bottle recovered from Walnut Grove has a champagne-style body, as does a complete mold-blown Dai Nippon bottle from the Asian American Comparative Collection (AACC) at the University of Idaho, and a similar Teikoku bottle in the reference collection at Simon Fraser University. One Dai Nippon specimen dating to the 1920s from the Seymour Valley logging camp, is machine made with an export body style (the Teikoku and Dai Nippon examples appear in Figure 1). Many bottles have embossed marks in Japanese or English on the shoulder and/or the body near the base, although marks on some fragmentary Dai Nippon bottles from Walnut Grove and Lion Island are acid etched (Costello and Maniery 1988; Ross 2009) (Figure 5, Table 2). Japanese bottle marks typically follow the pre-World War II convention of reading right to left, and characters presented in Table 2 conform to that practice.

The bottles from Chuuk (Truk) described by King and Parker (1984) are primarily machine-made with crown finishes, the majority coming from a Japanese World War II feature dating from 1941 to 1945. These bottles occur in both large and small sizes and in various shades of green and amber. Because the sample from earlier sites is so small, it is likely that pre-World War II bottles also vary in size and color. The two most common bottle types in the Chuuk assemblage are from Dai Nippon and Kirin, the

Figure 4. Stoneware *saka-bin* in the Asian American Comparative Collection at the University of Idaho, in one-liter (*left*) and half-liter (*right*) sizes (heights 28.5 cm and 21.7 cm). (Photo by author, 2006.)

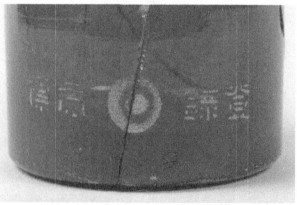

Figure 5. Embossed (*top*) and acid-etched (*bottom*) registered trademark for the Dai Nippon Beer Company. (Photos by author, 2008.)

former with an export body style and the latter a champagne body. Dai Nippon bottles are embossed in English or Japanese with a logo of the sun (a circle with a dot in the center), a monogram of the letters *DNB*, and a five-pointed star on the base, whereas Kirin bottles are embossed in Japanese and have the monogram *KB* (Figure 6a–c). Both styles are similar to specimens from the earlier Seymour Valley site. The Sakura bottle from Walnut Grove has the name embossed in English and Japanese, accompanied by a cherry blossom logo.

Soda Bottles

Japanese soft-drink bottles appear to occur only in the smaller size. Mitsuya (Three Arrows) cider bottles are commonly green and turn molded with a crown finish and an embossed ring around the neck. They have the name "Mitsuya" embossed in Japanese on the base, and a logo comprised of the fletching from three arrows (Figure 6d). One example from the Chinese bunkhouse on Lion Island also has the letter *B* inside a circle in the middle of the base, while another is machine made with the logo located on the body near the base (Ross 2009). Another green soft-drink bottle from Lion Island, blown in a three-piece cup-bottom mold and without a neck ring, has the name "Hirone Mineral Springs Company" embossed on the base. It bears a cherry blossom and wave crest above the shoulder (Figures 6e, 7a).

In addition to the well-known stoneware liquor bottles, Chinese medicinal liquor was sold in green or amber,

Table 2. Japanese Bottle Marks from the Chinese Bunkhouse on Lion Island.

Vessel	Color	Manufacture	Description	Mark	Translation
1	Amber	Indeterminate	Shoulder fragment	ルービ	Beer
				録登 (Toroku)	Registered
2	Emerald	Indeterminate	Base fragment	会式株 (part of Kabushiki Kaisha)	Company
3	Amber	Turn mold	Base fragment	造醸社会式 (part of Kabushiki Kaisha Jouzou)	Brewing Company
4	Amber	Turn mold	Base and partial body	造醸社会式株酒麦本日大 (Dai Nippon Bakushu Kabushiki Kaisha Jouzou)	Great Japan Beer Brewing Company
				標商録登+ sun (dot-in-circle) trademark	Registered Trademark
5	Amber	Mold blown	Base and partial body	——KOKU BEER (Teikoku Beer)	Imperial Beer
6	Olive	Turn mold	Partial base	Part of Three Arrows trademark	(Mitsuya cider)
7	Olive	Indeterminate	Body fragment	式株泉鉱(?) (part of Kosen Kabushiki Kaisha)	Mineral Springs Stock (Company)
8	Olive	Indeterminate	Shoulder fragment	内宮 (Miyauchi)	Company name?
9	Emerald	Mold blown	Partial base	Three Arrows trademark, backwards "5" on base	(Mitsuya cider)
10	Olive	Indeterminate	Body fragment	Dot-in-circle trademark	(Dai Nippon Beer Company)
11	Emerald	Turn mold	Base and partial body	矢ツ三 (Mitsuya) + Three Arrows trademark + *B*	Three Arrows (cider)
12	Olive	Turn mold	Base	矢ツ三 (Mitsuya) + Three Arrows trademark	Three Arrows (cider)
13	Olive	Three-piece mold	Nearly complete	社会式株泉鉱根広 (Hirone Kosen Kabushiki Kaisha) + waves and cherry blossom crest	Hirone Mineral Springs Company
14	Amber	Indeterminate	Partial base and body	本日大 (Dai Nippon) + sun (dot-in-circle) trademark	Great Japan (Beer Company)
				標商録 (part of Toroku Shyohyo)	Registered Trademark

Figure 6. Logos on Japanese beverage bottles: (*a*) and (*b*) Dai Nippon Beer; (*c*) Kirin Beer; (*d*) Mitsuya Cider; (*e*) Hirone Mineral Springs Company. (Drawing by author, 2008.)

Figure 7. (*a*) Hirone Mineral Springs Company bottle from Lion Island (height 23.4 cm). (Photo by author, 2008.); (*b*) Machine-made Chinese glass liquor bottle from the Asian American Comparative Collection, embossed with the name "Wing Lee Wai." (Photo by author, 2006.); (*c*) Deep aqua blue Asian bottle from Lion Island (turn mold, height 23.2 cm). (Photo by author, 2008.)

pint-sized glass bottles with or without embossed neck rings, similar to those used for Japanese soda (Figure 7b). Ritchie (1986:195–198) argues that these bottles may have been an early-20th-century alternative or successor to their ceramic counterparts. This may be why they are not reported from sites dating between the mid- and late 19th century, although further work is required to confirm the date of introduction. Some are embossed or have paper labels with "Wing Lee Wai," the name of a Chinese liquor producer. Unmarked bottles are difficult to distinguish from their Japanese counterparts, however, and specimens without neck rings could be Chinese, Japanese, or non-Asian. For example, six fragmentary bottles recovered from Lion Island comprising intact crown finishes and neck rings, three olive colored and three a deep aqua blue, could be either Chinese liquor or Japanese soda (Ross 2009) (Figure 7c). Base fragments with embossed marks suggest the olive bottles may all be from Mitsuya Cider, but the aqua blue specimens are more ambiguous. A common feature of many mold-blown Asian bottles, however, is an abundance of air bubbles in the glass and a tendency for them to be slightly asymmetrical.

Conclusions

Historical and archaeological data are providing important details on the functions and manufacturing histories of Japanese glass beverage bottles, which until now have received little attention in the archaeological literature. Further research in museums and archives in Japan will refine the interpretive potential of these Asian imports, especially the histories of individual companies and their manufacturing technology. Nevertheless, this brief overview offers a strong foundation for enhancing our understanding of the daily lives of Asian migrants in overseas contexts.

ACKNOWLEDGMENTS

A complete set of acknowledgments associated with this research accompanies my Ph.D. dissertation, but here I would like to highlight the individuals who made significant contributions to this particular component of my study. They are Scott Baxter, Leland Bibb, Ross Jamieson, Dana Lepofsky, Trelle Morrow, Bob Muckle, Takashi Sakaguchi, and Priscilla Wegars, all of whom shared valuable research data and expertise, or aided in shaping the ideas found herein. This research was funded in part by a Social Sciences and Humanities Research Council of Canada Doctoral Fellowship.

REFERENCES

Armstrong, Jane
1979   The Lovelock Bottles. In *Archaeological and Historical Studies at Ninth and Amherst, Lovelock, Nevada,* Eugene M. Hattori, Mary K. Rusco, and Donald R. Tuohy, editors, pp. 199–250. Nevada State Museum Archaeological Services, Carson City.

Burton, Jeffery F. (editor)
1996   *Three Farewells to Manzanar: The Archaeology of Manzanar National Historic Site, California.* Western Archaeological and Conservation Center, National Park Service, U.S. Department of the Interior, Publications in Anthropology 67, Tucson, AZ.

Copp, Stanley A.
1987   Excavation of the Marpole-Eburne Site (DhRs 25): An Urban Garbage Dump in an Early Vancouver Suburb. Report to the Heritage Conservation Branch, Victoria, BC, from Vancouver Community College, Langara Campus, Vancouver, BC.

Cort, Louise Allison
1979   *Shigaraki, Potters' Valley.* Kodansha International, Tokyo, Japan.

Costello, Julia. G., and Mary L. Maniery
1988   *Rice Bowls in the Delta: Artifacts Recovered from the 1915 Asian Community of Walnut Grove, California.* Institute of Archaeology, University of California, Occasional Paper 16, Los Angeles.

Dixon, Boyd
2004   The Archaeology of Rural Settlement and Class in a Pre-WWII Japanese Plantation on Tinian, Commonwealth of the Northern Mariana Islands. *International Journal of Historical Archaeology* 8(4):281–299.

Douglass E. Ross

Gauntner, John
2002   *The Sake Handbook.* Tuttle Publishing, Boston, MA.

2004   Sake in Glass Bottles. Sake World Sake e-Newsletter 53, John Gauntner's sake-world.com, Kamakura, Japan <http://www.sake-world.com/html/sw-2004_2.html>. Accessed 11 April 2008.

Godley, Michael R.
1986   Bacchus in the East: The Chinese Grape Wine Industry, 1892–1938. *Business History Review* 60(3):383–409.

Greenwood, Roberta S.
1996   Down By the Station: Los Angeles Chinatown, 1880–1933. *Monumenta Archaeologica* 18. Institute of Archaeology, University of California, Los Angeles.

Hakutsuru Sake Brewing Co., Ltd.
2008   Hakutsuru Sake. <www.hakutsuru-sake.com>. Accessed 22 May 2008.

Izumi, Sensuke
2005   *The Izumi Family: Seven Generations of Sake Making.* YS Publishing, East Setauket, NY.

Jahn, Gisela
2004   *Meiji Ceramics: The Art of Japanese Export Porcelain and Satsuma Ware 1868–1912.* Arnoldsche, Stuttgart, Germany.

Kanzaki, Noritake
1989   *Japanese Food: Customs and Traditions.* Understanding Japan No. 56, International Society for Educational Information, Tokyo, Japan.

King, Thomas F., and Patricia L. Parker
1984   *Pisekin Nóómw Nóón Tonaachaw: Archaeology in the Tonaachaw Historic District, Moen Island.* Center for Archaeological Investigations, Southern Illinois University, Occasional Paper No. 3, Carbondale.

Kondo, Hiroshi
1996   *The Book of Sake.* Kodansha International, Tokyo, Japan.

Laker, Joseph Alphonse
1975   *Entrepreneurship and the Development of the Japanese Beer Industry, 1872–1937.* Doctoral dissertation, Department of History, Indiana University, Bloomington. University Microfilms International, Ann Arbor, MI.

1980   Oligopoly at Home and Expansion Abroad: The Development of the Japanese Beer Industry, 1907–1937. *Proceedings of the Second International Symposium on Asian Studies, 1980,* pp. 313–324. Asian Research Service, Hong Kong.

Muckle, Bob
2001   The Seymour Valley Archaeological Project. *The Midden* 33(2):2–6.

Perez, Louis G.
2002   *Daily Life in Early Modern Japan.* Greenwood Press, Westport, CT.

Ritchie, Neville A.
1986   Archaeology and History of the Chinese in Southern New Zealand During the Nineteenth Century: A Study of Acculturation, Adaptation, and Change. Doctoral dissertation, Department of Anthropology, University of Otago, Dunedin, New Zealand.

Ross, Douglas E.
2009   Material Life and Socio-Cultural Transformation among Asian Transmigrants at a Fraser River Salmon Cannery. Doctoral dissertation, Department of Archaeology, Simon Fraser University, Burnaby, BC.

Schaefer, Jerry, and William McCawley
1999   A Pier Into the Past at Point Mugu: The History and Archaeology of a Japanese-American Sportfishing Resort. Report to U.S. Army Corps of Engineers, Los Angeles District, from ASM Affiliates, Encinitas, CA.

Slaughter, Michelle Ann
2006   An Archaeological and Ethnographic Examination of the Presence, Acquisition, and Consumption of Sake at Camp Amache, a World War II Japanese Internment Camp. Master's thesis, Department of Anthropology, University of Colorado, Denver.

Society for Historical Archaeology
2009   Historic Glass Bottle Identification & Information Website. Society for Historical Archaeology, University of Montana, Missoula <http://www.sha.org/bottle/index.htm>. Accessed 28 April 2009.

Stoltie, Bernard P.
1995   Tokkuri and Friends: A Salutation to the Japanese Sake Bottle. *Arts of Asia* 25(1):101–112.

Tamir, Orit, Scott C. Russell, Karolyn Jackman Jensen, and Shereen Lerner
1993   Return to Butte Camp: A Japanese-American World War II Relocation Center. Report to Bureau of Reclamation, Arizona Projects Office, from Archaeological Consulting Services, Ltd., Cultural Resources Report No. 82, Tempe, AZ.

Tanimoto, Masayuki
2006   Capital Accumulation and the Local Economy: Brewers and Local Notables. In *The Role of Tradition in Japan's Industrialization,* Masayuki Tanimoto, editor, pp. 301–322. Oxford University Press, Oxford, UK.

Yang, Zhiguo
2007   This Beer Tastes Really Good: Nationalism, Consumer Culture and Development of the Beer Industry in Qingdao, 1903–1993. *The Chinese Historical Review* 14(1):29–58.

Douglas E. Ross
Department of Archaeology
Simon Fraser University
8888 University Drive
Burnaby, BC Canada V5A 1S6

An Archaeologist's Guide to Nineteenth Century American Glass

DESSAMAE LORRAIN

The nineteenth century saw a vast increase in the amount and variety of glass produced in the United States. All of the manufacturing techniques used — freehand blowing, blowing into molds, pressing, drawing, and casting - and the coloring and decorating methods were known at the beginning of the century. The changes during the nineteenth century consisted of new ways to improve t h e known techniques to speed and simplify production. A major stimulus to the increased glass output was the development of mass transportation systems which opened new markets among the ever expanding and growing population. The invention of the steamboat in 1807, opening of the Erie Canal in 1825, and the tremendous increase in numbers of railroad lines after 1830 were important in fostering the increased demand for glass products.

In 1800 there were but nine glass houses operating in the United States. There were 108 glass houses in existence by 1837 but these were reduced to 78 by the depression of 1837-1840. With a return to prosperity, the years from 1846 to 1860 saw the establishment of 72 new glass factories in this country.

The types of articles produced by the glass works changed through the century. The earlier glass houses produced chiefly bottles and window glass with minor quantities of tableware for the local trade. As the century progressed, there was a tendency for increased specialization. Factories specializing in tablewares, such as the Boston and Sandwich Glass Co. at Sandwich, Massachusetts were able to transport their products far beyond the New England region via rail and barge. The bottle and window glass factories in turn ceased production of tablewares except for the occasional pieces turned out by the workers for their family and friends (McKearin and McKearin, 1948: 132-137).

The improvements and innovations in glass manufacture during the century resulted in observable changes in the glass products. Many of these changes are important for archeologists working with nineteenth century material. Some of the more important ones will be described. Others can be found in the date list. Emphasis is put on bottles because a survey of published and unpublished material from nineteenth century archeological sites showed that bottles constituted the bulk of excavated glass artifacts.

Before describing the changes during the nineteenth century, however, it is necessary to describe some of the manufacturing techniques in use by 1800 and the characteristics of the glass produced by each. The most common method for producing bottles and tableware was by blowing. The glass produced is called handblown, free-blown, or off-hand-blown. The form of the hand-blown objects is determined by the skill of the glass blower without the use of molds. Surfaces of handblown pieces are smooth and shiny and are without impressed designs or letters. Design may be cut, engraved, or etched into off-hand-blown pieces after they are cooled but these are not an intrinsic part of the glass. Decorative globs or threads of molten glass may be added to the object before it is cooled but they will also have smooth, shiny surfaces. The bases of off-hand-blown pieces will have a spot of rough glass, the pontil mark, in the center. The pontil rod is attached to the base with a glob of molten glass to hold the object while the blowpipe is struck off and the raw edge at the top is finished. Occasionally on fine wares the pontil mark is ground away or it may be smoothed over by fire polishing without completely removing it.

Another characteristic of blown glass is asymmetry. Free-blown bottles are frequently quite lopsided although a careful, skilled glass blower could make perfectly symmetrical pieces if he wanted to do so.

The most important thing to remember is that off-hand-blown glass will not have mold marks. Blown-in-mold bottles may or may not have mold marks but free-blown bottles cannot have them. Mold marks are the raised lines which result from blowing glass into hinged molds. The glass is forced into the seams where the sections of the molds are joined. These lines are rounded and feel quite smooth.

The form of mold-blown or blown-in-mold wares is determined by the mold rather than by the glass blower. Impressed design patterns or lettering are also effected by the mold. Two types of molds are used: full size contact m o l d s and partial size pattern molds. In using the latter the gather of molten glass is inserted in the mold and blown to impress the pattern into the glass. The glass is then removed from the mold and free-blown to full size. The common term for such wares is "pattern-molded and expanded". There will be no mold marks and the designs appear quite diffuse with rounded edges. Some articles with over-all patterns blown in full size contact molds may look very similar to pattern-molded and expanded pieces but they may be distinguished by feel unless the glass is too thick. On glass with an impressed design blown in a contact mold, the curvature of the inner surface is a negative image of the curvature of the outer surface; that is, it is concave on the inside where it is convex on the outside and vice versa (Fig. 1a). On pattern-molded and expanded glass, the curvature of the inner surface is a positive image of the curvature of the outer surface. It is convex on the inside where it is convex on the outside and concave on the

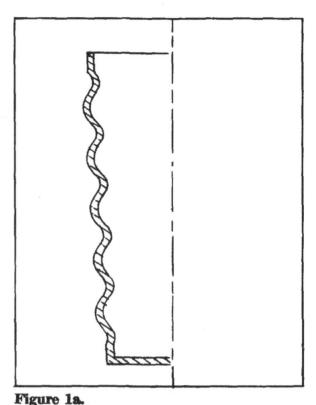

Figure 1a.

Cross-section of glass blown in contact mold.

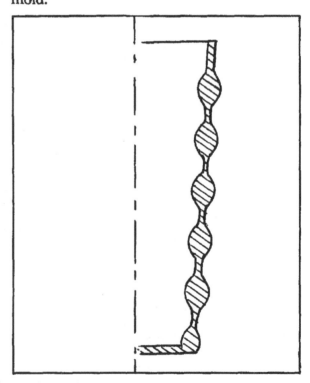

Figure 1b.

Cross-section of pattern-molded and expanded glass.

inside where it is concave on the outside (Fig. 1b). At the beginning of the nineteenth century, pattern molded and expanded glass was common but by 1850 it had practically disappeared in the United States. Modern pattern-molded and expanded pieces from Mexico have been imported in significant quantities into the border states recently.

In 1800 beads and glass tubing were produced by drawing as they had been for centuries and still are today. To draw a hollow tube the gaffer (glass blower) blows a small bubble in the gather to which the pontil rod is quickly attached by his assistant. The two men then walk rapidly in opposite directions pulling the glass bubble into a long thin tube. The hollow is extended throughout the length of the tube. The tube is then sliced into appropriate lengths for beads. Some beads were produced by pressing or other processes but these are quite rare in archeological sites. Beads in nineteenth century sites are less informative than other glass products.

Production of flat window glass in 1800 was by both the crown and cylinder methods. In the crown method a large glass bubble is blown, the pontil rod is attached, and the blowpipe removed. The bubble is reheated while the pontil is rotated rapidly. When sufficiently soft, the bubble is removed from the furnace and rapid rotation of the pontil continues until the glass bubble opens out into a large circular sheet. The size of the panes which can be cut from the sheet is restricted by the relatively small size of the sheet and the thick bull's eye of glass in the center where the pontil is attached. The bull's eye is translucent and cannot be used for transparent panes although it is sometimes used for decorative effect in windows or lamps. Crown glass varies considerably in thickness from the center to the edge of the sheet, so much so that the variation can usually be detected in sherds over an inch long. In larger sherds or whole panes, the curved distortion lines or waves can be seen in oblique light.

The cylinder method consists of blowing a large bubble of glass, then elongating it into a long cylinder by swinging. The closed distal end of the cylinder and the blowpipe are then removed, a lengthwise cut is made, and the cylinder is returned to the furnace and reheated until it falls

open into a flat piece of glass. Cylinder glass is more uniform in thickness and can yield larger panes. The distortion waves, which result from the unequal size of the inner and outer surfaces of the initial bubble, are straight in cylinder glass rather than curved as in crown glass. A sizeable sherd is necessary to detect them however. The usual tiny fragments from an archeological site are seldom identifiable as cylinder glass.

Another method for making flat glass is casting. The molten glass is poured onto a sand covered table and rolled out evenly. It is not transparent until it is ground and polished. The resulting product is plate glass. The cost of hand grinding plate glass in the nineteenth century made it so expensive that it was seldom used for anything except small mirrors. It is distinguishable from other flat glass by its clarity and lack of distortion.

Among the first of the changes in the

Figure 2a.

Bottle blown in a dip mold for body form with hand finished shoulders, neck, and mouth. The horizontal mold mark at the point where the shoulders start their inward slope does not show clearly in this photograph. The bottle has a pontil mark on a kick-up base.

nineteenth century was the use of hinged molds for bottles (Putnam, 1965: preface; McKearin and McKearin, 1948: 427, 428). Hinged molds were known previously but did not come into widespread use until about 1810. From 1790 until sometime after 1810, bottles were made by forming the body in a one piece dip mold and hand finishing the neck and shoulders (Fig. 2a). The three part mold, which was developed around 1810, consisted of a one piece body mold and a two piece hinged mold for the neck and shoulder (Figs. 2b, b¹). The lip continued to be hand finished throughout the century.

Another important discovery in 1810 was that of food processing by Appert in

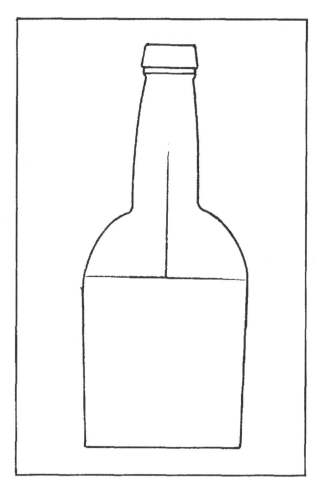

Figure 2b1.
Line drawing of bottle shown in 2b to emphasize the mold lines. Note their disappearance on the upper part of the neck due to reheating the neck to hand finish the mouth.

Figure 2b.
Bottle blown in a three piece hinged mold with hand finished mouth. Note that the horizontal mold line is lower on the body than the one on the preceeding bottle and that there are vertical mold lines above the horizontal one. The bottles shown in 2a and 2b both have a hammered metal appearance which does not show in the picture. The base of this bottle is dished with no pontil mark. A snap case was used to hold it while the mouth was finished.

France (Lief, n.d.: 6, 7; Wyatt, 1966: 14, 15). He found that foods would keep if they were bottled and cooked thoroughly. This greatly increased the demand for glass bottles and jars.

A major invention patented in 1827 was the pressing machine (McKearin and McKearin, 1948: 334). It enabled the glass houses to produce large quantities of attractive, inexpensive tableware. Pressed glass is identified by the sharply defined impressed patterns on the exterior and a smooth inner surface. The inner contour is produced by the plunger used to press the glass in the mold and thus has no one-to-one relationship to the outer curvature as in molded glass. Piece molds are used for pressed glass so it will have mold marks, usually three or four. If examined closely, they will be found to differ from those on mold-blown wares inasmuch as they are normally narrow and sharply ridged rather than smooth and rounded. The early pre-1850 pressed glass has a grainy finish and the background is usually stippled — these are the familiar "Lacy" patterns (Fig. 3a). Later pressed glass was fire polished to give a smooth reflective finish. The background stippling was then eliminated (Fig. 3b). By 1845 pressed glass was common in American households.

The two piece bottle mold began to re-

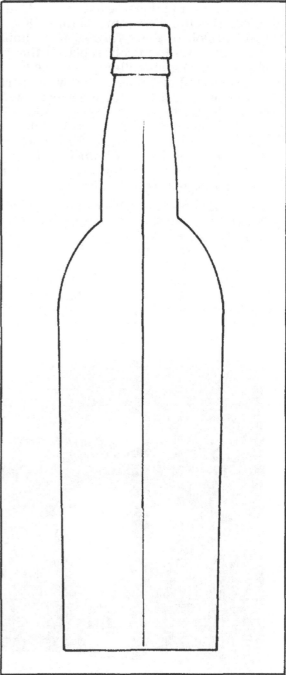

Figure 2c.
Bottle blown in a two piece hinged mold with hand finished mouth. Note that the vertical mold lines (2 of them on opposite sides) run the entire length of the bottle from base to neck. This bottle was made in a chilled iron mold and does not have the hammered metal look of the bottles shown in 2a and 2b. The base has no pontil mark; a snap case was used to hold it when the mouth was finished.

Figure 2c1
Line drawing of bottle shown in 2c to emphasize the mold lines and indicate their disappearance on the upper neck due to reheating when the mouth was finished by hand.

place the three piece mold between 1840 and 1850. The mold lines on a bottle made in a two piece mold run from the base up to the neck before fading out (Figs. 2c, c'). The disappearance of the mold lines on the upper neck is due to the reheating of the neck when additional glass was added to finish the lip. Sometime before 1850 an applied glob of glass formed by a lipping tool had almost entirely replaced the simple laid on ring of molten glass. The lipping tool consisted of a plug which was inserted in the neck and two forming arms which were clamped around the outside (Fig. 4a). The tool was then rotated so that the mold lines were removed and the glass was left with a swirled appearance. It is hoped that a firm date for the invention of the lipping tool will be established.

One of the most archeologically significant of the nineteenth century inventions was the snap case which was introduced around 1857 (Encyclopedia Britannica, 1949, Vol. 10: 410). This device replaced the pontil rod for holding bottles while the neck and lip were finished, therefore bottles held in a snap case will not have a pontil mark. The snap case consisted of four curved, padded arms which could be

Figure 3a.
Pressed glass bowl showing early "Lacy" type pattern with stippled background. (This is a modern reproduction.)

Figure 3b.
Pressed glass bowl with "peacock feather" design showing a typical later pressed glass design without background stippling.

clamped around the bottle (Fig. 4b). It occasionally left slight indentations on the side of the bottle but usually there is no mark. If a bottle has a hand finished lip and mold marks but no pontil mark, it can be assumed that a snap case was used.

The Mason jar for home canning was patented in 1858 (Lief, n. d.: 12). Most house sites occupied after that date should yield at least some Mason jars and their zinc caps.

About 1867 the first lettered panel bottles appeared (Moore, 1924: 255, 256). These were usually square or rectangular bottles with recessed panels on one or more sides on which were raised letters giving the name of the contents and frequently the city and state of the manufacturer of the contents. These bottles were most often used for patent medicines. The initials of the bottle manufacturer were sometimes impressed on the base but little work seems to have been done in tracking down the factories and determining when they operated and what years they used a particular imprint on their bottles.

Sometime around 1870 an improvement in the method of manufacturing the bottle mold resulted in the "chilled iron" mold (Ferraro and Ferraro, 1966:3; Watson, 1965:43). This process made it possible to

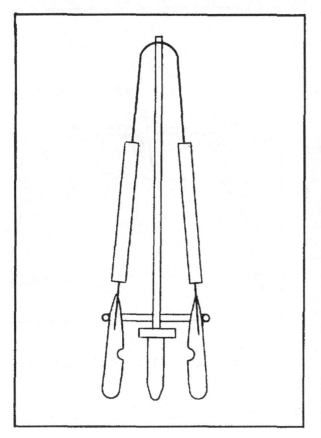

Figure 4a.
Line drawing of a lipping tool used for finishing bottle mouths. Note the central plug, the hinged patterned arms, and the band which clamped the arms together. When used the tool was rotated so no mold marks were left.

produce a very smooth interior surface on the mold and therefore a smooth exterior surface on the bottle. Before this, bottles blown in contact molds usually had an irregular surface resembling hammered metal. A bottle with a wavy or pebbly surface resembling hammered metal was blown in a contact mold whether mold lines can be found or not. Hand-blown or pattern-molded and expanded bottles never have such a surface but are instead smooth and shiny because all small irregularties are erased when the bubble is expanded to form the bottle.

Between 1860 and 1895 a large number of stoppers or closures were invented and patented. Most died a-borning but a few achieved widespread popularity and may be encountered in the excavation of nineteenth century sites. The almost universal

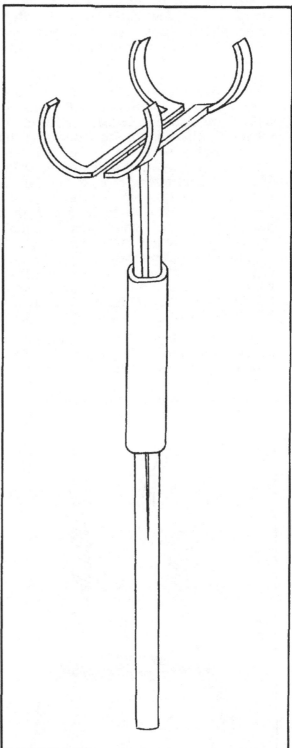

Figure 4b.
Line drawing of a snap case used to hold a bottle while the neck was reheated and finished by hand with the addition of molten glass. The snap case arms were closed around the bottle by the moveable ring clamp shown on the shaft.

closure before mid-century was the cork stopper. The few internal and external screw thread tops were produced would be rare and unexpected in an excavation. Some of the more popular closures invented in the second half of the century were the internal glass-ball stopper patented by Hiram Codd in England in 1860 (the U. S. patent was issued in 1873), the Hutchinson stopper consisting of an internal rubber gasket and a wire loop (Fig. 4c) which was a U. S. invention patented in 1872 or 1879; the Lightening stopper for jars and bottles which was patented in Europe by Charles de Quillefeldt in 1875 and an improved version of which was patented in the U. S. by Henry Putnam in 1882 (Fig. 4d), and the Crown cap — so common today on soft drink and beer bottles — which was patented by William Painter of Baltimore in 1892 (Fig. 4e), (Lief, n. d.: 13-19; Ferraro and Ferraro, 1966:15-18).

A semi-automatic bottle machine was developed in 1881 (Meigh, 1960:3). Bottles produced by this machine will have mold

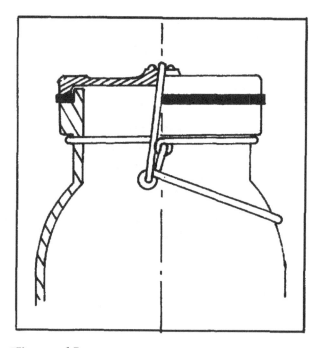

Figure 4d.
Lightening type closure with iron bail and lever.

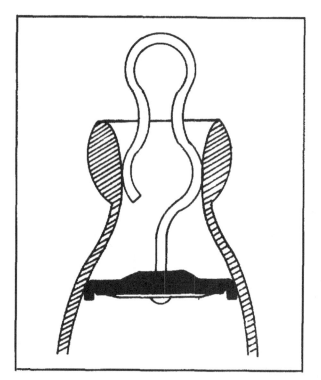

Figure 4c.
Hutchinson type stopper. To open a bottle so stoppered, the iron wire loop was struck sharply driving the stopper into the bottle. The resulting sound gave rise to the term "pop" bottles.

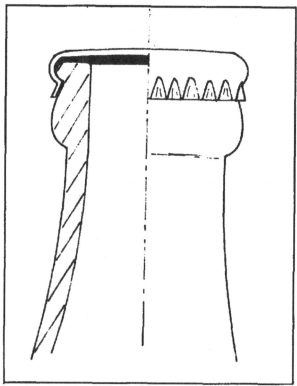

Figure 4e.
Crown type closure.

lines running up to the lip but not on the top of the rough lip. The machine was not widely distributed however, and the bottles produced were comparatively few in number.

A fully automatic bottle machine was patented in 1903 by Michael Owens (Meigh, 1960:7). Bottles produced by the automatic machine have continuous mold lines all the way up the sides and onto the top of the lip. By 1920 the changeover to automation by the commercial glass industry was complete. A few hand-blown or mold-blown bottles may still be produced as novelties by small glass houses but they cannot compete with the machine-made bottles in the commercial market.

The dateable changes in nineteenth century glass involve manufacturing techniques. It therefore behooves archeologists to learn the distinguishing characteristics of the products of these techniques so they can be identified and dated when encountered in the course of excavation. A description of glass pieces in a site report should include the manufacturing process used and the criteria used to determine it. This is often overlooked or ignored. Many descriptions list only the color and degree of patination and are virtually useless for identification and comparison. Throughout the nineteenth century all colors of glass were produced. Color should be mentioned in a description, preferably by using a standard color chart, but it should be considered one of the minor attributes. The degree of patination depends on the glass formula and the conditions of the environment to which the glass object is exposed (soil, water, air, sun, etc.). Some glass patinates very rapidly unless carefully protected; some will patinate hardly at all. Unless the glass formula is determined and the environment analysed, the degree of patination is not very informative but should, of course, be mentioned.

The following hierarchy of categories has been found useful for describing and classifying glass collections from archeological sites. It does depend on complete specimens or large segments of complete pieces. A handful of small sherds is not very informative and can be dismissed in a few short sentences in most cases.

I. **Storage Vessels** (or Table Service, Flat Glass, Beads, Miscellaneous Glassware)

II. **Bottles** (or Jars)

III. **Hand Blown** (or Blown in Contact Mold, Pattern Molded and Expanded, Machine Made)

IV. **Description** (manufacturing marks, form, design, color, patina, size, etc.) See Wilson (1961) for an example of a useful descriptive classification.

DATE LIST OF NINETEENTH CENTURY CHANGES

ca. 1810	Three piece hinged bottle mold introduced.
1810	Appert discovers how to preserve foods for storage, uses glass jars and bottles with wired on cork stoppers.
ca. 1820	First historical flasks.
ca. 1825	Octagonal medicine bottles, later followed by oval shapes, tooled lips.
1827	Pressing mold machine patented.
1827-1850	Period of Lacy pressed glass patterns
1830	No Masonic pictorial flasks after this date.
ca. 1840	Two piece hinged bottle mold.
before 1850	Lipping tool for finishing bottles (Ferraro and Ferraro, 1961, say 1850-1860 but I have seen earlier bottles finished with a lipping tool).

after 1850	Very little crown (flat) glass produced after this in U. S.
1857	Snap case introduced to replace pontil rod for finishing bottles.
1858	Mason jar patented.
1850-1880	Glass balls for trap shooting.
1860's	Kerosene lamps appear.
1861	First lead glass medicine bottles. Shortly after this "French squares" — tall, four-sided bottles with beveled edges — were put on the market.
1867	First lettered panel bottles.
1860-1900	Heyday of bitters (patent medicine) craze.
after 1868	Most figure bottles are post civil war.
ca. 1870	Chilled iron mold introduced.
after 1870	Historical flasks are rare.
1871	Pressed glass bottle fire extinguisher patented.
1872 or 1879	Hutchinson stopper patented.
1873	U. S. patent for internal glass ball stopper. (Patented in England in 1860).
1879	Edison's first light bulb — hand-blown.
1881	Semi-automatic bottle machine.
1882	Lightening fastener patented in U. S.
Mid 1880's	First milk bottles.
1892	Crown caps for bottles patented.
1891-1893	Safety glass with imbedded wire mesh produced.
1903	Owens automatic bottle machine patented.

References

ENCYCLOPEDIA BRITANNICA
1949 Glass. Vol. 10: 398-413.

FERRARO, PAT, and BOB FERRARO
1966 **A Bottle Collector's Book.** Western Printing and Publishing Company, Sparks, Nevada.

LIEF, ALFRED
n.d. **A Close-up of Closures.** Glass Containers Manufacturers Institute, New York.

McKEARIN, GEORGE, and HELEN McKEARIN
1948 **American Glass.** Crown Publishers, New York.

MEIGH, EDWARD
1960 **The Development of the Automatic Glass Bottle Machine.** Glass Manufacturers' Federation, London.

MOORE, N. HUDSON
1924 **Old Glass, European and American.** Frederick A. Stoles Company, New York.

PUTNAM, H. E.
1965 **Bottle Identification.** Jamestown, California.

WATSON, RICHARD
1965 **Bitters Bottles.** Thomas Nelson and Sons, New York.

WILSON, REX L.
1961 **A Classification System for 19th Century Bottles.** Arizoniana, Vol. II, No. 4: 2-6.

WYATT, VICTOR
1966 **From Sand — core to Automation: A History of Glass Containers.** Glass Manufacturers' Federation, London.

An Annotated Bibliography of Bottle Manufacturer's Marks

Bill Lockhart

Although most people are familiar with *Bottle Makers and Their Marks*, the epic volume by Julian Harrison Toulouse, there have been several other publications addressing manufacturer's marks used by glass factories producing bottles. To the best of my knowledge, this is a complete list of books and other reliable sources that attempt to classify marks of this type. These are reviewed in chronological order.

Knittle, Rhea Mansfield

1927   *Early American Glass*. Appleton-Century, NY.

Knittle's work is the earliest attempt at manufacturer's mark classification I have been able to find. The marks she addressed were almost all from the 19th century. On pages 441-442, she noted 46 marks arranged in alphabetical order in three columns that listed the marks, the manufacturing company, and the city of location. Knittle made no attempt to date the marks, and, like most of these early works, she made no attempt to cite her sources.

Jones, May

1963   *The Bottle Trail*, Volume 3. Nara Vista, NM.

May Jones is one of the true pioneers of bottle research. Despite her isolation in the small town of Nara Vista, NM, she built a network of bottle collectors that extended throughout the U.S. and included such noteworthy researchers as Grace Kendrick, author of *The Antique Bottle Collector*, itself a pioneer work in the field often cited by archaeologists and collectors, and Julian Harrison Toulouse, reviewed later in this bibliography.

Jones wrote a total of nine lengthy newsletters between September 1961 and February 1968. Because she was unlettered, rural, and wrote in a rambling, colloquial style, many dismiss her work. They are foolish. Jones collected information from her vast network of collectors, and wrote numerous letters to glass houses, breweries, food packagers, and others connected with glass containers. She was an inveterate reader and shared her knowledge freely.

Volume 3 of *The Bottle Trail* was her first look at manufacturer's marks. At this point, she made no attempt to be comprehensive but illustrated a number of marks along with her comments about them including a letter from a Mr. Caroll of Anheuser-Busch giving his opinions about marks that may have appeared on bottles used by that company.

Jones, May

1965   *The Bottle Trail*, Volume 5. Nara Vista, NM.

In 1965, Jones produced her first tables of manufacturer's marks. She included very few dates at that point but satisfied herself by attempting to match marks with factories. In this volume, she was also the first to illustrate the Owens-Illinois Glass Co. mark and correctly identify the meanings of the accompanying numbers by reproducing a six-page letter from Toulouse.

Jones, May

1966   *The Bottle Trail*, Volume 6. Nara Vista, NM.

In Volume 6, Jones began to make a serious contribution. She produced two tables; one of older marks (mostly from beer bottles) and the other of more recent logos. The table of newer marks identified 85 with appropriate companies, although she added very few dates. The table of older marks, however, included illustrations, company identification, and frequent dates for 38 marks along with several variations. Her illustrations were excellent and contained details often missing from archaeological reports and collectors' literature. Many of the dates were remarkably close to those used by Toulouse and ones we have subsequently discovered.

Jones, May

1968   *The Bottle Trail*, Volume 9. Nara Vista, NM.

Jones' final effort, Volume 9, concentrated on the marks shown in her older table from Volume 6 but presented all the information she had been able to amass. In some cases, the information was quite impressive for the time. It included information I have still not found in any other source. She produced, for example, a large volume of information on the Missouri Glass Co., including city directory data that placed the factory in business continuously from 1859 to 1911. Toulouse completely ignored this information when compiling his data for the M. G. Co. mark found on beer bottles from the 1880-1900 period. After Volume 9, however, Jones faded into obscurity.

Peterson, Arthur G.

1968   *400 Trademarks on Glass*. Washington College Press, Takoma, MD.

Peterson's small (54 pages) book is divided into three sections. The first "Trademarks on Glassware, 1860-1914" deals with marks registered for tableware. Section II "Lamps and Accessories" also deals with registered marks. The sections pertinent to this discussion are section III "Bottles and Jars" and an appendix entitled "Some Trademarks Introduced After 1914."

Although section III is useful, it should be noted that these are trademarks used by the company rather than marks appearing on bottles and jars. For example, Peterson illustrated the upside-down bottle superimposed over a "G" used by the Graham Glass Co., Evansville, IN, first used in 1914. The logo appeared extensively in company literature and advertisements; however, it was never used on glass bottles. Graham used an extensive and complex method of factory identification, date codes, and mold marks on the heels of its bottles but did not include the "Bottle-and-G" mark.

The final section is on trademarks after 1914 and describes(but did not illustrate) marks actually found on bottles along with the date each mark was first used. These dates are sometimes at odds with those found in Toulouse and are generally more accurate. Unfortunately, Peterson failed to include end dates and only listed 37 marks on pages 48-49.

Toulouse, Julian Harrison
1969   *Fruit Jars*. Thomas Nelson & Sons, Camden, NJ.

In this book, Toulouse made an attempt to catalog all known fruit-jar manufacturer's marks. The work is impressive. He arranged the marks in alphabetical order, a style that sometimes makes it difficult to find a mark and even more arduous to locate a company. This difficulty is exacerbated by the lack of a comprehensive index. He solved that problem to a certain extent, however, by including an index of sorts entitled "Fruit-Jar Manufacturers and Their Jars." This section lists all companies identified in the book and the marks on the jars; however, it fails to include page numbers. The main section of the book showed drawings (and occasional photographs) of marks found on fruit jars and a short description, date range, and discussion of each mark and the glass house that used it. Although he failed to include any company histories (an oversight he corrected in his second book), he included sections on "Men Who Made Fruit-Jar History," "Using the Jars," "Dating the Fruit Jar," "The Shape of the Fruit Jar," "Patent Chronology," and "Fruit Jar Seals." The added chapters are very useful, especially to a researcher unfamiliar with fruit jars.

Toulouse, Julian Harrison
1971   *Bottle Makers and Their Marks*. Thomas Nelson, NY.

Often considered the "bible" for manufacturer's marks, this epic work is astounding in its breadth. By his own count, Toulouse offered information on more than 1,200 different marks found on glass bottles and jars. The book is filled with information that could only have come from a factory "insider." Toulouse, in fact, spent his career in the glass manufacturing industry before he wrote his two books on marks for collectors.

The book is all the more remarkable when you consider that he accomplished his task without all the modern conveniences which are almost essential in compiling large databases today. He had no Internet, no email, and no access to eBay auctions (a great source for empirical bottle information). Often, his information about marks came from collectors writing in to organizations like that of May Jones (see above), another early pioneer in the field of marks on glass. He followed such information collecting with calls to glass manufacturers, letters to companies, a review of the available literature, and research in city directories. The sheer volume of information he presented is daunting. The study is arranged in alphabetical order by marks. While this enables a researcher to locate fairly easily a specific mark, it separates the various company histories into choppy sections and makes tracing histories or cross-checking references very difficult. It also resulted in frequent contradictions.

Toulouse's work, however, has a downside. It is riddled with typographical errors, especially in the recording of dates. He is frequently a century off, for example on page 317, he dates the mark LAMB from "1855 to 1964" - the dates are 1955 to 1964. He is often also a decade away from the correct date, such as his dating of the L-G mark from 1946 to 1954 (page 321). Other sources place the start at 1936, and empirical evidence backs the earlier decade as a more correct date. In another instance, Toulouse (page 263) had Christian Ihmsen bringing his two sons into the business in 1850, when his sources placed the date at 1860.

Toulouse frequently miscopied dates from his sources. An example is his statement (page 132) that W. Cunningham & Co. changed its name to Cunningham & Ihmsen in 1865; his sources both dated the change at 1857. Another example is when he placed Ihmsen's retirement (page 120) at 1879; his source provides a date of 1878. Toulouse also contradicted himself such as when he placed the closing of Cunninghams & Co. at 1909 on page 99 but at 1907 on page 120. Since he was not specific as to his sources, we do not know which date is correct. There are so many typographic errors in the book that most of his dates should be considered approximate.

He also missed the mark (pardon the pun) by accepting the identification of marks that apparently do not exist. Our research group has been unable to find several marks that are shown in *Bottle Makers and Their Marks* despite the use of archaeological databases, eBay, Internet searches, a large array of collectors networks, and numerous books and articles. These apparently bogus marks include IG on page 264, attributed to the Illinois Glass Co., C. C. Co. (page 117), supposedly used by C. Conrad & Co. (their actual mark is much more complex and interesting), and five out of the nine marks on pages 268 and 269 that he claimed were used by the Illinois Pacific Glass Company (or Corporation or Coast Co.). We have found only four marks used by the various incarnations of Illinois Pacific, one of which he did not list.

Another major failing of the work is the general exclusion of date codes and other marks on bottle bases and heels. These often provide helpful information and show specific dates of manufacture. In his introduction, he made it clear that he considered embossed numbers to be of little or no help in identifying or dating glass.

Bottle Makers and Their Marks is essential in any research into manufacturer's marks, but its information should be compared with other data as well as checking the sources used by Toulouse wherever possible.

Herskovitz, Robert M.
1978   *Fort Bowie Material Culture*. University of Arizona Press, Tucson.

Herskovitz only presented a short discussion (pages 7-11) about manufacturer's marks and only those associated with beer bottles. However, his disagreement with some of Toulouse's attributions and the assertion of alternative explanations makes this a worthwhile addition to a research library. On pages 8 and 9, Heskovitz offered a table of 76 marks found at Fort Bowie (1862-1894) that included the basemarks, the number of bottles or bases on which each mark was found, additional letters/numbers accompanying the marks, name of the manufacturer (where known), and date ranges. Many of his attributions, however, came from Toulouse.

11. An Annotated Bibliography of Bottle Manufacturer's Marks

Ayers, James E., William Liesenbien, Lee Fratt, and Linda Eure
1980 Beer Bottles from the Tucson Urban Renewal Project, Tucson, AZ. Unpublished manuscript, Arizona State Museum Archives, RG5, Sg3, Series 2, Subseries 1, Folder 220.

This unpublished manuscript is beyond a doubt the best and most comprehensive study of beer bottles that has been undertaken to date. The authors deserve a standing ovation for every aspect of the research except their failure to publish. I postponed citing the study in hopes of its publication, but it is time the work became more publicly known.

The study is divided into three untitled sections. The first of these, 60 pages in length, dealt with the history, variations, and manufacturing techniques pertinent to beer bottles. This section was well presented and is a must-read for anyone researching beer bottles. The second section (pages 1-44 plus five unnumbered pages) discussed specific manufacturing companies and the marks they used. The authors chose to present the information alphabetically by company instead of by mark. Although this makes it more difficult to locate a specific mark, the company information is condensed into a single section.

The manufacturers section is very helpful in that it corrects, contradicts, and offers alternative explanations for many of the marks, dates, and information set forth in Toulouse (see above). For example, where Toulouse offered only two possible companies for the use of the M. G. Co. mark (neither of which fit the date range for the bottle style and manufacturing techniques), Ayers and associates listed four additional possibilities and discussed their likelihood. Of great importance, the authors included specific citations for their sources. This is most helpful in any serious study of marks.

The final section consisted of unnumbered pages with drawings of bottle shapes, finishes, and manufacturer's marks. These are detailed and include heel marks along with numbers and letters accompanying the marks themselves. This section is helpful but is not referenced to the second section. I am certain the researchers intended to connect the two parts, but the report is incomplete in this respect. A final problem is that the references for the bottle section are not listed separately from those for the rest of the Tucson report.

Overall, this is a very important study, one that is almost essential for any subsequent research on beer bottles or any comprehensive study of bottle marks.

Giarde, Jeffery L.
1980 *Glass Milk Bottles: Their Makers and Marks*. Time Travelers Press, Bryn Mawr, CA.

Giarde specialized in milk bottles and addressed 201 marks used on them. He followed the style used by Toulouse, cataloging the marks alphabetically. Along with dates and historical information, he also discussed specific points about milk bottle manufacture that was not pertinent to other containers produced by the same company. He frequently listed marks not found in Toulouse along with the presence/absence of date codes and other marks specific to each company. He provided an especially comprehensive look at milk bottles produced by the Owens-Illinois Glass Co.

In a second section, Giarde addressed other marks (e.g. REGISTERED SEALED 1-11-14) and how to interpret them, pyroglazing (the applied color labeling used after 1933), war slogans, patent numbers, other dating elements, and color. Giarde's dates are frequently obtained empirically and are generally accurate, although he occasionally included marks and/or dates taken directly from Toulouse or Peterson. This is an excellent reference for anyone seeking information on milk bottles and their marks.

Wilson, Rex
1981 *Bottles on the Western Frontier*. University of Arizona Press, Tucson.

Wilson's section on manufacturer's marks was restricted to Appendix A, pages 113-130, although he included brief references to the marks, identification, and date ranges throughout the text. Except for a very short discussion on marks found on ceramic bottles, the section only discussed marks on bases of beer bottles found at Fort Union. Wilson explained, "The marks are depicted here because the bottles can be dated safely between 1863 and 1891 [the dates Fort Union was open]" (Wilson 1981:113). Wilson included no dates for each mark but attributed them to factories in most cases. He illustrated each mark found on the site along with accompanying letters, numbers, and symbols. Wilson provided an excellent study of mark variation.

Roller, Dick
1983 *Standard Fruit Jar Reference*. Privately published, n.p.

Although not a book about manufacturer's marks, Roller's fruit-jar identification manual deserves a place in the listing. The main section of the work used drawings, photos, and descriptions to identify different types of fruit jars and, where possible, to name the manufacturer and set the approximate date range. This is in alphabetical order by mark, maker, or name embossed on the fruit jar (e.g. STANDARD). In some cases, he included background information, although he did not cite his sources. Roller appended his book with sections of patents relating to fruit jars, relevant trademarks, biographical sketches of some "fruit jar pioneers," and company histories of the Keystone Glass Works, Sheet Metal Screw Company, Mason Manufacturing Company, Consolidated Fruit Jar Company, Hero Glass Works, Ball Brothers, Hazel Glass Company, and Kerr Glass Manufacturing Company. Unfortunately, he did not include an index. Although currently out of print and difficult to find, the book contains useful supplemental information.

Bethman, David
1991 *The Pioneer Drug Store: A History of Washington State Drug Stores and Their Bottles.* Privately printed, n.p.
    Although Bethman's book is a study of Washington State drugstore bottles, he included a seven-page section on manufacturer's marks found on drugstore bottles. Bethman addressed 26 marks specific to drugstore bottles, many of which are absent from Toulouse. Others, like the six marks used by Whitall Tatum and Company are expansions on the Toulouse information. Although the book is difficult to find, the information is well worth the effort if you are involved in the study of drugstore bottles.

Richardson, Lillian C., and Charles G. Richardson
1992 *The Pill Rollers: A Book on Apothecary Antiques and Drug Store Collectibles.* Old Fort Press, Harrisonburg, VA.
    The Richardsons only included a single page (page 162) that is pertinent to this bibliography. Their approach was to research dates for marks that identified pharmaceutical companies. They identified and dated 23 such marks and noted whether the marks were placed on bases, shoulders, or (in one case) sides of the bottles. Although only useful for pharmaceutical bottles, the list provides another level of identification available to researchers.

Creswick, Alice
1995 *The Fruit Jar Works, Vol. I, Listing Jars Made Circa 1820 to 1920's.* Douglas M. Leybourne, N. Muskegon, MI.
    Although this book is very specialized (fruit jars, as the title stated), it is a great identification guide—an attempt to catalog every fruit jar made during the 1820-1920 period. This book could have been devised with archaeologists in mind (it was not) because of the way it is formatted. Almost every jar is illustrated, including the lids, bases, and reverse sides where embossing is present. This is ideal for anyone dealing with fragmentary glass as well as complete jars. Not only does Creswick include major variations, she shows even minor discrepancies. For example, she shows illustrations of 21 variations in basal markings on one variety of Mason jar. In addition, she provides descriptions that included the identification of the manufacturer (when known) and the date range of production. She often identified manufacturers and date ranges not found in other sources.
    Creswick began her book with a brief history of canning and followed the identification section (the main body of the book) with an extensive appendix on patents and copyrights. A second appendix (although she did not use the term) was a 12-page list of fruit jar manufacturers that included many entries not found in any other sources I have reviewed. She finished with a brief history of jar makers from Allegheny County, PA, in 1876 and historical sketches of several jar makers. My only complaint about the work is that it is out of print and quite expensive. The two-volume set is generally priced from ca. $275. I have been unable to obtain a review copy of Volume II (fruit jars after 1920), but I suspect it contains the same high-quality information.

Porter, Bill
1996 *Coke Bottle Checklist.* Privately printed, n.p.
    Porter operated in another specialty area—the "hobble-skirt" Coca-Cola bottle. On pages 3 to 6, he enumerated all manufacturer's marks known to be found on Coke bottles along with specific information about marks that are only found on hobble-skirt bottles. Coca-Cola demanded that each manufacturer follow the Coke scheme for marking, so marks were sometimes different from those otherwise used by the same companies (e.g. CHATT for Chattanooga Glass Co. instead of the usual Circle C mark) and were placed in different locations on the Coke bottles. He continued (pages 6-8) by providing other useful information specific to Coke bottles including a discussion of date codes and locations for all marks. Although a specialty area, Porter's work is accurate and useful.

Whitten, David
2004 "Glass Factory Marks on Bottles." <http://www.myinsulators.com/glass-factories/bottlemarks.html>.
    This is one of the most useful and well-maintained Web sites for researchers of manufacturer's marks. Whitten has compiled an accurate list alphabetically ordered by marks. Generally, the site contains minimal factory information, although Whitten occasionally includes longer discussions and provides links to other pages for additional information on selected companies. These pages are updated on a regular basis. Unlike the other sources listed in this bibliography, this site is immediately accessible to almost anyone (requires a computer and Internet access). For a fast and accurate identification of manufacturer's marks, this is an excellent resource.

Postscript

    In 2003, a small research group gradually formed for the study of manufacturer's marks, other marks on glass containers, and bottles in general. The group has a mixed membership, composed of both archaeologists and bottle collectors, working together for a common goal. Currently the group consists of Bill Lockhart, Bill Lindsey, Carol Serr, and David Whitten, with occasional input from Mike Miller.
    The goals of the group are to correct many of the errors in Toulouse and other works and to locate information on marks that have not yet been identified. Within this process, we are also learning more about bottle making, what other marks on bottles can tell us, and innovative forms of research. The primary reporting mechanism for the group is a column written by this author called "The Dating Game" which appears in each issue of *Bottles and Extras*, the quarterly journal of the Federation of Historic Bottle Collectors. Occasional articles will also appear in the *SHA Newsletter* and other publications. The eventual goal of the group is to produce a new book on marks for use by archaeologists, collectors, and other interested researchers. At the time of this publication, the group has researched more than 150 marks, frequently discovering new date ranges not comprehensively recorded by any other source. Our research sharply disagrees with many of the previously-published data. In addition, we offer an element lacking in virtually all previous studies of marks—discussions on how we reached our conclusions. This allows the reader to decide whether to accept or reject our dates and identification.

Bill Lockhart

The Color Purple: Dating Solarized Amethyst Container Glass

ABSTRACT

From the late-19th century on, there was an increased production of colorless bottles for a wide variety of products. Producing colorless glass is not difficult if pure sand with a very low iron content is available. Iron in sand gives the glass a range of colors from light green to dark amber, depending on the amount of iron in the sand. To overcome this problem, some factories that used iron-bearing sands added manganese to their batch as a decolorizer. While this produces colorless glass, that glass will turn a light purple or amethyst color when it is exposed to sunlight. Dating of solarized glass by archaeologists has relied on information from a variety of sources, including books produced by bottle collectors. Some of this information is good and some of it, erroneous. The objective here is to provide a useful chronology of the development and use of manganese as a decolorizer and to dispel some of the myths that have crept into the literature.

Introduction

Historically, both container glass and window glass have generally been colored varying shades of green and aquamarine. This color was produced by the natural inclusion of iron impurities in the sand used to produce the glass (see detailed information below). Gradually, lead glass came to be used for fine tableware, but the process was too expensive for the general line of containers. Throughout the 19th century, a gradual trend occurred in the glass industry toward light shades of aqua and colorless glass. Relatively inexpensive means were sought to produce colorless bottles. One of the cheapest methods was to add manganese to the glass mixture to create a colorless environment. This additive generated an interesting side effect—the glass became purple with prolonged exposure to the sun.

The color purple (or amethyst), when created by the inclusion of manganese in the formula of container glass, has long been a source of fascination for the archaeologist and the bottle collector. Although scientists and collectors are often at odds over issues of curation, access, ownership, and techniques in dealing with historical bottles, both have contributed to the literature used by archaeologists in dating and researching glass containers. Often, collectors have been on the cutting edge of descriptive and historical research on the glass industry, local users and bottlers, and local/national containers (McKearin and McKearin 1941; Munsey 1970, 1972; Zumwalt 1980; Fowler 1986) and are frequently cited by archaeologists. In researching solarized amethyst glass, archaeologists and collectors alike have made contributions. Archaeological and collector literature as well as contributions by chemists, physicists, and the glass industry is examined to study the dating and use of manganese dioxide as a decolorizer for impure container glass.

Background

Chemical and Physical Properties of Manganese Decolored Glass

Sand is one of the basic ingredients in the manufacture of glass, and most sand contains iron impurities in varying types and quantities. These impurities impart a green, blue-green, blue, or yellow tint to the glass, depending on the percentage of iron in the glass mixture and whether the iron is ferrous (blue-green), ferric (yellow), or a combination of the two. Because container glass was generally made as cheaply as possible (especially prior to the 20th century), most bottles displayed the blue-green or greenish tints often referred to by archaeologists and collectors as aqua but known in earlier times as "common green" (Harrington 1952: 28). The use of the term was so prevalent that one of the unions was called The Green Glass Bottle Blowers' Association of the United States and Canada (Scoville 1948:201). In most cases, "the *colour* of the glass [was] nearly, or quite, immaterial so that the introduction of relatively large proportions of iron oxide [was] permissible [emphasis in original]" (Rosenhain 1908:96).

Colorless glass became important for use in windows and tableware before it was widely introduced to containers, requiring a method of eliminating the tint caused by the iron impurities. L. M. Angus-Butterworth (1948:64) suggested that there were three ways to overcome the problem of unwanted color: (1) use a pure grade of sand with as low a percentage of iron impurities as possible (the best solution, but frequently impractical); (2) use oxidation to reduce undesirable color; or (3) add complementary colors (usually purple or pink) to offset the green tint caused by iron. George Miller and Antony Pacey (1985:44) add that the color may be masked by adding "other metallic oxides, such as cobalt" to change the color, or the color could be accepted as is. Pure sand produces a glass without color, and some locations are noted for sands lacking in impurities. Glasshouses, located in such areas, generate colorless glass without the use of complementary colors or oxidizers. Benjamin Biser ([1899]: 28) noted, "American sands, especially, show supremacy over all others, many of them being free from excessive organic matter and in almost absolute state of purity, and the supply nearly always inexhaustible." He also notes that Minnesota, Missouri, Illinois, Pennsylvania, Maryland, New Jersey, and the New England states are especially good places to find pure sand.

Although the distinction is of little practical use to historical archaeologists (at least using currently practiced methods), chemically, glass is formulated in four basic ways: soda-lime glass, potash-lime glass, potash-lead glass, and lime glass. Each of these glass types can be produced in colorless form without the addition of decolorizers. Glassmakers of Venice discovered a method to create colorless soda-lime glass by the 13th century, and colorless potash-lime glass was produced by the 17th century (for a more detailed discussion, see Jones and Sullivan 1989:10–12). It is clear that colorless glass for containers (as well as other uses) has been available for some time.

Historically, the most common method used to produce colorless glass was to add complementary colors, often using the purple hue created by manganese dioxide (MnO_2). At the close of the 19th century, Biser ([1899]:

43) explained the decolorization process: "Manganese imparts to glass a pink or red tint, which being complementary to green, neutralizes the color and permits the glass to transmit white light." The required quantity of manganese varied with the amount of iron in the mixture along with the nature of other chemicals present. D. J. McSwiney (1925a:23) noted, "the desired results are actually achieved by adding more color to the glass instead of taking it away." F. W. Hodkin and A. Cousen (1925:133) noted, "manganese is a more successful decolouriser in potash glass than in soda glass," although that distinction is of little practical use to archaeologists. There is no doubt that manganese was the most successful decolorant used in the latter part of the 19th century and the early part of the 20th century (Rosenhain 1908:192–193; Scholes 1935:207). Manganese-decolored glass that has undergone a color change due to exposure to the ultraviolet rays of the sun is variously known as sun-colored amethyst (SCA), solarized amethyst, solarized purple, or irradiated glass.

Through the years, chemists have argued *why* mixing complementary colors green and purple result in (to the eye, at least) a colorless glass (Fettke 1918:83; Weyl 1959:500–507; Paul 1982: 260). For the archaeologist it is sufficient to note *that* the phenomenon takes place. For a more technical explanation of how manganese dioxide functions as a decolorant, see A. Paul (1982:260) and Woldemar Weyl (1959: 500–507).

J. F. White and W. B. Silverman (1950: 255,257) sliced thin layers of glass to reveal that the solarization of manganese-bearing glass extends through the entire body of the piece rather than just appearing on the surface. Although the color extends all the way through, C. R. Bamford (1977:51) records, "ultra-violet irradiation gives a purple colouration extending with decreasing intensity into the body of the glass from the glass surface." It is clear that direct sunlight (or artificial irradiation) is required to create the color change. In 1905, S. Avery (1905:910) noted that a partially-buried bottle "showed the greatest change of color where most exposed to the sun's rays." Charles Hunt (1959:10) also illustrated the phenomenon in a way that suggested solarization would not occur through soil packed into a bottle or fragment. Further confirmation was offered by Mary Zimmerman (1964:31) that "partially colored bottles, those that are half-purple-and-half-clear, are commonly found by bottle diggers."

The combining of manganese and the impure sand must be conducted under oxidizing conditions (in this case, exposure to ultraviolet light). As early as 1948, Angus-Butterworth (1948:58) noted, "reducing agents destroy the purple tint." Reducing may be accomplished by heating the glass to a temperature between 450° and 500° F. This reverses the chemical change created by the exposure to solar radiation, and sun-colored amethyst glass becomes colorless once more. It should be noted that these temperatures are perilously close to the point where glass becomes plastic and the sample can become damaged (Weyl 1959:508–509; Paul 1982:261).

Early Investigations, Gaffield's Observations, and Gortner's Experiment

Chemists have been interested in color changes in glass caused by solar irradiation since the early-19th century. Scientists began discussing the phenomenon at least as early as 1823, although the controversy at that time centered around window glass rather than containers. The change of color in British windows was already becoming obvious early in the century (Gaffield 1867:244–252, 1881:4; Weyl 1959:498–500).

Thomas Gaffield (1867) conducted what may be the first actual testing of the effects of solarization on window and plate glass. He first placed what he called "really *colored* glasses, red, green, yellow, blue, and purple [emphasis in original]," in the sun but noticed little change except for the purple glass which "became slightly darker" (Gaffield 1867:245). He then exposed "white" (colorless) glass and lightly tinted glasses to sunlight and was rewarded by an increase in tint, mostly to a light-bluish or yellowish color with some pinks. He did not test any container glass.

Gaffield began his second set of experiments in 1870 and presented his findings in 1880 to the American Association for the Advancement of Science meeting in Boston (Gaffield 1881:7). He exposed "rough and polished plate; crown and sheet window glass; flint and crown optical glass; glass ware and glass in the rough metal" to sunlight over a 10-year period. Gaffield "witnessed a perceptible change in a single hour of sunlight exposure upon the top of a post in a country garden, at noontime, on a clear and hot day of August." Other changes took place much more slowly. He observed changes in most types of glass except some "fine glass-ware and optical glass" (Gaffield 1881:4–5). Again, he did not test any container glass.

Gaffield (1881:5) observed a variety of color changes, including "from white [colorless] to yellow," colorless to purple, and several changes in lightly tinted glass of various shades. It is important to note that even prior to 1880, other decolorants (besides manganese) were in use. Gaffield (1881:7) indicated the presence of other decolorants (even prior to 1880) when he stated, "a yellowish or purple color was produced" when colorless glass was "painted by the magic pencil of the sun." Manganese does not create a yellowish color. Gaffield (1881:9) correctly attributed the cause of the aqua coloration in most glass to "the presence of oxide of iron" and "oxide of magnesium" as "the great colorist in all of these changes [solarization to a purple color]."

Gaffield (1881:6) also noted that sun-colored fragments of glass could be "restored to their original color by being placed in the kiln during a single fire." In other words, heating the glass would reverse the sun's action and alter the specimens back to a colorless form (see the chemical discussion of this phenomenon above). He noted that this phenomenon had been reported as early as 1867.

The discussions on solarization virtually ceased after 1881 only to be rekindled in the early-20th century in debates over the color change in container glass. Avery (1905:909–910) and Charles Rueger (1905:1206) each published brief notes that suggested the likelihood that color change was caused by irradiation from the sun among other possible explanations.

Such discussions spurred Ross Gortner (1908) to seriously study the phenomenon. On 9 July 1906, he attached 22 colorless glass containers and other colorless glass objects (including a glass funnel, a laboratory flask, and pieces of glass tubing) to a board atop his roof to assess their susceptibility to sunlight. Some of the containers were filled with various ingredients including manganese dioxide, lampblack, potassium permanganate, and other substances. After one month, five items had begun to turn purple. He did not check the experiment again for almost a year, at which time he discovered 17 items had turned purple, 4 remained unchanged, and 1 had been "blown away by the wind" (Gortner 1908:159).

Gortner's results showed that some contents retarded the solarization on the backs of the bottles (but not the fronts) and some (notably lampblack) eliminated the coloration from the backs entirely. Gortner ground up the samples of glass he had placed on the roof and tested them to obtain the chemical composition of each container. All but one of the test items that remained colorless contained no manganese, but the unaltered Jena glass (laboratory glass) flask had a manganese component (Gortner 1908:159–161).

In conclusion, Gortner (1908:1962) demonstrated that when glass is "colored violet by the action of sunlight, proof is furnished that the glass contains manganese." He further confirmed that even glass containing small amounts of manganese will turn violet or purple after prolonged exposure and that length of exposure will deepen the color intensity. Finally, he established that some glass (notably Jena glass) contains a chemical combination that inhibits color change during solarization despite the inclusion of manganese dioxide in its composition (although it is likely that only a very tiny percentage of glass fits into this category).

Dating Solarized Amethyst Glass

Background Literature

Until recently, bottle-collector literature has been the major source for information and dating of glass containers by historians, archaeologists, and collectors alike. Although some collectors' literature is well written and well researched, much of it is compiled without scientific methodology or accuracy. While some collector dating and wisdom have been disproved (for example, the idea that the proximity of mold marks to the lip of a bottle is relevant to its relative age), the dating and history of solarized, manganese-bearing glass has not been seriously researched by archaeologists.

The first collector to attempt dating purple glass was Grace Kendrick (1963:54–56). Kendrick dated the phenomenon of "sun-colored glass" as lasting from 1880 to 1914. Although she provided no justification for her beginning date, she stated, "[w]ith the advent of World War I, our main source of manganese (German suppliers) was cut off" (Kendrick 1963:56), thereby providing an end date that has been more or less accepted (along with her beginning date) ever since. Zimmerman followed Kendrick a year later, referencing solarized purple, flat (window) glass and tableware along with bottles as being used between 1850 and 1910 (Zimmerman 1964:7,19). She noted that many innovations in the glass industry began about 1890 (Zimmerman 1964:20–21), and the changeover to selenium was a process that continued from about 1910 until about 1930. Although Cecil Munsey (1970:55) cited Zimmerman as one of his sources, he accepted Kendrick's basic dating scheme and added, "around 1880, . . . the demand for clear glass forced the manufacturers to perfect the technique of decolorizing with manganese." Rick Baldwin (1985:23) combined the Kendrick and Zimmerman dating schemes to suggest a beginning date of 1880 and an end date between 1915 and 1930. T. Stell Newman (1970:74) modified that range by adding 10 years to all dates to allow for industry transition; Olive Jones and Catherine Sullivan (1989:13) and Miller and Pacey (1985:44) generalized it; and Richard Fike (1987:13) ignored it completely.

Kendrick was only partially correct in her reasoning for the industry's cessation of the use of manganese. In 1910, the United States imported 4,928 long tons of manganese from Germany, 2.03% of our total import for the year. By 1915 that was reduced to 258 long tons (0.08% of total import), followed by a reduction to zero in 1916. It was not until 1920 that the U.S. returned to German suppliers, and then the total import was only 11 long tons. In other words, Germany was never an important supplier of manganese during the period in question. Prior to World War I, British India supplied the most manganese to the U.S.: 58.2% of the total import in 1910, decreasing to only 11.4% by 1915. Brazil had contributed 22.2% of U.S. manganese imports in 1910, increasing to 85.9% in 1915.

The United States itself became an important manganese supplier by the end of the war, generating 31.4% of its supply (an increase from less than 1% in 1910) (U.S. Geological Survey 1913:207–208, 1919:734–736, 1922: 274–276). The United States Tariff Commission (1918a:13) stated that clay, not manganese was a major import from Germany.

Import records failed to tell the complete story. The U.S. Tariff Commission conducted two hearings concerning the effects of the war on the glass industry in 1917. In the second meeting, representatives from "65 flint-glass manufacturing firms" (not all bottle manufacturers) met with government officials in December 1917 to discuss the state of U.S. glass production. Despite the evidence produced above, glass manufacturers imported most of their manganese from Russia, although some was imported from Germany along with a small amount from France. It is clear that war disruption played a significant role in the importation of manganese (U.S. Tariff Commission 1918b:32).

It is instructive to note that the disruption produced a very complex reaction from the glass industry, rather than the simplistic response posited by Kendrick. Not counting plate glass manufacturers, 43 representatives discussed imports. Of those, 25 discussed manganese. Nine discussants continued to use manganese derived from other sources. Most of these used domestic manganese, although a few were dissatisfied with its quality. Two imported manganese from countries (like Canada) where shipping was unaffected by the war. Three discussants discontinued the use of manganese with no replacement; three others substituted selenium. A single glassmaker continued to pay higher prices and was still using imported manganese. The final nine were using other decolorants in place of manganese (Table 1). Five of them substituted a decolorizer manufactured by the Frink Laboratories, Lancaster, Ohio (U.S. Tariff Commission 1918b:32–37). The U.S. Tariff Commission hearing makes two points clear: (1) a significant number of manufacturers (36% of those who discussed manganese use) continued to use manganese as a decolorant in 1917; and (2) by that point, selenium was only one of a number of substitutes for manganese.

Beginning Dates

Manganese was used as a coloring agent at least as early as 660 B.C. in Egypt (Angus-Butterworth 1948:49) and in Roman glass from the 4th century B.C. to the 9th century A.D. (Werner 1968:34A). Helen McKearin and Kenneth Wilson (1978:10) note that the decoloring properties of manganese were demonstrated prior to 1662. Scholes (1935: 207) even claims that "it was used for hundreds of years as the only satisfactory decolorizer." Manganese appears in tableware at least as early as the 18th century (Jones and Sullivan 1989:13). Window glass that had solarized to a purple color was investigated in England as early as 1823 (Gaffield 1881:4) and 1825 (Weyl

TABLE 1
EFFECTS OF IMPORT DISRUPTION ON MANGANESE-USING GLASS MANUFACTURERS IN 1917*

Reaction to Import Disruption	N	%
Substituted other manganese sources (mostly domestic)	9	36.0
Discontinued use of decolorant	3	12.0
Substituted selenium	3	12.0
Continued to use existing imported supplies	1	4.0
Substituted various other decolorants**	9	36.0
Totals	25	100.0

* Data derived from U.S. Tariff Commission (1918b:32–37).

** Five glass manufacturers (20.0% of the total number) used a decolorant developed by Frink Laboratories, Lancaster, Ohio.

1959:498–500). Gaffield (1881:3) observed, "changes of some light colored plate glass to a purple" had been noted "after the beginning of this century [19th]," placing manganese use in flat glass about 1800 or shortly thereafter. Manganese-decolored flat glass was also in use in the United States prior to 1880. In his report for the 1880 census, Joseph Weeks (1883: 1062–1063) claimed,

> manganese is used to correct this greenish color, and is often termed "glass-maker's soap," but glass so decolorized is liable under the action of sunlight to acquire a purplish tint of "high color." Window glass in which manganese has been used often assumes this tint to such an extent as to lead to the belief that it was originally colored.

It becomes clear that manganese-bearing glass was in use long before 1880 and was used in the United States prior to that date.

Prior to the use of manganese-decolored glass, most containers were manufactured as cheaply as possible, a technique that retained the green, blue-green, aqua, yellow, or light blue colors associated with the presence of iron oxides in the glass mix. Contemporary sources that deal with glass colors (Fike 1987:13; Jones and Sullivan 1989:13) are strangely silent on the subject of the light blue bottles that appear primarily in pre-1917 contexts. Bamford (1977:51–52), Walter Rosenhain (1908:190), and Donald Sharp (1933:762) identify blue as a color associated with iron impurities in glass. In a 1929 experiment, B. Bogitch "obtained colours [of glass] varying from brown to blue according to the condition of the iron" (Gooding and Murgatroyd 1935:45). Biser ([1899]:13) described this glass as "coarse and inferior in quality, used extensively for the commonest grades of bottles and hollow-ware, and is usually of a greenish, amber, or black color."

Because color was often unimportant (Rosenhain 1908:196), certain types of bottles continued to be made from "naturally colored" (iron bearing) glass, notably soda and beer bottles. Although occasional beer bottles appear in light blue or colorless forms, most were amber from the last quarter of the 19th century. Soda bottles generally retained the green, aqua, or light blue tints caused by the iron impurities. Biser ([1899]:86) suggested that soda and beer bottles remained colored because of the fear that "the liquid contents of a flint glass [colorless] bottle were seriously impaired in strength and in color by the actions of light, which a green or amber bottle excluded, and thus protected its contents." The use of unaltered glass was so common in the manufacture of bottles that green glass was synonymous with "bottle glass" (*Harpers* 1889:257).

Two factors confound the selection of a single date as a beginning for the use of manganese as a decolorant in the United States: process and terminology. Process is a problem because manufacturers rarely (if ever) all switch to a new technology simultaneously or even in a relatively short time (Newman 1970:70). Weeks (1883:1062–1063) reported the use of manganese decolorization in 1880, but he was very unclear about the context.

When Gaffield (1881:5) examined the effects of sunlight on glass in 1867 and 1881, he reported that he used "rough and polished plate; crown and sheet window glass; flint and crown optical glass; glassware and glass in the rough metal" for his experiments. Like Weeks (above), the lack of reference to container glass is significant. Although not conclusive, these references create a lack of clear context for early manganese use in container glass.

The second problem is terminology. In their justification for the use of the term "colourless," Jones and Sullivan (1989:13) state that "terms like 'clear,' 'white,' 'flint,' or 'crystal' . . . have not been used consistently by contemporary authors or in historical documents." Originally, the term *flint* was used to mean lead glass (or potash-lead glass), highly prized for tableware because it was "colourless, heavy, and lustrous" (Jones and Sullivan 1989:11; also McKearin and McKearin 1941:8). Because the process was more expensive, its use in containers was limited, although *Harpers* magazine (1889:257) noted that it was used in the U.S. to manufacture "fine bottles." Later, the use of the terms grew more lax, and *flint* or *white* often meant glass made from pure sand, glass manufactured by techniques such as that developed by William Leighton in 1864 (Jones and Sullivan 1989:11) or glass made with a decolorant. Leighton, working for the glasshouse of Hobbs, Brockunier and Co., developed a soda-lime glass (often called "lime" or "lime flint" glass) that was colorless, of high quality, and much cheaper than lead-flint glass

(McKearin and McKearin 1941:8; Douglas and Frank 1972:40). Frank Gessner (1891:54–56) presented recipes for "flint hollow-ware" that all contained manganese as a decolorant.

George Griffenhagen and Mary Bogard (1999:20,35) note that imported "flint glass" medicine bottles were offered for sale in the U.S. as early as 1773 and American-made flint glass containers by the 1850s. Edward Perrish wrote in 1856, "flint vials are considerably more expensive than the green, though they are far more elegant for prescription purposes" (Griffenhagen and Bogard 1999:27). Although Perrish was most likely talking about lead flint glass, a more expensive process, his statement is important because it shows that people in the U.S. were showing a desire for colorless glass (at least in pharmaceutical containers) by the mid-19th century.

Although Leighton's "lime-flint" glass was well known for its use in pressed table glass (Jones and Sullivan 1989:11), no reference is found for its use in containers. Although Julian Toulouse (1971:369–370,387–388), mentions the company several times, it is always in connection with pressed tableware and never in a context connoting containers. It is obvious, that some form of colorless glass was used to produce medicinal containers in the U.S., possibly just glass made from essentially pure sand.

The combination of process and terminology creates a final hurdle that must be cleared before an understanding of when the use of manganese-decolored glass began among glassmakers can be achieved. The combined aspect centers around container type. Makers of different types of containers appear to have adopted glass decolorized by manganese at different times. Whitall Tatum & Co., for example, opened a "flint glasshouse" in 1864. Initially, the company used William Leighton's formula for colorless glass (without manganese), although it only met with limited success (Pepper 1971: 228–232). By 1870 the process had improved at Whitall Tatum through the use of manganese dioxide (Horner 1969:98). Personal communication with numerous collectors of drug store bottles indicates that, regardless of manufacture date, virtually all pre-1924 Whitall Tatum colorless drug store bottles (generally oval-shaped, pharmacy bottles with plate molds identifying local drug stores) will solarize to a light

amethyst color. Attempting to quantify collector data is difficult. The author observed one collection of about 1,850 drugstore bottles, about half of which were marked with the Whitall Tatum logo. All were solarized to a light amethyst. Various collectors have reported looking at hundreds of drug store bottles from Whitall Tatum that showed similar characteristics.

By 1904, Whitall Tatum had developed a semiautomatic machine for wide-mouth containers and had one for narrow-mouth bottles operational by 1912 (Toulouse 1971:544–547); however, these were not used for drug store bottles. Because of the use of plate molds, these bottles were available to local storeowners at a slight additional charge and were popular during the late-19th and early-20th centuries. For drug store bottles (and, presumably other medicinals) the beginning date is about 1870.

An examination of soft drink bottles shows a different pattern completely. As stated above, most soda bottles were allowed to retain whatever colors the natural impurities in the glass mix created. The use of manganese-bearing, colorless glass in soft drink bottles seems to have begun sometime in the mid-1890s (William Lindsey and numerous bottle collectors 2004, pers. comm.). Less information is available for other bottle types, although beer bottles, even today, are generally not colorless.

Personal communication with collectors also indicates that many of the early milk bottles, most of which were made of colorless glass, will solarize to varying shades of amethyst or purple. Although the record of the earliest milk bottles is unclear, when the Thatcher milk bottles were first made in 1886, they were formed of colorless glass (Tutton [1996]:6). Colorless glass continued to be the industry standard until glass milk bottles were almost completely replaced by waxed paper and plastic containers.

Apparently, at least with Hemingray Glass Co., jar manufacturers did not begin using manganese to any strong degree until after 1893. Although Hemingray was best known for the making of insulators, the company, like its predecessors Hemingray Brothers & Co. and Gray & Hemingray, made such items as tableware, tumblers, chemical apparatus, perfume bottles, pickle bottles, fruit jars, and other bottle types (Toulouse 1971:224–225,246). Bob Genheimer (2004, pers. comm.) described his excavation of the Hemingray Glass Co. in 1986. In a large excavation unit (2.5 × 2.5 m), Genheimer found sizeable quantities of broken glass discarded by the factory. Although 52.7% of the broken glass was colorless, only 0.9% was a solarized amethyst. This may suggest the beginning of manganese use as a decolorant by the company by 1893 (the date the factory moved and ceased production on the site). Alternatively, the small amount of manganese glass could be from *cullet* (broken glass used to "prime" the furnace) collected from other factories.

Despite the unsupported references to 1880 found in the early collectors' literature, documentary sources discuss the appearance of manganese-decolored glass as a part of a general trend toward technological improvement beginning about 1890. Although specific inventions were unmentioned, *Harpers* magazine (1889) touted the innovations and modern techniques then taking place within the glass industry. Biser ([1899]:86) noted, the "so-called 'lime flint' bottle glass" was becoming more common and "the past decade [since ca. 1889] has wrought a revolution in so far as to give flint glass bottles much prestige." Scholes (1935: 217) likewise stated: "From the first attempts to produce crystal glass in continuous tanks in the 1890's to the development of decolorizing by selenium twenty years later, glass makers struggled to maintain good color by manganese treatment." Zimmerman (1964:20–21) noticed the importance of the industrial development around 1890 but failed to link it to the early use of manganese in container glass. Although these sources are a bit unclear as to the date of entry of manganese-bearing glass, Gessner established the certainty that it was in use by 1891. In his *Glassmakers' Hand-Book*, Gessner (1891: 7) notes, "the use of manganese has, however, been largely abandoned in European factories during latter years, especially in the manufacture of window glass and fine flint ware" because it changed color. For bottle glass he included manganese in all of his "flint hollow-ware" recipes. Gessner (1891:54) also states:

> flint hollow-ware has grown to immense proportions during recent years, and in many cases has largely displaced green glass. Fruit jars, the use of which is growing more extensive each year, especially those of large size to displace the shape and color of the contents, are now, to a large extent, made of flint [manganese-decolored glass], which is preferred on account of its greater clearness and transparency.

This suggests that, by 1891, manganese-bearing glass had been in use for at least a few years and was growing in popularity.

Biser ([1899]:86) also noted another interesting development near the end of the 1880s, "For a long time flint glass bottles were regarded with disfavor, inasmuch as their cost alone excluded them from beer and soda trade, to say nothing of the current belief rife among the bottling fraternity that flint glass lacked the strength and resistance of green glass." The sentence implies that the resistance was by then no longer prevalent. Although this may suggest other new techniques as well, it seems to describe the process of conversion to manganese decolorization. The use of manganese as a decolorant would have left the glass as strong and resilient as its predecessor, green (or aqua) bottle glass.

Although developed by manufacturers of drug store bottles more than a decade earlier, use of the technique for manganese decolorization was therefore probably widely in use by the late 1880s. The actual dates of inception for the technique seem tied to container type. Three different methods, then, may be used for determining a beginning date for the use of manganese-decolored glass. First, the earliest known date for use in the United States is 1870 (at Whitall Tatum & Co.). Second, the most practical "general use" date is the late 1880s. Finally, more specific dates need to be researched for specific types of glass containers. Currently, that includes 1870 for drug store bottles (and probably other pharmaceuticals), the mid-1880s for milk bottles, and the mid-1890s for soft drink bottles.

A slight postscript about beginning dates must be added. In his excavation of the Johnson's Island Civil War Prison, David R. Bush (2004, pers. comm.) discovered "numerous examples of solarized glass from contexts that date from the Civil War." While this questions the veracity of the dates discussed above, there are two mitigating circumstances. First, manganese was used in tableware throughout much of the 19th century; second, manganese has also been used as a colorant. McKearin and Wilson (1978: 591) describe a style of flask that is found in both amethyst and deep amethyst (black) colors as well as various shades of green, blue, and yellow. A second style (McKearin and Wilson (1978:597) was colorless and "colorless, lavender tint." Although solarization is a possibility, the first bottle described was almost certainly made from amethyst glass intentionally, and the second probably obtained its tint accidentally through cullet or impurities. McKearin and Wilson (1978:592) also note a flask that is "amethyst and clear in striations, the overall effect being of brilliant amethyst." Other flasks are described as colorless, clear, or colorless with light shading of various colors ("clear light green" or "clear yellow green"). All of these are obviously not solarized. Future research should stress close observation of glass from the Civil War period for indications that might address solarization.

End Dates

As with a beginning date, the end date expresses a process. As noted above, the change from manganese dioxide to selenium and other decoloring agents was not caused by a shortage of manganese from Germany (although World War I did create a shortage of manganese, along with most other resources). The change was actually a result of technological improvements in the glass industry and is closely connected to the conversion to automatic bottle machines. McSwiney (1925b:53–57) and Miller and Pacey (1985:44–45) provide a concise summary of technological events that resulted in the transition to selenium usage, although they are vague as to the actual dating. Manganese dioxide performs best in crucibles, such as those used in the production of hand-blown glass, because of its need for an oxidizing environment. It is much less effective in open tanks, such as those required for the Owen Automatic Bottling Machine and others of its type. Even though manganese was more difficult to obtain during World War I, and selenium was cheaper to use, the improvement in technology (the popularity of semi-automatic and automatic bottle blowing machines) was the major reason for the change in decoloring agents. Because of the problem with manganese, many of the early machine-made bottles were aqua in color, a convenient way of avoiding the problem, as no decolorant was needed.

Scholes (1935:217) places the initial use of selenium about 1910. McSwiney (1925b: 53,55) suggests the earliest use of selenium at "a few years before the war" but adds, "up to ten years ago [1915] the only decolorizer used to any considerable extent for the production of colorless soda lime glass was manganese." Weyl (1959:283) contends that the use of selenium began in the early 1890s. Sources more contemporary with the change declared, "in 1917, selenium, a domestic by-product of copper, was substituted for manganese" (U.S. Tariff Commission 1918a:32) and "manganese is one of the important decolorizers employed by the glass manufacturer" (Fettke 1918:82). These sources indicate that selenium was in use by at least 1910 (possibly earlier) but did not become popular until about 1917.

The term *popular* needs to be clarified. Since the popularity of selenium use (and, therefore, the end of prominence for manganese) closely follows the development of the automatic bottle machine, the significance of the term concerning automation of the glass industry must be examined. The use of automatic bottle machines had increased in popularity to the point that, in 1917, approximately half of all bottles in the United States were made by the Owens Automatic Bottle Machine. Additional containers were made on a variety of semi-automatic machines. Although machine production increased in popularity, hand-blown bottles continued to be manufactured until the early 1930s (Miller and Sullivan 1984:86–89). Machines were more efficient for producing bottles in quantity, so the more popular container styles (beer, soda, and food bottles) were the earliest made by the new process. By approximately 1920, most of the popular types of bottles were machine made.

Also following the machine production trend, manganese use as a decolorant continued in the smaller, hand-production glasshouses and for specialty bottles in the larger plants. These small-run, specialty bottle producers still used crucibles and had no reason to make the transition to selenium. In 1926, Alexander Silverman (1926:897) commented, "selenium has also largely displaced manganese dioxide as a decolorizer." By 1933, Sharp (1933:763) noted, "selenium is almost invariably used as the decolorizer in bottle glass because of the relatively constant results to be obtained. Manganese is still employed for high-grade pot glass." Although manganese use continued past 1920, its widespread use had clearly come to an end.

End dating specific container types provides a postscript to the dating discussion. As with beginning dates, not all bottle types or glass houses adopted selenium or other decolorants at the same time. Drug store bottles (pharmaceutical bottles, usually oval in shape and containing embossed plate molds with the names of local druggists), probably the earliest to show the adoption of manganese as a decolorant, were also some of the last to abandon the technique. Whitall Tatum continued to make drug store bottles by hand blowing until about 1924 (beginning about 1924, all pharmaceutical bottles at Whitall Tatum were machine-made and embossed with a different logo) and therefore continued to use manganese as a decoloring agent until that time. Cost may have been a deciding factor for druggists. Machine manufacture required a minimum order. Often, that minimal requirement resulted in an order too large to fit the needs of most druggists (Miller and Pacey 1985:42). As a result, the machine manufacture of bottles created a cost beyond the practical reach of many businesses. The day of the individually marked drug store bottle was at an end.

Soft drink bottles rarely showed the presence of manganese after the advent of machine usage in that field, between about 1912 and 1915. Some of the pint- and fifth-size preprohibition liquor bottles with no manufacturer's mark and those with the *B* (with serifs) mark made by the Charles Boldt Glass Co. from 1910 to 1919 solarize to light amethyst color, indicating the use of manganese. Yet these same bottles have the distinctive Owens scars that indicate the use of the Owens Automatic Bottle Machine. According to Miller and McNichol (2002:3,6–7), only Boldt and the Illinois Glass Co. were issued licenses to make whiskey bottles prior to the cessation of the Owens patents in the mid-1920s. Because Boldt did not include date codes on his bottles, the date range when he discontinued the use of manganese is unknown. Many early milk bottles (ca. 1900–ca. 1912), including some made with Owens machines by the Thatcher Glass Manufacturing Co. as late as 1914 (by date code on the base), have solarized to varying shades up to a rich, dark purple.

Conclusion

Both historical and empirical evidence indicate that the previously accepted earlier date (1880) for the beginning of popularity of colorless glass container use in the United States as suggested by bottle collectors may be slightly incorrect. Popular use seems to have begun by at least the mid-1870s and was solidly in place by 1890. This dating cannot be generalized to all glass artifacts. Manganese was used in tableware by 1865 and in flat (window) glass in the U.S. long before 1880. A practical end date for manganese use in all but specialty bottles is about 1920, although some use continued until the early 1930s. The end of manganese use is generally concurrent with the end of mouth-blown bottle production.

Acknowledgments

I would like to particularly thank George Miller for his many suggestions and for recommending sources. An important group consists of archaeologists (especially Bob Genheimer) who shared their findings with me through the HISTARCH listserv and numerous bottle collectors who inspected their collections for solarized bottles and gave me their candid views. A bouquet of gratitude also to my wife, Wanda Wakkinen, for listening to my endless hours of speculation.

References

ANGUS-BUTTERWORTH, L. M.
    1948 *The Manufacture of Glass.* Putnam, New York, NY.

AVERY, S.
    1905 Changes of Color Caused by the Action of Certain Rays on Glass. *Journal of the American Chemical Society* 27(7):909–910.

BALDWIN, RICK
    1985 Decolorizing Glass with Manganese. *Crown Jewels of the Wire* 17(7):23–25.

BAMFORD, C. R.
    1977 *Colour Generation and Control in Glass.* Elsevice Scientific, New York, NY.

BISER, BENJAMIN F.
[1899] *Elements of Glass and Glassmaking: A Treatise Designed for the Practical Glassmaker, Comprising Facts, Figures, Recipes, and Formulas for the Manufacture of Glass, Plain and Colored.* Glass and Pottery, Pittsburgh, PA.

DOUGLAS, R. W., AND SUSAN FRANK
1972 *A History of Glassmaking.* G. T. Foulis & Co., Henley-on-Thames, Oxfordshire, England.

FETTKE, CHARLES REINHARD
1918 *Glass Manufacture and the Glass Sand Industry of Pennsylvania.* Report no. 12, Topographic and Geologic Survey of Pennsylvania, Harrisburg.

FIKE, RICHARD E.
1987 *The Bottle Book: A Comprehensive Guide to Historic, Embossed Medicine Bottles.* Peregrine Smith, Salt Lake City, UT.

FOWLER, RON
1986 *Washington Sodas: The Illustrated History of Washington's Soft Drink Industry.* Dolphin Point Writing Works, Seattle, WA.

GAFFIELD, THOMAS
1867 The Action of Sunlight on Glass. *American Journal of Science and Arts* 94:244–252.
1881 *The Action of Sunlight on Glass.* Salem Press, Salem, MA. [From a paper presented to the American Association for the Advancement of Science, Boston, 27 August 1880.]

GESSNER, FRANK M.
1891 *Glassmakers' Hand-Book: Containing Recipes for Making Flint, Bottle, Window, and Architectural Glass. Plain and in Colors: Plate Glass–American, French, Belgian, German, and Bohemian Formulas: Also Recipes for Strass and Artificial Gems.* George E. Williams, Pittsburgh, PA.

GOODING, E. J., AND J. B. MURGATROYD
1935 An Investigation of Selenium Decolorising. *Journal of the Society of Glass Technology* 19:43–103.

GORTNER, ROSS AIKEN
1908 Some Effects of Sunlight upon Colorless Glass. *American Chemical Journal* 34(2):158–162.

GRIFFENHAGEN, GEORGE, AND MARY BOGARD
1999 *History of Drug Containers and Their Labels.* American Institute of the History of Pharmacy, Madison, WI.

HARPERS
1889 Great American Industries, VIII, A Piece of Glass. *Harpers* 79:245–264.

HARRINGTON, J. C.
1952 *Glassmaking at Jamestown: America's First Industry.* Dietz Press, Richmond, VA.

HODKIN, F. W., AND COUSEN, A.
1925 *A Textbook of Glass Technology.* Constable & Company, London, England.

HORNER, ROY
1969 *Tempo, the Glass Folks of South Jersey.* Reprinted in 1985 by Gloucester County Historical Society, Woodbury, NJ.

HUNT, CHARLES B.
1959 Dating of Mining Camps with Tin Cans and Bottles. *Geo Times* 3(8):8–10,34.

JONES, OLIVE, AND CATHERINE SULLIVAN
1989 *The Parks Canada Glass Glossary for the Description of Containers, Tableware, Flat Glass, and Closures.* Parks Canada, Ottawa, Canada.

KENDRICK, GRACE
1963 *The Antique Bottle Collector.* Reprinted in 1971 by Old Time Bottle, Salem, OR.

McKEARIN, HELEN, AND GEORGE McKEARIN
1941 *American Glass.* Crown Publishers, New York, NY.

McKEARIN, HELEN, AND KENNETH M. WILSON
1978 *American Bottles & Flasks and Their Ancestry.* Crown Publishers, New York, NY.

McSWINEY, D. J.
1925a The Decolorization of Glass. *The Glass Industry* 6(2):23–26.
1925b The Decolorization of Glass. *The Glass Industry* 6(3):53–57.

MILLER, GEORGE L., AND TONY McNICHOL
2002 Dates for Suction Scarred Bottoms: Chronological Changes in Owens Machine-Made Bottles. Paper presented at the 2002 Annual Meeting of The Society for Historical Archaeology, Mobile, AL.

MILLER, GEORGE L., AND ANTONY PACEY
1985 Impact of Mechanization in the Glass Container Industry: The Dominion Glass Company of Montreal, a Case Study. *Historical Archaeology* 19(1):38–50.

MILLER, GEORGE L., AND CATHERINE SULLIVAN
1984 Machine-Made Glass Containers and the End of Production for Mouth-Blown Bottles. *Historical Archaeology* 18(2):83–96.

MUNSEY, CECIL
1970 *The Illustrated Guide to Collecting Bottles.* Hawthorn, New York, NY.
1972 *The Illustrated Guide to the Collectibles of Coca-Cola.* Hawthorn, New York, NY.

NEWMAN, T. STELL
1970 A Dating Key for Post-Eighteenth-Century Bottles. *Historical Archaeology* 4:70–75.

Bill Lockhart

PAUL, A.
1982 *Chemistry of Glass.* Chapman and Hall, New York, NY.

PEPPER, ADELINE
1971 *Glass Gaffers of New Jersey.* Scribner's Sons, New York, NY.

ROSENHAIN, WALTER
1908 *Glass Manufacture.* Archibald Constable & Co., London, England.

RUEGER, CHARLES E.
1905 Changes of Color Caused by the Action of Certain Rays on Glass. *Journal of the American Chemical Society* 28(9):1206.

SCHOLES, SAMUEL R.
1935 *Modern Glass Practice.* Reprinted in 1952 by Industrial Publications, Ind., Chicago, IL.

SCOVILLE, WARREN C.
1948 *Revolution in Glassmaking: Entrpreneurship and Technological Change in the American Industry, 1880–1920.* Harvard University Press, Cambridge, MA.

SHARP, DONALD E.
1933 Chemical Composition of Commercial Glasses. *Industrial and Engineering Chemistry* 25(7):755–764.

SILVERMAN, ALEXANDER
1926 Fifty Years of Glass-Making. *Journal of Industrial and Engineering Chemistry* 18(9):896–899.

TOULOUSE, JULIAN HARRISON
1971 *Bottle Makers and Their Marks.* Thomas Nelson, New York, NY.

TUTTON, JOHN
[1996]*Udderly Beautiful: A Pictorial Guide to the Pyroglazed or Painted Milkbottle.* Privately Printed, Front Royal, VA.

UNITED STATES GEOLOGICAL SURVEY
1913 *Mineral Resources of the United States, Calendar Year 1912, Part 1—Metals.* U.S. Geological Survey, Washington, DC.
1919 *Mineral Resources of the United States, Calendar Year 1916, Part 1—Metals.* U.S. Geological Survey, Washington, DC.
1922 *Mineral Resources of the United States, Calendar Year 1920, Part 1—Metals.* U.S. Geological Survey, Washington, DC.

UNITED STATES TARIFF COMMISSION
1918a *The Glass Industry as Affected by the War.* Tariff Information Series, No. 4. U.S. Tariff Commission, Washington, DC.
1918b *The Glass Industry as Affected by the War.* Tariff Information Series, No. 5. U.S. Tariff Commission, Washington, DC.

WEEKS, JOSEPH D.
1883 Report on the Manufacture of Glass. *Report on the Manufactures of the United States at the Tenth Census (June 1, 1880), Embracing General Statistics and Monographs on Power used in Manufactures, the Factory System, Interchangeable Mechanism, Hardware, Cutlery, etc., Iron and Steel, Silk Manufacture, Cotton Manufacture, Woolen Manufacture, Chemical Products, Glass Manufacture.* Bureau of the Census, Washington, DC.

WERNER, A. E. A.
1968 Analytical Methods in Archaeology. *Analytical Chemistry* 40(2):28A–42A.

WEYL, WOLDEMAR
1959 *Coloured Glasses.* Dawson's of Pall Mall, London, England.

WHITE, J. F., AND W. B. SILVERMAN
1950 Some Studies on the Solarization of Glass. *Journal of the American Ceramic Society* 33(8):252–257.

ZIMMERMAN, MARY J.
1964 *Sun-Colored Glass: Its Lure and Lore.* "Ole" Empty Bottle House, Amadore City, CA.

ZUMWALT, BETTY
1980 *Ketchup Pickles Sauces: Nineteenth-Century Food in Glass.* Mark West Publications, Fulton, CA.

BILL LOCKHART
DEPT. OF BUSINESS, HUMANITIES, AND SOCIAL SCIENCES
NEW MEXICO STATE UNIVERSITY AT ALAMOGORDO
2400 SCENIC DR.
ALAMOGORDO, NM 88310

Part II:

Metal and Small Finds

EDWARD L. BELL

The Historical Archaeology of Mortuary Behavior: Coffin Hardware from Uxbridge, Massachusetts

ABSTRACT

A popular cultural trend developed in late 18th- and 19th-century American mortuary practices. Called "the beautification of death," this Romantic movement idealized death and heaven through ideological, behavioral, and material transformations. The appearance of mass-produced coffin hardware in archaeological contexts throughout North America may be linked with this popular movement. Archaeological recovery of mass-produced coffin hardware and glass view plates, from cemeteries spanning a range of socioeconomic contexts, demonstrates that certain aspects of popular culture were so pervasive as to find expression, albeit dilute, at even the lowest level of society. The presence of decorated coffins at the Uxbridge Almshouse Burial Ground, as at other cemeteries associated with socioeconomically marginal groups, also suggests that archaeological interpretations that unquestioningly equate socioeconomic status directly to coffin embellishment need to be reviewed in light of socio-historical developments relating to mass consumption and popular culture in industrializing America.

Introduction

Cemetery investigations by historical archaeologists have brought to light an immediate and previously untapped source of data on American mortuary behavior. While historians have studied written accounts of funerals and have shown an interest in surviving examples of related material culture, archaeological evidence from the grave provides direct and compelling evidence of mortuary behavior among many social classes. Strides have also been made toward characterizing the nature of health, morbidity, and mortality among a range of social and economic groups (e.g., Lange and Handler 1985:19–22, 25–27; Reitz et al. 1985: 178–183; Rose 1985a; Parrington et al. 1986; Rose and Rathbun 1987; Wesolowsky 1988, 1989a, 1989b). The emphasis in this article, however, is on the larger socio-historical context of deathways shared among many American groups. Deathways encompasses the whole cultural system of mortuary behavior, involving emotion, ideology, symbolism, technology, and economy. Whether traditional, popular, innovative, or elite, deathways are the customs, rituals, etiquette, and material culture considered appropriate to the treatment and disposal of the dead (cf. Huntington and Metcalf 1979:17–20, 184–186).

The recovery of decorative coffin fittings from geographically and socially diverse archaeological contexts suggests a pervasive material shift that paralleled changes in popular attitudes toward death and burial in industrializing America. Similar forms of mass-produced coffin hardware have been reported throughout North America and are common at archaeological sites dating after the mid-19th century. This distribution testifies to developments in technology, marketing strategies, and transportation. More importantly, the ubiquity of coffin hardware indicates that similar material items were not only popular, but considered appropriate for the burial of the dead by many social and economic groups. The broad archaeological distribution of similar material items, specific to a mortuary context, not only suggests that a material shift had occurred in 19th-century America, but that these objects are the embodiment of a shared ideology.

A popular cultural trend, known as "the beautification of death," developed in the late 18th and 19th century. It was characterized by ritualized behavior and material objects that idealized death and heaven and prolonged the mourning and memorialization of the dead (Douglas 1975:56; Jackson 1977a:298; Stannard 1979:44; Farrell 1980:4–5; Pike and Armstrong 1980:16). Nevertheless, broad patterns of mortuary behavior, such as the beautification of death outlined by social historians, tend to exclude the interesting and significant differences in deathways of socially marginal classes and other divergent groups. Historical research that does address deathways out of the mainstream of American society is wanting for details in the few documentary sources available (Riis 1890: 177; Hoffman 1919:27, 41; Kleinberg 1977:202,

204–205; Buckley 1980:123; Ames 1981:651; Goodwin 1981; Clark 1987; Bell 1987:61–69). Archaeologically recovered mortuary assemblages can provide information, lacking in documentary history, on the deathways of many social and economic groups. Research on the Uxbridge Almshouse Burial Ground, for example, characterized the burial practices associated with a socially and economically marginal group dependent on political structures for economic relief (Elia and Wesolowsky 1989).

Archaeological investigations at historical American cemeteries, focused on traditional death practices among ethnic or economic groups, often fail to recognize the broad impact of popular culture that shaped specific material expressions of mortuary behavior. Mortuary and other behavioral phenomena are often described in terms of discrete, well-defined, and steadfastly maintained ethnic or economic boundaries. Such models often lack the means to show how groups interacted with, participated in, and contributed to larger cultural traditions. By viewing archaeological assemblages in the socio-historical context of 19th-century American mortuary behavior, archaeologists are uniquely able to define the parameters of popular culture of that era within the sphere of traditional deathways practiced by particular social or economic groups.

Mass-produced coffin hardware has been interpreted by historical archaeologists as an indication of socioeconomic rank (cf. Thomas et al. 1977: 410–417; Woodall 1983:17–19; Hacker-Norton and Trinkley 1984:51; Trinkley and Hacker-Norton 1984:13–15; Rose and Santeford 1985b: 135–136, 1985c:156; Bell 1987:15–18, 1989: 340–343; Parrington 1987:57–58; Owsley et al. 1988:90). Drawing from a common disciplinary background in prehistoric archaeology and anthropology, historical archaeologists have viewed coffin hardware as analogous to grave goods in preindustrial cultures. Variable mortuary assemblages are interpreted as evidence of differential rank. Mass-produced and mass-marketed coffin hardware, however, was inexpensive. It was utilized by many socioeconomic classes and not limited to middle-class or upper-class burials. The presence of coffin hardware at sites used to bury nutritionally deficient, physically stressed, low-status groups emphasizes the unsatisfactory and inconsistent conclusions that have been brought forward regarding coffin hardware as an unequivocal indication of high rank.

The beautification of death, an historical paradigm that might be considered equivalent to an archaeological horizon (Willey and Phillips 1958: 32–33), effectively summarizes a large-scale cultural trend. When regarded as an archaeological horizon, the beautification of death is reflected materially in the use of decorative, mass-produced coffin hardware. The interpretation of mass-produced coffin hardware as material evidence of the beautification of death is advantageous since it may serve as a point of departure for the archaeological study of a significant cultural trend.

Mass-produced objects may reflect an aspect of popular culture and function as a strategy of mediating or masking socioeconomic differences. Mass-produced objects are symbolic of apparent wealth; they serve to impart a sense of socioeconomic stature that was not otherwise attainable. Only the middle or upper classes could obtain actually expensive, hand-produced items (cf. Trachtenberg 1982:150; Williams 1982:92). The symbolic function of mass-produced objects, when cast against their role in the popular culture of 19th-century death practices, may account for the appearance of coffin hardware in the graves of low-status, 19th-century groups.

At the Uxbridge Almshouse Burial Ground, a 19th-century paupers' cemetery in southeastern Massachusetts, the recovery of decorative, mass-produced coffin hardware was initially viewed as an anomaly. No such decorative objects were expected at a paupers' cemetery containing the remains of people from the lowest social and economic class. Interpreting the variable mortuary assemblages at the Uxbridge site as a function of differential socioeconomic rank was considered unproductive, given the absolute poverty of the Uxbridge paupers. Interpretations of common coffin accouterments as culturally significant of rank obscure the real nature of socioeconomic disparity at cemeteries used by or for low-status people.

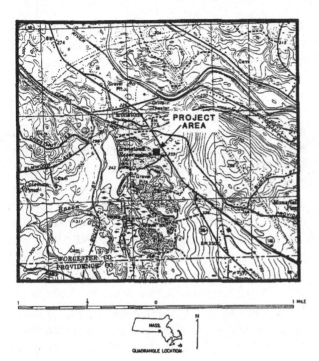

FIGURE 1. Location of the Uxbridge Almshouse Burial Ground (after United States Geological Survey [Blackstone, Massachusetts, Quadrangle] 1979).

Research into 19th-century mortuary behavior provided a context within which to understand the small sample of decorative, mass-produced coffin hardware and glass view plates from Uxbridge as evidence of a larger cultural trend related to the behavioral and material transformation of a way of life and death.

The opportunity for research, excavation, and analyses of materials recovered from the Uxbridge Almshouse Burial Ground was provided by the rediscovery of the site within the proposed right-of-way for the relocation of Route 146 through southeastern Massachusetts (Figure 1). The highway project was carried out by the Massachusetts Department of Public Works, with additional funding from the Federal Highway Administration. Under the direction of Ricardo J. Elia, the Office of Public Archaeology at Boston University excavated the Uxbridge site in 1985. Elia (1986, 1988, 1989a:1–15) has documented the background of the project in greater detail, and the research results are more fully described in the final report of investigations (Elia and Wesolowsky 1989).

Mortuary Behavior in 19th-Century America

A popular ideology, called the beautification of death, began in the late 18th century (cf. Douglas 1975:65–68; Jackson 1977b:5; Pike and Armstrong 1980:16). A related movement occurred in England and on the Continent (Jones 1967; Morley 1971; Gittings 1984). Closely aligned with the Romantic movement, the beautification of death was essentially an ideational shift accompanied by social and material transformations. Late 18th- and 19th-century Americans, unlike their 17th- and early to mid-18th-century counterparts, viewed death and heaven in a sentimental light (Douglas 1975:56; Jackson 1977a:298; Stannard 1979:44; Farrell 1980:4–5; Pike and Armstrong 1980:16). The movement was manifest in the creation of bucolic, landscaped cemeteries, such as Mt. Auburn Cemetery in Cambridge, Massachusetts, and Greenwood Cemetery in Brooklyn, New York (French 1975; Stannard 1979). Perhaps the best-known social expression of the beautification of death was the practice of high mourning among middle-class Victorians. Public mourning became protracted and increasingly formalized and expensive, reaching a pinnacle of ostentation toward the close of the 19th century. By the time this lugubrious period was on the decline (Farrell 1980:5), funeral reform societies began to appear (e.g., Hoffman 1919:26, 41).

The history of funeral directing describes the emergence of a full-time specialist from more generalized occupations. Death and burial involved not only friends and family, but also a number of skilled individuals. Among these were cabinetmakers (who made coffins); "layers out of the dead" (often women who prepared corpses for viewing and burial); sextons (who oversaw more public aspects of funeral ritual, such as supplying coffins and appropriate accouterments, tolling church bells, digging graves, and presiding over funerals and interment); and municipal officers such as coroners, superintendents of burial grounds, and registrars of deaths. Many of these tasks were often carried out by a single person (Habenstein and Lamers 1955: 227–249). The creation of the professional funeral director in the late 19th century capitalized on widely held public perceptions concerning faith in science, technology, and the need for specialized knowledge. The late 19th- and 20th-century popularity of embalming and the relocation of the dead from the family parlor to the funeral parlor reflected "an increased concern for appearances in a consumer culture, a strong and widely publicized sanitary movement, surgical pretensions in an age of respected medicine, [and] a privitization of the home" (Farrell 1980:7).

While the emergence of the funeral directing profession was in many ways responsible for fostering the elaborate nature of funerals into the late 19th century and beyond, the artifacts associated with late 18th- and 19th-century deathways provide evidence of change in popular attitudes toward death. The beautification of death appeared materially in the use of elaborate mourning clothes, decorative mortuary art, ornamental burial containers, and ornate memorial statuary. During this period, mortuary artifacts incorporated classical, biblical, natural, and Romantic motifs, such as seraphs, urns, draped columns, lambs, symbolic flora such as willows, oaks, and evergreens, and deeply grieving mourners. Such motifs departed from earlier depictions of skeletons brandishing scythes or holding hourglasses, as seen on gravestones, mourning rings, palls, and printed broadsides from the 17th and 18th centuries. Spoons and gloves given as funerary tokens in the 17th and 18th centuries also suggest antecedents to the profusion of late 18th- and 19th-century mortuary artifacts, but these earlier death-related artifacts lack the characteristic "melancholy beauty" (Farrell 1980:34) of the material culture associated with the beautification of death (cf. Concord Antiquarian Society 1967; Deetz and Dethlefsen 1967; Earle 1973:365; Schorsch 1976; Pike and Armstrong 1980; Fairbanks and Trent 1982:313–324).

The beautification of death created a social context for the production of funeral-related material culture. The combined forces of mass production and the professionalization of the funeral director eventually gave rise to a fully commercialized funeral industry. Mass-produced coffin hardware, including coffin handles, hinges, plaques, lid fasten-

ers, lid lifters, and tacks, were made specifically for use on coffins. The ornate styles of mass-produced coffin hardware paralleled the sentimental styles so typical of other objects associated with 19th-century mourning. The symbolic representation of the beautification of death inherent in mass-produced coffin hardware can be appreciated in contrast to the plain or restrained styles common to hand-finished handles and plaques made before the mid-19th century (e.g., Fellows n.d. [ca. 1850]). Handles, nameplates or escutcheons, and tacks used on coffins were not 19th-century innovations, but the degree of coffin embellishment peaked during that period with the use of both highly ornamented and specialized, mass-produced items (for earlier, especially 18th-century examples, see Habenstein and Lamers 1955:255–257; Watkins 1962:31; Concord Antiquarian Society 1967; Noël Hume 1969: 158; Bell 1987:54–55). In contrast to the 18th-century use of generalized hardware forms on coffins (i.e., tacks or hinges that would not be out of place on household furniture), 19th-century coffin builders used hinges, tacks, and other fittings that were specifically designed to be used in a mortuary context.

The ubiquity of mass-produced coffin hardware was the result of technological improvements in metal-working machinery that essentially replaced hand finishing; the appearance of inexpensive, malleable alloys such as white metal (also called paktong or German silver) and Britannia metal made decorative coffin hardware affordable to a larger market (Smith 1974:23–25). Illustrated merchandising or trade catalogues, which seem to have first appeared in the United States around the middle of the 19th century (Nelson 1980:iii–ix; McKinstry 1984:xi), influenced popular tastes in hardware styles. Improvements in transportation throughout the 19th century account for the wide geographical distribution of the objects. These transformations in technology, marketing, and transportation can only be fully understood, however, when viewed in the context of cultural changes that define the beautification of death. Stylistically and functionally, mass-produced coffin hardware was clearly a material aspect of the beautification of death. Molded in symbolic and sentimental decorative motifs and culturally specific for a mortuary context, mass-produced coffin hardware perpetuated the identity of the deceased with nameplates and more generic plaques; embellished burial containers; and provided a means to present and view the deceased by enabling hinged coffin lid sections to be lifted or removed. Memorialization and display of the dead in a beautified manner, such as in a decorative coffin, are characteristic of the beautification of death. See Pike (1980:642) for a useful typology.

The trend toward more decorative coffins can also be seen in the use of plate glass on coffin lids, through which the face of the deceased could be viewed. While this particular innovation was used as early as 1848 (Habenstein and Lamers 1955: 263, cited in Rose and Santeford 1985a:68), glass view plates are commonly found at cemeteries dating after the mid-19th century. Glass view plates may simply reflect efforts to ornament burial containers, or their use may be related to concerns about disease, fear of apparent death, or the increasing importance placed on display of the dead (Farrell 1980:7; Ariès 1982:397–404; Mytum 1989:288). Unlike the specially designed coffin hardware, mass-produced by machine, rectangular glass view plates could be fashioned by local coffin makers from windowpane stock. Oval or trapezoidal view plates recovered from some cemeteries may be more specialized forms.

Whether brought about through the persuasion of enthusiastic funeral directors or less formally by family members who saw mass-produced coffin trimmings in merchandising catalogs at the local general store, material aspects of the beautification of death became widely popular. Evidence for the popularity of mass-produced coffin hardware and glass view plates is found in their wide geographical distribution.

Similar styles of coffin hardware have been found at archaeological sites across the United States, including sites in Massachusetts (Faulkner et al. 1978:20–22; Bell 1987:106–137, 1989:351–370), New York (Olafson 1985; Spencer J. Turkel 1986, pers. comm.), Pennsylvania (Parrington 1984:10), Maryland (Rhodes 1987:7–8), Delaware

(Payne and Thomas 1988:18), North Carolina (Woodall 1983:8, 15), South Carolina (Combes 1974:54; South 1979:19, 23; Hacker-Norton and Trinkley 1984; Trinkley and Hacker-Norton 1984: 9–12; Orser et al. 1987, 1:398–413), Georgia (Thomas et al. 1977:416–417; Blakely and Beck 1982:192, 202; Garrow 1987), Arkansas (Rose 1985b), Louisiana (Owsley et al. 1988:29, 31, 38, 83), Texas (Fox 1984:40, 43; Taylor et al. 1986), Oklahoma (Ferguson 1983:11, 15), California (Leonardi 1986; Costello and Walker 1987:9, 14–15), Oregon (Brauner and Jenkins 1980:144–152, passim), and Washington (Wegars et al. 1983). Coffin glass view plates, in oval, trapezoidal, and rectangular shapes, have been recovered throughout the United States and in Canada (Combes 1974:54; Brauner and Jenkins 1980:30, 31, 148; Finnigan 1981:41, 45; McReynolds 1981:43–44, 50–51; Blakely and Beck 1982:188, 202; Parrington 1984:13; Rose and Santeford 1985a:58, 90, 114; Rose 1985b:189–193; Taylor et al. 1986: 41, 45; Bell 1987:128–129, 1989:368; Orser et al. 1987, 3:93–106; Payne and Thomas 1988:17, 18, 21). Whether or not glass view plates were simply decorative coffin features, they were popular objects, as shown by their archaeological distribution. The rectangular examples recovered from Uxbridge and from Saskatchewan (Finnigan 1981, James T. Finnigan 1986, pers. comm.) do not appear to be mass-produced, per se, but rather were possibly cut from windowpane stock and fitted by the coffin maker.

The context of late 18th- and 19th-century mortuary behavior has been linked to the advent of an industrialized way of life. "The nineteenth century brought dramatic change and extreme social stress. Struggling to live in an uncertain world, Americans retreated. They idealized and sanctified the home, the family, and the women who formed them" (Pike and Armstrong 1980:16; cf. Morley 1971:7). Similarly, death and heaven were idealized in popular literature. Heaven "became a domesticated haven, a place where all would be welcomed home" (Pike and Armstrong 1980:17; cf. Douglas 1975:65–68; Stannard 1979:44,46; Farrell 1980:5; Ames 1981:653). The transformation was linked closely with larger social changes:

While Heaven became a more comfortable place, earth had become a less comfortable one. The trauma of uncertainty and change affected the lives of all Americans in the nineteenth century. In the practice of increasingly ritualized mourning customs, they found themselves able to express not only their grief, but their moral and spiritual values as well (Pike and Armstrong 1980:17).

Morley (1971) traced the appearance of the beautification of death to the interplay of industrialization and socioeconomic upheaval:

> The Industrial Revolution brought wealth and death; impartiality in their distribution was not observed.
> . . . A new rural and urban middle class arose, accompanied by a new class of rural and urban poor.
> . . . An intense social competition was generated . . . [and] the urge towards visible display found ever more opulent expression.
> . . . [T]o secure the double crown of respectability in life, and salvation after it, became the aim of the typical Victorian.
> . . . [I]t was thought as necessary to maintain the standards of one's class in death as in life, and, if possible, even to use death as a means of further social advancement. This feeling was present with the lowest classes (Morley 1971:10–11).

Morley (1971:11) went on to give examples of these common concerns among England's poor, saving money to ensure against the disgrace of a pauper's grave. A similar anecdote can be related from Easton, Massachusetts (Chaffin 1886:449). To retain social respectability among the living, it was necessary to avoid the mortification of burial at public expense. Morley (1971:10) observed that "the connexion between death and poverty was close . . . [P]overty made it necessary to portray death as the only way to taste even the basic necessities of life."

In selecting decorative, sentimental trappings that represented the beautification of death, late 18th- and 19th-century Americans assimilated certain aspects of this popular movement into their traditional death practices. By transforming their way of death, the new ideology and material culture of the beautification of death allowed 19th-century Americans to find comfort in the loss of a way of life as it helped to overcome the grief naturally associated with the loss of the living. Traditional death practices reinforced group cohesiveness; funerals helped mend the social fabric torn by the loss of group members (cf. Goody 1975; Stannard 1975; Huntington and Metcalf 1979; Yentsch 1981; Brooke 1988:464). When controlled by authority, such as a town or the state, funeral ritual could be exclusionary, seeking to set off one group from another by reserving certain aspects of ritual for the elite. The selective interweaving of popular innovations in mortuary paraphernalia with long-standing, traditional rituals was one way that social groups participated in popular culture without relinquishing group identity. Similar responses in other social events contributed to a pluralistic American culture (cf. Burke 1978:23–64; St. George 1988:11).

"Fit, Proper and Rational": Poverty, Death, and Burial in Uxbridge, Massachusetts

The almshouse system was viewed by the Uxbridge Town Selectmen as a humanitarian effort to provide care for the poor and as a pragmatic means of supporting the poor at the lowest possible cost. One Uxbridge committee concluded in 1870 that "it seems fit, proper and rational, for the Town to have an Asylum for the Poor, a place for the Needy and destitute, it is a humane and laudable act, on the part of the Town" (Uxbridge, Town of, [1848–1870]:456). This passage captures much of the philosophy relating to the mortuary treatment of the Uxbridge paupers during the time that the burial ground was in use (1831–1872): the burial of the poor took place in a context that was "fit, proper and rational" in the eyes of the Overseers of the Poor, commensurate with the poor's marginal status. Poor relief in Uxbridge was shaped by the limitations of the state system of municipal reimbursement, as well as by what the town was willing to pay.

The structure of the poor relief system in Uxbridge, as in other 19th-century American communities, was influenced by many views, sometimes complementary, sometimes contradictory. The broad if somewhat vague notions of Christian charity or Yankee frugality, for example, were both present when decisions were made on how to provide for the "worthy" poor. In Uxbridge, the separation of the needy and the unfortunate into "worthy" and "unworthy" paupers related to the nature of economic support the town was willing to provide (Cook 1988:4–5, 1989:71–76) and mirrors the increasing segmentation of class in 19th-century America. Previous to the establishment of the almshouse, Uxbridge was able to support its poor by providing food, fuel, rent, and labor to residents who required assistance; people without housing were boarded with town families.

The industrialization of the Blackstone River Valley, in which Uxbridge is located, shifted the economic base from a labor, credit, and barter system to one based on labor and cash. Other aspects of regional industrialization played a role in the increasing demand for economic relief among many segments of the community. Cook (1989: 60–64) demonstrated that the development of the almshouse in Uxbridge followed the establishment of similar institutions across the Commonwealth and in other places, where a growing population of the poor put a strain on existing structures of support. The creation of a "poor farm," "town farm," or "poor house," terms by which the Uxbridge Alsmhouse was also known (Elia 1989a: 15), perhaps also embodied certain Romantic values: the idealization of the home and the therapeutic benefits of work at a rural farm while living with other inmates and the superintendent as in a fictive family (Cook 1989:81–82). A centralized institution allowed more efficient control over the unworthy poor and their attendant expenses. Only the worthy poor continued to receive assistance away from the town farm (Cook 1988:5). The Uxbridge Almshouse, like many Massachusetts almshouses, was located away from the town center, near the town's legal boundary (Cook 1989:64; Ricardo J. Elia 1987, pers. comm.). The unworthy poor were institutionalized, kept literally at the margins of town society, and symbolically excluded at their death by burial in a pauper's grave.

Pauper burials were meant to provide decent, Christian interments for those who could not afford them (Hoffman 1919:23–26). According to Hoffman (1919:20) in his treatise on *Pauper Burials and the Interment of the Dead in Large Cities,*

pauper burials were simply "interment[s] at public expense" and were generally but not exclusively characterized by minimal funerary treatment (see Elliot 1858:205–211; Earle 1977:34; Bell 1987: 61–69). Interments were often made in plain and simple wooden coffins, brought in a wagon rather than in a hearse to sections of cemeteries set aside for paupers or buried in "potters' fields" in urban areas. The locations of paupers' graves were often indicated by simple markers such as those made of wood (e.g., Hoffman 1919:47–51; Wigginton 1973:318; Leveillee et al. 1981:11; Jordan 1982: 41–43). Pauper burial grounds, wrote Ames (1981:651), were "symbolic and visible manifestations of hierarchical social order." Kleinberg (1977:203) concurred that areas set aside in cemeteries for the burial of paupers "reflected and perpetuated class differences by relegating the poor to undesirable sections and by denying to paupers the right to memorial of their death or resting place."

Paupers who were interred at the Uxbridge Almshouse Burial Ground came from disparate backgrounds. Wesolowsky's (1988, 1989a, 1989b) analyses indicated the presence of at least two blacks and one Native American among the mostly white majority. The cemetery population is an institutional sample, represented by a bimodal distribution of elderly and infirm adults and pre-adolescent children and infants. People who died destitute at the almshouse, and likely other people (such as an unidentified vagrant) who could not pay the costs associated with burial, were interred by the Town of Uxbridge (Cook 1989:75).

The economic and humanitarian rationale of Uxbridge's poor relief system, to provide care for the poor at the lowest possible cost, is embodied in the minimal funerary treatment of paupers. The mention of watching, washing, and dressing the dead in town documents identifies traditional mortuary activities that were carried out in certain cases. Tantalizingly short references found by Cook (1989:106; see Bell 1987:93–95) to "digging graves" and "attending funerals" may have summed up what were possibly quite perfunctory graveside ceremonies.

Burial containers for the poor were purchased by

the town, mostly from a man who also made and repaired furniture for the almshouse (Uxbridge, Town of, 1841–1868:18 February 1847, 20 February 1852). These Selectmen's records indicate that coffin prices varied from a low of less than $2.00 in 1845 (the figure given was for "dig[g]ing [a] grave & [for] a box") to a high of $6.00 in 1867. The usual figure between 1841 and the 1860s was $4.50. (The rise of coffin prices in the mid-1860s was probably the result of widespread economic change during and after the Civil War.) Minor differences in coffin prices evident in town records may also reflect variations in coffin size or style, may indicate discounts given on volume purchases, or may be related to price variations that could be expected when different purveyors supplied coffins to the town. The fact that the person who provided most of the coffins for the town also supplied and repaired furniture for the almshouse, as well as Hansen's (1989:489) identification of wood used for coffin construction, strongly suggests that the chestnut, pine, and yellow poplar coffins were made locally.

Considering the economic stricture imposed by Uxbridge and the limited level of reimbursement set by the Commonwealth in the care and burial of the poor (Cook 1988:4–5, 1989:71–76), it comes as no surprise that paupers were generally interred at the site in simple, inexpensive coffins. In the austere context of pauper burials, the more ostentatious expressions of the beautification of death would have, in fact, been considered a ludicrous, if lamentable, situation (Elliot 1858:209–211).

The Archaeological Evidence of Burial in Uxbridge

Of the 31 graves at the Uxbridge site, 16 were marked with granite quarry spalls or unmodified fieldstone. The permanent commemoration of individuals was not generally followed at this burial ground since a little under half of the graves appear to have been unmarked, and all but one of the graves were marked anonymously. Only one traditional headstone, carved from white limestone,

was present at the site (Elia 1988:11–14, 1989b:34–36).

The range of variation in the artifacts recovered from the graves at the Uxbridge site is remarkable only for the general lack of highly ornamented burial containers. By and large, the coffins provided for the pauper burials at Uxbridge were quite plain. With the exception of two rectangular burial containers, the graves contained coffins that were hexagonal or roughly so (Figure 2). While in a majority of cases the shape of the container was apparent to excavators, smaller details eluded observation. Deterioration of the coffin wood obliterated carpentry details, save for the fortuitous preservation of a single coffin lid fragment with a beveled edge. Consequently, the hardware from the graves provided most of the data for an analysis of burial practices at the site.

The mortuary assemblages from 17 of the graves (55%) consisted simply of wooden coffin fragments, a handful of cut nails (and sometimes a half dozen or fewer screws), and often one or two common brass hinges (Figure 3d-g). Fourteen graves (45%) contained stylistically specialized, or otherwise unusual, hardware fittings. These items included mass-produced coffin hardware, such as white metal coffin hinges and white metal coffin lid screws and tacks molded in complex designs; white metal coffin hardware was found in 12 graves or nearly 39 percent of the graves (Graves 1, 2, 3, 4, 5, 11, 14, 16, 17, 20, 28, and 30; see Figure 2). Other artifacts found at the site included two rectangular glass view plates (from Graves 1 and 12); five brass tacks (from Grave 27); a brass hook-and-eye fastener (from Grave 12); and five coffin fabric-lining (or covering) tacks, one of white metal (Grave 2), three possible lining tacks of iron or alloy (Graves 12 and 20), and one possible lining tack made of copper or alloy (Grave 4). Straight pins and clothing fasteners were found at the site, as were a few brick fragments and small sherds of refined white earthenware and redware.

The cast plate glass used to fashion coffin view plates and the hardware recovered during excavation were commonly available at general merchandise stores (cf. Clark 1964:228–229; Hacker-Norton and Trinkley 1984). Hacker-Norton and

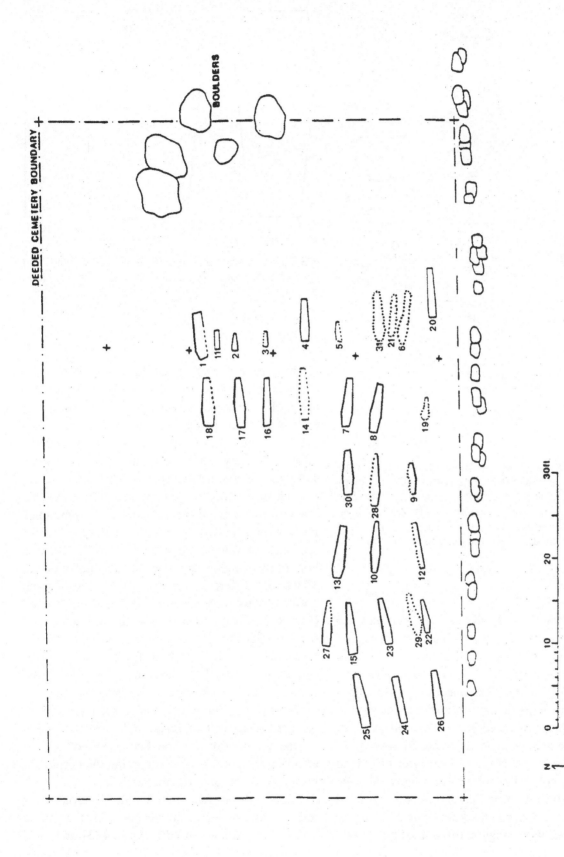

FIGURE 2. Site plan showing outlines of the 31 burial containers at the Uxbridge Almshouse Burial Ground, Uxbridge, Massachusetts. (Courtesy of Office of Public Archaeology, Boston University.)

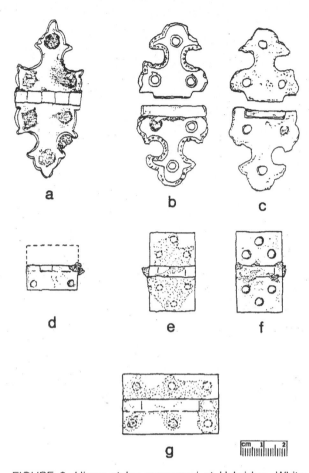

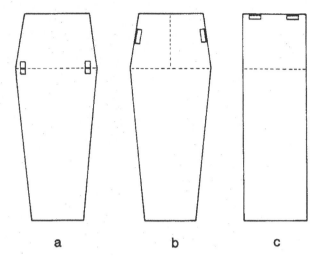

FIGURE 4. Conjectural reconstruction of hinged and divided burial container lid styles based on in situ hinge positions.

FIGURE 3. Hinge styles recovered at Uxbridge. White metal hinges: a, coffin butt hinge (Grave 1); b-c, dowel-type hinge (Grave 30) [b, obverse; c, reverse]. Brass butt hinges: d, Grave 12 (this example is rusted closed); e, Grave 19 (with iron wood screws); f, Grave 10 (with brass brads); g, Grave 8 (with iron wood screws).

Trinkley (1984:35–37) list wholesale prices for coffin screws and tacks at less than half a cent each (cf. Peck and Walter Manufacturing Company 1853:31; Orser et al. 1987, 1:413), probably what they cost in Uxbridge. The materials used for Uxbridge coffin construction were not expensive, but the cost of labor involved in building coffins is not known. The archaeologically recorded position of hinges suggests that at least three styles of hinged and divided coffin lids were made (Figure 4). One form of coffin lid opened up and forwards toward the feet (Figure 4a); another kind opened like a pair of window shutters (Figure 4b); a third type of lid

seems to have opened up and back toward the head of the coffin (Figure 4c). Two of these forms (Figure 4a-b) are known historically from surviving examples, from patent models, and from depictions in 19th-century documents (Concord Antiquarian Society 1967:Catalogue No. 57; Jones 1967:75; Pike and Armstrong 1980:151).

A close scrutiny of the container fittings reveals that coffins for the Uxbridge poor were sometimes made with a limited attention to detail and a general lack of fine craftsmanship. Two coffin lids bore only a single hinge (Graves 8 and 30); Grave 10 had two different sized hinges; the slots of some coffin screws were severely damaged or stripped (Figure 6e); and, most telling, the articulation of some bodies strongly suggests that decedents were frequently provided with ill-fitting coffins. Wesolowsky (1989a:183) has suggested that "the practice may indicate that coffins were not custommade to fit the individual, but rather more or less standard sizes were on hand; and if the coffin was a little too narrow for the late departed, a little effort on the part of those preparing the corpse for burial would resolve the matter."

None of the artifacts found with the burials contradicts the historical evidence that the burial ground was probably used between 1831 and 1872

(Cook 1989:58–60, 63–71; Elia 1989c:381–383); diagnostic features of grave markers, nails, wood screws, coffin hardware, clothing fasteners, and the few small ceramic sherds all indicate that the interments span the middle of the 19th century. Attempts to seriate the graves based on general manufacturing dates of these items proved unsuccessful, as the presence or absence of certain artifacts may have resulted from factors other than date of interment, e.g., the use of whatever hardware and coffins were on hand (cf. Habenstein and Lamers 1955:243–244; Hacker-Norton and Trinkley 1984:44, 48–50). White metal coffin hinges (Figures 3a-c and 5), in particular the styles recovered from Uxbridge, are depicted in hardware catalogues as early as 1861 to as late as 1904 (Sargent and Company 1861:107, 1866:129, 1869:155, 1871:277, 1904:46; Russell and Erwin Manufacturing Company 1865:332; Hawley Brothers Hardware Company 1884:409). Coffin screws and tacks (Figures 6 and 7), some identical to the Uxbridge examples, are described or illustrated in manufacturers' trade catalogues from as early as 1853 (Peck and Walter Manufacturing Company 1853:31) until at least 1877 (Hacker-Norton and Trinkley 1984:49–50). Since the styles of mass-produced coffin hardware recovered from Uxbridge appeared in the mid-19th century, only the burial containers manufactured after ca. 1850 would evidence such items. This factor, the *terminus post quem* of mass-produced coffin hardware, certainly modified the incidence of embellished coffins, given the limited temporal span of the Uxbridge series (ca. 1831–1872).

Among all the mortuary assemblages from the site, three graves (Graves 1, 12, and 30) contained the remains of more elaborate coffins. Cluster analyses run on the cemetery sample consistently singled out Graves 1, 12, and 30 for the above-average amount of coffin furniture. Coffin furniture from Grave 1 included two white metal hinges mounted onto a divided lid outfitted with a rectangular glass view plate. The coffin had 16 white metal coffin screws and 29 matching coffin tacks. The coffin from Grave 12 originally had two small brass hinges on a divided coffin lid with a rectangular glass view plate. The Grave 12 coffin also

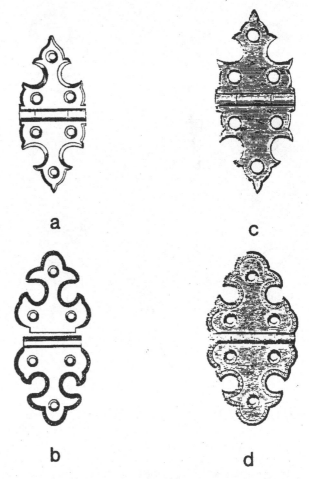

a   c

b   d

FIGURE 5. White metal coffin hinges, identical to Uxbridge forms, illustrated in 19th-century hardware catalogues (a-b, Russell and Erwin Manufacturing Company [1865:332]; c-d, Sargent and Company [1871:277]. Illustrations identical to c-d can also be seen in Sargent and Company [1866:129, 1869:155]. An illustration identical to d also appears in Hawley Brothers Hardware Company [1884:409] and in Sargent and Company [1904:366]).

had a brass hook-and-eye fastener. Ferrous tacks were possibly used to fasten a fabric lining or covering. Grave 30 contained a single white metal coffin hinge, six white metal coffin screws, and 42 matching coffin tacks. Wesolowsky's (1989a:183) observations of skeletal position for Graves 1, 12, and 30 did *not* indicate that the coffins for these individuals were noticeably ill-fitting. Such a circumstance might support the idea that the three more elaborate coffins were not simply available stock, but may have been specially commissioned

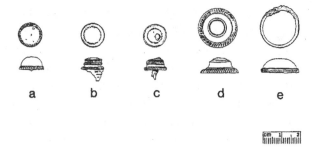

FIGURE 7. Coffin tack styles recovered at Uxbridge: a-d, white metal coffin tacks, plan and profile; e, brass tack, plan and profile. (a, Grave 1; b, Grave 11; c, Grave 2; d, Grave 30; e, Grave 27.)

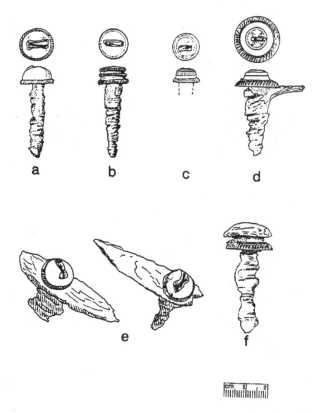

FIGURE 6. White metal coffin screw styles from Uxbridge: a-d, white metal coffin screws, plan and profile (a, Grave 1; b, Grave 4; c, Grave 2; d, Grave 30); e, coffin screws with stripped slots (Grave 1); f, one example of a wood fragment adhering to the top of a coffin screw (Grave 30), possibly indicating the use of "grave arches" or planks placed laterally across the coffin lid to forestall collapse (cf. Blakely and Beck 1982:188).

for the individuals interred therein. Then again, the normal dimensions of the coffins may only have been fortuitous.

Attempts to interpret intrasite variation in coffin decoration as evidence for differential status positions relating to age, sex, and/or racial categories were unconvincing and subsequently abandoned when faced with a nexus of conundrums that complicate the observation of differentially embellished coffins. Speculation in this regard revolved around a concatenation of events that could have resulted in decedents being provided with whatever burial containers were on hand, and not provided with coffins that matched their (hypothetically) variable status. Considerations included the

practice of using ready-made, stockpiled coffins; the different forms of hardware available at a given time (a function of the vagaries of technological innovation, marketing, supply, and demand [cf. Hacker-Norton and Trinkley 1984:49–51]); the documentary evidence that the Town of Uxbridge paid little money for paupers' coffins; and that particular discrepancies in the relative cost of paupers' coffins may not be directly related to status or decoration but to competitive prices negotiated between coffin purveyors and the town. The lack of internal evidence of a relative chronology among the graves (Elia 1988:17, 1989c:384) further confounded attempts to link coffin embellishment with differential status, as plain coffins may simply date earlier than coffins with decorative hardware. Other variables studied and found to be independent of age, sex, race, and coffin embellishment included grave marking, type of grave markers, and grave location. In sum, interpretations of intrasite variation at Uxbridge were so excessively qualified as to be inconclusive. The socioeconomic baseline of poverty of the almshouse inmates had been established through documentary evidence and later reinforced by conclusions drawn from the osteological data, indicating an institutional sample, generally consisting of "abandoned or orphaned children and . . . the destitute elderly bereft of family" (Elia 1989c:382). Provided with this socioeconomic background of misfortune, the research was not compelled by a search for status among the artifacts from the site. It was clear that relative status in such an adverse socioeconomic situation is culturally meaningless. It was possible, however, to understand the nature of death and burial at the site (generally minimal mortuary treatment) and to characterize the presence of embellished coffins in the cemetery as an aspect of 19th-century popular culture.

Elliot (1858:217), in his sentimental novel *New England's Chattels: or, Life in the Northern Poorhouse*, lamented the conditions under which a pauper's burial took place, saying, "the whole thing was economically arranged." It is widely known that pauper burials were modest (e.g., Elliot 1858: 205–211; Chaffin 1886:449; Hoffman 1919:12, 23–26, 51; Kleinberg 1977:203; Ames 1981:651). The relative paucity of coffin embellishment observed at the Uxbridge site is generally consistent with what one would expect from a paupers' cemetery. The coffin remains studied archaeologically reinforce historical data on the Uxbridge poor relief system: paupers in Uxbridge were generally provided with minimally decent care at low cost. Certainly, economic considerations played a large role in the treatment of the Uxbridge poor, both during life and at death.

The evidence of embellished coffins, however stylistically attenuated, can be understood in the context of the beautification of death movement. The apparent anomaly of embellished coffins in the Uxbridge paupers' burial ground is understandable when the absolute low cost and popularity of mass-produced coffin hardware is taken into consideration. Rectangular glass view plates, white metal hardware, brass tacks, and the brass hook-and-eye were inexpensive and readily available items, and regardless of their low cost, were present on burial containers for the poor. The presence of coffin hardware, such as white metal coffin fittings and glass view plates, demonstrates that the carpenters responsible for coffin construction were familiar with popular, marketable, decorative styles. The presence of these items on 45 percent of the coffins from the Uxbridge Almshouse Burial Ground, then, does not suggest an elevated economic or social status—the sum of evidence from the site denotes just the opposite. The people buried at town expense were, at death, a socially and economically marginal class. Archaeological evidence was invaluable to understanding the material manifestations of death practices accorded a marginal group. The significance of the data, reflecting a popular trend in American death practices, was drawn out by reference to historical and archaeological studies of American deathways. The results of complex social, political, economic, and technological factors were manifest in the mortuary assemblages uncovered at the site.

Implications for Status-Based Approaches to Historical Mortuary Assemblages

Decorative coffin hardware at historical cemetery sites has been considered as evidence to infer rank or status of decedents (cf. Thomas et al. 1977: 410–417; Woodall 1983:17–19; Hacker-Norton and Trinkley 1984:51; Trinkley and Hacker-Norton 1984:13–15; Rose and Santeford 1985b: 135–136, 1985c:156; Bell 1987:15–18; Parrington 1987:57–58; Owsley et al. 1988:90). Nonetheless, such hardware at the Uxbridge site, a paupers' burial ground, suggests that status-oriented archaeological approaches to historical mortuary data need to be reexamined.

First, by comparing the Uxbridge assemblages to sites used by black Americans, the roles of ethnicity and economic or social marginality as they affected material expressions of mortuary behavior can be considered. Next, a comparison of Uxbridge with other marginal burial sites and with a cemetery used by wealthy whites shows that the inference of social status solely based on the presence or absence of coffin furniture may not agree with known historical socioeconomic contexts. The resulting analysis suggests that the unqualified use of status-based interpretive frames is not a tenable approach to surviving material vestiges of historical funerary behavior. Intrasite differences in coffin embellishment may not be solely related to economic factors; a particular grave assemblage may or may not include particular forms of coffin hardware or even any hardware at all, depending on the state of technological development at the time, the vagaries of marketing and supply, the nature of burial (e.g., by a public institution rather than by family, neighbors, or friends), and a host of other factors. Given the nexus of variables that should be considered at the site-level of analysis, status-based approaches alone are not highly productive means to draw out the complexity of mortuary behavior.

Comparisons with Black American Cemeteries

While a little under half of the burial containers at Uxbridge had some decorative elements, even the decorative elements from the three most elaborate coffins from Graves 1, 12, and 30 appear minimal compared to burial containers recovered from most other 19th-century cemeteries, especially those (e.g., Oakland, Cedar Grove, and Mount Pleasant cemeteries) used by blacks. Consider the elaborate coffin handles and oval glass view plates recovered from the Oakland Cemetery in Atlanta, Georgia (Dickens and Blakely 1979; Blakely and Beck 1982:192, 202), or the frequent appearance of coffin handles, engraved plaques, thumbscrews, and escutcheons (lid fasteners), and oval glass view plates at the Cedar Grove Cemetery in Lafayette County, Arkansas (Rose 1985b). The Mount Pleasant Cemetery (38CH778) in Charleston County, South Carolina, yielded ornate coffin handles, decorative thumbscrews, studs, escutcheons, seven stamped brass coffin plaques and a single engraved, tin-plated copper coffin plaque (Trinkley and Hacker-Norton 1984:6, 9, passim). Similar types and quantities of hardware and glass view plates were also noted at the Millwood Cemetery in Abbeville County, South Carolina, possibly used by both black and white tenant farmers (Orser et al. 1987, 1:398–414; 3:93–106). In addition to the assemblages from Oakland, Cedar Grove, Mount Pleasant, and Millwood, compared above, archaeological excavations at other North American and Caribbean black cemeteries have uncovered similarly complex mortuary assemblages, both with and without mass-produced hardware (e.g., Combes 1974; Lange and Handler 1985:25–27; Parrington and Wideman 1986).

In contrast to the mortuary assemblages from other cemeteries, the Uxbridge site contained no coffin handles and no engraved coffin plaques. The two glass view plates were rectangular, unlike the oval or trapezoidal forms found elsewhere. And, while it seems to be a function of the date of the Uxbridge burial ground (cf. Hacker-Norton and Trinkley 1984:46–47), the site contained neither the thumbscrews nor escutcheons common at sites dating to the end of the 19th century. Furthermore, the Uxbridge coffins display none of the ostentation of the high-quality, mass-produced caskets that appeared in the late 19th century (e.g., Crane, Breed & Company 1867; Columbus Coffin Company 1882; National Casket Company 1891).

Deathways, Ethnicity, and Economy

Excavations at black American cemeteries provide insight to mortuary practices and beliefs among some segments of the population. Because at least some of these groups shared a low socioeconomic status (relative to other segments of American society), it is likely that some other factor or factors besides status played a role in the choice of elaborate coffins among some 19th-century blacks, such as persistent traditional beliefs in appeasing peripatetic spirits (cf. Pollak-Eltz 1974; Thompson 1984:132–142; Bell 1987:61–69).

The strength of ethnicity in directing material and social aspects of burial practices (Goodwin 1981; Koch 1983; Parrington and Wideman 1986: 59; Clark 1987:394–395; Thomas 1988) may have had a deciding impact on the presence of ornate burial containers at some black cemeteries. Among others (e.g., Schuyler 1980:viii), Parrington and Wideman (1986:59) recognized the difficulty of "distinguish[ing] between the culture of ethnicity and the culture of poverty," especially as those two "cultures" relate to the material manifestation of burial practices. Their point is most relevant when attempting to differentiate between documentary and material vestiges of ethnic-specific burial practices and mortuary treatment based on economic exigencies. It may be specious, therefore, to compare the artifact assemblages from black cemeteries (presumably used by both the richer and the poorer from more or less *separate* social groups) with the Uxbridge assemblages (from a burial ground used by a municipality to bury only the poor from *many* social groups). Paupers, by definition, occupied the lowest position on the economic scale, but their ranks were made up of people drawn from many social corners.

The selection of decorative coffin trimmings by both mainstream and marginal groups communicates much about these people's perception of their place in the society and economy of 19th-century America. Williams (1982) suggested that mass consumption of mass-produced items, imitative of expensive objects, reinforced a need among some to display the appearance of wealth and to impart a tenuous sense of security. "The outpouring of new commodities . . . created a world where the consumer could possess images of wealth without actually having a large income" (Williams 1982:92; cf. Trachtenberg 1982:130). Williams (1982:58–66) illuminated how this consumer revolution, where most people could acquire objects symbolic of apparent wealth and belonging, actually accentuated the real social and economic distances between classes. Conspicuous and mass consumption are dialectical; while attempting to mask socioeconomic inequality, they reveal larger social conflicts (cf. Douglas and Isherwood 1979:12, 89; Trachtenberg 1982:150–153).

Archaeological reports of burial sites supposedly used exclusively for people on the fringes of society described even sparser burial containers than those recovered from Uxbridge (cf. Dailey et al. 1972; Dethlefsen et al. 1977; Dethlefsen and Demyttenaere 1977; Leveillee et al. 1977; Sargent 1977; Thomas et al. 1977:398–412; Burnston and Thomas 1981; Lutz and Rubertone 1982; Kelley 1984; Piper and Piper 1987; Brian Nagel 1989, pers. comm.). The presence of plain burial containers held together by simple fasteners at these sites is a complex issue, best approached through the site-specific historical contexts. As at Uxbridge, some of the interments at these sites probably predate the introduction of mass-produced hardware. The social contexts of these sites—sometimes difficult to characterize for lack of documentary information—are also important factors to consider. The Catoctin Furnace Cemetery (Burnston and Thomas 1981) and Cunningham Mound (Thomas et al. 1977) were probably used by or for slaves. Dailey et al. (1972), Piper and Piper (1987), and Kelley (1984) reported on cemeteries used or overseen by the military or the government. Testing at the Bridgewater, Massachusetts, Correctional Institution found areas used to reinter the remains of inmates at a facility that had various uses as an almshouse, an insane asylum, and a prison (Leveillee et al. 1977; Lutz and Rubertone 1982). Brian Nagel (1989, pers. comm.) discussed the excavation of over 300 interments at the Highland Park Cemetery in Rochester, New York, associated with an almshouse and asylum between 1837 and 1862. Only two coffins had brass hinges, and the broken glass in one grave could not be definitively interpreted as a view plate because of disturbance. Personal and religious items—a brass ring, two crucifixes, and two sets of rosary beads—are notably present. A report on limited excavations of burials associated with an almshouse in Montgomery County, Maryland, operating continuously since the late 18th century, indicated that "far more grave goods [including coffin hardware] and differential burial patterns were discovered than expected" (Rhodes 1987:8).

The nature of interment at these sites, reflecting in many cases burial overseen by institutions and not by family or friends, confounds any attempt to interpret the social status of the decedents simply from an observation of plain or embellished coffins. The critical relationship between the historical information of decedents unable to pay burial costs and the observation of minimal burial treatment illuminates the material correlates of poverty, exploitation, and social distance.

To complicate the issue of class and burial treatment, Parrington's reports on the 18th- and 19th-century interments of a group of wealthy white Philadelphians described "various burial techniques . . . from interment in plain wooden coffins with simple iron handles to coffins with metal liners and elaborate and ornate cases and handles" (Parrington 1984:14; see also Parrington 1987:61–62). Again, intrasite differences in coffin styles are related to the dates of interment (Parrington 1987: 62), and the presence of plain containers may also be a function of consumer choices not to purchase elaborate coffins. Perhaps secure in their social and economic positions, and reflecting their Protestant beliefs, members of the Old St. Paul's Episcopal Church may not have been inclined to display the appearance of wealth through ornate burial containers for their dead. As Parrington (1987:62) indicated, however, interment in vaults at Old St. Paul's was more expensive than burial in earth graves and considered to be more prestigious and sanitary.

While the quality or quantity of coffin decoration was often obviously a function of what those responsible were able and willing to pay, the embellishment, per se, of a coffin with fancy hardware does not necessarily correlate with prominent social or economic status of the interred individual. The presence or absence of coffin hardware in a particular grave is a function of a complex chain of events related to date of burial, technological innovation, marketing and supply, stylistic change, and consumer preference (cf. Hacker-Norton and Trinkley 1984:49–51). Intrasite mortuary variability can be approached with explicit reference to the specific socio-historical context of individual cemeteries and the general context of death and burial in historical America. Documents and other kinds of material evidence may complement comparisons of mortuary practices within and between cemeteries and among socioeconomic groups. Grave markers, for example, commemorating individuals or family groups at 19th-century cemeteries conspicuously display relative expenditures in their material and dimensions (Ames 1981; Clark 1987; McGuire 1988). Because grave markers are on display to a community far longer than coffins, the symbolic representation of differential status is more permanently communicated through grave markers than through extravagant burial containers.

Status-Based Interpretations of Historical Mortuary Assemblages

One aspect of recent archaeological investigations at historical cemeteries is the observation of subtle and interesting distinctions in coffin decoration. Hacker-Norton and Trinkley's (1984; Trinkley and Hacker-Norton 1984) influential research on this aspect of material culture persuaded historical archaeologists that formal aspects of coffin hardware represented a productive area of mortuary research. Garrow (1987), for example, seriated coffin hardware in Georgia, providing guidance for synchronic dating of cemeteries and suggestive information on diachronic change in stylistic preferences. Interpretive difficulties are posed, however, by the inference that qualitative or quantitative intrasite differences in coffin hardware may be directly related to the social or economic rank of interred individuals (cf. Thomas et al. 1977:410–417; Woodall 1983:17–19; Hacker-Norton and Trinkley 1984:51; Trinkley and Hacker-Norton 1984:13–15; Rose and Santeford 1985b:135–136, 1985c:156; Bell 1987:15–18; Parrington 1987:57–58; Owsley et al. 1988:90). The unqualified application of status-based interpretive frames to archaeological remains of complex, industrialized cultures is problematic (cf. Beaudry 1988), as many of the researchers just cited have realized, but some have not explicitly acknowledged. The advent of mass production, for example, blurred socioeconomic distinctions based on the possession and control of certain objects because previously expensive articles could be cheaply imitated and globally distributed (Trachtenberg 1982:150–153; Williams 1982:92).

Interpretive models to infer rank at prehistoric mortuary sites (e.g., Bartel 1982) possess only a highly restricted utility when applied in an analogous manner to mass-produced coffin hardware. Mass-produced, inexpensive coffin hardware does not seem analogous to status symbols or grave goods that marked high ranking interments at prehistoric sites. Status symbols in prehistoric mortuary contexts are generally regarded as "exotic material items" (Tainter 1978:120), requiring a great energy expenditure to acquire or produce, and presumably restricted to an elite faction. Traditional mortuary analyses by prehistorians are geared toward inferring rank differentiation, determining descent or affinity groups, characterizing social organization, and elucidating details of emic belief systems (Tainter 1978; Bartel 1982). Tainter (1978:121) was unsatisfied with the "extensive reliance archaeologists place on grave associations", and echoed Brown's (1971) call for more rigorous studies that place the description and explanation of mortuary assemblages within the larger context of mortuary behavior. Brown and Tainter's position on the value of a comprehensive archaeological approach to mortuary behavior is embraced in this analysis. The beautification of death, considered as an archaeological horizon, is particularly apposite to this interpretive vein. Exclusive attention to historical grave assemblages, disregarding the socio-historical context of death and burial, creates some of the same interpretive difficulties addressed by modern pioneers of archaeological mortuary study (see Brown 1971; Tainter 1978; Bartel 1982). Accordingly, rank-based approaches to historical mortuary sites merit reexamination.

Hacker-Norton and Trinkley (1984:51; Trinkley and Hacker-Norton 1984:13–15) suggested that the amount and cost of coffin hardware in a grave are directly related to the decedent's rank. While it is clear that Hacker-Norton and Trinkley were interested in quantifying intrasite mortuary variability, relating the observation to variable cost and linking relative expenditures to differential status (Trinkley and Hacker-Norton 1984:13–15), it is also true that their pioneering research offered a considerably more complex view of coffin hardware in the economic world of the late 19th- and early 20th-century South than their status-based approach suggested. Technological innovation, marketing, supply, and demand in rural communities affected the availability—and, hence, the archaeological representation—of coffin hardware (Hacker-Norton and Trinkley 1984:44). Parrington (1987:57–58), Rose and Santeford (1985b: 135–136, 1985c:156), and Thomas et al. (1977: 410–417) tempered their traditional mortuary analyses by explicitly recognizing that factors other than status (e.g., technological development and pooling group resources to meet burial expenses) can account for variable mortuary assemblages at historical American sites. Consumer preferences, ethnicity, and the institution or group responsible for burial are other mitigating factors

in the nature of coffin embellishment within and between sites. Some investigators (e.g., Woodall 1983:19; Bell 1987:57–58, 65; Owsley et al. 1988: 90) acknowledge the possibility of using elaborate burial containers or personal items interred with the deceased as some measure of status at 19th- or 20th-century sites, but turn to other sources for this information. For example, Bell (1987:15–26, 79–95) gleaned socioeconomic information from primary historical documents and secondary sources as a point of departure for interpretations relating to death and burial of a marginal class; Owsley et al. (1988) focused on variations in grave assemblages, not for identifying status, per se, but as a means to differentiate civilian and military burials; Woodall (1983:7, 17–19) proposed that the relative depth of meticulously dug grave pits, certainly representing considerably effort on the part of grave diggers working in the hard clay of the Carolina Piedmont, is positively correlated to the status of the interred when interpreted in a systemic framework of relative energy expenditure.

Physical evidence of nutritional inadequacy, trauma, and high mortality among 19th-century black American cemetery populations has been detailed using skeletal remains (Rose and Rathbun 1987) at some of the same sites where high rank of individuals has been inferred using coffin hardware. Such evidence accentuates the unsatisfying conclusions drawn from a reductive reliance on status-based models; as Thomas (1988:115) concluded in his overview of mortuary variability in 16th- and 17th-century Spanish Florida, "it is clear that simplistic categorizations such as 'high status' and 'low status' serve to obscure considerably more than they clarify." Lange and Handler (1985), Parrington et al. (1986), Rose (1985a), and Rose and Rathbun (1987) made critically important links between physical evidence from black cemeteries regarding nutrition, health, and mortality with the historical fact of exploitation and discrimination experienced by 19th-century black Americans. Relating these findings to surviving material vestiges of mortuary behavior shows that black Americans, along with other marginal social groups, actively participated in popular cultural traditions. The limited use of coffin hardware in adult graves by two early 20th-century Choctaw families in Oklahoma may be a case in point (Ferguson 1983:7, 11, 15). Even within communities struggling under social, economic, and physical stress, funeral ritual, shaped by popular culture, was used to distinguish highly regarded individuals at their deaths (cf. Bell 1987: 42, 61–68). That such efforts may have included the use of decorative coffin hardware, symbolic of apparent wealth, is likely. Yet, such practices among marginal classes underscore their desires to bridge the real socioeconomic distance between classes by relying on cheap but highly symbolic objects.

Advances in mass production and distribution of coffin fittings, the continuity of local coffin construction after the appearance of ready-made, mass-produced coffins, and consumer strategies (e.g., fraternal burial insurance) followed by different social classes could work alone or in tandem essentially to mask economic distinctions in coffin styles. Toward the end of the 19th century, some firms produced high-quality caskets and silver coffin trimmings that could, one supposes, enable those who wished to reinforce class distinctions to do so through ostentatious display of an expensive casket (Crane, Breed & Company 1867; Columbus Coffin Company 1882; National Casket Company 1891; Bell 1987:17, 42, 57, 63). While an expensive casket can function as conspicuous display, mass-produced coffin hardware was inexpensive and used in the burials of many low-status groups.

Hacker-Norton and Trinkley (1984:50–51) observed that by reducing the number of items on a coffin or using less-expensive hardware styles, coffins could retain a decorative, richer appearance but actually cost less. Such saving measures are one aspect of Hacker-Norton and Trinkley's (1984: 51) understanding that coffin hardware could be used to "denote 'apparent' status as well as 'real' status." Inexpensive coffin hardware, however, did not denote real socioeconomic status at all. Rather, like many mass-produced items, coffin hardware was embraced even by the lower socioeconomic classes in an effort to conceal their real socioeconomic disparity. In Douglas and Isherwood's (1979:11–12) perspective, poverty is not defined by a want or lack of goods, it is defined by a lack of social involvement: "goods are neutral, the issues are social." The profusion of goods created by mass production did not ameliorate socioeconomic distance between classes.

Instead of viewing archaeological assemblages from mortuary sites as directly equated with status, the surviving material evidence from 19th-century cemeteries provides richer interpretations when seen in light of popular changes in mortuary ritual. In the case of the Uxbridge Almshouse Burial Ground, this interpretive angle helped to explain the apparent anomaly of embellished coffins in a paupers' burial ground. The observation that similar material items related to mortuary behavior have been recovered from archaeological contexts throughout North America, coupled with what is known about deathways in 19th-century America, leads to the conclusion that some aspects of a popular movement regarding proper burial of the dead were shared, in various ways, among many social and economic groups. When cast against the technological and social transformations of 19th-century industrialization, mass production and mass consumption can be acknowledged, dialectically, as a means to mediate persistent socioeconomic disparity.

Conclusions

Coffin builders who used popular decorative elements were responding to changes taking place in American deathways, a transformation marked by the increasing commercialization of death-related paraphernalia. Decorative coffin hardware is a small but definite embodiment of the beautification of death, a major cultural phenomenon that had a profound effect on the context of death and burial among most social groups in 19th-century America.

Funerary treatment accorded to some paupers in Uxbridge was consistent with the humanitarian and pragmatic rationale for the support of the poor. Pauper burials were meant to provide minimal Christian burial rites for those who could not pay for them. Decisions by many levels of the town and state government, however, restricted the amount of money available to bury the poor. Unlike the deathways of other social groups, the Uxbridge paupers had no choice in the nature of their funeral rituals. The mortuary assemblages from the site reflect the minimal funerary treatment accorded a marginal group dependent on policial structures for economic relief. Such minimally decent treatment enabled the Town of Uxbridge symbolically and literally to exclude the dependent poor from the community, while reconciling Christian ethics and political mandates. While the town seemingly fulfilled its Christian duties by what it perceived to be "humane and laudable" treatment of the Uxbridge poor, treatment that was "fit, proper and rational," the minimal nature of the burials is a clear testimony of the status accorded the poor, a group that the town made no effort to remember and who were, in fact, forgotten (cf. Cook 1989:48–49; Elia 1989a:5–8).

The absence of any indications of extravagant preparations for burial and the lack of any efforts to memorialize individual deaths suggests that the better known, elaborate aspects of the beautification of death had a negligible role in the death practices associated with the Uxbridge poor. The Uxbridge Almshouse Burial Ground, with its rude markers of quarry waste and fieldstone, stood in stark contrast to the landscaped "rural" cemeteries that were veritable statuary gardens. The Uxbridge coffin builders only expressed their contact with popular culture in the few fittings and minor departures in coffin styles observed at the site.

In comparison to most archaeological grave assemblages at other cemeteries, the Uxbridge examples reinforce the historical conclusions that pauper burials in Uxbridge were minimal. Nonetheless, the presence of any coffin hardware at a paupers' burial ground emphasizes the problematic nature of archaeological inferences directly linking coffin hardware with socioeconomic status. Economic factors alone do not account for the presence of decorated coffins at Uxbridge or at other cemeteries used to inter low-status 19th-century Americans. Given the limitations of status-based approaches to historical mortuary data, less confidence should be placed on the reliability of mass-produced coffin hardware as an unequivocal indication of socioeconomic rank of interred individuals.

In applying a template of traditional archaeological mortuary analyses, originally formulated to discern rank and descent in preindustrial cultures, historical archaeologists must consider the larger historical and cultural context of death and burial in industrializing America. The application of status-based mortuary analyses seems to be confounded by the recognition that coffin hardware is not strictly analogous to grave goods in a prehistoric context. The concomitant development of mass production, mass marketing, and mass consumption, along with advances in distribution systems, allowed inexpensive, decorative coffin hardware to be used in the burials of the socially and economically marginal. As with other inexpensive, mass-produced objects, symbolic of apparent wealth, coffin hardware was embraced by socially disenfranchised groups to mask the real nature of socioeconomic distance between classes.

In tandem, historical and archaeological studies of mortuary behavior can explore traditional deathways among historical America's disparate groups, seeking out the effects of popular culture and mass consumption on behavior and taste. Historical mortuary sites represent a unique source of data on deathways and may provide the only detailed information about the influence of popular culture on American death practices along the social spectrum.

ACKNOWLEDGMENTS

Principals on the Uxbridge Almshouse Burial Ground project included Ricardo J. Elia (Principal Investigator), Al B. Wesolowsky (Physical Anthropologist), and Lauren J. Cook (Project Historian). Some of the research presented in this article was accomplished for the Office of Public Archaeology (OPA) at Boston University under contract with the Massachusetts Department of Public Works. The research benefited from communication among the author, the principals, and the many scholars who generously shared their interest in and knowledge of American death practices. The figures accompanying the article were provided by courtesy of the OPA. The author expresses his appreciation to the staff of the OPA and the Department of Archaeology, in particular Mary C. Beaudry and Ricardo J. Elia, for their guidance and support. Thoughtful comments by three reviewers clarified many points in the article. Responsibility for the interpretations presented here remains solely with the author.

REFERENCES

AMES, KENNETH L.
1981 Ideologies in Stone: Meanings in Victorian Gravestones. *Journal of Popular Culture* 14(4):641–656.

ARIÈS, PHILIPPE
1982 *The Hour of Our Death,* trans. Helen Weaver. Random House, New York.

BARTEL, BRAD
1982 A Historical Review of Ethnological and Archaeological Analyses of Mortuary Practice. *Journal of Anthropological Archaeology* 1(1):32–58.

BEAUDRY, MARY C.
1988 Introduction. In *Documentary Archaeology in the New World,* edited by Mary C. Beaudry, pp. 1–3. Cambridge University Press, Cambridge.

BELL, EDWARD L.
1987 The Historical Archaeology of Mortuary Behavior at a Nineteenth-Century Almshouse Burial Ground. Unpublished M.A. thesis, Department of Archaeology, Boston University, Boston.
1989 Artifacts from the Uxbridge Almshouse Burial Ground. In *Archaeological Excavations at the Uxbridge Almshouse Burial Ground in Uxbridge, Massachusetts,* edited by Ricardo J. Elia and Al B. Wesolowsky, pp. 337–378. Report of Investigations No. 76. Office of Public Archaeology, Boston University, Boston.

BLAKELY, ROBERT L., AND LANE A. BECK
1982 Bioarchaeology in the Urban Context. In *Archaeology of Urban America: The Search for Pattern and Process,* edited by Roy S. Dickens, Jr., pp. 175–207. Academic Press, New York.

BRAUNER, DAVID R., AND PAUL CHRISTY JENKINS
1980 *Archeological Recovery of Historic Burials within the Applegate Lake Project Area, Jackson County, Oregon.* Department of Anthropology, Oregon State University, Corvallis.

BROOKE, JOHN L.
1988 "For Honour and Civil Worship to Any Worthy Person": Burial, Baptism, and Community on the Massachusetts New Frontier, 1730–1790. In *Material Life in America, 1600–1860,* edited by Robert Blair St. George, pp. 463–485. Northeastern University Press, Boston.

BROWN, JAMES A.
1971 Introduction. In *Approaches to the Social Dimensions of Mortuary Practices,* edited by James A. Brown, pp. 1–5. Memoirs of the Society for American Archaeology No. 25. Society for American Archaeology.

BUCKLEY, P. G.
1980 Truly We Live in a Dying World: Mourning on Long Island. In *A Time to Mourn: Expressions of Grief in Nineteenth Century America,* edited by Martha V. Pike and Janice Gray Armstrong, pp. 107–124. Museums at Stony Brook, Stony Brook, New York.

BURKE, PETER
1978 *Popular Culture in Early Modern Europe.* Harper and Row, New York.

BURNSTON, SHARON ANN, AND RONALD A. THOMAS
1981 *Archaeological Data Recovery at Catoctin Furnace Cemetery, Frederick County, Maryland.* Mid-Atlantic Archaeological Research Associates, Newark, Delaware.

CHAFFIN, WILLIAM L.
1886 *History of the Town of Easton, Massachusetts.* John Wilson & Son, Cambridge, Massachusetts.

CLARK, LYNN
1987 Gravestones: Reflectors of Ethnicity or Class? In *Consumer Choice in Historical Archaeology,* edited by Suzanne M. Spencer-Wood, pp. 383–395. Plenum Press, New York.

CLARK, THOMAS D.
1964 *Pills, Petticoats and Plows: The Southern Country Store.* University of Oklahoma, Norman.

COLUMBUS COFFIN COMPANY
1882 *Illustrated Catalogue.* Columbus Coffin Co., Columbus, Ohio. [1984 facsimile edition (microfiche). In *Trade Catalogues at Winterthur,* compiled by E. Richard McKinstry, Item 618. Clearwater Publishing Co., New York.]

COMBES, JOHN D.
1974 Ethnography, Archaeology, and Burial Practices among Coastal South Carolina Blacks. *The Conference on Historic Site Archeology Papers, 1972* 7: 52–61. Columbia, South Carolina.

CONCORD ANTIQUARIAN SOCIETY
1967 *Memento Mori: Two Hundred Years of Funerary Art and Customs in Concord, Massachusetts.* Concord Antiquarian Society, Concord.

COOK, LAUREN J.
1988 A Family of Strangers: Documentary Archaeology and the Uxbridge Town Farm. Paper presented at the 21st Annual Meeting of the Society for Historical Archaeology, Reno, Nevada.
1989 The Uxbridge Poor Farm in the Documentary Record. In *Archaeological Excavations at the Uxbridge Alms-*

house Burial Ground in Uxbridge, Massachusetts, edited by Ricardo J. Elia and Al B. Wesolowsky, pp. 48–107. Report of Investigations No. 76. Office of Public Archaeology, Boston University, Boston.

COSTELLO, JULIA G., AND PHILLIP L. WALKER
1987 Burials from the Santa Barbara Presido Chapel. *Historical Archaeology* 21(1):3–17.

CRANE, BREED & COMPANY
1867 *Wholesale Price List of Patent Metallic Burial Cases and Caskets* . . . Crane, Breed & Co., Cincinnati. [1984 facsimile edition (microfiche). In *Trade Catalogues at Winterthur*, compiled by E. Richard McKinstry, Item 621. Clearwater Publishing Co., New York.]

DAILEY, ROBERT C., L. ROSS MORRELL,
AND W. A. COCKRELL
1972 *The St. Marks Military Cemetery (8WA108)*. Bureau of Historic Sites and Properties Bulletin No. 2. Florida Department of State, Tallahassee.

DEETZ, JAMES, AND EDWIN S. DETHLEFSEN
1967 Death's Head, Cherub, Urn and Willow. *Natural History* 76(3):29–37.

DETHLEFSEN, EDWIN S., L. CABOT BRIGGS,
AND LEO P. BIESE
1977 The Clement Site: Analysis of Skeletal Material. *Man in The Northeast* 13:86–90.

DETHLEFSEN, EDWIN S., AND NANCY DEMYTTENAERE
1977 The Clement Site: Features and Artifacts. *Man in the Northeast* 13:90–96.

DICKENS, ROY S., JR., AND ROBERT L. BLAKELY
1979 Preliminary Report on Archaeological Investigations in Oakland Cemetery, Atlanta, Georgia. *The Conference on Historic Site Archeology Papers, 1978* 13:286–314. Columbia, South Carolina.

DOUGLAS, ANN
1975 Heaven Our Home: Consolation Literature in the Northern United States, 1830–1880. In *Death in America*, edited by David E. Stannard, pp. 49–68. University of Pennsylvania Press, Philadelphia.

DOUGLAS, MARY, AND BARON ISHERWOOD
1979 *The World of Goods*. Basic Books, New York.

EARLE, ALICE MORSE
1973 *Customs and Fashions in Old New England*. Charles E. Tuttle Co., Rutland, Vermont.
1977 Death Ritual in Colonial New York. In *Passing: The Vision of Death in America*, edited by Charles O. Jackson, pp. 30–41. Greenwood Press, Westport, Connecticut.

ELIA, RICARDO J.
1986 Death and Burial at a 19th-Century Almshouse. *Context* 5(1-2):1–4. Center for Archaeological Studies, Boston University.
1988 "Forgotten and Unknown till the Judgement Morn": Discovery and Excavation of the Uxbridge Almshouse

Burial Ground. Paper presented at the 21st Annual Meeting of the Society for Historical Archaeology, Reno, Nevada.
1989a The Uxbridge Almshouse Burial Ground Project. In *Archaeological Excavations at the Uxbridge Almshouse Burial Ground in Uxbridge, Massachusetts*, edited by Ricardo J. Elia and Al B. Wesolowsky, pp. 1–15. Report of Investigations No. 76. Office of Public Archaeology, Boston University, Boston.
1989b Archaeological Context. In *Archaeological Excavations at the Uxbridge Almshouse Burial Ground in Uxbridge, Massachusetts*, edited by Ricardo J. Elia and Al B. Wesolowsky, pp. 16–47. Report of Investigations No. 76. Office of Public Archaeology, Boston University, Boston.
1989c Conclusions and Recommendations. In *Archaeological Excavations at the Uxbridge Almshouse Burial Ground in Uxbridge, Massachusetts*, edited by Ricardo J. Elia and Al B. Wesolowsky, pp. 379–400. Report of Investigations No. 76. Office of Public Archaeology, Boston University, Boston.

ELIA, RICARDO J., AND AL B. WESOLOWSKY
(EDITORS)
1989 *Archaeological Excavations at the Uxbridge Almshouse Burial Ground in Uxbridge, Massachusetts*. Report of Investigations No. 76. Office of Public Archaeology, Boston University, Boston.

ELLIOT, SAMUEL HAYES
1858 *New England's Chattels: or, Life in the Northern Poor-house*. H. Dayton, New York.

FAIRBANKS, JONATHAN L., AND ROBERT F. TRENT
(EDITORS)
1982 *New England Begins: The Seventeenth Century*. 3 vols. Museum of Fine Arts, Boston.

FARRELL, JAMES J.
1980 *Inventing the American Way of Death, 1830–1920*. Temple University Press, Philadelphia.

FAULKNER, ALARIC, KIM MARK PETERS, DAVID P.
SELL, AND EDWIN S. DETHLEFSEN
1978 *Port and Market: Archaeology of the Central Waterfront, Newburyport, Massachusetts*. Interagency Archaeological Services, National Park Service, Atlanta.

FELLOWS, F. P.
n.d. [ca. 1850]
Untitled catalogue. F.P. Fellows, Wolverhampton, England. [1984 facsimile edition (microfiche). In *Trade Catalogues at Winterthur*, compiled by E. Richard McKinstry, Item 1095. Clearwater Publishing Co., New York.]

FERGUSON, BOBBIE
1983 *Final Report on the McGee Creek Cemetery Relocations, Atoka County, Oklahoma*. Bureau of Reclamation, U.S. Department of the Interior, Ferris, Oklahoma. Microfiche.

FINNIGAN, JAMES T.
1981 St. Barnabas Burials: Salvage Excavations at a Late 19th Century Cemetery. *Na'Pao: A Saskatchewan Anthropology Journal* 11(12):41–48.

FOX, ANNE A.
1984 *A Study of Five Historic Cemeteries at Choke Canyon Reservoir, Live Oak and McMullen Counties, Texas.* Choke Canyon Series No. 9. Center for Archaeological Research, University of Texas at San Antonio, San Antonio.

FRENCH, STANLEY
1975 The Cemetery as Cultural Institution: The Establishment of Mount Auburn and the "Rural Cemetery" Movement. In *Death in America,* edited by David E. Stannard, pp. 39–48. University of Pennsylvania Press, Philadelphia.

GARROW, PATRICK H.
1987 A Preliminary Seriation of Coffin Hardware Forms in Late Nineteenth and Early Twentieth Century Georgia. Paper presented at the Annual Meeting of the Eastern States Archaeological Federation, Charleston, South Carolina.

GITTINGS, CLARE
1984 *Death, Burial and the Individual in Early Modern England.* Croom Helm, London.

GOODWIN, CONRAD M.
1981 Ethnicity in the Graveyard. Unpublished M.A. thesis, Department of Anthropology, College of William and Mary, Williamsburg.

GOODY, JACK
1975 Death and the Interpretation of Culture: A Bibliographic Overview. In *Death in America,* edited by David E. Stannard, pp. 1–8. University of Pennsylvania Press, Philadelphia.

HABENSTEIN, ROBERT W., AND WILLIAM M. LAMERS
1955 *The History of American Funeral Directing.* Bulfin, Milwaukee.

HACKER-NORTON, DEBI, AND MICHAEL TRINKLEY
1984 *Remember Man Thou Art Dust: Coffin Hardware of the Early Twentieth Century.* Chicora Foundation Research Series No. 2. Chicora Foundation, Columbia, South Carolina.

HANSEN, JULIE
1989 Analysis of Uxbridge Coffin Wood. In *Archaeological Excavations at the Uxbridge Almshouse Burial Ground in Uxbridge, Massachusetts,* edited by Ricardo J. Elia and Al B. Wesolowsky, pp. 488–495. Report of Investigations No. 76. Office of Public Archaeology, Boston University, Boston.

HAWLEY BROTHERS HARDWARE COMPANY
1884 *Price List and Illustrated Catalogue of Hardware and Agricultural Implements* . . . Hawley Brothers, San Francisco.

HOFFMAN, FREDERICK L.
1919 *Pauper Burials and the Interment of the Dead in Large Cities.* Prudential Press, Newark, New Jersey.

HUNTINGTON, RICHARD, AND PETER METCALF
1979 *Celebrations of Death: The Anthropology of Mortuary Ritual.* Cambridge University Press, Cambridge.

JACKSON, CHARLES O.
1977a American Attitudes to Death. *Journal of American Studies* 11(3):297–312.

JACKSON, CHARLES O. (EDITOR)
1977b *Passing: The Vision of Death in America.* Greenwood Press, Westport, Connecticut.

JONES, BARBARA
1967 *Design for Death.* Bobbs-Merrill, Indianapolis.

JORDAN, TERRY C.
1982 *Texas Graveyards: A Cultural Legacy.* University of Texas Press, Austin.

KELLEY, JEFFREY A.
1984 Skeletal Remains from Chelsea: The U.S. Marine Hospital. Typescript on file, Massachusetts Historical Commission, Boston.

KLEINBERG, SUSAN J.
1977 Death and the Working Class. *Journal of Popular Culture* 11(1):193–209.

KOCH, JOAN K.
1983 Mortuary Behavior Patterning and Physical Anthropology in Colonial St. Augustine. In *Spanish St. Augustine: The Archaeology of a Colonial Creole Community,* edited by Kathleen A. Deagan, pp. 187–227. Academic Press, New York.

LANGE, FREDERICK W., AND JEROME S. HANDLER
1985 The Ethnohistorical Approach to Slavery. In *The Archaeology of Slavery and Plantation Life,* edited by Theresa A. Singleton, pp. 15–32. Academic Press, New York.

LEONARDI, THOM
1986 Casket Furniture from Monroeville. Paper presented at the 19th Annual Meeting of the Society for Historical Archaeology, Sacramento.

LEVEILLEE, ALAN D., BRUCE J. LUTZ, AND DUNCAN RITCHIE
1981 *An Archaeological Assessment of Historic Cemeteries on the Grounds of the Massachusetts Correctional Institution, Bridgewater.* Public Archaeology Laboratory, Department of Anthropology, Brown University, Providence.

LUTZ, BRUCE J., AND PATRICIA E. RUBERTONE
1982 *Archaeological Investigations Relating to Cemeteries Within the Bounds of the Perimeter Fence, Massachusetts Correctional Institution, Bridgewater.* Public Archaeology Laboratory, Department of Anthropology, Brown University, Providence.

McGuire, Randall H.
1988 Dialogues with the Dead: Ideology and the Cemetery. In *The Recovery of Meaning: Historical Archaeology in the Eastern United States*, edited by Mark P. Leone and Parker B. Potter, Jr., pp. 435–480. Smithsonian Institution Press, Washington.

McKinstry, E. Richard (editor)
1984 *Trade Catalogues at Winterthur: A Guide to the Literature of Merchandising, 1750 to 1980*. Garland, New York.

McReynolds, Mary Jane
1981 *Archaeological Investigations at the Laredo Cemetery Site (41WB22), Webb County, Texas*. Reports of Investigations No. 11. Prewitt & Associates, Austin.

Morley, John
1971 *Death, Heaven, and the Victorians*. University of Pittsburgh Press, Pittsburgh.

Mytum, Harold
1989 Public Health and Private Sentiment: The Development of Cemetery Architecture and Funerary Monuments from the Eighteenth Century Onwards. *World Archaeology* 21(2):283–297.

National Casket Company
1891 *National Casket Company, Buffalo, N.Y., 1891*. National Casket Co., Buffalo. [1984 facsimile edition (microfiche). In *Trade Catalogues at Winterthur*, compiled by E. Richard McKinstry, Item 638. Clearwater Publishing Co., New York.]

Nelson, Lee H.
1980 Introduction. In *Illustrated Catalogue of American Hardware of the Russell and Erwin Manufacturing Company*, pp. iii–xi. Association for Preservation Technology, n.p.

Noël Hume, Ivor
1969 *Historical Archaeology*. Alfred A. Knopf, New York.

Olafson, Peter
1985 Breaking Backs for Bones. *Times-Herald Record*, November 10:5, 92. Middletown, New York.

Orser, Charles E., Jr., Annette M. Nekola, and James L. Roark
1987 *Exploring the Rustic Life: Multidisciplinary Research at Millwood Plantation, A Large Piedmont Plantation in Abbeville County, South Carolina, and Elbert County, Georgia*. 3 vols. Russell Papers 1987. Archaeological Services, National Park Service, Atlanta. Mid-Atlantic Research Center, Loyola University of Chicago, Chicago.

Owsley, Douglas W., Mary H. Manhein, and Ann M. Whitmer
1988 *Burial Archaeology and Osteology of a Confederate Cemetery at Port Hudson, Louisiana (16EF68), Report of Investigations*. Division of Archaeology, Louisiana Department of Culture, Recreation, and Tourism, Baton Rouge.

Parrington, Michael
1984 *An Archaeological and Historical Investigation of the Burial Ground at Old St. Paul's Church, Philadelphia, Pennsylvania*. John Milner Associates, Philadelphia.
1987 Cemetery Archaeology in the Urban Environment: A Case Study from Philadelphia. In *Living in Cities: Current Research in Urban Archaeology*, edited by Edward Staski, pp. 56–64. Special Publication Series No. 5. Society for Historical Archaeology.

Parrington, Michael, S. Pinter, and T. Struthers
1986 Occupations and Health Among Nineteenth-Century Black Philadelphians. *MASCA Journal* 4(1):37–41. Museum Applied Science Center for Archaeology, University Museum, University of Pennsylvania, Philadelphia.

Parrington, Michael, and Janet Wideman
1986 Acculturation in an Urban Setting: The Archaeology of a Black Philadelphia Cemetery. *Expedition* 28(1): 55–62. The University Museum, University of Pennsylvania, Philadelphia.

Payne, Ted M., and Ronald A. Thomas
1988 *Relocation of the Nowell Family Cemetery, (7K-E-174, CRS K-6395), Harrington, Delaware, Final Report*. Mid-Atlantic Archaeological Research Associates, Newark, Delaware.

Peck and Walter Manufacturing Company
1853 *Price List*. Peck and Walter Mfg. Co., n.p.

Pike, Martha V.
1980 In Memory Of: Artifacts Relating to Mourning in Nineteenth Century America. *Journal of American Culture* 3(4):642–659.

Pike, Martha V., and Janice Gray Armstrong (editors)
1980 *A Time to Mourn: Expressions of Grief in Nineteenth Century America*. Museums at Stony Brook, Stony Brook, New York.

Piper, Harry M., and Jacquelyn G. Piper
1987 Cultural Response to Stress: An Example from a Second Seminole War Cemetery. Paper presented at the 20th Annual Meeting of the Society for Historical Archaeology, Savannah.

Pollak-Eltz, Angelina
1974 *El concepto de múltiples almas y algunos ritos fúnebres entre los negros americanos*. Instituto de Investigaciones Historicas, Universidad Católica, Caracas.

Reitz, Elizabeth J., Tyson Gibbs, and Ted A. Rathbun
1985 Archaeological Evidence for Subsistence on Coastal Plantations. In *The Archaeology of Slavery and Plantation Life*, edited by Theresa A. Singleton, pp. 163–191. Academic Press, New York.

RHODES, DIANE LEE
1987 *Report on Archeological Investigations at the Poor Farm Cemetery, Montgomery County, Maryland, Summer 1987.* Applied Archeology Center, National Park Service, Rockville, Maryland.

RIIS, JACOB A.
1890 *How the Other Half Lives: Studies among the Tenements of New York.* Charles Scribner's Sons, New York.

ROSE, JEROME C.
1985a Cedar Grove and Black American History. In *Gone to a Better Land: A Biohistory of a Rural Black Cemetery in the Post-Reconstruction South,* edited by Jerome C. Rose, pp. 146–152. Arkansas Archeological Research Series No. 25. Arkansas Archeological Survey, Fayetteville.

ROSE, JEROME C. (EDITOR)
1985b *Gone to a Better Land: A Biohistory of a Rural Black Cemetery in the Post-Reconstruction South.* Arkansas Archeological Research Series No. 25. Arkansas Archeological Survey, Fayetteville.

ROSE, JEROME C., AND TED A. RATHBUN (EDITORS)
1987 Afro-American Biohistory Symposium. *American Journal of Physical Anthropology* 74(2):177–273.

ROSE, JEROME C. AND LAWRENCE GENE SANTEFORD
1985a Burial Descriptions. In *Gone to a Better Land: A Biohistory of a Rural Black Cemetery in the Post-Reconstruction South,* edited by Jerome C. Rose, pp. 39–129. Arkansas Archeological Research Series No. 25. Arkansas Archeological Survey, Fayetteville.
1985b Burial Interpretations. In *Gone to a Better Land: A Biohistory of a Rural Black Cemetery in the Post-Reconstruction South,* edited by Jerome C. Rose, pp. 130–145. Arkansas Archeological Research Series No. 25. Arkansas Archeological Survey, Fayetteville.
1985c Proposed Research Directions for Analysis. In *Gone to a Better Land: A Biohistory of a Rural Black Cemetery in the Post-Reconstruction South,* edited by Jerome C. Rose, pp. 156–157. Arkansas Archeological Research Series No. 25. Arkansas Archeological Survey, Fayetteville.

RUSSELL AND ERWIN MANUFACTURING COMPANY
1865 *Illustrated Catalogue of American Hardware . . .* Russell and Erwin Manufacturing Co., New Britain, Connecticut. [1980 facsimile edition. Association for Preservation Technology, n.p.]

ST. GEORGE, ROBERT BLAIR
1988 Introduction. In *Material Life in America, 1600–1860,* edited by Robert Blair St. George, pp. 3–13. Northeastern University Press, Boston.

SARGENT AND COMPANY
1861 *J.B. Sargent & Co., New Britain, Conn., Sargent & Co., No. 85 Beekman St., New York, New York 1861.* Sargent and Co., n.p.

1866 *Prices of Hardware. . . .* Tuttle, Morehouse, & Taylor, New Haven.
1869 *Illustrated Catalogue and Price List of Hardware and Mechanics' Tools Manufactured and Sold. . . .* Sargent and Co., n.p.
1871 *Price List of Illustrated Hardware Manufactured and for Sale. . . .* Sargent and Co., n.p.
1904 *Coffin and Casket Trimmings. . . .* Sargent and Co., New Haven and New York.

SARGENT, HOWARD R.
1977 The Clement Site: Field Investigation. *Man in the Northeast* 13:79–86.

SCHORSCH, ANITA
1976 *Mourning Becomes America: Mourning Art in the New Nation.* Main Street Press, Clinton, New Jersey.

SCHUYLER, ROBERT L.
1980 Preface. In *Archaeological Perspectives on Ethnicity in America,* edited by Robert L. Schuyler, pp. vii–viii. Baywood Monographs in Archaeology No. 1. Baywood Publishing Co., Farmingdale, New York.

SMITH, CYRIL STANLEY
1974 Reflections on Technology and the Decorative Arts in the Nineteenth Century. In *Technological Innovation and the Decorative Arts,* edited by Ian M.G. Quimby and Polly Anne Earl, pp. 1–64. University Press of Virginia, Charlottesville.

SOUTH, STANLEY
1979 *The General, The Major, and the Angel: The Discovery of General William Moultrie's Grave.* Research Manuscript Series No. 146. University of South Carolina, Institute of Archeology, Columbia.

STANNARD, DAVID E.
1975 Introduction. In *Death in America,* edited by David E. Stannard, pp. vii–xv. University of Pennsylvania Press, Philadelphia.
1979 Calm Dwellings. *American Heritage* 30(5):42–55.

TAINTER, JOSEPH A.
1978 Mortuary Practices and the Study of Prehistoric Social Systems. In *Advances in Archaeological Method and Theory* 1, edited by Michael B. Schiffer, pp. 105–141. Academic Press, New York.

TAYLOR, ANNA J., ANNE A. FOX, AND I. WAYNNE COX
1986 *Archaeological Investigations at Morgan Chapel Cemetery (41 BP 200), A Historic Cemetery in Bastrop County, Texas.* Archaeological Survey Report No. 146. Center for Archaeological Research, University of Texas at San Antonio, San Antonio.

THOMAS, DAVID HURST
1988 Saints and Soldiers at Santa Catalina: Hispanic Designs for Colonial America. In *The Recovery of Meaning: Historical Archaeology in the Eastern*

United States, edited by Mark P. Leone and Parker B. Potter, Jr., pp. 73–140. Smithsonian Institution Press, Washington.

THOMAS, DAVID HURST, STANLEY SOUTH, AND
CLARK SPENCER LARSEN
1977 Rich Man, Poor Men: Observations on Three Antebellum Burials from the Georgia Coast. *Anthropological Papers of the American Museum of Natural History* 54(3):393–420.

THOMPSON, ROBERT FARRIS
1984 *Flash of the Spirit: African and Afro-American Art and Philosophy.* Random House, New York.

TRACHTENBERG, ALAN
1982 *The Incorporation of America: Culture and Society in the Gilded Age.* Hill and Wang, New York.

TRINKLEY, MICHAEL, AND DEBI HACKER-NORTON
1984 *Analysis of Coffin Hardware from 38CH778, Charleston County, South Carolina.* Chicora Foundation Research Series No. 3. Chicora Foundation, Columbia, South Carolina.

UNITED STATES GEOLOGICAL SURVEY
1979 Blackstone, Massachusetts, Quadrangle (7.5 minute series). United States Geological Survey, Washington, D.C.

UXBRIDGE, TOWN OF
1841– Selectmen's Records, 1841–1868. Bound ms. vol-
1868 ume. Town Clerk's Office, Uxbridge, Massachusetts. [1848–Town Meetings, etc. Vol. 5 [1848–1870]. Bound ms. 1870] volume. Town Clerk's Office, Uxbridge, Massachusetts.

WATKINS, LURA WOODSIDE
1962 Middleton Buried Its Dead. *Essex Institute Historical Collections* 98(1):26–34.

WEGARS, PRISCILLA, RODERICK SPRAGUE, AND
THOMAS M. J. MULINSKI
1983 *Miscellaneous Burial Recovery in Eastern Washington, 1981.* University of Idaho Anthropological Research Manuscript Series No. 76. Laboratory of Anthropology, University of Idaho, Moscow, Idaho.

WESOLOWSKY, AL B.
1988 "A Sort of Journey I Never Thought to Go": The Bones of the Uxbridge Paupers. Paper presented at the 21st Annual Meeting of the Society for Historical Archaeology, Reno, Nevada.
1989a Osteological Analysis. In *Archaeological Excavations at the Uxbridge Almshouse Burial Ground in Uxbridge, Massachusetts,* edited by Ricardo J. Elia and Al B. Wesolowsky, pp. 173–302. Report of Investigations No. 76. Office of Public Archaeology, Boston University, Boston.
1989b The Osteology of the Uxbridge Paupers. In *Archaeological Excavations at the Uxbridge Almshouse Burial Ground in Uxbridge, Massachusetts,* edited by Ricardo J. Elia and Al B. Wesolowsky, pp. 303–336. Report of Investigations No. 76. Office of Public Archaeology, Boston University, Boston.

WIGGINTON, ELIOT (EDITOR)
1973 Old-Time Burial Customs. In *Foxfire 2,* edited by Eliot Wigginton, pp. 304–323. Anchor Press/Doubleday, Garden City, New York.

WILLEY, GORDON R., AND PHILIP PHILLIPS
1958 *Method and Theory in American Archaeology.* University of Chicago Press, Chicago.

WILLIAMS, ROSALIND H.
1982 *Dream Worlds: Mass Consumption in Late Nineteenth-Century France.* University of California Press, Berkeley.

WOODALL, J. NED
1983 *Excavation and Analysis of the Vawter-Swaim Cemetery, 31FY714, Forsyth County, North Carolina.* Archeology Laboratories, Museum of Man, Wake Forest University, Winston-Salem.

YENTSCH, ANNE E.
1981 Death, Misfortune, and Communal Responsibility in Seventeenth Century New England. Paper presented at the 41st Conference on Early American History of the Institute of Early American History and Culture, Millersville, Pennsylvania.

EDWARD L. BELL
MASSACHUSETTS HISTORICAL COMMISSION
80 BOYLSTON STREET
BOSTON, MASSACHUSETTS 02116

LESTER A. ROSS
JOHN D. LIGHT

A Guide to the Description and Interpretation of Metal Files

Introduction

Files can often be identified as a discrete artifact class, due in part to their composition and surviving stylistic attributes. Oxidation of the ferrous alloys will obscure many important attributes. After physical brushing or careful chipping of a limited amount of the corrosive encrustation and rust, most significant attributes can be identified. Comparisons of these attributes with historical illustrations, and the identification of historical manufacturers, provides useful information for functional, geographical, and temporal interpretations.

Files are originally constructed as tools for specific tasks and functions. These functions can be inferred from the files themselves and from the contexts in which they are found. For example, a smooth, 3-square file recovered from a fur trade site probably represents a gun-working tool (Karklins 1983:139, 155, 159). Rough, coarse, and bastard files recovered from a site may represent the tools of a stone mason or sawyer. An assemblage of smooth and second-cut files may indicate the presence of an instrument maker or cutler. Functional interpretations are often speculative, due to the lack of an adequate assemblage of tools and by-products or to limited historical evidence. To extract interpretive data and comparative information from the files recovered from historical sites requires a common lexicon for file attributes, types, sizes, and historical equivalents. The first requirement should be the adoption of a standard terminology for describing stylistic attributes.

There are nearly as many artifact cataloguing systems as there are archaeological research organizations. It is not the intention of this guide to put forward any one system as superior, but rather to provide terminology by which archaeologists can communicate their findings.

Many historical trades used files. Some file shapes (such as flat files) had universal applications, so they cannot be given a specific functional attribution. Frequently, however, files were designed to do a particular job, but because they were so task-specific, they were rare; e.g., a wood carver's rifflers or a shoemaker's channel file (a tool for cleaning out a channel cut in leather so that stitches may be recessed). These files often had unique trade names. Occasionally, however, names were given to trade-specific tools without reference to other usage, so the same word might refer to two or more quite different objects, as is the case with a farrier's, shoemaker's, and marble worker's float. This guide represents a rudimentary introduction for the description of files. It cannot replace the hard task of understanding (as opposed to knowing about) the tool itself (Nicholson File Co. 1956); but in metal research, it is unfortunately still a case of: "One foot up and one foot down, That's the way to London town."

File Description

File Definition

A file is the generic name for any metal tool with raised teeth or ridges on one or more of its surfaces which is used to reduce, smooth, or sharpen the surface of another material through abrasion (Figure 1). The word can be used as a verb, not only to describe the action of reducing the surface of something, but also as a direct synonym for the verb "sharpen," as in, to file an axe. All files have two attributes in common: one or more working faces and multiple cutting teeth. Included within this category are tools commonly identified as the burnishers, floats, rasps, rifflers, and steels used for abrading wood, metal, stone, leather, hooves and fingernails, bone, and teeth. Since files could also function as fine cutting implements when used on edge, they were occasionally utilized for scoring or incising bone, glass, shell, etc. From descriptions available in early historical accounts, files were primarily associated with metal working activities, presumably reflecting their historical

Lester A. Ross and John D. Light

development within the metal trades (Biringuccio 1540:216, 307, 363; Moxon 1703:15-17; Appleton 1851:760ff; Ure 1864:708ff).

Historical Development

Metallic files in Europe were probably introduced during the initial years of the "metal age." Archaeological examples of ferrous files have been recovered from 1st- to 3rd-century Roman camps in Britain, and based upon the diversity of styles during that period, prior temporal development must have been extensive. Functionally, files appear to have been initially developed as metal working tools (I Samuel 13:21), but by the "Age of New World Explorations," functional variations included at least wood-working tools as well. As such usages imply, files had to be strong, relatively durable, and manufactured from materials harder than the material upon which they were used.

General Features and Methods of Manufacture

Since files were intended for hard usage on relatively inflexible substances, they were commonly manufactured from steel. Prior to the introduction of special alloy steels in the late 19th century, ferrous metals which were considered suitable for files were carburized (casehardened) wrought iron, blister steel, shear steel, and crucible or cast steel. Methods for manufacturing files from these carbon steels were known by most blacksmiths, but because of the precise skills and specialized tools required to produce good-quality steel files with uniformly spaced teeth, a specialized class of smiths were soon recognized–the filesmiths. By the 18th century in Great Britain, filesmiths had established their own society, and by the 19th century, specialists within the profession included file forgers, file grinders, file cutters, and file harden-

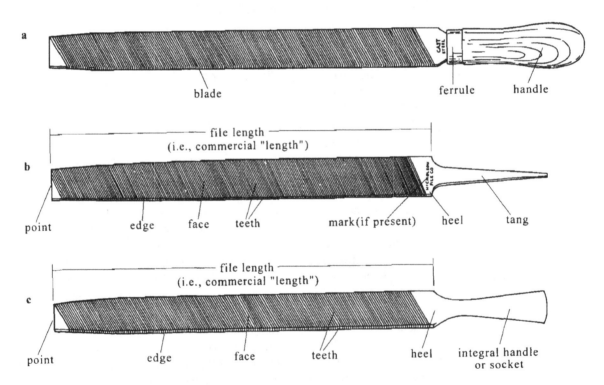

FIGURE 1. Metal file terminology and types: *a*, metal file showing major parts; *b*, single-pointed file showing major attributes (J. H. Ashdown Hardware Company 1904:91); *c*, single-pointed file showing tang variation.

ers (Tomlinson 1854:643-645; Lloyd 1913:58-61, 317).

Prior to the late 19th century, files were generally hand made. Wrought iron or steel bars were forged into variously shaped file blanks. Steel bars were annealed to soften their surfaces for teeth cutting. These blanks were next ground to attain the proper shape and smoothness, and each tooth was individually cut with a hand chisel and hammer. Exact precision was required by the file cutter in order to stamp each tooth precisely parallel to, and only a fraction of an inch beyond, the preceding tooth. Whether the file was flat or round, a flat chisel was used to cut the teeth. For round files, as many as 22,000 individual cuts had to be made. After cutting, the maker's or factory mark was stamped into the file, usually on its heel, tang, or center. Wrought-iron files were case hardened. Next, the steel file was coated with a thick saline solution in order to prevent oxidation and cracking, heated, straightened, and quench-tempered to an exact hardness. Finally, each file was tested, cleaned, oiled, and shipped to awaiting suppliers (Tomlinson 1854:643-645; Spon 1898:76-77).

To fulfill various functional requirements, files were manufactured with a wide variety of cross sections; came in a multitude of shapes, sizes, and weights; and had many teeth configurations and spacings. Variations in shape and cross section were indicative of the shape of the surfaces being abraded, whereas variations in size and teeth attributes were related to the surface area being abraded and to the degree of abrasion desired. Most files (file blades) could be utilized without additional accessories, but handles were often desired by tradesmen who relied daily upon the use of files. The exception is the butchers' steel which always appear to have had handles, and sometimes guards.

Associated File Accessories

File blades were commonly used with attached wooden handles which could be removed when a blade became worn and placed on the tang of another blade (Figure 1a). Such handles normally required the use of brass or iron ferrules for reinforcement, but non-reinforced handles were also used, though usually these were homemade by the user. Occasionally, for convenience of working, a file holder (Nicholson File Co. 1878:66-68) was employed, but such items were rare.

The only other commonly associated articles found with file blades are their cleaning tools. All files tend to clog with the material they are abrading, and they must be kept clean for optimum use. Tapping, carding, brushing, or rubbing the file on an apron are common ways of keeping a file clean. More difficult cleaning jobs call for special techniques. Oil is removed by wiping off the excess, rubbing the file with chalk, charcoal, or any soft non-clogging substance which will absorb the oil, and carding. This was, in fact, a common procedure as new files were factory oiled before they were shipped. Soft substances like wood can be removed by immersing the file in boiling water and carding. Heating the file in order to burn off the clog runs the risk of drawing temper.

Three articles were manufactured for cleaning the spaces between the teeth: file brushes, file cards, and file picks. File picks were used for removing heavily encrusted material or for cleaning between coarse teeth, and such picks were normally stored in the handle of a file brush or card. File brushes (Figure 2) had two working sides for medium and fine cleaning; one side with coarse bristles and the other with fine wire bristles. File cards (Figure 2) had only fine wire bristles for cleaning between closely spaced teeth.

File Stylistic Types and Attributes

Stylistically, files can be classified into four basic shapes: single-pointed files, double-pointed files, self-handled double-pointed files, and double-handled files (Figures 1b-c, 3). The earliest and most common style was the single-pointed file, which served as the basic model for later stylistic variations. File attribute terminology, originally developed for single-pointed files, remained consistent for all subsequent stylistic variations.

Single-pointed Files

Single-pointed files (Figure 1b-c) came in many stylistic variations, but generally all had

Nicholson Files.
EXTRA X. F. FINE SWISS PATTERN.
SLITTING.

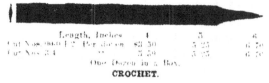

CROCHET.

ASSORTED NEEDLE FILES.
Round.

Half-Round.

Flat.

Oval.

Knife.

Square.

Three-Square.

Equaling.

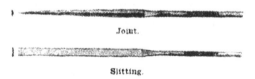

Barrette.

Joint.

Slitting.

Marking.

ASSORTED NEEDLE FILES.
Round Handle.

File Cleaners.

NICHOLSON CARD.

With Scorer.

NICHOLSON BRUSH.

With Card and Scorer.

COMMON CARD.

FIGURE 2. File cleaners and uncommon files advertised in The George Worthington Company catalogue (1916:250).

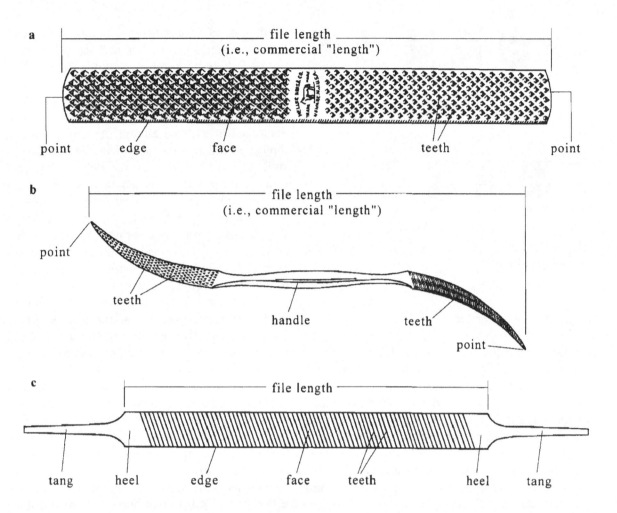

FIGURE 3. Metal file types: *a*, double-pointed rasp showing major attributes; *b*, self-handled, double-pointed file showing major attributes; *c*, double-handled file showing major attributes. (Drawing by Dorothea Larsen.)

a tang (also called a spike) intended for insertion into a socketed wooden handle (Figure 1a). Occasionally, socketed file blades were manufactured (Figure 1c), but this variation is exceedingly rare. Maker or factory marks were generally placed on or near the heel, either perpendicular or parallel to the file length. When placed parallel, marks generally occurred on the upper portion of the tang. This is the most common sort of file.

Double-pointed Files

Double-pointed files (Figure 3a-b) required no attached handle, thus no tang was present. Usually, such files were divided into two symmetrical portions with maker or factory marks placed in the center. Teeth on each portion were not always identical, and thus such files could serve dual purposes such as for roughing as well as for finishing. A typical file of this type is the farrier's horse rasp (Figure 3a).

Self-handled, Double-pointed Files

Self-handled, double-pointed files (Figure 3b) are generally known as rifflers or riffler files and rasps. As a rule, opposing ends of such files had totally different teeth configurations, and were thus intended as dual purpose tools. As with the double-pointed files, maker or factory marks were stamped in the center of the tool, in this case, on the handle. Files used by wood carvers were typically rifflers.

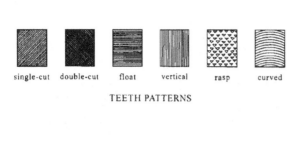

TEETH PATTERNS

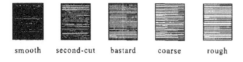

TEETH SPACING GRADES

FIGURE 4. File teeth patterns and spacing grades. (Drawing by Dorothea Larsen.)

Double-handled Files

Double-handled files (Figure 3c) came either with two self-handles or with two tangs for socketed wooden handles. Such files were generally homemade, and were rarely stamped with a maker's mark. Designed as two-man files, they were commonly quite long, reaching a length of up to 4 ft. (1.2 m), and were "occasionally found in wheelwright's and coachsmith's workshops" where they were used to file hot metal (Salaman 1975:390).

Attributes

In addition to having one or more working faces and multiple cutting teeth, there may be additional attributes present on files. These attributes include: one or more edges with or without teeth (so that one may file into a corner or a dovetail without affecting one edge) a heel and tang (on single-pointed files only), and one or two handles or points. Functionally, the most important attributes of a file are the configuration and spacing of its teeth, together with the shape and cross section of its faces.

Teeth Configurations

Teeth configurations on file faces consist of six basic patterns: single-cut, double-cut, float, vertical, rasp, and curved (Figure 4). Such configurations are the result of variations in tooth types (continuous ridge vs. discrete barbs),

tooth angles (diagonal, horizontal, vertical, or curved) and presence or absence of overlapping teeth (single-cut vs. double-cut). Size of teeth vary according to both the spacing between individual teeth and the depth to which each tooth has been cut. The decline of hand manufacture and the advent of mechanization, though it did not cut down on the number of styles offered for sale by the industry, did cut down on the minute eccentricities which one may encounter in a close examination of spacing or depth or angle of cut. These differences should enable one to determine whether a file is machine- or hand-made, although file cutters were highly skilled and this can often be difficult to detect. Nevertheless, despite the idiosyncratic nature of hand-made tools, various grades of tooth size were historically acknowledged. There were at least five major grades recognized: smooth, second-cut or middle, bastard, coarse, and rough (Figure 4). Occasionally, a finer grade, known as dead or dead smooth, was utilized, but its use was rare because emery and tripoli or crocus took over from files as fine abrasives. Determining exact historical sizes for archaeological files is currently impossible, but relative sizes can be inferred by matching specimens with known historical illustrations. Sizes determined by this method, however, must be considered somewhat inaccurate. Blending various combinations of teeth patterns and spacing grades produced a wide variety of styles which were referred to by such descriptive terms as single-cut bastard, double-cut smooth, rasp coarse, etc. (Figure 5). When such styles were combined with file shapes and cross sections, the resulting product was a distinctive file type.

File-Blade Shapes

File-blade shapes were extremely variable, and no consistent classification system has yet been recognized. Numerous catalogues and mechanical dictionaries contain file classifications, but there are usually slight disagreements between them (Chambers 1738; Smith 1816; Ure 1848; Tomlinson 1854; Knight 1867; Orr and Lockett Hardware Company 1898; J. H. Ashdown Hardware Company 1904; Wood, Vallance 1911; George Worthington 1916; Smith 1916; Simonds Canada Saw Company 1952; Roberts 1976;

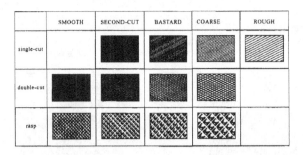

	SMOOTH	SECOND-CUT	BASTARD	COARSE	ROUGH
single-cut					
double-cut					
rasp					

FIGURE 5. File teeth styles. (Drawing by Dorothea Larsen.)

Lee Valley Tools 1986). Shapes historically identified as pillar, tapering, knife, etc., appear to have been defined by a polythetic set of attributes including face shape, cross section, relative length, and teeth configurations. Presently, face shapes cannot be adequately defined by referencing historical terminology. Apparently, shape definitions would only be possible through exhaustive research into shape variability, and such research has not been undertaken. Presently, the only method for recording face shapes is the complete description of file attribute variations: parallel-edged faces; slightly tapering edges; face formed with one straight and one curved edge; etc. Somewhat similar in its difficulty to be classified is a file's cross section (Tomlinson 1854:640-642; Nicholson File Co. 1878).

File-Blade Cross Sections

Historical terms for file cross sections are relatively common, but they vary and no exhaustive classification system has been recognized. Styles of cross section have been defined (Figure 6), but their historical usage has been somewhat inconsistent.

In order to create a distinctive file style, the manufacturer had to combine all the attributes mentioned above into a single tool. The total possible number of styles which could have been produced is extremely high, and no extensive research has been completed on the number of styles known historically or archaeologically, although it is highly probable that before the industrial revolution, the variation in styles was more limited than after.

Historical Archaeological Interpretations

Historical Varieties

SHAPE

Stylistic variations for files were exceedingly numerous because they were often designed for very specific tasks. Among the more common names applied to files were the terms burnishers, files, floats, rasps, rifflers, and steels. Examples of a few of the terminological and stylistic variations within these groups are shown in Figures 2, 7-8.

Unusual or odd shapes can often be ascribed to a particular trade or function, whereas the more common shapes tended to be used freely for handiwork or other assorted purposes and by separate trades.

SIZES

Files were customarily sold by length. For single-pointed files, length implied the length of the working face, whereas for double-pointed

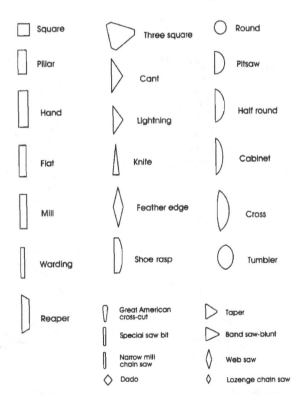

FIGURE 6. File blade cross sections. (Drawing by Dorothea Larsen.)

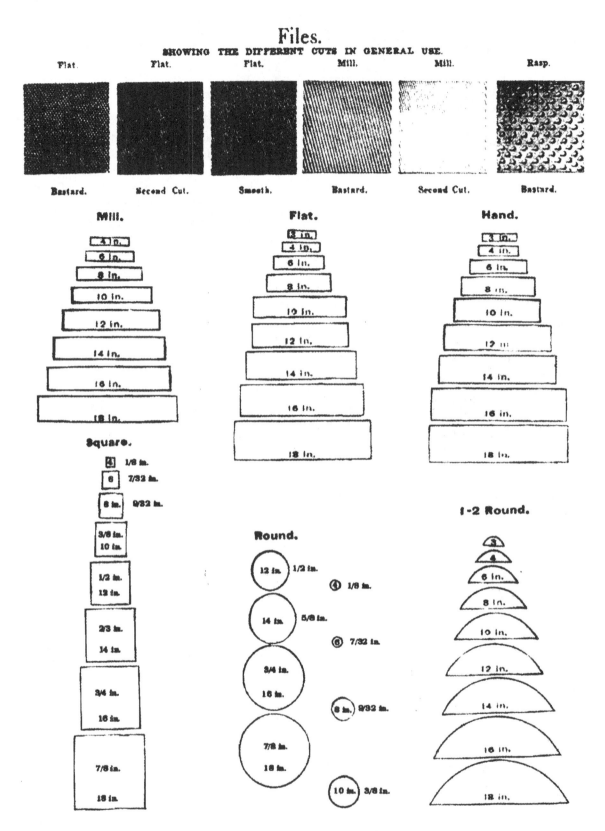

FIGURE 7. File teeth patterns, cross sections and sizes in The George Worthington Company catalogue (1916:242).

Files.

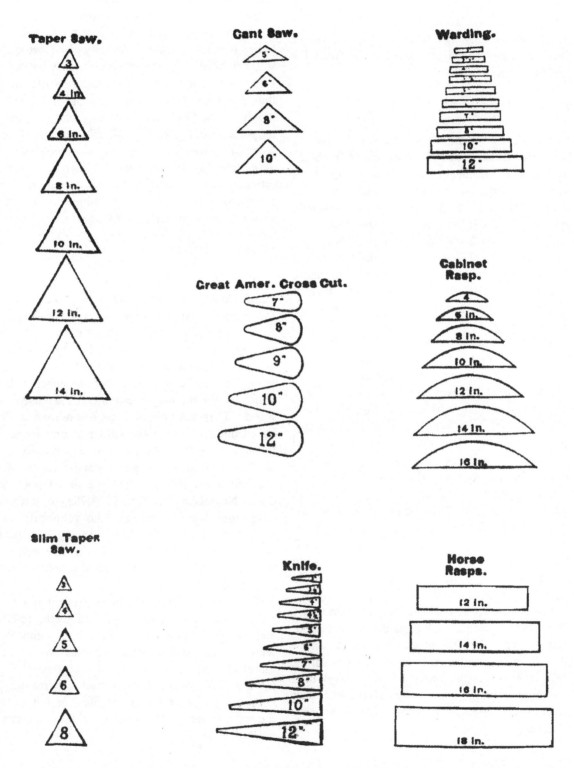

FIGURE 8. Additional file cross sections and sizes in The George Worthington Company catalogue (1916:243).

files, length implied the total file length. The more common sizes ranged between 3 and 20 in. (7.5 and 51 cm), but larger sizes were also manufactured. Occasionally, extremely large files were sold according to their weight. A large blacksmith's rubber might be denoted as an 84 lb. (2.4 kg) file. Generally, larger files are coarser, and are therefore intended for rougher jobs.

File-Blade Use

Every archaeological assemblage is unique, so it is difficult to discuss the question of file-blade use without pre-judging a particular collection, but some suggestions may be made without presupposition. Some idea of the probable specific uses of individual sizes, forms, etc., may be gained from Nicholson File Company (1956) and Salaman (1975), even though they are nearly contemporary works. This is because the nature of the tool itself, and hence the job which it is capable of performing, has not changed in many centuries.

The problem faced by archaeologists is to identify, if possible, how the files in a site assemblage were used. In many cases this may not be possible. Nevertheless, context may provide important, and even definitive, clues. The presence of a warding file in a general smithy along with a key blank and several smaller bits of lock hardware, for example, is convincing evidence that locksmithing was a normal part of the activities of the smith (Light and Unglik 1987:18-20). A broken half round bastard file in the same context, however, reveals little; not because it was a useless tool, but because it was *too* useful, for there were a multitude of applications for which it could have been used.

Even negative information may be informative. Files are so useful, and therefore so common, that not to find them in an expected situation should raise comment. Not to find warding files in a locksmith's shop, or wood rasps in a carpenter's shop, should raise eyebrows. Not to find *any* files in a smithy would be *very* bizarre.

FILE-BLADE USE-WEAR

Normal file wear generally consisted of the gradual wearing down of the teeth, with such wear resulting in the flattening of each tooth through abrasion. Excessive usage resulted in the breakage of teeth, with single teeth generally being partially broken. Usually such breakage was exhibited as a line or space across the teeth. Files were manufactured of hard, brittle steel, thus excessive pressure or abnormal usage commonly resulted in blades snapping into two parts, or portions being broken off file points. When worn or broken files were no longer considered as suitably sharp, they were either used for a different task, discarded, recut, reconditioned, or reworked into other types of objects, the latter option being extremely common.

FILE-BLADE REUSE

Worn files can be reused in many ways. Their owners may assign them to new duties, as for example when a smith used his dull horse rasp (actually the coarse file portion) as a hot rasp (a blacksmith's term used to refer to the action of smoothing the end of a forging or workpiece while it is still hot) or when a file which could no longer cut metal was used on wood. It is also possible to recondition a file by cleaning it with a file card and immersing it in an acid bath. The process was usually not worth the effort, but it was common enough for the Nicholson File Co., in one of its publications (Nicholson File Co. 1878:79), to threaten litigation against anyone who reconditioned their files and resold them leaving the mark intact. Eventually, however, the file became useless and it had either to be discarded, recut, or reworked.

To re-cut a file, it must be annealed (softened), ground to remove the old teeth, re-cut, and tempered (hardened). There were companies which specialized in recutting files. After the material revolution in the steel industry following 1860, however, it became increasingly uneconomical to recut worn files, and it is no longer practiced. Re-cut files were sometimes marked as such.

FIGURE 9. Files reworked into combination tools: *a*, chisel/saw set; *b*, half-round file/chisel; *c*, rasp/hoof knife; *d*, bastard file/saw set. (Photograph by Rock Chan.)

Most commonly, files served as the raw material for new tools (Figure 9). Since files were manufactured from high-quality steels, they were highly regarded for reuse by local blacksmiths. The practice was ubiquitous, and virtually every archaeological assemblage from excavated smithies contains reworked files. Even after tool steel became readily available, the habit continued and is still prevalent today among the few remaining smiths. A worn file could be reforged into any number of other shapes, and once properly retempered, the metal could serve a wide variety of purposes. Known examples of reworked files include such tools as chisels, gouges, knives, scrapers, and hammers (Light 1991). Normally, such reworked tools can be detected by the presence of distorted and flattened file teeth, but another sign of such reworking is a discarded hot-cut tang. Such reworking should be noted as part of artifact discussions and descriptions.

Finally, there is a special case which requires comment. It sometimes happens that a user needs a file and another tool for a particular job. Rather than deal with two tools, he may have the file reworked into a combination tool (Figure 9) (Light 1991). For example, the file/saw set illustrated in Figure 9d allows the user both to sharpen and set saw teeth without putting down one tool in order to pick up another. These combination tools are uncommon but not rare.

Conclusion

As an important, readily recognizable class of artifacts containing a multitude of shapes and functions, files are virtually ubiquitous. It is frequently possible, either through its context or the tool itself, to discern the use of a file. It is highly desirable for archaeologists to be able to properly describe and interpret files because of their intelligibility, importance, diversity, and ubiquity. This work is intended to guide the way to this end.

REFERENCES

APPLETON AND CO.
1851   *Appleton's Dictionary of Machines, Mechanics, Engine-work, and Engineering.* D. Appleton, New York, NY.

BIRINGUCCIO, VANNOCCIO
1540   *Pirotechnia.* Venice. Reprinted 1959, M.I.T. Press, Cambridge, MA.

CHAMBERS, EPHRAIM
1738   *Cyclopaedia: or, An Universal Dictionary of Arts and Sciences,* 2nd edition. Midwinter, Bettesworth, et al., London, England.

GEORGE WORTHINGTON COMPANY
1916   Catalogue. George Worthington Company, Cleveland, OH.

J. H. ASHDOWN HARDWARE COMPANY
1904   *Wholesale Hardware Catalogue.* J. H. Ashdown Hardware Company, Winnipeg, Ontario.

KARKLINS, KARLIS
1983   Nottingham House: The Hudson's Bay Company in Athabasca, 1802-1806. Parks Canada, *History and Archaeology* 69:3-281. Ottawa, Ontario.

KNIGHT, EDWARD H.
1867   *Knight's American Mechanical Dictionary.* Hurd and Houghton, New York, NY.

LEE VALLEY TOOLS LTD.
1986   *File Catalogue 1986.* Lee Valley Tools Ltd., Ottawa, Ontario.

LIGHT, JOHN D.
1991   Recycled Files. Parks Canada, *Research Bulletin* 285. Ottawa, Ontario.

LIGHT, JOHN D., AND HENRY UNGLIK
1987   A Frontier Fur Trade Blacksmith Shop, 1796-1812, revised edition. Parks Canada, *Studies in Archaeology, Architecture and History.* Ottawa, Ontario.

LLOYD, G. I. H.
1913   *The Cutlery Trades: An Historical Essay in the Economics of Small-scale Production.* Frank Cass, London, England. Reprinted 1968, Augustus M. Kelley, New York, NY.

MOXON, JOSEPH
1703   *Mechanick Exercises: or the Doctrine of Handy-works.* Midwinter, London, England.

NICHOLSON FILE COMPANY
1878   *A Treatise on Files and Rasps.* Nicholson File Company, Providence, RI. Reprinted 1983, The Early Industries Association, South Dartmouth, MA.
1956   *File Filosophy and How to Get the Most Out of Files.* Nicholson File Company, Providence, RI.

ORR & LOCKETT HARDWARE COMPANY
1898   *Catalogue of Mechanics' Tools.* Orr & Lockett Hardware Company, Chicago, IL. Reprinted 1975, Robin Hood Publications, Berkeley, CA.

ROBERTS, KENNETH D.
1976   *Tools for the Trades and Crafts: An Eighteenth Century Pattern Book. R. Timmins and Sons, Birmingham.* Kenneth D. Roberts, Fitzwilliam, NH.

SALAMAN, R. A.
1975   *Dictionary of Tools Used in the Woodworking and Allied Trades, ca. 1700-1970.* Allen and Unwin, London, England.

SIMONDS CANADA SAW COMPANY
1952   American Pattern Files and Rasps [Catalogue]. Simonds Canada Saw Company, Montreal, Quebec.

SMITH, JOSEPH
1816   *Explanation or Key, to the Various Manufactories of Sheffield, With Engravings of Each Article.* Reprinted 1975. The Early American Industries Association, South Burlington, VT.

SPON, E., AND F. N. SPON
1898   *Spons' Mechanics' Own Book.* E. and F. N. Spon, London, England.

TOMLINSON, CHARLES (EDITOR)
1854   *Cyclopaedia of Useful Arts.* James S. Virtue, London, England.

URE, ANDREW
1864   *Dictionary of Arts, Manufactures, and Mines.* D. Appleton, New York, NY.

WOOD, VALLANCE, LTD.
1911   *Wholesale Catalogue of Shelf and Heavy Hardware; Bar Iron and Steel; Cutlery; Guns; Ammunition; Fishing Tackle; Factory, Mill, Miners' and Lumbermen's Supplies.* Wood, Vallance, Toronto, Ontario.

LESTER A. ROSS
2667 GARFIELD STREET
EUGENE, OREGON 97405

JOHN LIGHT
MATERIAL CULTURE RESEARCH
ONTARIO SERVICE CENTRE
PARKS CANADA
1600 LIVERPOOL COURT
OTTAWA, ONTARIO K1A 0M5
CANADA

JANE BUSCH

An Introduction to the Tin Can

ABSTRACT

The tin can has played a significant role in American history and can play a significant role in archaeology. Beginning with the food can, the author traces developments in canning and can-manufacturing, and briefly discusses can shape and labelling. The narrative continues with the beer can, the center of can-manufacturing innovation after 1935. There are obstacles facing archaeologists interested in tin cans. One is corrosion; another is the lack of archaeological and documentary research on this artifact.

The early rising cow-boys were off again to their work; and those to whom their night's holiday had left any dollars were spending these for tobacco, or cartridges, or canned provisions for the journey to their distant camps. Sardines were called for, and potted chicken, and devilled ham; a sophisticated nourishment, at first sight, for these sons of the sage-brush. But portable ready-made food plays of necessity a great part in the opening of a new country. These picnic pots and cans were the first of her trophies that Civilization dropped upon Wyoming's virgin soil (Wister 1902:31).

The tin can has always been a pioneer. It went west with the settlers, south with the Union troops, and overseas with the G.I.'s. The portable, ready-made character of canned food was valuable to explorers and soldiers, who did the tin can a service in turn by accepting it. Once canned food gained trust, it became instrumental in cultural change as well as cultural expansion. The tin can was a packaging pioneer, a leader in the change from bulk selling to individualized packaging that has grown into the modern packaging industry. As more foods were canned and shipped, the regional and seasonal barriers that defined American foodways broke down. Food preparation changed, affecting the role of women. Today we know the tin can as a symbol of American wastefulness, but it has meant much more. Robert Ascher, in his article "Tin Can Archaeology," singled out the tin can when he wrote, "the urgency of archaeology will appear when its study leads to insight, or at least an awareness of the world around us" (Ascher 1974:14).

Another characteristic of the tin can has special value for archaeologists: its disposability. This does not apply to fancy biscuit or tea tins, but there are few uses for an open tomato can once the tomatoes are gone. Immediate disposal makes the food can a valuable dating tool for archaeologists. Cans also provide information on trading patterns, eating habits, and economic circumstances; any description of these characteristics based on bottles alone when cans are present is incomplete. Tin cans at a campsite might even indicate which way the camper was travelling. Walter Webb wrote: "if he is going west, the camp is surrounded by tin cans and paper sacks, if he is going east it is littered with fieldlark feathers and rabbit-fur," (Webb 1931:320). In the West that Owen Wister described in *The Virginian*, tin cans are nearly as ubiquitous on the landscape as sagebrush. So prominent a cultural artifact merits the attention of archaeologists.

Origin

Metal cans are commonly called tin cans although many have no tin and even tin cans are actually tin-plated. Modern tinplating technology began in Bohemia in the early Middle Ages and tinplate was first marketed officially in England in 1730. The word "can" is an American abbreviation of the English "canister," a word for box derived from the Greek "kanastron" which was a reed basket (Fontana et al. 1962:67; Hedges 1964:154). Captain John Stedman, in a diary published in 1796, wrote of sending roasted beef in "a block-tin box or cannister" from Europe to Dutch Guiana, a valuable present on account of the inferiority of the beef in Guiana (Anonymous 1968a:1). The Captain's canisters were not hermetically sealed, however, a method perfected in France by Nicholas Appert in 1809. Appert's method, the foundation of modern canning, was to pack food in glass jars tightly sealed with cork and wire and cook them in boiling water, a successful technique even though it was not correctly understood until Pasteur's work in 1860 (Clark 1977:13). An Englishman, Peter Durand, took out a patent for canning in tin canisters in 1810. Tinplate then was tinned iron sheet. When the English firm of Donkin and Hall began producing tin-canned food commercially in 1812 their first big customer was the British army, establishing military use of canned foods at the start. Explorers followed suit; canned food went with Sir Edward Parry on his Arctic expeditions in the 1820s (Hedges 1964:153–55).

Commercial canning in America began in 1819, with William Underwood canning fruit in Boston and Thomas Kensett canning seafood in New York. Both canners used glass. In 1825, Kensett was granted a patent for preserving food in tin vessels, but the first recorded use of tin cans was in 1839, when Underwood and Kensett switched to tin because of the rising price of glass (National Canners Association 1963:6, 17; Hedges 1964:157). By then canneries were spreading in the U.S.; one opened in Baltimore in 1840 and sardine canning began in Eastport, Maine, in 1841 (Bitting 1916:14).

The Hole-And-Cap Can

The cans of this era were manufactured completely by hand. To make the body, a piece of tinplate was bent into shape on a roller and the overlapping edges were soldered together. Two round disks were cut for the ends, their edges were bent down, or flanged, and they were soldered to the body. The top could be soldered on after the can was filled, but more common was the hole-and-cap can. A top with a circular hole about an inch in diameter was soldered on before the can was filled, food was pushed through the hole, then a cap with a small venthole was soldered over the opening. During processing, when a sufficient amount of steam had escaped, the venthole was closed with a drop of solder (Figures

1 & 2; Singer et al. 1958:43–44; Clark 1977:14). The soldered hole-and-cap can changed little in style through the 19th century, but even before the Civil War its manufacture was partially mechanized. In 1847 Allen Taylor patented a drop-press to flange the edges of the end disks. In 1849 Henry Evans patented a foot-powered pendulum press to cut out the ends and William Numsen patented a combination die that cut out the ends, flanged them, and cut out the filler holes in the tops (May 1938:28; Fontana et al. 1962:69–70).

Two important developments in canning occurred just in time for the Civil War. In 1856, Gail Borden was granted a patent for vacuum processing canned condensed milk.

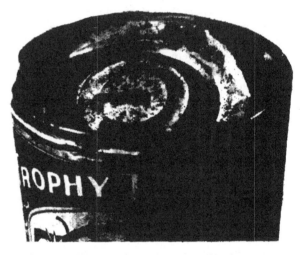

FIGURE 1. Top of hole-and-cap can, ca. 1880. Diameter 4 1/4 inches.

FIGURE 2. Folded end seam of hole-and-cap can. Lapped side seam just visible above label.

In 1861, American canners learned to add calcium chloride to their cooking water, which raised the temperature of the water and increased the reliability of the canning process. During the Civil War canned foods were used extensively for soldiers' rations. Borden's milk, purchased in large quantities by the government, is credited with saving lives and convincing the public that canned foods were safe. The war marked a turning point in the canning industry; the post-war annual output of canned food was thirty million cans, compared to five million in the pre-war years (Can Manufacturers Institute 1978; Clark 1977:17; National Canners Association 1963:7).

The salmon canning industry began in 1864 on the Sacramento River in California, a portent of the expansion and diversification of the canning industry in the next three decades. By 1892 pineapple was canned in Hawaii (Hedges 1964:156–57). Advances in canning and can manufacturing accompanied expansion. The pressure cooker, used earlier in Europe, was introduced in Baltimore in 1874 (Fontana et al. 1962:69). Systematic studies of bacteria in canned foods that were undertaken in the 1890s led to more efficient cooking methods (Singer et al. 1958:42–43). In can manufacturing, the introduction of the open-hearth steel process in 1875 initiated the replacement of iron with steel for tinplate, allowing a thinner coating of tin (Kloap 1971:232; Clark 1977:10). In 1876 can making was mechanized further, with the Howe floater which automatically soldered on can ends by rolling the can at an angle in a bath of solder. The Merriam "Little Joker" of 1880 was an improvement on the Howe floater. When the Norton Brothers introduced a semi-automatic machine to solder side seams in 1883, all the processes of can making could be done by machine (May 1938:28–29; Fontana et al. 1962:70). The Norton Brothers factory produced cans at the rate of 2500 an hour, compared to 60 cans an hour in the 1870s and 5 or 6 cans an hour by hand-manufacturing methods in the early 19th century (Clark 1977:18).

The Sanitary Can

The most radical change in can history was the switch from the hole-and-cap to the sanitary can. The sanitary or open-top can was initially developed in Europe, where can ends were attached to the body by hand crimping the edges together, with a rubber gasket in between to make the seam airtight. In 1896, in the United States, Charles Ams patented a sealing compound of rubber and gum to replace the rubber gasket. By 1897, the Ams Machine Company brought out a machine that applied this compound to can ends automatically and crimped the ends to the body in a double seam, an improvement over the single seam used in Europe (Figure 3; May 1938:438, 439; Collins 1924:36–38). With the crimped, or locked, double end seam, locked side seams replaced lapped side seams. For a lapped seam, solder was applied to the body edges which were lapped over each other while hot. The lapped side-seam fit the flanged, soldered-on top better than the locked side-seam, which was not perfected until the 1900s. For a locked side-seam the edges are crimped together and

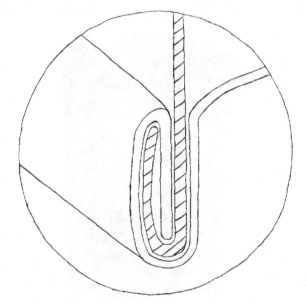

FIGURE 3. Cutaway view of locked, double end seam (bottom).

soldered on the outside only, leaving no external ridge (Figure 4; Fontana et al. 1962:70; Collins 1924:35).

The new can was considered more sanitary because it was soldered on the outside only. Because the top was crimped on after filling, it could hold larger pieces of food than the hole-and-cap can (National Canners Association 1963:8). George Cobb of the Cobb Preserving Company bought Ams can-making machinery in 1899 and in 1904 organized the Sanitary Can Company to market fruit in the "Sanitary Enamel Lined Can." The enamel lining was a combination of resins and linseed oil that prevented bleaching of red fruits and vegetables in contact with tin (May 1938:259–60, 440). The search for protective internal lacquers had begun in 1868 but was not satisfactorily solved earlier. "R" enamel for red fruits became a standard can lining and was joined by "C" enamel in the 1920s, which protects against the corrosive effects of citrus fruits and juices, first successfully canned in that decade (May 1938:440; Clark 1977:32).

In 1908 the Sanitary Can Company was absorbed by American Can, the can-manufacturing giant formed in 1901 through the merger of 60 independent firms. By the early 1920s the sanitary can was generally accepted by the public and had almost completely replaced other types of food cans (Clark 1977:18, 31). The condensed milk can has been an outstanding exception; even today most condensed milk cans are similar in construction to the old hole-and-cap can (Figures 5 & 6). The modern sanitary food can is basically the same as it

FIGURE 5. Condensed milk can from a lumbering camp used ca. 1912–1915. Note folded edge (Courtesy of Archaeological Consultants).

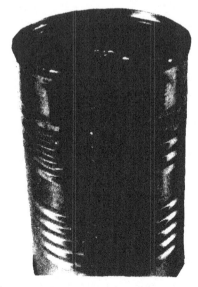

FIGURE 4. Modern sanitary can, showing locked end and side seams. Height 4 inches, diameter 2 5/8 inches.

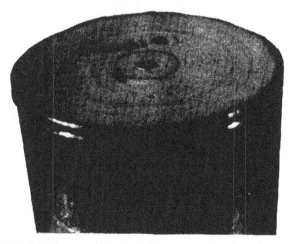

FIGURE 6. Detail of modern condensed milk can, showing folded edge and soldered vent hole. Diameter 2 7/8 inches.

was at the beginning of the century. The major trend has been decreasing its weight through techniques such as the cold rolling of steel, which reduces thickness, and electrolytic tin plating, introduced commercially in 1937, which uses less tin (National Canners Association 1963:18). The tin can of 20 years ago required 20% more steel and 50% more tin than the tin can of today (Can Manufacturers Institute 1978).

Identity

Can labelling has a history of its own. In the first half of the 19th century labelling methods included handpainting, stenciling, and embossing the container itself, attaching paper labels, and soldering on embossed labels. Transfer printing on tin was pioneered in London in the 1860s. The image was printed in reverse on paper then transferred to a flat sheet of tinplate (Clark 1977:22–25; Blanc 1972:13). In America, the lithographed container seems to appear in the 1860s (Can Manufacturers Institute 1978; Davis 1967:77). The invention of the offset lithographic press by Barclay and Fry of London in 1870 made metal lithography easier and multicolor metal lithography appeared in the 1880s. The rotary offset lithographic press, patented in 1903, introduced the principle used in most tinplate printing today (Clark 1977:11, 27–28, 31; Blanc 1972:13).

Metal lithography was more complicated than paper lithography, which appears earlier. Nineteenth century paper labels were often fanciful, identifying product and canner but with little additional information (Figure 7). The first uniform federal law to establish labelling standards was the Pure Food and Drug Law of 1906. Because it was ineffective, this law was superseded in 1938 by the Federal Food, Drug and Cosmetic Act, requiring all labels to bear the legal name of the product, the net contents, and the name and address of the packer, manufacturer or distributor (Mullin 1960:12, 20–26).

Most food cans had paper labels which are

FIGURE 7. Tomato can with red, blue and yellow lithographed paper label, ca. 1880. Height 4 7/8 inches.

not preserved in normal archaeological circumstances. Metal lithography was the norm for cans that were not hermetically sealed, containing tea, spices, gunpowder, drugs, and other products. These types of tin containers predate the appearance of the hermetically sealed food can; the oldest known American tins held gunpowder (Davis 1967:77; Clark 1977:19, 21). Many of these decorative tins had reclosable openings and were designed for secondary use. Today, they are the province of collectors more than archaeologists. Tobacco tins, the most numerous collectibles, are normally found at archaeological sites (Fontana et al. 1962:77; Suzanne Baker 1979, pers. comm.). The pocket tobacco tin, often concave to fit a back pocket, was the equivalent of the cigarette package, and tobacco lunch pails, made between 1901 and 1925 were also popular (Figure 8). Tobacco containers may be dated by the date on the paper tobacco tax stamp when it survives (Clark 1977:90–102).

Shape may be a more informative characteristic for archaeologists than label, since

Jane Busch

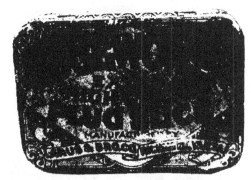

FIGURE 8. Pocket tobacco tin, ca. 1930. 2 1/8 by 3 1/8 inches.

shape is recognizable when all detail is obscured by corrosion. Many characteristic shapes developed in the 19th century. The flat, oblong can was used early for seafood. By 1880, the base and body of this shallow can were drawn in one piece, a technique that became more important later (Fontana et al. 1962:72). Another distinctive can, the tapered meat can, was developed in Chicago in 1875. The tapered shape of this corned beef can allowed the meat to slide out in one piece (May 1938:212, 437).

The Beer Can

The historical archaeologist who ignores the beer can at his site is like the prehistoric archaeologist who ignores historic pottery. Beverage cans are difficult to avoid; in 1969, an estimated 1,809 million cans were littered along U.S. roads, most of which were beverage cans (Bingham and Mulligan 1972:26). Since the beer can appeared in 1935, the center of innovation in can manufacturing has been in the beverage can industry. A can for beer had to withstand greater pressure than a food can and needed a lining to keep the liquid from combining with the tin. By 1935 these problems were solved, and the American Can Company brought out the flat-top beer can, followed by the Continental Can Company with the cone-top beer can in the same year

(Figure 9). The cone-top can, capped with a bottle-cap, was designed to be used with existing bottle-filling equipment. The flat-top can was easier to make, fill, and store. Initially a can-opener was given away with every purchase and instructions for opening were printed on each can (Clark 1977:32, 124).

Stiff competition and rising material costs have induced rapid progress in beer can technology since 1935. High sales volume has also aided change. In 1950, 5.1 billion beer cans were produced in the United States, a figure which increased to 24 billion by 1973 (Beer Can Collectors of America 1976:10). In 1976, 40 billion cans were used for beverages in the United States, which translates to a per capita consumption of 190 cans a year (Anonymous 1976:12). But, in its early years, the new canned beer industry had to confront World

FIGURE 9. Cone-top beer can.

War II, with metal shortages that curtailed the use of tin cans for many products. The beer can almost disappeared from the domestic mârket, but more than one billion were shipped overseas for the army. Acceptance of canned beer by soldiers meant increased popularity for beer when the war ended. The cone-top beer can had a higher spout after the war, and in the early forties a new two-piece cone-top beer can appeared. The body and cone of this can, the "Crowntainer" were drawn in one piece, with no side seam; the bottom and cap were added. But the convenience of the flat top for filling and stacking won out, and the cone top disappeared by the mid-fifties (Beer Can Collectors of America 1976:16, 19–21, 203).

Soda pop was first marketed in cans in the early 1950s but canned pop did not catch on as quickly as canned beer. Canned Coke was not sold on the open market in the United States until 1959 (Anonymous 1959:226). By that time beer canners had advanced from the aluminum-top can of the late fifties to the first all-aluminum canned beer, Primo beer in Hawaii in 1958 (Anonymous 1958:106–07). On the mainland, Coors was first with the all-aluminum beer can in 1959, a two-piece can with no side or bottom seam (Beer Can Collectors of America 1976:23). Primo cans and other aluminum cans through the early sixties were impact-extruded from an aluminum slug (Anonymous 1958:107). In 1963 the drawn and ironed (D & I) method of aluminum beverage can manufacture was perfected (Kloap 1971: 232). In this method a cup is punched out of a metal sheet, then the sides of the cup are drawn out and ironed to about 1/3 their original thickness (Anonymous 1968b:103; Clark 1977:11, 33).

In 1971, the D & I process was adapted for tin-plated cans, and more recently for tin-free steel cans (Barry and Evans 1974:14; Can Manufacturers Institute 1978). But in the early sixties the two-piece aluminum can had the advantage. Seamless construction allowed all-around lithography, and aluminum took

printed labels more clearly than tinplate. Aluminum cans were lighter and chilled faster. In 1964, many breweries switched to aluminum, and by 1967, 10% of beer cans were aluminum (Beer Can Collectors of America 1976:23).

Can manufacturers countered the aluminum companies with the tin-free steel can in 1965. Tinless steel plate had been used for non-food cans since the tin shortages of World War II. These containers were lacquered or coated with an alloy of tin and lead called terne plate (Fontana et al. 1962:75; Anonymous 1942: 254). As early as 1956, a tinless food can, with an aluminum coating and welded side seams was shown at a canners convention (Anonymous 1956:200). The two types of tin-free steel (TFS) introduced for beer cans in 1965 were electrochemically treated or electrolytically coated to resist environmental and product corrosion. Since tin is needed for soldering, two new seaming processes were developed for the TFS can. American Can Company used a cemented seam, with the edges overlapped 1/4 of an inch and sealed with a thermoplastic adhesive. Continental Can devised a welded seam with an overlap of 1/16 of an inch. The lightness of tin-free steel and the thinness of the solderless side seam emulated the advantages of the aluminum can (Anonymous 1968b:103; Clark 1977:11, 33).

These technological advances have been important to can manufacturers and brewers but a simpler, mechanical innovation has had the greatest impact on the consumer and on American culture. Aluminum-top cans with pull tabs were test marketed in 1962. By 1965, 70% of all beer cans featured the easy-open tab top and the proportion was nearly 100% in 1975. The original pull tab has been changed and refined; most popular today is the "ring-pull," introduced in 1965 (Beer Can Collectors of America 1976:22–23). The convenience of the easy-open, throwaway tab has had a tremendous effect on the popularity of canned beverages (Anonymous 1976:12). The throwaway tab is the most ubiquitous artifact of contemporary American culture; in other words, it is the biggest litter problem in America today. State laws against non-returnable beverage containers ban the throwaway tab. In response, can companies have been testing new easy-open tops. One type is a peel-back tab which is secured at one end; another consists of two raised buttons which are pushed inwards to open a venting hole and a pouring hole (Anonymous 1976:12). The throwaway pull tab is on its way out, and future generations may look at this artifact as the index fossil of a throwaway society which reached its peak in the years between 1962 and 1972, when Oregon was the first state to ban the throwaway tab.

The aerosol can, a spin-off of beer-can technology, deserves mention for its prominent place in modern society. The first aerosol was a high pressure bug bomb developed during World War II for the Army overseas (Anonymous 1944:98). The high pressure aerosol insecticide was marketed commercially in 1945 and in 1947 the conventional beer can was adapted as a low pressure aerosol. Aerosol shaving cream was introduced in 1950. By 1967, aerosol cans contained insect sprays, deoderants, paints, laundry products, polishes, hair sprays, perfumes, and food products. In that year, 1,681,798,000 aerosol cans were produced (Anonymous 1954:320; Anonymous 1970:11-12).

The Tin Can Archaeologist

In the past, archaeologists ignored tin cans, which were not relevant to the 18th and early 19th century sites where they worked. But the increase in excavation at later sites has not brought about a corresponding increase in tin can studies, as it has for bottle studies. This is partly because cans do not preserve as well as bottles. Tin cans are tinned on the inside and outside to prevent environmental and product corrosion. Lacquers and paint provide additional protection. But all these measures are designed to protect the can only until it reaches the consumer. Tin does not rust, but all tin-plate has tiny imperfections where the steel is exposed and begins to rust. The presence of tin actually accelerates the rusting of steel because of a reaction between iron and tin. Corrosion is retarded by a drier environment and by a thicker coating of tin (Mantell 1949:485; Hoare and Hedges 1945:246). Lacquers also help, as evident in the better preservation of well-lacquered beer cans from the thirties and forties (Beer Can Collectors of America 1976:98).

Another problem is that the lack of tin can studies has perpetuated itself, as archaeologists have preferred to study artifacts for which they could find references. There are two noteworthy discussions of tin cans in the archaeological literature. Charles B. Hunt published "Dating of Mining Camps with Tin Cans and Bottles" in 1959. Hunt uses tin cans in the dumps of western mining camps, along with other artifacts to establish four periods of habitation for the sites. The first period, before 1900, is characterized by soldered tin cans, as is the second period, from 1900 to World War I. In the third period, the early 1920s to early 1930s, cans are crimped rather than soldered, and the last 20 years is the era of the beer can. The only reference on cans listed by Hunt is the 1910 edition of *Encyclopedia Britannica* (Hunt 1959:8-9, 34), which may account for the ambiguities of his four periods. In particular, the soldered-can period from 1900 to World War I is oversimplified. The locked-seam can was first manufactured in 1897, even though it was not fully accepted until the 1920s. It should also be noted that the locked side-seam is soldered on the outside, although it differs in appearance from the older soldered seam. Nevertheless, Hunt's work is a step in the right direction. His dating scheme for mining camps could be refined, and information on eating habits and trading patterns could be gleaned from the cans as well.

A more extensive discussion of tin cans is found in "Johnny Ward's Ranch: A Study in Historic Archaeology," by Bernard Fontana and others, published in 1962. Johnny Ward's Ranch is located in southeastern Arizona and was occupied between 1859 and 1903. A number of tin cans were found during excavation there in 1959 and 1960, and the published report contains a detailed history of the tin can with a good bibliography. Treatment of the cans actually found at the site, however, is brief. Because the site was disturbed, and because the excavators felt the artifacts could not be dated with much refinement, all the artifacts were lumped together for analysis. The cans are described as dating mostly to the late 19th century and are divided into nine types, including rectangular hole-in-top cans for meat, round soldered hole-in-top cans, condensed milk cans, tobacco cans, and sardine cans. The author notes that the cans came from manufacturing centers outside of Arizona; one can top has the trade mark of a Cincinnati distributor (Fontana et al. 1962:1, 9, 67, 77, 115).

It is unfortunate that, even though for good reason, analysis of the tin cans was not more refined. It would have been interesting to know if any of the cans were associated with the store that was added to the ranch in 1882 (Fontana et al. 1962:24). More exact dating could have provided clues to distribution and consumption of different canned foods at different times, whereas written sources tend toward information on manufacture. But it is significant that the excavators of Johnny Ward's Ranch felt tin cans were worth attention and research.

Historical sources can only take archaeologists so far. Histories of the canning industry are social and economic histories with minimal information on the actual can. Even when sources describe physical characteristics, they are not necessarily the characteristics that are most important or evident to archaeologists, especially after a can has been buried for seventy-five years. If archaeologists want to know how a hand-soldered hole-and-cap can differs from a machine-soldered specimen they will have to find, identify and compare

them. Excavation reports and typological analyses are needed. Hopefully, this introduction to the tin can will soon be surpassed by surveys based on archaeologically recovered samples.

> The cow-boy is now gone to worlds invisible; the wind has blown away the white ashes of his campfires; but the empty sardine box lies rusting over the face of the western earth (Wister 1902:31).

TABLE 1
CAN CHRONOLOGY

1809	Nicholas Appert perfects canning in France
1812	Tin-canned food first marketed in England
1819	Beginning of commercial canning in America
1825	Thomas Kensett granted U.S. patent for canning food in tin
1847	Drop-press automatically flanges can ends
1856	Gail Borden granted patent for canned condensed milk
1876	Howe floater solders on can ends automatically
1897	Ams machine company begins manufacturing locked, double-seamed can
1901	Formation of American Can Company
1904	Sanitary Can Company markets double-seamed can as the sanitary enamel lined can
1935	Introduction of the beer can
1945	First aerosol cans marketed
1958	First all-aluminum beer can
1962	Introduction of the beverage can pull-tab
1965	Introduction of the tin-free steel beverage can

ACKNOWLEDGMENTS

I would like to thank John L. Cotter and Robert Schuyler of the University of Pennsylvania, the Tin Container Collectors Association, and Suzanne Baker of Archaeological Consultants in San Francisco for assistance in the research and writing of this article. The line drawings are by Michael Mouri.

REFERENCES

ANONYMOUS
1942 Tin Cans and Packages. *Modern Packaging Encyclopedia*: 254–60.

1944   Bug Bomb: Pressure Package for Self-Dispensing Product. *Modern Packaging* 18(2):98–102.

1954   Aerosols. *Modern Packaging Encyclopedia*: 320–26.

1956   Tinless Food Can. *Modern Packaging* 29(5):200–01.

1958   First Aluminum Canned Beer. *Modern Packaging* 32(1):106–10.

1959   Coke in Cans. *Modern Packaging* 33(2):226.

1968a   Canned Beef Before 1777. *Tin and Its Uses* 80:1–2.

1968b   Look at the Action in Metals. *Modern Packaging* 41(2):100–105.

1970   Pressurized Packaging. *Tin and Its Uses* 84:11–12.

1976   Beverages—From the Tinplate Can to the Pewter Tankard. *Tin and Its Uses* 107:12–14.

ASCHER, ROBERT
1974   Tin Can Archaeology. *Historical Archaeology* 8:7–16.

BARRY, B. T. AND C. J. EVANS
1974   D & I Cans—A Can-Making Revolution. *Tin and Its Uses* 100:12–15.

BEER CAN COLLECTORS OF AMERICA
1976   *The Beer Can: A Complete Guide to Beer Can Collecting*, edited by Larry Wright, Cornerstone Library, New York.

BINGHAM, TAYLOR H. AND PAUL F. MULLIGAN
1972   *The Beverage Container Problem: Analysis and Recommendations*. U.S. Environmental Protection Agency, Washington, D.C.

BITTING, A. W. AND K. G.
1916   *Canning and How to Use Canned Foods*. National Canners Association, Washington D.C.

BLANC, J. P.
1972   100 Years of Decorated Tinplate Containers. *Tin and Its Uses* 92:12–15.

CAN MANUFACTURERS INSTITUTE
1978   *The Can: Yesterday, Today and Tomorrow*. Washington, D.C.

CLARK, HYLA M.
1977   *The Tin Can Book: The Can as Collectible Art, Advertising Art and High Art*. New American Library, New York.

COLLINS, JAMES H.
1924   *The Story of Canned Foods*. E. P. Dutton & Company, New York.

DAVIS, ALEC
1967   *Package and Print: The Development of Container and Label Design*. Faber & Faber, London.

FONTANA, BERNARD L., J. CAMERON GREENLEAF, CHARLES FERGUSON, ROBERT WRIGHT AND DORIS FREDERICK
1962   Johnny Ward's Ranch: A Study in Historic Archaeology. *The Kiva* 28 (1–2).

HOARE, W. E. AND E. S. HEDGES
1945   *Tinplate*. Edward Arnold & Company, London.

HEDGES, ERNEST S.
1964   *Tin in Social and Economic History*. Edward Arnold Ltd., London.

HUNT, CHARLES B.
1959   Dating of Mining Camps with Tin Cans and Bottles. *Geo Times* 3(1):8–10, 34.

INTERNATIONAL TIN RESEARCH AND DEVELOPMENT COUNCIL
1936   Tin Plate and Tin Cans in the United States. *Bulletin of the International Tin Research and Development Council*: 4.

KLOAP, JOHN M.
1971   Progress of the Metal Can. *Modern Packaging Encyclopedia*: 232–35.

MANTELL, C. L.
1949   *Tin: Its Mining, Production, Technology and Applications*. second edition. Reinhold Publishing Company, New York.

MAY, EARL CHAPIN
1938   *The Canning Clan: A Pageant of Pioneering Americans*. The MacMillan Co., New York.

MULLIN, JAMES A.
1960   *Influences on the Use of Labels for Canned Foods*. Unpublished M.B.A. thesis. University of Pennsylvania.

NATIONAL CANNERS ASSOCIATION
1963   *The Canning Industry: Its History, Importance, Organization, Methods and the Public Service Value of its Products*. fifth edition. Washington, D.C.

SINGER, CHARLES, E. J. HOLMYARD, A. R. HALL, TREVOR I. WILLIAMS, EDITORS
1958   *A History of Technology* (Vol. 5). The Clarendon Press, Oxford.

WEBB, WALTER PRESCOTT
1931   *The Great Plains*. Ginn, Boston.

WISTER, OWEN
1902   *The Virginian*. The MacMillan Co., New York.

JANE BUSCH
DEPT. OF AMERICAN CIVILIZATION
UNIVERSITY OF PENNSYLVANIA
PHILADELPHIA, PENNSYLVANIA 19104

JAMES T. ROCK

Cans in the Countryside

ABSTRACT

The mining frontier was "a curious blending of the new and the familiar, of innovation and imitation" (Paul 1963:7). The truth of this assertion is reflected in the artifacts present in early Anglo sites found in northern California. One artifact class that documents this blending of the familiar with the new is the tin can.

   The study of tin cans and their associations with other artifacts can provide a key to understanding the dependence of settlers on the outside world. The same artifacts, of course, also mirror technological advances in the canning industry. This study discusses one example of the mutual ties that settlers in northern California maintained with the larger, industrialized society from which they had come.

Introduction

The material culture remains left by those who came to northern California between 1825 and the early 1900s is ample proof (if such is needed) that these settlers also brought their socio-cultural "baggage" with them. The material remains reflect the supply and transportation systems that maintained contact with homeland areas left behind. Material evidence for connections between the larger parent society and its offspring in northern California are exemplified by the "tin can."

The relationships maintained with the outside world as settlement, communication and supply systems developed in Siskiyou County, California, form the central focus of this article. Of equal interest are the technological and industrial stages that the canning industry achieved as the direct result of increased demand created by western expansion and national industrial growth. The physical evidence suggests that between 1825 and 1900 eastern industry responded to demand from those who migrated to the Far West by increasing both the quantity and quality of the goods they supplied. The positive feedback system between suppliers and consumers must be examined to understand the interplay among the social, technological and economic forces operating in this period.

The tin can is a perfect example of an artifact type that reflects the interrelationship between man and one attribute of his material culture. Detailed analysis of such mundane artifacts can contribute to a wider understanding of the ways in which mankind adapts to new and challenging social and natural environments while retaining many elements of an already familiar cultural repertoire.

Settlement of the American Far West depended to a large degree on the established culture of the East. The demand for eastern goods triggered a response in an individual society adjusting to meet new needs and markets. Relationships between East and West were dynamic; the development of the American West was always closely linked to the production capacities of the American East.

The Area

The first recorded Anglo contact in Siskiyou County, California, was via the trappers and traders of the Hudson's Bay Company who brought trade goods with them in their quest for pelts. In the 1820s and 1830s a number of trapping parties explored this area of California exchanging beads, knives, axes, blankets, etc., with the Shasta and Karok Indians in return for beaver pelts and the skins of other animals.

By the 1850s, a new group of Anglos had arrived who had not come to trade but to search for gold. The first miners brought very little with them to the Klamath, Scott and Salmon rivers and withdrew when winter weather became too severe. Beans, flour, sugar and coffee were frequent dietary staples, but liquor and tinned goods did not lag far behind in frequency of use. Prospectors needed these supplies to live, and this need was met by the development of trade routes and supply systems (Figure 1).

In the early 1850s, steamboats carried supplies into the northern part of the central valley of California. The goods were transferred from boats to mule trains which journeyed north into the mountains, mining camps and towns of Siskiyou

James Rock

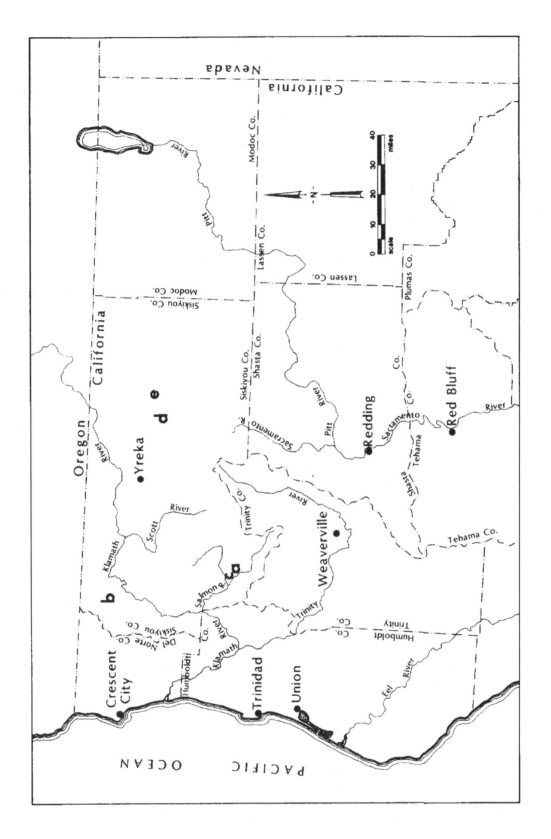

FIGURE 1. Far northern California. Letters indicate locations of sites discussed in Table 2. a. Wadstein mining claim. b. Classic Hill mine. c. White Bear mine; d. Abner. e. Kellum railroad logging camp.

County. Some supplies also came from the coast; they were shipped by sea to Trinidad, Union and Crescent City and were then brought inland by packers. Mule trains brought the tents, gold pans, shovels, picks and foods such as fruits, vegetables, flour, sugar and coffee into the county. Consumer practices by the time of the Gold Rush assured that northern California's immigrants were already familiar with canned goods. Many necessities were packaged in tin when this chapter in the expansion of the American frontier opened.

Settlement of the northern California gold fields was hastened by many who originally came for gold but who quickly turned to ranching, homesteading, logging or supply occupations. Towns such as Yreka, California, developed into inland supply centers from which pack trains conveyed stores to more remote areas. By the late 1850s, prospecting as well as individual small–scale placer mining were on the wane; large–scale operations were replacing them. Larger mining operations required increased capital, labor and material goods that could be met only by increased interaction with the "outside" world.

Steamboat and coastal trade were greatly affected when railroad transportation reached Siskiyou County from the Sacramento Valley in the mid–1880s. The railroad's arrival promoted a marked population increase. Supply shipments became more predictable at the same time that shipment predictability itself became more critical. Of course, rail transportation also meant that a new class of bulk goods could be brought into the county and that products could also be exported efficiently.

Large–scale logging began in northern California in the 1890s as mining activity continued to expand. Operations of larger scope naturally employed more people who had to be supplied with non–perishable foods. Industrialized logging and mining businesses thereafter became a part of Siskiyou County's economic and social milieu (Anonymous 1886; Cox 1974; McDonald 1979; McGown 1949; Reichman 1957; Rock 1980; Schrader 1949; Stumpf 1979; Wells 1881).

The Canning Industry

As the Far West continued to industrialize, complementary changes were occurring in those parts of the country that already had experienced this economic, technological and social revolution. This is exemplified in the canning industry and in the manufacture of tin cans (Table 1). Originally, metal food can bodies were cut out by hand; shaping and soldering of the side seam and ends were operations also performed by hand. The finished products had flush ends or ends that were crimped by hand and plumb or lap side seam joints (Figure 2). The cans were almost always filled through an opening in the center of one end. Once filled, a cap was soldered into place to close the can which, logically enough, became known as the hole–and–cap can (Busch 1979:3, 1981:96; Cobb 1919:5; Collins 1924:32; Fontana et al. 1962:69–70; Hunt 1902:464; May 1937:28, 435; MacNaughtan and Hedges 1935:41; Stevenson 1914:92; Woodward 1958:37).

An improvement to the hole–and–cap can was the addition of a small hole in the center of the cap; this was known as the hole–in–cap can (Figure 3). Hole–in–cap cans allowed filled containers to be closed and then heated to drive off excess moisture and air through the small hole. Sealing by this process reduced the number of "leakers," i.e., cans that swelled or burst. The "match–stick" filler hole in the center of the cap was closed and sealed by a drop of solder after the can and its contents had been heated. These cans were made by a slow, labor intensive process that produced only 60 crude cans per day per tinsmith (Sacharow and Griffin 1970:9).

The hole–in–cap can served a need, but manufacturers worked to improve both its dependability and availability. By the 1840s, large–scale canneries were in operation in both Baltimore, Maryland, and Boston, Massachusetts. If folklore is correct, it was at the William Underwood Company's Boston plant that bookkeepers shortened the term *cannister* to *can* (Fontana et al. 1962:67; May 1937:12; Woodward 1958:35).

TABLE 1
CAN CHRONOLOGY AND TERMINOLOGY

Term	Description	Approximate Date for Onset of Manufacture	Comments	References
tin cannister	containers made from tin plate or iron plate	1810	Augusta de Heine and Peter Durand patented iron and tin plated containers in England at this time. Durand patented his tin plate containers in the United States in 1818. Thomas Kensott patented an improved tin canister in 1825.	Clark 1977:13; Sacharow and Griffin 1970:9.
hole-and-cap	cans with a filler hole in one end that is closed by a cap	1810	These cans were used for a very brief period and were quickly improved upon. They often swelled or burst.	Collins 1924:34; MacNaughtan and Hedges 1935:40; Sacharow and Griffin 1970:9.
hole-in-cap	tin containers with a filler hole in one end sealed with a tin plate cap that has a pinhole vent in its center (see Figure 3)	By 1820	The introduction of the pinhole vent in the filler hole cap greatly reduced can failure. The terms hole-in-cap, hole-in-top and hole-and-cap are often used interchangably in the literature.	Clark 1977:14; Fontana et al. 1962:68; Sacharow and Griffin 1970:9.
stamped can ends	machine made can ends with extended edges that fit over the can body (see Figure 4)	1847	Allen Taylor invented a drop press to convert flat discs into vertically flanged caps. In 1849, Henry Evans invented a machine for pressing can tops and bottoms, rendering them more quickly and efficiently made.	Collins 1924:32; May 1937:28, 435; MacNaughtan and Hedges 1935:41.
key-wind opened	This is a closure mechanism in which a scored band on the side	1866	The sardine can is the most familiar example of this closure method in which nearly the	MacNaughtan and Hedges 1935:42–44; Sacharow and Griffin 1970:10.

Term	Date	Description	References
tapered tin	1875	entire can end is removed. There are many variations on this theme. or top of a can can be removed by rolling or tearing it away with the use of a key (see Figure 10) The base of this tin is larger than its top. The original tapered tins were rectangular in shape. Arthur A. Libby and J. Wilson of Chicago, Illinois, purchased the patent rights for this container in 1875 and began using it for their processed meat products.	May 1937:437; Pulati 1973:16.
double side seam	1888	This is a seam that locks the parts of a can together (see Figure 9). Max Ams of the Max Ams Machine Company of New York, New York, invented and produced tin products using this seam.	Sacharow and Griffin 1970:9.
key-wind opened tapered tins	1895	This is a closure mechanism in which a scored strip was placed on the can body near its larger end. The scored strip was removed with a key (see Figure 6). Edwin Norton of Chicago, Illinois, perfected this closure method which soon was in use on tapered tins. Later, the key-wind mechanism was most frequently found on cylindrical coffee cans.	Cobb 1914:94; Lee 1914:44.
Ams can	1898	This term denotes cans without internal solder and which have their side seam, top and bottom closed by double seams. The Max Ams Machine Company first produced these cans for the Cobb Preserving Company of Fairport, New York, at this time. Ams' employees called these containers ''sanitary cans.''	Collins 1924:39; May 1937:88.
hole-in-top	After 1900	This is a can with a single pinhole or ''match-stick'' filler hole no larger than $1/8$ inch in the center of one end. This hole is closed by a drop of solder (see Figure 8). By ca. 1920, evaporated milk tins were almost exclusively hole-in-top cans. These cans were also known as venthole cans.	Hunziker 1914:90; Pulati 1973:28–29.
sanitary can	1904	Sanitary cans are made using double seams. They are airtight and need no solder to fasten the side seam, top, or bottom (see Figure 11). Sanitary Can Company cans were completely made by machines; the interiors were lacquered to prevent chemical reaction of the product with the metal. American Can Company took over the four Sanitary Can Company plants in 1908.	Clark 1977:18; Collins 1924:36–37; Cruess 1948:37–38; Kopetz 1978:879; May 1937:91–95, 440.

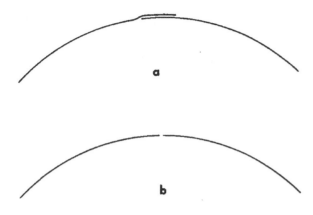

FIGURE 2. Can side seam types. a. lap side seam. b. plumb joint. The lap side seam was the dominant side seam type on cans until 1888.

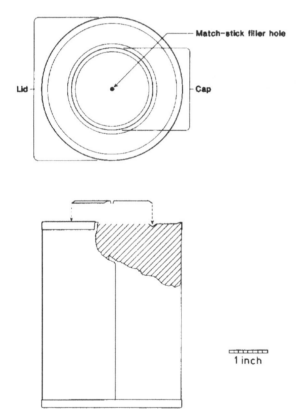

FIGURE 3. Hole–in–cap can. These were the first cans used for commercially produced food in the United States.

A major technological improvement in the tin can was the process that permitted stamping the can ends (Figure 4). Allen Taylor patented a drop–press to flange the edges of can ends in 1847. In 1848, William Numsen and Son of Baltimore, Maryland, improved the machine that stamped flat discs into can tops and bottoms. Numsen and Son patented their foot–powered pendulum press in 1849. This machine consisted of a "combination die" that not only formed flanged can ends but also cut the filler hole in the cap at the same time (Busch 1981:96; Clark 1977:13; Fontana et al. 1962:69–70; May 1937:12, 28; Sacharow and Griffin 1970:9).

An example of the variety of foods available in cans by 1863 is apparent by examining a list of the foodstuffs packaged by Ezra A. Edgett of Camden, New York, who was then a supplier for the Union Army. These products included sweet corn, chickens, turkey, ducks, geese and beef (May 1937:24).

At the same time that soldiers in the Civil War were learning of the existence of canned foods, a demand for fish was being met at the opposite end of the country by William Hapgood and the Hume Brothers. They established a salmon cannery in Sacramento, California, in 1864 (Collins 1924:140; May 1937:103, 436; Stevenson 1899:512). Cans for the Hapgood and Hume cannery were cut out and shaped by hand; however, the ends of their cans were stamped. All seams were hand–soldered (Figure 5). The interior of

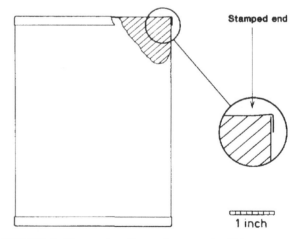

FIGURE 4. Stamped or flanged can ends. This process was patented in 1847.

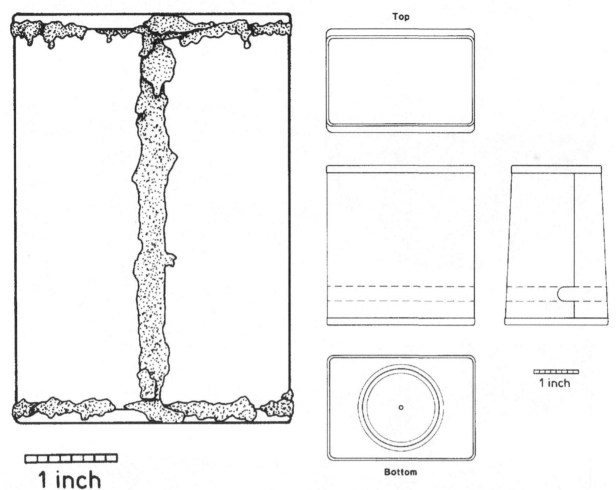

1 inch

FIGURE 5. Hand–soldered hole–in–cap can. This can type was common until the 1880s.

Top

Bottom

1 inch

FIGURE 6. Tapered tin. A patent for the tapered tin was obtained by Libby and Wilson of Chicago in 1875.

these hole–in–cap cans was painted with a mixture of red lead paint, turpentine and linseed oil in an attempt to prevent the fish from chemically reacting with the tin (Bitting 1937:850).

In 1875, Arthur A. Libby and W. J. Wilson of Chicago, Illinois, obtained rights to use a rectangular can for their products (Figure 6). This tapered tin allowed removal of the can's contents in a single piece. Libby and Wilson's canned corn beef rapidly gained popularity (Collins 1924:153; Fontana et al. 1962:73–74; May 1937:437).

Labor problems stimulated improvements in can soldering techniques during the 1870s. The "Howe Floater" system was introduced to canneries in 1876. This system rolled the cans at an angle in a solder bath and sealed the ends (Busch

1981:97; May 1937:28–29; Fontana et al. 1962:70).

The Norton Brothers of Chicago, Illinois, introduced a semi–automatic machine for soldering can side seams in 1883. This improvement meant that all processes of can–making could now be done by machines (Figure 7). Automatic can construction permitted up to 2500 cans to be made per machine in a single hour (Busch 1979:5, 1981:97; Clark 1977:18; Hunt 1902:464; May 1937:351; Stevenson 1914:92; Woodward 1958:37).

John B. Meyenberg began to use hermetically sealed cans for evaporated milk in 1885 (Bitting 1937:737; Hunziker 1914:9, 13; May 1937:184; Rock 1983). Many of Meyenberg's cans had a flush profile and a small (½ inch or ¾ inch) cap

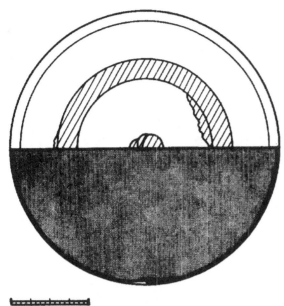

1 inch

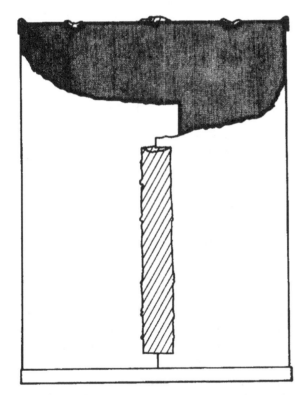

FIGURE 7. Machine-soldered side seam hole–in–-cap can with flush profile, ca. 1883.

with a ''match–stick'' filler hole in the center of the top. The tops and bottoms of Meyenberg's cans had lips that overlapped the can body (Fontana et al. 1962:74). After 1900, Carnation introduced the

hole–in–top can which has stamped ends and a match–stick filler hole in one end. This can is still dominant in the evaporated milk industry today (Figure 8).

Until the mid–1880s, can-making was a part of the canning business itself and was linked to the processing plant. The demand for tin cans had be-

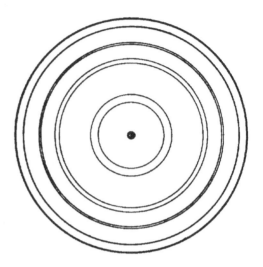

1 inch

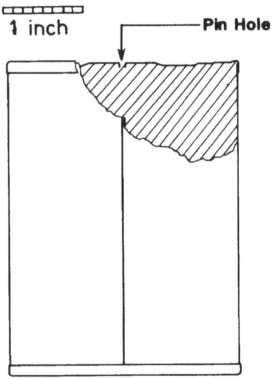

FIGURE 8. Hole–in–top can with a so-called match–stick filler hole. This is an example from an evaporated milk can, post-1900.

come sufficiently great by about 1885 that a separate can–producing industry became necessary. Many technological advances in can manufacture were made as a result of this specialization. Such businesses could focus on the problems of can production, improving their products and advancing their position in the marketplace without the added responsibility of undertaking successful foodstuff processing (Collins 1924:36; Fontana et al. 1962:74–75; Pulati 1973:28–29).

Max Ams of the New York based Max Ams Machine Company made a major technological breakthrough for the canning industry in 1888. He introduced the double seam method for side seaming cans. This locking seam held the sides of a can together far more satisfactorily than the earlier plumb and lap seams had been able to do (Figure 9). Can failure during the build–up of internal pressure was greatly reduced (Sacharow and Griffin 1970:9).

The key–opened, rolled, scored strip can was used by Edwin Norton in Chicago in 1895 (Figure 10). This can opening method had been known previously, but it was not employed to any great extent until Norton adapted it for his processed meat tins (Cobb 1914:94; Fontana et al. 1962:71, 73–74; Lee 1914:44; MacNaughton and Hedges 1935:43–44; Teague 1980:107).

In 1897, Charles Ams and Julius Brenzinger improved their can sealing equipment by crimping both the top and bottom thus forming a sealed double seam. In 1896 Charles Ams had patented a

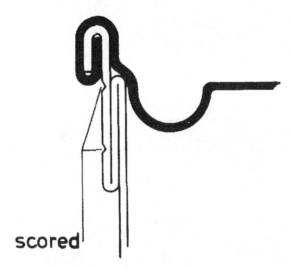

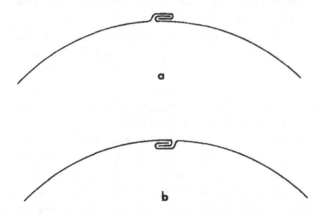

FIGURE 9. Double side seams. a. external. b. internal. Double side seams were introduced in 1888 and were being commercially produced by the late 1890s.

FIGURE 10. Cross section of key-opened tin introduced by Edwin Norton of Chicago in 1895.

liquid sealing compound of rubber and gum that replaced the rubber gaskets previously used. The combination of Am's double side seam method of closure, the double seam crimp top and bottom, exterior solder and automatically applied sealing compound produced what became known as the ''solderless can'' (Collins 1924:38; May 1937:439).

The first so–called solderless cans were under production at the Max Ams Machine Company for the Cobb Preserving Company of Fairport, New York, by 1898 (May 1937:88). The solderless can also became known as the ''Ams can.'' Between 1900 and 1902 Cobb's Fairport cannery shifted from using the older hole–in–cap can to the open–top can (May 1937:90) which by this time had become a commercially viable commodity.

The Sanitary Can Company was formed in Fairport, New York, in 1904, and thereafter sanitary cans rapidly replaced hole–in–cap cans. Sanitary cans were the first tin–plated cylindrical food containers that were air–tight and did not use solder for sealing and fastening their side seam, top and bottom (May 1937:91). Sanitary cans replaced the Ams can when the double seam process became completely mechanical. By 1904, sanitary cans were being made at the rate of 25,000 in a 10–hour day (Figure 11). The American Can Company purchased and took over the plants of the Sanitary Can Company in 1908.

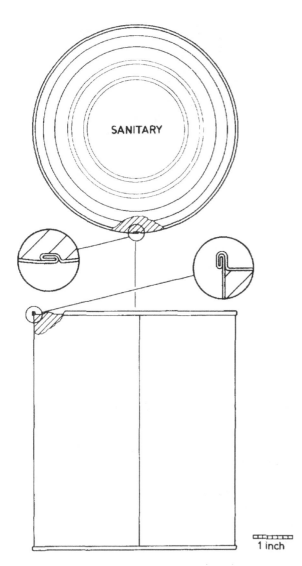

SANITARY

1 inch

FIGURE 11. The double seam or sanitary can commercially produced in 1889. The illustrated example is *from a Weed Lumber Company camp in Siskiyou County,* California, and dates between 1910 and 1914.

By 1910, California canners were incorporating into their production new elements in canning technology developed in the East. The sanitary can dominated the West Coast industry by the end of 1911 (Busch 1979:6, 1981:98; Clark 1977:11, 18; Cobb 1914:94, 96; Collins 1924:36–40; Cruess 1948:37, 38; Fontana et al. 1962:72–75; Kopetz 1978:87; May 1937:91–95).

Northern California Evidence

Material culture remains left by the settlers of northern California between 1825 and the early 1900s indicate that frontier development was accompanied by the extension of products and processes already developed in the East. The first Anglos in the area left only trade goods including Hudson's Bay Company axes, beads, traps, buttons and an occasional musket. Clearly, the traders and trappers who came to northern California were themselves part of a larger social and economic unit, the international trading company.

The first miners brought with them very little but their clothes, gold pans and shovels, but as time went on, there is material evidence of greater contact with other segments of American culture. One example, and one that reflects an outside source of supply, is the hand–formed, hand–soldered hole–in–cap can with lap side seams. Soldering on the California specimens is ordinarily quite crude even though the tops and bottoms usually had been manufactured by stamping (Table 2).

Supplies of all kinds were imported into northern California in increased amounts to meet growing demand in the 1870s and 1880s. The logging industry was still comparatively small but grew throughout this period. Mining continued as the major occupation in northern California. Artifact inventories from the sites of small–scale operations frequently contain recycled tin cans. Cans were made into cups by adding a handle or were punctured to form strainers.

As a rule, big mining operations required more goods and more complex equipment. Population in northern California increased rapidly, and this is at times seen not only in the extensive alteration of the land but in the greater variety and increased quantity of consumer goods found on sites occupied after the time of initial exploration.

Distinguishing features of larger, more complex mining and logging sites are tins of greater volume than those on sites of individual habitations or small–scale businesses. The No. 10 tin and the evaporated milk can are quite common artifacts on sites where big mines and logging operations fed large numbers of workers (Figure 12).

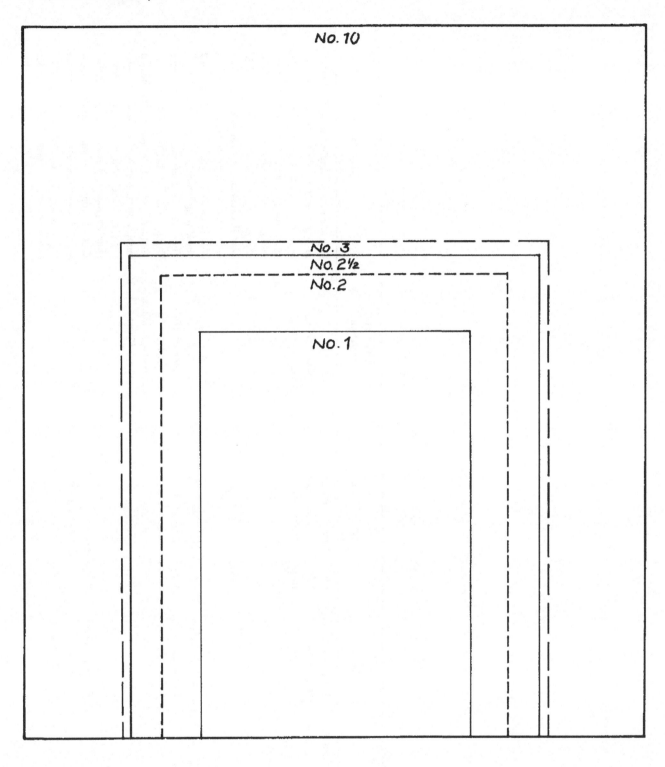

FIGURE 12. Numerical designations for tin cans and their profile sizes.

TABLE 2
EXAMPLES OF ARCHAEOLOGICAL SITES PRODUCING CANS IN SISKIYOU COUNTY, CALIFORNIA

Site Name Number	Location	Other Names	Years of Operation	Comments
Wadstein Mining Claim (three archaeological sites)	Eddy Gulch (Figure 1a)	Burnes Brothers Placer John Frank 1&2 Placer Mines Judge Hydraulic Mine	ca. 1870s ca. 1900–1920 ca. 1920–1940	One site in this complex has yielded hole-in–cap evaporated milk tins, several sizes of lap side seam hole–in–cap cans, and opium tins, in addition to shoe parts, cooking utensils, ceramics, etc. The other two sites in the complex include a post-World War II cabin and a hydraulic mining pit with crane, single drum, beam and box hydraulic balance, sluice boxes, flume, and plank wing dams.
Classic Hill Mine	Indian Creek (Figure 1b)	Classic Claim 1873 Howard Placer Mine	land patented 1877 by Classic Hill land patented 1880 by Howard Placer	The site includes the collapsed James Camp cabin, the dwelling of the original claimant, as well as mining ditches, a dump with fragments of lap seam hole–in–cap cans, wine bottle fragments, ironstone plate fragments, porcelain, and cut nails.
White Bear Mine	Callahans Gulch (Figure 1c)	White Bear May Land Mining Co.	1890 1920s	This site consists of Adits, office, domestic, and work buildings, and a five stamp mill location, 15 structures in all, in addition to an ore car track. Various powder

cans, cooking and washing containers, sanitary cans, evaporated milk hole–in–top cans, vegetable cans of various sizes, including No. 10 tins in association with bottles and bottle fragments, wire nails, corrugated iron, etc. The mine dump is quite large and diffuse rather than concentrated in one area.

Abner — Grass Lake (Figure 1d) — Weed Lumber Co. Abner Camp — 1908–1911

This site has yielded several thousand cans, about one-half of which are No. 10 tins. The remainder are dominated by hole–in–cap evaporated milk tins and rectangular tins in association with bottle fragments, handleless white ceramic cups, plates, saw-cut cattle bones, lumber, horseshoes, etc.

Kellum — Butte Creek (Figure 1e) — Weed Lumber Co. Kellum Wye — 1917–1920

This railroad logging camp site has yielded amethyst glass, a sanitary can with the letter "C" embossed on one end, ca. 100 small hole–in–cap food cans, a H. J. Heinz octagonal bottle base, white ceramics marked "Grindley Hotel Ware, England, Vitrified," and Lea & Perrins machine made bottles, tobacco tin lunch pail, etc. There are no No. 10 tins present. Sanitary cans are the dominant can type present in the artifact inventory.

From the preceding discussion, it is clear that cans made after the 1880s reflect a major technological change in soldering techniques. The hole–in–cap can predominated, but more uniform application of solder to the can ends and to the side seams is apparent in more recent specimens. The cap and vent hole in the 1880s were still hand–soldered. Many hole–in–cap can sizes are represented at northern California sites of this time period.

After 1890 and into the early 20th century, industrial improvements in northern California continued as the railroad opened a two–way flow of products and the lumber industry established large camps. Cookhouse foods in the lumber camps came out of large–volume containers and were served on ironstone plates. Concentrations of No. 10 tins, evaporated milk cans and condiment tins with double side seams are often all that remain at logging camp sites. For recreation, it appears from the evidence of empty cans that the men smoked or chewed tobacco. Pocket tobacco tins and tobacco tins designed for reuse as lunch boxes are common. Mining sites and other company-controlled operations reflect similar artifactual components. As noted above, the tin can was improved in this time period by the introduction of the open top, by the adoption of double seam side seams and finally by the development of double seam ends. Sanitary cans dominated can production in the United States by 1910, and by the mid–1930s, the hole–in–cap can had all but passed from the scene.

Conclusions

The humble tin can formed one important link between the developing western frontier of the United States and the industrialized East which supported the expansion of that frontier. The technological, economic and social significance of the tin can is recognized only by examining the material culture record within a theoretical framework that acknowledges the dependence of the West on the products of the East. The artifacts left by miners, settlers and others who moved into far northern California after 1825 clearly reflect the level of this dependence. The canning industry is but one example of rapid technological development in response to increasing demand for canned products. The effect of market on producer is reflected in both the increased variety and the types of tins recovered in northern California archaeological contexts. In the final analysis, the tin can and its development is but one key to understanding larger anthropological problems of the interrelationships and mutually reinforcing feedback mechanism that existed between East and West, that is, between producer and consumer. Ultimately, it is those behind the can—the makers of the products and the consumers—whose behavior and motivations one may hope to fathom by the systematic study of these physical remains.

ACKNOWLEDGEMENTS

The author would like to thank Joseph W. Hopkins III for his help in developing the symposium we held in 1981 at the Society for American Archaeology meetings in San Diego, California, from which this paper developed. Thanks also are extended to Tim Nilsson for creating the illustrations.

REFERENCES

ANONYMOUS
1886 *List of Names on the Great Register of Siskiyou, State of California*. Yreka Semi–Weekly Journal Book and Job Office, Yreka, California.

BITTING, A. W.
1937 *Appetizing or the Art of Canning: Its History and Development*. The Trade Pressroom, San Francisco.

BUSCH, JANE
1979 Sardines to Beer: An Introduction to the Tin Can. Ms. on file, Klamath National Forest, Yreka, California.
1981 An Introduction to the Tin Can. *Historical Archaeology* 15(1):95–104.

CLARK, HYLA M.
1977 *The Tin Can Book*. New American Library, New York.

COBB, GEORGE W.
1914 *The Development of the Sanitary Can*. In *A History of the Canning Industry*, edited by Arthur I. Judge, pp. 94–97. The Canning Trade, Baltimore.

COBB, JOHN N.
1919   *The Canning of Fishery Products*. Millen Freeman, Seattle.

COLLINS, JAMES H.
1924   *The Story of Canned Foods*. E. P. Dutton and Company, New York.

COX, THOMAS R.
1974   Mills and Markets; *A History of the Pacific Coast Lumber Industry to 1900*. University of Washington Press, Seattle.

CRUESS, WILLIAM V.
1948   *Commercial Fruit and Vegetable Products*. McGraw–Hill, New York.

FONTANA, BERNARD L., J. CAMERON GREENLEAF, CHARLES FERGUSON, ROBERT WRIGHT AND DORIS FREDERICK
1962   Tin Cans. In Johnny Ward's Ranch: A Study in Historic Archaeology. *The Kiva* 28(1–2):67–78.

HUNT, ARTHUR L.
1902   Canning and Preserving, Fruit, Vegetable, Fish and Oysters. In *Twelfth Census of the United States, Part III*, pp. 463–513. Washington, D.C.

HUNZIKER, OTTO F.
1914   *Condensed Milk and Milk Powder*. Privately published, Lafayette, Indiana.

KOPETZ, ARNOLD A.
1978   Metal Cans: Types, Trends and Selected Factors, Modern Packaging 1978/1979. *Encyclopedia and Buyers Guide* 51(12):87–91.

LEE, C. T.
1914   A History of the Canned Meat Industry. In *A History of the Canning Industry*, edited by Arthur I. Judge, pp. 40–42. The Canning Trade, Baltimore.

MACNAUGHTAN, D. J. AND ERNEST S. HEDGES (EDITORS)
1935   The Evolution of the Sealed Tinplate Container. *Bulletin of the International Tin Research and Development Council* 1:40–56.

MAY, EARL CHAPIN
1937   *The Canning Clan: A Pageant of Pioneering Americans*. The MacMillan Company, New York.

MCDONALD, JAMES A.
1979   Cultural Resource Overview. Ms. on file, Klamath National Forest, Yreka, California.

MCGOWN, JOSEPH A.
1949   *Freighting to the Mines in California 1849–1859*. Unpublished Ph.D. dissertation, Department of History, University of California, Berkeley.

PAUL, RODMAN
1963   *Mining Frontiers of the Far West, 1848–1880*. Holt, Rinehart and Winston, New York.

PULATI, EVALENE
1973   *Illustrated Tin Container Guide*. Privately published, Santa Ana, California.

REICHMAN, GUS
1957   The Farmers Mill. *The Siskiyou Pioneer* 2(8):3–8.

ROCK, JAMES T.
1980   *What's Out There: Railroad Logging's Material Culture Remains*. A Paper Presented at the Society for California Archaeology Meeting, Redding, California, April 4.
1983   *The Swiss Connection*. A Paper Presented at the Society for Historical Archaeology Meeting, Denver, Colorado, January 8.

SACHAROW, STANLEY AND ROGER G. GRIFFIN
1970   *Food Packaging: A Guide for the Supplier, Processor and Distributor*. The AVI Publishing Co., Inc., Westport, Connecticut.

SCHRADER, GEORGE R. (EDITOR)
1949   *Yearbook* 1(4). Siskiyou County Historical Society, Yreka, California.

STEVENSON, CHARLES H.
1899   The Preservation of Fishery Products for Food. In *Bulletin of United States Fish Commission*, edited by George M. Bowers, pp. 335–563. U.S. Government Printing Office, Washington, D.C.

STEVENSON, W. H. H.
1914   Cans and Can-Making Machinery. In *A History of the Canning Industry*, edited by Arthur I. Judge, pp. 92–93. The Canning Trade, Baltimore.

STUMPF, GARY D.
1979   Gold Mining in Siskiyou County 1850–2900. *Siskiyou County Historical Society Occasional Paper* 2.

TEAGUE, GEORGE
1980   Reward Mine and Associated Sites. *Western Archaeological Center Publications in Anthropology* II.

WELLS, HARRY L.
1881   *History of Siskiyou County, California*. D. J. Stewart & Co., Oakland, California.

WOODWARD, ARTHUR
1958   Appendices to the Report on Fort Union 1851–1891. Ms. on file, Western Archaeological Center, Tuscon, Arizona.

JAMES T. ROCK
KLAMATH NATIONAL FOREST
YREKA, CALIFORNIA 96097

D.B.S. MAXWELL

Beer Cans: A Guide for the Archaeologist

ABSTRACT

Beer cans are potentially useful as tools for dating later components in historical sites, and for determining the time of intrusion into prehistoric sites. Changes in major and minor design features are sufficiently documented to yield age estimates accurate to within five years of production. Even in cases of poor can preservation, general trends in shape and construction should provide an estimate accurate to within a decade. This article details both morphological and stylistic changes for the purpose of providing a basic guide to the dating of beer cans.

Introduction

Busch (1981) provides an overview of the history of the tin can. The research herein serves to expand her work on a specific subject—the beer can. Beer cans are of potentially great value for dating both later historic sites and intrusive components in prehistoric sites. Changes in beer can morphology and design are well documented, meaning that determining the age of a beer can to within a few years of production is a distinct possibility. Beer can collectors have done a great deal of research into the history and development of the beer can, and much of the terminology used in this article is taken from beer can collecting literature.

Origins

In 1909, a brewer in Montana first suggested that beer be put in cans. The American Can Company of Greenwich, Connecticut, experimented with this idea briefly, but had little success (Beer Can Collectors of America [BCCA] 1985:3). The technology available at that time simply made canned beer an impossibility. While ordinary tin cans are designed to withstand internal pressure of between 24 and 35 p.s.i., the pasteurization process used on beer creates pressures of 80 p.s.i. and requires a more sturdy container (BCCA 1976a:1). Another obstacle to canning beer was the necessity of developing an internal coating for the can (Martells 1976).

With the coming of prohibition in 1920, further canning experiments were discontinued. However, towards the end of prohibition the American Can Company resumed its experiments in making a stronger container (*Fortune* 1936). The weakness problem was solved by using rephosphorized steel for the can top and bottom, and by soldering each layer of metal in the fold of the side seam.

The second problem was that beer reacts with metal, producing precipitated salts—referred to by brewers as metal turbidity (*Fortune* 1936)—rendering the beer discolored and undrinkable (BCCA 1985:3). To address this problem, a number of experimental can linings were tried, and several proved to be suitable. The American Can Company had settled on a combination of enamel and brewer's pitch, similar to a keg, which was trademarked "Keglined." The trademark lasted although the material itself was replaced by a synthetic vinyl (known as "vinylite") prior to large-scale production. The Continental Can Company of New York City and the Cork, Crown, and Seal Company of Philadelphia both developed wax coatings, while National Can and Pacific Can each developed enamel coatings for their containers (BCCA 1985:4).

The first cans filled were "Kruger's Special Beer," a 3.2 percent alcohol beer made during the partial lifting of prohibition in 1933 (Christensen 1976:3). Two thousand of these cans were filled, but none was sold. On 24 January 1935, in Richmond, Virginia, Kruger Cream Ale became the first brand of canned beer sold commercially. These cans were the standard 12-oz. size, similar in design to cans sold today.

Dating Cans

Unfortunately, there are few foolproof guides for dating beer cans. Very few brewers ever in-

TABLE 1
CHRONOLOGY OF STYLISTIC DEVELOPMENT OF THE BEER CAN

Date	Feature Introduced
1980s	–UPC computer codes standard feature on all cans.
	–Multiple neck-in chimes present on cans produced in the early years of the decade.
	–Single, longer neck-in chimes prevalent during latter years of the decade.
1989	–Government alcohol warning labels introduced.
1984	–Straight-sided steel cans cease production.
1983	–Production of ring-pull cans ceases.
1970s	–Production of 11-oz., 15-oz., and gallon cans ceases.
	–UPC computer codes introduced.
1977	–Coors phases out push-button cans.
1975	–American Can Company begins producing push-button cans.
1974–1979	–Cans issued commemorating the U.S. bicentennial.
1972	–Oregon bans the use of ring-pull cans. Push-button can openings introduced by Coors.
	–Cans with specialized shapes first marketed.
1967	–Tin-free steel (TFS) cans introduced.
1966	–Welded-seam cans introduced.
	–"Neck-in chime" cans (lid smaller than can body) introduced.
1965	–First "ring-pull" can marketed.
1964	–Continental Can's "U-tab" design introduced.
	–Tab-tops with "smile" beads introduced.
	–Gallon cans introduced.
1963	–In January, Schlitz becomes first national brewer to use tab-top cans. By August, 65 brands are available in this design.
	–First 12-oz. all-aluminum can issued.
	–Plastic six-pack holder (yoke) introduced.
1962	–First self-opening can ("snap-top" or "tab-top") introduced by Pittsburgh Brewing Company.
1960	–Cones completely phased out by this time.
1950s	–Crowntainers phased out by mid-decade.
	–Cones largely phased out by mid-decade.
	–Odd-size cans marketed include 7-, 8-, 10-, 11-, 14-, and 15-oz. sizes.
	–Aluminum lids used on steel-bodied cans. These are often described on can labels as "soft-tops."
	–Pastels and metallic colors become common features of can labels.
1959	–Coors markets 7-oz. all-aluminum can.
1958	–Primo markets 11-oz. paper-labeled, all-aluminum can.
1954	–Schlitz markets the first 16-oz. punch-top can.
1950	–"Internal Revenue Tax Paid" marking removed from can (and bottle) labels, March 30.
1942–1947	–Domestic canned beer production ceased due to World War II. Over 18 million cans of beer produced for military use.
	–Military beer cans are silver or olive drab in color.
	–Military cans are not marked "Internal Revenue Tax Paid" but, rather, "Withdrawn Free of Tax for Exportation."
1940	–J-spout cans phased out of production.
	–Introduction of crowntainer, which replaces the J spout.
1930s	–Most cans feature heavy paint and lacquer, resulting in good label preservation.
	–The word "beer" is usually as prominent as the brand name, owing to the novelty of having beer in cans.
	–Opening instructions, usually with illustrations, are included as part of the label (usually near the seam).
	–Contents are often described as "contains 12 fluid ounces—same as a bottle."
1937	–Cones produced after this date have concave bottoms and long cones ("high-profile").
	–J-spout cans introduced.
	–Quart-size cones introduced in July.
1935	–First can marketed on January 24 in Richmond, Virginia. Eighteen breweries are canning beer by end of year.
	–Beginning June 28, all cans produced are marked "Internal Revenue Tax Paid."
	–Cone-top cans first marketed in September. These have flat bottoms and short cones ("low-profile").

Note. It is often difficult (if not impossible) to document the dates when various features are eliminated or removed from use, due primarily to the fact that old stock is frequently utilized after changes have been made. The presence of multiple suppliers (and in some cases, brewery locations) will also result in the simultaneous usage of different styles of cans (i.e., a single brewing company may produce aluminum and crimped-steel cans in different plants).

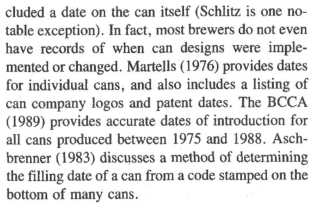

FIGURE 1. A standard 12-oz., punch-top beer can.

FIGURE 2. "Internal Revenue Tax Paid" (IRTP) marking on a pre-1950 can.

cluded a date on the can itself (Schlitz is one notable exception). In fact, most brewers do not even have records of when can designs were implemented or changed. Martells (1976) provides dates for individual cans, and also includes a listing of can company logos and patent dates. The BCCA (1989) provides accurate dates of introduction for all cans produced between 1975 and 1988. Aschbrenner (1983) discusses a method of determining the filling date of a can from a code stamped on the bottom of many cans.

The techniques and information utilized by these authors may not always be obtainable from a beer can, owing to problems such as preservation. However, there are a number of guidelines for determining the age of any given can to within a few years. The majority of this information comes from BCCA (1976a, 1985, 1989), Martells (1976), and from personal observation and experience. Table 1 summarizes the major events in the beer can's history.

The Pre-World War II Era

Pre-World War II era cans are divisible into three primary categories: punch tops, cone tops, and crowntainers. Each category is discussed below.

Punch-Top Cans

The 1930s and 1940s saw the greatest variety of types of beer cans. The first type marketed was

Figure 3. Cone-top can depicting side seam and "Cap-Sealed" logo.

FIGURE 4.   A short cone or "low-profile" can, produced only prior to World War II.

American Can's "punch-top" or "flat-top"—so named because its flat top required a punch opener. An early punch-top can stands 12–12.5 cm (5 in.) high, has a diameter of 7 cm (2¾ in.), and a soldered side seam 2.5 cm (1 in.) wide. Cans produced by the American Can Company all bear the trademark "Keglined" (Figure 1). Continental Can, National Can, and Pacific Can all marketed similar 12-oz. cans.

By the end of 1935, 18 breweries were canning beer in punch-top cans; by the late 1930s, at least 78 breweries were doing the same (Garard 1978). Cans first appeared on the west coast in late 1936 (Maloney 1973:4).

All cans (and bottles), with the exception of those designated for military use, produced be-tween 28 June 1935 and 30 March 1950 were marked "Internal Revenue Tax Paid" (IRTP) (Figure 2). The IRTP marking is an important horizon for determining the production date of a can.

Cone-Top Cans

Cone-top cans were manufactured by the Continental Can Company, and were trademarked "Cap-Sealed" (Figure 3). These were first marketed in September of 1935 by the Schlitz Brewing Company of Milwaukee, Wisconsin (BCCA 1985: 9).

Cone-top cans have been described as looking like tin bottles—complete with a cap—and thus as

Cone-top cans came in three sizes: 12 oz., 16 oz. (rare), and 32 oz. (U.S. quart). There are three varieties of cones on standard 12-oz. cans: short cone, referred to as "low-profile" (Figure 4) which stands a total of 14 cm (5½ in.) high (12 cm [4¾ in.] to the base of the cone); a standard long cone or "high-profile" (Figure 5), which also stands 14 cm (5½ in.) high (11.5 cm [4½ in.] to the base of the cone—see Garard 1981:18); and a type produced by the Crown, Cork, and Seal Company referred to by collectors as a "J spout" because of its straight, narrow neck which flares into a wide base (Cameron 1983b:28). These cans all have a basal diameter of 7 cm (2¾ in.), and a soldered side seam that is 2.5 cm (1 in.) wide.

FIGURE 5.   A long cone or "high-profile" can, produced after World War II.

being more likely to be accepted by beer drinkers. In fact, early advertisements claim that "the public preferred the shape of the Continental can two to one over American's flat-top can" (BCCA 1976a: 41). Indeed, the appeal of the can to both brewers and beer drinkers does appear to have been its familiar bottle-like shape. However, Clark (1977: 32) feels that this attraction was primarily for the brewer, as the shape of this can meant that it could be filled with only minor modifications to existing bottling lines, thus eliminating the need to purchase American Can's expensive (ca. $25,000) flat-top canning line. As a result, smaller brewers tended toward using cone-top cans. Garard (1981) lists 102 breweries using cone-top cans by the end of 1939. Only one of these, Schlitz, was a national brewer.

FIGURE 6.   The silver crowntainer lacks a side seam.

FIGURE 7. Early Brown Derby can (ca. 1937) shows the word "beer" as prominently as the brand name.

FIGURE 8. Early cans often had opening instructions as part of their label.

Crowntainers

In 1940, the Crown, Cork and Seal Company introduced a new and very distinctive can design. This was known as the crowntainer (Figure 6), and was often referred to as a "Silver Growler" or "Silver Bumper" (BCCA 1985:21). This design replaced the "J spout" described above. The crowntainer "was formed by drawing the sides and top from one piece of steel sheet, and attaching the concave bottom by the standard rolled flange method" (BCCA 1985:21). The method of drawing involved would not allow for the use of tin-plated steel, and plating the can after forming was very expensive, so an aluminum coating was used on the steel body. The bottom was tin-plated, and the internal lining was wax (BCCA 1985). A crowntainer stands 13 cm (5 in.) high, and has a 7.2 cm (2¾-in.) diameter at the base and no side seam. Crowntainers were used by a number of brewers until the mid-1950s, when they were phased out. These cans were either silver- or cream-colored and were available only in the 12-oz. size and east of the Rocky Mountains.

Dating Cans from Prior to 1950

Because of Internal Revenue tax laws, beer cans from prior to 1950 can be easily distinguished from those produced after this date. Developments prior to this date are described subsequently.

FIGURE 9.   An early 16-oz. can (ca. 1958).

FIGURE 10.   Two different versions of the 8-oz. can (ca. 1980).

fluid ounces—same as bottle.'' Many of these practices had been discontinued by the early 1940s.

Cone Tops

Many of the stylistic label variations found on cone-top cans are similar to those found on punch tops made at the same time. However, some features are unique to cones.

Cones made prior to 1937 have flat bottoms. Those produced after this date have concave bottoms. Cones produced prior to World War II are described as ''low-profile''—that is, they have a short cone (Figure 4). Post-war cones are called ''high-profile,'' because the cone is longer (Figure 5). J-spout cones were produced only from 1937 to 1940 (Cameron 1983a). The quart-size cone was introduced in July 1937 (White 1978:17) and continued until the early 1950s.

Crowntainers

Crowntainers and growlers have a much more limited history, having been produced only be-

Punch Tops

Cans of this time period have a number of distinguishing features. Both the paint and the lacquer used on the can were very heavy, especially during the 1930s, as can manufacturers did not know exactly how much of each was necessary to preserve the label. Thus, early cans often have very good paint preservation.

Can labels from the 1930s often display the word ''beer'' as prominently as the brand name (Figure 7), because the idea of canned beer was still unfamiliar to many customers. Cans produced up to the early 1940s usually had opening instructions (Figure 8) along the seam of the can (Cameron 1983b). Also common on early cans was the practice of describing the contents, e.g., ''contains 12

FIGURE 11. Ten-oz. can.

FIGURE 12. Eleven-oz. can (ca. 1960).

tween 1940 and the middle 1950s. The presence or absence of an IRTP marking should differentiate these two time periods. There were no major changes in the construction of crowntainers (BCCA 1976a). As is mentioned earlier, most cone-top cans and all crowntainers were obsolete by the mid-1950s.

The World War II Era

Canned beer production for the U.S. domestic market ceased in 1942 because of restrictions in the availability of tin plate, which was reserved for military use (Martells 1976; Rock 1980). However, the military purchased huge quantities of canned beer—at least 18 million cans (BCCA 1976b:29)—for overseas consumption. According to the BCCA (1985:21), over one billion cans of beer were supplied to the armed forces. Military cans, which were produced by 40 different breweries, have two distinct features that set them apart from other cans. First, rather than reading ''Internal Revenue Tax Paid,'' all military beer cans read ''Withdrawn Free of Tax for Exportation.'' Second, these cans are camouflaged—olive drab (or grey) in color, with the brand's standard logo in black. Advertisements of the time describe these cans as ''lusterless—will not reflect the sun's rays—and of olive-drab color, like tanks, army trucks, etc.'' (Beer Cans Monthly 1979:26). A number of olive-drab cans have turned up in North

FIGURE 13. Fourteen-oz. can.

FIGURE 14. Fifteen-oz. can (late 1950s).

America (California, Texas, and Washington State), suggesting that not all were shipped overseas (Kirkpatrick 1980:4). Domestic production of canned beer resumed in 1947.

The 1950s

On 30 March 1950, the U.S. Bureau of Alcohol, Tobacco, and Firearms lifted the regulation of paying internal revenue tax on beer prior to shipping it from the brewery (Henderson [1976]:2). Thus, the words "Internal Revenue Tax Paid" were re-moved from the labels of all beer packages including cans, which is an important guide for dating cans. Most beer cans lacking these words (or "Withdrawn Free of Internal Revenue Tax") were produced after this date, as discussed above.

The 1950s also saw the demise of cone-top cans and crowntainers. Most brewers canning beer had reached the point where sales revenue exceeded the expense of installing canning lines. Since cone-

FIGURE 15. Schlitz can with "Super Softop" logo advertizing an aluminum top for easier opening (1960).

FIGURE 16. Two varieties of 7-oz. cans (mid-1970s).

top cans and crowntainers were slower to fill than punch-top cans, they became too costly and thus obsolete (Martells 1976:9; BCCA 1985:22). The Rice Lake Brewing Company was the last brewer to use cone-top cans, which were completely phased out of the brewing industry by 1960 (BCCA 1985). Cone-top cans continued to be used for oil and gasoline additives until the 1980s.

While punch-top cans were the standard of the 1950s, the 12-oz. size was by no means universal. Schlitz issued 16-oz. cans (Figure 9) in 1954, in an effort to make up revenue lost during a 1953 Milwaukee strike (Martells 1976). Other sizes were also introduced: Goebel of Detroit began marketing beer in 8-oz. cans; and 10-, 11-, 14-, and 15-oz. cans were also brought to market (Figures 10–14). Eleven- and 15-oz. cans were used in the western states, while 10- and 14-oz. cans were popular in the southern states. Thirty-two-oz. cans continued to be produced on a small scale (e.g., New York's Ballentine brewery made quart punch-top cans). Many of these sizes continue to be produced at present.

Aluminum also found its way into beer cans during the 1950s. The Adolf Coors Company of Colorado began to use cans with aluminum tops; these were billed as "soft-tops" and were designed to make opening the can easier. Schlitz and a number of other brewers continued this practice beginning in 1960 (Figure 15). All-aluminum cans followed shortly. Primo, a Hawaiian brewer, marketed an 11-oz. paper-labeled, all-aluminum can in 1958 (Martells 1976:100). Coors issued an all-aluminum 7-oz. can in 1959 (Figure 16; BCCA 1985: 22).

Another distinctive change found in the 1950s was a wider variety of label colors, as can manufacturers exploited improved printing methods. Pastels and metallic colors were quite common.

The 1960s

The decade of the 1960s was a time of great innovation in the canning industry, and a number of new types of cans became available.

FIGURE 17.   Hamm's produces the first all-aluminum 12-oz. can.

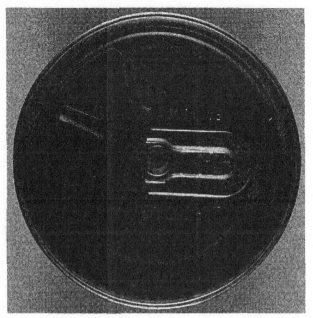

FIGURE 18.   An early version of the "tab-top," with the tab still in place (can unopened). Occasionally early tab-top cans will be found with the tab in place, and holes punched either through the tab or the bottom of the can, apparently by a beer-drinker who did not approve of the new innovation.

In the early years of the decade, soft-top cans became very common, in an attempt to increase convenience for the buyer (*Modern Packaging* [*MP*] 1962a:33–34, 1963a:159–160). The presence of the soft-top was usually advertized on the cans label using words such as "super soft-top."

All-aluminum cans also became an important part of the market. While such cans had been introduced in the 1950s, they were available only in the 7-oz. size (Primo notwithstanding). In 1963, 12-oz. aluminum cans became a reality. Hamm's beer was the first brand available in this package (Figure 17) and was quickly followed by Budweiser (*MP* 1963b:150, 1963c:210). These are two-piece aluminum cans. In 1966, aluminum cans with a lid smaller than the body of the can (known as a "neck-in chime") appeared on the market (*MP* 1966a). Many early aluminum cans include slogans such as "New! All-Aluminum Can" on their labels.

The single most significant change in beer cans during the 1960s was the introduction of the self-opening can, frequently described as the "pop-top" or "snap-top" can (Figures 18, 19), first used in 1962 when the Pittsburgh Brewing Company test-marketed their "Iron City" label with the new self-opening device (BCCA 1985:22). *Modern Packaging* (1962b:102, 1963d:66–67) also treats this type, which met with immediate popularity. Schlitz was the first national brewer to use the device, beginning on 17 January 1963 (BCCA 1973:6), and by March 1963, the "tab-top" was used on all cans produced by Schlitz and Pittsburgh. Forty brands were using "tab-tops" by July of that year, 65 by August, and by 1965, 70 percent of all canned beer featured this item (BCCA 1985:22).

The actual design of the "tab-top" underwent a

D.B.S. Maxwell

FIGURE 19. Early "tab-top" can, after the tab is removed and the can opened.

FIGURE 21. The "ring-pull" or "pull-ring" opener.

FIGURE 20. Continental Can's "U-tab."

FIGURE 22. A "tear-drop shaped" opening, with "smile" beads along the side to prevent spillage.

considerable number of changes over the years. These changes were primarily associated with convenience and safety for the consumer. Early tabs were quite sharp, often resulting in cut fingers, and

so, by early 1964, the American Can Company had introduced a tab that had no sharp edges (*MP* 1964a:58). Continental Can produced an almost identical version, called the "U-Tab" (Figure 20),

FIGURE 23. Iron City can has both a welded side seam and neck-in chimes (crimps at top and bottom) (ca. 1980).

FIGURE 24. A tin-free steel (TFS) can with wrap-around graphics, known as MiraForm II. Seam can be seen along the center line of the can (ca. 1978).

later that year (*MP* 1964b:back cover). Also at this time, both companies introduced "smile beads," raised lines alongside the opening which helped to prevent spillage (*MP* 1964c:60).

In 1965, Continental Can introduced the first "ring-pull" can (Figure 21) (*MP* 1965:back cover). This opening design allowed the consumer to insert a finger into the ring and pull open the can. The initial version of this device produced a rather narrow opening which was soon expanded from a tear-drop (Figure 22) to a more triangular shape (*MP* 1966b:back cover). Martells (1976) provides an excellent pictorial overview of the development of the tab-top and pull-ring. It is interesting to note that although self-opening beer cans were not produced until 1962, the idea had been well developed and patented as early as 1943 (Gordon 1984:22–23).

In 1961, the Continental Can Company began experimenting with a welded side seam (Figure 23) for their steel cans. This seam is narrower than the conventional soldered seam that had been in use up to that time (Kelsey 1961:147). Welded-seam cans did not appear on the market until 1966 (*MP* 1966c:54). Roth (1981:158) provides an illustrated comparison of seam types. At the time, this seam was only used on 12-oz. cans, although other sizes such as 8- and 16-oz. cans followed shortly.

In 1967, tin-free steel (TFS) cans first appear on the market (*MP* 1967). TFS cans allow the side seam to be cemented, rather than soldered or welded (although welding was still possible),

D.B.S. Maxwell

FIGURE 25. Hamm's Draft barrel can, the only widely produced beer can with a custom shape.

FIGURE 26.   Standard and tall 12-oz. cans.

which allows for wrap-around graphics (Figure 24). TFS cans were produced under different trade names by different companies, including American Can's "Miraseam" and Continental Can's "Conoweld" (*MP* 1968a). TFS cans were available in both the traditional straight-sided style, and the neck-in chime style (*MP* 1968b).

The ubiquitous plastic six-pack holder (yoke) was first introduced by Anheuser-Busch in 1963 (*MP* 1963e:121–124, 199).

A final innovation of the 1960s was the introduction of U.S. gallon-sized cans, beginning in 1964 (*MP* 1964d:119).

The 1970s

Aluminum cans became most common during the 1970s, due primarily to the fact that aluminum cans weigh less than steel cans and so are more economical for the brewer to ship. To combat this situation, steel can manufacturers began to market "crimped-steel" cans (Figure 23)—cans with end pieces smaller than the body of the can (*MP* 1970). These cans are lighter in weight and require less shipping space than straight-sided steel cans. "Crimped-steel" cans also have a more narrow side seam (5 mm) than most straight-sided steel cans (those which are not welded).

The "Miraform" can (Figure 24) was developed by the American Can Company in 1972 (BCCA 1972a:2), as an attempt by steel manufacturers to regain the market lost to aluminum. This was a two-piece, drawn-steel can, referred to by collectors as "seamless steel" (BCCA 1985). It resembles an aluminum can in appearance but is more robust, and thus less likely to dent.

A short-lived phenomenon was the use of specialized shapes for beer cans. The idea of having different can shapes dates at least to the late 1960s (*MP* 1968c:back cover). In 1972, the Theodore Hamm Brewing Company of Minnesota introduced their draft beer in a 12-oz. can shaped like a

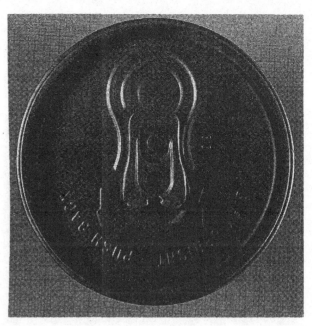

FIGURE 27. The push-button can lid. This design was implemented in Oregon after pull-rings were banned for creating excess litter.

FIGURE 28. The StaTab. This early design was replaced because it was difficult to open.

barrel (Figure 25) (BCCA 1972b:3). These cans were quite popular, but production costs were higher than the profit made from selling the beer, and they were gone from the market by 1978. At least two other brands were produced in cans of this shape, although these were never marketed (Cameron 1982). Some brewers, including Schlitz, began to use a taller, more narrow version of the standard 12-oz. can (Figure 26). This practice continued until the mid-1980s.

A number of types of self-opening cans became available during the 1970s. Pull-rings were common throughout most of the decade, although they were phased out beginning in the late 1970s as a response to lobbying by environmentalists who objected to the additional litter created by the rings. In 1972, Oregon banned the use of pull-rings on cans (BCCA 1972c:20). This law meant that canners needed to develop a new type of self-opening can without a separate pull tab.

That same year, Coors of Colorado introduced a push-button can lid (Figure 27) (BCCA 1972d:2). This type of lid found a wider market in 1975, when the American Can Company began to produce a similar style of opening device (BCCA 1975:4). Coors phased out the push-button top in late 1977 (BCCA 1977:40).

Later, the "StaTab"—an opening device that remained with the can—was introduced (BCCA 1985:23) by the Reynolds Aluminum Company, and it has become the standard of today's canned beverage. A number of varieties of "stay-with-the-can" openers were used during the 1970s, and many of these are pictured in Martells (1976) (Figures 28, 29, 30).

The 1970s also saw the widespread production of beer cans which commemorated both local and national events (Figure 31). These cans will often bear the date of the event on their label. However, it may be misleading to assume that all cans produced for an event were used at the time of the event itself. For example, cans commemorating the U.S. bicentennial were produced from 1974 until 1979, widely bracketing the event itself.

The production of 11-oz., 15-oz., and gallon-sized cans ceased by the mid-1970s.

FIGURE 29. StaTab's second stage, with solid tab structure.

FIGURE 30. StaTab's current design, with a ring-like tab structure.

FIGURE 31. One of Falstaff's bicentennial commemorative cans.

The 1980s

During this decade, the brewing industry changed to the exclusive use of cans with "stay behind" tops (although pull-ring cans were produced as late as 1983), which have a less detrimental effect on the environment, theoretically cutting in half the amount of litter produced by cans.

Production of straight-sided steel cans—the same design as the original beer can—ceased in 1984 (BCCA 1985:23). Crampton (1988:119) suggests that steel cans may make a comeback in the next few years, owing to improvements in the manufacturing of thin steel cans (comparable in strength to aluminum) combined with the escalating cost of aluminum.

A phenomenon occurring throughout the 1980s is decreasing the diameter of the can lid. It is less expensive to produce a can with a small diameter lid and a tapering neck than to produce a can lid

FIGURE 32. Multiple neck-in chimes.

FIGURE 33. Single, long neck-in chimes.

equal in diameter to the base of the can. Early tapered cans featured a number of neck-in chimes (Figure 32), while those from the later years of the decade (1985 and later) feature a single, longer neck-in chime (Figure 33).

Cans produced in the 1980s are also notable for the presence of UPI computer codes and, beginning in 1989, government warning labels detailing the harmful effects of drinking alcoholic beverages (Figure 34).

Conclusion

Changes in beer can design are sufficiently well documented to render this artifact very useful as a dating tool. Its presence on virtually all parts of the landscape also suggests that it should be employed by archaeologists interested in inferring the age of historic deposits, or the date of intrusion on prehistoric sites. While it may not be possible to determine the exact production date of the can, it should be well within the abilities of anyone to provide an age range within about five years. This range, combined with other datable materials from sites, should provide abundant information for firmly establishing the age of a given deposit.

ACKNOWLEDGMENTS

The author gratefully thanks Michael B. Schiffer, William L. Rathje, Tim Jones, David V. Burley, Jim Rock, and two anonymous reviewers for their comments and suggestions regarding this manuscript.

FIGURE 34. Computer price code and government warning about alcohol consumption.

However, omissions and errors remain entirely the responsibility of the author. Thanks also to W. Karl Hutchings for his invaluable darkroom assistance. Special thanks is due to Thomas, Sheilah, and Susan Maxwell for their continued encouragement and enthusiasm. Partial funding for this research was provided by the Educational Fund, Department of Anthropology, University of Arizona, Tucson.

REFERENCES

ASCHBRENNER, LEIGH
 1983   Cracking the Code. *Beer Can Collectors News Report* 13(1):4–5.

BEER CAN COLLECTORS OF AMERICA [Fenton, Missouri] (BCCA)
 1972a   American Can Announces Patented Two-Piece Can. *Beer Can Collectors of America News Report* 2(3):2.
 1972b   ConCan's Conoweld Making News. *Beer Can Collectors of America News Report* 2(3):3.
 1972c   Oregon Cans the Can! *Beer Can Collectors of America News Report* 2(4):20.
 1972d   Coors to Introduce Revolutionary New Can. *Beer Can Collectors of America News Report* 2(1):2.
 1973   10 Years Ago Today. *Beer Can Collectors of America News Report* 3(2):6.
 1975   Next: Beer Can with Buttons. *Beer Can Collectors of America News Report* 5(5):4.
 1976a   *The Beer Can; A Complete Guide to Beer Can Collecting*. Great Lakes Living Press, Matteson, Illinois.
 1976b   Million Camouflage Cans? *Beer Can Collectors of America News Report* 6(5):29.
 1977   New Tab Junked by Coors Beer. *Beer Can Collectors of America News Report* 7(6):40.
 1985   The Golden Anniversary. *Beer Can Collectors News Report, Special Edition*. St. Louis, Missouri.
 1989   *American Beer Cans, 1975–1987*. Pressworks, Denver, Colorado.

BEER CANS MONTHLY [Buckner, Missouri]
 1979   Gangway for G.I. Beer. *Beer Cans Monthly* 1(11): 26–32.

BUSCH, JANE
 1981   An Introduction to the Tin Can. *Historical Archaeology* 15(1):95–104.

CAMERON, JEFFREY C.
 1982   *The Class Book of U.S. Beer Cans*. Class, Souderton, Pennsylvania.
 1983a   J Spouts. *Brewery Collectibles* 1(3):28–31.
 1983b   Opening Instruction Cans. *Brewery Collectibles* 1(4):32–36.

CHRISTENSEN, BILL
 1976   The Prewar Krueger Cans or the Riddle of the "World's First Beer Can" Resolved. *Beer Can Collectors of America News Report* 6(3):3–9.

CLARK, HYLA M.
 1977   *The Tin Can Book*. Tree Communications, New York.

CRAMPTON, NORM
 1988   *Complete Trash; The Best Way to Get Rid of Practically Everything Around the House*. M. Evans, New York.

FORTUNE [New York]
 1936   Beer into Cans. *Fortune* 13(1):75–80.

GARARD, MICHAEL
 1978   The Early Flats—1935. *Beer Cans Monthly* 1(1): 12–13.
 1981   Early Cone Tops. *Beer Cans Monthly* 3(7):18–19.

GORDON, DENNIS W.
 1984   Early "No Opener Needed" Cans. *Beer Can Collectors of America News Report* 14(4):22–23.

HENDERSON, BILL
[1976] Why They Did That. *Beer Can Collectors of America News Report, New Member Issue*. Beer Can Collectors of America, St. Louis.

KELSEY, ROBERT J.
1961 Continental Can Experimenting with Welded Seam. *Modern Packaging* 35(1):147.

KIRKPATRICK, ROGER
1980 OD Military Cans Revisited. *Beer Can Collectors of America News Report* 10(4):4.

MALONEY, JOHN
1973 Homage to the Beer Can. *Beer Can Collectors of America News Report* 3(5):4–5.

MARTELLS, JACK
1976 *The Beer Can Collectors Bible*. Ballantine, New York.

MODERN PACKAGING [New York City] (*MP*)
1962a Advertisement for Alcoa Aluminum. *Modern Packaging* 36(2):33–34.
1962b New Importance of Convenience. *Modern Packaging* 36(3):101–107.
1963a Advertisement for Alcoa Aluminum. *Modern Packaging* 36(7):159–160.
1963b Hamm's Beer First in the New 12-Ounce All-Aluminum Can. *Modern Packaging* 37(4):150.
1963c 12-oz. Aluminum Cans Now Used for Beer. *Modern Packaging* 37(4):210.
1963d Advertisement for Alcoa Aluminum. *Modern Packaging* 36(9):66–67.
1963e All-Plastics Multipack that Saves Thousands. *Modern Packaging* 36(11):122–124, 198–199.
1964a Improved Beer-Can Tear-Tab Top. *Modern Packaging* 37(7):58.
1964b Advertisement, Continental Can Company. *Modern Packaging* 37(10):back cover.
1964c Equipment and Materials. *Modern Packaging* 37(12):60.
1964d Gallon Can of Beer Converts to Refrigerator-Storage "Keg." *Modern Packaging* 38(1):119.
1965 Advertisement, Continental Can Company. *Modern Packaging* 39(1):back cover.
1966a Neck-in Chime on New Aluminum Cans (Equipment and Materials). *Modern Packaging* 39(11):66.
1966b Advertisement, Continental Can Company. *Modern Packaging* 40(4):back cover.
1966c Welded-Seam Can Is Now Commercially Available to Packagers (Equipment and Materials). *Modern Packaging* 39(12):54.
1967 Here Comes the Tin Free Steel Can (Ideas in Action). *Modern Packaging* 40(9):96.
1968a Look at the Action in Metals. *Modern Packaging* 41(10):100–105.
1968b Advertisement, Continental Can Company. *Modern Packaging* 41(4):back cover.
1968c Advertisement, Continental Can Company. *Modern Packaging* 41(7):back cover.
1970 New Economy in Shrink-Wrapped Six-Packs for Double-Neck-In TFS Beer Cans. *Modern Packaging* 43(1):71.

ROCK, JAMES
1980 Beverages: Canned Beer and Soda Notes. Ms. on file, U.S. Forest Service, and with the author, Yreka, California.

ROTH, LASZLO
1981 *Package Design; An Introduction to the Art of Packaging*. Prentice-Hall, Englewood Cliffs, New Jersey.

WHITE, KEN
1978 Collecting Quart Conetops. *Beer Cans Monthly* 1(6):17.

D.B.S. MAXWELL
DEPARTMENT OF ANTHROPOLOGY
UNIVERSITY OF ARIZONA
TUCSON, ARIZONA 85721

The Archaeology of Mass-Produced Footwear

Adrienne Anderson

During the past year the Arizona State Museum has been conducting extensive archaeological investigations within t h e eighty acres of Tucson's urban renewal area (Ayres 1968). This problem oriented archaeological salvage project is unique not only in its geographic size, but in the quantity of artifacts being recovered. Among the numerous items excavated from latrines, wells, and trash areas are the remains of hundreds of boots a n d shoes. Archaeologists digging in post-1850 frontier and nonaborginal sites should expect to find a great deal of leather, principally shoe leather. However, an examination of the literature reveals that to a great extent shoe remains from such sites have been disregarded, glossed over, simply categorized as soles or uppers, or discarded as too fragmentary to handle. This source of archaeological data h a s been ignored. With careful study, shoes, even in a fragmentary condition, can be a source of chronological, technological, and economic information.

TREATMENT AND PRESERVATION

Unless leather has been preserved in continual dampness or in complete dryness it will be in various stages of decay when recovered. Most excavated leather is split, rotten, and friable. Without immediate treatment much of the data which can be derived from even fragmentary pieces will be lost as the items disintegrate.

The large amount of shoe leather from Tucson's urban renewal area required a practical and inexpensive means of initial treatment and preservation. Some fragments were very dry and crumbly, while others were brittle and stiff (Fig. 1). We decided that the majority of the pieces could be d i s c a r d e d after careful

study. The problem was to prevent further decay until the leather could be handled and analyzed beyond the point of simple categorization.

Shoe leathers occur in two forms. The soles, counter, and occasionally the reinforced toe, are thick and relatively firm. The uppers are thin and pliable, while the thicker parts of the shoe are friable and powdery. We used two methods to clean the shoe fragments in the laboratory. Initially, all pieces were dry brushed to remove any soil adhering to them. The shoe uppers and extremely dirty sole fragments were washed under gently-running warm

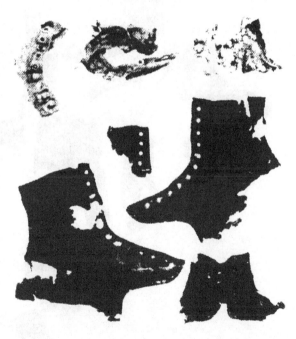

Figure 1.

Upper shoe leather before treatment (top row), and after treatment.

water. In the case of uppers and other relatively thin and fine items of leather, water actually reduced the brittleness and added temporary flexibility. These pieces, when washed, became very pliable and could be carefully unfolded and returned to their original form. Before drying they were painted with Lexol (a commercial preparation obtainable in most leather craft stores), then flattened and pinned to a thick piece of cardboard much as an entomologist pins down an insect (Fig. 2). This flattened the bent and curling pieces and restored their original shape. When necessary, additional Lexol was painted in thin coats on the pinned leather.

The remaining pieces of leather, the soles and reinforcings, were rinsed in water if they were extremely dirty. Otherwise, they were only dry brushed. Once these pieces were cleaned, we conducted experiments using a variety of solutions and techniques recommended by conser-

vationists to prevent the further drying and crumbling of the leather (Burns n. d.: 123-24; Plenderleith 1957: 32-33; Keel 1963: 49-50). Various solutions of glycerine, neetsfoot oil, castor oil, and mineral oil were used. Each preparation was used in a 60% alcohol solution and again as a 60% water emulsion. In addition, the oils were used undiluted. Lexol was also used.

The soles and reinforcings were painted with a thin coat of the mixtures. The following day they were painted with a thin coat of the undiluted oil. In cases of extreme dryness the oil was absorbed rapidly and more coats were applied as needed. It was far more satisfactory to apply two or three thin coats than to apply one thick coat or to soak the leather overnight in the undiluted oil. For the thicker parts of the shoe, painting with castor oil proved to be superior, although nothing actually made the leather pliable. Lexol worked equally well, but it is far more expensive.

Figure 2. Treated shoe uppers pinned for flattening.

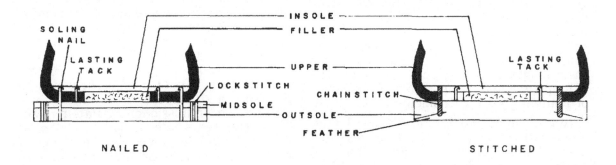

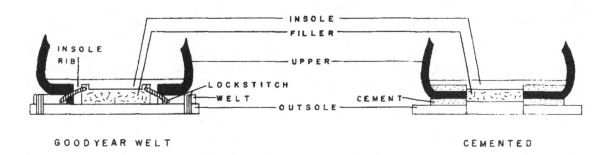

Figure 3. Types of sole construction.

After six months the pieces treated with glycerine, neetsfoot oil, and mineral oil were in various stages of decomposition through dryness. Fragments treated with castor oil or Lexol were intact and could be easily handled for study. Lexol was most effective on shoe uppers. It made them pliable and stopped disintegration without the undue greasiness caused by castor oil.

THE EVOLUTION OF SHOE TECHNOLOGY

A few attempts were made in Europe during the early 1800's at making shoe machinery, but it was the American shoemaker who created the first successful machine for shoe manufacture (United Shoe Machine Corporation 1966: 4). The first invention which materially changed the method of the shoemaker was the use of wooden shoe pegs. Around 1811 a machine which actually made tiny wooden pegs was developed, thus freeing the shoemaker from having to whittle them by hand (Dooley 1912: 257). In 1829 a hand-operated pegging machine was patented by

Nathan Leonard of Merrimack, New Hampshire (Burke 1847: 295). These two developments made possible the use of wooden pegs in large quantities.

Before this time most footwear was hand-sewn, the heavier shoes welted and the lighter ones turned (Figs 3 and 4a). A few shoes were nailed. Wooden pegs were used only to attach the heel and heel lifts to the sole (Fig. 5). The leather lifts were stitched around the edges and fastened in the center with wooden pegs. Occasionally a peg was used at the heel breast to attach the sole to the upper (Townsend 1958: 7). By 1843, pegging by machine had been generally adopted.

In the 1830's patterns were developed for cutting out shoe pieces, thus eliminating reliance on the skill of the cutter. The manufacture of counters as quarter reinforcing accompanied this. Counters are stiff, thick pieces of leather that fit around the back of the heel between the upper and the lining. Because it is sturdier than the other upper pieces, frequently the counter is the only archaeological evidence of footwear that remains (Figs. 6g, h).

After automatic pegging the next successful application of machinery to shoe manufacture was the rolling machine. Developed in 1845, this was used to compress rapidly the sole fibers in order to increase their longevity. It replaced the centuries-old lapstone and hammer as well as hours of pounding by the cobbler.

Rubber appeared in shoes around mid-nineteenth century. Charles Goodyear discovered the process of vulcanization and patented it in 1844 (Burke 1847: 358). During the 1850's rubber was used in shoes in the form of a small protruding insert in an otherwise all-leather heel. It wasn't until 1895 that an all-rubber heel appeared (Wilcox 1948: 138). It was a hard, heavy heel attached with screws.

In September, 1846, Elias Howe, Jr. patented a sewing machine (Burke 1847: 87). This was the major invention leading to mass-produced footwear. A machine immediately followed which, sewing with waxed thread, made it possible to stitch the uppers in a far more rapid, reliable, and satisfactory manner (Dooley 1912: 258). This process sped up shoemaking, although soles were still attached by hand.

Power began to be used in the shoe industry about 1855. In that year William F. Towbridge used horsepower on his machines. By 1860 there were very few factories not driven by steam or water power (Dooley 1912: 258).

As late as 1860 most shoes were formed on "straight" lasts. This meant that the shape of the instep was not considered and no distinction was made between right and left feet. In addition, lasts came only in two widths, "slim" and "wide." A piece of leather padding was simply placed over a "slim" last to made a "wide" shoe. During the Civil War "crooked" shoes as opposed to "straights" were developed. In 1888 the Retail Boot and Shoe Dealers National Association established criteria for shoe sizes known as "The Standard Measurement of Lasts" (United Shoe Machinery Corporation 1966: 21). This standard is used by shoe manufacturers today.

The first true shoe making machine, the Davey Pegging Machine, was developed in 1854 (United Shoe Machinery Corporation 1966: 4). It mechanically fastened the sole to the upper with small wooden pegs and revolutionized the manufacture of boots and shoes. In a few years, however, the pegging machine was replaced by a machine invented by Lyman R. Blake of Abington, Massachusetts. This machine sewed soles to uppers. Blake patented the result in 1860 calling it "a new article of manufacture, a boot or shoe in which the bottoms and uppers are united with stitches" (Commissioner of Patents 1861: 587). Two years later Colonel Gordon McKay patented an invention "designed as an improvement upon the invention for which patents were granted to L. R. Blake" (Commissioner of Patents 1964: 311). The next month McKay wrote another patent application saying, "The object of this invention is to enable the seam to be made completely around the shoe, thus facilitating the sewing and making a stronger seam" (Commissioner of Patents 1864: 322-23). Blake's machine left a loop stitch and ridge of thread on the foot side of the insole, and did not stitch the heel or the toe. These still had to be finished by hand. The McKay method of construction lightened the shoe a n d made possible the use of thread instead of pegs and nails. It also left a unique characteristic: stitching on the foot side of the insole (Figs. 3 and 7).

At the time the "McKays" were becoming popular, two other machines for attaching soles to uppers were introduced. The cable nailing machine produced a cable of nails, the head of one joined to the point of another. The machine cut off each nail and drove it automatically into the shoe. A second machine, this one patented by Eugene Lemercier in 1862, formed a screw from a continuous brass wire, forced it into the leather, and cut it o f f automatically (Commissioner of Patents 1864: 707). This was the prototype of the standard screw machine, perfected around 1880, which was popular into the early 20th Century. G. W. Parrot invented one of the first machines designed to use nails instead of wooden pegs. Similar machines for nailing soles to uppers rapidly developed. However, they did not drive finished nails into the shoes. Instead, they forced wire which was then cut off and finished by the machine. Until this time shoemakers preferred wooden pegs to iron or brass nails because they could be applied rapidly by machine.

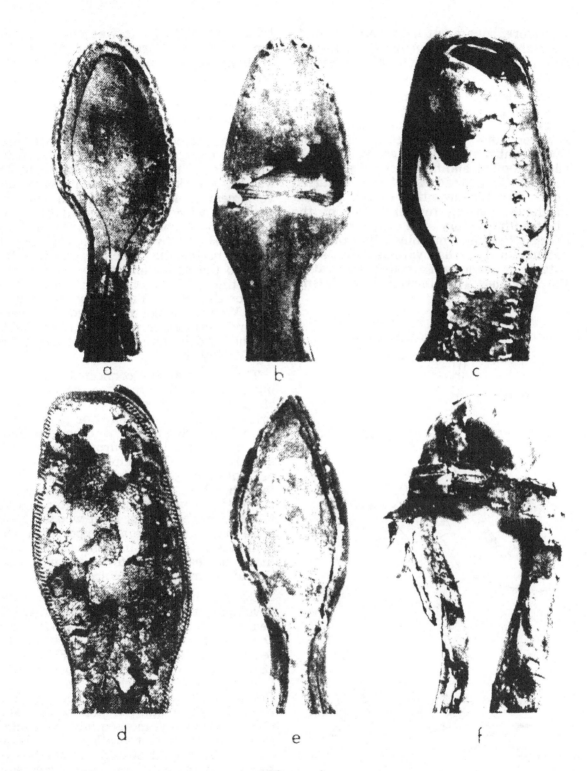

Figure 4.

Shoe soles showing evidence of different types of construction: a) top view of turned shoe; b) bottom view of outsole showing early machine stitching with channeling, feathering, and nailed toe; c) top view of machine nailed shoe; d) top view of standard screwed shoe; e) bottom view of insole showing rib for Goodyear Welt construction; f) top view of cemented shoe. All shoes are from Tucson's urban renewal area except C which is from Gila Bend Stage Station.

Therefore, square cut nails found in footwear that has not been resoled generally date shoes before the time of wire nailing machines.

There is some confusion in the literature concerning pegs and pegging terminology. Pegs refer only to wooden pegs (John Houston 1968: personal communication). Today nails are classed as soling nails, clinch, top-lift, and hold-fast nails, but not as pegs. Widespread use of pegs occurred only after the invention of the pegging machines, making the first half of the nineteenth century the era of pegged shoes. Pegging machine improvement patents in 1858 list various devices for cutting or sawing off wooden pegs within the machines (Commissioner of Patents

1859: 398, 412-13). It was not until the time of G. W. Parrot's 1862 patent for "nailing soles of boots and shoes to the upper leather . . ." that actual nailing machines were developed (Commissioner of Patents 1864: 568). Nails were driven by hand until this time.

While pegging and nailing shoe machines were gradually being replaced by the McKay stitcher, Charles Goodyear, Jr. was busy working on an even greater development in shoe stitching. In 1875 he came out with an improvement based on the idea by Auguste Destouey for making turned shoes by machine. Utilizing a curved needle, his machine stitched the welt to the upper and to the sole at the same time. This required a rib on the bottom of the insole (Figs. 3 and 4e). Goodyear Welt construction utilized this insole rib and thus eliminated the uncomfortable stitches which were present on the inside of a McKay shoe.

The first machine connected with heeling came out shortly after the Goodyear stitcher. It compressed the heel lifts and pricked holes for the nails or pegs which were still being used. Another machine which automatically drove heel nails quickly followed, making the production of footwear completely automatic. The fact that heel attachment was automatic led to the return of high heels to women's fashions in the 1880's. Most wooden heels were made in France and exported to the United States. Heels in this country were made of leather, cottonwood, oak, and Canadian brasswood (Wilcox 1948: 142).

During the thirty years following the development of McKay's stitcher, of Goodyear's machines, and of related devices, the shoe making business was disrupted by feuds, suits, and injunctions. Finally, in 1899, the three major companies, the Goodyear Sewing Machine Company, the Consolidated and McKay Lasting Machine Company, and the McKay Shoe Machinery Company, merged into the United Shoe Machinery Corporation. The USMC in turn purchased outright a number of smaller manufacturers. Each company within the corporation made and leased machines adapted to a particular class of operations. Therefore, no shoe machinery manufacturer competed with another, and every shoe manufacturer had to patronize all three companies.

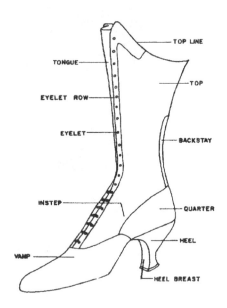
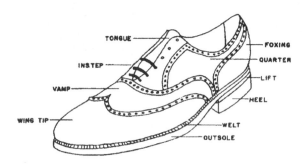

Figure 5.
Shoe terminology on 1920 woman's high laced shoe and man's brogue.

By 1912 the principal methods of shoe manufacture were the Goodyear Welt, Mc-Kay, turned, standard screw, and nailed (Dooley 1912: 103). Since this time there have been few developments in the technology of shoe manufacture. Cement shoe production became practical in 1926 through the development of a superior type of glue. Attempts to cement the upper to the sole were made in the 1850's, but due to lack of a strong glue, these were unsuccessful. The modern process, used almost exclusively on light women's and children's shoes, gradually replaced the turned shoe manufacture.

SHOES IN AMERICAN ARCHAEOLOGY

During the industrialization of the nineteenth century a number of important technological innovations took place within the shoe industry (Table 1). Each development was marked by some distinctive feature which provides the archaeologist with valuable technological data. The twentieth century has been a period of stylistic experimentation and innovation, but today's shoes are manufactured by the same methods used in 1912 and are processed by the same types of machines.

There are two basic types of shoes: turned shoes and shoes whose upper is attached to the insole and reinforced by the outsole and heel. The upper of a turned shoe is sewn inside out to a single, thin sole. Then it is turned right side out. Today turned shoe manufacture has generally been replaced by the cementing process, but archaeologically this form abounds and can be easily recognized (Fig. 4a). The single sole has a thin, feathered strip of leather on the inside of the sole. The upper is stitched to this strip when inside out.

Any mass-produced shoe can be further placed into one of three groups based on the method of attaching the outsole to the upper. A shoe is nailed (or pegged or screwed), sewn, or cemented (Fig. 3). Even fragmentary pieces of sole leather generally betray the method of manufacture. Nails may still be intact, or their corroded remains visible in a nailed shoe. If the nails are gone, the round hole remains. There are no channels, feathered ridges or ribs. Thread from a stitched shoe

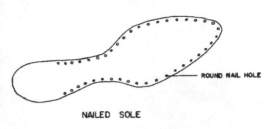

NAILED SOLE — ROUND NAIL HOLE

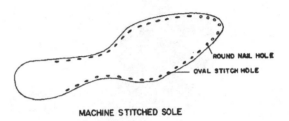

MACHINE STITCHED SOLE — ROUND NAIL HOLE — OVAL STITCH HOLE

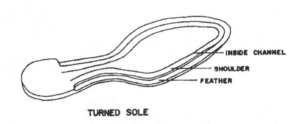

TURNED SOLE — INSIDE CHANNEL — SHOULDER — FEATHER

Figure 7.
Upper surface of insole showing evidence of different types of construction.

will probably be gone, but small needle holes remain. These are generally much smaller than those left in nailed shoes and are slightly oval (Fig. 7). There may be indentations in the leather between the holes, indicating tightly pulled thread. Sewn shoes will have an outsole channel where the stitching occurs to keep the thread from being worn. They may also have a feathered edge on the bottom of the outsole with the stitching underneath (Fig. 4b). Feathering was a method used around the turn of the century for protecting stitches from wear. Often this feathering is worn off at the ball of the outsole, but will still be present on the shank. A McKay shoe will have stitching on the inside of the insole. If the stitching does not include the toe and heel, it may

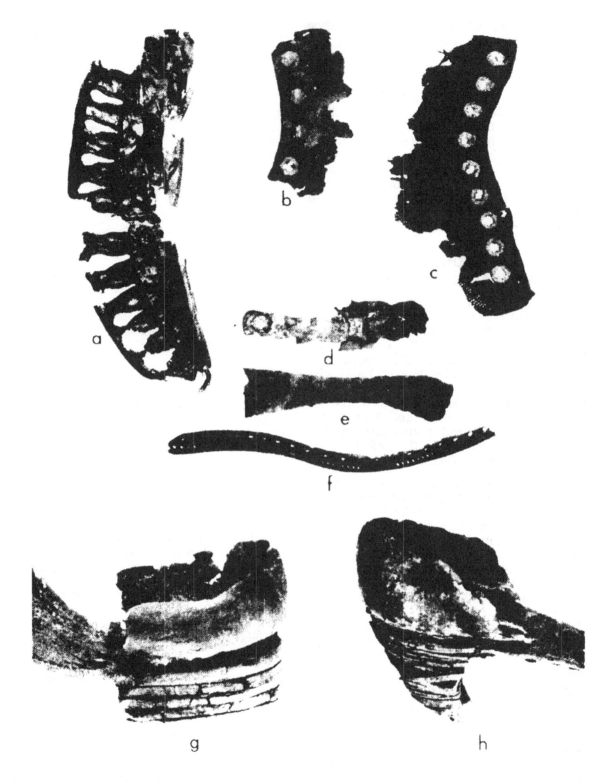

Figure 6.
Shoe fragments preserved in archaeological context: a) button hole row from woman's high button shoe; b) lace hook and eyelet row from high lace shoe; c) lace eyelet row from high lace shoe; d) metal shank; e) leather shank; f) welt; g) man's heel and counter; h) woman's heel and counter.

be dated before McKay's 1862 patent (Fig. 4b). Goodyear Welt shoes are recognized by the unique rib on the underside of the insole (Fig. 4e). Cemented shoes occur late and are distinguished by the fact that the part of the upper cemented to the insole will be intact (Fig. 4f). This glued piece may be the only remaining fragment of a cement shoe's upper.

A study of fashions and stylistic changes provides another source of chronological information. However, consideration of styles is outside the scope of this paper. Reports on shoes should utilize the terminology for shoe parts and manufacturing processes that are standard within the shoe industry. Primary sources, including shoe manufacturers' guides, trade catalogues, and patent records should always be consulted. Archaeological and other reports have relied on secondary sources containing factual errors which are prepetuated in the literature.

Footwear can be dated by technology alone. Archaeologists working in post-1850 sites need to be aware of the information that can be derived from old shoes.

CHRONOLOGY OF MASS-PRODUCED FOOTWEAR

circa 1811 — machine manufacture of wooden pegs

1829 — hand operated pegging machine

1830 — patterns for cutting shoe uppers; manufacture of counters

1844 — vulcanization process patented by Goodyear

1845 — rolling machine

1846 — Elias Howe's sewing machine

1854 — Davey Pegging Machine

circa 1860 — L. R. Blake's stitching machine; power driven manufacture of shoes; lasts for right and left shoes

circa 1862 — McKay's patent of Blake's process, stitching completely around shoe eliminating nail reinforced toe; cable nailing machine; standard screw machine

circa 1875 — Goodyear Welt stitcher; automatic heeling machine

1888 — standardization of shoe sizes

1899 — United Shoe Machinery Corporation

circa 1912 — methods of manufacture standardized: Goodyear Welt, McKay, turned, screwed, nailed

1926 — cement shoe production practical

ACKNOWLEDGMENTS

I wish to thank William Wasley, Bernard Fontana, and James Ayres for reading the working copy of this paper and offering valuable comments and criticisms. I am also indebted to Walter Birkby who aided with the preservation experiments and John Houston of Johnny's Shoe Shop who helped with the shoe identification and terminology. All photographs are courtesy of the Arizona State Museum.

REFERENCES

AYRES, J. E.
1968 "Urban Renewal Salvage Archaeology in Tucson, Arizona." Paper presented at the 33rd annual meeting of the Society for American Archaeology, Santa Fe.

BURKE, EDMUND
1847 **List of Patents 1790-1847.** J. and G. S. Gideon, Washington.

BURNS, N. J.
n. d. **Field Manual for Museums.** National Park Service, Washington.

COMMISSIONER OF PATENTS
1859 **Report of the Commissioner of Patents for the Year 1858,** Vol. I. James B. Steedman, Washington.
1861 **Report of the Commissioner of Patents for the Year 1860,** Vol. I. George W. Bowman, Washington.
1864 **Report of the Commissioner of Patents for the Year 1862,** Vol I. Washington.

DOOLEY, W. H.
1912 **A Manual of Shoemaking and Leather and Rubber Products.** Little, Brown, and Company, Boston.

KEEL, B. C.
1963 The Conservation and Preservation of Archaeological and Ethnological Specimens. **Southern Indian Studies,** Vol. 15. The Archaeological Society of North Carolina and the Research Laboratories of Anthropology, University of North Carolina, Chapel Hill.

PLENDERLEITH, H. J.
1957 **Conservation of Antiquities a n d Works of Art.** Oxford University Press, London.

TOWNSEND, RAYMOND
1953 The Mystery of the Shoe Peg. **The Chronicle of the Early American Industries Association,** Vol. 8, No. 1, pp. 5-7.

UNITED SHOE MACHINERY CORPORATION
1966 **How American Shoes are Made.** United Shoe Machinery Corporation, Boston.

WILCOX, R. T.
1948 **The Mode in Footwear.** Scribner's Sons, New York.

CARTRIDGES, CAPS, AND FLINTS:
A PRIMER FOR ARCHAEOLOGISTS

By Peter J. Gleichman and Dock M. Teegarden

ABSTRACT

Gunflints, percussion caps, cartridge cases, and bullets are durable artifacts that may provide temporal and functional data. Loaded metallic ammunition was introduced in the 1860s and quickly replaced muzzle loaded flintlock and caplock ammunition. Loaded or self-contained metallic cartridges consist of a metal case, primer, powder charge, and bullet. The American caliber identification or cartridge designation standards are a complex, confusing, and inconsistent series of nonsystematic conventions. The development and changes in cartridge cases, ignition or priming systems, powder, and bullets are documented, and some of the changes are time markers. Cartridge cases with or without headstamps can be identified, and the process for doing so is presented. Once identified, the date of introduction, period of manufacture, intended use, and firearm(s) for which the cartridge was designed can be determined.

INTRODUCTION

The archaeological recovery of elements of firearm use from field surveys and excavations on historic era sites is not uncommon. Artifacts such as gunflints, percussion caps, spent bullets, cartridges, and cartridges cases are durable and potentially diagnostic. Identification and description of these firearm elements, particularly cartridge components, using proper terminology can be a vexing problem.

This paper addresses this problem, with an emphasis on the loaded or self-contained metallic ammunition period from the advent of such cartridges in the 1860s through World War II. Most commercial ammunition loading was halted during World War II for the war effort. Subsequent to World War II, cartridge design has become more standardized. The archaeological recovery of firearms, i.e., parts or fragments of guns, is not common. Unlike information about cartridges, an astounding amount of detailed information has been published about firearms. Even with the amount of information available, accurate identification of gun parts may best be left to an expert. Summaries of firearms used in the West, including Indian trade guns, are in Hamilton (1960), Mails (1972), Markham (1991), Rosa (1985), Russell (1977), and numerous other sources.

Firearms have obviously had a substantive and dramatic impact on cultural developments and historical events in America. Wallack (1977:71) asserts that the American Industrial Revolution developed around two industries, firearm manufacture and textile machinery, with firearms being the earliest industry. The archaeological presence of firearm elements has the potential to provide functional and temporal information regarding the site. The

Peter J. Gleichman ▪ Native Cultural Services, P. O. Box 357, Ward, CO 80481

Dock M. Teegarden ▪ Native Cultural Services, P. O. Box 357, Ward, CO 80481 assemblage of cartridge cases or bullets at a particular site or component can provide direct data regarding what types of activities were occurring, as well as information about the socioeconomy of the inhabitants (e.g., Horn et al. 1986; Scott 1989).

Gunflints, percussion caps, and loaded metallic cartridges also provide temporal data. Period of use for flintlock and caplock guns is well established. Date of introduction or period of manufacture of a particular cartridge can be ascertained. Since the brand and model of firearm used can be determined from spent cartridges, the period of manufacture of that firearm can also be documented. Date of use is more difficult, particularly in light of the practice of handloading or reloading. Commercial production of cartridges often continues for many years after the gun they are made for is obsolete, i.e., no longer manufactured. Cartridges may be used many years after manufacture. Cartridge cases can be reloaded and reused long after they were manufactured, even long after commercial manufacture has ceased. The particularly American practice of handloading adds complexity to the interpretation of archaeological cartridges. The issue of lag time—the time between manufacture and deposition in the archaeological record—is compounded by handloading. An assemblage of cartridge components at a site may provide data pertaining to the advent and length of occupation (Berge 1968, 1980; Fontana et al. 1962; Smith 1954, 1955). Cartridge cases and bullets can also be intrusive at a site, occurring from transitory reuse of the locale. Caution must be used in the interpretation of archaeological cartridges.

Identifying and documenting the archaeological occurrence of self-contained metallic cartridges is also important to understanding the evolving technology of firearms and loaded metallic ammunition. As Barnes (1989:11) points out regarding cartridge types, "Cartridges don't just happen, they evolve in response to some need or use requirement." Moreover, archaeological studies will provide detailed knowledge and specific understanding of the access, spread, and use of this technology. For example, while no gun parts were found during the excavation of Johnny Ward's Ranch in Arizona, the recovery of 31 identifiable cartridge cases, representing 16 types of ammunition, indicated the number and types of firearms used. At least four kinds of rifles, five kinds of handguns, and two kinds of shotguns were used to fire the cartridges (Fontana et al. 1962:79–83). Thus, a distinct record of firearm use at a Southern Arizona ranch between 1854 and 1903 was constructed.

Accurate identification of cartridge components is integral to battlefield studies. Such studies include determining the type of ordnance used, defining the location of events, and understanding the sequence of events. Examples are the studies of the Sand Creek Massacre locale (Dawson 1999; National Park Service 2000), and the Battle of the Little Big Horn (Scott 1989; Scott et al. 1989).

The brand and model of firearm used can also be ascertained from bullets recovered archaeologically. The firearm leaves signature marks on the fired bullet, from the lands and grooves and type of rifling. Signature marks are also left on cases from the firing pin and extractor. Using forensic ballistic techniques devised for law enforcement, the number of firearms can be determined, and individual firearms can be identified and typed by an expert (Scott 1989).

FIREARM DEVELOPMENT

Firearms are basically pipes which use gunpowder to propel a projectile. When the gunpowder is ignited, the powder is converted to a rapidly expanding greater volume of gas. The expanding gas exerts pressure, projecting the bullet out of the muzzle of the firearm. The original powder used was black powder, a mixture of potassium nitrate (saltpeter), charcoal, and sulfur. Black powder has been used for centuries, perhaps millennia. The date and place of origin are unclear. Incendiary mixtures were used by the Greeks and Romans in war. True gunpowder was apparently developed in China, and explosive devices were used there by AD 1000. Written references to gunpowder occur in Europe in the 1200s (Barnes 1976; Logan 1959). By the late 1300s gunpowder, guns, and cannons were well-known.

A variety of ignition systems has been used to ignite the powder and fire the bullet. Muzzle-loading firearm ignition evolved from matchlock in the late 1400s, to wheellock by 1530, to flintlock by around 1630. Matchlocks used a burning wick to ignite the powder. Wheellock and flintlock guns used sparks. Flintlocks were the standard until the caplock system was developed in the early 1800s. Loaded metallic cartridges were in use by the 1860s. There are two principal types of loaded rifle/pistol cartridges, centerfire and rimfire. Rimfire cartridges have the primer compound contained in the folded rim of the case. Centerfire cartridges have a separate component, the primer, pressed into a receptacle in the center of the case head. Caplock firearms and loaded cartridges use percussion to explode the primer, igniting the powder. The difference is that caplocks use a separate element, the percussion cap, as the primer, while loaded cartridges contain the primer in the cartridge (self-contained).

Firearms evolved from smoothbored muzzle loaders, termed muskets, to rifled muzzle loaders to breechloaders. Muzzle loaded firearms were extant by the late fourteenth century. Rifling refers to spiral grooves in the gun barrel which impart a rotational spin to the projectile, increasing accuracy. Rifling was in use by about 1500. Muzzle loaded flintlock rifles were developed and used from the early to mid 1600s, until the first half of the nineteenth century, when the percussion "cap and ball" muzzle-loaded system was used. Smoothbored muskets continued to be manufactured until at least 1842. While there were earlier breechloaders, the development of effective breech loaded firearms went hand-in-hand with the development of loaded metallic cartridges. The development of shotguns is discussed at the end of this paper.

Muskets and rifled muzzle loaders used lead balls as bullets, and until 1844 all military arms used a round or spherical ball (Sharpe 1987:28). Loading spherical balls into rifled barrels required the ball to be wrapped in a cloth or leather patch. The problem was to have a bullet that would fill the rifling grooves and prevent the loss of the propellant gas. The problem was solved by Chas. Minié of France, who devised a conical bullet with a hollow base in 1846.

The bullet was sized slightly under-bore for easy muzzle loading, and the hollow base expanded under powder gas pressure, filling the rifling. Minié balls became the standard for cap and ball rifles, and the Civil War was fought primarily with Minié bullets.

Elongated or conical bullets, sometimes termed slugs, have far superior ballistics than spheres. Round balls are now used almost exclusively in shotgun shells and muzzle-loaded replicas. Note that the term "ball" does not refer solely to spherical bullets.

FLINTS AND CAPS

Archaeological manifestations of firearm use prior to the self-contained metallic cartridge era are limited in the Western United States. Use of flintlock and caplock firearms may result in the deposition of gun flints, black powder containers, percussion caps and cap containers, and bullets. Such artifacts may be present at the earlier historic sites, and sometimes co-occur with self contained metallic cartridges from sites dating to the 1860s or 1870s.

Flintlocks used a flint clamped in a hammer, which when released struck sparks into a flash pan containing a priming charge of loose powder. The flash from the priming powder ignited the main charge. The flint was a square to rectangular piece of cryptocrystalline stone. Gunflints usually have a steep edge angle or a bevel, and are readily identifiable by their square shape. Holland, France, and England were major producers of flints, with French flintknappers dominating the trade from 1750–1800, and English flints becoming prevalent after 1800. French flints were characterized by a blond or honey color and a sub-angular or rounded edge or heel. English flints were dark colored and had four distinct corners. Almost equal numbers of French and English flints were recovered from Bent's Old Fort in southeast Colorado (Moore 1973:99–100).

Flints varied in size according to the intended gun. Musket flints ranged from 1.25″ in length and width to 1.5″. Rifle flints ranged from slightly under to just over an inch square (Moore 1973:101). The pistol gunflints in Figure 1 range from .530 ×.585 in. to .645 × .780 in.

Use of fulminate of mercury mixed with other compounds as a priming device began in 1807. The fulminate was detonated by a blow, igniting the gunpowder. Efforts to place the fulminate mixture inside a tiny metal cup were first made in 1814. Originally the cups were iron or steel, then pewter, and in 1816 copper cups or caps were devised, and patented in 1822 (Sharpe 1987:19). Commercial percussion caps were marketed by 1830, and most gun makers were producing percussion cap arms around that time. The cuplike portion of the cap fit on a nipple attached to the breech. When the hammer struck the cap, the fulminate exploded and the flame flashed through a hole in the nipple to the powder charge and fired the gun. The ignition system was so superior to flintlocks that by the early 1840s flintlocks were obsolete (Rosa 1985:34), although the U.S. government did not manufacture copper caps on a large scale until 1845. Many flintlock guns were converted to caplocks in the 1840s. American Indians often continued to use flintlocks, since they could make their own gunflints and not have to procure percussion caps. (It was not unusual for

FIGURE 1. Percussion caps and gunflints. Caps at left are musket caps, on right are pistol/rifle caps. Cap at upper right has been fired. Bottom row of gunflints are at the small end of the range of flint sizes. Scale in inches.

old Indian guns sold at gun shows before World War II to contain a fragment of an arrowhead as the gunflint).

Percussion caps were produced in at least 25 sizes, from large musket caps 0.24″ diameter to pistol caps 0.16″ diameter (Figure 1). Large musket or "hat type" caps are no longer produced in the United States. The percussion cap ignition system was used for about 35 years, marking the transition from flint-locks to self-contained metallic cartridges. Markham (1991:90) asserts that caplocks were used by some civilians in remote parts of western America almost into the twentieth century. Bullets from the flintlock/caplock era were primarily spherical balls or conical Minié balls.

CARTRIDGES

Prior to the adoption of loaded metallic cartridges, "cartridges" were produced consisting of a measured charge of black powder and a round lead ball, wrapped in a paper cylinder. These were used by biting off the end, pouring a bit of the powder into the priming pan and the rest down the barrel, and ramming the bullet and paper down the muzzle. Paper cartridges were introduced in Sweden about 1600, but loose powder and ball remained standard, except for the military, until the 1800s. In the first half of the nineteenth century combustible cartridges were made for caplocks, using conical bullets and a powder charge contained in nitrated material such as paper, linen, or skin. In 1845 the

Frenchman Flobert introduced his BB (bullet breech) Cap. This led to the development of the .22 Short by Smith & Wesson in 1857.

This was the first really successful U.S. metallic cartridge. This rimfire with a copper case was designed for use with the Smith & Wesson First Model revolver in .22 caliber. This invention revolutionized the firearm industry. Other metallic cartridges had been developed and were briefly used. They are described in the section on primers, below.

The nomenclature of a loaded metallic cartridge, also called fixed ammunition, is as follows: A complete unit, out-of-the-box and ready to fire, is a cartridge, or round in military language. This unit consists of a metal case, primer, powder charge, and bullet (or shot). The term "shell" for a cartridge case applies *only* to shotgun shells and artillery shells. A shotgun cartridge is called a shell even if it is metallic.

Caliber

Cartridges may be commercially manufactured in standard calibers, or they may be created by individual designers or handloaders, termed wildcat cartridges. Cartridge identification or caliber designation is perhaps one of the most confusing, least consistent nomenclature systems extant. There is absolutely *no* rhyme or reason for the American cartridge identification system, even up to the present. Caliber designation can be defined by several different methods, including bore (land) diameter of the barrel, groove diameter of the barrel, bullet diameter, inside diameter of the cartridge case mouth, or an arbitrary figure chosen by the manufacturer (White and Munhall 1948, 1949; as referenced in Bearse 1966:15).

Caliber is designated in 100ths or 1000ths of an inch in the United States and British Commonwealth countries. Cartridge designations often include caliber compounded with other information, such as powder load of the cartridge case, case length, date of adoption, proprietor, muzzle velocity, etc.

Generally the centerfire black powder cartridges used caliber and powder weight in grains (7,000 grains/lb.) as the .45-70, .38-55, etc. A .45-70 cartridge means a .45-caliber bullet with 70 grains of black powder. Some black powder cartridges appended a third figure, bullet weight. A .45-70-500 was a .45-caliber cartridge with 70 grains of black powder and a 500 grain bullet. Some early rimfires used only caliber and a name, such as .44 Henry, .56-56 Spencer, or caliber and relative length, such as .32 Short, .32 Long, etc.

Then came the smokeless powder era, at the end of the nineteenth century, and with it more confusion. Some new calibers were designated by the British system—bore diameter, such as the .405 WCF (Winchester Center Fire), .348 Winchester, etc.

There was a race by manufacturers to push proprietary cartridges resulting in duplication and utter confusion in cartridge designations, especially in centerfires. For example, there were so many .45 caliber cartridges that further differentiations were necessary for example, .45-78 Wolcott, .45-70 Morse, .45-100 Ballard Everlasting, etc. (Logan 1959:140–146).

Some cartridges were designated by the caliber × case length, which is similar to the European system, resulting in .40 × 2¹/₂ Remington-Hepburn, .40 × 3¹/₄ Sharps, etc. The European system uses bullet diameter, case length and type, given in millimeters.

In 1903 the United States adopted a new service rifle designated the Springfield model 1903 with a new smokeless bottlenecked cartridge with a round nose jacketed bullet of .30 caliber, called .30-03. It was not successful and was redesigned and adopted in 1906, and was and still is known as the .30-06.

In the 1920s came more trouble: Savage Arms Co. introduced a new cartridge and started a new trend. The .250-3000 was a .25 caliber bore diameter bullet, and the first cartridge to reach a velocity of 3,000 ft/sec. The cartridge became known as the .250 Savage, and descriptive names entered the picture along with bore or bullet diameter for cartridge designation, resulting in the .22 Savage Hi-Power, .22 Hornet, .218 Bee, .219 Zipper, etc. Caliber and designer's name were used, such as the .220 Swift, .256 Newton, .257 Roberts, etc, and of course caliber and proprietor or manufacturer, like the .351 Winchester Self Loading, .35 Remington, etc.

In 1912 the .375 H&H Magnum was introduced (O'Brien 1994). The Holland & Holland (H&H) Magnum was a British round which featured more power and higher velocity that found favor in the United States during the 1920s. Magnum rifle cases have a "goiter" or belt around the base of the case, for headspacing. After World War II "Magnumitis" hit the country, and the big belted case started a family that is still growing. The magnum craze caught on with handguns too. The first was the .357 Magnum in 1935 by Smith & Wesson, still popular today. Belted magnum rifle cases are distinctive and easily identified. Magnum pistol cases are not belted.

Some cartridges with different names or caliber designations will interchange with some guns. For example, the .50-100-450 Winchester Express and the .50-110-300 Winchester Express used the same case, only the powder charge and bullet weight differed. The .30-40 Krag was the same as the .30 US Army, as another example.

The same caliber bullet may be used in several different cartridge cases. The same case may be used for several different bullet weights or powder charges (Figure 2). A cartridge may have several different designations; e.g., Bearse (1966:15) points out that there are nearly 40 synonyms for the .44-40 Winchester.

The above discussion of caliber/cartridge designations hopefully points out the lack of systematics. There are exceptions and variances from all of the cartridge designation standards or conventions. Even the orthography for designating cartridges is not consistently applied or agreed on. Knowing what any given caliber designation means relies on personal knowledge of the cartridge or a thorough reference book.

Cases

Rimfire and centerfire cases may be made of copper, brass, nickel-plated brass, or (rarely) steel or aluminum; and contain the primer, powder charge, and the bullet. The case usually bears a headstamp (manufacturer's identifica-

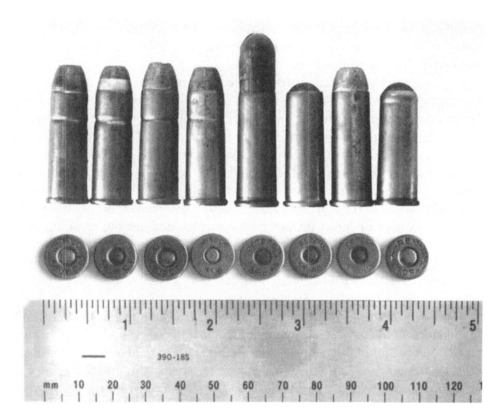

FIGURE 2. Example of variety of cartridges in the same caliber. These are all .44-40 caliber. Note differences in bullets, cases, and headstamps. Two cartridges on left are the same, except the bullets are jacketed in different metals. Cases at right and third from right are loaded with round balls. Case fourth from right has shot enclosed in a paper "bullet."

tion) and nearly all military cases have a date of manufacture. The body of the case may be straight, as in the 22 L.R. rimfire, or taper slightly from the base to the mouth, as the .45-70, or bottlenecked with a distinct shoulder, like the .30-30.

Cases are further classified by rim type, which are rimmed, rimless, semi-rimmed, and belted. The rim is the edge of the head of the case. Rimmed cases have a rim that is of greater diameter than the rear or base of the case, to stop the case from propelling forward into the chamber, and for the extractor to grip. All rimfires and some centerfires are rimmed. Rimless centerfires have a base or head the same diameter as the case, with an extractor groove machined around the base. In between these two types are semi-rimmed, with the case body just slightly smaller than the rim, and an extractor groove. A belted case has a thickened strip or belt around the base of the case, above the extractor groove. A rebated rim case exists, used by one modern American cartridge, the .284 Winchester, introduced in 1963, with the rim smaller than the case body.

The original United States centerfire cartridge was a copper "folded head" case with an interior primer, used from about the late 1860s to the 1880s (Wallack 1977). These cartridges look like rimfires, since the primer can't be

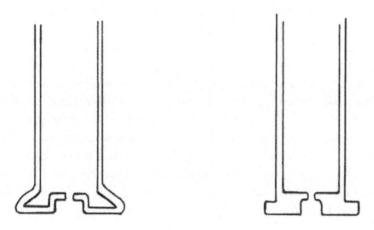

FIGURE 3. Case head types: left, solid head; right, balloon head.

seen. They can be distinguished from rimfire cartridges by the presence of crimps in the case just above the rim, which hold the primer in place.

Early external primer centerfire cases had a primer pocket that ballooned or extended into the powder chamber of the cartridge (Figure 3). As smokeless powder succeeded black powder around the turn of the century, the increased pressures in the popular old cartridges, including revolver loads, necessitated replacing the old folded head "balloon head" cases with stronger solid heads. The thicker solid heads have the primer pocket limited to the case head, so the powder chamber is flat at its base (Figure 3). Some examples of cartridges produced with folded head cases and subsequent solid head cases are the .45-70 and .38-55 rifle cartridges, and the .44-40, .32-20 and .38-40 which were used in both revolvers and rifles and are still made today.

Folded head cases are easily distinguished from solid head cases by looking at the inside of the case head, through the case mouth. The balloon head will have a rounded, raised platform with the flash hole centered in it while the solid head case will have a flat, solid base with the centered flash hole.

The early cartridge cases were copper. Brass cases began to be commercially produced in the early 1870s, and some brass cases were purchased by the government for military use in the mid 1870s. Copper cases remained prevalent in the military, but the failure of the copper cased, inside primed .45-55 cartridge at the Battle of the Little Big Horn in 1876 led the military to convert to brass cases and external centerfire primers. The case failure was because the soft copper folded head case with inside primer often lost its head when fired, and fouled chambers caused extraction problems (Bearse 1966:156; Rosa 1985:110–113).

Commercial use of brass cases pre-dated government military production by 10 years, and brass alloy cases became standard, comprised of 70 percent copper and 30 percent zinc. Centerfire primers became standard in brass cases except for some low powered copper cased pistol cartridges such as the .22 rimfire line, the .32 rimfire, .41 rimfire, and a few odd rifle rimfires like the .25 Stevens and the .41 Swiss copper case bottleneck rimfire cartridge; all now obsolete (no longer manufactured) except the .22 line.

The .22 rimfire copper cases gave way to brass and nickeled cases in 1927 (Warner and Shrader 1971:17) as smokeless powder and higher pressures made stronger cases necessary. Nickel plated cases were originally used for .22 caliber, and then were used for pistol cartridges, particularly premium quality cartridges. In the last 10 years they have been produced for rifle cartridges.

Steel was used during World War II when brass shortages occurred. After World War II, aluminum cases were produced. Aluminum cases are cheap but too weak to be safely reloaded and reused. CCI currently manufactures a complete line of aluminum cased centerfire handgun cartridges, but uses the Berdan primer to stymie reloading.

Headstamps

Headstamps are elements of information stamped onto the case head by the manufacturer. Early rimfire cartridges were copper cased with no head stamps or a single letter or symbol stamped in the center of the head. Winchester used an H, in honor of B. Tyler Henry, Winchester's chief engineer. Union Metallic Co. used a U early on, then a UMC until its merger with Remington.

Most commercial American centerfire cartridges have been headstamped from before the turn of the twentieth century. Commercial cartridges usually have the initials or symbol of the manufacturer and the caliber designation. Sometimes other elements of information are present, such as the letters S H, indicating a solid head case. American military cartridges are identified by the code of the arsenal or ordnance plant of manufacture and usually the last two numerals of the year of manufacture.

Headstamps varied over the years as manufacturers changed and new loads developed, and as copper cases and black powder loads were dropped. Thus Union Metallic Cartridge Co. (UMC) became REM-UMC, Remington and Peters merged and became REM-PETERS, Winchester bought the Western Cartridge Co. (WCC) and became WIN-WESTERN, etc. Few dates are available for advent or duration of particular headstamps. Data regarding manufacturer's use of headstamps has generally not been gathered, and many ammunition manufacturers may not have records of initial use for headstamps. The same manufacturer's mark may be used for numerous different cartridges, with only the caliber designation changing. A headstamp and caliber can lead to data about the period of manufacture for that cartridge, or period of manufacture for the firearm(s) chambered for that cartridge.

Barnes (1989:419) states that there are at least 400 commercial headstamps and over 800 military headstamps worldwide. Logan (1959) provides a list of over 200 headstamps. Cartridges for a given caliber may be produced by numerous manufacturers or have different headstamps for variations in powder charge or bullet weight. For example, Bearse (1966:104) lists over 70 headstamps for .30-06 caliber cartridges.

A headstamp alone should not be relied on for caliber determination. The case may have been reformed by a handloader to a different standard caliber or to a wildcat caliber. Measurements should be taken to confirm the caliber. Presence of a headstamp is not necessary to identify a cartridge. A list of common and useful commercial headstamps is presented in Table 1, military headstamps in Table 2. Illustrations of headstamps are presented in Figures 4 and 5.

Primers

Rimfire ignition cartridges contain the priming compound in the rim of the case head, and ignition comes from pinching or hitting the rim with the firing pin. After the introduction of the .22 Short in 1857, the development of the rimfire advanced rapidly.

The Civil War made the advantages of a self-contained, waterproof cartridge quite evident. The .44 Long was developed by 1860, as was the .56-56 Spencer round, used by the Union from 1862. The .44 Henry cartridge was manufactured by the New Haven Arms Company in 1861, for the Henry lever action repeating rifle, forerunner of the Winchester rifles. The rimfire cartridge made repeating rifles practical. Pistol cartridges such as the .30 Short, .32 Long, .38 Short , .38 Long, and .41 Short were all available by the early to mid-1860s (Barnes 2003). The military had used some loaded metallic rifle cartridges during the Civil War, but despite the availability of revolver cartridges, caplock pistols were used throughout the Civil War. It wasn't until 1871 that the Ordinance Department decided to introduce cartridge pistols for the military (Rosa 1985:70).

Some 75 rimfire cartridges have been loaded by American companies, but only about 42 were still around by the turn of the century. By the 1930s only 17 survived, and after World War II the count was down to 10 or fewer (Barnes 1989:356). Most had been replaced by centerfires or made obsolete by smokeless powders. Rimfire cartridges are still manufactured and used worldwide—mostly in .22 caliber.

The folded head and copper case of rimfires made a weak container for the pressures involved with high velocity loads, and limited cartridge development. More importantly, rimfire cartridges cannot be reloaded. These problems were solved by the brass centerfire case. There are two principal types of centerfire primers. The Boxer primer was invented by Col. Edward Boxer of the British Army in 1867. The Berdan primer was invented by Col. Hiram Berdan of the American Army in 1866 (Barnes 1976:301). The Boxer primer is self-contained, with a cup, priming compound, and anvil. The Berdan primer does not contain an anvil, but uses a small projection in the bottom of the primer pocket, a part of the cartridge case (Figure 6).

The centerfire system as we know it today was developed by the 1880s. Prior to the adoption of the Boxer and Berdan primer systems, a variety of experimental primer/case head configurations were patented. Logan (1959: 77–87) illustrates and describes several.

The (British) Boxer system is the easiest and most practical for reloading,

TABLE 1. Headstamps

STAMP	MANUFACTURER
Acorn (symbol)	Gustav Genschow (Germany)
Diamond (symbol)	Western Cartridge Co. (rimfire cases)
C (raised)	Kynoch Cartridge Co. (England)
C (impressed)	Creedmore Cartridge Co. (1890–1892)
ELEY	Eley Brothers (England)
F. (impressed)	Federal Cartridge Co. (rimfire cases)
H.	Winchester Repeating Arms (rimfire cases)
H (raised)	Winchester Repeating Arms (rimfire, ~1860–late 1880s)
P. (raised)	Phoenix Cartridge Co.
P (impressed)	Peters Cartridge Co. (rimfire); (Peters, 1887–1934, merged with Remington)
P	Peters Cartridge Co. (centerfire)
PC	Peters Cartridge Co. (centerfire)
P.C.	Peters Cartridge Co.
PCCO	Peters Cartridge Co.
PETERS	Peters Cartridge Co.
PETERSHV	Peters Cartridge Co. (rimfire)
R-P	Remington–Peters (adopted 1960)
REM	Remington Arms Co.
RAH	Remington Arms Co.
REM-UMC	Remington Union Metallic Co. (adopted 1911)
R	Robin Hood Ammunition Co.
RHA	Robin Hood Ammunition Co.
R.H.A. Co	Robin Hood Ammunition Co.
S.A.W.	Sage Ammunition Works
S.A. CO	Savage Arms Co. (1897–1917)
SAVAGE	Savage Arms Corp. (1921–1963)
S.R.A.C.O.	Savage Repeating Arms Co. (1895–1897)
SUPER SPEED	Winchester Repeating Arms (about 1930 on)
super speed	Winchester–Western (about 1930 on)
SUPER X	Western Cartridge Co.
SUPER-X	Western Cartridge Co.
U	Union Metallic Cartridge Co. (1867–1911, merged with Remington)
UMC/U.M.C.	Union Metallic Cartridge Co.
U HiSpeed	Remington Union Metallic Co. (rimfires since WW II)
U.S.	United States Cartridge Co. (company existed from 1869–1936)
US (raised)	United States Cartridge Co. (stamp used from 1869–1875)
U.S.C. CO	United States Cartridge Co.
WCC	Western Cartridge Co.
W.C. Co.	Western Cartridge Co. or Winchester
Western	Western Cartridge Co.
W	Winchester or Western
WRA	Winchester Repeating Arms
WRA CO/W.R.A. CO.	Winchester Repeating Arms
W-W	Winchester–Western
XL	Federal Cartridge Co. (rimfire cases)

and thus became the most popular type in the United States, supplanting the Berdan system. The (American) Berdan system is easier and cheaper to manufacture, and is used in most foreign nations. The Berdan primer is difficult to remove and those cases are seldom reloaded. Barnes (1976:302) states that

TABLE 2. United States Arsenal Headstamps

STAMP	ARSENAL
Den (plus date)	Denver Ordnance Plant (1941–1944)
DM (plus date)	Des Moines Ordnance Plant (1941–1945)
EW (plus date)	Eau Claire Ordnance Plant (1942–1943)
ECS (plus date)	Evansville Ordnance Plant (1942–1945)
CF (plus date)	Frankford Arsenal (.45 Govt. in 45-55-405 load)
F (plus date)	Frankford Arsenal (pre-1902)
FA (plus date)	Frankford Arsenal (1902 on)
KS (plus date)	Alleghany Ordnance Plant (1942–1943)
LC (plus date)	Lake City Arsenal (1941–1944, 1950s on)
LM (plus date)	Lowell Ordnance Plant (1942–1943)
M (plus date)	Milwaukee Ordnance Plant (1942–1943)
RF (plus date)	Frankford Arsenal (.45 Govt. in 45-70-500 load)
SL (plus date)	Saint Louis Ordnance Plant (WW II)
TW (plus date)	Twin Cities Ordnance Plant (1943 on)
U (plus date)	Utah Ordnance Plant (1941–1943)
UT (plus date)	Utah Ordnance Plant (1941–1943)

Note: Dates are given as the last two numbers of the year, e.g., "44" = 1944. If a third number is present it is the month of manufacture. The elements are equally spaced around the head, with the month on the left and the year on the right of the head (Figure 5). The month designation was discontinued in late 1917.

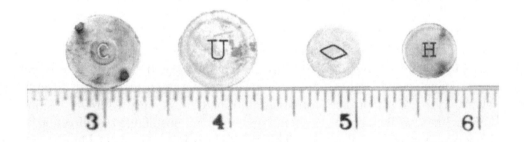

FIGURE 4. Examples of rimfire headstamps, left to right: C = Kynoch Cartridge Co. (England); U = Union Metallic Cartridge Co.; Diamond symbol = Western Cartridge Co.; H = Winchester Repeating Arms. Scale in inches.

FIGURE 5. Examples of centerfire headstamps. Headstamp at right indicates cartridge manufactured at Frankford Arsenal (F) in February (2) of 1892 (92). Scale in inches.

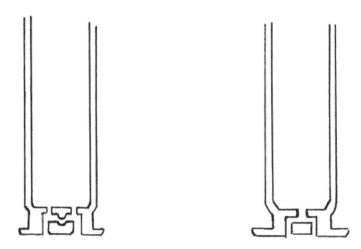

FIGURE 6. Primer types: left, Boxer; right, Berdan.

Berdan primers have not been manufactured in America since the 1920s. This may have changed with the recent production by CCI of aluminum cased revolver ammunition with Berdan primers.

Identification of the primer type is simple. The Boxer system has a single hole from the primer pocket through the head of the case to ignite the powder charge. The Berdan system requires two small holes through the case head. By looking down inside the case the holes, single or double, may be seen on the inside of the head at the bottom of the case.

Centerfire primers may be copper, brass, or plated steel. Early primers were copper cased, and some copper primers continued to be used through World War I. Early primers contained fulminate of mercury. Mercury residue attacks brass, weakening the cases and making them unsuitable for reloading. A later priming mix was potassium chlorate, which leaves a salt residue in gun barrels, causing corrosion. In the late 1920s non-corrosive lead styphnate was substituted for chlorate, and by the 1950s even the military stopped using corrosive primers (Wallack 1977:143). Currently all primers are non-mercuric and non-corrosive, labeled NM-NC. Current primers are standardized sizes; large rifle and large pistol are .210″, small rifle and small pistol are .175″. While the large rifle and large pistol primers are the same size, they are different in priming charge, as are the small rifle and small pistol primers. Unfortunately, primers of a given size are visually indistinguishable as to being designed for rifle or pistol. Obsolete and discontinued primer types and sizes are listed in Barnes (1976:306).

Shotgun shells made of paper or plastic with a brass head use a separate brass cup, the battery cup, which contains the primer cap and anvil. For reloading the primer cap alone may be replaced, or the entire battery cup removed and replaced.

Primers may be recovered archaeologically, particularly spent primers if the site was inhabited by handloaders.

Oddities

Rarely an old case or cartridge may turn up that is neither rim- nor centerfire. These variations in the quest for an ignition system for self-contained cartridges include the following, which may be found in any good reference book.

1. Maynard — early 1860s Maynard cases had large flat disk with pin hole covered by wax paper. Primer was paper type like modern cap pistol (Figure 7). Later Maynard cases were centerfire with a distinctive bulging head (Figure 7).

2. Pin fire — the primer is inside the case and is actuated by a pin protruding from side of base of the case (Figure 7).

3. Burnside — a very early brass case, tapered with an annular receptacle for lubricating grease, which shows as a bulge around bullet, has no head or rim.

4. Teat fire — mouth of case flared out with bullet totally contained and the priming was in a teat protruding from the base, has no head or rim (Figure 7).

5. Mule Ear or Flop Ear — head of brass case has no rim, instead there is a flange protruding from one side of the head like a tab. There is a pinhole in center of case head for ignition from paper or percussion cap.

FIGURE 7. Oddities, left to right: .32 teatfire patent 1864; .50 Maynard 1865; .44-60 Maynard Model 1873 (centerfire); 7mm pinfire; .32 pinfire. Scale in inches.

Powder

Black powder was used in self-contained metallic cartridges until the development of smokeless powder. The saltpeter, charcoal, and sulfur are generally mixed in a 75-15-10 proportion, although other proportions have been used.

Barnes (1976:310) has the discovery that the burning rate of black powder was affected by compressing the powder into grains of various sizes occurring in 1860. Finer granulations burn faster, while coarser granulations burn slower. The burning speed of powder affects the rate of formation of the explosive gas, thus controlling the velocity of the projectile. However, Rosa (1985:16) states that frontiersmen using Kentucky-type rifles manufactured their own powder by the late 1700s, and were aware that different granulations of gunpowder burned at different rates. They used fine grained powder for priming, and coarse grained powder for the main charge. During the Lewis and Clark Expedition, Meriwether Lewis, in his journal entry for February 1, 1806, mentions the supplies of best rifle powder, common rifle powder, glazed powder, and musket powder (DeVoto 1953:317). It is unclear what the difference is. It may refer to proportional mix, purity of the ingredients, or quality of production.

Black powder is currently manufactured in a variety of grain sizes, with the larger grain used for larger caliber cartridges. At the turn of the century a number of special purpose black powders were marketed, none of which are now manufactured. The resurgence of interest in black powder firearms has stimulated the manufacture of different powders.

Smokeless powder is cellulose nitrate, created by the chemical action of concentrated nitric and sulfuric acid on cellulose fiber such as cotton. The nitrated cellulose can be compounded with other chemicals to control the burn time. Straight nitrocellulose powder is termed single base, and nitrocellulose colloided with nitroglycerin are double base powders.

Nitrated compounds were developed in the 1840s. Alfred Nobel created dynamite in 1867. European chemists spent considerable time and effort in developing nitrated organic compounds with controllable burning speeds. Single base smokeless powder existed by the early 1860s, and Nobel created a double base smokeless powder in 1887. Smokeless powder began to replace black powder in the 1890s (Barnes 1976:311).

European militaries had replaced large-bore black powder cartridges with small-bore smokeless cartridges using metal jacketed bullets before 1890, when United States Army Ordinance began experimenting with smokeless .30 caliber cartridges (Bearse 1966:107). The .30-40 Krag, a military round loaded with smokeless powder, was introduced in 1892. The 1894 Winchester Lever Action rifle, designed by Browning, was created for smokeless powder cartridges (Markham 1991:142). The .30-30 WCF and .25-35 WCF, designed for this rifle, were introduced in 1895, and were the first sporting smokeless cartridges developed in the United States.

Use of black powder cartridges dropped off after 1910 (Barnes 1976:69). Commercial production of some black powder cartridges continued until the mid 1930s. Many popular old black powder cartridges were loaded with smokeless powders into the 1920s and 1930s, with jacketed bullets, and a few originally black powder cartridges, such as the .45 Colt, are still active, manufactured with smokeless loads.

Smokeless powder is manufactured in different grain types, including flake, disc, ball, and tubular. The grain types are made in different sizes. The chemical content of the grain as well as its size and shape affect the burning speed. There are several manufacturers of smokeless powder, and each brand makes several types of powder for specific use with different cartridges.

Smokeless powder came into general use after 1900 (Smith 1954:25). At that time, Boxer centerfire primers, brass bottleneck cases, swaged (pressure formed) crimp, and jacketed bullets were the norm, and case headstamps were standard, except on some rimfires.

Gunpowder may be recovered archaeologically in unfired cartridges, or powder containers may be recovered. The powder in a cartridge can be identified as black or smokeless and to grain type, but smokeless powder decomposes over time, turning to dust.

Bullets

Here things get interesting. The projectile or bullet is after all what firearms are about. Cartridge cases, primers, and powders have been fairly standardized since the development of smokeless powder and the Boxer primer, but development of the bullet continues yet today, trying to find the ultimate in efficiency as to trajectory, accuracy, and expansion.

Early lead bullets were made by pouring melted lead into a mould. The mould was usually made with two mating blocks, and mould and sprue marks are sometimes visible on the bullet. The sprue is the mark where the stem, from the filler hole in the mould, was cut off. Lead bullets commonly have one or more cannelures, or grooves, around the circumference for grease lubricant to reduce leading and help prevent black powder fouling the bore. A narrow groove near the top of the bullet, and above the grease grooves was common to crimp the mouth of the case to prevent the bullet from "jumping" forward in the case under recoil in repeaters and revolvers.

Bullets had flat bases, hollow bases, and convex bases. Some of the old large caliber black powder bullets were "paper patched," i.e., had a strip of stiff paper around the body of the bullet and under the mouth of the case to fit the bore, shoot cleaner, and facilitate reloading in the field. The famed "Buffalo" Sharps .45-120-550 was one of these.

Later lead bullets were swaged in dies from lead wire instead of poured into moulds, and are yet today, such as the .38 Special revolver cartridge. Pure lead gave way to lead alloys. Lead bullets declined in usage except for .22 rimfires and centerfire revolvers. Lead bullets often have a gilding metal (a copper and zinc alloy) base attached, called a gas check, to prevent the lead from melting from the hot propellant gas.

Bullets were retained in the mouth or neck of the case by crimping, which was accomplished by several methods. A "stab" crimp was common early on and consisted of three or four indentations, as with a center punch, spaced around the circumference of the case neck to secure the bullet in the case. This system was used primarily on lead bullets. Later a rectangular flat punch was used, instead of the round punch. A rolled cannelure was also used but the cannelure was more commonly used to establish bullet seating depth and still is—especially in handgun cases. The final and present crimp is swaging the case mouth to the bullet.

By the 1880s, rifle action had been made stronger and longer, allowing higher velocities that caused lead bullets to strip in barrels. This severe leading impaired accuracy and made gun cleaning difficult. Accordingly, efforts were started to cover the lead bullet with a metal "jacket." The first metal jacket bullet was developed in Switzerland in 1880 (Logan 1959:9). By the mid-1880s jacketed bullets, using a copper and nickel alloy, were produced in the United States (Wallack 1977:156). The switch to smokeless powder hastened the change to jacketed bullets. After World War I the continued acceleration of muzzle velocities stimulated switching jacketing material to gilding metal. Mild steel, brass, and other alloys are also used for jackets. This jacketing helped the issue of barrel leading, but at a cost of bullet efficiency, constraining bullet expansion.

To rectify this, jackets were designed to have lead exposed at the front of the bullet. Bullets with a rounded point of lead exposed at the nose are termed "soft points," bullets with the exposed lead truncated or flattened are "flat noses" and bullets with a hollow cavity in the nose are "hollow points." A fully jacketed bullet with a sharp point is termed a "spitzer" (Figure 8). In the 1920s the base of the jacketed bullet was tapered to reduce drag and increase velocity, termed "boat tails." A spitzer boat tail was usually a military bullet.

SHOTGUN SHELLS

Shotguns have been used for hunting and sport shooting, as well as for military and law enforcement purposes. Double barreled shotguns, mainly 10 gauge but some 12 gauge were commonly used by stagecoach guards, and Colt produced shotguns termed "Coachguns." The phrase "riding shotgun" is still used by teenagers today. Shotguns were also used by gunfighters and lawmen in the West and by the military during the Indian Wars.

Single and double barrel muzzle loaded flintlock shotguns were prevalent in the late eighteenth and early nineteenth centuries. Shot of uniform size and quality was produced by the late 1700s. When the percussion system was developed, single and double barrel muzzle loaded percussion shotguns were manufactured and popular until the early twentieth century. A pinfire shotshell was patented in France in 1836, and is still used in Europe today. Breech loaded shotguns were developed and appeared between the late 1840s and 1870s. The shotgun was the first firearm to use smokeless powder. Smokeless powder made from nitrated wood pulp was commercially loaded into shot shells in 1864.

The shotgun gauge system is a throwback to muzzle loaded muskets centuries ago. The "gauge" of muskets referred to the number of lead balls of the bore diameter that weighed a pound. A 10 gauge gun thus had a bore diameter

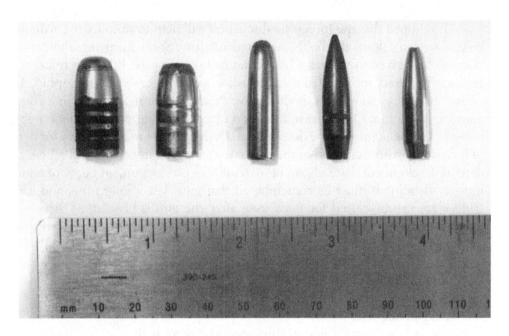

FIGURE 8. Bullet types, left to right: unjacketed lead bullet; flat nose; soft point; spitzer boat tail; hollow point.

that a lead ball weighing 1/10 pound would enter the barrel; a 12 gauge gun has a bore that allows a lead ball weighing 1/12 pound, etc. The system is still used, for shotguns only. Exceptions to the gauge system are the 410 gauge, which is actually a caliber (.410-inch), and the 9mm rimfire shotshell, also a caliber.

Shotguns were manufactured in every gauge from 1 gauge down to 32 gauge, however commercial American shells are no longer loaded larger than 10 gauge. Barnes (1989:375) states that prior to World War I the different combinations of shot size, loads, shell length, and powder resulted in 6,500–7,000 different factory loads, and the custom, special-order, and wildcat loads doubled that figure. After 1920 the number of commercial loads was greatly reduced, and now some 160 commercial loads are available.

Self contained shot shells for breech-loaded guns were made of paraffin-impregnated paper with a crimped-on brass head and center-fire primer. All-metal shells were also made, of brass or aluminum. Metal shells are superior for preventing moisture from entering the shell, and make reloading practical. Remington introduced plastic shells in 1958, and most shells are now plastic with metal heads. All-metal shells are still made, and were used during the Vietnam War, for example, where paper and plastic were inferior.

Rifled slugs for shotguns were introduced in Germany in 1898, termed the Brenneke. The American or Foster type rifled shotgun slug was introduced by Remington about 1936.

CARTRIDGE CASE IDENTIFICATION PROCEDURES

How do we identify specimens found in the field and come by an approximation of age? Here is where the fun starts!

It is hoped that the foregoing discussion will help to simplify the arduous task of tracking down the field specimen's identity. Some immediate information can be derived from even a basic examination of a case; however, reference texts are necessary for detailed data regarding a cartridge (see bibliography). To be *sure* of a very old artifact, it should be checked against a sample in a comparative collection. Once a case has been identified, date of introduction and period of manufacture can be determined. Discrepancies of a few years for date of introduction are common in the reference texts, due in part to differences in date of development, date of patent, date of trial production, and date of common availability. It must be remembered that guns last a long time, and cartridges are manufactured for guns long after the gun is obsolete. Cartridges may be used years or even decades after manufacture, and may be reloaded after manufacture has ceased.

Useful Equipment
- Micrometers or dial caliper graduated in thousandths
- Magnifying lens
- Six-inch scale graduated in thirty-seconds of an inch
- Log sheet

Identification Log
Determine and log the following:
- Ignition type: rimfire or centerfire
- Centerfire: internally primed or externally primed
- External primer: Berdan or Boxer; copper, brass, or steel
- Case: shape, rim type, material (copper, brass, steel, nickel)
- Head Stamp
- Measure *all* dimensions: Measurements are the primary key to identifying a case. Measure length, body diameter at head (base), head diameter (rim), body diameter at mouth (neck), and shoulder diameter (if bottle-necked). Careful measuring is important but a variance of a few thousandths of an inch in dealing with old cases must be expected, compared to book specifications, because of looser tolerances in manufacturing long ago and lack of standards between factories.

Refer to Barnes (2003:504–520), Cartridge Identification by Measurement, for identification (see bibliography).

Three examples are given: 1) a case without a headstamp; 2) a case headstamped with a maker's mark but no caliber; and 3) a case headstamped with maker and caliber.

Example 1: 5BL2712, case: copper, corroded and bent; rimfire, no head stamp
case length: .912″
body diameter at head: .555″
body diameter at mouth: indeterminate
head diameter: .645″ approx.

FIGURE 9. Example 1: .56-56 Spencer, case and comparative cartridge. Scale in inches.

The specs match the .56-56 Spencer, original cartridge for the first Spencer rifle, patented 3-6-1860. Manufactured in quantity beginning in 1862. Frankford Arsenal made ca. 50,000 in 1864–1865. Cartridge was commercially loaded until 1920. Loaded with a 350 grain conical, pointed, lead bullet, .540-.555″ diameter, using 42-45 grains of black powder (Figure 9).

Example 2: case: copper, rimfire, with a headstamp SAW
case length: 1 5/32″ with a slight taper
body diameter at head: .555″
body diameter at mouth: .545″ average, not perfectly round
head diameter: .646″
mouth of case crimped into bullet
interrupted cannelure around circumference of case, consisting of three rectangular punch marks, evenly spaced, about 5/16″ long, and about 5/16″ below mouth of case

The specs match .56-50 Spencer, loaded with a 350 grain conical, flat-nose, lead bullet, using 45 grains of black powder. SAW is the stamp of Sage Ammunition Works, Middletown, Conn. The cartridge was used in the Spencer Repeating Carbine, Model 1865, used in the Indian Wars, including by Custer in the Battle of Washita, 1868 (Figure 10).

Example 3: case: brass, tapered, rimmed, centerfire, boxer primer without markings
headstamp: WRA CO, 40-65 WCF
case length: 2.105″
rim diameter: .600″–.603″
rim thickness: .063″–.065″
base diameter: .500″–.503″
neck diameter: .430″ average (not round)

FIGURE 10. Example 2: .56-50 Spencer, case and comparative cartridge. Scale in inches.

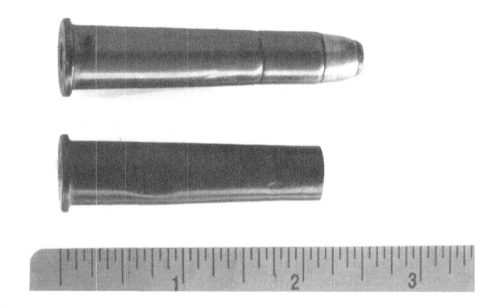

FIGURE 11. Example 3: .40-65 Winchester Center Fire, case and comparative cartridge. Scale in inches.

Surface find on sage flats, purple-brown patina, excellent condition. This case has a solid head, and lack of corrosion indicates it was loaded with smokeless powder, thus dates post-1900. Measurements confirm it was a .40-65, not reformed. The .40-65 W.C.F. (Winchester Center Fire) was introduced in 1887, used a .404″ diameter, 260 gr bullet, and was loaded with black and then

The Historical Archaeology Laboratory Handbook

smokeless powder. It was used in the Model 1885 Winchester, 1886 Winchester, and 1895 Marlin rifles. It was not manufactured after World War II (Figure 11).

CONCLUSIONS

Elements of firearm use recovered from archaeological contexts have the potential to provide a variety of important information. Bullets, gunflints, percussion caps, and cartridge cases, when correctly identified and analyzed, provide temporal and functional data. They also serve to document the adoption and use of firearm technology. Gunflints and percussion caps are elements of the ignition systems of, respectively, flintlock and caplock guns. Flintlocks were used through the 1840s, and later by indigenous people into the 1870s or 1880s. Caplocks replaced flintlocks, were prevalent from about 1830 until the late 1860s or early 1870s, and were used later in some remote Western areas. Caplocks were replaced by firearms using loaded or self-contained metallic ammunition, which was developed rapidly from the early 1860s.

The cartridge case of loaded metallic ammunition developed from copper cased black powder rimfire to copper cased black powder centerfire to brass cased smokeless powder centerfire, with a number of other changes in primer, bullet, and case, some of which are time markers. Cartridge designation conventions are complex, inconsistent, and nonsystematic, but cartridge cases can be identified by using headstamps and taking measurements. With a reference book, date of introduction and period of manufacture of a cartridge can be determined. Determination of caliber is possible from spent bullets, including spherical balls, and the type of firearm used to fire the bullet can often be deduced. Advent and period of manufacture of a firearm can be ascertained. Temporal interpretation of cases and bullets is made more complex by the American practice of handloading, and suitable caution is necessary.

ACKNOWLEDGEMENTS

The authors thank Kevin Black for his support and editorial suggestions, and two anonymous reviewers for their helpful comments and corrections. Photographs and drawings, Figures 1–3, 6–8, and 11 are by Christopher Allen Photography—our thanks to Chris and Sandy Allen. Thanks to Bob Hinton for photos, Figures 4 and 5. Thanks to Tom Meier for photos, Figures 9 and 10. Any errors are the fault of the authors.

REFERENCES CITED

Barnes, Frank C.
1976   *Cartridges of the World*. 3rd ed. DBI Books, Northbrook, Illinois.
1989   *Cartridges of the World*. 6th ed. DBI Books, Northbrook, Illinois.
2003   *Cartridges of the World*. 10th ed. Stan Skinner, editor. Krause Publications, Iola, Wisconsin.

Bearse, Ray
1966   *Centerfire American Rifle Cartridges, 1892–1963*. A. S. Barnes and Co., South Brunswick, New Jersey.

Berge, Dale L.
1968   The Gila Bend Stage Station. *Kiva* 33(4): 169–243.
1980   *Simpson Springs Station, Historical Archaeology in Western Utah*. Cultural Resource Series No. 6. Bureau of Land Management, Salt Lake City, Utah.

Dawson, William F.
1999   Ordnance Artifacts at the Sand Creek Massacre Site: A Technical and Historical Report. Ms. on file, Intermountain Regional Office, National Park Service, Denver.

DeVoto, Bernard (editor)
1953   *The Journals of Lewis and Clark*. Houghton Mifflin Co., Boston.

Fontana, Bernard L., and J. Cameron Greenleaf, with collaboration of Charles W. Ferguson, Robert A. Wright, and Doris Frederick
1962   Johnny Ward's Ranch. *Kiva* 28(1–2):1–115.

Hamilton, Theodore M. (editor)
1960   Indian Trade Guns. *The Missouri Archaeologist* 22 (December), Columbia, Missouri.

Horn, Jonathon C., Gary Matlock, and Duane A. Smith
1986   Archaeological Investigations of an Historic Cabin Near Durango, Colorado. *Southwestern Lore* 52(3):1–33.

Logan, Herschell C.
1959   *Cartridges—a Pictorial Digest of Small Arms Ammunition*. Bonanza Books, New York.

Mails, Thomas E.
1972   *The Mystic Warriors of the Plains*. Doubleday & Co., Garden City, New York.

Markham, George
1991   *Guns of the Wild West: Firearms of the American Frontier, 1849–1917*. Arms and Armour Press, London.

Moore, Jackson W., Jr.
1973   *Bent's Old Fort, An Archaeological Study*. Colorado Historical Society, Denver, and Pruett Publishing, Boulder.

National Park Service
2000   *Sand Creek Massacre Project. Volume 1: Site Location Study*. Intermountain Regional Office, National Park Service, Denver.

O'Brien, Bill
1994   What Makes A Magnum? *Guns & Ammo* 38(2):50–55.

Rosa, Joseph G.
1985   *Guns of the American West*. Crown Publishers, Inc., New York.

Russell, Carl P.
1977   *Firearms, Traps, and Tools of the Mountain Men*. University of New Mexico Press, Albuquerque.

Scott, Douglas D.
1989   Firearms Identification for the Archaeologist. In *From Chaco to Chaco, Collected Papers in Honor of Robert H. Lister and Florence C. Lister*, edited by Meliha S. Duran and David T. Kirkpatrick, pp. 141–151. Bulletin of the Archaeological Society of New Mexico No. 15.

Scott, Douglas D., Richard A. Fox, Jr., Melissa A. Connor, and Dick Harmon
1989   *Archaeological Perspectives on the Battle of the Little Big Horn*. University of Oklahoma Press, Norman, Oklahoma.

Sharpe, Phillip B.
1987   *The Rifle in America*. Reprinted. Wolfe Publishing Co., Prescott, Arizona. Originally published 1938, Wm. Morrow & Co., New York.

Smith, Carlyle S.
1954   Cartridges and Bullets From Fort Stevenson, North Dakota. *Plains Anthropologist* 1(1):25–29.

1955 An Analysis of Firearms and Related Specimens From Like-A-Fishhook Village and Fort Berthold I. *Plains Anthropologist* 4(July):3–12.

Wallack, Louis R.

1977 *American Rifle Design and Performance*. Winchester Press, Tulsa, Oklahoma.

Warner, Ken, and Jan R. Shrader

1971 The Long and Short of .22's. *The American Rifleman* (June). National Rifle Association, Washington, D.C.

White, Henry P., and Burton D. Munhall

1948 *Cartridge Identification, Volume I. Centerfire Metric Pistol and Revolver Cartridges*. A. S. Barnes and Co., New York.

1949 *Cartridge Identification, Volume II. Centerfire American and British Pistol and Revolver Cartridges*. Sportsman's Press, Washington, D.C.

BIBLIOGRAPHY FOR CARTRIDGE IDENTIFICATION

There are three principal references for cartridge identification. These compilations are rather amazing, because manufacturers do not provide data on cartridge measurements.

* Barnes (various editions), *Cartridges of the World* has been the basis and stimulus of this paper. Each edition of Barnes provides the same encyclopedia of data about cartridges, and each edition has chapters on cartridges unique to that edition. The tenth edition is in print, and contains a comprehensive table of cartridge identification by measurement, as well as historical notes and comments, illustrations, loading data, and ballistics for over 1500 cartridges, current and obsolete.

* Bearse (1966), *Centerfire American Rifle Cartridges, 1892–1963*. Out of print. Bearse provides information on centerfire smokeless rifle cartridges, including outline drawings of the case, dimensions, synonyms, bullet data, representative headstamps, rifles adapted to, history and development, and notes and comments.

* Logan (1955), *Cartridges*. Out of print. Logan provides a list of chronology of cartridge development; information about paper, combustible, and early metallic oddities; drawings of cartridges and headstamps; dimensions, and some history of each cartridge; illustrations of caps, primers, and bullets; and a partial list of manufacturers' headstamps.

Other cartridge identification references exist, such as White and Munhall (1948, 1949), cited above, but the authors have been unable to obtain copies.

ERRATA

In the Fall 2005 issue of *Southwestern Lore* (Vol. 71, No. 3), the article "Cartridges, Caps, and Flints: a Primer for Archaeologists," by Peter J. Gleichman and Dock M. Teegarden was published with incorrect captions on two figures. The captions for Figures 3 and 6 identify cartridge feature types in reversed order. For Figure 3 on page 11 the correct caption is, "Case head types: left, balloon head; right, solid head." For Figure 6 on page 16 the correct caption is, "Primer types: left, Berdan; right, Boxer." We regret the errors.

China or Prosser Button Identification and Dating

Roderick Sprague

ABSTRACT

China buttons or "small chinas," glass-like ceramic buttons, are one of the most often misidentified artifacts in 19th and 20th century sites. These buttons, manufactured by the Prosser process, date after 1840. The common varieties are characterized by the top side being quite smooth, the under side with an "orange peel" surface, and a noticeable seam around the edge. Fancy examples include such varieties as calicoes, ginghams, igloos, bird cages, and pie crusts. Button collectors have not only known for many years that these are ceramic not glass, but have created an excellent classification system that should be utilized, in a modified form, by historical archaeologists. This is a prime example of how costly it can be when archaeologists ignore the collectors and their published body of knowledge. For the sake of clarity it is suggested that china buttons be referred to as Prosser buttons in the archaeological literature.

Introduction

One of the more ubiquitous historic artifacts in archaeological sites is the button. While buttons can be made of bone, shell, plant materials, various metals, hard rubber, plastics and other synthetics as well as numerous other materials, the most enduring are those made of glass and ceramic. High-fired ceramic buttons—the "chinas" or "small chinas" of the button collectors—while glass-like in appearance, are ceramic, made by the Prosser or "dust" process.

The historical archaeology reports in which these buttons are identified as glass are so numerous that there is no need to cite examples. One report goes to the opposite extreme and labels all such buttons as porcelain but again without mentioning chinas or Prosser and setting up a completely unique classification (Coleman 1990:155–158). This confusion is also apparently a problem in Australia according to Lindbergh (1999). It cannot be emphasized enough that china buttons must be identified in archaeological reports as ceramic, *not* glass.

For the historical archaeologist the question becomes one of how to tell the two materials apart. Fortunately, the collectors have already faced this dilemma. Several authors have suggested that the back of a china or Prosser button has the well-known pebbly or orange-peel surface, a surface which is clearly rough and pitted (Figure 1b, d, i). The back of a glass button will have a very smooth or mirror-like surface sometimes with a meandering hair line or very regular, fine lines in concentric circles or segments. If a button is broken, under magnification, the surface of a china will show minute crystals while the glass will be absolutely smooth. Both Prosser and glass buttons can have a noticeable peripheral seam at the outer edge, thus this is not a defining trait.

Lisa Young (Bromberg, et al. 2000:472) has recently suggested that ceramic buttons "fluoresce deep purple under UV [short wave] light (like any hard paste porcelain), while the glass buttons do not fluoresce." This distinction is of questionable value when applied to any buttons because both glass and hard paste ceramics will fluoresce or not fluoresce, depending on their chemical constituents. Furthermore, experiments carried out on Prosser buttons in the author's collection showed fluorescence to be random. Such variability in the fluorescence of buttons may be of help in determining the time or location of manufacture but all Prosser buttons by definition are ceramic.

In the process of identifying Prosser porcelain buttons, the archaeologist can benefit by consulting the collectors and their literature and thus avoid the "plowing of old ground." Not only have the collectors known that these buttons are ceramic not glass but as will be shown, they have an excellent, fairly logical, and readily available system for the description of ceramic buttons. The introduction of Prosser buttons is one of the more precisely dateable events in the area of common personal items and gives an excellent *terminus post quem* of 1840.

The Prosser process of button manufacture involved the preparation of fine clay with the addition of quartz or finely ground ceramic wasters, a small amount of moisture, and then pressing this mixture into cast-iron molds. After being turned out of the mold, the buttons were fired in a muffle furnace at a temperature sufficient to transform the clay into a highly fired

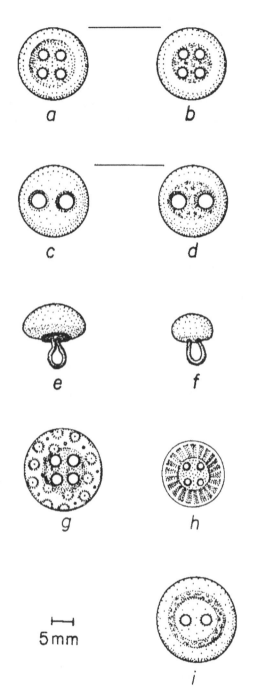

FIGURE 1. Common Prosser button styles: *a*, four-hole dish type button, front; *b*, four-hole dish type button, back; *c*, two-hole panty-waist button, front; *d*, two-hole panty-waist button, back; *e*, domed gaiter button, note the shank plate; *f*, domed shoe button; *g*, calico button; *h*, pie crust button; *i*, back of fisheye button showing typical back rough surface only on the raised ring. (Line drawings by Sarah Moore from samples in the author's collection.)

ceramic button, approaching or even achieving the level of porcelain. After the first firing, the buttons could be glazed with any color, including metallic lusters, and fired again. They also could be treated much as transfer-printed ceramics to produce calico buttons or treated with other techniques of decorating to create ginghams and stencils.

The term china button should not be confused with buttons made from common potters clay that have been fired at low temperatures. In the 19th century, Prosser buttons were known in England and the United States as "agate" buttons (Prosser 1881:62; U.S. Tariff Commission 1918). Sears Roebuck and Company catalogs listed agate buttons *at least* until 1909 (Feinman 1979:1026). Someone with better eyesight than the author should research the exact date in the microfilm series of catalogs. As noted below, one of the Prossers himself not only used the term agate for these buttons but also the term "dry process." The term agate was still in use in 1945 in the bead collector's literature (Adams 1945:184).

Luscomb (1972:627) in one of her many unsigned articles, in her journal *Just Buttons*, takes the position that while agate may be the proper term at an earlier date, "small chinas" is the term coined by the collectors and should be used. She says:

> There is no attempt being made here to change the well known term "Small Chinas." This term was coined by button collectors for the family of calicoes, pie crusts, saw-tooth, ringers, deep wells, and the other small china or porcelain cuties. It is probably best at this late date to just know the favorite "Small Chinas" were once sold as "Agates."

Her article also lists a Boston dry goods store ledger from 1871 that used the term agate for all types of Prosser buttons.

In discussing beads and buttons, Jargstorf (1993:67) says: "Towards the end of the 1870s, the European market was flooded with what were known as 'agate' buttons and beads which would eventually be called 'Oriental beads,' 'Bapterosse [sic] beads,' or 'Porcelain beads'. . . ." She does not clearly indicate if any of these terms were also applied to buttons. These are not accurate terms even for beads—Oriental is far too general, not all Prosser products are true porcelain, and Bapterosses was neither the first nor the only manufacturer of Prosser buttons and beads.

Chamberlain, a competing manufacturer in England during the decade of the invention called them both "agates" and "cornelians" (Godden 1982:225). Peacock (1978:54) adds the term " pressed clay" and further notes that "agate and carnelian were British manufacturers' terms to denote whether the buttons were made from earthernware or porcelain," but she does not explain if the names are related to the type of ceramic and if so, which is which. To call them all porcelain, as Coleman (1990) has done, is contrary to the modern laboratory evidence. Even the junior Richard Prosser (1881:60–64) described numerous porcelain buttons but always referred to the 1840-invention buttons as "agate," never porcelain. The term of the collectors—chinas or small chinas—has precedence but as any ceramic analyst can verify, china is a very imprecise term used in a number of different ways by equally knowledgeable authorities. It is suggested, for the sake of precision, that this class of buttons, in the archaeological literature, be called Prosser buttons with a secondary reference to "chinas" as the term of the collectors.

Manufacturing and Chronology

Much of this discussion on manufacturing is found in an earlier work on Prosser *beads* (R. Sprague 1983). That work was limited to a specialized audience and was also more limited in its application hence it seems appropriate to repeat portions of it here. Also many of the references are now known to be available in a single bound source (Albert and Adams 1970; Lamm et al. 1970) rather than scattered throughout years of the *National Button Bulletin*, a very popular and, at times, scholarly source for collectors but difficult to find in full runs in libraries. Much of what follows, thus was later found in the book form, a very disheartening situation for one who has already located and researched the many separate articles. Often what was excised for the book was the very information pertinent to this study hence the originals are sometimes referenced. Also when a source becomes separated from the true author due to incorporation into the book form, the

original may be referenced. All too often, work by Jane Ford Adams is referenced in the literature as Albert and Adams (1970) or Lamm, et al. (1970).

The chronology of the development of the Prosser process has yet to offer any real help in dating any specific artifact other than to the century following 1840. It is necessary, however, to make such a beginning by determining just what information is in the literature and how it may eventually give both the collector and the archaeologist a series of identifiable traits for the more precise dating of Prosser buttons. The several descriptions may at first appear to be redundant but a careful reading will show changes through time that may eventually help in this dating process.

The first patent for the Prosser process was issued on 17 June 1840 as No. 8548 (published in error in 1853 as No. 8637) in London to Mr. Richard Prosser. Adams (Albert and Adams 1970:6) has republished the entire patent. The first paragraph refers to the production of "knobs, rings, and other articles." It further states "the materials are clays and clayey earths, flint and felspar, separate or mixed together according to the quality of the article to be made." These materials are "ground to powder" and are used "without the addition of any water." A sieve having 200 meshes to the square inch is required for a smooth surfaced object. The second paragraph describes the "machine and tools" for the manufacturing process. "The machine is a press comprising bed, bolt, bolster, treadle, and handle." The tools are the two halves of the die which are then forced together after filling with the proper mixture to a pressure of 200 lbs. to the square inch. The rest of the patent description is concerned with the hole in the back of the button for the attachment of a metal shank. Tiles made by the Prosser system at this time were compressed to one-third the original thickness "with a pressure which may amount to 400 tons" (Tomlinson 1852:[2]459).

The year following Richard Prosser's patent, his bother Thomas Prosser, of Patterson, New Jersey, took out a patent in the United States on 30 June 1841 (Patent No. 2199) for "improvement in the manufacture of buttons." Again, Adams (Albert and Adams 1970:7) has republished the complete patent. Thomas Prosser's patent reads:

My improvement in the manufacturing of buttons consists, first, in making them of materials not heretofore used for or applied to that purpose—to wit, such clay-earths or other earthy materials and metallic oxides as are now commonly used by potters in the manufacture of domestic earthenware; and, secondly, in making them in metallic molds, in which the materials are compressed with considerable force by means of a common fly screw-press, or any other suitable mechanical contrivance, after being reduced to a fine powder. The pressure given must be sufficient to cause the powdered clay to cohere and retain the form of the buttons which is impressed upon it in the mold, after which it is to be fired and glazed in the potters kiln in the usual manner, and also painted or printed similar to ordinary porcelain, if required. Such buttons as have holes in them for the purpose of sewing them on the clothing are then complete; but those requiring shanks of metal have them stuck into a recess made in the buttons for that purpose by means of shellac or other cement; or they attach to a shell which covers the whole of the back of the button and turns a little over the front, the front of the button only appearing set in a metallic frame or shell, and at the back is the shank.

Little is known about the Prosser brothers other than that Richard was a successful civil engineer and industrialist in the ceramic and metal industry, in Birmingham, England. Richard had 11 patents for the manufacturing of metal tubes and nails between 1831 and 1852 (Prosser 1881:75, 210–212; Dutton 1984:159). There was contentious debate between the brothers as to who actually invented the process with both laying claim to being first. Thomas is reported to have said "that it was he, not his brother, who discovered the compressed powder technique. According to him, he had the idea as early as 1832 and 'the first button that was ever made by that process was made by me in 1837'" (Albert and Adams 1970:4).

Perhaps in response to this claim, an excellent summary of the Prosser or "agate" button industry was written by Richard B. [Bissell] Prosser of the Patent Office in Birmingham concerning the inventions registered in Birmingham. It is likely that this was the inventor's son or possibly a nephew as he refers to the "late" Richard Prosser several times and lists his death as 1854 (Prosser 1881:97). The book was a compilation of newspaper articles published together in a limited edition book of only fifty copies. Prosser (1881:64) summarized the history of the industry thus:

Amongst what may be termed the miscellaneous processes of button-making there is one which was invented by a Birmingham man, although it was never carried out here, nor, indeed, in this country at all to any great extent, except for a short time. We refer to Mr. Richard Prosser's "agate" buttons, as they were, not unhappily, called, for which a patent was granted in 1840. The process, which was exceedingly simple, consisted in pressing a finely-powdered mixture of clay, felspar, flint, &c.—the proportions of which vary according to circumstances—between dies of the shape of the button required. A single pressure only was requisite, and the buttons were then fired and glazed in the usual manner of treating porcelain articles. The process was taken up by Mr. Minton, of Stoke-on-Trent, and at the beginning of the year 1852 a make of 5,000 gross per week was found insufficient to supply the demand. For a few years the process was successfully carried on at Stoke, and shortly afterwards the manufacture was commenced in France. M. Bapterosses took out several patents for improved machinery by which he was enabled to make no less than 500 buttons at a single operation of the press, and, in consequence of the low price of labour in France, the "agate" buttons could be sold here for less than it cost to sew them on to the cards at Stoke. This, of course, ruined the home trade, and they have ceased to be made here for many years past. There is, however, a very large establishment at Briare, about forty miles from Orleans [France], where they are manufactured in enormous quantities. Mr. Prosser's patent included also a claim for a new form of button with two holes connected by a channel for the thread to lie in, which had the effect of protecting it from wear. At the suggestion of Mr. Blashfield the process was applied to the making of tesserae and tiles, and the foundation of a most important industry was thus laid. An early use of the patent tessellated pavement in Birmingham was for the steps of Mr. Prosser's house, No. 18, Broad Street. We have ventured to digress thus far from the subject in hand to place on record a few facts, which seem in danger of being forgotten, relating to the origin of the "dry clay" process of making tiles and buttons.

Adams (Albert and Adams 1970:5) and Atterbury and Batkin (1990:46) report Prosser buttons manufactured in England by the Minton Company as early as 1840 but that they had ceased manufacture in 1846 (Albert and Adams 1970:5) or 1848 (Atterbury and Batkin 1990:46). Other English firms beside Minton producing buttons included Maw (Watkins 1950:228); Turley and J. M. Blashfield (Celoria 1973:44); and W. Chamberlain and Co. of Worcester, "some Birmingham companies," and Boyle (Peacock 1978:50).

A report in 1851 by a London exhibition awards committee (Argyll 1852:539) reported that the French had "beat the English manufacturers entirely out of the market." Chamberlain's production of buttons "continued to at least September 1850" (Godden 1982:225). Chamberlain was apparently involved in a lawsuit with Richard Prosser over patent infringement by Chamberlain (Godden 1982:224). R. W. Binns in 1865, as quoted in Godden (1982:224), said that "the lawsuit . . . disgusted the patentee [Prosser] and he no longer cared to protect his licensees from the competition of French manufacturer [Bapterosses] who had improved upon the invention and were producing a superior article at lower prices; the trade was therefore shortly after given up." Godden (1982:224–225) also clearly shows, with production records, the proof of the claim often made, as by Prosser above, that in England the carding of the buttons cost more than the total cost in France.

Barber (1909:348, 386) notes that the Prosser process was applied to tiles by J. M. Blashfield (Barber's Blachfield) in his English plant sometime after 1858. Ure (1861) gives a detailed description of the tile manufacturing process as well as illustrating the screw press and mold used for making buttons. The technique was also applied to tiles in this country by Hyzer and Lowellen of Philadelphia (Barber 1909:345). Watkins (1950:228) further mentions John G. Low, a New England company making "dust tiles." It is not known if these manufacturers also made buttons by the Prosser method.

Barber (1909:444) states that the Charles Cartlidge & Co., of Greenpoint, Long Island, New York, manufactured buttons by the Prosser process starting at least by 1844 (Ketchum 1987:72). He made over 100 designs, including highly decorated styles. An illustration of two calico buttons from the Cartlidge factory is dated 1848 by Barber (1895:16, 1909:444). Luscomb (1967:31) claims that these were the first United States manufactured calicoes. Barber (1895:17) said that Cartlidge was "probably the first to introduce this method of button making into the United States. . . ." but later he (Barber 1909:164) said simply that this is "definitely the time of the first appearance of this class of ceramic productions in this country." The Cartlidge factory closed in 1856 (Barber 1909:164). Torley (1962:174), without any source, country,

or factory name, but implying the United States, says that calicoes "continued to be made until about 1910." This date appears too early for Europe and too late for the Unites States.

As already noted, the Prosser process was also utilized in France by Jean-Felix Bapterosses (1813–1885). An eight page pamphlet produced by the Musée de la Mosaïque et des Emaux (1999), in Briare, provides a brief history of Bapterosses' career and the company he founded. He apparently traveled to England in 1843 where he worked in the Minton factory long enough to learn the Prosser process. As noted above, Minton made Prosser buttons only from 1840 to 1846 or 1848. On returning to France, Bapterosses developed and patented, on 4 November 1844, a machine for the production of buttons far in excess of what the English could produce. In July 1845 he set up the first of several factories that ultimately, by 1851, placed him in Briare. Additional patents included various steps in the process such as a new coal burning furnace design in 1847 and an improved shank button process. He is also credited with the first use of milk, rather than water, as the wetting agent (Bourry 1926:461). According to Peacock (1978:54) this was about 1855. The added benefit of using casein as a binder or glue in the dry dust process is obvious. The Museum in Briare indicates that milk was used earlier than 1855 and that it was to improve the plasticity of the paste ("Il améliore la plasticité de la pâte en y incorporant du lait."). By 1848 and 1849 buttons in pink, ochre, gray, blue, and black, in addition to white, were being produced. Bapterosses essentially killed the English ceramic button industry with his cheaper labor and improved technical processes. An ending date for button manufacture is not given but it is stated that plastic buttons delivered the fatal blow ("le coup fatal") in the 1950s and 1960s.

Without any referenced source, Torley (1962:174) claims that "calicoes and similar buttons were first made in 1840 in France." The French patent records have not been systematically searched for Prosser button patents but according to Albert and Adams (1963:133) and Schuler and Lamm (Lamm et al. 1970:21) button cards from the Bapterosses Company indicate that the process was clearly patented in France (Figure 2). One button card described by Albert and Adams (1963) translates from the French as

"Mineral-like Buttons" which the authors state was used by Bapterosses:

> almost as a brand name to identify solid-color china buttons. It corresponds to the English adjective "iron-stone" and suggests what fine qualities the buttons possess in durability and strength, because they have feldspar in them. For us, "rock-like" or "stone-like" conveys the image better than the literal translation "mineral-like."

FIGURE 2. Button card with the F. B. trade mark of Felix Bapterosses. (Author's collection.)

An even more likely source of the Bapterosses terminology was the then-current English term "agate" which was also used by Bapterosses as early as 1845. Based on exposition awards and medals listed or not listed on the button card, Albert and Adams (1963:133) date the card between 1849 and 1851. A series of Bapterosses cards being sold by a peddler in 1855 contained bull's-eyes, pie crusts, and calicoes (Luscomb 1952:273) but it is also claimed that the cards had exposition medals dated as late as 1862, hence the suggested date of 1855 is suspect. Behrbaum (2001) has illustrated a large button card with numerous styles from Bapterosses with the title "Agate Buttons."

Adams (Albert and Adams 1970:10) reprinted an excerpt from the 28 July 1866 issue of the *Working Man*, a London weekly which described the Bapterosses plant that, by that time, had already developed the "wet process" for handling the clay. A more recent source (Bourry 1926:460) mentions the addition of oil to the basic clay formula to give it plasticity. The buttons were made of moistened clay pressed in molds, after which they were placed on boards to dry and then biscuit or bisque fired. No further processing was done on some uncolored ones while others were painted or received transfer-printing nearly identical to that utilized for ceramic dinnerware. The buttons were then glazed by a process "which is the same as that used for common porcelain." It is inferred from the literature and inspection of numerous samples that the plain buttons were fired at a high enough temperature to result in self-glazing while the decorated one had to be fired at a lower temperature to protect the decoration and thus required a second glazing process and final firing.

It appears that the difference between the so-called dry and later wet process was more a matter of patent protection or avoidance rather than a real change in the actual process. After the initial patent, moisture was always mentioned as a part of the process.

The transfer-printed buttons included the type known today as calicoes. Adams and Albert (1952:81), imply that they observed or were told at the Bapterosses factory that "The escossals [éscossals = French for plaid, i.e. gingham] patterns involved a more complex operation. The area to be colored must be covered with a sticky medium and the color must then be sifted over in powdered form. When more than one color is employed, each one must be separately fired." Obviously, the added labor would have made these buttons more expensive.

A clear distinction between calico and gingham is that "cross-bars and plaids are typical of ginghams" and "tiny repetitive details are characteristic of calico" (Lamm et al. 1970:123). Some of the transfer-printed designs included among calicoes are clearly not traditional calico cloth designs, such as the vermiculated (worm) designs (Snell 1955). Ferguson (1978) presents a clear, more detailed, and fairly accurate explanation of the differences among calicoes, ginghams, and stencils

One source (Bourry 1926:460) mentions decoration by gilding and "chromo-lithography with vitrifiable colours." The chromo-lithography probably was for the color printing of decalcomania (decals). Collectors have suggested that the stencil type of buttons may have been made by applying decals. The decal process was invented in 1860 which places it within the stencil period. Under magnification, however, stencils—especially poor examples—appear to have had the decoration applied by a spray, fine splatter, or stiff brush process, but never with a decal. The suggestion by Arndt (1993:63) that also calico decorations were applied as decals is not supported by the historical chronology, historical sources, or physical evidence.

Stencil decorated buttons in some cases, besides the stencil application, also have added brush strokes. Splatter, in one or two colors, is also defined as a specific technique said to be "sponged, sprinkled or sifted" (Adams and Albert 1952:81). Tarbox (1949) and Adams (1971:316–317) report a card of stenciled buttons labeled in German as "Bemalte Knöpfe" (painted buttons). Stencils obviously could be described as painted. No authority has discussed the method of applying the color to ringers (Lamm et al. 1970:50) and bull's-eye gaiter buttons (Lamm et al. 1970:23–25). Gold pattern calicoes and gold ringers are described by Albert and Adams (1963) but nothing is mentioned about the techniques involved in producing them.

On 25 September 1872, the United States Patent Office issued patent No. 141,749 to Bapterosses for "improvement in machines in making buttons." The major improvement in this new press was a moveable middle section of the die that permitted easier removal of the buttons after being compressed. Also the press utilized a series of gears thus avoiding the necessity of a screw press for each set of buttons. The invention included a series of interchangeable dies so that buttons with a hole partially through for the attachment of a shank as well as buttons with the holes clear through for sewing, could be made on the same machine. The drawings accompanying Bapterosses' patents are far superior to those submitted with the Prosser brothers' patents.

As was typical of 19th-century encyclopedias, writers for Spon's Encyclopedia (Lock 1879) lifted the description of what they call porcelain buttons almost verbatim from an 1866 description. Since it is an excellent summary of later developing mechanization it is quoted in its entirety:

> *Porcelain Buttons.*—The process of manufacturing porcelain buttons resembles that of making small ornamental articles of earthenware. The moistened clay is pressed into plaster of Paris moulds, carefully placed on boards to dry, and then taken to the "biscuit-oven," where it undergoes the first firing or baking. The baked clay is now called "biscuit," and is ready for the painter or printer. A great number are made uncoloured; but many also, both with holes and shanks, are partly or wholly painted, some with simple, others

with complicated designs. The painting is effected either by hand or by transfer printing: in either case, the colours are "fixed" by the articles being baked in a muffle furnace or enamel kiln. In transfer printing, the design required is printed from copper plate, by means of a peculiarly prepared ink, on thin tissue paper, which is then placed, while the impression is still moist, upon the biscuit ware and allowed to dry, after which it is removed, the design having become transferred from the paper to the biscuit ware. The design is then burnt into the article in a muffle furnace. This baking effectually removes the oil used in preparing the colour, and leaves the button ready for the glazing process. Each muffle furnace is furnished with a little tramway, which traverses the interior of the furnace and projects forwards into the bakehouse. This tramway is provided with small, flat, movable iron platforms, on which the "frames" containing the buttons are carefully piled and then wheeled into the oven, around which a steady fire is kept constantly circulating. When the baking has been completed, the button is subjected, if required, to the glazing process, which is the same as that used for common porcelain, after which the shanks are added (Lock 1879:[2] 559).

This description is the earliest to mention the use of plaster of paris molds replacing cast iron, a change in manufacturing that defies logic and has not been explained in the literature, only repeated. Plaster of paris molds, as used for large dinnerware, would not seem practical for highly compressed clay used in buttons, beads, and tiles. A French description dated to 1889 does not mention plaster of paris molds yet does go into detail concerning the furnace and firing process (Knab 1889:881).

Morey (1940:23), as is typical of the collector's literature, describes the transfer-print process for calicoes in great detail with absolutely no sources or references. She states that after being fired for an unlikely 36 hours (most description specify minutes):

> The buttons are then in a state known as biscuit ware—that is, not glazed. The calico figures are then printed on large sheets of paper which are in turn applied to the surface of the buttons in the molds before the ink is dry. The biscuit ware absorbs the enamel ink and the paper is removed by water. The calico designs in the colors must be fixed by washing with a fixing solution and glazed by dipping in a solution of ground feldspar, ground flint, sal soda, boric acid, and cobalt blue mixed with water.
>
> The buttons must then be placed in the baking oven again where the glazing solution fuses and flows evenly over the button, making a coating of glassy smoothness.

The cobalt blue was not part of the transfer-printing process but rather was undoubtedly to give the glaze a whiter appearance.

No further information has been found concerning another French manufacturer of Prosser buttons, Lebeuf-Milliet and Company (Albert and Adams 1970:11). The French encyclopedia, *La Grande Encyclopédie* (Knab 1889:881) lists ceramic button production at Creil and Montereau as well as at Briare in France. Two different reports in the same publication from 1867 list Lebeuf-Milliet and Co. as being from two different locations in France: Creil (Johnson 1969:269) and Montereau (Richards 1969:279).

Jargstorf (1993:67) says the famous glass manufacturing region of Gablonz caught up with the ceramic bead industry about 1885 with production from the Redhammer brothers, Albert and Eduard. Most bead producers at this time were also producing buttons. Röntgen (1981:371, 404, 406) lists one Bohemian and two German ceramic button makers with the city, dates, and trade mark thus: Gebr. [Brothers] Redhammer (Gablonz, 1872-unknown, GR); Ferdinand Schmetz Porzellanknopffabrik (Aichen, 1851–1959, F.S.); and Risler & Cie [French abbreviation for Company] (Freiburg, 1847–1927, R & C). A report from 1867 (Johnson 1969:269) also lists Risler and Co. as a manufacturer of buttons.

Jargstorf (1993:67) apparently erroneously lists the Freiburg manufacturer as Rister & Co. and says they were a competitor of Bapterosses in the late 1870s, thus the name, city, and dates agree with Röntgen's (1981:404) Risler & Co. except for the one letter in the name. The formerly unidentified button cards marked R & C as shown in Lamm at al. (1970:134–138) are undoubtedly Risler and Cie. Sample cards of Prosser beads observed by Karlis Karklins in the van der Sleen collection at the *Instituut voor Zuid-Aziatische Archeologie* in Amsterdam, have the following explanatory notes:

> These are sample cards from the firm of *Riesler* in Herzogenrath [town in Germany near the Netherlands border]. These beads were made by pressing pastils with a hole through the centre from powdered glass, to which was added a little clay as a binder so that the beads kept their shape better [italics in original, brackets represent a footnote].

It is not known if they also manufactured buttons but it was noted that this plant ceased using this process around 1957, a date which coincides with Bapterosses. The similarity between Risler and Riesler, suggests the possibility of confusion in the recording of names or a long-term family tradition of ceramic manufacturing in Germany.

No additional information could be gathered on button cards reported as having been made in Germany by A. & R. Co. as reported by Beatrice Lorah (Lamm et al. 1970:107). As noted above, Tarbox (1949) and Adams (1971:316–317) report on a card of stenciled buttons labeled in German as Bemalte Knöpfe (painted buttons). Adams questions whether this is a trade name or a descriptive name. The cards have a trademark of an anchor and F. S., the same initials as Ferdinand Schmetz used on their porcelain dinnerware. The one illustrated is card (Karte) 16 and pricelist (Preisblatt) 16 so obviously the company was producing numerous styles.

An unsigned article in the *National Button Bulletin* (1985:108–110) mentions the "Albert Parent Sample book" and "the Parent Company." So far, no country of origin or other information has been discovered for this company. Without any reference or authority, George Adams (1944) uniquely lists Spain as a country for the manufacture of "agate" buttons.

Chemical and Physical Properties

The most recent description of the manufacturing of Prosser buttons is concerned with the chemistry of the process and comes from the final paragraph of Bourry's (1926:461) *A Treatise on Ceramic Industries*:

> The body is formed of felspar, which is powdered and treated with sulphuric acid to separate part of the impurities (iron oxide). To the purified felspar is added some colouring oxides, or sometimes a little bone ash or chalk. Milk or an emulsion of caseine in a solution of boracic acid is next added, so as to give the material a consistency firm enough for it to be moulded in a press. Five hundred buttons are moulded with one stroke. They are arranged automatically on a sheet of paper, which is used to carry them on to a fireproof plate. This is first heated, so that the paper is burnt up; then the plate is put into a muffle, where it remains for about ten minutes. It is then drawn out, the buttons on it are taken off with one stroke of a rake, and it is covered with a fresh sheet of paper. As many as thirty muffles are sometimes arranged in a rectangular down-draught kiln. The burned buttons fall into a series of boxes fastened to a pivot, where they finish cooling, and from which they are taken out through a movable bottom.

Historical and contemporary research was not completely satisfactory in answering all of the questions concerning the materials used in Prosser beads, thus laboratory analysis was applied (R. Sprague 1983). This work is also of interest here because the samples included both buttons and beads. A series of samples including Prosser buttons and tile beads of several colors and drawn glass beads of similar colors were analyzed by non-destructive energy dispersive x-ray fluorescence The analysis, while not as precise as some other chemical analyses, does have the advantage of being relatively inexpensive and non-destructive.

The results were startling and rewarding. The buttons and tile beads were found to be essentially identical in chemical composition. It was also found that the coloring agents in some cases tended to mask the basic ingredients so additional work was done with strictly white materials. Not only were the Prosser buttons and the tile beads found to be identical but these were also chemically identical to white drawn glass beads. It was the opinion of Charles R. Knowles, the geological physicist involved in the analysis that "to call Prosser buttons and tile beads anything but glass [chemically] is splitting hairs" (R. Sprague 1983:172).

The conclusion derived from this laboratory work is that Prosser-made objects are chemically identical to glass but are physically very different because they possess a crystalline structure lacking in glass. Further discussion of the ceramic/glass question can be found in R. Sprague (1983, 1988) and Francis (1988). Once again, the important point is that Prosser buttons should be described in the archaeological literature as ceramic not glass.

Two theories have been advanced for the orange-peel surface on the back of buttons. One states that the appearance is due to the striking off of the clay at the top of the metal mold. The appearance of Prosser tile beads tends to support this theory. The other explanation is that the rough surface is caused by the button resting on that surface while it is being fired. One type of large fisheye button has a raised ring on the back which is the only part of the back that is roughened (Figure 1i), thus supporting the second theory. Given the improvements in the mechanical technique and the low profile of a typical button, the second theory is much

more likely for all but the very early buttons. This, however, is only a speculation based on the detailed inspection of numerous samples.

Attachment and Shape

A ready-made classification of china buttons is found in articles by members of the National Button Society (NBS) most of which were published first in the *National Button Bulletin* (*NBB*) and later collected in a book with the cover title of *Guidelines for Collecting China Buttons*. The true authorship of this small hardbound volume (1970; soft bound reprint 1994) is very difficult to establish. The title page again has the same title as the cover with "by Ruth Lamm, Beatrice and Lester Lorah, and Helen W. Schuler" and below that another title, *Essential Data Concerning China Buttons* "by Lillian Smith Albert and Jane Ford Adams." Chapter One has a title page listing the second title with the same two authors. This is the chapter with much of the information on the manufacturing of china buttons. The remainder of the book is directed at collecting, hence it is assumed that the two titles on the title page are in reverse order of how they are presented. This conclusion is also supported by the names of the authors on the original articles in the *National Button Bulletin* which, strangely, are not always listed in the book.

The classification system assembled by the authors of the china button volume is based on major categories followed usually by a body style number, a color or combination of colors designated by a capital letter (A is usually solid white), a lower case letter for the decoration (often i for calico, j for gingham), and numbers for variations in the decoration. This system is not universal due to variations in the number of levels but with minor modification it should serve to designate any archaeological specimen.

The major area of non-mutually exclusive categories is the highest level in which shape (including number of holes), manufacturing method, and decoration are mixed as the determining criteria. This could pose a problem, however, since the manufacturing techniques, shapes, and the number of holes are all simply ways of categorizing how the buttons are attached to the clothing they can logically be all grouped together. This highest level of clas-

Rick Sprauge

sification could thus be called "attachment" with the same terms as used by the original authors such as gaiter, shoe, three-hole, etc.

The other problem with this highest level is the inclusion of transfer-printed and other applied decoration. There has been an attempt by Lamm et al. (1970) to solve this problem, for example the listing of calicoes and other decorated types as a special color variety yet calicoes in their system are a separate classification equivalent to three-hole or gaiter. A better solution and one that does little violence to the system as published would be to simply place the transfer-print and other decorative description at one level below the attachment level and above color. The decoration designation of "none" would thus be the most common but still a legitimate category.

The order of the number of holes—two, four, and three—is probably based on the number of samples available to collectors rather than logic, but in spite of these defects, the system is established, widely used, and should be easily applied and understood by archaeologists. The advantage of using such a system is obvious—it provides a consistent and available method for archaeologists to begin the process of placing specific buttons in dated contexts and thus move forward in the process of creating a more precise dating tool. A collector knows exactly what a "two-hole panty-waist button" is and can find numerous illustrations in the literature. The archaeological report, which uniquely calls it a "two-way sew-through pant type," is only compounding the problem of identification. It is also important to be able to cross reference archaeological specimen types with the collector's literature. For example the collectors report that small three-hole buttons are usually associated with doll or baby clothing, not an unimportant piece of information for the archaeologist. The effort devoted to classifying Prosser buttons by a modified Lamm et al. system would quickly become well worth-while. As always, it is quicker, easier, and safer to use an established system than to create a new and untested one.

The four-hole, smooth beveled rim, body style 1 or dish type, in white probably accounts for 98% of the reported archaeological speci-

mens (Figure 1a-b). The most common four forms—four-hole dish, panty waist, calicoes, and pie crust (Figure 1a-b, c-d, g, h)—comprising over 99% of the archaeological finds illustrated in the literature, are marked below with an asterisk. Many other types have been found archaeologically, however, including from just one site: gaiters in white and brown; two-hole in white; four-hole in white, pink, blue, and black; and white pie crust (L. Sprague 1983) or in another example from one site a pie crust, a calico, and a rare whistle (Schuetz 1969:40). In addition to the common white, another frequently recovered variety is the panty-waist button (Figure 1c-d), a two-hole variety with a simple lenticular shape and noticeably larger holes to accommodate the cloth tape used for attachment to children's underwear, not as one archaeological report noted above states: "called the pant type, which is associated with trousers." The gaiter and shoe buttons are found in a variety of shapes, the most common being domed. Gaiter buttons (Figure 1e) are larger than shoe buttons (Figure 1f) and always have a shank plate while the shoe buttons do not. These terms do not necessarily identify the actual use, for example, so-called gaiter buttons were most often used on women's and children's clothing (Luscomb 1967:76) or as ornamental buttons used on coat cuffs (anonymous reviewer 2001, pers. comm.).

Kohrs (1998) suggests that shoe buttons, smock buttons, and calico pinshanks should be classified together as pinshank buttons. Lamm et al. (1970:28) indicate that shoe buttons can have attached shank or pinshanks. The best source with drawings to define all shank types, even beyond chinas, remains Adams (1966). For excellent color illustrations of calicoes and other decorated buttons on the web see Behrbaum (2001) and Stewart (2000).

The NBS classification system with appropriate page numbers from Lamm et al. (1970), as well as other references, is freely paraphrased in outline form below (* = more common archaeological types). This is a system that is available in print and it works, hence it is strongly endorsed for use by archaeologists.

The last three factors; applied decoration, color, and size; are discussed in more detail below.

Lamm et al. 1970 (or other reference)

I. Attachment
A. Metal shanks — 20–29
1. Gaiter — 20–27
   a. bull's-eye — 23–25
   b. hobnail rim — 26–27
2. Shoe buttons — 28
3. Smock/lab coat — 29
4. Calico pinshanks — Kohrs (1998) lists 2, 3, & 4 as pinshanks
5. Calico jewels — Behrbaum 2001
B. Complex Construction — 30–32
1. Bird cage
  or inserted 4-way self shank — 30–32
2. Inserted 2-way self-shank — 33–37
3. Whistles — 38–43
4. Igloos — 44–45
C. Two-Hole — 47–75
1. Hollow eye — 49–57
2. Deep well — 58–59
3. Smooth beveled rim — 60
4. Tire shaped — 61
5. Radiating-line rim — 62–63
6. Oval-eye — 64–70
7. Fisheye — 71–72
8. Panty-waist * — 73
9. Pattern eyes — 74–75
D. Four-Hole — 77–94
1. Smooth beveled rim — 79–82
2. Dish * — 79–81
3. Ink well — 82
4. Saucer — 83–84
5. Rolled rims — 85–87
   a. tire — 85
   b. tire variants — 86–87
6. Radiating-line rim — 90–92
   a. pie crust * — 90
   b. saw-tooth — 91–92
7. Hobnail — 93–94
E. Three-Hole — 95–104
1. Dish — 97–98
2. Ink well — 99
3. Saucer — 100
4. Tire — 101
5. Plate — 102
6. Scalloped edge — 102
7. Radiating-line rim — 103
8. Hobnail — 104
II. Applied Decoration
A. Calicoes * — 107–122, 127–129
B. Ginghams — 123–124
C. Stencils — 139–150
D. Marbled — Stewart 2000
E. Spattered — Stewart 2000
F. Rimmed Calicoes — Behrbaum 2001
1. Plain rim
   a. flat rim
   b. smooth rim
   c. rolled rim
   d. angled rim
2. Fancy rim
   a. scroll

III. Color
A. Paste
B. Glaze
C. Decoration
IV. Size
A. Metric
1. Diameter
2. Thickness
3. Holes
B. English diameter
C. Line diameter

Applied Decoration

The style of design can easily be referred to in the several pages of black and white line drawings by Adams (Lamm et al. 1970:111–121) for calicoes; Lamm et al. (1970:123–124) for ginghams; and Lamm et al. (1970:24) for bull's-eyes. Unfortunately, only photographs rather than line drawings are used for the ginghams and not all of the known designs are shown. For stencils, the preferred source remains Lamm et al. (1970:141–150) which is based on work by H. A. Washburn (1944) and George Adams (1944). Washburn (1944) suggested the unlikely situation that all cream-colored buttons with stencils were vegetable ivory, not ceramic. The term stencil is imprecise but as Lamm et al. (1970:141) say: "Since these buttons are known to all of us as 'stencils,' they cannot be rechristened, desirable as a more accurate name would be." When colored designs on buttons are described they require designations for both the background color and the design color(s) plus a code number for the design.

Rimmed chinas are most often calicoes but also can be white or colored four-hole. They are simply a metal ring around a button with the attachment still through the ceramic button holes. The only published works on rimmed chinas thus far are Ferguson and Ferguson (1979) and especially Behrbaum (2001) who provides clear drawings of the several rim types and a table of known combinations of rims, patterns, colors, and sizes. None is known from an archaeological context. While not in Lamm et al. (1970) they can easily be inserted into that system.

Jewel calicoes differ from rimmed chinas in that the ceramic portion does not have holes for attachment, rather the attachment is formed by a ring and solid metal back. Behrbaum

(2001) does not classify jewel calicoes as true calico buttons but they would fall in the metal shank group with apparently all known examples having calico decoration. The Fergusons (1979) argue that calico jewels "are not, in the strictest sense, china buttons, but instead, are metal buttons with porcelain-disk settings." They are of some concern to archaeologists who might find them with the outer ring eroded away and thus have what appears to be a calico button with no holes. Again Behrbaum (2001) provides drawings of the rim types and known combinations of rims, patterns, and colors. She also lists the known back markings including a circle of six five-pointed stars (Ferguson and Ferguson 1979:21), "FEINE QUAL," and "EXTRA FEIN." These written markings imply a German-speaking country of origin.

Any calico buttons with a blue or black script or cursive "L" (𝓛) or currently with an embossed script "L" are modern reproductions by Lindy Miller (2000, pers. comm.) made since 1997. Her fairness and honesty in marking her work is a model for anyone making reproductions of any kind. Those interested in obtaining samples should check the Behrbaum (2001) web site.

Color

The colors used in the making of Prosser buttons include variations in the clay body (also known as the matrix or fabric), the glaze, and the applied decoration. Any one of these, according to the literature, can be the final treatment. No examples of buttons with a truly unglazed biscuit surface are reported in the modern collector or archaeological literature, implying a very high firing temperature for the single fired buttons. The biscuit fired buttons were then heated enough to set the transfer-print or paint, and then glost fired with a glaze as described above or apparently in one description, fired to set the decoration as well as to create a self-glaze at the same time. The result is that all Prosser buttons have a glaze but the technique employed in each case must be based on inference. The clays used were usually white or cream resulting in unglazed white or cream colored buttons. The glazes used could result in a vast variety of colors including a fairly common iridescent white and numerous metallic colors.

Based on experience with glass trade beads and Prosser beads, it is strongly recommended that the colors be given both a generally understood and culturally neutral common name *and* a Munsell color designation. Metallic colors are not covered by the Munsell charts, hence it is suggested that the Pantone Metallic Color Guide© be used when these colors are encountered. In contrast to glass buttons there is virtually no variation in surface luster within a color and all buttons observed have been opaque with transparent and translucent examples not present. Some collectors and analysts claim to have found translucent buttons but none has been verified in the laboratory.

Size

For reasons that will become clear, size designations for the diameter should be listed in English, metric, and lines. The line was a standard measure for buttons including the time period when Prosser buttons were being manufactured. The line is defined as 1/40 (0.025) in. Most of the western world used the English line except the French used the ligne which equals 12 to the French (pre-metric) inch thus 1 line = 0.635 mm and 1 ligne = 2.256 mm (1 ligne = 3.55 lines and 1 line = 0.28 ligne). For tables of equivalency of the two different lines and lines to older English coins see Luscomb (1971:129–130). George Adams (1943:6) states that "the English line is usually marked in multiples of two and the French ligne in consecutive numbers, whole and half, 2, 2½, 3, etc." Collectors have found that buttons should be measured in both inches and millimeters to aid in finding modal diameter size groupings. Without a large sample of archaeological materials researchers must depend upon the collectors' data to assign buttons to a proposed size cluster. Luscomb (1971:130), in contrast to archaeological convention, states that buttons should be measured at the largest diameter, for example from corner to corner on square buttons. The modern collector's measuring devices (the Lindley and the NBS flat measure) which classify buttons for competition as diminutive, small, medium, and large (Harris

1972:137) are of no value in the archaeological laboratory.

Generally, collectors have not been concerned with the thickness of china buttons, however, until more is known about dating buttons, this dimension should be recorded. Luscomb (1971:130) again notes that the height of buttons should be measured "from the highest point on the face to the lowest point on the base." As yet, no one in either the collectors' ranks or in historical archaeology has investigated the meaning of the hole size in common Prosser buttons. With careful research, these could be found to indicate the date and/or location of manufacture. It appears that the perforation size in Prosser *beads* has significance with holes becoming smaller with improved technology, hence this trait in buttons should not be dismissed out-of-hand.

Luscomb (1971:129) gives the suggested size in lines of buttons for various types of clothing as follows:

> Certain sizes have become recognized for specific purposes on men's wear garments, etc. Umbrella buttons are normally 14 lines. Shirt buttons 18 lines. Pajama buttons (jackets) are 30 lines. Trouser buttons are 23 lines on the fly with 27 lines on the brace [suspender attachment]. Men's jackets are normally secured by 30 line buttons, with 22 lines on the sleeves and on the waistcoat. Men's overcoats are normally fastened by 45 line buttons. Warehouse coats and overalls usually call for 30 line buttons.

This information should be used with caution as there is no clear indication of the time period for these suggestions. Fashions and the uses of various button sizes change through time. Just this type of reliable information, however, is exactly what archaeologists need to find, refine, and publish.

Chronology

One obvious interest of any archaeologist in a discussion of an artifact type is how useful is it for dating their site. With a long history of improvements in production machinery, techniques, and materials, one might expect something more than a *terminus post quem* of 1840. The dating of buttons is vital to the interests of the button collectors yet even they have given up and said "the only sound course is to catalogue [chinas] without regard to age" (Lamm

et al. 1970:151). Thus far the evidence for dating by decoration alone is not encouraging with Mintons in England reputed to have made calicoes by 1842 (Albert and Adams 1970:8), Cartlidge in the United States by 1848 (Barber 1909:444), and Bapterosses in France until at least the 1950s (Musée de la Mosaïque et des Emaux 1999). Without any references to support her conclusions, Johnston (1949) dates bulls eyes, pie crusts, ringers, and whistles as 1840 to 1880 but stops calicoes at 1870 and extends stencils to 1942.

Dating special shapes has some possibility when patents are involved. For example, a patent (apparently French) for a "vertical hole" button, better know as a "whistle" button was issued to Pierre Eugene Richardiere of Paris in 1863 (Luscomb 1970:55). He did not limit the material to ceramic but also listed horn, india-rubber, and metal.

With more research in the actual European records, those which may still exist in spite of two world wars, it should be possible to determine the differences in decoration or size that possess chronological meaning. Obviously there are differences in chemical content, manufacturing traits, or decorative elements among English, French, and Bohemian/Czechoslovakian buttons.

So far the raised dot in the exact front center of some buttons has not been given an age or origin. One collector has stated that this is a trait of Bapterosses buttons but there is no proof of this contention. Likewise the raised ring on the back of some buttons "may someday provide the clue to where buttons with it were made" (Schuler and Lamm 1961:265) (Fig. 2g). These are just two traits where spectrographic or other analyses might lead to conclusions concerning the country of origin.

Conclusions: Function, Use, and Meaning

With the *form* identified, now it is possible to look at the cultural factors: the *function, use,* and *meaning* in Ralph Linton's (1936:401–421) terms. A more general discussion of one biased view of form, function, use, and meaning can be found in Sprague (1981).

The *use* of buttons might include to keep clothing in place, closed, or decorated. The use can often be determined from the form. Obviously shoe buttons are usually used on shoes, panty-waist buttons on underwear, and common buttons on outer clothing. Very small buttons in the common varieties (especially three-hole) may be from doll or baby clothing, while fancy buttons of the smaller sizes probably indicate women's garments. Large, massive plain buttons were most likely used on coats. These are all logical speculations that any historical archaeologist could or should make. The archaeologist must also be careful of assigning use based on modern collector's terms such as gaiter buttons which Luscomb (1967:76) considers a modern term for a type of button generally used on women's and children's clothing and only rarely on gaiters. (How many students today even know what gaiters are?) When buttons are associated with burials, the location on the body may be indicative of the use.

The *function* might include keeping warm, for modesty, to be attractive, or in the case of dolls to entertain or teach. A cache of gaiter buttons, with the lead shanks melted out due to a fire, was excavated from a Hudson's Bay Company warehouse at San Juan Town, San Juan Island, Washington (L. F. Sprague 1983:261). Except for the warehouse, San Juan Town consisted of mostly bars and brothels. The gaiter buttons appear to have been a commercial shipment that did not reach the intended ultimate users. In Linton's terms the use was still to attach clothing but the function in this case was in commerce, not to keep warm or look good.

The *meaning* of elaborate or expensive buttons might be associated with the validation of status. For example, in the case of San Juan Town, fancy buttons would mean you were of low status as a prostitute. The military buttons associated with the fancy women's buttons in San Juan Town would have a very different meaning.

One final consideration is the meaning of Prosser buttons to the dress of the population from this time period. Prior to Prosser buttons, buttons were largely made by hand from bone, wood, shell, clay, glass, or metal. The mass production of buttons in lots of 500 at a time in 30 muffles, all day long, day after day would and did bring the price down so low that everyone could afford to use them. This is but one small facet of the introduction of industrialization to western Europe and some of

its colonies but it is one which shows up clearly in the archaeological record and is worthy of more study.

The factors such as use, function, and meaning can more easily be determined when the archaeologist knows the relative cost or frequency of the specific button types found. Fortunately this is information already known but not necessarily published by the collectors but from which the archaeologist could benefit. Too often the artifact analyst ignores the collectors' knowledge to the detriment of historical archaeology. The example of Prosser buttons is one that should be consider carefully and then perhaps mend our ways.

ACKNOWLEDGEMENTS

Many of the ideas and much of research and text comes from previous work with Prosser beads thus the acknowledgments found in R. Sprague (1983:172) should be repeated here. Especially helpful have been George R. Hamell, Charles F. Hayes III, Greg Laden, Linda Ferguson Sprague, Charles F. Wray, and three anonymous reviewers. DiAnn Herst then of Parks Canada, Ottawa, first introduced me to the Prosser brothers and their buttons. The chemical analysis of samples was through the courtesy of Charles R. Knowles of the Idaho Bureau of Mines, Moscow. Karlis Karklins and Lester Ross, long-time colleagues in bead studies encouraged me to add Prosser buttons to my writing and gave many helpful suggestions. Les was especially helpful in the discussion of clay firing technology. Also providing help and comments since the publication of the Prosser bead paper are Linda Ferguson Sprague, Peter Francis, Annalies Corbin, Mark Warner, and Laurie Burgess. Lindy Miller generously provided details concerning her modern reproductions. As usual, Jennifer O'Laughlin and the Interlibrary staff at the University of Idaho Library served pleasantly and beyond normal duty in finding items all too often from poor or corrupt references. Pamela J. Cressey kindly provided help and information on buttons at Alexandria Archaeology. Jean Corcoran of Portland, Oregon, bravely served as the first Oregon Archaeological Society "archival research volunteer" and copied numerous articles on china buttons. Without her help this article would never have gotten off the ground. Alison Helms of Rochester, New York generously provided sources, comments, and a critique of several drafts. Jody Behrbaum, through her web site <http://home.pon.net/Behrbaum/> and personally, provided encouragement, information, and innumerable copies of sources not available elsewhere. Especially important was the original and translation of the *Musée de la Mosaïque et des Emaux* and *Le Grande Encyclopédie*. Jody is truly a professional button researcher. My sister, Anne Sprague Geaudreau, provided much needed information and samples, files of button journals, and made a gift of the hard-bound edition of the China book for this research. The three anonymous reviewers and Judy Tordoff have suggested numerous improvements and found many errors all of which is appreciated. Thanks to all and all remain blameless.

REFERENCES

ADAMS, GEORGE E.
1943 Stencil Buttons. *Just Buttons,* 2(2):6.
1944 *A Stencil Check List.* The Delmo Press, Pascoag, RI.
1945 The Porcelain Family. *National Button Bulletin,* 4(3):184–185.

ADAMS, JANE FORD
1966 A Glossary of Shank Names. *National Button Bulletin,* 25(1):12–17.
1971 Another Sample Card of China Buttons. *National Button Bulletin,* 30(6):316–318.

ADAMS, JANE FORD, AND LILLIAN SMITH ALBERT
1952 A Sample Case from Bapterosses. *National Button Bulletin,* 11(2):81.

ALBERT, LILLIAN SMITH, AND JANE FORD ADAMS
1963 Calico Buttons with Designs of Gold. *National Button Bulletin,* 22(3):132–134.
1970 *Essential Data Concerning China Buttons.* Bound with *Guidelines for Collecting China Buttons* by Ruth Lamm, Beatrice Lorah, Lester Lorah, and Helen W. Schuler. National Button Society of America, Boyertown, PA. Reprinted 1994 by NBS.

ARGYLL, DUKE OF (REPORTER)
1852 Report on Ceramic Manufacturers. In *Exhibition of the Works of Industry of All Nations, 1851, Report of the Juries,* Duke of Argyll, reporter, pp. 538–543. W. Clowes and Sons, London, England.

ARNDT, NANCY
1993 Calico Buttons. *Piece Work,* (March/April):63.

ATTERBURY, PAUL, AND MAUREEN BATKIN
1990 *The Dictionary of Minton.* Antique Collectors' Club, Woodbridge, Suffolk, England.

BARBER, EDWIN ATLEE
1895 *Historical Sketch of the Green Point (N. Y.) Porcelain Works of Charles Cartlidge & Co.* The Clay Worker, Indianapolis, IN.
1909 *The Pottery and Porcelain of the United States.* G. P. Putnam's Sons, New York, NY.

BEHRBAUM, JODY
2001 Calicoes Web Site. <http://www.pobox.com/–behrbaum>.

BOURRY, EMILE
1926 *A Treatise on Ceramic Industries, a Complete Manual for Pottery, Tile, and Brick Manufactures,* 4th revised English edition, Alfred B. Searle, translator. Scott, Greenwood & Son, London, England.

BROMBERG, FRANCINE W., STEVEN J. SHEPARD, BARBARA H. MAGID, PAMELA J. CRESSEY, TIMOTHY DENNÉE, AND BARNARD K. MEANS
2000 "To Find Rest From All Trouble" The Archaeology of the Quaker Burying Ground, Alexandria, Virginia. *Alexandria Archaeology Publication,* No. 120. Alexandria, VA.

CELORIA, FRANCIS
1973 Ceramic Machinery of the 19th Century in the Potteries and Other Parts of Britain. *Staffordshire Archaeology,* 2:11–48.

COLEMAN, ROGER E.
1990 Archeological Investigation for Construction of a Pedestrian Trail and Identification of Laundress Row, Fort Smith Historic Site, Arkansas. National Park Service, *Southwest Cultural Resource Center, Professional Papers,* No. 30. Santa Fe, NM.

DUTTON, HAROLD IRVIN
1984 *The Patent System and Inventive Activity During the Industrial Revolution, 1750–1852.* Manchester University Press, London, England.

FEINMAN, JEFFREY (EDITOR)
1979 *Sears Roebuck and Co., 1909 Catalog.* Ventura Books, New York, NY.

FERGUSON, BOB
1978 Ginghams, Calicoes and Stencils. *Just Buttons,* 36(10&11):193–194.

FERGUSON, JO, AND BOB FERGUSON
1979 Calico Jewels. *Just Buttons,* 37(8 & 9):19–21.

FRANCIS, PETER, JR.
1988 Rocaille Beads. *The Bead Forum,* 12:17–21.

GODDEN, GEOFFREY A.
1982 *Chamberlain-Worcester Porcelain, 1788–1852.* Barrie & Jenkins, London, England.

HARRIS, MYRTLE
1972 The Tools of the Trade. *National Button Bulletin,* 31(3):137–139.

JARGSTORF, SIBYLLE
1993 *Baubles, Buttons and Beads: The Heritage of Bohemia.* Schiffer Publishing, Atglen, PA.

JOHNSON, THOMAS
1969 Buttons. *National Button Bulletin,* 28(5):267–271. Originally published in 1867 in *Report of Artisans* by the Society for the Encouragement of Arts, Manufacturers and Commerce, London, England. First published in *NBB* in 1947.

JOHNSTON, MARGARET
1949 A B C's of Button Collecting. *Just Buttons,* 7(11):275–276.

KETCHUM, WILLIAM C.
1987 *Potters and Potteries of New York State, 1650–1900.*
Syracuse University Press, Syracuse, NY.

KNAB, L.
1889 Bouton. In *Le Grande Encyclopédie Inventaire Raisonné des Sciences, des Letteres et de Arts,* Camille Dreyfus, Secrétary géneral, Vol. 7, pp. 876–882. H. Lamirault et Cie, Paris, France. (Volume date from Library of Congress.)

KOHRS, CECILE T.
1998 Plain Jane Buttons? No, Not REALLY! Button Bytes Light, No. 10, (www.tias.com/articles/buttons).

LAMM, RUTH, BEATRICE LORAH, LESTER LORAH, AND HELEN W. SCHULER
1970 *Guidelines for Collecting China Buttons.* Bound with *Essential Data Concerning China Buttons* by Lillian Smith Albert and Jane Ford Adams. National Button Society of America, Boyertown, PA. Reprinted 1994 by NBS.

LINDBERGH, JENNIE
1999 Buttoning Down Archaeology. *Australasian Historical Archaeology,* 17:50–57.

LINTON, RALPH
1936 *The Study of Man.* Appleton-Century Crofts, New York, NY.

LOCK, CHARLES G. WARNFORD (EDITOR)
1879 *Spon's Encyclopedia of the Industrial Arts, Manufactures and Commercial Products.* E. & F. N. Spon, London, England.

LUSCOMB, SALLY C.
1952 Boutons Fantaisie. *Just Buttons,* 10(12):273.
1967 *The Collector's Encyclopedia of Buttons.* Crown Publishers, New York, NY.
1970 Vertical Hole Buttons. *Just Buttons,* 29(2):55.
1971 Button Measurements. *Just Buttons,* 29(5):129–130.
1972 Agates, 1871. *Just Buttons,* 30(11):627.

MOREY, DOROTHY L.
1940 The Manufacture of Porcelain Calico Buttons. *Hobbies,* 45(1):23.

MUSÉE DE LA MOSAÏQUE ET DES EMAUX
1999 *Musée de la Mosaïque et des Emaux (Historique).* Musée de la Mosaïque et des Emaux, Briare, France.

NATIONAL BUTTON BULLETIN
1985 A Great Find! *National Button Bulletin,* 44(3):108–110.

PEACOCK, PRIMROSE
1978 *Discovering Old Buttons.* Shire Publications, Dyfed, England.

PROSSER, RICHARD B.
1881 *Birmingham Inventors and Inventions: Being a Contribution to the Industrial History of Birmingham.*
The "Journal" Printing Works, Birmingham, England. Reprinted with a new forward by Asa Briggs, 1970 by S. R. Publishers, Wakefield, England.

RICHARDS, S. W.
1969 On Buttons. *National Button Bulletin,* 28(5):275–282. Originally published in 1867 in *Report of Artisans* by the Society for the Encouragement of Arts, Manufacturers and Commerce, London, England. First published in *NBB* in 1947.

RÖNTGEN, ROBERT E.
1981 *Marks on German, Bohemian and Austrian Porcelain, 1710 to the Present.* Shiffer Publishing, Exton, PA

SCHUETZ, MARDITH K.
1969 The History and Archeology of Mission San Juan Capistrano, San Antonio, Texas. Texas State Building Commission, Archeological Program, *Report,* No. 11. Austin.

SCHULER, HELEN W., AND RUTH LAMM
1961 Catalog of Fisheye China Buttons. *National Button Bulletin,* 20(6):264–265.

SNELL, RUTH E.
1955 The Vermiculated Design. *National Button Bulletin,* 14(3):139.

SPRAGUE, LINDA FERGUSON
1983 Artifact Summary Old San Juan Town, 65-SJ-290. In *San Juan Archaeology,* Roderick Sprague, editor, Vol. 1, pp. 249–283. Laboratory of Anthropology, University of Idaho, Moscow.

SPRAGUE, RODERICK
1981 A Functional Classification for Artifacts from 19th and 20th Century Historical Sites. *North American Archaeologist,* 2(3):251–261.
1983 Tile Bead Manufacturing. In Proceedings of the 1982 Glass Bead Conference, Charles F. Hayes III, editor, pp. 167–172. *Rochester Museum and Science Center, Research Records,* No. 16. Rochester, NY.
1988 More on Tile Beads. *The Bead Forum,* 13:3–4.

STEWART, JUDYE
2000 Collectible China Buttons. <http://www.geocities.com/Heartland/Cottage/5399>.

TARBOX, ALICE T.
1949 Stencils. *Just Buttons,* 7(12):292–293.

TOMLINSON, CHARLES
1852 *Cyclopaedia of Useful Arts, Mechanical and Chemical, Manufactures, Mining, and Engineering.* James S. Virtue, London, England.

TORLEY, LAVONNA
1962 Ceramic Buttons. *Just Buttons,* 20(9):171–174.

U.S. TARIFF COMMISSION
1918 The Button Industry. *Tariff Information Series,* No. 4. Washington, DC.

URE, ANDREW (EDITOR)
1861   Tiles and Tesserae. In *Ure's Dictionary of Arts, Manufactures, and Mines, Containing a Clear Exposition of their Principles and Practice*, 5th edition, pp. 884–888. Longman, Green, Longman, and Roberts, London, England.

WASHBURN, H. A.
1944   *Stencils in Chart and Description*. Clyde W. Kennedy, Shelbyville, IN

WATKINS, LURA W.
1950   *Early New England Potters and Their Wares*. Harvard University Press, Cambridge, MA.

RODERICK SPRAGUE
SOUTH FORK PRESS
625 NORTH GARFIELD
MOSCOW, ID 83843-3624

GÉRARD GUSSET

A Preliminary Annotated Bibliography on Electrical Artifacts

Introduction

Devices which produce or use electricity do not often spark an archaeologist's enthusiasm. They often look unusual and hard to identify, and no one seems to know much about them. While some, like the ubiquitous insulator, are often simple to identify, others are far more intriguing and complex. Since expertise is not available and most archaeologists do not have the time or resources to learn about them, these objects often do not get the same degree of attention that other artifacts do. At the end of many excavations, they are often piled together and eventually classified and recorded as "electricals."

Electrical artifacts can tell us a lot; not only about the production and use of electricity in a specific context, but also about the way a specific electrically driven activity or trade was organized and conducted. These artifacts are useful because of their highly specialized nature: most of them were designed and manufactured for a very specific purpose or a very limited number of uses. For example, a "barrel-shaped glass jar Edison primary battery" was probably used for railway signaling purposes; a "200-ampere, 125-volt angled dial rotary switch" was likely used in a heating appliance, such as a cooking range. Electricals are generally found well preserved because they are often made of stable or durable materials such as porcelain, stoneware, glass, bakelite, gutta-percha, copper alloys, and aluminum. They are also relatively easy to identify and date since most of them were patented and well described in catalogues.

This short bibliography is intended to guide the user to a basic corpus of information on those electrical artifacts most often found in archaeological sites. It includes products manufactured or sold in Canada, and emphasizes source documents that meet the following criteria: (1) published material widely available and relatively easy to find; (2) well illustrated to assist with identification and dating; (3) not too technical; and (4) plentiful detailed information with direct relevance to the interpretation of domestic and small industrial archaeological sites. Machinery and supplies from large industrial plants and highly specialized equipment could obviously not be covered here. Documents are grouped under thirteen headings: Bibliographies; Patents; History, Sociology, and Economics; Trade Catalogues; Power Production and Distribution; Batteries and Accumulators; Insulators; Fixtures, Receptacles, and Wiring; Lighting; Domestic Appliances; Motive Power; Electroplating; and Communication and Recording.

The section on trade catalogues is the largest. These documents are a major source of information on brand name electrical supplies. They normally contain detailed illustrations, manufacturers' names, standard trade names and marks, model numbers, materials, dimensions, specifications, and prices. They also often provide useful information in the form of wiring diagrams, technical descriptions of innovative products, directions for installation, explanations of intended purpose and use, and safety precautions. Catalogues from large companies were generally published yearly. By consulting them chronologically, one easily gets a sense of the improvement and evolution of supplies and machines through time. The present selection covers the vast majority of general domestic and industrial supplies marketed from the 1880s to about 1950. Monographs provide a more in-depth explanation on how devices work and how electrical components are put together to function in properly designed setups.

This bibliography is intended for the beginner who wants to learn the basics of electrical technology as it was understood from the 1880s to the 1940s. As the second half of the 20th century unfolded, electricity was no longer a separate alternative in technology. It permeates most modern trades and many new technical activities. Electrical and electronic machinery can no longer be described and understood on the basis of a limited number of discrete electrical components and circuits. Due to the higher degree of specialization and integration, and because of the huge amount of information that has been published, a different approach becomes necessary. Each activity, field, and subfield should then presume a separate and specific quest for information.

Bibliographies

LOWOOD, HENRY
1992 Current Bibliography in the History of Technology (1990). *Technology and Culture* 33:1-211.
Energy conversion: hydraulic engineering, steam-electrical stations, power transmission, lighting, heating and ventilation, refrigeration, and direct-conversion power plants. Electronics and electro-mechanical technology: tools, machines, instruments, timekeepers, and automatic controls. Communication and records: telegraph, telephone, radio, phonographs and recorders, and photography.

THE SOCIETY FOR THE HISTORY OF TECHNOLOGY
1991 An Annotated Index to Volumes 1 through 25 of Technology and Culture 1959-1984. *Technology and Culture* 32(2).
Lighting, railroads, communications, engineers and scientists, industry, power production and transmission, electrical technology and science, electrochemical technology, electrocution, electrohorticulture, and electronics industry.

Patents

FISET, RICHARD
1993 *Record of Canadian Patents 1824-1891– Electricity.* Nessy Publications, Quebec, Quebec.
Canadian patent numbers 1,670 to 37,956, with line illustrations, list of inventors, and index by subject.

History, Sociology, and Economics of Electricity

DENIS, LEO G.
1918 *Electric Generation and Distribution in Canada.* Commission of Conservation Canada, Ottawa, Ontario.
Electrical plants by province, with a brief description of equipment, power, fuel, value of assets, rates, and the distribution network, photos, drawings, maps, and index.

HALL OF HISTORY FOUNDATION
1989 *The General Electric Story: 1876-1986.* Schenectady, NY.
Illustrated history of the company, history of electrification, bibliography, and index.

HAUSMAN, WILLIAM J., AND JOHN L. NEUFELD
1989 Engineers and Economists: Historical Perspectives on the Pricing of Electricity. *Technology and Culture* 30(1):83-104.
The economics of the electrical utility industry, contrasting view of engineers and economists, cost and fare structures, fixed costs, and differential rates.

HUNTER, P. V.
1916 Development of Electric Power Stations. *The Electrician* 77(24):838.
A concise history of power production in Europe.

INSTITUTE OF ELECTRICAL AND ELECTRONICS ENGINEERS-CANADIAN REGION
1985 *Electricity: The Magic Medium.* The Institute of Electrical and Electronics Engineers, New York, NY.
Commemorates the achievements of the Canadian electrical industry over the past 100 years or so. Historical highlights, electrical engineering and technology education, and production of electricity; past, present, and future.

NYE, DAVID E.
1990 *Electrifying America: Social Meanings of a New Technology.* Massachusetts Institute of Technology Press, Cambridge.
Social and economic impacts of electrification.

SCHURR, SAM H., CALVIN C. BURWELL, WARREN D. DEVINE, AND SIDNEY SONENBLUM
1990 *Electricity in the American Economy: Agent of Technological Progress.* Greenwood Press, Westport, CT.
A history of the technological and economic impacts of electrification on many fast-evolving trades in the United States, such as mining, transportation, and entertainment.

WALKER, DAVID F., AND JAMES H. BATER
1974 *Industrial Development in Southern Ontario.* University of Waterloo, Waterloo, Ontario.
Many chapters on the electrification of various manufacturing processes.

Trade Catalogues

AMALGAMATED ELECTRIC
1956 *Wiring Supplies Catalogue, Bulletin No. 1–Wiring Devices.* Amalgamated Electric Corporation Limited, Montreal, Quebec.
Wiring devices, domestic lighting, and switches.

ARMY AND NAVY STORES
1969 *Yesterday's Shopping: The Army and Navy Stores Catalogue 1907,* introduction by Alison Adburgham. David and Charles, Newton Abbot, Devon, England.
Domestic appliances, batteries, bells, games, fans, heating, flashlights, lamps and parts, time pieces, medical supplies, shaving mirrors, hair brushes, toys, machine models, electricians' tools, telephones, and electroplated goods.

BENJAMIN ELECTRIC MANUFACTURING COMPANY OF CANADA

1926 *Benjamin Electric Products–Catalogue C25.* Benjamin Electric Manufacturing Company of Canada, Toronto, Ontario.

General catalogue; domestic and industrial supplies.

CANADIAN GENERAL ELECTRIC

[1915] *Electrical Supplies–Catalogue No. 15.* Canadian General Electric Company, Toronto, Ontario.

General catalogue; all domestic and industrial supplies with index.

1927 *The CGE Farm Book–Electricity in the Farm.* Canadian General Electric Company, Toronto, Ontario.

Lighting, motors, dairy machines, brooders, ranges, irons, and other domestic appliances; battery chargers, radios, and wiring devices.

1929 *Electrical Merchandise–Catalogue No. 29.* Canadian General Electric Company, Toronto, Ontario.

General catalogue; all domestic and industrial supplies; index.

1940 *Motors. Catalogue 40M.* Canadian General Electric Company, Toronto, Ontario.

Illustrations of all CGE motor types, applications of motors and controls, DC generators, and induction motor-generators.

1949 *Wiring Devices–Catalogue 49WD.* Canadian General Electric Company, Toronto, Ontario.

Lampholders and accessories, wiring devices, switches, signaling, terminals and boards, indoor bus supports, power line hardware, fluorescent lighting, and insulators.

1952 *Wiring Supplies, Power Apparatus–Catalogue 53G.* Canadian General Electric Company, Toronto, Ontario.

Air conditioning, domestic appliances, aviation equipment, power tools, water treatment, conduits and fittings, electronic equipment, flashlights, batteries, generators, rectifiers, welding equipment, insulators, meters, lighting, locomotives, motors, controls, magnets, power line hardware and tools, raceways, signaling equipment, switches, transformers, wires and cables, and wiring devices.

CANADIAN WESTINGHOUSE ELECTRIC COMPANY

1960 *Canadian Westinghouse Industrial Apparatus–Catalogue H-30-000.* Canadian Westinghouse Electric Company, Hamilton, Ontario.

Descriptions, specifications, and illustrations of motors, controls, switches and breakers, ducts, panelboards, transformers, and lighting devices.

GENERAL ELECTRIC

1930 *General Electric Catalogue GEA-600A.* General Electric Company, Schenectady, NY.

Generators, converters, motors, domestic and industrial fuses, switches, lighting, resistors, wiring devices, steel furnaces, controls, conduits, and glazes for crucibles.

[1935] *Electric Equipment for Industry. Catalog GEA-621.* General Electric Company, Schenectady, NY.

Motors types, generators, and specifications.

GRAYBAR ELECTRIC COMPANY

1948 *General Catalog No. 103.* R. R. Donnelly & Sons, Chicago.

Domestic and industrial supplies.

NORTHERN ELECTRIC COMPANY

[1917] *General Catalogue No. 3–Wire and Cables, Telephone Apparatus, Electrical Supplies.* Northern Electric Company, Montreal, Quebec.

Domestic and industrial supplies; index.

[1921] *General Catalogue No. 4–Electrical Supplies.* Northern Electric Company, Montreal, Quebec.

Domestic and industrial supplies; index.

[1925] *General Catalogue No. 5.* Northern Electric Company, Montreal, Quebec.

Domestic and industrial supplies; index.

1937 *Electrical Supplies–Catalogue No. 7.* Northern Electric Company Limited, Montreal, Quebec.

Domestic and industrial wiring, lighting, and insulators.

1940 *Electrical Supplies–Catalogue No. 2241.* Northern Electric Company, Montreal, Quebec.

Domestic and industrial supplies and their specifications.

1953 *Illumination–Industrial: Catalogue I-53.* Northern Electric Company, Montreal, Quebec.

Incandescent, mercury, and fluorescent tubes and bulbs.

n.d. *Materials and Tools for Line Construction and Maintenance, Overhead and Underground.* Northern Electric Company, Montreal, Quebec.

Power lines: tools, wiring, insulators, and poles.

SEARS, ROEBUCK & CO.

1897 *Sears Roebuck Catalogue 1897.* Sears, Roebuck & Co., Chicago, IL. Reprinted 1993, Chelsea House, New York, NY.

Electrical bells, motors, batteries, rings, switches, and other goods; index.

1908 *The Great Price Maker, Catalogue no. 117–1908.* Sears, Roebuck & Co., Chicago, IL. Reprinted 1971, Digest Books, Northfield, IL.

Domestic appliances, toys, batteries, small motors, telephony, bells, wiring supplies, magnets, electricians' tools, insulators, meters, lightbulbs, and lightning arresters; index.

1927 *The 1927 Edition of the Sears Roebuck Catalogue.* Reprinted 1970, Crown Publishers, New York, NY.

Domestic appliances and accessories; index.

T. Eaton Company

1927 *Eaton's Spring and Summer Catalogue 1927.* T. Eaton Co. Toronto, Ontario. Reprinted 1971, Musson Book Company, Toronto, Ontario.

Lightbulbs, cookers, wiring devices, lamps, sewing machines, curling tongues, and washing machines; index.

Westinghouse Electric & Manufacturing Company

[1906] *Detail and Supply Apparatus–Perpetual Catalogue No. 3001* (1906-1916). Westinghouse Electric & Manufacturing Company, Pittsburgh, PA.

All domestic and industrial supplies, their description and specifications; index.

1939 *General Catalogue 1939-1940.* Westinghouse Electric & Manufacturing Company, East Pittsburgh, PA.

Specifications, technical information and prices for domestic insulators, fuses, motors, wiring, lighting (bulb and tubes), domestic appliances, batteries, medical supplies and X-ray equipment, power line equipment, switches, speed reducers, vacuum tubes, battery chargers, rectifiers, and radios; index.

Wood, Alexander & James

[1923] *Jobbers of Electrical Supplies–Catalogue No. 23.* Wood, Alexander & James, Hamilton, Ontario.

General catalogue of industrial supplies.

[1938] *Wholesale Electrical Supplies–Catalogue No. 38.* Wood, Alexander & James, Hamilton, Ontario.

General catalogue of domestic and industrial supplies.

Power Production and Distribution

Blackwell, F. O.

1906 The Power Plant of the Electric Development Company of Ontario. *The Electrician* 57(19):746.

General technical description of the plant; construction, equipment, and operation.

Buck, H. W.

1906 The Electrical Plant of the Canadian Niagara Power Company. *The Electrician* 57(19):738.

General technical description of the plant; construction, equipment, and operation.

U.S. Department of Agriculture

1956 *Description of Units, Specifications and Drawings for 7.2/12.5 KV Line Construction.* Washington, DC.

Many drawings of aerial lines: poles, cables, guy wires, insulators, and related equipment.

Batteries and Accumulators

Crawter, Frank

1916 Some Accumulators of the Past. *The Electrician* 77(24):829.

Principles and operation of some types of chemical accumulators.

Schallenberg, Richard H.

1982 *Bottled Energy–Electrical Engineering and the Evolution of Chemical Energy Storage.* American Philosophical Society, Philadelphia, PA.

The evolution of the technology and industry of batteries and accumulators in the U.S. between 1880 and 1970. Commercialization, the role of batteries in transportation, electrical cars, and alkaline batteries.

Insulators

Brown, Gerald

1972 *Collectible Porcelain Insulators.* Gerald Brown, Two Buttes, CO.

Insulators for power lines and telegraph, mainly pin-type insulators, notes on electrical porcelain, drawings for each specimen, dimensions, model numbers, some descriptions from trade catalogues, and marks.

Canada, Department of Energy, Mines and Resources

1968 *Ceramic Plants in Canada.* Mineral Resources Division, Department of Energy, Mines and Resources, Ottawa, Ontario.

A listing of ceramic plants and their products; mostly insulators.

Cranfill, Gary G.

n.d. *The Collectors' Guide for Glass Insulators–Revised,* 2 volumes. Gary G. Cranfill, Sacramento, CA.

Various types of glass insulators: markings, dimensions, and drawings.

n.d. *Dictionary of Glass–Ceramic Insulators.* Gary G. Cranfill, Sacramento, CA.

Various types of ceramic insulators: markings, dimensions, and drawings.

Cranfill, Gary G., and Greg A. Kareofelas

1973 *The Glass Insulator–A Comprehensive Reference.* Gary G. Cranfill and Greg A. Kareofelas, Sacramento, CA.

Glass insulators: markings, dimensions, and drawings.

Lauckner, Mark

1995 *Canadian Railway Communications Insulators: 1880-1920.* Gyote Publishing, Mayne Island, British Columbia.

A brief history of Canadian railway communications, insulator design, glass insulator manufacturing, glass mold development, porcelain insulator manufacturing, threading, numbering system, marks, color pictures for classifying colored glass insulators, other references, bibliography, rarity, and value guide.

McINTOSH, COLIN
n.d. *Canadian Insulators & Communication Lines.* Colin McIntosh, n.p.
Descriptions, drawings, and photographs of several types of telegraph and power insulators. Short notes on companies across the country.

MILHOLLAND, MARION C.
n.d. *Glass Insulator Reference Book.* Marion C. Milholland, Sequim, WA.
Various types of insulators: markings, dimensions, and drawings.

MILLS, BRENT
1970 *Porcelain Insulators and How They Grew.* Canfield and Tack, Rochester, NY.
Various insulators: markings, dimensions, and drawings.

PARMELEE, CULLEN W.
1951 *Ceramic Glazes.* Industrial Publications, Chicago, IL.
Insulating properties of glazes, electrical porcelains, and leadless glazes.

WOODWARD, N. R.
1988 *The Glass Insulator in America–1988 Report.* N. R. Woodward, Houston, TX.
Discusses most common brands of American insulators from about 1865. Short histories of Brookfield, early Boston-area production, Hemingray, Witall, Tatum, Armstrong and Kerr, Gayner and Lynchburg, Pyrex insulators, production in the Denver area, and production on the West Coast. Identification of and basic information on little-known company names, telegraph and telephone company names, high-voltage insulator names, supply companies, glass insulators in Canada and other countries, and insulator styles and marks. Section drawings and dimensions of selected models, and U.S. Patents for molded glass insulators.

Fixtures, Receptacles, and Wiring

BLACK, ROBERT M.
1983 *The History of Electric Wires and Cables.* Peter Peregrinus/Museum of Science, London, England.
Early telegraph cables, lighting cables, paper insulated cables, three-phase cables, house-wiring cables, telephone cables, enameled wires, special purpose cables, etc.

COOK, ARTHUR L.
1933 *Electric Wiring for Lighting and Power Installation.* John Wiley & Sons, New York, NY.

Lighting systems, power systems, and interior wiring.

GRAHAM, FRANK D.
1946 *Audels Handy Book of Practical Electricity with Wiring Diagrams–Ready References for Students and All Electrical Workers.* Audels, New York, NY.
Electrical theory, batteries and cells, wires, cables, insulators, electrolysis, electroplating, transformers, converters, rectifiers, DC apparatus (internal and external), underground wiring supplies, marine wiring, signs, lighting (fluorescent and neon), AC and DC motors, dynamos, alternators, winding and repairs, power stations, power tools, welding, ignition, vehicles, pumps, elevators, cranes, bells, telegraphs, telephones, radios, motion picture projectors, heating and refrigeration, compressors, and resuscitation equipment.

SCHROEDER, FRED E. H.
1986 More 'Small Things Forgotten': Domestic Electrical Plugs and Receptacles 1881-1931. *Technology and Culture* 27(3):525-543.
Domestic wiring (1881-1931): accessories, plugs, and receptacles.

UNDERWRITERS' NATIONAL ELECTRIC ASSOCIATION
1908 List of Electrical Fittings that have been Examined and Approved by the Underwriters' National Electric Association for Use under the Rules and Requirements of the National Board of the Fire Underwriters for the Installation of Electric Wiring and Apparatus. Underwriters' National Electric Association, Chicago, IL.
Product names for many wiring devices, model numbers for approved products, American manufacturers, and UL labels.

Lighting (Incandescent Lamps, Arc Lamps, Gas Discharge Lamps)

ANDREWS, LEONARD
1906 Long Flame Arc Lamps. *The Electrician* 57(3):87; 57(4):51; 57(4):129; 57(5):164.
A series of short articles on the development of arc-lamp machines.

BOHM, C. R.
1906 Modern Forms of Electrical Incandescent Lamps. *The Electrician* 57(23):894.
A brief survey of the latest bulb designs, bulb shapes, and filament material.

BRIGHT, ARTHUR
1949 The *Electric-Lamp Industry: Technological Change and Economic Development from 1800 to 1947.* Macmillan Company, New York, NY.
Technological evolution in the manufacture of incandescent, arc, and ionization lighting in America.

COX, HENRY BARTHOLOMEW
1979 Hot Hairpin in a Bottle: The Beginning of Incandescence. *Nineteenth Century* 5(3):45-49.
History of incandescent lighting in the United Kingdom and the United States; discusses the various substances used for filaments.

DAVIS, PEARCE
1949 *The Development of the American Glass Industry.* Harvard University Press, Cambridge, MA.
Brief history of the technology and manufacturing of lightbulbs.

DUBUISSON, BERNARD
1968 *Encyclopédie Pratique de la Construction et du Bâtiment*, Tome 2. Librairie Aristide Quillet, Paris, France.
General and industrial engineering, public works, public lighting, and public transportation.

THE ELECTRICIAN
1903 Westinghouse Bremer Arc Lamps. *The Electrician* 51(15):615.
Development of a new type of arc lamp.

O'DEA, W. T.
1958 *A Short History of Lighting.* Science Museum, London, England.
History and construction of lighting devices: incandescent, arc, and ionization lamps.

PATERSON, CLIFFORD C.
1916 The Evolution of the Electric Lamp. *The Electrician* 77(24):822.
A short technological history of early-20th-century incandescent lamps. Discusses bulb shapes and new material for filaments.

PHILLIPS, CHARLES JOHN
1960 *Glass–Its Industrial Applications. Reinhold*, New York, NY.
Technology and manufacture of various types of electrical lightbulbs and electron tubes: incandescent, vapor discharge, projection, photography, heating, radio receiving, power tubes, cathode ray, and television.

SHAND, E. B.
1958 *Glass Engineering Handbook.* McGraw-Hill, New York, NY.
Technology, manufacture, and properties of glass for lightbulbs, electron tubes, and insulators.

STEINMETZ, P.
1903 The Mercury Arc. *The Electrician* 51(4):171.
Brief description of the design and operation of the mercury vapor lamp.

WOODHEAD, E. I., C. SULLIVAN, AND GÉRARD GUSSET
1984 Lighting Devices in the National Reference Collection, Parks Canada. Parks Canada, *Studies in Archaeology, Architecture and History.* Ottawa, Ontario.
A short history of lighting devices; description of operating principles; terminology of components; and incandescent, arc, and ionization lamps. Some archaeological specimens included.

Domestic Appliances

ARTMAN, E. TOWNSEND
1996 *Toasters 1909-1960.* Schiffer, Atglen, PA.
Describes and illustrates many forms by type: perchers, pinchers, flatbeds, floppers, etc. Includes novelties and discusses all major brands and some rarities.

GORDON, BOB
1984 *Early Electrical Appliances.* Shire Publications, Aylesbury, England.
Photographs and drawings of appliances for heating, refrigeration, cooking, water heating, cleaning and washing, health and beauty, etc., with brief descriptions and historical comments.

MILLER, GARY, AND K. M. SCOTTY MITCHELL
1991 *Price Guide to Collectible Kitchen Appliances.* Wallace-Homestead, Radnor, PA.
Coffee makers, combination appliances, cooking appliances, irons, mixers and whips, novelties, toasters, waffle irons, sandwich grilles, and bibliography; index.

PEET, LOUISE J., AND LENORE E. SATER
1934 *Household Equipment.* John Wiley & Sons, New York, NY.
Description and illustration of common electrical equipment in the standard household including ranges, small equipment, refrigerators, cleaning equipment, and lighting; index.

Motive Power

FYNN, V. A.
1906 The Classification of Alternate-Current Motors. *The Electrician* 57(6):204; 57(8):284; 57(9):329.
Series of articles on the design and operation of the best known types of AC motors, with wiring diagrams. Lists advantages and disadvantages of each type.

KLINE, RONALD
1987 Science and Engineering Theory in the Invention and Development of the Induction Motor, 1880-1900. *Technology and Culture* 28(2):283-313.

Theoretical background and invention of the induction motor, engineering, research, and development from 1888 to 1891.

PARSHALL, H. F.
1916 Electric Traction. *The Electrician* 77(24):824.
Motive power and transportation.

PENN, E.
1987 Fifty Electric Motors. *Electronics & Technology Today* (Sept.):11-13.
Short discussion of the various type of electric motors normally found in a typical modern home with some theory.

WALKER, MILES
1916 Dynamo-Electric Machinery, 1878-1916. *The Electrician* 77(24):817.
New developments in direct-current machines.

WORMELL, R.
1897 *Electricity in the Service of Man–Popular and Practical Treatise on the Application of Electricity in Modern Life.* Cassell and Company, London, England.
Many engravings and descriptions of machines and apparatus, both domestic and industrial, including the history of power producing machines for AC and DC, dynamos, alternators, transformers, batteries, accumulators, lighting, motive power, electrochemistry and metallurgy, and telephone and telegraph.

Electroplating

HASLUCK, PAUL N.
1908 *Electroplating–With Numerous Engravings and Diagrams.* Cassell and Company, New York, NY.
Illustrates and describes shop equipment such as vats, batteries, dynamos, measuring devices, shop machines and accessories, and hand tools; also explains procedures.

REETZ, HENRY C.
1911 *Electroplating–A Treatise for the Beginner and for the Most Experienced Electroplater.* Popular Mechanics Company, Chicago, IL.
Principles and apparatus, shop equipment, cleaning, copper-, nickel-, silver-, and gold-plating.

Communication and Recording (Telegraphy, Telephony, Wireless, Sound and Picture Recording)

BRIGHTS, CHARLES
1916 The Story of the Submarine Cable. *The Electrician* 77(24):801.

A short history (including new developments) of submarine cables for communication.

COHEN, B. S.
1916 Long-Distance Telephony. *The Electrician* 77(24):814.
The operation of long-distance telephone systems; new designs and schematic diagrams.

FLEMING, J. A.
1916 Radiotelegraphy: A Retrospect of Twenty Years. *The Electrician* 77(24):831.
A short history of technological advances in early-20th-century wireless telegraphy transmitters, receivers, and related apparatus.

HARRISON, H. H.
1916 The Story of Land Telegraphy. *The Electrician* 77(24):798.
Overview of telegraph systems on land including technical descriptions and schematic diagrams.

KINGSBURY, J. E.
1916 The Story of the Telephone. *The Electrician* 77(24):812.
Overview of telephone systems with technical descriptions and schematic diagrams.

KNAPPEN, RON, AND MARY KNAPPEN
1978 *History and Identification of Old Telephones.* R. Knappen, Galesville, WI.
Terminology, history, description, and illustrations of typical phones; description and identification by parts; switch boards; bell boxes; index of manufacturers many period illustrations.

MARCONI, ELECTRONIC TUBES AND COMPONENTS DIVISION
1951 *Radiotron Characteristics Manual.* Marconi, Electronic Tubes and Components Division, Toronto, Ontario.
Interpretation of technical data, classification, characteristics, and ratings of receiving tubes, special-purpose tubes, television picture tubes, non-standard tubes, outline drawings of tubes and tube sockets, and typical circuits.

READ, OLIVER, AND WALTER L. WELCH
1959 *From Tin Foil to Stereo.* Howard W. Soms, Indianapolis, IN.
Description and illustration of electrical apparatus and machines for telegraphy, telephony, radio, motion pictures, and sound recording.

GÉRARD GUSSET
MATERIAL CULTURE RESEARCH
ONTARIO SERVICE CENTRE
PARKS CANADA
1600 LIVERPOOL COURT
OTTAWA, ONTARIO K1A 0M5
CANADA

Telling Time for the Electrified: An Introduction to Porcelain Insulators and the Electrification of the American Home

Adrian T. Myers

ABSTRACT

As archaeologists increasingly survey and excavate at sites from the late 19th to the mid-20th centuries, they more commonly encounter artifacts that the standard guides do not consider. Included in this class of "too recent" artifacts are the material remnants of the early electrification of the American household. Particularly ubiquitous electrical artifacts are the small white porcelain knobs, tubes, and cleats used in "knob and tube" wiring systems. Meticulous research by insulator collectors, notably Jack Tod and Elton Gish, is a significant boon to the archaeologist, and their work shows that these artifacts can often be dated and provenanced. This article introduces some of the social and material aspects of electrification that are particularly relevant to the archaeologist, and elaborates on electrical porcelain used in the wiring of buildings—one class of artifacts out of several related to electrification.

Introduction

During the period of approximately 1880–1930, rapid developments in materials and distribution technologies transformed electricity from a feared and, for some, ostensibly magical novelty into a widely available, much-discussed, and must-have commodity. Scientists had experimented with electricity since the 17th century, but it was not until late in the 19th century that they would manage to generate and deliver it in a viable manner to people who would have practical uses for it (Edison 1885). Electrification's spread followed the precepts of modern capitalism: it was privately owned and delivered to paying customers. These customers were primarily in urban centers: beginning with municipalities (for street lighting) and wealthy home owners in the 1880s, trolley companies in the 1890s, and factories and department stores in the 1900s. The gimmick of attracting shoppers to electrically lighted store displays lost some momentum once electricity became more affordable and widely available to the average urban homeowner in the 1910s. See Table 1 for "milestones in electrification."

Most American townspeople and farmers lived with the now seemingly archaic oil and gas lighting for some time longer. Although some homes and farms had personal generators or battery-operated appliances, for the most part rural areas, except for settlements and buildings fortuitously located near existing transmission lines, stayed "in the dark" until the second half of the 1930s. It would take federal government action in the form of Roosevelt's 1935 New Deal-inspired Rural Electrification Administration to kick start the unprofitable process of providing electricity to the country's planters and townspeople. The impact of the arrival of electricity to the American home should not be underestimated. As Schroeder (1986) suggests, electrical technology led to the "conversion of our nation's households from hand labor and inconvenient fuels to automation and boundless flexibility."

This period, as archaeologists of the more recent past are well aware, is part of an extended moment that saw a formidable increase in the amount of things designed, patented, manufactured, distributed, discarded, and generally available to the discerning consumer. A second industrial revolution—this time electrical—was under way. The moving assembly line was perfected by about 1915, and with it Model T automobiles and many other products were being manufactured at faster rates and in greater numbers than ever before. The industry producing the infrastructure for electrification was no different from any other industry of this period. Once the electrification of the average American household became the norm, competing companies produced many competing products.

The variability of available products, however, does not stop productive analysis of the material culture of turn-of-the-century electrification. Patterns of use do emerge. Some forms were more successful than others, and those became standardized. When Thomas Edison experimented

Table 1. Electrification milestones.

Year	Event	Source(s)
1865	Production of pin-type glass electrical insulators begins	Miller 2000:15
1876	Arc lighting first used in public areas and streets	Woodhead et al. 1984:75
1879	First practical incandescent light bulb	Devine 1983:354
1882	Direct current (DC) first marketed as a commodity	Devine 1983:354
1882	Incandescent light bulb commercially available	Nordhaus 1997:37
1882	Introduction of cords, plugs and receptacles	Schroeder 1986:526
1883	First electric motors used in manufacturing	Devine 1983:353–354
1884	First steam powered electric turbine	Devine 1983:354
1886	Alternating current (AC) available for lighting	Devine 1983:354
1888	First electric trolley	Hilton 1969:124
1888	First AC motor	Devine 1983:354
1890	Edison first mass manufactures light bulbs	General Electric 2010
1891	First AC power transmission for industrial use	Devine 1983:354
1897	National Electrical Code (NEC) first published	Tod 1977:15
1904	Invention of the parallel two-blade plug	Schroeder 1986:531–532
1904	Introduction of appliances connected to lamp sockets	Schroeder 1986:542
1904	First electric underground trolley (subway)	Hilton 1969:127
1917	Sockets standardized to two-blade style and T-shaped	Schroeder 1986:536, 542
1922	Red neon lights appear in commercial advertising	Woodhead et al. 1984:77
1931	End of lamp-socket appliances	Schroeder 1986:542
1935	Sports played under lights at night for first time	General Electric 2010
1935	Rural Electrification Administration (REA) established	Nye 1990:24
1950s	High intensity incandescent lights used in public areas	Woodhead et al. 1984:75
1962	First three-pronged (grounded) plug	Schroeder 1986:542

with different methods for connecting a light bulb to its power source, his screw-in base approach was only one idea from a field of competitors vying to solve this potentially lucrative problem. Edison's 1881 screw-in base did become the standard, and remains the same to this day. (Edison's success also created the social space for decades of bad jokes.)

The light-bulb socket struggle was an early "format war," akin to the later battles of the 8-track tape versus the compact cassette in the 1970s, and of Blu-ray DVD versus HD DVD in the 2000s (the compact cassette winning the former, and Blu-ray the latter). Even in Edison's lifetime there were format battles fought over everything from the shape of plugs and sockets—parallel two-blade versus T-shaped (Figure 1)—to whether direct current (DC) or alternating current (AC) would most efficiently and safely deliver electricity to the consumer (Schroeder 1986).

Confusion over competing formats would come to be lessened significantly through Herbert Hoover's drive for standardization in industry and technology (Hoover 1924).

Early American Electrification and the First Electrical Porcelain

For effective generation, transmission, and end use of electricity to occur, every electric circuit requires an arrangement of conductors and insulators. The *conductors* allow electricity to flow, and the *insulators* block that flow. A copper ingot, for example, makes an excellent conductor, and a piece of glass or plastic makes an excellent insulator. Electrical wire might be described as an *insulated conductor*, since the inner conducting material (metal wire) is sheathed in an outer insulating material (generally paper, cloth, or plastic). A light switch is a great conductor when toggled

Figure 1. T-shaped plug receptacle (General Electric 1925:34).

to the "on" position. A *resistor* is any component that, by design, introduces a resistance to the flow of electricity. The filament in an incandescent light bulb, though not a resistor per se, is more resistive than the electrical wire leading to it. It resists the flow of electricity in the circuit and thus turns electrical energy into heat and light energy.

Electrical potential is most simply defined as the difference in electrical charge (measured in volts) between two points in a circuit, and a *short circuit* may be defined as an unintentional, and potentially damaging, connection between two points in a circuit. If there is ever insufficient insulation or very low resistance between two points of different potential in any electrical system, there will be a flow of excess current and a short circuit will occur; thus, if the two metal wires bringing electricity to a household are improperly insulated from each other and come into contact, there will be a short circuit. Since a short circuit marks the end of the successful transmission of electricity, it is paramount that electrical wires and components be

sufficiently insulated wherever the system calls for it. It is, of course, equally important that the conductors conduct. See Powell (1995:10–39) for a general introduction to electricity and electric circuits.

Some early experimentation in delivering electricity to customers used insulators made of wood and other materials to separate wires from each other and wires from poles and building materials. This practice, common during the period of approximately 1880–1890, seemed perhaps a logical extension of the use of wooden insulators in wiring for telegraphs. Wood is, in fact, a decent electrical insulator, but only when it is perfectly dry. Wood is a porous material and thus absorbs water easily; and since water is a good conductor, a wet wooden insulator will likely short circuit. A second problem with using wood as an insulator is that, though dry wood is an adequate insulator of electrical current, it catches fire at a relatively low temperature. A short circuit in an unfused or poorly fused circuit will quickly generate significant heat, and heat emanating from metal wires attached to wooden insulators leads to fires. An article in an 1892 trade magazine discussed the fact that fire insurance companies were beginning to demand that insulators be made of porcelain rather than "wood, now in general use" (Tod 1977:12). Initially, individual insurance companies set their own standards for electrical wiring. In 1895 there were at least five recognized standards (Grant 1995:95). This changed in 1896, when insurers cooperated to form what is now known as the National Fire Protection Association, which released the first National Electrical Code in 1897. Porcelain, as was soon acknowledged, is cheap, strong, nonflammable, and highly resistive to the flow of electricity; and thus with the support of the insurers it found many electrical applications, as indeed it still does today.

During the mid-1890s, pressure from fire insurance companies resulted in increased regulation and standardization of electrical components. This, combined with a general increase in the number of customers eager for electricity, created significant demand for insulators made of porcelain, or "electrical porcelain." This marked the beginning of what would come to be known as "knob and tube" wiring, the predominant method of wiring buildings from about 1890 to 1930 (Figures 2–14). In knob-and-tube wiring, "knobs" (Figures 2–6) and "cleats" (Figures 3 and 7–9) were used to run wiring along walls, ceilings, and beams, and "tubes" (Figures 6, 10, and 11) were used to run wires through beams. The simple principle of the three forms is that they insulated flammable wooden building materials from the electrical and heat potential inherent in the electrified wires. Excerpts from a 1917 textbook on electrical wiring are useful here:

The cheapest form of concealed wiring is the knob and tube system. The wires are run beneath the floors or in the partitions and are supported on porcelain insulators or knobs where the wires are run parallel to the floor joists or studding, and pass through porcelain tubes where crossing beams, partitions, etc. (Cook 1917:206).

The system is used chiefly in frame buildings (dwellings, etc.), where a cheap piece of work is desired. The use of the knob and tube system is prohibited by the local rules of many large cities. It cannot be used for fire-proof buildings or for damp places. With this system, the wires are not protected from mechanical injury, and there is always the possibility that they may be damaged by workmen during construction or by rats after the house is in use. The wires may sag against beams, lath, etc., or they may be covered by shavings or other inflammable material during construction so that an overheating of the wires or a short circuit might start a fire (Cook 1917:207).

The knobs may be either solid or split … and must keep the wires at least 1 in. above the surface wired over. Knobs are generally held by wire nails using a leather washer or nail head to prevent breaking the knob. The tubes have a head at one end to prevent their being displaced. The wire used must be rubber-insulated (Cook 1917:207).

In running the circuits, the wires must be kept as far apart as possible, separated at least 5 in. and run on different studding wherever possible. The wires must be supported at least every 4.5 ft and at shorter intervals if they are liable to be disturbed (Cook 1917:208).

This system is used for small branch circuits, where appearance is of no importance, as in cellars, and also used frequently for heavier circuits, for factories (Cook 1917:209).

The advantages of open wiring are that it is cheap and accessible and can be easily changed as required. On the other hand, the wires are not protected, and are liable to mechanical injury (Cook 1917:209).

Being the cheapest and easiest form of electrical wiring, knob and tube ruled the electrification of America through the 1920s. The knob-and-tube boom, however, ended abruptly with the onset of the Great Depression in 1929, when new construction halted and another round of more rigid building codes was widely instituted (Grant 1995). Interestingly, changing perceptions and standards of fire safety mark both the beginning and the end of knob-and-tube wiring. Knob-and-tube wiring continued to be used in some, especially rural, areas until about the 1950s, and remnants of this type of wiring system are to this day commonly seen in basements and attics across America (Figure 2).

Electrical Porcelain Manufacture

Electrical porcelain was manufactured either by the "wet" process or the "dry" process. The wet process used wet clay and either multipart molds (for knobs and cleats) or extrusion (for tubes), and the dry process used drier clay and multipart molds. The dry process produced porcelain that was more porous, and thus less insulating, than the wet process, the result being that only wet process–produced porcelain was used for high-voltage applications. Knobs were almost always finished with a white or clear glaze, and cleats were sometimes glazed and sometimes unglazed. Early tubes were glazed brown or a grayish white, and later tubes, typically after 1900, were mostly unglazed. Additionally, in some catalogs glazed tubes cost about 50% more than unglazed tubes. The porcelain was kiln fired, most commonly in beehive-style kilns.

Research to date suggests that ascertaining the method of manufacture of electrical porcelain artifacts is not useful for identifying the manufacturer or for dating these artifacts. Spurred on by companies in competition with each other, over time innovation seems to have occurred more in the features and functions of electrical porcelain items than in their composition or method of manufacture. The brief summary of manufacture above is based on Tod (1977:63–67), and the reader is directed to that reference for a more in-depth treatment of this topic.

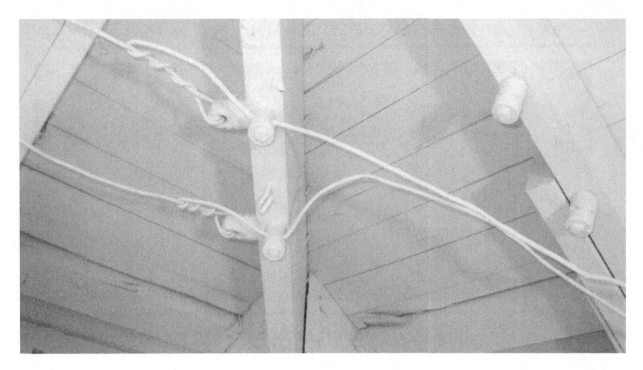

Figure 2. Disused knob-and-tube open wiring above the author's desk at the Stanford Archaeology Center. (Photo by author, 2010.)

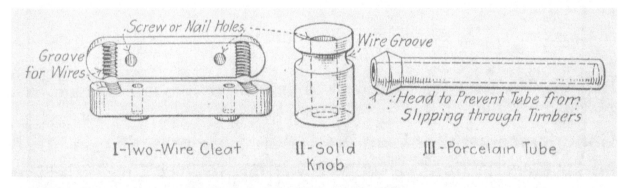

Figure 3. Illustration of a cleat, a knob, and a tube (Croft 1920:172).

Figure 4. Nail knob with nail still present, excavated at Stanford University, courtesy of Laura Jones. (Photo by author, 2010.)

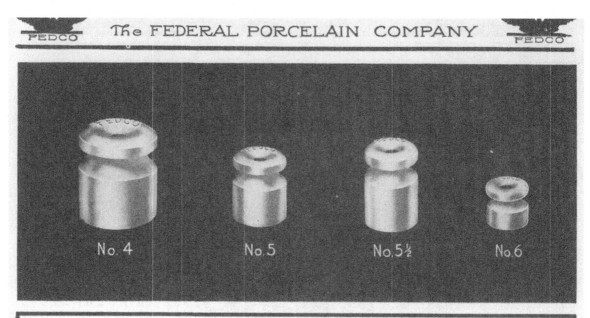

The FEDERAL PORCELAIN COMPANY

SOLID KNOBS
WHITE GLAZE STANDARD

Catalog Number	Height, Inches	Diameter, Inches	Hole, Inches	Groove, Inches	Quantity per Barrel	Shipping Weight Lbs. per Barrel	Code Word	Price per 1,000
4	1 11/16	1 1/2	3/8	3/8	2,200	490	Abroad	$22 00
4, 2-groove Tel. Knob	(See Telephone Knobs, page 13.)							
*4 1/2	1 7/8	1 1/2	3/8	7/16	1,900	475	Abscond	25 00
5	1 1/4	1	1/4	5/16	6,000	480	Absence	13 00
5 1/2, Old Code	1 9/16	1	1/4	5/16	5,300	500	Abstract	13 00
5 1/2, New Code	1 3/4	1 1/8	1/4	5/16	4,500	500	Accede	16 00
6	7/8	13/16	7/32	1/4	13,000	490	Accept	11 00
7	3/4	7/8	1/4	7/16	15,500	425	Acceptance	13 00
8	15/16	1	1/4	5/16	9,000	475	Access	13 00
9	1 1/8	5/8	3/16	3/16	15,000	475	Accident	16 00
10	1 3/4	1 5/8	3/8	3/8	2,000	490	Accommodate	30 00
*10 1/2	1 7/8	1 5/8	3/8	3/8	2,000	490	Accompany	30 00

* At request of the Government, manufacture will be discontinued after stock on hand is exhausted.

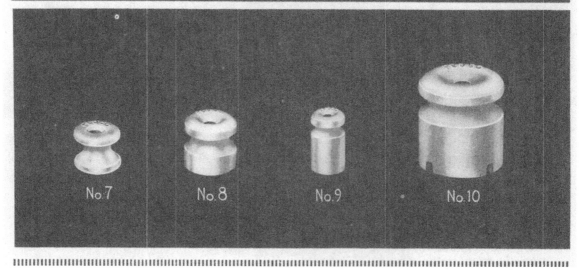

Figure 5. Page from a porcelain-knob supply catalog (Tod 1977:44).

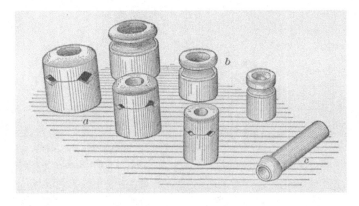

Figure 6. Split knobs *(a)*, solid knobs *(b)*, and a tube *(c)* (Cook 1917:209).

Figure 7. Two-wire *(a)* and three-wire *(b)* cleats (Cook 1917:211).

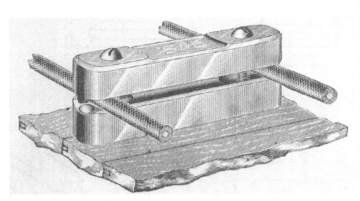

Figure 8. Illustration of cleat with wires in use (Tod 1977:28).

Figure 9. Three cleats excavated at Stanford University, courtesy of Laura Jones. (Photo by author, 2010.)

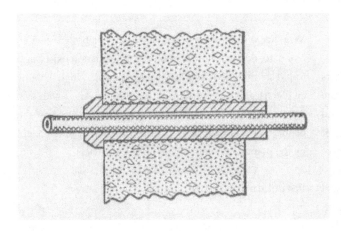

Figure 10. Illustration of the placement of a tube through a stud (Cook 1917:212).

Figure 11. Four tubes excavated at Stanford University, courtesy of Laura Jones. (Photo by author, 2010.)

1,042,372   1,061,620   1,218,181   1,290,540

1,048,850   1,079,239   1,232,354

1,049,405   1,217,315   1,273,313   1,302,158

Figure 12. Example of drawings of knobs available in Tod (1977:132).

Dating Electrical Porcelain

The key to dating household electrical porcelain artifacts is through the combination of identifying the style of the porcelain artifact and the maker's mark, when present, and cross-referencing this information with the known dates of introduction of styles and the known start and end dates of use of particular makers' marks. Additionally, companies' trademarks were registered with the U.S. Patent Office and appeared in advertising and catalogs, and sometimes on the insulators themselves; and thus at times these can provide a date of introduction for a particular item (Tod 1977:168–169).

Whether one can find only a start date, or both a start and end date, depends entirely on what information exists and is found about a particular company and its markings. Although an electrical porcelain artifact can often be dated with some accuracy, it must be noted that the precision of dating sites and contexts conclusively based on electrical porcelain is hindered by the potentially long use life of these artifacts.

Porcelain Insulator Styles

The history of electrical porcelain during its peak popularity is one of rapid invention and continuous patenting, as

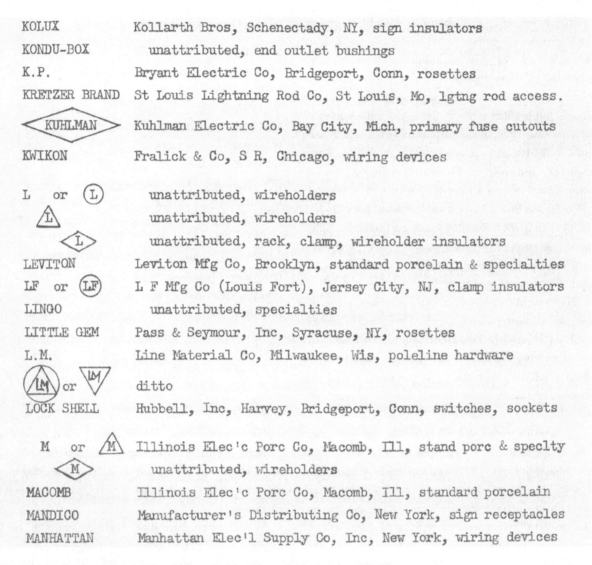

KOLUX	Kollarth Bros, Schenectady, NY, sign insulators
KONDU-BOX	unattributed, end outlet bushings
K.P.	Bryant Electric Co, Bridgeport, Conn, rosettes
KRETZER BRAND	St Louis Lightning Rod Co, St Louis, Mo, lgtng rod access.
◁ KUHLMAN ▷	Kuhlman Electric Co, Bay City, Mich, primary fuse cutouts
KWIKON	Fralick & Co, S R, Chicago, wiring devices
L or Ⓛ	unattributed, wireholders
△L	unattributed, wireholders
◇L	unattributed, rack, clamp, wireholder insulators
LEVITON	Leviton Mfg Co, Brooklyn, standard porcelain & specialties
LF or ⒧	L F Mfg Co (Louis Fort), Jersey City, NJ, clamp insulators
LINGO	unattributed, specialties
LITTLE GEM	Pass & Seymour, Inc, Syracuse, NY, rosettes
L.M.	Line Material Co, Milwaukee, Wis, poleline hardware
⊛ or ▽	ditto
LOCK SHELL	Hubbell, Inc, Harvey, Bridgeport, Conn, switches, sockets
M or △M	Illinois Elec'c Porc Co, Macomb, Ill, stand porc & speclty
◇M	unattributed, wireholders
MACOMB	Illinois Elec'c Porc Co, Macomb, Ill, standard porcelain
MANDICO	Manufacturer's Distributing Co, New York, sign receptacles
MANHATTAN	Manhattan Elec'l Supply Co, Inc, New York, wiring devices

Figure 13. Example of electrical porcelain makers' marks available in Tod (1977:110).

Figure 14. Factory worker "turning" knobs for uniformity (Tod 1977:39).

dozens of competing manufacturers aimed to enter the market, each with its own slight variation on the standard shapes and sizes of porcelain insulators. Sometimes the approximate dates of introduction (TPQs) of these different styles of insulators are accessible through patent records and product catalogs. Exhaustive information on the dates of introduction of various styles is available from two excellent sources: a website maintained by insulator researcher and collector Elton Gish (<http://www.r-infinity.com>), and *A History of the Electrical Porcelain Industry in the United States,* a self-published book by Jack Tod (1977). Tod's book is the most comprehensive published collection of ceramic insulator styles (Figure 12). Note that these sources are principally, if not exclusively, applicable to the United States.

The patents themselves can, of course, also be searched directly, a task that has been made incomparably easier with the advent of internet-based patent searching (insulator patents are compiled at <http://reference.insulators.info/patents>, and all patents are available at <http://www.google.com/patents> and <http://www.uspto.gov>). Some of the variants of the standard porcelain knob accessible through patent records, for example, are the split knob (1884) and the reversible split knob (1902); and variants of the porcelain cleat include the one-piece cleat (1883), the multipiece cleat (1885), the reversible wire cleat (1891), and the two-wire cleat (1892). For some examples see Figures 7–8 and Table 2, which compile some of the milestones of diagnostic traits of electrical porcelain useful to the archaeologist.

Patent dates should be used with caution. Without a second source of evidence (in other words, if relying on a patent alone), it is always an open question whether the date of patenting is close to the date a product actually reached the market. Many patents were never realized in products, or their releases were delayed. As with all artifacts encountered, time lags between design, manufacture, commercial availability, in-context use, and discard must always be considered.

Porcelain Insulator Markings

For insulators that do not have markings of any kind on them, identifying the style as described above will usually be the only way that approximate dates of manufacture can

Table 2. Electrical porcelain milestones.

Year	Artifact / Event	Source
1880	Beginning of porcelain cleats boom era	Tod 1977:14
1883	One-piece cleat	Tod 1977:129
1884	Split-knob	Tod 1977:13
1885	Crossover style knob	Tod 1977:141
1885	Multipiece cleat	Tod 1977:127
1889	Self-tying knob	Tod 1977:137
1890	Beginning of knob-and-tube boom era	Tod 1977:7
1891	Reversible wire cleat	Tod 1977:126
1892	End of use of wood for wiring insulators	Tod 1977:12
1892	Two-wire cleats	Tod 1977:13
1892	First wall tube	Tod 1977:15
1897	Standardization of electrical porcelain	Tod 1977:15
1901	Insulating bushing on knobs	Tod 1977:156
1902	Reversible split-knob	Tod 1977:134
1907	Cleat for corner edges	Tod 1977:128
1910	End of porcelain cleats boom era	Tod 1977:14
1932	End of knob and tube boom era	Tod 1977:9

be obtained. Many insulators, however, do have stamped markings on them, and these markings, when present, are invaluable for dating. Note, though, that markings found on insulators are not always makers' marks: a marking might refer to an item's catalog number, size, patent number, or patent date.

As with the insulator styles discussed above, the reader is again referred to the exhaustive cataloging work done by collectors—in particular, Tod's 1977 work, which lists over 400 electrical porcelain makers' marks (Figure 13), and the website maintained by Elton Gish cited above. Up to three separate sections of Tod's book might be needed to find the dates of a particular marking: the listing of manufacturers and their dates of operation, pages 69–101; the listing of stamped marks and the names of their associated manufacturers, pages 103–115; and the listing of manufacturers' trademarks, pages 168–169.

Conclusion

While this article seeks to provide an introduction, aimed at archaeologists, to the social and material aspects of the early electrification of the American household, it is not intended to provide exhaustive coverage of all artifacts related to electrification, or even of a single class of artifacts within this grouping. This discussion of electrical porcelain used in the wiring of buildings is only introductory; and many other artifacts are worthy of exploration beyond the scope of this article, including glass insulators, light bulbs, fuses, wire, plugs and receptacles, junction boxes, personal generators, batteries, and home appliances. Preliminary research suggests, perhaps surprisingly, that each of these other classes of artifacts is a large topic that warrants a topic-specific article.

Electrical artifacts in late-19th- and early-20th-century contexts are evidence of a period of rapid technical and social change related to the electrification of America. Research suggests that these electrical artifacts will, in many cases, be useful for dating sites and contexts. Archaeologists are encountering these artifacts in excavations but have not always seen their potential for contributing to dating and interpretation. This, together with a paucity of writing on the topic directed at archaeologists, is perhaps why few archaeological reports discuss electrical artifacts more than cursorily. In the case of household electrical porcelain, the class of artifacts discussed in this article, the potential for dating comes both from morphology, since this is often documented through patents, product catalogs, and other records, and through the makers' marks, many of which have been painstakingly cataloged by collectors.

ACKNOWLEDGMENTS

This article draws on previous research by avocational insulator enthusiasts and, in particular, the extensive work of Elton Gish and Jack Tod. The content was much improved thanks to close readings provided by Elton Gish, Michael Schiffer, Barbara Voss, Larry McKee, Kathy LaVergne, and Erica Gibson. For bringing sources to my attention, thanks are due to Carol Serr, Jakob Crockett, and Liz Clevenger. The idea for this article came about as I was working on excavations at the Stanford University men's gymnasium ruin (Cain et al. 2009), and a special thanks is owed to Laura Jones both for inviting me to work on that project and for obliging my side interest in electrical artifacts while on the clock.

REFERENCES

Cain, Julie, Laura Jones, Tara Laidlaw, and Katrinka Reinhart
2009   The Stanford University Men's Gymnasium Ruin: Archaeological Testing and Evaluation for the Concert Hall Project. Report to the County of Santa Clara Office of Planning and Community Development, from Stanford University, Stanford, CA.

Cook, Arthur
1917   *Electric Wiring for Lighting and Power Installations.* John Wiley & Sons, New York, NY.

Croft, Terrell
1920   *Wiring for Light and Power.* McGraw Hill, New York, NY.

Devine, Warren
1983   From Shafts to Wires: Historical Perspectives on Electrification. *Journal of Economic History* 43(2):347–372.

Edison, Thomas
1885   Electricity Man's Slave. *Scientific American* 52(12):185.

General Electric
1925   *The Home of a Hundred Comforts.* General Electric Company, Bridgeport, CT.

2010   Innovation Timeline. General Electric <http://www.ge.com/innovation/timeline/index.html>. Accessed 9 December 2010.

Grant, Casey
1995   Movers and Shakers: The Men Who Made the NFPA. *NFPA Journal* 89(3):97–102.

Hilton, George
1969   Technology and the Urban Pattern. *Journal of Contemporary History* 4(3):123–135.

Hoover, Herbert
1924   Industrial Standardization. In *Scientific Management Since Taylor*, Edward Hunt, editor, pp. 189–196. McGraw-Hill, New York, NY.

Miller, George
2000   Telling Time for Archaeologists. *Northeast Historical Archaeology* 29:1–22.

Nordhaus, William
1997   Do Real Output and Real Wage Measures Capture Reality? The History of Light Suggests Not. In *The Economics of New Goods*, Robert Gordon and Timothy Bresnahan, editors, pp. 29–66. University of Chicago Press, Chicago, IL.

Nye, David
1990   *Electrifying America: Social Meanings of a New Technology*. MIT Press, Cambridge, MA.

Powell, Ray
1995   *Introduction to Electric Circuits*. Arnold, London, UK.

Schroeder, Fred
1986   More "Small Things Forgotten": Domestic Electrical Plugs and Receptacles, 1881–1931. *Technology and Culture* 27(3):525–543.

Tod, Jack
1977   *A History of the Electrical Porcelain Industry in the United States*. Jack Tod, Phoenix, AZ.

Woodhead, Eileen, Catherine Sullivan, and Gérard Gusset
1984   *Lighting Devices in the National Reference Collection, Parks Canada*. Parks Canada, Ottawa, ON.

Adrian T. Myers
Stanford Archaeology Center
PO Box 20446
Stanford, CA 94309

Common 20th Century Artifacts: A Guide to Dating

Cathy Spude

Historical archeologists and others trying to date historical sites by means of the artifacts found on them are increasingly interested in common items manufactured during the lifetimes of people still living. This dating guide is intended to provide a simple source for the most common artifacts found in archeological or historic contexts.

Aluminum Foil

1825: Aluminum first isolated
(Encyclopedia Britannica 1973 (1): 693).

1855: Introduced in Paris Exposition
(Encyclopedia Britannica 1973 (1): 693).

1886: Modern electrolytic method of producing aluminum discovered by Charles Martin Hall in the United States and Paul L. T. Heroult in France (Encyclopedia Britannica 1973 (1): 693).

Ca. 1920: Beginning of commercial production of aluminum foil; used to wrap tea, candy, gum and cigarettes (Sacharow 1978:111).

1939: Aluminum foil being used to wrap dried fruit, cream cheese, and for beer labels (Sacharow 1978: 111).

1940-1945: Increased demand for aluminum foil packaging
(Sacharow 1978: 112).

1947: Upward trend in world production of aluminum begun
(Encyclopedia Britannica 1973 (1): 694).

Bottles, General

1820-1925: Tooled finish
(Jones and Sullivan 1985: 165).

1877-1920: Vent marks (Jones and Sullivan 1985: 165).

1886: The first machine to make narrow-mouthed bottles was developed. This was a semi-automatic Ashley machine. It involved the hand-gathering of glass (Douglas and Frank 1972: 178).

1889-Present: Machine-made bottles
(Jones and Sullivan 1985: 165).

Post-1892: Crown finish. Originally made with a finishing tool (Jones and Sullivan 1985).

1905-1982: "Owen's" mark on bottle base
(Miller and McNichol 2002).

1905-1920: 6 oz, 7 oz, and quart soda pop bottles standardized (Kaplan 1982).

1905: Owen's mark first appears on beer, porter, ale, soda water, wine, brandy, milk and patent medicine bottles (Miller and McNichol 2002: 3).

1906: Owen's mark first appears on catsup bottles (Miller and McNichol 2002: 3).

1908: Owen's mark first appears on vinegar, grape juice, narrow mouth food bottles and European bottles (Miller and McNichol 2002: 3).

1910: Owen's mark first appears on fruit jars, packers ware, prescription ware, ammonia bottles, and Heinz bottles (Miller and McNichol 2002: 3).

1911: Owen's mark first appears on whiskeys, gallon packers, and small bottles from one-half to six ounce capacity (Miller and McNichol 2002: 3).

1912: Owen's mark first appears on carboys (Miller and McNichol 2002: 3).

1914: Blue glass, primarily Bromo-Seltzer bottles, first produced by Owens machine (Miller and McNichol 2002: 8).

1917: Half of all bottles produced in the United States are made on Owens machines (Miller and McNichol 2002: 3).

1920-1930: 8 oz. bottles standardized (Kaplan 1982).

1924: 9 oz, 10 oz bottles standardized (Kaplan 1982).

Pre-1925: Hand-blown bottles
(Jones and Sullivan 1985: 165).

1929-1931: Pepsi introduces the 12 oz. bottle (Kaplan 1982).

1934: Square paper milk container introduced (Busch 1987: 76).

1935: Non-returnable beer bottles introduced (Busch 1987: 77).

1935: "FEDERAL LAW FORBIDS SALE OR RE-USE OF THIS BOTTLE" mandated for all liquor bottles (Busch 1987: 75).

1948: Non-returnable soda bottles introduced (Busch 1987: 77).

1955: Coca-Cola introduces the 26 oz. bottle (Kaplan 1982).

1955-1960: 16 oz. bottle introduced (Kaplan 1982).

1958: Introduction of plastic 6-pack carriers (Kaplan 1982: 127).

1965: Non-returnable bottles or One Way
   bottles introduced (Kaplan 1982:106).
1970: Plastic soft drink bottles introduced
   (Kaplan 1982: 106).
1971: Plasti-shield bottles introduced by Owens-Illinois
   (Kaplan 1982:106).
1977: Introduction of PET bottle
   (polyethylene terathalate) (Kaplan 1982: 113).
1978: Wide-spread adoption of plastic pop bottles
   (Kaplan 1982: 109)
1978: 62% of soft drink bottles, 89% of beer bottles
   and 98% of milk containers were non-returnable
   (Busch 1987: 77).

Bottles, Beer

1895-1910: Applied crown finish (Kroll 1976: 7).
1935: Introduction of stubby bottles as a response to the
   space-saving advertisements of can manufacturers
   (Cady 1976: 15; Kroll 1976: 7).
1939: "NO DEPOSIT, NO RETURN, NOT TO
   BE REFILLED" (Kroll 1976: 7).
1950: Only 2.6% of all packed beer was disposable
   (Kroll 1976: 7).

Cans, General

1934: Applied color label that could not wash off
   became commercially available (Kaplan 1982: 114).
1936: Soft drinks begin to appear in cans. Not
   very popular (Kaplan 1982: 114).
1940: Because tin became unavailable during World
   War II, the tin-free can was developed. Aluminum,
   tin-free steel, fiber/foil laminates were all developed
   during this period. A method for the very thin
   coating of tin was also developed. At least 9 different
   resins were also developed to coat steel cans
   (Sacharow 1978: 127).
1940-1945: Composite cans: foil lined paper
   board cans capped with metal were used for
   biscuits and motor oil (Sacharow 1978: 131).
1945: Aerosol sprays developed out of need for effective
   insecticides during jungle fighting
   (Sacharow 1978: 17; Kaplan 1982: 124).
1948: Resurgence in use of cans for soft drinks
   (Kaplan 1982: 114).
1950: Paper labels eliminated by applied color labels
   (Kaplan 1982: 114).

1953: Adoption of flat-top can for soft drinks
   (Kaplan 1982: 114).
1958: Only 17% of soft drink manufacturers using cans
   (Kaplan 1982: 117).
1959: Pepsi, Coca-Cola using cans (Kaplan 1982: 117).
1960: The last cone top cans were sold in the
   United States
   (BCCN 1985: 22; Sacharow 1978: 139).
1962: ALCOA introduced the pull tab opener:
   open ring design (Kaplan 1982: 117).
1963: Pull tab on aluminum can invented
   by Ermal Fraze (Petroski 1993: 199).
1963: Introduction of drawn and ironed aluminum can
   (Kaplan 1982: 120).
1969: 5% of cans aluminum (Kaplan 1982: 120).
1970: 90% of all soft drink cans had pull tab openers
   (Kaplan 1982: 117).
1971: Necked-in, soldered side seams, double decked
   (Kaplan 1982: 120).
1972: Two piece steel cans developed
   (Kaplan 1982: 124).
1974: Introduction of non-removable opener
   (Kaplan 1982: 120).
1974: 46% of beer cans aluminum; 20% of soft
   drinks are aluminum (Kaplan 1982: 120).
1978: Introduction of the "paper" can: plastic-coated,
   foil-lined, steel bottom, aluminum top
   (Kaplan 1982: 120).
1980: 66.1% of all soft drinks are sold in cans
   (Kaplan 1982: 120).
1980: Pull tab that does not separate from the can
   (Petroski 1993: 203).
1981: triple-necked cans (Kaplan 1982: 120).

Cans, Beer

1935: First beer cans. Produced by the American Can
   Company, and used by Pabst Brewery. By end of the
   year, 36 companies were selling canned beer
   (BCCN 1985: 1, 5-6).
1940-1955: "Crowntainer" aluminum coated steel can,
   painted outside, hot wax inside, cone topped can
   (BCCN 1985: 21).
Pre-1942: Large letters "BEER" or "ALE" on cans
   (Cady 1976: 44).
1942-1945: Tin-plated cans reserved for exclusive use
   by the military. Words "WITHDRAWN FREE OF
   TAX" Olive drab or gray cans (BCCN 1985: 21).
1942: End of production of beer cans for civilians
   (Cady 1976: 15).

1950: Dropped use of IRTD statement on cans "INTERNAL REVENUE TAX PAID" (BCCN 1985: 22 Cady 1976: 43).

1953: One fourth of all beer sold in cans (Cady 1976: 15).

1954: Appearance of 16 oz. Beer can, as well as 10, 11, 14, and 15 oz. Cans (BCCN 1985: 22; Cady 1976: 15).

1959: Introduction of all-aluminum can by Coors (Wright 1976: 22).

1959: Introduction of the 7 oz. Coors can (BCCN 1985: 22).

1963: Hamm's, Budweiser, Busch aluminum cans (Wright 1976: 22).

1963: First use of pull tabs (BCCN 1985: 22; Bull, et al. 1984: 10).

1964: Large number of breweries using all aluminum cans (Wright 1976: 22).

1965: Ring top pull tab. 65% of all beer cans had pull tabs (BCCN 1985: 22; Bull, et al. 1984: 10).

1965: Begin of gradual change to crimped cans (BCCN 1985: 23).

1969: Canned beer outsells bottled beer (Bull, et al. 1984: 10).

1975: Nearly 100% of all beer cans were easy-open tops (Wright 1976: 22).

1975: "Sta Tab" top (Reynolds Aluminum) (BCCN 1985: 23).

1984: Last straight-sided can (BCCN 1985: 23).

Cigarettes

(For additional dates and history, see the [website] Cigarette History compiled by Michael Pfeiffer.)

1850s: Widespread use during the Crimean War (Encyclopedia Britannica 1973 (5): 767-768).

1853: First manufactured in Havana (Encyclopedia Britannica 1973 (5): 767-768).

1853-1900: Cigarettes handmade (Encyclopedia Britannica 1973 (5): 767-768).

1860s-1880s: Patents for machines to make cigarettes. Not used widely until 1880s (Encyclopedia Britannica 1973 (5): 767-768).

1920: Cigarette consumption equaled cigars (Encyclopedia Britannica 1973 (5): 767-768).

1938: Half of all tobacco consumption was in cigarette form (Encyclopedia Britannica 1973 (5): 767-768).

Ca. 1942: Deletion of green coloring behind Lucky Strike bulls-eye (Sacharow 1978: 20).

1950: Three-fourths of all tobacco consumption was in cigarettes (Encyclopedia Britannica 1973 (5): 767-768).

1952: 1.4% of all cigarettes had filters (Encyclopedia Britannica 1973 (5): 767-768).

1960: 80% of all tobacco consumption was in cigarettes (Encyclopedia Britannica 1973 (5): 767-768).

1964: Surgeon General's Advisory Committee found link between cigarettes and lung cancer (Encyclopedia Britannica 1973 (5): 767-768).

1966: Surgeon General's warning appears on tobacco products (Encyclopedia Britannica 1973 (22): 46-47).

1969: Introduction of the disposable cigarette lighter (Pfeiffer 2002).

1970: 33% of all cigarettes had filters (Encyclopedia Britannica 1973 (5): 767-768).

1971: Health warning appears on all tobacco products (Encyclopedia Britannica 1973 (22): 46-47).

Closures, Bottle

1857-1912: Hutchison stopper (Kaplan 1982: 128).

1892: Patent for the crown cap was awarded to William Painter (Kaplan 1982: 123).

1909: Introduction of crown-like closure with no corrugations in the skirt (Everette 1982: 168).

1909: Invention of composition cork for use as liner in crown caps (Lief 1965:25).

1912: Widespread adoption of the crown cap (Kaplan 1982).

1927: Charles E. McManus developed a way to granulate cork, for use in crown cap (Kaplan 1982: 124).

1930: Spot crowns (plastic lined) (Kaplan 1982: 125).

1933: Pilferproof roll-on closure for use on alcohol bottles (Everette 1982: 185).

1955: Introduction of solid, molded polyvinyl chloride lined crown. 0.235" I.007" skirt (Everette 1982: 168, 174; Ward et al. 1977: 239).

1956: Short-skirted crown cap (7/32") introduced (Ward et al. 1977: 239).

1957: Plastic liners in crown caps instead of cork were first used (Kaplan 1982: 124).

1965: Twist-off crown cap (Kaplan 1982: 131).

1965: Roll-on closure (Kaplan 1982: 131).

Ca. 1965: Elimination of cork-lined crown cap (Everette 1982: 168).

1966: Introduction of the "turn-off" crown cap, 4-threaded finish (Everette 1982: 168).

Cathy Spude

1966: Aluminum roll-on closure for beer bottles. 28 mm only size used for beer (Everette 1982: 182).
1977: Plastic bottle cap introduced (Kaplan 1982: 131).

Plastics and Synthetics

1866: Polystyrene invented (fake rubber). Not used on a wide scale until the mid – 1950s. Is most familiar to us as foam cups and other thermofoam products (Sacharow 1978: 93).
1869: First semi-synthetic plastic, celluloid, invented by John Wesley Hyatt (Friedl 1987; King 1991: 3).
1900: Invention of cellulose acetate, the "improved" cellulose. Glossy jewelry, toothbrush handles, eyeglass frames, soda straws, cellophane, and rayon. Many of these products are produced today (King 1991: 4).
1909: Bakelite invented by Leo H. Baekeland (King 1991: 5).
1918: First plant for production of cellulose acetate (celluloid), the first plastic (Sacharow 1978: 17).
1924: Beginning of production of cellophane (Sacharow 1978: 86).
1929: Urea-formaldehyde plastics, the first transparent synthetic plastics. Known as "Beatl" and "Beetleware." Included tablewares, cases for shavers and hair dryers, buttons, tabletops, and lampshades. Brittle, warps easily and fades (King 1991: 6).
1930s: The Great Depression was largely responsible for the boom in packaging materials of all kinds, due to government subsidy of package designers; subsidies were meant to stimulate consumer interest in products through attractive packaging (Sacharow 1978: 19).
1930: First use of cellophane as a wrapping material (King 1991: 4).
1930: Scotch tape (adhesive-coated cellophane) invented and produced by 3M (Allen 1995: 51).
1934-1976: Pliofilm introduced commercially by Goodyear. Rubber hydrochloride film. Thermoplastic film used as a heat sealing medium for flexible packaging; e. g. Saran Wrap (Sacharow 1978: 93).
Ca. 1935: Waterproof cellophane invented by DuPont (Sacharow 1978: 19).
1936: Acrylic plastics introduced by Rohm and Hass Company, called "plexiglass." In 1937, DuPont introduced "Lucite," another form of acrylic plastic (King 1991: 6).

1937: Introduction of melamine-formaldehyde plastic, called Melamine. Still used widely today (King 1991: 6).
1938: Nylon plastics developed by DuPont, for bristles in toothbrushes, hosiery and undergarments (King 1991: 7).
1940: Discovery of polyethylene (flexible plastic) (Sacharow 1978: 88).
1945: Tupperware developed (King 1991: 7).
1946: Introduction of Saran Wrap; PVDC copolymer film (Sacharow 1978: 95).
1954: Wide scale manufacture of polyester films, dimensionally stable, temperature resistant, barrier to odors and gases (Sacharow 1978: 94-95).
1957: Polypropylene invented. Used to laminate paper products (like potato chip bags) (Sacharow 1978: 91)
1961: Scotch Brand Magic Tape on acetate rather than cellophane (Allen 1995: 52).

Other Artifacts

Ca. 1928: Toothpaste tubes were developed (Sacharow 1978: 154).

References

ALLEN, OLIVER E.
1995   "Sticky Business," Invention and Technology (winter): 48-52.

BCCN
1985   "50 Years of Canned Beers," Beer Can Collectors' News Report Special Edition.

BULL, DONALD, MANDRED FREIDRICH, AND ROBERT GOTSCHALK
1984   American Breweries. Bullworks, Trumbull, Connecticut.

BUSCH, JANE
1987   "Second Time Around: A Look at Bottle Reuse." Historical Archaeology 21(1):67-80.

CADY, LEW
1976   Beer Can Collecting: America's Fastest Growing Hobby. Grosset and Dunlap, New York.

DOUGLAS, R. W. AND SUSAN FRANK
1972   A History of Glassmaking. G. T. Foulis, Henley-on-Thames, Oxfordshire.

ENCYCLOPEDIA BRITANNICA
1973   "Aluminum," Encyclopedia Britannica (1): 693-694, Chicago.

1973   "Cigarette," Encyclopedia Britannica (5): 767-768, Chicago.

1973   "Tobacco," Encyclopedia Britannica (22): 46-47, Chicago.

EVERETTE, J. F.
1982   "Bottle Closures," in Beer Packaging: A Manual for the Brewing and Beverage Industries, edited by Harold M. Broderick. Master Brewers Association of the Americas, Madison, Wisconsin.

FRIEDEL, ROBERT
1987   The First Plastics. American Heritage of Invention and Technology (Summer): 18-23.

JONES, OLIVE AND CATHERINE SULLIVAN
1985   The Parks Canada Glass Glossary for the Description of Containers, Tableware, Flat Glass and Closures. Studies in Archaeology, Architecture and History. Parks Canada, Ottawa.

KAPLAN, SAMUEL R. (EDITOR)
1982   Beverage World: 100 Year History 1882-1982 and Future Probe. Keller Publishing, Great Neck, New York.

KING, ROBERT
1991   Plastics in Archaeological Sites: A Brief History. Paper presented to the Alaska Anthropological Association, Anchorage, Alaska.

KROLL, WAYNE L.
1976   Badger Breweries, Past and Present. Wayne L. Kroll, Jefferson, Wisconsin.

KYVIG, DAVID E.
1979   Repealing National Prohibition. University of Chicago, Chicago.

LIEF, ALFRED
1965   A Close-up of Closures: History and Progress. Glass Container Manufacturers Institute, New York.

MILLER, GEORGE L. AND TONY MCNICHOL
2002   Dates for Suction Scarred Bottoms: Chronological Changes in Owens Machine-Made Bottles. Paper presented at the 2002 Annual Meeting of the Society for Historical Archaeology, Mobile, Alabama.

PETROSKI, HENRY
1993   The Evolution of Useful Things. Alfred A. Knopf, New York.

PFEIFFER, MICHAEL
2002   Personal Communication. Email to Catherine H. Spude dated December 30, 2002. "I first saw a totally disposable cigarette lighter in 1969. My father had a plastics factory and he was given it as example to bid on making more. It was the summer I was home on leave from the army and was supposed to be going to Viet Nam. I think that is why he gave it to me. I still have that one in my collection."

SACHAROW, STANLEY
1978   A Packaging Primer. Magazines for Industry, New York.

WARD, ALBERT E., EMILY K. ABBINK AND JOHN R. STEIN
1977   Ethnohistorical and Chronological Basis of the Navajo Material Culture. In Settlement and Subsistence along the Lower Chaco River: The CGP Survey. University of New Mexico, Albuquerque.

WRIGHT, LARRY (EDITOR)
1976   The Beer Can. Great Plains Living Press, Matteson, Illinois.

Made in the USA
Las Vegas, NV
25 April 2024